COMPUTER EDUCATION *for* TEACHERS

VICKI SHARP
CALIFORNIA STATE UNIVERSITY, NORTHRIDGE

Madison, Wisconsin • Dubuque, Iowa • Indianapolis, Indiana
Melbourne, Australia • Oxford, England

Book Team

Editor *Paul L. Tavenner*
Developmental Editor *Sue Pulvermacher-Alt*
Production Editor *Carla D. Kipper*
Visuals/Design Developmental Consultant *Marilyn A. Phelps*
Publishing Services Specialist *Sherry Padden*
Visuals/Design Freelance Specialist *Mary L. Christianson*
Marketing Manager *Pamela S. Cooper*
Advertising Manager *Jodi Rymer*

A Division of Wm. C. Brown Communications, Inc.

Vice President and General Manager *Thomas E. Doran*
Editor in Chief *Edgar J. Laube*
Executive Editor *Ed Bartell*
Executive Editor *Stan Stoga*
National Sales Manager *Eric Ziegler*
Director of CourseResource *Kathy Law Laube*
Director of CourseSystems *Chris Rogers*
Director of Marketing *Sue Simon*
Director of Production *Vickie Putman Caughron*
Imaging Group Manager *Chuck Carpenter*
Manager of Visuals and Design *Faye M. Schilling*
Design Manager *Jac Tilton*
Art Manager *Janice Roerig*
Permissions/Records Manager *Connie Allendorf*

Wm. C. Brown Communications, Inc.

Chairman Emeritus *Wm. C. Brown*
Chairman and Chief Executive Officer *Mark C. Falb*
President and Chief Operating Officer *G. Franklin Lewis*
Corporate Vice President, President of WCB Manufacturing *Roger Meyer*

Cover design by Matthew Doherty Design
Cover photo by Robert Lightfoot III
Copyedited by Mary Waddell

Library of Congress Catalog Card Number: 91–78163

ISBN 0–697–11702–2

Printed in the United States of America by Wm. C. Brown Communications, Inc.,
2460 Kerper Boulevard, Dubuque, IA 52001

10 9 8 7 6 5 4 3 2 1

For David, Dick, Bobbie, and Paul, with love

Brief Contents

Contents

Preface

The author first became involved with computers in 1969 when she learned Fortran. In the early eighties, she bought pocket computers and taught programming off campus. At that time, educational software was limited, inadequate, and the rage was teaching BASIC, followed shortly thereafter by Logo.

During the last ten years, the author has been gathering material for a computer book. In the meantime, there have been many technological changes, and the computer has emerged as an important tool in society. With the production of quality software, the computer's role has changed from a device used for computer programming to an instrument that can be efficiently integrated into the curriculum. Furthermore, an increasing number of teachers utilize the computer for such tasks as word processing, data base management, graphics generation, and desktop publishing. With this renewed interest in computers, computer literacy is becoming as necessary as reading literacy in the schools. Because computers are so commonplace, teacher education programs are requiring students to take computer literacy courses. Emerging trends in education, as reflected by the California and New Mexico State guidelines, make a course of this nature mandatory. In order for teachers to use computers, they must acquire operational competency and the skills to evaluate and use the software that is being produced and marketed.

Computer Education for Teachers, which assumes no prior experience with computers, is designed to meet these needs in a thorough and clear manner. It is written for the undergraduates and graduate students who need an up-to-date, readable, practical, concise introduction to the computers. It is not intended to make students computer programmers, but to help them acquire the knowledge and skills to use computers effectively in the classroom.

The content of the text is arranged in a logical teaching order. However, the chapters are not dependent on each other and can be taught in the order the instructor requires. This book has the following salient features:

- **Chapter objectives.** Using the objectives at the beginning of each chapter, the reader has a map of the chapter's contents, thus knowing the direction to travel.
- **Clear illustrations.** There are over three hundred illustrations used to highlight pertinent points, facilitate understanding, and explain software.

- **Contents not specific to a particular system.** The book discusses general concepts and principles that are applicable to any personal computer.
- **Chapter mastery tests.** According to sound learning principles, the student answers questions at the end of each chapter to ascertain if s/he understands the material presented in the chapter.
- **Recommended annotated software listing.** Having a complete up-to-date annotated listing of software, the reader can make a more informed decision when purchasing it.
- **Classroom activities and projects.** The book has an assortment of learning activities and projects to motivate students, enhance learning, and help integrate the computer in the classroom.
- **Summary of current computer research.** With an understanding of past and current research, the reader knows what is an effective use of the computer, what is not, and what is a promising new direction for further research.
- **Exposure to state of the art technology developments.** By exploring advances in computer technology, the student is aware of up-to-date developments and is on the cutting edge of knowledge.
- **Extensive Bibliography.** The reader can use the selected bibliography to investigate other topics and explore in depth subjects and issues that cover a wide spectrum.
- **A chapter on desktop publishing.** Using one of the primary applications for the computer, desktop publishing (DTP), the student can create such products as a newspaper, bulletins, or signs that can enrich the curriculum.
- **A chapter on hypermedia.** This chapter introduces the student to ways of using the computer to combine text, graphics, and sound into a multimedia presentation that can enhance instruction.
- **A teacher's manual.** This manual supplies the teacher with chapter summaries, lecture outlines, answers to mastery test questions, suggested activities and projects, transparency masters, additional test items, and sample software evaluations.

It is with great appreciation that I acknowledge the assistance of many of the people and companies who contributed to the completion of this textbook:

Advanced Ideas, Gary Schwartz
Aldus Corporation, Freda Cook
AV Systems, Adrian Vance
Apple Computer
Bank Street Writer, Frank Smith
Baseline, Diane Cavazos
Baudville, Debbie Sikanas
Brittanica, Lynn Batts
Brøderbund Software, Jessica Switzer, Karen Omholt
California State University, Northridge:
Dr. Bonnie Ericson,
Dr. Richard M. Sharp
CCIE, Robert Allen Sachs
Claris Corporation, Stephen F. Ruddock
CompuTeach, Lynn Rushing
Connors and Associates, Angelique d'Addario
Davidson, Julie Gibb, Sue Marshall, Delina J. Roberts
Data Description, Inc.- Paul Velleman
Didatech Software Limited, Darren K. Francks, David J. Young, Brian Sellstedt
Dubl-Click Software
E.M.A. Bob Enenstein
GifConverter, Kevin A. Mitchell
Hartley, Cathy Carres
Hi Tech, David Summer
Jay Klein Productions, Jay A. Klein
Jeff Friedman
Keith Boudreau
Larry Woodard
Lawrence Productions, Susan Wiltse
Learning Company, Debbie Aube, Mimi Cockall, Frances Roseblade
Logo Computer Systems Inc.(LCSI), Lea M. Laricci
MacValley
Mainstay, Brain T. Coleman
MECC, Patricia Kallio
Mike Devlin
Mindplay
Mindscape(SVE)- Kelly J. Town, Dena Kareotes
Optimium Resources, Inc. Sally Carr Hannafin
Pelican Software, Joel Free
Projac, Bob Mayall
Roger Wagner Inc. Garland Buchingham, Roger Wagner
Queue, Lynn Gadarowski
Reference Software, Sigrid A. Metson
Santa Barbara Softworks, Gordon Morrell
Scholastic Software, Geri Zabitz Badler, Susan Beecher
Softswap, Hal Gibson
Spinnaker, Priscilla Seuss
Springboard, Tom Kuder
Sunburst Communication Clair Kubasik
Superschool, Robert L. Barbosa
Tom Schneider Productions
Terrapin Logo, Dorothy M. Fitch, Tricia Donahue
Timeworks, Donna Graen
True Basic Inc. Norm Chapman
The Writing Tools

A special thanks to **Patricia Kallio, MECC, Jessica Switzer, Brøderbund, Susan Beecher, Scholastic, Julie Gibbs, Davidson and Associates, Angelique D'Addario, Connors and Associates, Sally Carr Hannafin, Optimium Resources, Inc., Clair Kubasik, Sunburst, and Larry Woodard, Nest Software, Inc.,** for their extra time and effort.

Bonnie Ericson deserves special recognition for a well-written teacher's manual that can serve as an excellent resource for the instructor. She did an outstanding job and it is greatly appreciated.

I want to express my appreciation to **Paul Tavenner** at William C. Brown for his invaluable assistance and direction. I am indebted to **Sue Pulvermacher-Alt** for her hard work, and constant help and encouragement on this project, and **Carla Arnold,** a skillful production editor. Last, but not least, I wish to thank the following individuals for their invaluable contributions in reviewing and critiquing my manuscript:

Alice A. Christie, Arizona State University;
B. Keith Eicher, University of Richmond
Clyde Greve, University of Wisconsin, La Crosse;
Romaine Jesky-Smith, Geneva College
Seymour Metzner, California State University, Northridge
Ronald F. Pauline, Gannon University
Terry L. Shoup, California State University, San Bernardino & San Bernardino City Unified School District
Neal Strudler, University of Nevada-Las Vegas.

Finally, special thanks to my family, my husband, **Dick,** who spent many hours critiquing the manuscript, and making sure I met my deadlines, my son, **David,** who became a computer expert, my mother, **Bobbie,** who entertained David, my dad, the late **Paul Friedman,** and my brother, **Jeff Friedman,** for his time and effort in reviewing my book.

History of the Computer

1

Objectives

Upon completing this chapter the student will be able to:

1. Identify and place in proper sequence five of the major inventions in the history of computing.
2. Discuss succinctly each of the following six individual's contribution to the field of computing:
   a. Herman Hollerith
   b. Joseph Marie Jacquard
   c. Charles Babbage
   d. John Atanasoff
   e. Howard Aiken
3. Differentiate among the generations of computers by their technological advances.

Early Times

Primitive man found it necessary to count and the natural instrument to use was his fingers. He could show how many animals he killed on a hunt or the number of people in a village. To indicate large numbers he used all ten fingers; thus ten became the basis of our number system today. As time passed, man needed a way to keep track of his possessions because life became more complex. He began to use rocks as a way to store information, using one rock to represent each animal he owned. Later, wanting a record of this information, he carved notches and symbols in stone or wood, an effective record keeping method until the abacus was invented.

The Abacus

The **abacus** was different from any recording device that came before it because it allowed manipulation of data. Historians are not sure who invented this tool or the date of its invention. The abacus probably existed around 3000 B.C. and originated with the Babylonians.

In 1854, at Senkereh, near Babylon, archaeologists found a clay tablet resembling a primitive abacus, which, they believed, is nearly 4,000 years old (J. M. Pullan, 1968). The discovery of this artifact indicates that some form of calculation existed in Babylon about 3,000 B.C. (The tablet now resides in the British Museum.) Records show that ancient civilizations, like India, China, Egypt, and Mesopotamia, were using calculating devices several thousand years ago. About five hundred years B.C. the Greeks used the abacus in the form of a plain board or counter on which a few lines were drawn to mark the places. A few hundred years later, the Romans developed a device for calculating called the calculi, which consisted of a smooth board or table marked with lines. Even though no boards have survived from these times, stones have been found at many archaeological sites. The stones found in China, Japan and Russia are similar to the stones used in the Roman bead-frame which suggests that the use of these instruments spread from Rome to China to Japan and then to Russia. However, without concrete evidence, it would be difficult to establish this as irrefutable fact. What is known is that the Chinese devised rules for the abacus in the thirteenth century, and they are often given credit for perfecting its use.

The abacus (Figure 1.1) user manipulates beads in a wood frame to keep track of numbers and place values. People who use it can do calculations almost as quickly as someone who uses a calculator. Of all the early aids to calculation, the abacus is the only one used today.

In the following paragraphs, the author will discuss the pioneers and their inventions prior to the computer. Some of these inventions made mathematical calculation and tabulation faster and simpler, while others gave access to ways of inputting information into computers and controlling more complicated data processing.

The Pioneers

John Napier

Our first pioneer, **John Napier,** a Scottish mathematician, invented **Napier's Rods** or **Bones** in 1617. The rods shown in Figure 1.2 were sometimes carved out of ivory in the form of an Arabian lattice. The user was able to multiply large numbers by manipulating these rods. These devices simplified tedious calculations, and they were faster and more accurate. Napier rods preceded the Oughtred's slide ruler by nearly four decades.

Wilhelm Schickard

Around 1623, **Wilhelm Schickard,** a German mathematician, was the first to attempt to devise a computer. He built a mechanism that could add, subtract, multiply, and divide. Later he intended to send his friend, Johannes Kepler, a copy of his invention, but fire

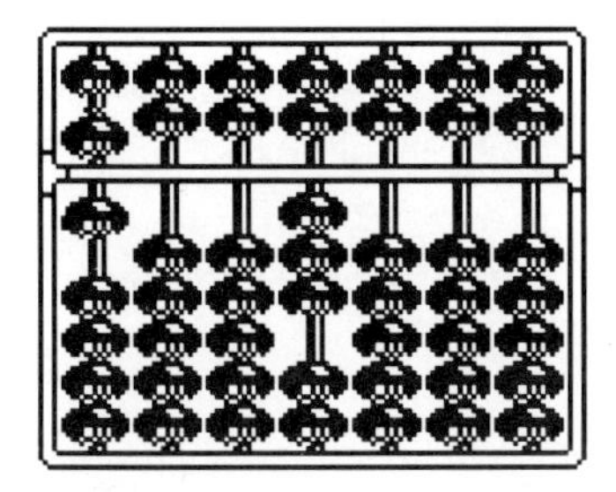

Figure 1.1
Abacus
Courtesy Brøderbund Software. Graphics created using the Print Shop. Copyright © Brøderbund Software, Inc., 1984.

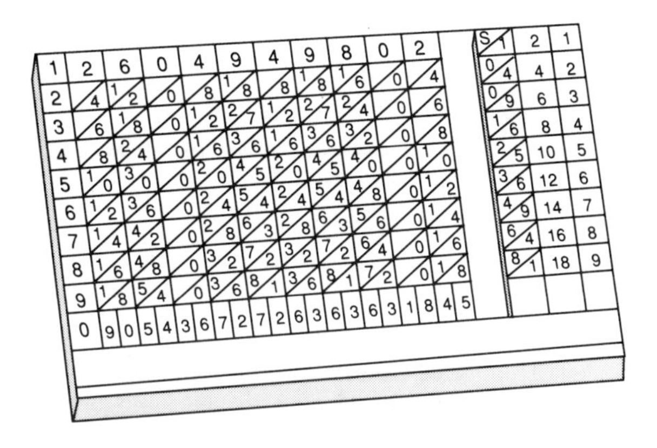

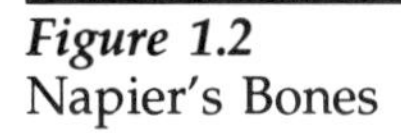

Figure 1.2
Napier's Bones

destroyed the parts before they could be assembled. Kepler died soon after the fire, and the prototype was never found, but a rough sketch of this machine survived and a model was built in the 1970s. It was too late, however, to help Pascal, who devised a calculator similar to Schickard's.

Blaise Pascal

Blaise Pascal, a child prodigy, was born in France in 1623. Before he had reached thirteen, Pascal had discovered an error in Descartes's geometry. At the age of sixteen he wanted to study mathematics, but his father, a tax collector, insisted young Pascal spend his time performing additions by hand. He was probably aggravated by the whole exercise, and he reacted by building a calculating machine. He built the first operating model of his calculating machine in 1642, which he called the **Pascaline** (Figure 1.3). During the next ten years, he built 50 more of these machines.

The Pascaline was a shoe-size brass box that operated with a system of gears and wheels. Since Pascal's machine was devised for English currency, the two right wheels were numbered for shillings and pence while the other wheels were numbered from 1 through 9 for pounds. The wheels could be read through holes at the top of the machine, and when a wheel made a complete turn, a notch caused the next wheel to the left to move up one number, thus performing addition. By reversing the revolutions, one could do subtraction. Considered the first mechanical calculator, the

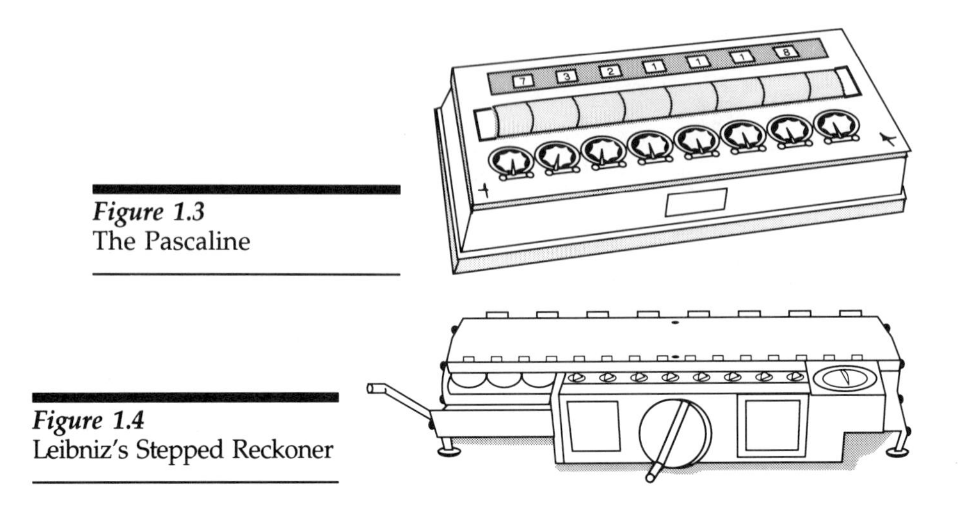

Figure 1.3
The Pascaline

Figure 1.4
Leibniz's Stepped Reckoner

Pascaline could handle numbers up to 999,999.99. Because of the expense to reproduce it, and because people feared it would put them out of work, the Pascaline was not a commercial success.

Gottfried Wilhelm Von Leibniz

Pascal's machine was the standard until Leibniz, a German mathematician, designed an instrument called the **Stepped Reckoner,** which he completed in 1694. **Baron Gottfried Wilhelm Von Leibniz's** machine was more versatile than Pascal's because it could do multiplication and division as well as addition and subtraction and it used cylinders instead of gears to do its calculations.

Unfortunately, the Stepped Reckoner and the Pascaline were not reliable machines because the technology at the time could not produce parts with the necessary precision. Leibniz's most important contribution to the computer's evolution was not this machine, but his notes on binary arithmetic—a system of counting that uses only two digits, 0 and 1. (For example, in the base 2, 0 is zero, 1 is one, 2 is represented by one and zero, 3 is represented by one and one and 4 is represented by one, zero and zero and so forth.) In Leibniz's Universe, the symbol 1 would represent existence and the symbol 0 nonexistence. Unfortunately, Leibniz never completed his work on binary arithmetic.[1]

In 1854, nearly two centuries later, George Boole devised a system of logic based on the binary system called Boolean Algebra. However, it wasn't until the late 1930s

1. Refer to Chapter 2 for a discussion of the binary code.

that inventors built a computer that used this binary system, the standard internal language of today's digital computers.

Joseph Marie Jacquard

Though not a calculating device, Jacquard's loom was the next invention of great significance in the development of the computer. In 1790, **Joseph Marie Jacquard** used punched cards to create patterns on fabric woven on a loom. The cards had holes punched in patterns, and these hole punches directed the threads up or down, thus producing the patterns. Jacquard's device was the forerunner of the key-punch machines (Figure 1.5).

All the mechanical gadgets discussed in the previous paragraphs were calculators that could do only arithmetic, but the first individual to conceptualize a real computer was Charles Babbage, a Cambridge mathematics professor.

Figure 1.5
Jacquard's Loom

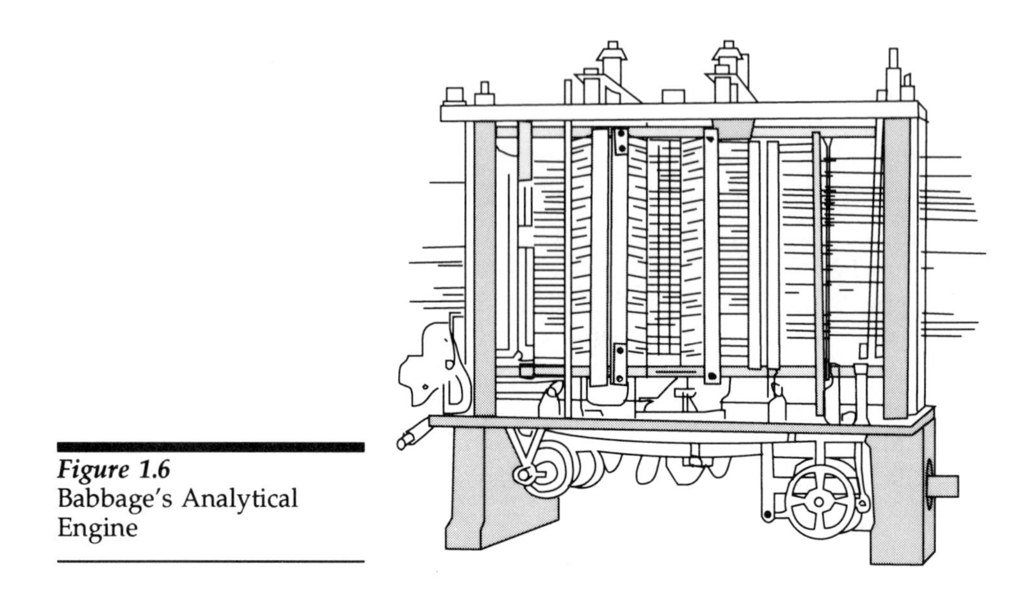

Figure 1.6
Babbage's Analytical Engine

Charles Babbage

Aggravated about the errors in the mathematical tables that were being printed, Babbage resigned his position at Cambridge to work on a machine that would solve this problem. He called this machine the "Difference Engine" because it worked on solving differential equations. Using government funds and his own resources, he labored on the computer for nineteen years, but was unable to complete it. Babbage constructed only a few components, and people referred to his engine with derision, calling it "Babbage's Folly."

After the government withdrew its funding, Babbage preceded to work on still another more sophisticated version of this machine which he called the **Analytical Engine.** A close personal friend of his, **Lady Agusta Ada Lovelace,** only daughter of Lord Bryon, tried to help him. She raised money for his invention and wrote a demonstration program for the Analytical Engine. Because of this program, she is considered the first computer programmer.

In 1835 Babbage designed a system with provision for printed data, a control unit, and an information storage unit. The Analytical Engine was never completed because of engineering problems and financial difficulties (Figure 1.6). Babbage was not able to see his dream realized because the construction of the machine required precision tools that did not exist then. He did not publish many details of his work although there were some notes from a lecture given at the British Association. Luckily, he did leave behind enough detailed drawings with a notebook and a portion of the machine. In 1906 Henry P. Babbage, Charles's son, was able to take these items and complete part of the engine, get it to compute, and publish samples of its work.

The logic of Babbage's machine was important for other computer inventors. Babbage is responsible for the two classifications of the computer: the "store," or memory, and the "mill," a processing unit that carries out the arithmetic calculations for the machine. For this achievement, he is called the "father of computers." Some historians have even said that all modern computers were descended directly from Babbage's Analytical Engine, the mechanical counterpart of today's electronic digital computer. It is, however, ironic that today historians hold Babbage in high esteem, but in his day he was considered a failure. Babbage died in poverty; his vision of a computer that would solve any number of problems would not be realized until the 20th century. However, just 19 years after he died, the punched card aspect of the Analytical Engine appeared in a working machine—a tabulator built by Herman Hollerith.

Herman Hollerith

No history would be complete without talking about the American inventor, **Herman Hollerith.** When Hollerith worked at the Census Bureau, he met Colonel John Shaw Billings, who was the director of the division of vital statistics. They became friends, and during an evening discourse, Billings discussed the possibility of a hypothetical machine that could do the mechanical work of tabulating the population. Billings envisioned the possibility of using cards with notches punched on the edges, and these notches would represent the individual's description. Hollerith was so fascinated with the idea he decided to leave his job at the Census Bureau to go to MIT to teach and work on this tabulating machine. Many years later Hollerith applied for several patents on punched-card data processing, and he devised several experimental test systems.

When Hollerith took out a patent for the first punch card calculator, he was offered a job in the Census Department by Robert Porter. He refused this offer because he was interested in winning the contract to do the 1890 census. In 1889, there was a contest held and Hollerith's system won by a landslide against two competing systems.

Hollerith's innovative tabulating machine (Figure 1.7) relied heavily on Jacquard's punched card idea. Hollerith designed his machine so that it pushed pins against cards that were the size of an old fashioned dollar bill. He had information on each person in the census punched on the cards. These holes represented characteristics of the population, such as sex, birthplace, number of children, etc. If a pin went through a hole, it made contact with a metal surface below and a circuit was completed. This census item was then counted and added to the total. If there was no hole, the census item was not counted and there was nothing added to the total. The census office bought fifty-six of Hollerith's machines and commissioned him to repair them. Because of Hollerith's invention, the census was completed in just two years as compared to seven years for the 1880 census.

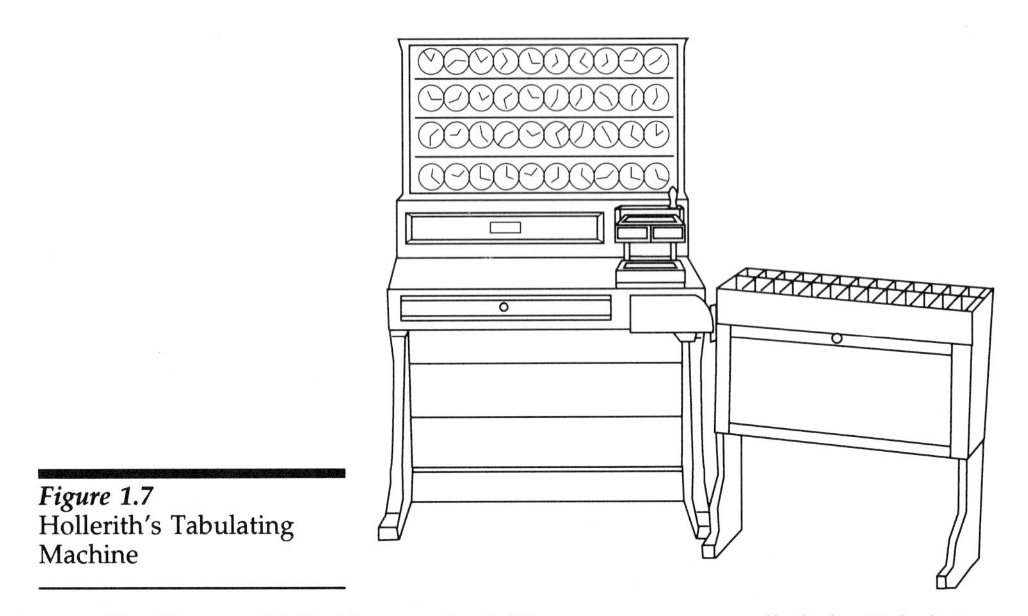

Figure 1.7
Hollerith's Tabulating Machine

Eventually, Herman Hollerith organized his own company called the Tabulating Machine Company. In the 1900s he rented out his more sophisticated tabulating machines for the census. His business prospered and merged with other companies. The company went through a series of name changes and the last name change came in 1924 when it became known as International Business Machines or IBM.

Let's conclude our discussion of these early pioneers with a summary of their achievements in Table 1.1:

Table 1.1 Computing Devices Before the 20th Century

Inventor	Invention	Year
Unknown	Abacus	3000 B.C.?
John Napier	Napier's Bones	1617
Wilhelm Schickard	Mechanical Calculator	1623
Blaise Pascal	Pascaline	1642
Gottfried Leibniz	Stepped Reckoner	1672
Joseph Marie Jacquard	Punched Card Loom	1804
Charles Babbage	Analytical Engine	1835
Herman Hollerith	Tabulating Machine	1887

During the 20th century, the Census Bureau quit using Hollerith's machines and bought a machine designed by James Powers. Powers founded a company called Powers Accounting Machine Co., which merged with others to become known as Remington Rand, then Sperry Rand. Today these companies are part of the conglomerate Unisys. During this time, Hollerith's Company and Powers' Company produced machines that primarily served the business community. However, the scientific community still needed machines that could do more complex processing and therefore there was a demand for scientific data processing machines.

The Modern Computer

In 1944 the age of the modern computer emerged. World War II created a need for better data handling that spurred on advances in technology and the development of computers. While the War was going on, a brilliant team of scientists and engineers (among them were Alan Turing, Max Newman, Ian Fleming, and Lewis Powell) gathered at Bletchley Park, north of London, to work on a machine that could solve the German secret code. They worked with electronic decoders to decipher the Germans' electromechanical teleprint, the Enigma. Unfortunately this innovative work was secretive, and much of it still remains classified.

Howard Aiken

During this period, **Howard Aiken** was working at Harvard to complete his research for his Ph.D. Because he had to do tedious calculations on non-linear, differential equations, he decided that he needed an automatic calculating machine to make the chore less arduous. In a memo written in 1937, he proposed to create a computer. Initially Aiken found little support at Harvard for his machine so he turned to private industry. Fortunately, IBM was taken with Aiken's idea and agreed to help back him in the production of the Mark I. Aiken headed a group of scientists whose task was to build a modern equivalent to Babbage's Analytical Engine. In 1943 the **Mark I,** also called the IBM Automatic Sequence Controlled Calculator, was completed at IBM Development Laboratories at Endicott, New York. It was 51 feet long, 8 feet high, and 2 feet thick, and it had 750,000 parts, 500 miles of wire, and weighed 5 tons. Noisy, but capable of three calculations per second, it accepted information by punched cards, then stored and processed this information. The results were printed on an electric typewriter. The first electromechanical computer was responsible for making IBM a giant in computer technology. Howard Aiken and IBM shortly afterwards parted company because of Aiken's arrogance. As documented, IBM had invested over one half a million dollars in the Mark I and in return for their investment, Thomas J. Watson, who was the head of

IBM, wanted the prestige of being associated with Harvard University. At the dedication ceremony for the Mark I, Dr. Howard Aiken boasted about his accomplishments without referring to IBM. This intentional oversight infuriated Watson, who shouted some blasphemies at Aiken before abruptly leaving the ceremony. Watson ended his association with Harvard. After the completion of the Mark I, IBM produced several machines that were similar to the Mark I, and Howard Aiken also built a series of machines (the Mark II, Mark III, and the Mark IV).

Besides building computers, Howard Aiken had many publications in the "Annals of Harvard Computation Laboratory Series." Perhaps his biggest contribution was the environment he helped to create at Harvard, enabling this institution to develop an illustrious program for computer scientists. Another interesting aside on Aiken pertains to the coining of the word *debug*. Aiken's computers had their share of bugs, so the use of this word was not uncommon. In 1945 the Mark II was housed in a building without air conditioning. Because it generated tremendous heat, the windows were left open. Suddenly this giant computer stopped working, and everyone was frantically attempting to discover the source of the problem. Grace Hooper and her co-workers found the culprit was a dead moth in a relay of the computer. They removed the moth with a tweezer and placed it in the Mark II logbook. When Aiken came back to see how things were going with his associates, they told him they had to debug the machine. Today the Mark II logbook is preserved in the Naval Museum in Dahlgren, Virginia.

After the Mark II, the computers were much faster because the moving parts were replaced by electrical circuits. There was a need now for computers that would operate faster and more efficiently.

John Atanasoff

In 1939 **John Atanasoff** designed and built the first electronic digital computer while working with **Clifford Berry,** a graduate student. Atanasoff built a prototype of an electronic computer at Iowa State. Atanasoff and Berry then went to work on an operational model called the ABC, the Atanasoff-Berry Computer. This computer, completed in 1942, used binary logic circuitry and had regenerative memory. No one paid much attention to Atanasoff's computer except John Mauchly, a physicist and faculty member from the University of Pennsylvania. In 1941 he took a train to Ames, Iowa, to learn more about the ABC. He stayed five days as Atanasoff's house guest where he had an opportunity to read Atanasoff's handbook explaining the electronic theories and construction plans of the ABC (Mollenhoff, 1990). Mauchly then returned home to the Moore School of Electrical Engineering at the University of Pennsylvania where he became involved in a secret military project with J. Presper Eckert, an astronomer. (He never told Eckert of his visit with Atanasoff in Ames Iowa.)

John Mauchly and J. Presper Eckert

With the emergence of World War II, the military wanted an extremely fast computer that would be capable of doing the thousands of computations necessary for compiling ballistic tables for new Naval guns and missiles. Mauchly and Eckert believed the only way to solve this problem was with an electronic digital machine so they worked on this project together. In 1946, **Mauchly and Eckert** completed an operational electronic digital computer called the **ENIAC** (Electronic Numerical Integrator and Calculator). This machine was not only based on the work of Mauchly and Eckert, but also derived from the ideas of Atanasoff's unpatented work.[2] It worked on a decimal system and had all the features of today's computers. The ENIAC, shown in Figure 1.8, was tremendous in size, filling up a very large room and weighing 30 tons. It conducted electricity through 18,000 vacuum tubes, generating tremendous heat.

This computer had to have special air conditioning to keep it cool and operated at a rate that was 500 times faster than any electromechanical computer of that day. A problem that took an electromechanical machine thirty to thirty-two hours to calculate this machine solved in three minutes. The ENIAC's limitations were a small memory and a problem in shifting from one program to another. When the user wanted to shift to another program, the machine had to be rewired. These problems might have taken years to solve if it hadn't been for a meeting between Herman Goldstine, a mathematician and liaison officer for the ENIAC project, and **John Von Neumann,** a famous logician and mathematician. Because of that meeting John Von Neumann joined the Moore team which was about to embark on a new computer called the **EDVAC,** the Electronic Discrete Variable Automatic Computer.

John Von Neumann

After **John Von Neumann's** arrival in Philadelphia, he helped the Moore group get the contract for the EDVAC. He also assisted the group with the logical make-up of this machine. As a result of the Moore team's collaboration, a major break through came in the form of the stored-program concept. Until this time, a computer stored its program externally, either on plugboards, punched tape, or cards. The ENIAC used 18,000 vacuum

2. Atanasoff's work was ignored for years; he was rejected by IBM, Remington Rand and Iowa State. He was unheard of until 1973 when Atanasoff received recognition as one of the fathers of computing. At this time, Sperry–Rand brought a suit against Honeywell and Federal District Judge Earl R. Larson invalidated the ENIAC Patent. Judge Larson said that Eckert and Mauchly had derived some of their ideas from Atanasoff's unpatented work.

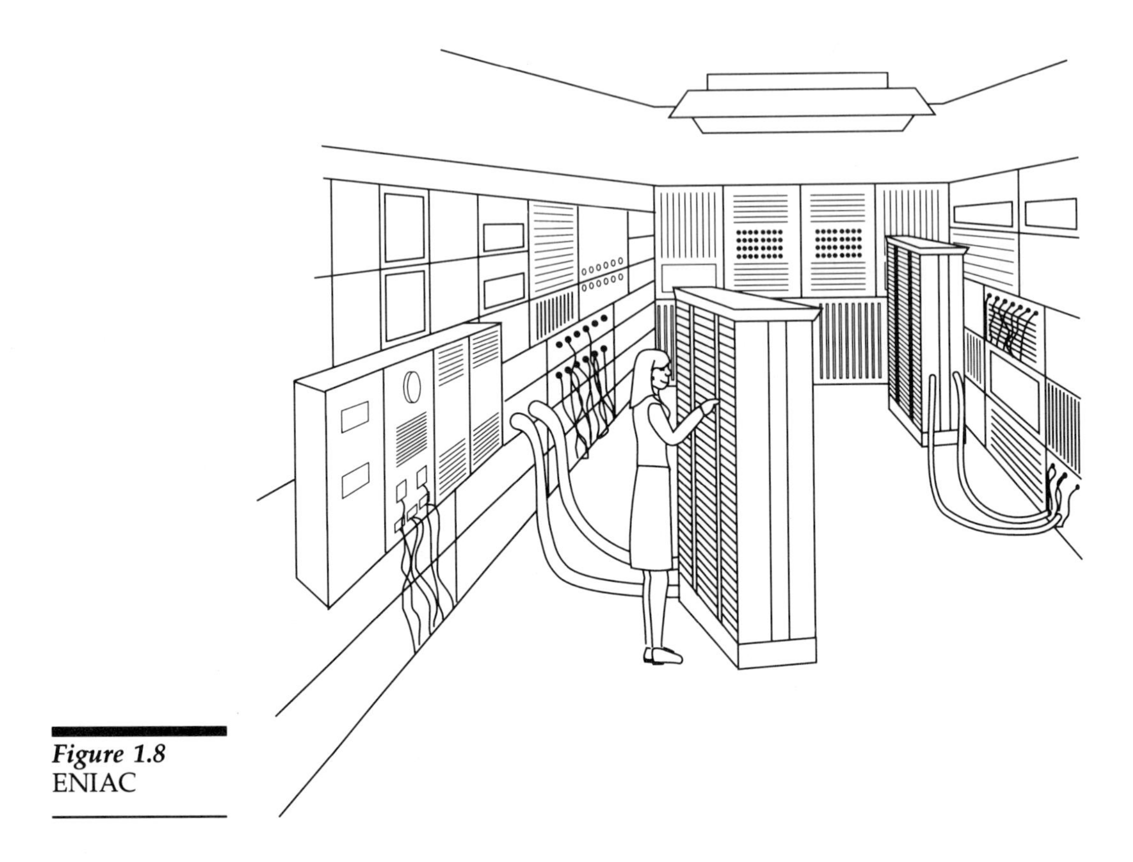

Figure 1.8
ENIAC

tubes and required a pair of these tubes joined in a particular manner to hold in memory a single bit of data.

Mauchly and Eckert discovered that one mercury delay line could replace dozens of these vacuum tubes. They figured that the delay lines would mean a gigantic savings in cost of tubes and space. The tiny racks of delay lines replaced the vacuum tubes; this enabled the computer's memory to take up very little space. This advance contributed to the design of the EDVAC Computer.

Using the EDVAC, a computer user stored his information in memory in the same form as data. The machine then manipulated the stored information. Von Neumann was a member of this group that spent hours discussing the stored-program concept. Though he was not the sole creator, there is no question that it was Von Neumann's original idea to have the computer store its numbers serially and process them that way—an innovation that made the EDVAC design much faster, simpler, and smaller. However, the machine could still do only one thing at a time.

In 1945 a controversy arose involving Von Neumann and the Moore Group. Von Neumann offered to write a report on EDVAC, an idea supported by the EDVAC staff. He finished the first draft, without references, and sent it to Goldstine, a member of the ENIAC group. In the report, Von Neumann did not give credit for the stored-program idea to the Moore Group. Unfortunately, Goldstine, without Mauchly and Eckert's knowledge, put a cover on Von Neumann's first draft report, and called it "Report on the EDVAC." Goldstine put Von Neuman's name down as the sole author and distributed it. This angered Mauchly, Eckert, and others because the paper contained almost no reference to the Moore Group. They feared that credit would go completely to Neumann, and that it would violate their rights for a patent. In retrospect, Von Neumann probably never intended to take credit for what he didn't do. He merely sent out a first draft that Goldstine prematurely distributed. However, Von Neumann did not try to rectify the situation by disavowing credit. This paper created a sensation, for it contained a model for computer structure and operation that was really the theoretical basis for the modern digital computer. Although Von Neuman and his group were credited with using the stored-program concept, theirs was not the first machine. Those honors go to a group at Cambridge University in England who developed the EDSAC, Electronic Delay Storage Automatic Computer. Moreover, the EDSAC and the EDVAC computers were the first to use binary notation.

Before 1951 the computer had been built on an individual basis and not manufactured on a larger scale. In 1951, with the arrival of the UNIVAC, the era of **commercial** computers began. Only two years later IBM started shipping their IBM 701, and other companies manufactured computers such as the Burrough E 101 and the Honeywell Datamatic 1000. The computers that were developed during the 1950s and 1960s were called "first generation computers" because they had one common feature, the vacuum tube.

Generations of Computers

Since its inception, the computer has gone through several stages of development. Generally writers classify these technological advances in generations, a marketing term. Even though there is some overlap, it is convenient to view the computer's technological development in this manner.

The First Generation of Computers

The **first generation** of computers began in the 1940s and extended into the 1950s. During this period, computers used **vacuum tubes** extensively, like the one in Figure 1.9, to conduct electricity.

The employment of vacuum tubes made the computers big, bulky, and expensive because the tubes were continually burning out and having to be replaced. At this time, computers were classified by the main memory storage device they used. The Univac I used an ingenious device called the "mercury delay line" that relied on ultrasonic pulses. Mercury delay line storage was a reliable device, but it was very slow as compared to modern storage devices. Another storage device, an electrostatic one based on the Williams Tube from Manchester University in England, stored data in patterns of electric charges on the face of a cathode ray tube. There was a debate over the reliability of this storage method, causing it to disappear quickly.

During the first generation, pioneering work was done in the area of magnetic storage. Data were recorded on magnetic tapes and magnetic drums, and these storage devices were used for auxiliary memory. In magnetic tape storage, the data were recorded on tapes like the audio cassette tapes used today. Data were held on the tapes in serial manner, which meant the user could not access the information directly, resulting in slower access time. Similar to magnetic tapes were magnetic drums where data were recorded on spinning drums. These two means of storage were important until magnetic disks appeared in the third generation.

The Second Generation of Computers

The **second generation** of computers began when the **transistor** (Figure 1.10) replaced the vacuum tube in the late 1950s. In 1947, Bardeen, Brattain, and Shockley, a team of physicists working at Bell Labs, invented the transistor. In 1956 they shared the Nobel Prize for this invention. The transistor, an electrically operated switch similar to an old-fashioned relay, was a landmark in the development of the computer. "When the transistor is activated it bridges the gap between two wires and allows current to flow," (Freedman, 1991). The transistor is created by melting silicon, an element found in common sand. The transistor conducts electricity more efficiently, consumes less energy, needs less space, and generates less heat. Since transistors do not heat up like vacuum tubes, they did not have a serious burn-out problem. The computer with transistors became smaller, more reliable, faster, and a less expensive machine than a computer with vacuum tubes.

Small and medium size businesses now found it more economical to buy computers. A new development that started in the early 1950s then came to fruition during the second generation. Magnetic-Core Memory was responsible for data being retrieved and stored

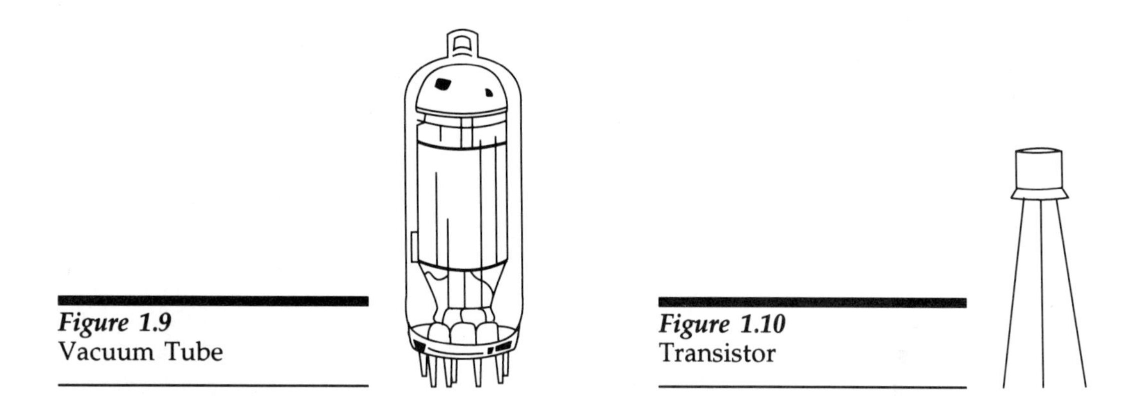

Figure 1.9
Vacuum Tube

Figure 1.10
Transistor

at a millionth of a second. Core memory became synonymous with the main memory of the computer.

The Third Generation of Computers

The **third generation** of computers began in 1964 with the introduction of the IBM 360, the computer that pioneered the use of **integrated circuits** on a chip. In that year computer scientists developed tiny integrated circuits and installed hundreds of these transistors on a single silicon chip, which was as small as a finger tip. The computer became smaller, more reliable, and less expensive than ever before. The integrated circuit chips made it possible for minicomputers to find their way into classrooms, homes, and businesses. They were almost 1000 times faster than the first generation of computers, and manufacturers mass produced them at a low price, making them more accessible to small companies.

The integrated circuits were now used as main memory, and magnetic disks replaced magnetic tape as auxiliary memory. These disks allowed information to be retrieved nonsequentially, speeding up access time. Computer terminals flourished, and an increasing number of individuals used them to communicate with computers at other locations. In the beginning the terminal was like a typewriter and produced a printed output. As time went on, the video display terminals replaced the punched cards for entering data and programs into the computer. Hollerith's cards became obsolete.

The 1970s began with the development of **large-scale integration (LSI).** It was a method that put hundreds of thousands of transistors on a single silicon chip. This chip was as minute as a speck of dust and so delicate that miniature scientific instruments were devised to create it. The development of the LSI led to embedded computers inserted in cameras, television sets, and cars. Another result of LSI was the arrival of the personal computer.

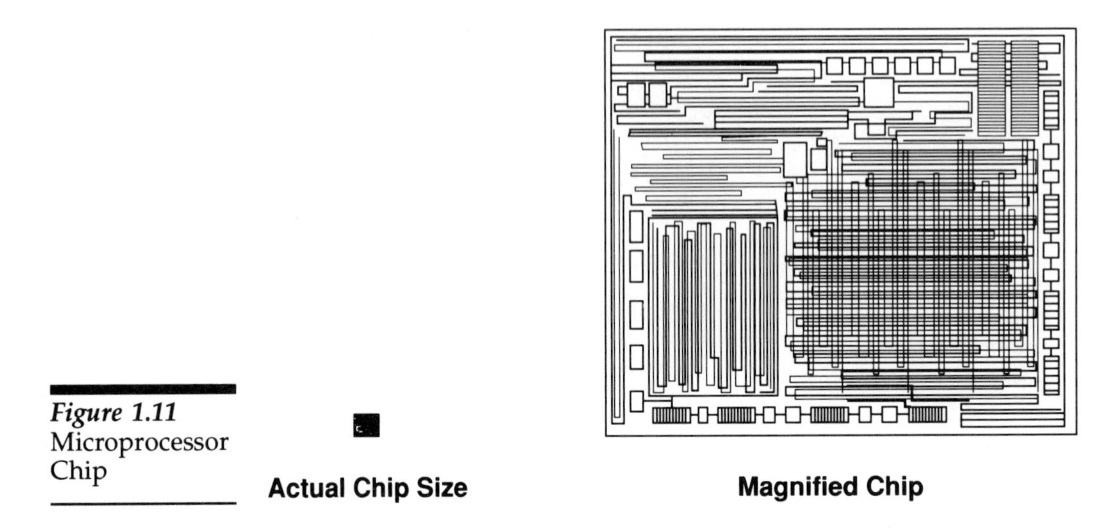

Figure 1.11 Microprocessor Chip

The Fourth Generation of Computers

The development of microprocessor technology resulted in the **fourth generation.** The microprocessor chip is a central processing unit, the brains of the computer, built on a single chip. It is hard to believe, but on this single chip the processing and computing take place. In the future, there will probably not be more circuits added to the surface of this chip, but the chip will be built in overlapping layers.

In 1968 Gilbert Hyatt designed a computer to fit on a silicon microchip the size of a fingernail. Hyatt wanted the world to recognize him as the inventor who made the computer revolution occur. After a legal battle lasting 20 years, the U.S. patent and trademark office gave Hyatt patent No. 4,942.516 for a "Single Chip integrated Circuit Computer Architecture" (Takahashi, 1990). In 1971 a group of individuals working at Intel introduced the 4004 microprocessor. They intended that this chip be used in items such as the calculator because the chip lacked the power needed to run a microcomputer. Three years later they introduced the 8080 version that was capable of running the processing unit of a computer. Radio Electronics, in 1974, published an article on a home built computer using this technology. Subsequently, *Popular Electronics* ran a story on Altair, a computer that had the 8080 chip. In the article, the writers mentioned that Micro Instrumentation Technology Systems was selling kits for this computer. The response to this article was overwhelming and it inspired other companies to develop new products.

Apple computers came into being in the 1970s. Steve Wozniak and Steve Jobs worked out of a garage where they began selling Apples for the price of $666.66. Figure 1.12 shows the Apple I. Wozniak and Jobs placed ads in hobbyist publications with the money that they raised from selling their personal possessions. This duo

Figure 1.12
Apple I Computer
Courtesy of Apple Computer Inc.

provided software for their machines free of charge and they achieved a modicum of success. They hired professional help and support and in 1977 introduced a new fully assembled version of their Apple machine called the Apple II, a historic moment for computers. The Apple II was the first computer accepted by business users because of a spreadsheet simulation program called VisiCalc. It was a compact desktop computer with 4K of memory, priced at $1, 298, with a clock speed of 1.0.

Four years later, IBM entered the computer market with the IBM personal computer, referred to as the *IBM PC.* This computer was tremendously successful and became a best seller. Because of IBM's successful entrance in the field, other computer makers chose to capitalize on its popularity by developing their own clones. These personal computers had many of the same features as the IBM machines and could run the same programs. The widespread use of the personal computers now became a reality.

The Fifth Generation of Computers

For the **fifth generation,** there will be computer chips that are unbelievably fast. In 1991, Cal Tech unveiled their Touchstone Delta Supercomputer that can perform 8.6 billion calculations per second (Hamilton, 1991). Presently the large Japanese firms control 90% of the world market. The dominance of Japan in the chip market has been a major concern of the U.S. However, current trends indicate further advances in chip design by U.S. companies such as IBM and Intel.

As the power of the computer builds, inventors will have to find new ways to deliver information to the machine. In the 1990s the erasable optical disks will become a viable alternative to the magnetic disk. Optical disks have much greater capacity for storage than the magnetic disk, and they will probably replace all the magnetic tape and disk media. The data storage system may come in the form of laser cards the size of a small plastic credit card that could hold gigabytes of information.

Now there are computers that carry out thousands of operations simultaneously, and the execution rates of these machines are measured in "teraflops." A teraflop is equivalent to one trillion floating-point operations per second. A one teraflop machine could lead to a suitcase size computer that is as powerful as today's fastest supercomputers. These powerful computers can solve the most complex problems in science, finance, and technology. The next generation of computers will be based on logical inference. There will be extensive use of **artificial intelligence.** "Artificial Intelligence is a broad range of applications that exhibit human intelligence and behavior . . ." (Freeman, 1991). The machine is able to do such things as make decisions, draw conclusions, understand everyday speech, and learn from experience. There are already some accomplishments today in this area. To name a few, there are medical programs that aid in diagnosing various diseases and mining programs that help mining companies in their explorations. Artificial intelligence has been directed to board games such as chess and backgammon. Some of the chess and backgammon programs defeat the people who created them. Alan Turing proposed a test in 1950 that could determine if a computer was reasoning like a human being. Some computers are getting close, and who knows—in years to come people might prefer talking to a computer rather than a real person.

In the next generation of machines, computers will communicate in English or Chinese rather than a computer language. They will respond to a human voice, not a keyboard or disk drive. Today some machines use voice synthesizers and computers are beginning to talk more like people. The earlier models were ridiculous because of the zombielike quality of their speech.

Computers keep decreasing in size and there is no limit to how small they could become. Many systems will have handwriting recognition software that will let the user employ a pencil-like stylus as the input device, along with touch screens. Many portable computer makers are coming out with pen devices for their machines. NEC introduced the first active matrix thin film transistor color notebook computer. This notebook computer, the UltarLite, weighs 7.4 pounds, uses Intel's 25-MHZ 386SL chip set and has superior color capabilities (Barr, 1992). Voice and data will probably be transmitted by a built-in cellular radio. Printers, projectors, and video cameras will probably communicate through an infrared interface similar to television's remote devices that exist today. The author can only speculate on what other amazing innovations the fifth generation of computers will bring. After all, it took thousands of years and many inventions to arrive at the first electromechanical computer and then only a short time later the UNIVAC appeared on the scene. The development of the computer has become like a stone rolling down a hill, gathering other stones and creating an explosion in technology. It is such a rapid changing field that when a user buys a computer today, tomorrow it is out of date.

Summary

In the beginning inventors who were interested in processing information wanted devices to simplify tedious arithmetic calculations. In the 1800s, Jacquard used punched cards in his loom to produce beautiful patterns, an invention that inspired Charles Babbage; he used the concept of the punched card in his Analytical Engines. Babbage's work was forgotten and only looked at again by the inventors in the 1900s. Near the end of the 1800s Herman Hollerith improved upon Jacquard's idea and pioneered processing of statistical data in the 1890 census. Today this application is a major one for the computer. In the 1900s inventors constructed the earliest electromechanical computer, quickly replaced by the faster electronic computer.

The machines that superseded the early experimental machines were classified in generations. In the first generation, computers used vacuum tubes to conduct electricity. In the second generation, transistors replaced tubes, followed in the 1970s by integrated circuits in the third generation. The fourth generation saw the advent of large scale, integrated circuit chips. For the fifth generation of computers, the reader will probably see the development of artificial intelligence, computers based on logical inference and parallel processing.

Let's test for chapter comprehension by taking a short mastery test and doing some classroom activities. After these activities, there are some suggested readings and references.

Chapter Mastery Test

1. Discuss briefly the contributions made to the computer field by the following individuals:
   a. Howard Aiken
   b. Charles Babbage
   c. Blaise Pascal
   d. Herman Hollerith
   e. John Atanasoff
2. Identify and place in correct order five of the major inventions in the field of computing.
3. Differentiate among the generations of computers by their technological advances.
4. Explain the significance of punched cards and vacuum tubes in the development of earlier computers.
5. Explain the importance of transistors and microprocessors in the development of modern computers.
6. What was George Boole's lasting contribution to computer history?
7. What computer opportunities would a sixth grader have in 1953 as opposed to a sixth grader in 2000?
8. Compare two early mechanical calculators and their inventors.
9. Why was Hollerith's tabulating machine for the 1890 census significant for the future of computing?

10. What was the connection between Herman Hollerith and Joseph Jacquard?
11. Explain the importance of the discovery that made it possible for us to have personal computers.
12. Discuss the contribution of Dr. John Von Neumann to computer technology.
13. Explain why Charles Babbage was born in the wrong time.
14. What were some of the problems of first generation computers?
15. What are Steve Jobs' and Steve Wozniak's major achievements, in the computer field?

Classroom Projects

1. Prepare a paper on the 1973 court trial between Sperry Rand and Honeywell. In this case Judge Larson ruled that, "Eckert and Mauchly did not themselves invent the electronic digital computer, but instead derived the subject matter from one John V. Atanasoff."
2. Investigate three computer magazines for recent developments in computer technology during the last 5 years. Write a brief summary of the findings.
3. Using a computer timeline program like Tom Snyder's TimeLiner, list at least ten significant, important, computer events from 1863 to 1989.
4. Prepare an in-depth research report on the life of an important inventor and his/her contribution to the history of computers.
5. What are today's schools covering in terms of computer history? What are second or seventh graders learning?

Suggested Readings and References

Austrian, G. *Herman Hollerith: Forgotten Giant of Information Processing.* New York: Columbia University Press, 1982.

Asimov, Isaac. *How Did We Find Out About Computers?* New York: Walker, 1984.

Aspray, William. "John Von Neumann's Contributions to Computing and Computer Science." *Annals of the History of Computing,* 11,(3), p. 189.

Barr, Christopher. "First Active-Matrix Color in a Laptop Dazzles." *PC Magazine* Vol. 11 No. 1 (January 14, 1992): 40.

Bernstein, J. *The Analytical Engine.* New York: Morrow, 1981.

Burks, A., and Burks, A. "The ENIAC: First General-Purpose Electronic Computer." *Annals of the History of Computing.* (October 1981): 310–400.

Diebold, John, ed. *The World of the Computer.* New York: Random House, 1973.

Evans, Christopher. *The Micro Millennium.* New York: The Viking Press, 1979.

Evans, Christopher. *The Making of the Micro: A History of the Computer.* New York: Van Nostrand Reinhold, 1981.

Feigenbaum, Edward A., and Pamela McCorduck. *The Fifth Generation.* Reading, Ma: Addison-Wesley Publishing Company, 1983.

Flynn, L. "Apple Boosts CD ROM Market With New Drive." *INFO World.* (March 1988): 31.

Freedman, A. *The Computer Glossary.* 15th ed. New York: Amacom, 1991.

Hamilton, Denise. "New Supercomputer at Caltech Ranks as the World's Fastest." *Los Angeles Times,* Business Section, B2, June 1, 1991.

Gardner, David, W. "Will the Inventor of the First Digital Computer Please Stand UP?" *Datamation 20* (February 1974): 84–90.

Goldstine, H. *The Computer from Pascal to Von Neumann.* Princeton, N.J.: Princeton University Press, 1972.

LaPlante, A. "IBM Details Claims It Has Developed the World's Fastest DRAM Chip." *INFO World. 11,* (23).

Metropolis, N., J. Howlett, and G. C. Rota, eds. *A History of Computing in the Twentieth Century.* New York: Academic Press, 1980.

Mollenhoff, Clark R. "Forgotten Father of the Computer." *The World & I.* (March 1990): 319–332.

Moreau, Rene. *The Computer Comes of Age: The People, the Hardware, and the Software.* Translated by J. Howlett. Cambridge, Massachusetts: MIT Press, 1984.

Morrison, P., and E. Morrison, eds. *Charles Babbage and His Calculating Engines.* New York: Dover, 1961.

Naisbitt, John. *Megatrends: Ten New Directions Transforming Our Lives.* New York: Warner Books, 1982.

Naisbitt, John. *Megatrends 2000: Ten New Directions for the 1990s.* New York: Morrow, 1990.

Niemiec, Richard P., and Richard J. Walberg. "From Teaching Machines to Microcomputers: Some Milestones in the History of Computer-Based Instruction." *Journal of Research on Computing in Education.* 21, (3) (Spring 1989): 263.

Pullan, J. M. *A History of the Abacus.* New York: Praeger Publishers, 1968.

Ralston, Anthon, and C. L. Meek, eds. *Encyclopedia of Computer Science.* New York: Petrocelli, 1976.

Ritchie, David. *The Computer Pioneers: The Making of the Modern Computer.* New York: Simon and Schuster, 1986.

Rochester, J., and J. Gantz. *The Naked Computer.* New York: Morrow, 1983.

Rosenberg, J. M. *The Computer Profits.* New York: MacMillan, 1959.

Smarte, Gene, and Andrew Reinhardt. "15 Years of Bits, Bytes and Other Great Moments: A Look at Key Events in Byte, the Computer Industry." *Byte 15, (9), (September 1, 1990): 369–400.*

Slater, Robert. *Portraits in Silicon.* Cambridge, Massachusetts: MIT Press, 1987.

Takahashi, D. "A Dogged Inventor Makes the Computer Industry Say: Hello, Mr. Chip." *Los Angeles Times,* Business Section, October 21, 1990.

Zorpette, Glen. "Science and Medicine." *Los Angeles Times,* December 30, 1991, page B-5.

Getting Started on the Computer

2

Objectives

Upon completing this chapter the student will be able to:

1. Discuss how the basic components of a computer system operate.
2. Explain the following terms: Random Access Memory (RAM), Read Only Memory (ROM), bit, byte, kilobyte, American Standard Code for Information Interchange (ASCII).
3. Be familiar with the Macintosh operating system and how it works.
4. List three precautions the user should follow when handling floppy disks.
5. Give the procedure involved in
   a. formatting or initializing a disk
   b. making a backup copy of a disk
   c. copying or deleting a file

Computer Classification

Computers are frequently divided into categories: the mainframes, the minicomputers, and the microcomputers. In the past, there was a technical distinction among these computers, but today the differences refer to cost and speed. These categories have become blurred because many new microcomputers have the same capabilities of the old mainframes and the classification system is convenient for discussion purposes only.

In the early 1960s all computers were called mainframes because the term referred to the cabinet that held the central processing unit. As time progressed, a very large computer was called a mainframe computer. Costing many thousands of dollars, mainframes with enormous memory and speed took up the space of standard size classroom. Because of the machine's memory, it could dispatch complex programs very quickly and it could execute these programs while many individuals utilized the computer simultaneously. A team of specialists usually managed the machine at a prepared site and large corporations or financial institutions used this computer. Mainframes were usually connected to terminals that resembled small computers. These terminals sent information to the mainframe and received information from the mainframe in the same building or even in another city. If the terminals were in another city, they used the telephone as a means of communication with the mainframe.

The largest and fastest of the mainframe computers are called **supercomputers.** These machines are produced by the United States and Japan and have the most advanced processing abilities. They are state of the art machines costing millions of dollars and able to execute hundreds of millions of instructions in a second. In the mid-1990s this processing speed will be one trillion calculations per second (Cray Research Incorporated). In the early days, government laboratories developed these computers under top secrecy. For years the U.S. government was the only market for these supercomputers and only a few scientists had access to these machines. These individuals did not develop the machine's capabilities aggressively because the government did not allow it. In the 1980s access to the supercomputers increased, and today they are used worldwide.

Cray Computers was the only American company to manufacture supercomputers until this company divided into two companies in May of 1989 to become Cray Research Incorporated and Cray Computer Corporation. Cray Research Incorporated produces the standard silicon technology with eight multiprocessors, currently having an installed systems base of 287 machines, while Cray Computer corporation, led by Seymour Cray, is working on a Gallium Arsenide base computer. Because the supercomputers are so expensive, the Aerospace industry, the military, the National Weather Service, and oil conglomerates are the primary users. According to technology analysts, eventually the supercomputers will take over the mainframe industry.

In 1965, Digital Equipment Corporation (DEC) introduced the **minicomputer.** Universities and large companies needed a machine that did not require a staff of professionals or additional room space, and the minicomputer met this need. This machine was smaller and less costly than the mainframes and usually fit in a large size cabinet in one corner of a room. The minicomputer did not have the diversified input/output devices of the Mainframe or its memory capacity. Like the mainframe, the minicomputer could handle more than one task at a time, but its terminals were usually in the same building or room. They were used in small businesses and by school districts. The minicomputer was still too expensive and too sophisticated for most individuals. Because it cost less than the mainframe, this computer was prevalent until the microcomputer came on the scene in the mid–1970s.

The **microcomputer** came into being because the computer engineers were able to etch many circuits on a single chip. This advance in computer technology produced a computer that was less costly, more powerful, and smaller than the minicomputer. Today the microcomputer is a powerful piece of equipment, small enough to go on a desk or fit in a briefcase. Because of its accessibility, this machine can be used by anyone who wants to take the time and effort to learn how to use it.

A microcomputer was usually called a *personal computer* or a *business computer*. Personal machines had a predominance of educational software developed for them: home management, computer literacy, and word processing programs. For instance, the Apple IIGS, Apple IIC+, and the Apple IIe had an abundance of education software. Business machines, however, like the IBM, IBM compatibles, and the Macintosh had an abundance of business software. The business software consisted of complex spreadsheets, elaborate data bases, professional word processing programs, statistical applications, and scientific programs. Now these distinctions are not as clear cut and educational software and business software are developed for all machines.

This computer book is about microcomputers, so whenever the word *computer* is used, it is referring to a microcomputer. To appreciate the beauty and sophistication of these machines, let's spend a little time explaining what a computer is and how it operates.

What is a Computer?

A computer is a machine that can handle huge amounts of information at an incredible speed. Computers do not have brains, feelings, or the ability to solve their own problems; they can only solve problems that people instruct them to solve. A typical computer system might have a monitor, keyboard, printer, mouse, internal disk drive and a hard disk drive. Figure 2.1 is an example of a Macintosh and its components.

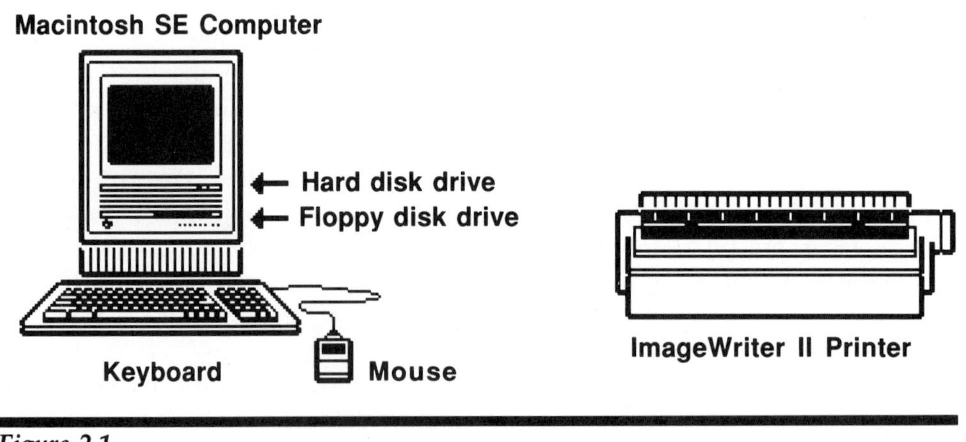

Figure 2.1
Macintosh SE Computer and its Components
Copyright T/Maker Company.

A computer performs four tasks:

1. Receives input such as figures, facts, or a set of instructions.
2. Stores information by placing it in its memory.
3. Processes the data, meaning the computer acts on this information.
4. Outputs the information by generating the results of the processing.

Professor Friedman's research study serves as a concrete example of how the computer performs the preceding four tasks. The Professor is conducting a research study and she has collected her data carefully. She now wants the computer to do some statistical analysis on it, so she loads her statistical program into the computer and chooses analysis of variance. Next, she enters her data into the computer by using the keyboard. The computer stores the data she enters in memory and then processes this information by performing the necessary statistical calculations. The central processing unit of the computer, discussed later in this chapter, does this analysis. The professor sees the results of the analysis on the screen or as a print out from the printer.

From this example, the reader should have some idea of how the computer works, so let's continue by examining the computer in more detail. A computer system is just interconnected components consisting of a central processing unit and the peripheral devices connected to it, along with the computer's operating system. The central processor, or CPU, is contained on one single chip called a *microprocessor.* The memory or RAM (Random Access Memory) and ROM (Read Only Memory) of the computer are also contained on computer chips. Before discussing these various chips, let's define the term *computer chip.*

The Computer Chip

A computer chip (Figure 2.2) is a silicon wafer, approximately 1/16 inch square and 1/30th of an inch thick, which holds from a couple dozen to several million electronic components. (The term *chip* is synonymous with *integrated circuit.*) Computer chips are encased in plastic to protect them, and metal pins enable these chips to be plugged into a computer circuit board. Figure 2.3 shows a chip encased in its plastic protection. Looking carefully at this chip, the reader can see tiny circuits etched on the metal. On one of these chips there are thousands of circuits connected to each other. The process of putting these circuits on one chip is called *Large Scale Integration (LSI) or Very Large Scale Integration (VLSI).* This complex procedure, which involves engineers, plotters, photography, baking, and magnetism is responsible for silicon chips being produced in large quantities at a very low cost. Today there are several million transistors on a single chip, and eventually wafer scale integration will exist with these circuits built in overlapping layers. The microcomputer has computer chips

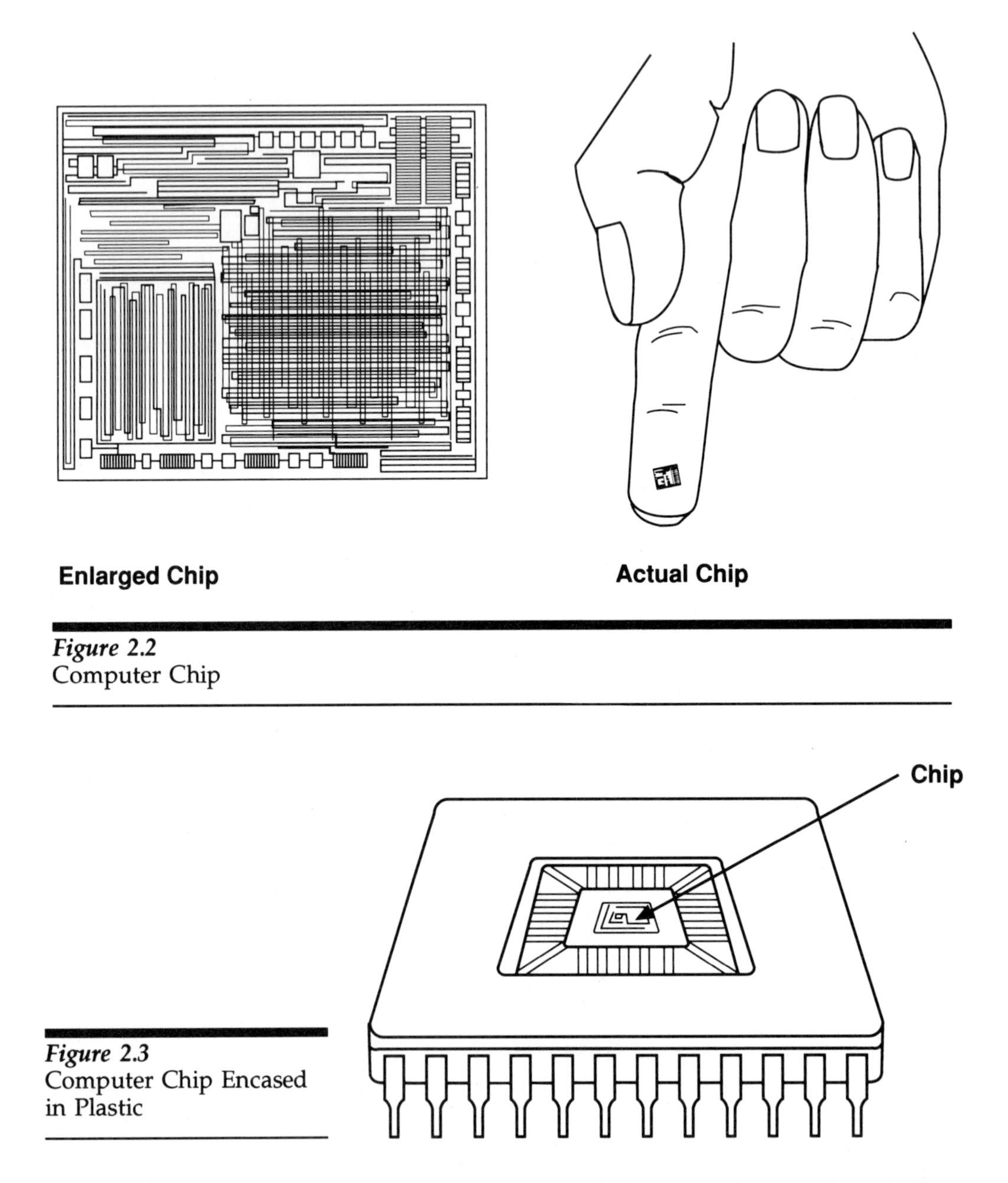

Figure 2.2
Computer Chip

Figure 2.3
Computer Chip Encased in Plastic

and other components mounted on a flat board called a printed circuit board (Figure 2.4) and the RAM chips, ROM chips, and the CPU chip are plugged into this board.

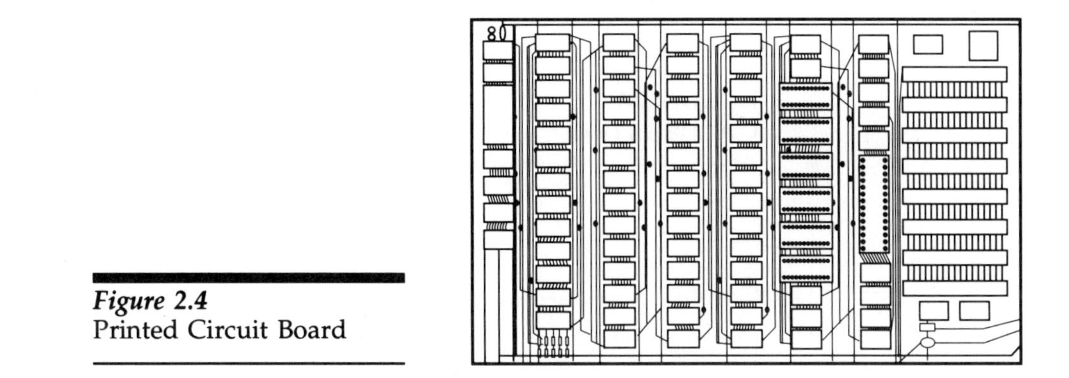

Figure 2.4
Printed Circuit Board

The other side of this board is printed with electrical conductive pathways between the components. A circuit board in 1960 connected discrete components together, while the boards in the 1990s connect chips together with each one containing hundreds of thousands of elementary components (Freedman, 1991). Computer systems have different components on their boards and their is no standard way of designing them. Nevertheless, the main component of any computer system is the Central Processing Unit, the brain of the computer.

Central Processing Unit

The central processor, also called the processor, is the computing part of the computer. A personal computer's central processor, or CPU, is contained on one single chip called a *microprocessor,* which is smaller than a fingernail. This unit is essential because it controls the way the computer operates. Whenever a programmer gives instructions to the computer, the processor executes these instructions. The central processor gets instructions from memory and carries out the instructions, then goes back to get the next set of instructions. This procedure is repeated until the task is completed. The processor carries out the instructions alone or it tells other components to follow the instructions.

The Central Processing Unit (Figure 2.5) consists of three components: the control unit, the arithmetic unit, and the logic unit. For most microcomputers, the arithmetic unit and the logic unit are combined and referred to as the *Arithmetic Logic Unit, ALU.*

The control unit verifies that the instructions are carried out by the computer; it acts like an officer who directs traffic. It has the power to transfer instructions to the main memory for storage and takes the information that is being processed from the main memory. The control unit sends information to and from the arithmetic logic unit. The Arithmetic Logic Unit carries out all the arithmetic operations and logical decisions. Since the central processing unit can work only on small amounts of

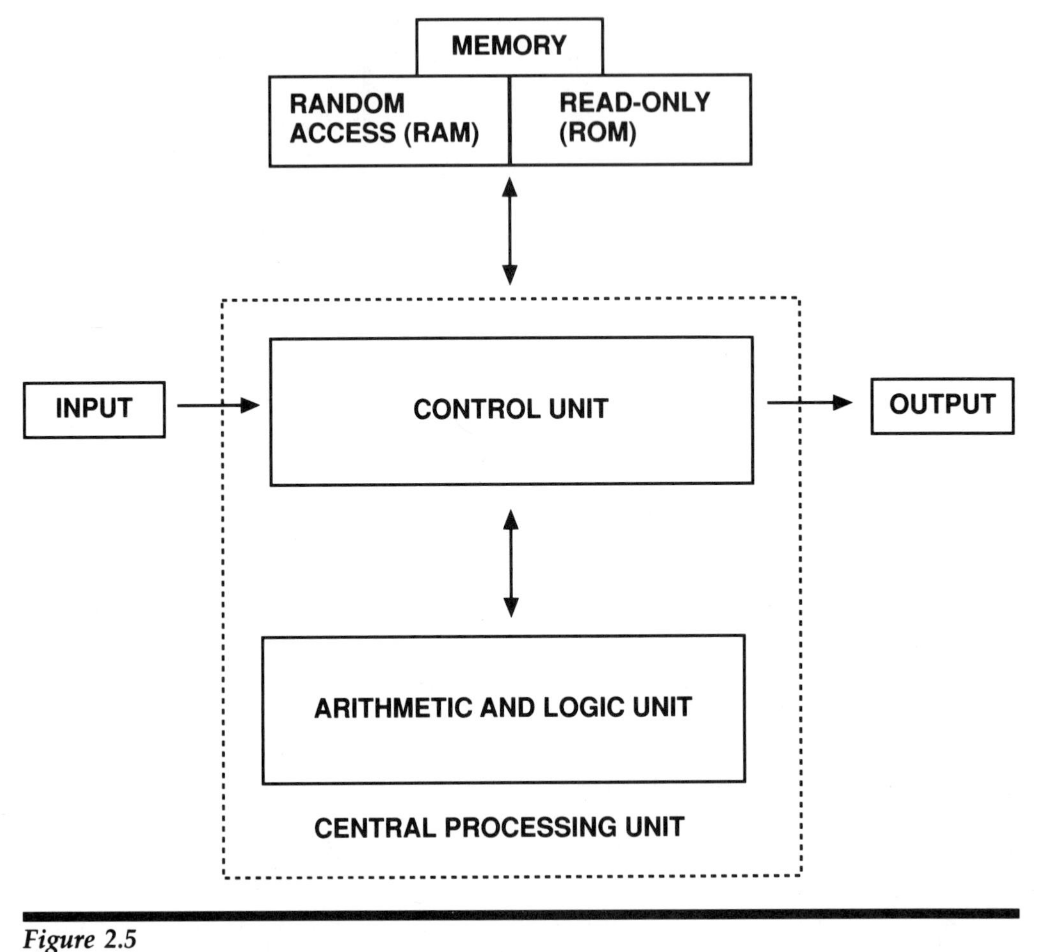

***Figure* 2.5**
Central Processing Unit

information at a time, it needs a way to store information while it is not being processed. It needs memory.

Memory

There are two types of chips that take care of the computer's internal memory, the *Read Only Memory Chips (ROM)* and the *Random Access Memory Chips (RAM)*.

The ROM chips store information permanently in the computer's memory and this memory supplies the computer with a list of operating instructions. These instructions are burnt into the computer during the manufacturing process. ROM is called *nonvolatile memory* because it does not disappear when the computer is turned off. There is nothing an ordinary computer user can do to remove or replace the instructions of ROM because the computer can only read information on these ROM chips. Most computers do have a program in ROM that puts symbols on the screen such as a cursor (usually in the form of a blinking square or line). BASIC is stored in the ROM of the Apple II line of computers and there are ROM chips in Microwave ovens.

In contrast to ROM, a computer user can *write, read* and *erase* information on RAM chips. However, the problem with this type of memory is it needs a constant power supply so that the data are not lost. In the literature, RAM is referred to as *volatile memory* because of its temporary nature. Whenever an individual turns off the computer s/he loses whatever information is in RAM. The basic unit for RAM storage is a *byte*, the space available to hold letters, numbers and special characters.[1] Because a computer user normally manipulates thousands of characters at a time, the RAM size is usually specified by a number followed by K *(kilobytes)* which is the symbol for 1,000. For example, a computer that has 512K is capable of holding approximately 512,000 numbers, symbols and letters.[2]

The amount of RAM chips a computer has determines the amount of information that can be retained in memory. A user's RAM need determines the size and number of programs that can be run instantaneously and the number of data that will be processed immediately. Programs vary in their memory requirements, and they will not run if the computer lacks this memory. For example, Appleworks GS needs 1.1125 MB (Million Bytes of RAM memory to operate). Fortunately, the RAM size of most computers can be expanded by adding RAM chips. In the early 1980s the computers purchased usually had a memory size of 64K, then considered more than adequate for a personal computer. Today, the RAM size of a computer is usually described in terms of millions or *megabytes* and tomorrow, it will be in billions or *gigabytes.*

Questions frequently asked about memory are, "How does the computer store this information since it cannot store it as a printed page? What does it use to translate information?" The fundamental principle behind digital computers' storage is binary notation.

Binary Notation

All computer input is converted into binary numbers consisting of two digits, 0 and 1. An instruction that is read as a 1 tells the computer to turn on a circuit, and an instruction read as a 0 tells the computer to turn off the circuit. The two digits symbolized by 0 and 1 are called bits, short for *b*inary dig*its*. The computer can represent letters, numbers, and symbols by combining these individual bits into a *binary code*. The most

1. Byte is discussed in more detail in the Binary Notation section of this chapter.
2. The accurate number is 524,288 (512 x 1024) because the computer uses powers of 2, and 210 is 1024. A kilobyte then represents 1024 or approximately 1,000 bytes.

common binary codes use eight–bit combinations, and each eight bit combination is called a **byte.** Each character or letter typed is translated into a byte by turning circuits off and on.[3] This whole procedure happens at lightening speed whenever a user hits a key on the computer keyboard. For example, when the user types the letter z, the computer translates it into 01011010 and the number 1 is translated into 00110001. Every character on the keyboard has a different eight bit combination or special code.

There are several coding systems, but the most commonly used one is the *American Standard Code for Information Interchange* (ASCII—pronounced "ask–ee"). This coding system uses seven bits to store as one byte, with one bit unused. It represents each character 2^7 times or with 128 possible codes. These codes represent the uppercase and lowercase letters of the alphabet, the digits, the most used punctuation marks, math signs, and control characters, such as carriage return and line feed. The letter A is the ASCII code 65 or 01000001 in binary notation. The ASCII code 66 represents the letter B, 67 represents the letter C, 48 represents 0, 49 represents 1, etc. Table 2.1 shows a partial listing of the ASCII Code.

Before leaving memory, let's look briefly at how the computer user stores his or her data permanently.

Table 2.1 ASCII Code (Partial Listing)

Character	Binary Notation	ASCII Code
A	01000001	65
B	01000010	66
0	00110000	48
a	01100001	97
b	01100010	98
?	00111111	63
>	00111110	62

Courtesy of Apple Computer

3. The letter A, represented by 65, would mean circuits 7 and 1 are on and the rest of the circuits are turned off. Refer to page 8.3 of *Computer Fundamentals with Application Software* by Shelly and Cashman, Boyd & Fraser, 1986, for a technical explanation.

Disks

The most common method of storage is still the disk. There are three commonly used methods of storage, pictured in Figure 2.6, the 5 1/4 inch, a single round disk of flexible, tape-like material encased in a square envelope, the 3 1/2 inch disk, flexible tape-like material encased in a firm plastic cover, and a hard disk positioned in a sealed unit. A recent development is Integral Peripherals subminiature hard disk that weighs only 3.3 ounces and is 1.8 inches (Barr, 1992). All of these disks store data in the same way; the disk spins on a surface that can be magnetized or demagnetized.

The disk drive is able to decode the information that it finds on a disk and send it to the computer. The number of tracks that are on a disk is a function of how accurately the disk is constructed, how fast the disk spins, how sensitive the disk is to magnetization, and so forth. It is for this reason that the 3 1/2 disk holds more information than the 5 1/4, and the hard disk is capable of holding more information than either one.

The hard disk is made of metal and covered with a magnetic recording surface. This disk is fixed or removable and can hold from ten to hundreds of megabytes of information. This is greater storage capacity than a floppy disk that holds anywhere from 800K to 2 megabytes of information. Presently the 40 megabyte hard disk is common place and larger sizes are available. The read/write head, an electronic device that records and reads the information from the disk electromagnetically, travels across this disk via an air cushion, without touching the disk.

Covered with a magnetic coating, such as iron oxide, a floppy disk (or diskette) looks like a small phonograph record divided into tracks invisible to the human eye. The information is sorted on the disk's cylindrical tracks on the surface. Whenever the user records or reads from the disk, the disk revolves at a constant speed inside its disk drive and the slightest separation between the drive head(s) and the disk surface can lead to the loss of data. The storage capacity of this disk depends upon whether data can be stored on both sides of the diskette and the storage density on each side of the disk. A floppy disk is very delicate, and a user should protect this disk from damage by adhering to the following eight suggestions.

1. Always hold a disk by its label, and do not touch the recording surface or exposed surface of the disk. (Refer to Figure 2.1.)
2. Store the 5 1/4 inch disks in paper envelopes or, at the least, in a box to avoid dust. Never store 3 1/2 disks in plastic envelopes because of the static.
3. When the red "in use" **light** is on, or the disk drive is working, *do not* remove or insert a disk.
4. Never bend the disk or use rubber bands or paper clips.
5. Keep the disk away from the television, magnets, or severe heat.

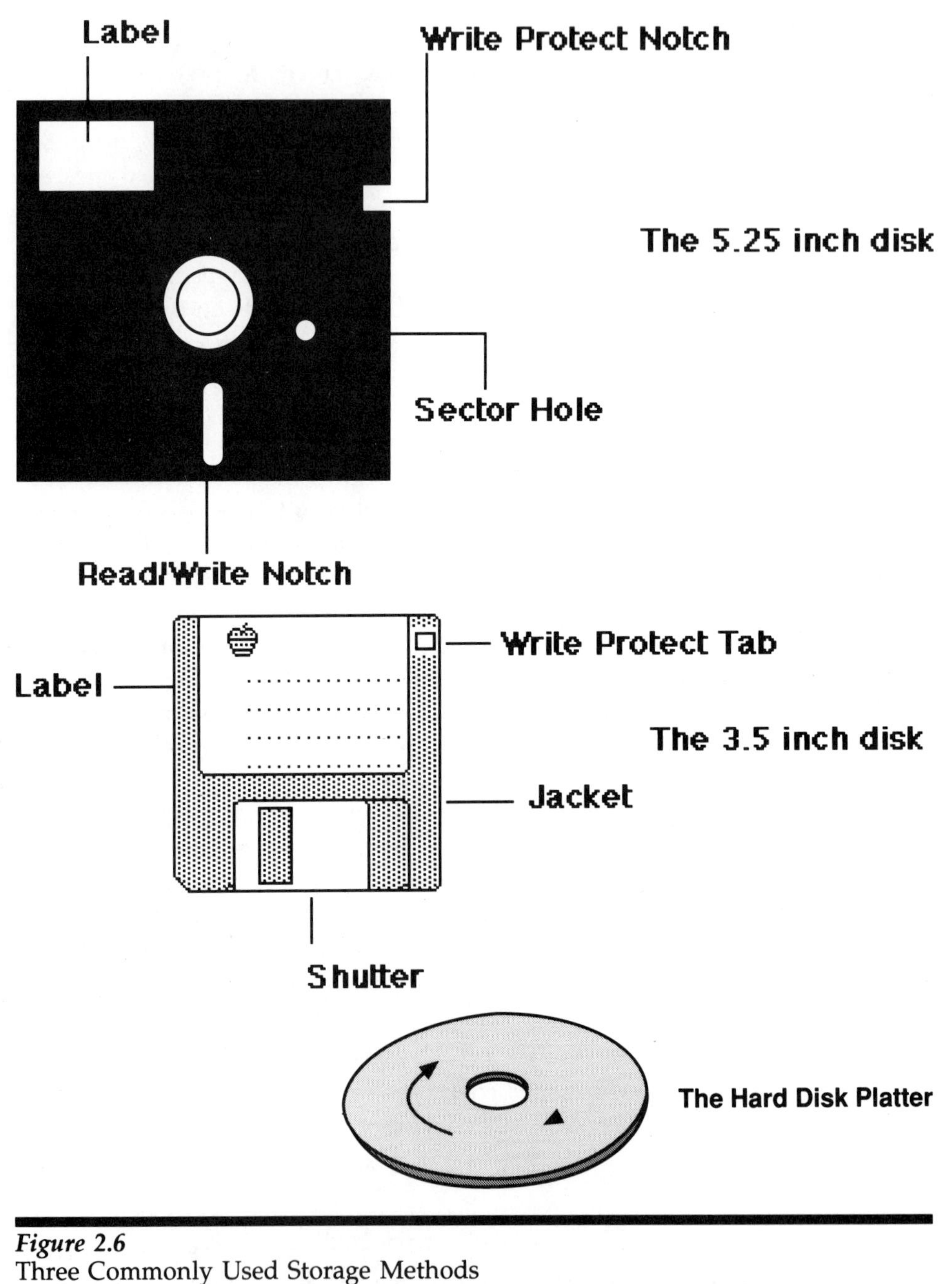

Figure 2.6
Three Commonly Used Storage Methods
The 3 1/2 inch disk is a graphic created using the Print Shop. Copyright Brøderbund Software Inc., 1984.

6. Do not smoke, eat, or drink near a disk.
7. Do not write on the disk label with a ball point because it will leave impressions. Always use a felt tip pen.
8. Stand the disks up in the container and put nothing on top of it.

In summation, disks are important because of their ability to store data and they must be handled in the proper manner.

Formatting a Disk

A disk cannot store information unless it has been formatted. Formatting a disk refers to letting the computer record some magnetic reference marks on the disk. These reference marks define the number and size of the sectors on a soft-sectored disk. The storage layout of the disk is determined by the computer operating system's access method. Disks must be formatted with the particular operation system of the computer, which means, operation system A cannot use a disk from operation system B. The user formats once unless s/he wants to erase everything on his or her disk.

Operating Systems

In the early days of computing, a person controlled the operation of a computer by using an elaborate control panel. Later computer programmers designed a program that would allow the computer to control its own operation. This control program is the operating system of the computer, and its major task is to handle the transfer of data and programs to and from the computer's disks. The operating system makes it possible to enter and run programs. It can display a directory showing the names of programs stored on the disk; it can copy a program from one disk to another; it can display and print the contents of any file on the screen. The operating system controls the computer components and allows them to communicate with each other. (The term DOS is an abbreviation for *disk operating system.*) There are many other functions that an operating system supplies and the computer's system manual enumerates them.

Different computers have different operating systems. The same computer, moreover, may have more than one operating system available to it. For example, the Apple IIGS computer uses DOS 3.3, ProDos, and OS/GS operating systems. Some other well-known operating systems are MS-DOS, UNIX, OS/2, and System 6.07 and System 7 for the Macintosh. Lacking a standard operating system for every computer, all computers are not compatible. IBM and Apple, in a joint venture, are currently working on a standard operating system that could make computers compatible (Gantz, 1992). Also, different models of computers vary in the way the operating system is supplied to the computer. Some computers have the entire operating system built into the ROM of the machine while others have their operating system placed on a separate disk that the user loads into the machine.

When the operating system is stored on a disk, the user turns on the machine and it begins running a small program usually stored in the ROM of the computer. This program's purpose is to load the operating system into the main memory of the computer and then turn over its authority to the operating system. The procedure of starting the computer is known as **booting** the system, a term that has interesting origins. In the beginning when a user first loaded the operating system into main memory, the small program that helped him to do this was called a bootstrap loader because the initial loading was analogous to "lifting yourself by your own bootstraps." As time went on, computer experts began referring to the procedure of starting the computer system as "booting the system."

How does one physically boot a system? If the operating system is on a disk, the user simply puts it in a disk drive, turns on the machine, and waits for it to boot. Some computer's operating systems request that the user supply information, such as date or time of day, before the operating system responds to the person's commands.

Before proceeding to the next chapter, let's get acquainted with a computer's operating system. For illustrative purposes, the author will show how to use version 6.07 for the Macintosh operating system. In the appendix there is a brief summary of the following operating systems: GS/OS, DOS 3.3, ProDos, MS/PC DOS, and Apple Macintosh's system 7. With the exception of the Macintosh system 7.0, these systems are most commonly found in the schools.

Of all the computers available, the Macintosh has the easiest, most workable operating system—a characteristic that distinguishes it from other systems. If a person learns how to operate a Macintosh, practically every application program uses the Macintosh user interface. This means that the user does not have to relearn commands each time after using a different application. The Macintosh is a popular computer because of this feature. The success of the Macintosh Interface led Microsoft to introduce Windows for the IBM, which is a graphical user interface with the look of the Macintosh Operating System. In the following paragraphs, the reader will see how the Macintosh displays a directory, formats a disk, makes a backup copy of a disk, and copies and deletes files.

Getting Started on the Macintosh Computer

First, let's learn the accepted sequence for turning on any computer, a sequence that provides a safeguard against electrical problems. Here is a computer safety list:

Computer Checklist

1. Turn on the printer.
2. Turn on the monitor.
3. Turn on any other peripherals.

4. Turn on the computer.
5. When the user is finished working, remove the disk from the disk drive.
6. Turn off the computer.
7. Turn off printer, monitor, and peripherals.[4]

Now that the reader is aware of the proper order for turning on the equipment, let's follow this procedure. Switch on the computer and let's learn the basics of the operating system. When booting the Macintosh computer, there is a beep sound and a picture representing the Macintosh appears with a short message, "Welcome to Macintosh." After that the following screen appears:

Macintosh Desktop

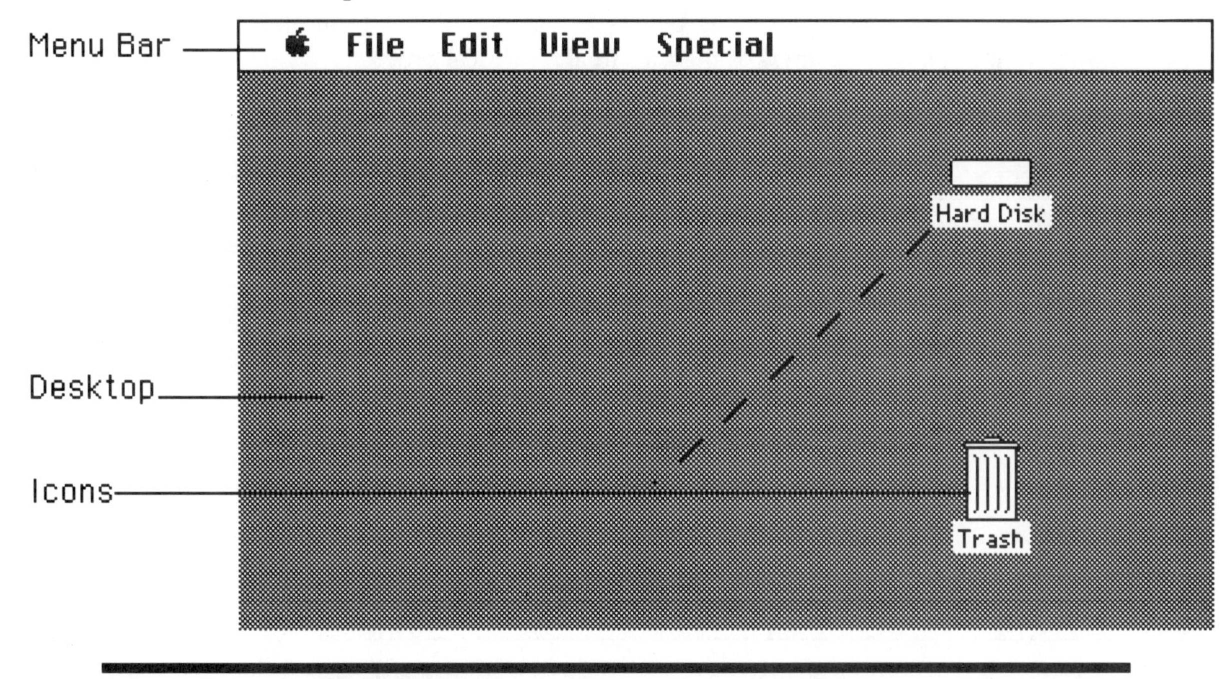

The menu bar is located at the top of the screen. Each title in the menu bar is a pull down menu consisting of many options. An Icon representing the hard disk is

4. An alternative method of turning on equipment is to have it plugged into a power surge strip and turn it on and off by simultaneously flipping the on-off button on the power strip.

located at the top right side of the screen and an icon representing the trash is on the bottom right side. (If the user had a computer without a hard disk the icon would be a floppy disk instead.) The screen represents the desktop that, in turn, represents the working memory (RAM) of the computer.

Directory

To view the contents of the hard disk, the user can either use the keyboard shortcut command⌘**0** or use the mouse. When a person moves the mouse, it moves the cursor represented by an arrow. The user moves this cursor to the hard disk icon and clicks on the mouse button twice. The hard disk icon opens and displays the contents of the disk. The directory shows the names of the files, their size, kind, date, and the time each file was modified. Going to the menu bar, and selecting *View,* the user can see the directory by large or small icon, by date, size, name, etc. For example, the directory shown next displays the names of the files in alphabetical order.

Directory

Hard Disk

Name	Size	Kind	Last Modified	
Chapters	--	folder	Fri, Jan 4, 1991	8:01 AM
Correct Grammar	--	folder	Sat, Nov 10, 1990	2:18 PM
Current Outline	7K	Microsoft Word d...	Thu, Jan 3, 1991	10:17 AM
GIFConverter	--	folder	Sat, Jun 30, 1990	7:42 PM
MacPaint Files	--	folder	Thu, Sep 20, 1990	12:23 PM
PICTViewer	9K	application	Mon, May 8, 1989	7:00 PM
Pyro Folder	--	folder	Wed, Jan 2, 1991	10:06 AM
Quick Access	59K	application	Thu, Dec 10, 1987	3:47 PM

If the user wants to see some of the options that are available under the File's Pull Down Menu, s/he goes to the Menu Title **File** and opens it by positioning the pointer over the word file and holding down the mouse button. The following menu appears:

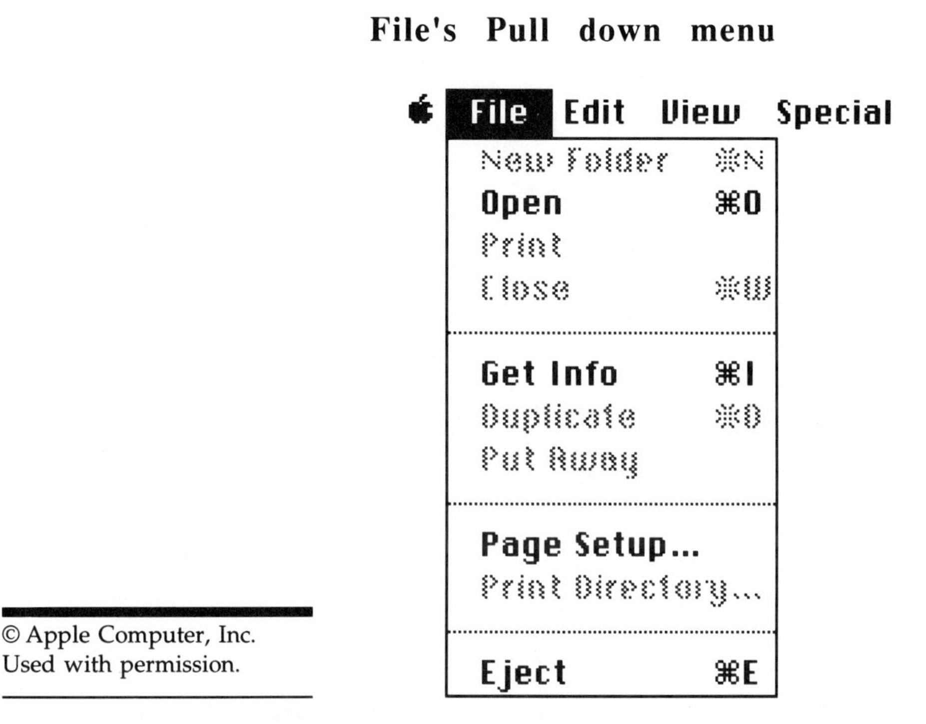

The boldfaced commands like **Open, Get Info, Page Setup,** and **Eject** are the ones that are currently available, whereas the dimmed commands are not usable. When the user releases the mouse button he or she is ready for the next operation, formatting a disk.

Formatting a disk

1. When a user inserts a blank disk in the disk drive s/he will see the following screen:

2. S/he moves the mouse until the cursor is positioned over two-sided, then clicks once on the mouse button. The next screen shot shows that formatting will erase all information on the disk. This safeguard allows the user to cancel or move the mouse so that the cursor is over the erase button and then click once.

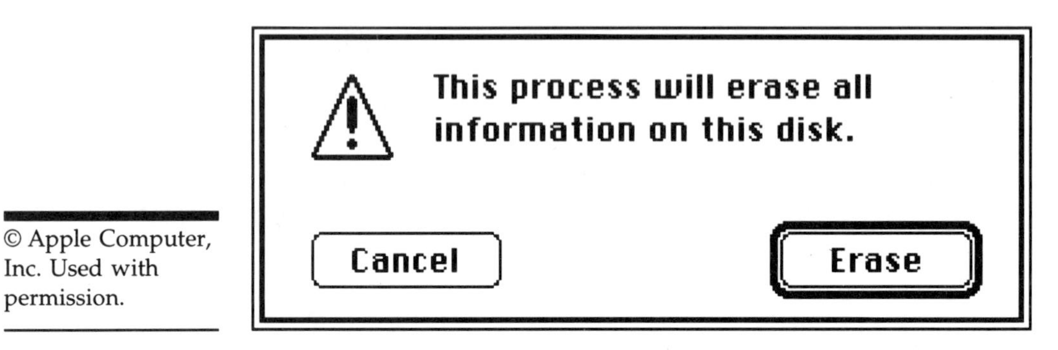

3. If the user clicks **Erase,** another screen appears that asks the person to name the disk, and for this example the name chosen is *Computer Disk.* Finally, the user moves the cursor over **OK** and clicks the mouse button once.

The disk drive goes through the process of formatting the disk, verifying the format, and creating a directory. At the end of the process, the following icon or picture appears on the desktop.

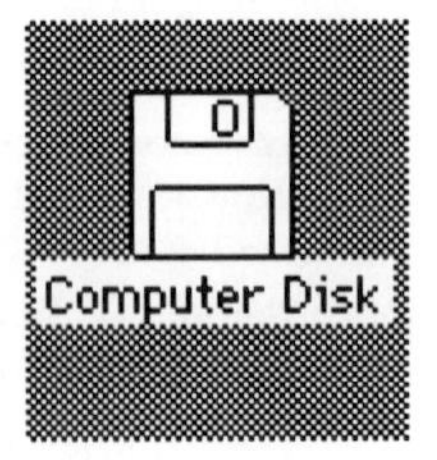

Backup Copy

The user should always make computer backup copies of a disk. There is always the chance that work could get accidentally erased or the disk could go bad. Regardless, make at least two extra copies and place one of these copies on the hard disk and the other one on a floppy disk.

The following example shows the process involved in making a copy of the Graphics-1,2 disk and placing it on the hard disk.

1. The user selects the disk Graphics-1,2 by moving the mouse so that the cursor is positioned on the disk. Now s/he clicks on the mouse so the disk is highlighted as illustrated:

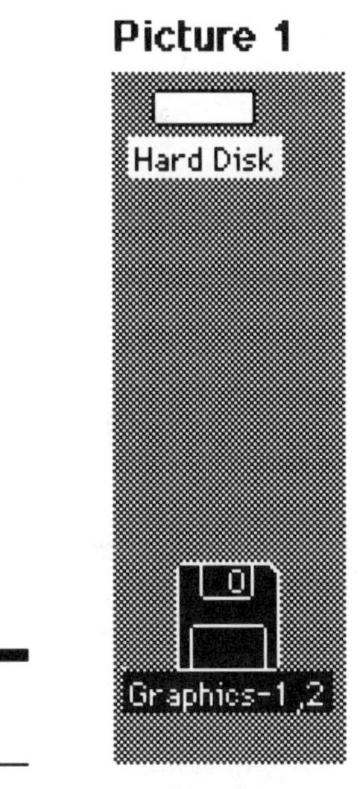

2. Next the user holds down the mouse button and drags the mouse so that the outline of the icon moves onto the hard disk icon as illustrated (top of page 40).
3. The following screen appears with a message that the two disks are different types and the contents will be placed on the folder on the hard disk. The user then clicks on the word **OK** to place a backup copy on the hard disk (middle of page 40).
4. The computer then proceeds to make the copy by displaying a screen that shows that it is reading, writing, and updating the desktop file. Look at the directory to verify that this backup copy exists (bottom of page 40).

Using the Macintosh operating system, let's see how to make a copy of an individual file and then how to delete this file.

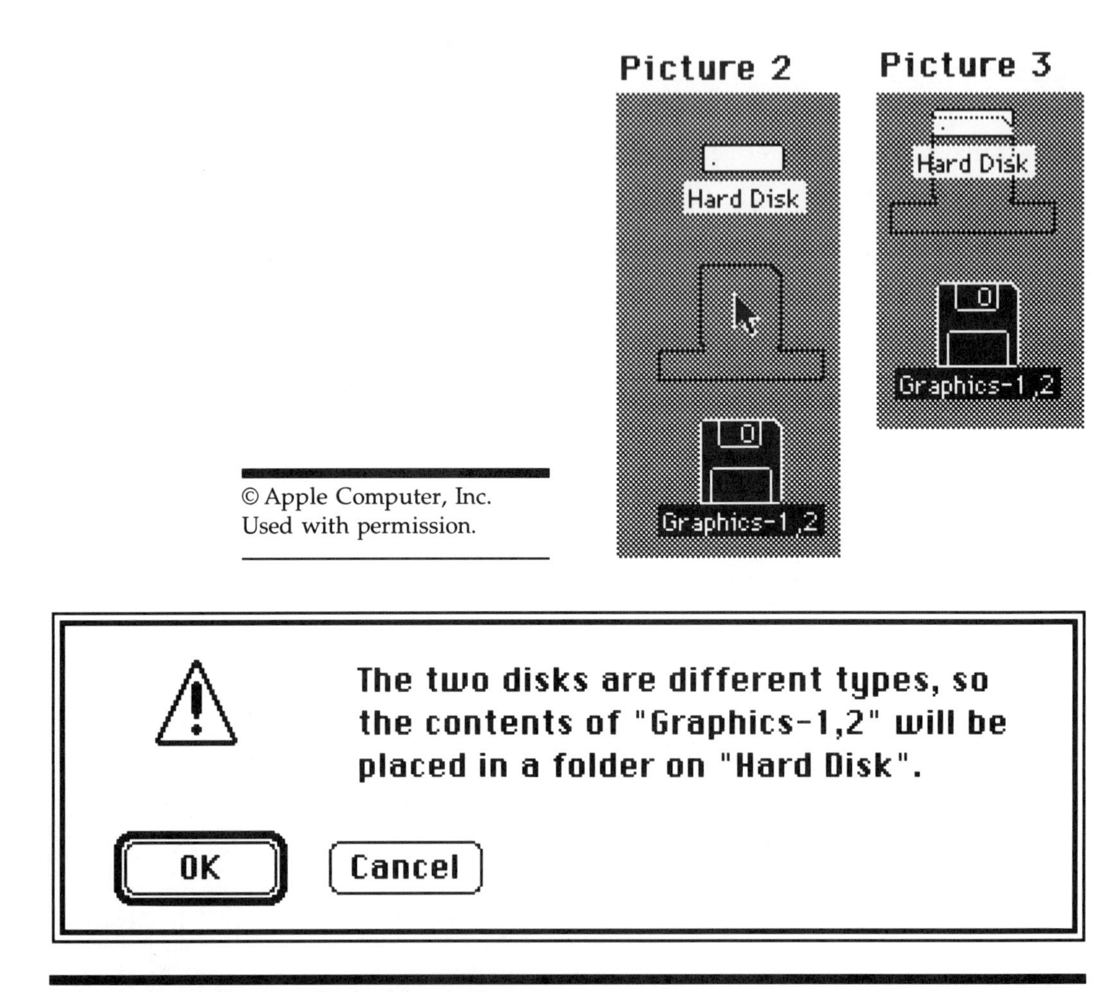

Hard Disk

Name	Size	Kind
Chapters	--	folder
Correct Grammar	--	folder
Current Outline	7K	Microsoft Word
GIFConverter	--	folder
Graphics-1,2	--	folder

Copying a File

The user will copy the file, Current Outline, by selecting it and clicking once on the mouse button.

Hard Disk

Name	Size	Kind
Chapters	--	folder
Correct Grammar	--	folder
Current Outline	7K	Microsoft Word
GIFConverter	--	folder
MacPaint Files	--	folder

Next the user opens the File Menu and drags the mouse down to click once on **Duplicate**. An alternate to the mouse procedure is the keyboard shortcut ⌘ **D**.

The computer proceeds to copy this file by showing it is reading, writing, and updating the desktop file. At the completion of the procedure, a copy of the current outline is listed on the hard disk.

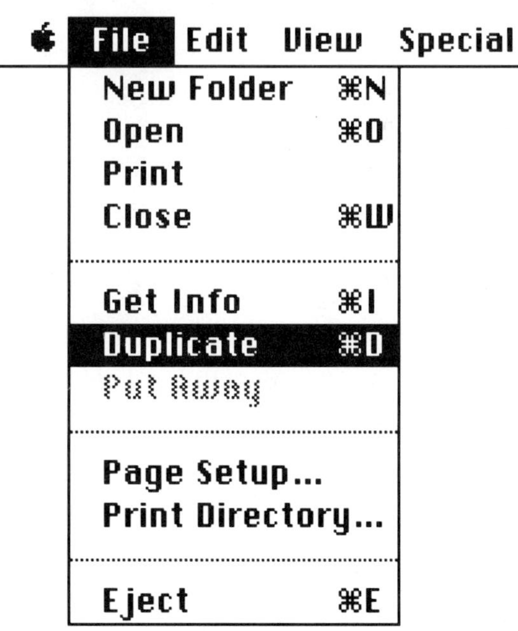

Deleting a File

If the user decides that s/he no longer wants the copy, it is a simple matter to delete the file.

1. First the user selects Copy of Current Outline as shown.

Hard Disk

Name	Size	Kind
Chapters	--	folder
Copy of Current Outline	7K	Microsoft Word
Correct Grammar	--	folder
Current Outline	7K	Microsoft Word
GIFConverter	--	folder

2. The user then drags the mouse until the copy of Current Outline goes into the trash can and the can bulges.

3. Next, open the special menu and select empty trash by clicking on the mouse button once (top of page 43).

Notice that the trash can is back to normal size (it is empty) and the directory contains the current outline but the *copy of Current Outline* is not there (middle of page 43).

Deleting a file is the last operating procedure. Let's conclude this chapter with a Summary, Chapter Mastery test, Classroom Projects, and Suggested Readings and References.

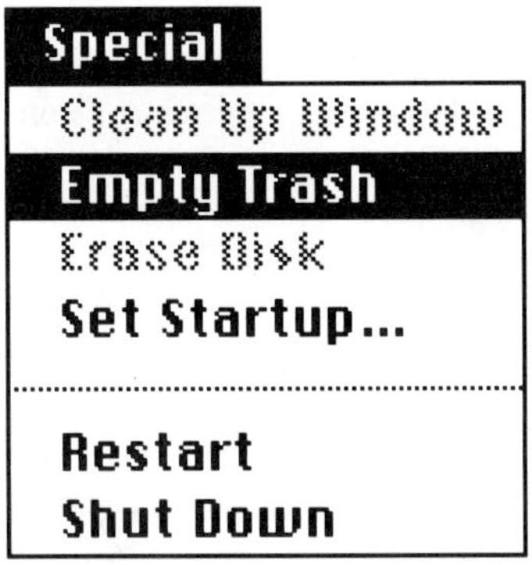

© Apple Computer, Inc.
Used with permission.

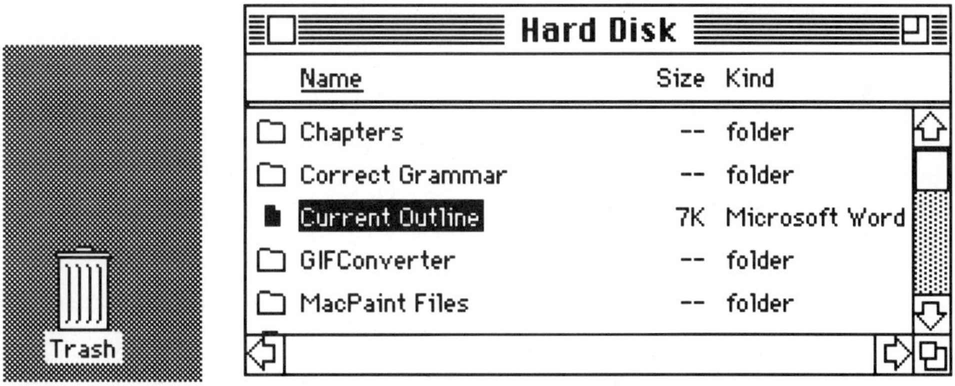

© Apple Computer, Inc. Used with permission.

Summary

Even though advances in technology have blurred the distinctions, computers are classified by memory capacity, speed, capability, price range, and size. The three classifications are mainframe, minicomputer, and microcomputer. In education, the student uses the microcomputer, and therefore this computer is the one that deserves the most attention. The microcomputer performs three functions: logic comparisons, arithmetic operations, and storage and retrieval. It accomplishes these functions at high speed, storing huge amounts of data in a binary format.

The central processing unit, the brain of the computer, consists of a control unit, which controls what is happening, the arithmetic/logic unit (ALU), which does the arithmetic and logic operations, and primary memory, ROM and RAM, which stores all data and instructions that are necessary to operate. ROM, Read Only Memory, cannot be changed and is hard wired into the machine. RAM, Random Access Memory, is temporary memory that stores data and programs that need processing. Because of its erasable characteristics, RAM allows a program to be executed as many times as the user needs. Since RAM is temporary, disks are very important, permanent storage media.

The floppy disk is delicate and requires special handling, as detailed earlier. The operating system, the control program that handles the transfer of data and programs to and from computer disks, makes it possible to enter and run programs. The Macintosh Operating System illustrates how a computer's operating system displays a directory, formats a disk, makes a backup copy of a disk, copies and deletes files.

Chapter Mastery Test

1. What is an operating system and what function does it perform?
2. Give some pointers on how to protect a floppy disk from harm and why this is a concern.
3. Compare and contrast RAM and ROM.
4. Explain how the different components of a central processing unit work.
5. Detail the differences and similarities between a mainframe, minicomputer, and a microcomputer.
6. Describe the use of ASCII code and binary code.
7. Discuss the microprocessor, the CPU, and memory, and explain how they function independently and as a complete unit.
8. Explain what K is and why it is important to have enough K in RAM.
9. When is it permissible to format a disk?
10. Define and explain the following terms: bit, byte, and kilobytes.
11. What does it mean "to boot a computer?"
12. How is a supercomputer different from any other computer?

Classroom Projects

A. Classroom Lab Activities

The student should be able to do the following operational procedures:

1. Boot the computer.
2. Initialize or format a disk.
3. Make a backup copy of a system disk.
4. Copy a file.
5. Delete a file.

B. Classroom Activities

1. Write a paper on the history of computer memory and in this paper explain the following:
   a. how the data was stored
   b. the speed and cost of memory
   c. the limitations and advantages of the system used
2. At the library, find a recent article on microchips and discuss recent developments in this technology.
3. Compare and contrast two operating systems, their differences and their similarities.

Suggested Readings and References

American National Standards Institute. *American National Standard Code for Information Interchange.* New York:

Alessi, S. M., and Trollip, S. R. 1977. *Computer-based Instruction: Methods and Development.* Englewood Cliffs, NJ: Prentice-Hall, 1985.

Barr, Christopher. (January 14, 1992). "First Sub-Mini Hard Disk." *PC Magazine* Vol. 11 No. 1, page 30.

Decker, James F. (1988). "The Role of the U.S. Federal Government in the Past, Present and Future of Supercomputing." *Supercomputer Review,* Myrias Research Corporation, San Diego, California, 22–25.

Downing, D. and Covington, M. *Dictionary of Computer Terms. Second Edition.* Barron's Business Guides, New York, 1989.

DeVoney, Chris. *PC Dos User's Guide.* Indianapolis: Que Corporation, 1984.

Eoyang, Christopher. "The Second Generation of Japanese Computers." *Supercomputer Review,* Myrias Research Corporation, San Diego, California, 1988, pages 26–27.

Edelhard, Mike. *The Complete Computer Compendium.* Addison Wesley: Reading, Massachusetts, 1984.

Evans, Richard. Processing Power in a Second. *Euromoney,* January 1, 1991, 88.

Freeman, Alan. The Computer Glossary, fifth edition. Amacom: New York, 1991.

Gantz, John. (December 30, 1991/January 6, 1992). "Pen Computers will usher in the next PC revolution." *Infoworld,* Vol. 13, issue 52/Vol. 14, issue 1, p. 107.

Godman, A. *The Color-coded Guide to Microcomputers.* Barnes and Noble: New York, 1983.

Harold, Fred G. *Introduction to Computers.* St. Paul, Minn.: West Publishing Company, 1984.

Laurie, Peter. *The Joy of Computers.* Little, Brown: Boston, 1983.

Lechner, Pieter, and Don Worth. *Beneath Apple DOS.* Chatsworth, California: Quality Software, 1985.

Long, Larry E. *Computers,* 2nd ed. Prentice Hall: Englewood Cliffs, N.J., 1990.

McMullen, John. "The New Breed of Mac Databases." *Datamation. 36,(23), December 1, 1990, 75.*

Patton, Peter. "Survey Forecasts Super Computer Market Growth at 35% to 40%." *Supercomputer Review*: Myrias Research Corporation, San Diego, California, 1988, pp. 26–27.

Poole, Lon, Martin McNiff and Steve Cook. *Apple II User's Guide*: Third Edition. Berkeley, California: Osborne/McGraw-Hill, 1986.

Ralston, Anthon and C. L. Meeks, Eds. *Encyclopedia of Computer Science,* New York: Petrocelli, 1976.

Richman, Ellen. *Spotlight on Computer Literacy.* Revised Edition. Random House, 1982, p. 27.

Rollwagen, John A., Cray Research Inc. Annual Report. Cray Research Inc., Eagan, Minnesota, February 27, 1991.

Rubin, Paul. "Watchdog Computer Verifies Shuttle Simulations." *Aerospace America,* 29, (1), January 1, 1991, 32.

Strom, Bruce. "Strange in a MAC Land." *Computers in Accounting,* 7, (4), June 1, 1991, 46.

Waite, Mitchell, John Angermeyer and Mark Noble. *DOS Primer for the IBM PC and XT*. Plume/Waite Books: New York, 1984.

Woodcock, Jo Anne (Senior Contributor). *Computer Dictionary*. Microsoft Press: Washington, 1991.

Zorpette, Glenn. "Science and Medicine." *Los Angeles Times (30 December 1991): B-5.*

Word Processing

3

Objectives

Upon completing this chapter the student will be able to:

1. Define the term *Word Processor.*
2. Describe the features and functions of a word processor.
3. Be familiar with a word processing program and how it operates.
4. Evaluate word processing software based on standard criteria.
5. Utilize and create a repertoire of word processing activities for the classroom.

Historical Background

How did word processing evolve? At the onset, there were simple typewriters, that eventually led to the development of sophisticated ones. In 1961, IBM introduced the elite Selectric typewriter, a fast electric model with changeable print balls, typefaces, and type sizes. Ten years later, Wang Laboratories, Inc. inaugurated its Wang 1200, a small-screen typing workstation capable of reading output and storing information on a cassette tape. A system user could recall his document whenever needed and could do simple editing.

Wang expanded and improved this marvel by developing a disk storage system that could store approximately 4200 pages. Altair 8800, a microcomputer kit introduced in 1974, was the first commercially successful microcomputer. This computer could store a small amount of data in memory; however, it had neither a keyboard nor a monitor screen. The user entered data and programs by flipping small toggle switches. The microcomputer did not have disks as a workable storage medium until 1976 when Digital Research Corporation introduced the Computer Program Management (CP/M) operating system. Three years later, Seymour Rubenstein created *WordStar,* a word processor for the CP/M operating system, and in 1980 Alan Ashton and Bruce Bastian produced *WordPerfect,* another word processor for the Data General minicomputer. Dedicated word processors, machines designed solely for word processing, dominated the office market.

This situation changed in 1981 when IBM introduced its personal computer, the PC. Simultaneously, Unlimited Software announced the first piece of software to run on this new machine; it was a word processor program called *EasyWriter*. However, a few months before the announcement, Lifetree Software had developed a program called *Volkswriter*.[1] From 1981 to 1985 there was a burgeoning of word processing programs such as *MacWrite* (Apple), *Microsoft Word* (Microsoft Corporation), *Bank Street Writer* (Scholastic), *PFS Write* (Software Inc.) and *Appleworks* (Apple)[2] *Appleworks*, introduced in 1983, was a combination word processor, data base, and spreadsheet. Today the computer field has hundreds of word processing programs, the most widely used computer application in the office, classroom, and home. In a study of teacher's perceptions, word processing was ranked as the primary need for the students and teachers (Woodrow, 1991). Now that we have some background into the evolution of word processing, let us define the term *word processing* and see what it involves.

Word Processing

A word processor is a software program designed to make the computer a useful electronic writing tool that can edit, store, and print documents. Before the computer, the typewriter was the principle means of writing reports, and a typist took great pains not to make mistakes because correcting and revising were tedious tasks. Word processing changed all that because the user can make changes quickly and more efficiently by pressing a few keys on the keyboard. This computer user can easily save the document on a disk, make multiple copies, and put the disks away for safe keeping.

Whenever a writer discusses word processing, it is automatically assumed s/he is discussing a personal computer with software that lets the user do word processing. The person usually buys this software program at a local software store in a 3 1/2 inch floppy disk format. (The 5 1/4 inch size is being phased out, even though many schools still use this size disk.) After the buyer loads the program into the computer, the writer types, edits text, underlines, deletes, and moves and removes words.

There are, however, two other forms of word processing programs that are different from the one just described.

1. There are computers designed primarily for word processing which have a special keyboard where the keys are programmed to do such things as underline, and change

1. *Lifetree* is now called *Writing Tools Groups* a Subsidiary of *Wordstar International.*
2. *PFS Write* is now owned by Spinnaker and Claris now produces *Appleworks.*

to italics. A person should buy this less expensive machine dedicated to word processing if the need is for typing only.

2. For a large organization it makes sense to buy mainframe processing software. The buyer purchases the software once, as opposed to buying software for each separate computer. This system allows many users to employ the same word processing software at computer terminals, saving a university or business considerable money.

Components of Word Processing

A word processor usually involves the interaction of the components pictured in Figure 3.1.

The user enters the text on the keyboard, views it, and changes it on the monitor screen. This person uses the word processing software to control the computer's operation, and the word processing software saves the document on the disk and prints it on the printer.

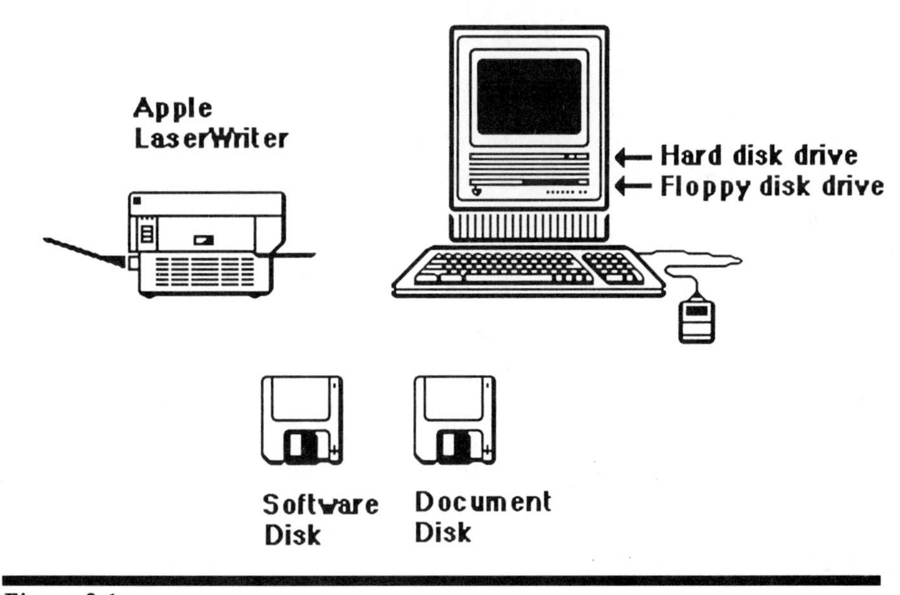

Figure 3.1
Word Processing Components
Copyright T/Maker Company.

Since word processing is a primary reason for using a personal computer, a user must exercise care in choosing the right package. The next section explains the factors a buyer should look at before purchasing this software. Before continuing on to the next section, the reader should experiment with a word processor package. After s/he is comfortable with this package, the reader can learn how to select a word processor for the classroom.

How to Select a Word Processor for the Classroom

There are hundreds of word processing packages on the market today, complete with every imaginable feature. Among these hundreds, there are word processors that are better for classroom use. Some word processing programs that fit into this category are: *Kidtalk, Muppet Slate, Bank Street Writer, Magic Slate II, The Writing Workshop, MECC Write, Easy Working, The Writer, Appleworks,* and *MacWrite. Word Perfect,* and *Microsoft Word* are for the advanced high school and college students. The software reviewers recommend programs such as *Magic Slate II* (20 column version) and *Muppet Slate* for the primary grades, *Bank Street Writer III* (40/80 column version) and the *Writing Workshop* for the middle grades, *Microsoft Works,* (Macintosh), and *Appleworks* (Apple II) for tenth grade and above. The word processors for the primary grades have fewer features and are easier to use. The features chosen for inclusion are the ones that will help the students the most such as delete, which removes unwanted text, and insert, which inserts lines or passages.

Choosing software for the classroom consists of the following five-step process: (1) Determine the hardware compatibility. (2) Study the program's general features. (3) Examine its standard editing features. (4) Review formatting functions. (5) Look at instructional design, cost effectiveness, and technical support.

Hardware Compatibility

Check out the computer brand the school is using. Is this computer an Apple IIe, an Apple IIGS, an old Commodore 64, an Apple Macintosh LC, or an IBM P.C.? How much memory does this machine have? Does the computer have 64K, 128K, 256K, 1 megabyte or 2 megabytes of RAM? How many disk drives are available for each machine and what kind? Generally, it is recommended that the user employ two disk drives with a word processing program. Although in many instances one drive is enough for the simpler word processors, the more advanced ones require two floppy disk drives or a hard disk drive and a floppy. One drive is used to hold the program while the other holds the data disk. What is the size of the disk drives? Are these disk drives 3 1/2 inch drives or 5 1/4 inch drives or does the hard disk drive contain 105 megabytes of storage space? What other equipment is available? For instance, does the district have a CD ROM Player or a Videodisc player?

General Features

Most word processors have cursor control, word wrap, and page break. Since cursor control is an important feature, it warrants discussion first.

Cursor Control A cursor (Figure 3.2) is usually in the form of a blinking white block of light which shows the position of a character. It is a place marker that lets the computer user quickly find his place to correct an error or enter new data.

Cursor control is critical because it makes it easier to move within the text and handle editing functions faster. As the individual types, the cursor moves ahead or under each character that is on the screen. The cursor moves with the keys or special equipment like the mouse. The cursor can move one character at a time, line by line, or over a block of text.

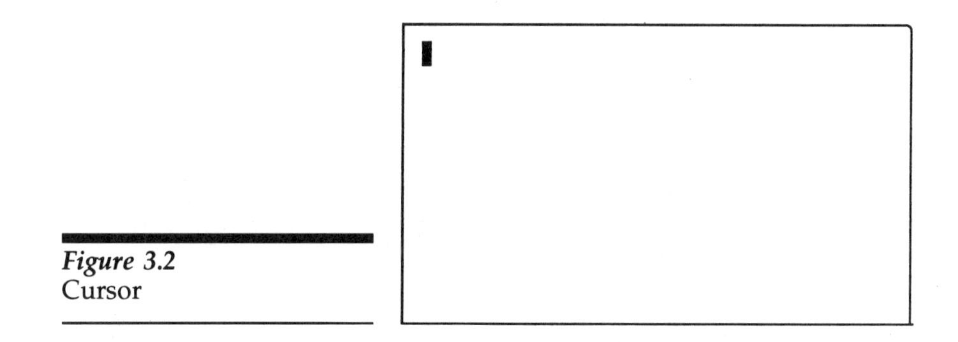

Figure 3.2
Cursor

Word Wrap Word wrap lets the individual type as much as he or she wants without paying attention to the end of lines. In this instance, the user does not have to press the RETURN Key. When s/he reaches the right hand margin, the cursor automatically moves to the beginning of the next line. If the word does not fit on a line, it automatically moves to the next line. When the same individual uses a typewriter, this typist has to hit the RETURN Key after each line. The word processor user hits the RETURN Key only to show a new paragraph or to move down a line.

Page Breaks Most word processors display some mark on the screen that tells where the page breaks in the document are. This is very helpful because the user can see where the page breaks are before printing the document.

Standard Editing Features of a Word Processor

Word processors vary in their editing capabilities because some are more powerful than others. However, they all usually have the same basic editing features: insert, delete, find and replace, and block operations.

Insert The **insert** function allows an individual to insert lines of text, words, and paragraphs anywhere in the document. The person does not need to retype any information preceding or following the inserted material.

Delete The **delete** function allows an individual to erase words, lines, or paragraphs of text. The remaining text arranges itself so that the layout is proper, after the material is deleted.

Find and Replace. When a student uses the **find** and **replace** function (Figure 3.3) s/he searches a document for a word or phrase and replaces it. For example, if the student misspells the word **their** the computer will find every incident of **their** and replace it when necessary.

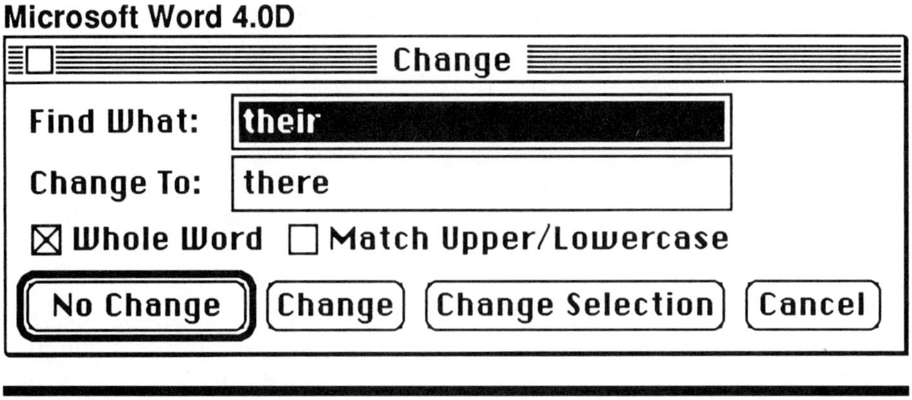

Microsoft Word 4.0D

Change

Find What: their

Change To: there

☒ Whole Word ☐ Match Upper/Lowercase

No Change | Change | Change Selection | Cancel

Figure 3.3
Find and Replace
Screen Shot Microsoft® Word© 1984–1989 Microsoft Corporation. Reprinted with permission from Microsoft Corporation.

This function also allows the software user to do a global search. In this case, a writer who has misspelled a word can have the computer change all entries of this word to the correct spelling without seeing each incident of the misspelled word. This particular function is extremely useful for editing a manuscript, because it makes locating corrections a simple matter.

Block Operations A block is a part of text found between two marked points. The advantage of working with blocks is that instead of deleting, inserting, or copying one line at a time the user can do these operations on blocks of text. This user can **cut (delete), cut and paste,** or **copy** by employing block operations. To delete a block of text, the word processor user applies the **cut** function. The user marks the beginning of the block of text or paragraph that will be cut and the end of the block of text. Next, employing the cut function, the person eliminates that portion of the text. The **Cut** and **Paste** function allows the user to **move** segments or blocks of text from one point to another. In the past, when a writer wanted to change the order of the paragraphs, s/he *really* had to cut and paste the original typewritten sheet of paper in the new sequence. Today, thanks to modern technology, the writer uses the cut and paste function by following these steps

1. **S/he signifies the beginning of the block of text or paragraph that will be moved and the end of the block of text or paragraph by selecting it.**
2. Using the cut function, the writer can remove the specified portion of text.
3. The computer user positions the cursor where he or she wants this material moved and uses the paste or insert function to place it. Like magic, the text will automatically arrange itself with the proper spacing.

Copy The **copy** function works similarly. The person chooses some text or a picture from one place by marking it and uses the copy function to copy it. Next, the person pastes or inserts it in a new location in the document. The user can duplicate a drawing or line of text elsewhere in the document or in another document.

Standard Formatting Functions

Besides editing features, there are numerous formatting functions. The discussion will handle only a few of the more pertinent ones such as spacing, justification, margins, etc. Formatting pertains to the way the text appears on the printed page. For this textbook, the category will be subdivided into functions concerned with space and those concerned with form.

Space Functions The most common space functions are: margins, tabs, justification, centering, headers and footers, and line spacing.

Margins The margin is the spacing between the edge of the page and the main text area. A margin is set for the entire document, whereas an indent is set for individual paragraphs. Margins should be easily adjustable to meet the writer's needs.

Tabs Tabs are similar to the tabs on a typewriter which position text precisely within a line in a document or within a column in a table. When the user presses the tab key, it moves the cursor across the page quickly to some predetermined point.

Justification Justification aligns the lines of text on the left, right side, center, and on both sides of the page. Left justified text has the left margin lined up and the right margin uneven. This is the most common type of justification, and word processing programs usually have this as their default. Right-justified text has the right margin lined up, and the left margin is uneven. Fill-justified, or right and left justification, aligns the text equally on the right and left side of the page. The computer achieves this type of justification by inserting spaces between words to spread the lines so that they flush with the right margin as well as with the left margin. Center-justified text aligns all the lines of text in the center and is often used to make headings more attractive on a page. Figure 3.4 shows examples of each type of justification.

The *Microsoft Word* and *MacWrite* word processing programs use icons identical to the ones shown in Figure 3.5 to let the writer select the type of justification s/he wants to use. If an individual wants fill-justified text, s/he highlights the icon on the extreme right; then the word processor arranges the text so that the lines are even on the right and left side of the page.

Header A header is text that appears at the top margin of each page of manuscript, while a **footer** is text that prints in the bottom margin of a page of the manuscript. Headers and footers usually include descriptive text; for instance, page numbers, titles, and dates.

Line Spacing "Line spacing is the vertical space that defines the height of the lines." (*Microsoft*, 1989) When an individual uses the Line spacing functions, he or she can single, double, or triple space text in the document.

Form Functions Under the form functions, the following terms are defined: boldface, underlining, superscripts, subscripts, fonts, and numbering.

A. Left Justified Text

Suddenly this giant computer stopped working, and everyone was frantically attempting to discover the source of the problem. Grace Hooper and her co-workers found the culprit was a dead moth in a relay of the computer. They removed the moth with a tweezer and placed it in the Mark II logbook.

B. Right Justified Text

Suddenly this giant computer stopped working, and everyone was frantically attempting to discover the source of the problem. Grace Hooper and her co-workers found the culprit was a dead moth in a relay of the computer. They removed the moth with a tweezer and placed it in the Mark II logbook.

C. Fill-Justified Text

Suddenly this giant computer stopped working, and everyone was frantically attempting to discover the source of the problem. Grace Hooper and her co-workers found the culprit was a dead moth in a relay of the computer. They removed the moth with a tweezer and placed it in the Mark II logbook.

D. Center Justified Text

Suddenly this giant computer stopped working, and everyone was frantically attempting to discover the source of the problem. Grace Hooper and her co-workers found the culprit was a dead moth in a relay of the computer. They removed the moth with a tweezer and placed it in the Mark II logbook.

Figure 3.4
Justification Types

Figure 3.5
Justification Icons
Screen Shot Microsoft® Word© 1984–1989 Microsoft Corporation. Reprinted with permission from Microsoft Corporation.

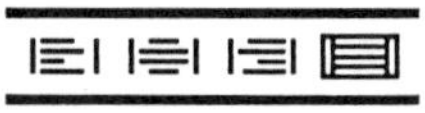

Boldface Boldfacing darkens words or sentences and slightly enlarges the text in a document. **This sentence is a perfect example of boldfaced text.** Some programs show boldfacing on their screen while others use special characters. When a program shows it with special characters, the words that are emphasized are not seen until printed.

Underlining Underlining is simply putting a line under a word or sentence. Some software programs will show the word underlined; other programs will use special characters and the actual underlining is not seen until the product is printed.

Superscripts and Subscripts Superscripts and Subscripts are typically used in mathematical formulae. "They position arguments above and below the baseline." (*Microsoft Word,* 1989) For example, 2^8 is a superscript while an A_1 is a subscript. They are generally marked with special characters and not shown on the screen.

Font "A set of type characters of a particular design and size." (Freeman, 1991) For example, courier is a popular font used for desktop publishing. Fonts can be printed bit map, a pattern of dots, or as outline defined by a mathematical formula. A font has many different characteristics, for example, typeface, spacing, pitch, point size, style. Typeface refers to design like Times, pitch represents characters per inch, point size is the height of characters, style changes the appearance by *italicizing,* **bold facing,** etc. Programs vary in the number of fonts that can be used. Figure 3.6 shows examples of different fonts, sizes and styles that can be generated on a Macintosh computer.

Figure 3.6
Font Sizes and Styles
Screen Shot Microsoft® Word© 1984–1989 Microsoft Corporation. Reprinted with permission from Microsoft Corporation.

Number Finally, many word processors automatically **number** the pages in a document and let the user change these numbers easily. After examining formatting functions, the software buyer should look carefully at the instructional design and features of his or her program. The next few pages should give the reader an idea of what to scrutinize.

Instructional Design and Features

At the lowest grade levels, the word processor that a person chooses can insert, delete, center, underline, double space, save text and print the document. A word processor program should be easy for the student to learn and not require hours of instruction. *Muppet Slate,* a word and picture processing program for Grades K-2, has large, easy- to-read letters, simple editing features, and 126 pictures of animals, bugs, and muppets for beginning writers. This software works with a specially designed muppet learning keyboard or the regular Apple keyboard. The application that has its functions displayed at the top of the screen is also ideal for beginners because they do not have to remember these functions. *Bank Street Writer* (Figure 3.7) has always had the program designed in this manner. In the past this program has been

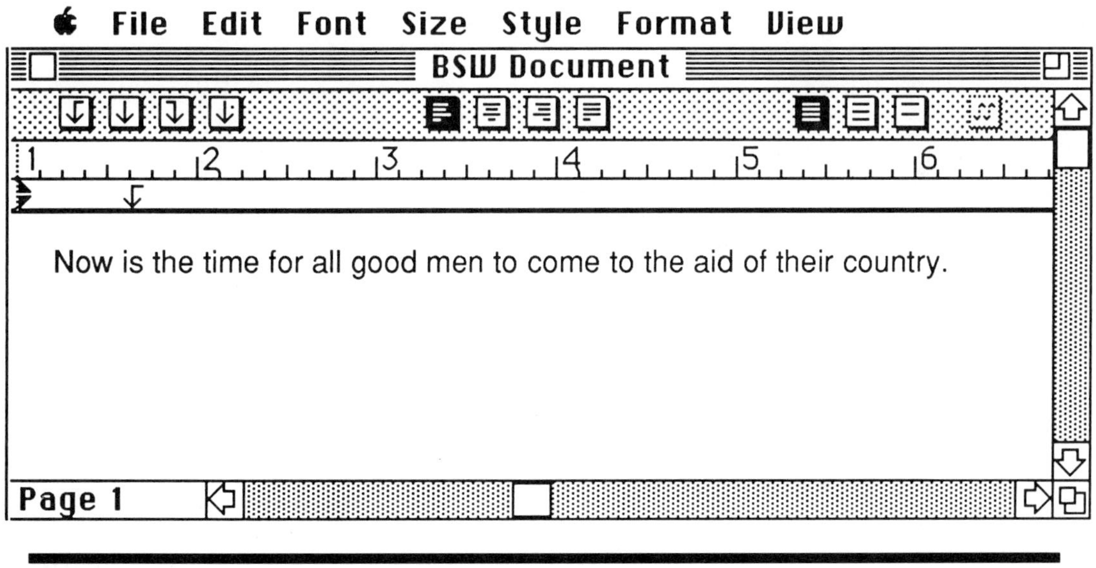

Figure 3.7
Bank Street Writer
Scholastic, Inc.

tremendously popular because of its on-screen prompts and tutorial disk. The most recent version for the Macintosh (pictured) has a spell-checker, thesaurus, and desktop capabilities.

This version has the major functions at the top of the screen in a menu title format that is almost self explanatory. When the user pulls down the menus, s/he gets a list of options. Figure 3.8 shows the list of options that are available under the **Edit** menu. Since these are editing functions, the list includes such items as cut, paste, copy, and undo typing.

Edit Font Size Style

Undo Typing ⌘Z

Cut ⌘X
Copy ⌘C
Paste ⌘V
Clear
Select All ⌘A

Find/Replace... ⌘F
Check Spelling... ⌘K
Search Dictionary...
Find Synonyms... ⌘Y

Preferences...

Figure 3.8
Bank Street Writer Edit Menu Options
Scholastic, Inc.

Muppet Slate and *Magic Slate II* have picture or icon based menus that make them intuitive programs. The following Main Menu Screen from *Magic Slate II* 40 column version (Figure 3.9) shows the intuitive nature of this type of program.

When the user first loads this program into memory, he or she encounters eight icons. The student chooses the **EDIT** to write, change something, or just see what is written. S/he chooses the **LOAD** to load a file from the data disk, the **PRINT** to print a file, and the **NEW** to create a new file. S/he uses the **SAVE** to save files on the data disk. The **DELETE** command displays a list of files that are on the disk and lets the user erase the ones desired. The student chooses **MAKE** to create and format a new data disk and chooses the **QUIT** command to stop the program.

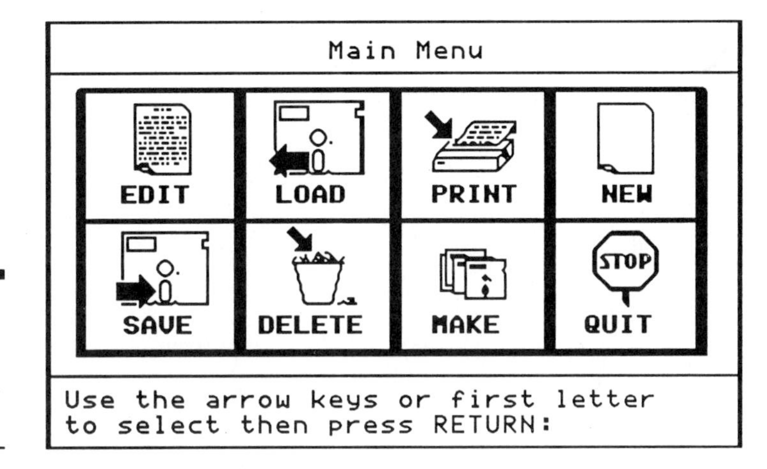

Figure 3.9
Magic Slate II
40 Column Main Menu
Sunburst Communications, Inc.

Appleworks is a menu-driven program that lets the user select options to command the program. Figure 3.10 shows the main menu folder and its contents as represented by 1 through 6. At the very top of the screen, the word, "Main Menu" tells the user where s/he is in the stack of folders. When the user chooses different options, this changes the folders listed.

Instructions that tell the user how to progress appear at the very bottom of the screen. If the user is confused s/he can hold down the open apple and question mark to receive on-screen help.

In looking for word processors, the buyer should examine only those that have simple to remember keys for functions. For example, P for Print is easier to remember than other combination of keys. Ask how the word processor does simple functions. While *Macwrite* is a simple program when it comes to underlining, *FrEdWriter* and *Bank Street III* send the user to a printer's manual to figure out the code for the printer to start and stop underlining. The word processor's design should allow the user to write and edit the text in the same mode. The original *Bank Street Writer* was not that simple: It had an edit, writing, and transfer mode. If the writer made a mistake, he or she had to switch from the writing mode to the edit mode. Next, the writer made the correction and then switched back to the writing mode to continue writing. If the *Bank Street* user wanted to save or print the material, s/he had to choose another mode called the Transfer mode. Switching back and forth was very tedious, and the newer versions of *Bank Street Writer* let the user do simple editing and writing in the same mode.

In the advanced grade levels, students make considerable use of word processing so they need more advanced features such as outlining, footnoting, glossary, indexing, graphic insertion, mail merge, and table of contents. An instructor must know what the

```
Disk: Disk 1 (Slot 5)          Main Menu

    Main Menu

    1. Add files to the Desktop
    2. Work with one of the files on the Desktop
    3. Save Desktop files to disk
    4. Remove files from the Desktop
    5. Other Activities
    6. Quit

Type number, or use arrows, then press Return     ⌘-? for Help
```

Figure 3.10
Appleworks Main Menu
Appleworks is a trademark of Apple Computers, Inc., registered in the U.S. and in other countries.

students' requirements are and the word processing features that are available. The higher end word processors have more depth and complexity.

Safety Features

Are there safety devices that prevent a student from making a mistake? If the student is about to format a disk and wipe out all data, is there a screen that cautions this student not to proceed? *The Bank Street Writer III* (Apple II version) handles problems like this with questions. ARE YOU SURE YOU WANT TO CONTINUE? DO YOU WANT TO CLEAR ALL OF YOUR TEXT(Y/N)? These types of queries warn both the novice and advanced users that they may be making errors. Many word processing programs try to insure that the user saves the data by automatically saving material intermittently. Other programs remind the user to save the document. *Bank Street Writer* (Macintosh Version) displays the following screen when the user is about to

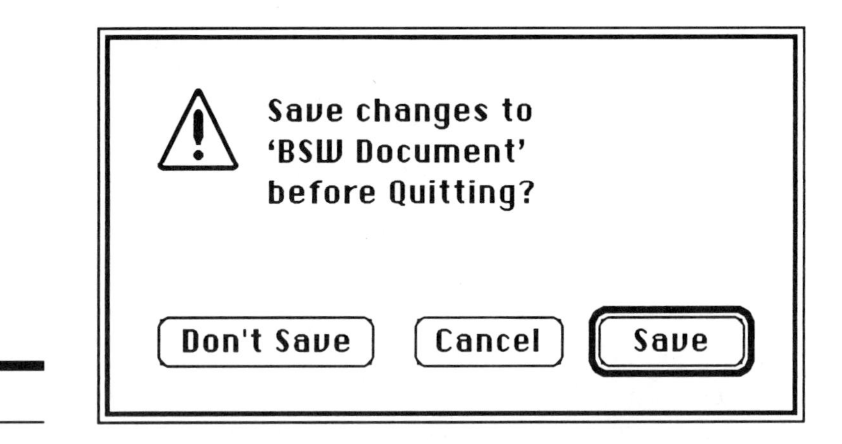

Scholastic, Inc.

quit an application without saving the changes. (The user then has three options—not to save, to cancel, or to save.)

Most word processing programs have undo features that reverse the last action performed on the document. *Nisus,* an advanced level word processor program designed for the Macintosh, has unlimited undos. It is important to have as many of these safeguards as possible, especially when the user is about to format a disk, delete a file, or save material.

Screen Display

When a teacher looks at the screen display, there are two primary concerns: **What You See Is What You Get** (**WYSIWYG**) and the column size. **WYSIWYG** is a feature that is common place on many word processors. It is a method of display that shows the document on the screen as it will appear when printed. WYSIWYG tries to duplicate the printout as closely as possible, but it is not always exact. For example, the Apple Macintosh displays font size and graphic images that approximate the printed copy.

The **column size** is determined by the software's purpose. A primary teacher usually finds a column size of 20 more appropriate for this age group, while the intermediate teacher usually chooses a 40 column size for his or her grade level. The visually handicapped student might need the 20 column type of display while the upper grade student needs only the 80 column display. The following *Magic Slate II* screen shows the 20 column size (example 1) and 40 column size (example 2) superimposed on one screen.

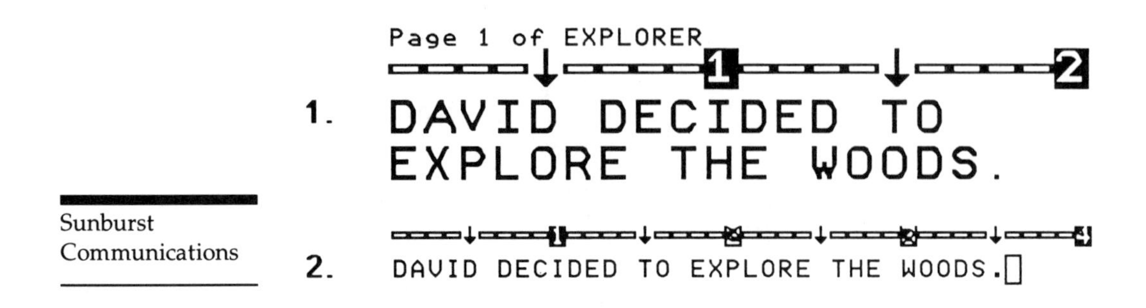
Page 1 of EXPLORER
1
2
1. DAVID DECIDED TO EXPLORE THE WOODS.
2. DAVID DECIDED TO EXPLORE THE WOODS.
Sunburst Communications

Consumer Value

Software is expensive, so cost is a consideration and that is why a program such as *FrEdWriter* (SoftSwap) is great. (The *Fr* represents free and the *Ed* represents Education.) FrEdWriter is a public domain software package that can be bought for a minimal price and duplicated as often as the user wants for his needs. There is one catch: The buyer cannot sell the program to anyone. Usually, commercial software is more expensive, but there are exceptions. Programs such as *Easy Working, The Writer* (Spinnaker) and *Swift Word Processor* (Cosmi) can be bought for under $10.00. Be sure to find out if the software that is purchased comes with a backup copy or allows the buyer to make a backup. If the software is protected, ask if the purchaser can buy an extra copy for a minimum charge.

Ease of Use

A major consideration for buying a word processor is how easy is it to learn this program. It is immaterial what features it has if it is difficult to learn. Ask the following questions:

(1) "Can a person sit down and in a reasonable amount of time use this program?" *The Writing Workshop* (Milliken), pictured on the following page, is a very intuitive program that is exceptionally easy to use. The majority of the instructions are on the screen so the student does not have to read a large manual. S/he chooses H for help, W to write, F to store information, and T to type or print. There are icons every step of the way to remind the student what each option does.

(2) "Are there help screens that tell the student what to do each step of the way?"

(3) "Is there a tutorial disk that takes the person through the program? Is the printer set up easy, and is the printer ready to print immediately?"

Support

Any reference to support means personal as well as written help. Can the software user call someone on the telephone at the software company and get immediate help, or does the person sit through a series of messages and wait an unbearable amount of time? Is the technical support toll free, or is it a pay call? Does the software package

Milliken Publishing

have tutorial lessons in the manual or on disk that help the user learn the program? Is the manual readable with activities and lesson plans and an index? Is there a spelling checker, grammar checker or thesaurus? The new advanced programs and revised ones are packaged with all three.

Spell Checkers

The **Spelling Checker** has become common place for the majority of word processors. It can come as an add-on package, or it can be built into the word processing program. The spelling checker looks for spelling and typing errors by checking the spelling of the words in the person's report against a dictionary that is stored on the disk. If a word in the document does not agree with the dictionary, the spelling checker will display the word in question and give the individual the opportunity to accept this word as spelled right, or accept an alternative. In the picture on the following page, the word **looks** is misspelled; the spell checker suggests two alternatives—looks and locks.

If the word in question is spelled right, the user can add it to the spelling checker's dictionary. The good spelling checker always lets the user see the misspelled word in context or in the sentence where there are problems. The spelling checker does not inform the user about incorrect word usage because this is the job of the grammar checker.

Grammar Checkers

Because of the rapidly increasing demand for grammar checkers, these programs are widely available. Grammar checkers help the writer with grammar, style, punctuation, and even spelling errors. The checkers identify problems such as inconsistencies, awkward

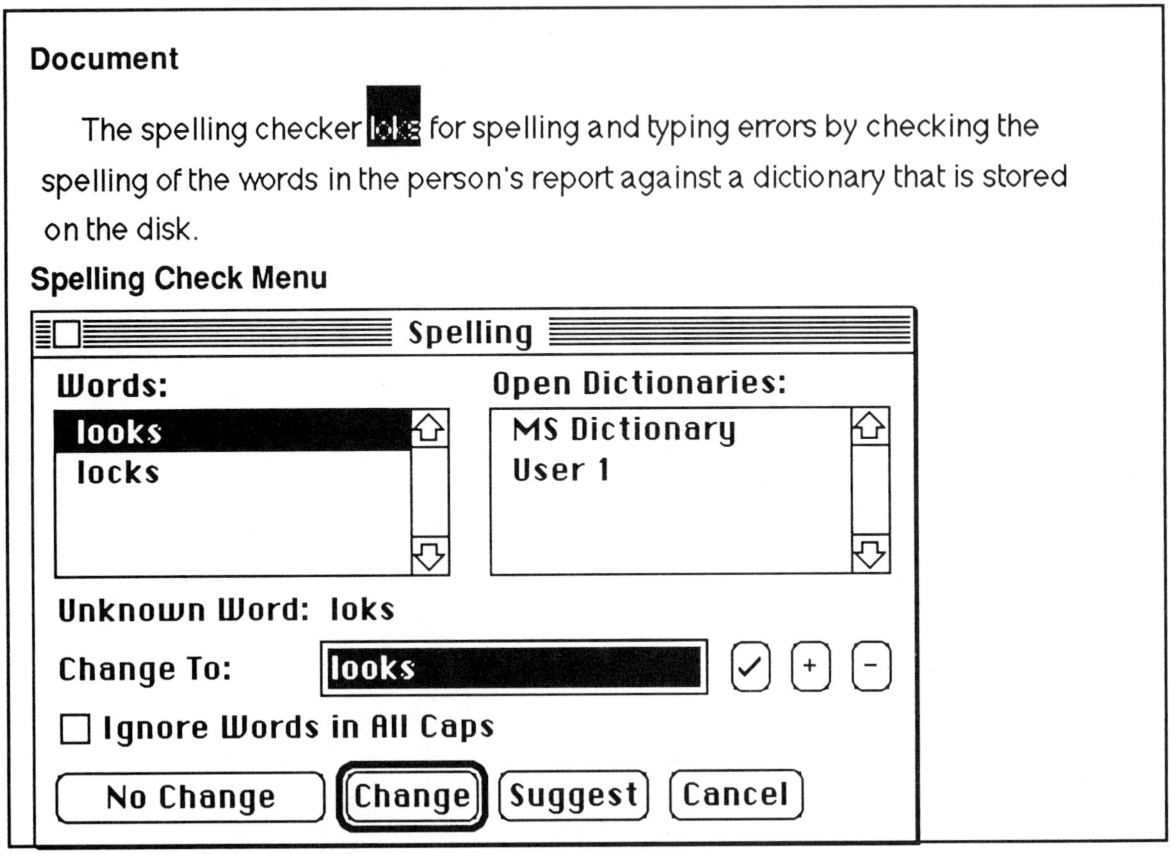

Document

The spelling checker loks for spelling and typing errors by checking the spelling of the words in the person's report against a dictionary that is stored on the disk.

Spelling Check Menu

Spelling

Words:
looks
locks

Open Dictionaries:
MS Dictionary
User 1

Unknown Word: loks

Change To: looks

☐ Ignore Words in All Caps

No Change | Change | Suggest | Cancel

Screen Shot Microsoft® Word© 1984–1989 Microsoft Corporation. Reprinted with permission from Microsoft Corporation.

phrases, clichés, and wordiness. After it identifies the problem, it makes suggestions on how the software user can correct it and provides an on-line tutorial explaining the grammar rule that applies. The user usually makes the correction with a click of a mouse. The user also has the option of rewriting the incorrect sentence or leaving it just as it is. The screen from *Correct Grammar* (Writing Tools Group) on the following page, shows a dialog box that offers a correction or suggestion to the writer.

The top of this box display offers a suggestion when an error is found. In this case it tells the author that the sentence should have "programs" instead of "program." The middle portion of the dialog displays buttons. The highlighted buttons are available to handle this particular problem while the dimmed ones are not currently available. The *correct* button lets the program correct the sentence, and the *ignore* button ignores the

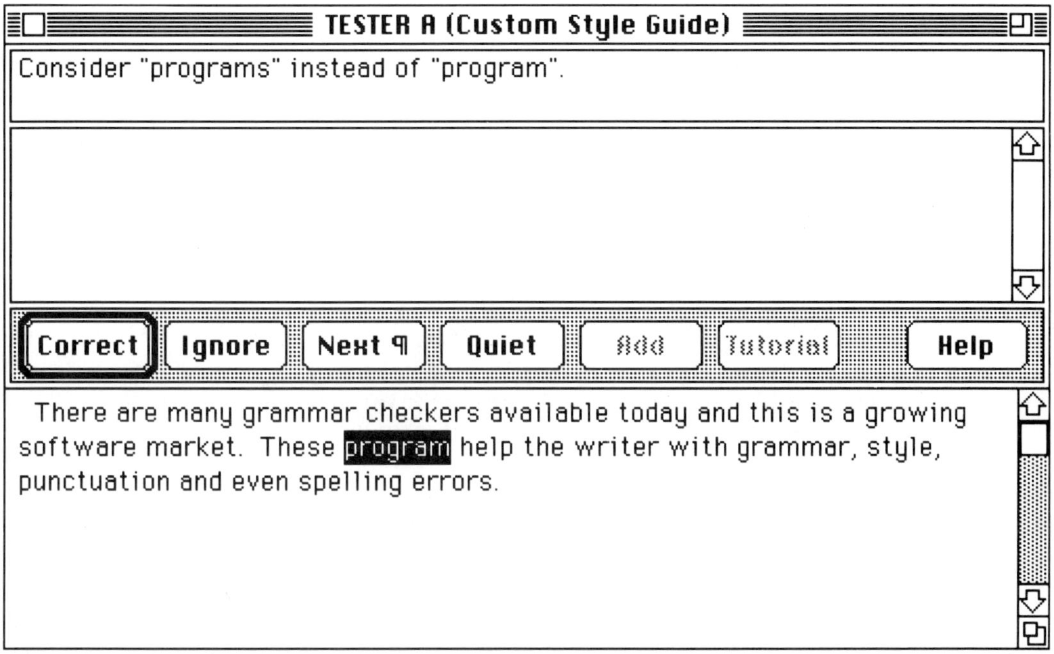

TESTER A (Custom Style Guide)

Consider "programs" instead of "program".

Correct | Ignore | Next ¶ | Quiet | Add | Tutorial | Help

There are many grammar checkers available today and this is a growing software market. These program help the writer with grammar, style, punctuation and even spelling errors.

Reprinted by written permission of Wordstar International Incorporated.

suggestions. The *next* button lets the person skip the paragraph entirely, while the *quiet* button turns off the rule that was used for the current suggestion. Finally, the help button explains procedure. At the bottom of the dialog box, Correct Grammar displays the pertinent part of the writer's document and lets the user type the corrections in this edit box.

Early grammar checks were limited because of their emphasis on mechanical and stylistic errors, but the new programs are more versatile. The grammar checkers do not restrict the writer to one writing style, but offer a choice, depending upon the writer's purpose. For example, *Correct Grammar* gives the user the choice of ten different writing styles, from Academic to Technical. This program also compares the readability of the writing, sentence by sentence, to the educational level of the audience. If a particular sentence is too difficult for that audience to understand, the checker tells the writer immediately.

There are more grammar checkers becoming available. Some accompany the word processing packages while others are built into the word processing software. For example, *Grammatik*, IBM Version (Reference Software) is now an integral part of the word processing package *Professional Write 2.2.* (Spinnaker).[3] Even though there have been advances in the last two years, the grammar checkers are still in the process of evolving.

3. In 1991 Software Publishing Corporations sold its PFS line to Spinnaker.

Thesaurus

Similar to a dictionary of synonyms, the thesaurus has the capacity of generating synonyms for any word that it has in its dictionary. For example, if the user wants a different word for **peculiar,** Microlytics's *Word Finder* lists such words as: **charming, funny, odd, old fashioned, picturesque.** Figure 3.11 shows Microlytic's *Word Finder* screen.

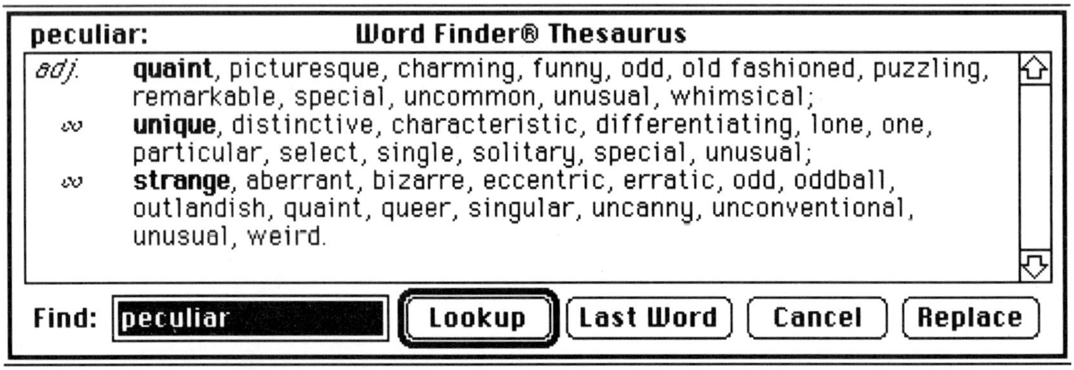

peculiar: **Word Finder® Thesaurus**

adj. **quaint**, picturesque, charming, funny, odd, old fashioned, puzzling, remarkable, special, uncommon, unusual, whimsical;
∞ **unique**, distinctive, characteristic, differentiating, lone, one, particular, select, single, solitary, special, unusual;
∞ **strange**, aberrant, bizarre, eccentric, erratic, odd, oddball, outlandish, quaint, queer, singular, uncanny, unconventional, unusual, weird.

Find: peculiar | Lookup | Last Word | Cancel | Replace

Figure 3.11
Microlytic's Word Finder
Microlytics

The user selects the synonym s/he wants , clicks on **Replace,** and the program automatically substitutes the new word. Thesauruses are different from spelling and grammar checkers because they work at an optimum level as a person is writing.

From reading the lists of features, the reader can see that word processing has certainly come a long way from the *Wang 1200.* A teacher now weighs many factors in order to select one of these word processing programs. Refer now to **Appendix A** for an annotated bibliography of highly rated word processing software programs for the classroom. Next examine one of these programs using the following simple checklist and evaluation rating instrument.

Word Processor Checklist

Directions: Examine the following items and determine which ones you feel are important for your class situation

Product Name ____________ **Manufacturer** __________ **Grade Level** ___________

A. Hardware
- __ 1. Memory Needed
- __ 2. Computer Compatibility
- __ 3. Printer Compatibility
- __ 4. Number of Disk Drives

B. Standard Editing Features
- __ 1. Cursor Control
- __ 2. Insert and Delete
- __ 3. Find/Replace
- __ 4. Block Operations
  - __ a. Delete Block
  - __ b. Copy Block

C. Standard Formatting Functions
- __ 1. Margins
- __ 2. Tabs
- __ 3. Justification
- __ 4. Centering
- __ 5. Headers and Footers
- __ 6. Line Spacing
- __ 7. Boldfacing
- __ 8. Underlining
- __ 9. Superscripts and Subscripts
- __ 10. Automatic Numbering

D. Advanced Features
- __ 1. Split Screen
- __ 2. Footnoting
- __ 3. Automatic Indexing
- __ 4. Outlining
- __ 5. Glossary
- __ 6. Mail merge

E. Safety Features
- __ 1. Undo Last Move
- __ 2. Undo Last Erase
- __ 3. Warning Questions
- __ 4. Automatic Save
- __ 5. Formats Disk Anytime

F. Screen Display
- __ 1. WYSIWYG
- __ 2. 20–40–80 Columns

G. Ease of Use
- __ 1. Help Screens
- __ 2. Tutorial Disk
- __ 3. Printer Setup

H. Support Features
- __ 1. Technical Support
- __ 2. Tutorial Material
- __ 3. Readable Manual
  - __ a. Activities and Lesson Plans
  - __ b. Tutorial
  - __ c. Index
- __ 4. Spelling Checker
- __ 5. Grammar Checker
- __ 6. Thesaurus

I. Consumer Value
- __ 1. Cost
- __ 2. Free backup disk

Rating Scale

Excellent ____ **Very Good** ____ **Good** ____ **Fair** ____ **Poor** ____

Comments

Learning to Use a Word Processor

The following exercises are meant to be used in conjunction with any word processor. If a computer lab is not available, the reader can just follow this section to get a feel for what is involved in using a word processor. Let us begin by loading a word processing program into the computer. Be sure to format one or more data disks with the word processing program so that the floppy disk can store files. After this process is completed, the reader is ready to begin writing on the word processor. Anytime the text appears on the screen, the cursor shows where the next letter or number will appear. The DELETE key will move the cursor to the left and delete letters. The RETURN key, when pressed, moves down the page like the carriage return on a typewriter. After the reader does the following preliminary exercises, then s/he can handle the six subsequent classroom activities.

Now type the jumbled sentence just as it is.

"LIS NOT THERE PRIZES HARD DIFFICULT WORK."

Do **not** press the RETURN key because it will move the cursor down a line.

1. Use the delete key in this instance to (a) delete the L in LIS (b) the T in not and (c) delete the word DIFFICULT. (The delete key deletes characters, words or paragraphs, depending on the writer's purpose.)
2. Now insert the word **FOR** between prizes and hard.
3. Next, learn to use the **MOVE** function and position the word **THERE** at the beginning of the sentence.
4. Use the FIND/REPLACE FUNCTION to replace the word **PRIZES** with **SUBSTITUTE.** If the word processing task is completed correctly, the following quotation appears:

"THERE IS NO SUBSTITUTE FOR HARD WORK."[4]

Before continuing with the next exercise, learn how to save the material just typed and how to erase the screen. In order to practice some basic word processing functions, let's unscramble a famous poem. First type this poem exactly as it appears on the next pages.

4. This quotation is by Alva Edison from *Life*.

Bananas

Stories are made by fools like me,
But only God can make a boy.

A boy whose hungry mouth is prest;
Against the earth's sweet flowing breaset

A boy that looks at God all day,
And lifts his strong arms to pray;

A boy wear
A nest of robins in his hair;

Upon whose boosom snow has lain;
Who intimately lives with rain.

My love he is the one for me;
He is bound to me for eternity.

I think that I shall neever see
A poem lovely as a boy.

1. Use the FIND/REPLACE option to exchange the word **Bananas** with the word **Trees.** Now exchange the word **strong** with the word **leafy,** and the word **stories** with the word **poems.** Use this option to exchange every instance of the following: the word **boy** with the word **tree,** and the word **his** with the word **her.**
2. Center the Word **Trees** as the title of the poem.
3. Use the **CUT AND PASTE** option to exchange lines one and two of the poem with lines 13 and 14. Proceed by cutting lines 1 and 2.

Poems are made by fools like me,
But only God can make a tree.

Move these lines to the very end of the poem.

Cut and Move lines 13 and 14 to the top of the poem. These lines will fill the empty spaces left.

I think that I shall never see
A poem lovely as a tree.

4. Use the **DELETE** Option to delete the 11th and 12th line:
   My love he is the one for me;
   He is bond to me for eternity.

   Now there are two blank lines, so hit the DELETE key twice and that will get rid of these lines. Next insert four words in the poem by putting the cursor on line seven, after the word **tree** and before the word **wear** and then typing the following words:
   that may in Summer
   Use the spacebar to create a space where one is needed.
5. Use the spelling checker to find any spelling errors in the poem. The first word the spelling checker finds is "neever." Since the word is misspelled, change it to "never." The second word the checker finds is "prest"; this word exists, so don't change it; instead add the word to the dictionary. The next word is "breaset;" correct it by typing "breast." The last word the checker finds is "boosom." Correct it by typing "bosom."
6. Now save the poem on the formatted disk.
7. As a final activity print the poem. The print out is the beautiful poem, *Trees,* written by Sergeant Joyce Kilmer[5].

Trees

I think that I shall never see
A poem lovely as a tree.

A tree whose hungry mouth is prest
Against the earth's sweet flowing breast;

A tree that looks at God all day,
And lifts her leafy arms to pray;

A tree that may in Summer wear
A nest of robins in her hair;

Upon whose bosom snow has lain;
Who intimately lives with rain.

Poems are made by fools like me,
But only God can make a tree.

---

5. Reprinted from *Trees and Other Poems* by Joyce Kilmer, George H. Doran Company. Copyright 1914.

8. To finish this exercise, learn how to retrieve a saved file, then reboot the computer and retrieve the poem that was just saved. Finally, learn how to **boldface** and underline the work of art.

The following six ready-to-use classroom activities test the student's ability to use successfully the different features of the word processor.

Classroom Applications

▼ I. Math Race ▼

Objective

The students can improve their math skills and, in the process, practice editing on the word processor.

Procedure

1. The teacher creates a list of math problems from the work that the class is currently doing.
2. The teacher develops a race sheet similar to the following:
3. On this race sheet, the teacher varies the horizontal distance and the vertical spaces between the problems and diversifies the missing parts of the problems.
4. The teacher then saves the race sheet on the disk under the name *Math Race.*
5. Next, the students load this program into their computers.
6. When the teacher gives the signal, the students race to solve the problems. They must use their arrow keys to reach each problem, delete the question mark, replace it with the correct response, then cross the finish line. The student who has the fastest time and correct answers will win the competition.
7. The teacher records a time after each student's name and checks each problem, taking 10% off for each problem not solved correctly.

Math Race

Starting----Position

4 * 5 = ?

8 * ? = 64

54 / 9 = ?

? * 8 = 40

25 / 5 = ?

8 * 8 = ?

72 / 9 = ?

6 * 7 = ?

? / 8 = 3

12 * 9 = ?

Finish----Line

Variation

The instructor can make this a group activity by dividing the class in half and creating two competing teams, Team A and Team B. The class follows the same procedure as before and records the time score for each student. Next, the teacher computes Team A's score; by adding together all the individual scores for Team A and deducting 10% for each problem not solved correctly. Then the teacher computes Team B's score in the same manner. The winning team is the one with the lowest combined time with correct answers. There is no end to the math races an instructor can create for a class.

▼ II. Unscramble the Story ▼

Objective

Upon completing this activity, the student will improve reading comprehension and learn how to use the word processor's MOVE/BLOCK function.

Procedure

1. Choose a story that the students are currently reading.
2. Type the story or part of the story into the computer.
3. For instance, type "The Hare and the Tortoise," an Aesop Fable.

The Hare and the Tortoise

A hare was once boasting about how fast he could run when a tortoise, overhearing him, said, "I'll run you a race." "Done," said the hare and laughed to himself, " but let's get the fox for a judge." The fox consented and the two started. The hare quickly outran the tortoise, and knowing he was far ahead, lay down to take a nap. "I can soon pass the tortoise whenever I awaken." But, unfortunately, the hare overslept himself; therefore when he awoke, though he ran his best, he found the tortoise was already at the goal.

Slow and steady wins the race.[6]

---

4. Save this story under something close to its title like **Hare/Tortoise.**

---

6. An Aesop fable from *The Children's Treasury,* edited by Paula S. Goepfert, Gallery Books, New York, 1987, p. 229.

5. Now scramble the story on the computer screen and use the Move/Block functions on the word processor to rearrange the story. The scrambled Tortoise and Hare story could look like the following:

The Scrambled Hare and the Tortoise

The hare quickly outran the tortoise, and knowing he was far ahead, lay down to take a nap. "Done," said the hare and laughed to himself," but let's get the fox for a judge." The fox consented and the two started. But, unfortunately, the hare overslept himself; therefore, when he awoke, though he ran his best, he found the tortoise was already at the goal. A hare was once boasting about how fast he could run when a tortoise, overhearing him, said, "I'll run you a race." "I can soon pass the tortoise whenever I awaken."

---

6. Save this scrambled fable under AERH—that is Hare scrambled.
7. Load the AERH or scrambled version of the fable into each student's computer.
8. The students must use their word processors to rearrange the story correctly.
9. Record each student's score by writing down the time to complete the activity and number of sentences arranged correctly.
10. The winner is the student who finished first and arranged all the sentences correctly.

Variation

1. Divide the class into two Teams, A and B.
2. Team A is responsible for scrambling a story.
3. Team B then rearranges the story.
4. Team B's score is determined by the time it takes to rearrange the story and the number of sentences correct on completion.
5. Team B then types a scrambled story and Team A tries to rearrange it.

▼ III. The Editor ▼

Objective

Upon completion, the students will gain practice in their basic word processing skills and in using their spell checker.

Procedure

Enter two or three paragraphs into the computer from a story the students have been reading in class and deliberately make four or five spelling errors. For purposes of illustration, let us use the following paragraphs on calculators. Now create five or six editing activities at the top of the paragraphs. An activity sheet sample follows:

Editor

1. Find and Replace the word *calculator* with the word *computer.*
2. In paragraph two for the second line, insert the sentence, "A programmer defines precisely what has to be done in each succeeding step."
3. Delete the last sentence in paragraph two: "The computer is a very useful device."
4. In the last sentence of the first paragraph after the word *stored* insert the words, "and recalled on command."
5. In the second paragraph, take the last sentence of the paragraph and make it the first sentence of that second paragraph.
6. Switch the titles of the paragraphs with each other.
7. Use the spelling checker to correct the six spelling errors.

"Programming the Calculator

Most people regard the calculator as an electrenic marvel, yet the principle on which it works is relativly simple. The heart of the calculator is an arithmetic and logical unit (which adds, subtracts, multiplies, divides, and compares numbers at highe speed by electronic means) and a memory unit, in which many thousands of numbers can be electornically stored

How Calculators Work

The value of the calculator over the human beiing lies in its ability to work without error and at immense speed; it can carry out hundreds of thousands of calculations every second, storing intermediate results in its memory and recalling them instantly when required. The various instrucitons for the stages in the program are stored in the computer memory in numerical form for instant access."[7] The use of the calculator is based on the technique known as programming—the conversion of the problem the calculator is to solve, or the tasks it is to perform, into the simple steps the calculator can carry out. The computer is a very useful device.

---

1. Save these paragraphs under the name *Editor.*
2. Have the students compete with each other and record the time it takes each student to complete the editing activities.
3. The numerical score is the time it takes each student to complete all six directions, plus a penalty for any incorrectly done items. The student with the fastest time and most correct items wins.

Variation

The teacher can design this activity for two groups by dividing the class in half. Team A would design a paragraph and create a set of directions. Team B would take Team A's paragraph and follow the directions, while being timed by Team A. After Team A finishes its tasks, the roles are reversed, and Team B designs the paragraph and creates a set of directions. The team with the fastest time and most correct responses wins.

▼ IV. Punctuation Exercise ▼

Objective

Upon completion of this activity, the student will improve punctuation skills and will practice using the FIND/REPLACE function.

Procedure

1. The teacher designs an activity sheet for the students. S/he types six to ten sentences, eliminating all punctuation marks and putting in asterisks instead. A sample sheet follows:

---

7. *The Random House Encyclopedia.* James Mitchell, Editor in Chief, "How Computers Work." New York, 1977. p. 1672.

Punctuation Exercise

1. The sun is shinning*
2. I bought a computer* a monitor* a printer* and a modem at the computer store*
3. Mom asked* *When will you clean your room?*
4. I have to teach a class at 1*30 this afternoon.
5. "I am going to lunch," said Dick*
6. The computer cost $3*700*

---

2. The instructor saves the Punctuation Exercise in a file with a name like *Punct* and loads this file into each student's computer.
3. The students then use their FIND/REPLACE function to find each asterisk and replace each with the correct punctuation mark.
4. When the students finish, they save their corrected work under their initials. For example, Martin Smith would save it as *Punct.MS.*
5. Later the teacher corrects the students activities and returns the results.

▼ V. Insert the Adjectives ▼

Objective

Upon completion of this activity, the student improves the ability to recognize adjectives and practices using the Find/Replace function of the word processor.

1. The teacher designs a sheet with missing adjectives similar to the following sample sheet.

Insert the Adjective

1. The * mansion sat on top of the hill in a remote end of the forest.
2. The * professor gave a very * lecture to the class.
3. Jim flew the * plane into the sunset.
4. The * horses raced to the end of the glen to see the * man.
5. An * individual visited the classroom yesterday.
6. She was a * * woman with * blue eyes.

---

2. The instructor saves this file under the name, *Adj.* and loads it into each student's computer. S/he then saves this file in the student's computer under the name *Adj.*
3. The student searches for the asterisk before each noun by using the FIND/REPLACE function of the word processor. The student then replaces this asterisk with an adjective.
4. After the student finishes the task, the student should save the work under a name with initials. For example, Vicki Sharp would save her work as *Adj. VS.*
5. Whenever the teacher wants, s/he can print the student's work out to check its accuracy.

▼ VI. Replace the Sentences ▼

Objectives

The student will improve his or her writing skills and, in the process, use the MOVE/BLOCK and FIND/REPLACE functions.

Procedure

1. The students independently create random sentences for a story file.
2. Each student writes his sentence on a piece of paper and the class examines the sentences, correcting grammar errors.
3. The students, one at a time, enter their sentences into the computer.
4. When the sentences are entered, they are separated by a blank line and numbered in the order received.
5. A student then saves these sentences under a name, for example, *Story 1.*
6. The students take turns giving random numbers and verify that these numbers go no higher than the number of sentences that were recorded for Story 1.
7. The teacher recalls *Story 1* from the computer and records this random sequence of numbers at the top of the screen. A sample activity sheet follows.
8. The students now take turns using the FIND/REPLACE function to locate the proper sentences.
9. The students use the MOVE/BLOCK function to move the sentences where they belong.
10. The class selects a Title for the story and a member prints a copy for the entire room.
11. A class member reads the story for the room's amusement.

Story 1

Use the FIND/REPLACE and MOVE/BLOCK Functions to create a story from the sentences that follow. Arrange the sentences in the following sequence.

1 4 8

2 3 5

6 9 7

1. Do not judge food on calories alone.
2. The professor was frustrated with the paper work he had to turn in next week.
3. The student was eagerly awaiting an exciting lecture on computers.
4. The wind blew a bee into the room
5. "Don't forget to pick up the groceries at the store," said Paul.
6. "Did the emergency rations arrive? " asked David.
7. There were many children on the playground.
8. The center fielder could not catch the ball.
9. The sound came from another room.

Summary

This chapter traced the historical beginnings of word processing. In the process, the readers learned the merits of word processing over the standard typewriter. They discovered how easy it was for users to change and edit documents by using word processors. They became familiar with the basic features of word processing and gained insight into what features to consider when selecting a word processor. The author presented a checklist and evaluation scale to facilitate this decision making process, along with specific ideas on how to incorporate the word processor into the classroom situation. There were six word processing activities shown that covered a range of curriculum areas.

Let's continue by taking the mastery test, and referring to the suggested readings and references. **Be sure to review the award winning annotated word processing list in Appendix A.**

Chapter Mastery Test

1. What is word processing and why is it important in education?
2. What distinguishes a typewriter from a word processor?
3. Identify and describe five features that are common to all word processors.
4. Discuss three different ways a word processor would be useful in the classroom?
5. Distinguish among a thesaurus, a spell checker and a grammar checker, and explain why a sixth grader and a tenth grader would prefer one over the other.
6. Select two standard editing features and justify their use.
7. Explain the concept of justification as it relates to the computer and give two examples.
8. Discuss the factors involved in selecting a word processor for a school district. Use Appendix A for an annotated list of word processing software.
9. Define the following terms:
   a. Font
   b. Cut
   c. Block function
   d. Text insertion
   e. Find/replace
10. In designing a word processor, what safety features should be included and why?

Classroom Projects

1. Create a word processing activity for any grade level.
2. Use a word processor with a thesaurus and develop a classroom activity for this feature.
3. Write a story with misspelled words and have the spelling checker find the words that are incorrect.
4. Compare two word processors on the basis of their features; then review each one separately.

Suggested Readings and References

Abbott, Chris. "Microcomputers Software Word Processing for All." *British Journal of Special Education,* 18(1) March 1, 1991, 8.

Adams, C. "Composing with Computers." *Computers in Education,* November, 1985, 18.

Allen, Philip A. "Adult Age Difference in Letter-Level and Word-Level Processing." *Psychology and Aging,* 6(2) June 1, 1991, 261.

Balajthy, E. "Keyboarding, Language Arts, and the Elementary School Child." *The Computing Teacher,* February, 1988, 40–43.

Bradley V. "Improving Students' Writing with Microcomputers." *Language Arts,* October, 1982, 732–43.

Calkins, L. M. "The Art of Teaching Writing." Portsmouth, NH: Heinemann, 1986.

Collier, R. M. "The Word Processor and Revision Strategies." *College Composition and Communication,* 34(2), 1983, 149–155.

Cochran-Smith, Marilyn. "Writing Processing and Writing in Elementary Classrooms: A Critical Review of Related Literature." *Review of Educational Research,* 61(1), Spring 1991, 107.

Daiute, C. "Writing and Computers." Reading, MA: Addison-Wesley, 1985.

Eiser, L. "I Luv To Rite." *Classroom Computer Learning,* November/December 1986, 50–57.

Feldman, P. R. "Personal Computers in a Writing Course." *Perspectives in Computing,* Spring 1984, 4–9 .

Jarchow, E., "Computers and Computing: The Pros and Cons." *Electronic, Education,* June 1984, 38.

Joslin, E. "Welcome to Word Processing." *The Computing Teacher,* March 1986, 16–19.

Howie, S. H. *Reading, Writing, and Computers: Planning for Integration.* Needham Heights, MA: Allyn & Bacon, Longwood Division, 1989.

Howell, R., and P. Scott. *Microcomputer Applications for Teachers.* Scottsdale, Ariz.: Gorsuch, 1985.

Laframboise, Kathryn L. "The Facilitative Effects of Word Processing on Sentence-Combining Tasks With At-Risk Fourth Graders." *Journal of Research and Development in Education,* 24(2), Winter 1991, 1.

Marcus, Stephen. "Word Processing: Transforming Students' Potential to Write." *Media and Methods,* 27(5), May 1, 1991, 8.

Microsoft Word Reference to Microsoft Word. Microsoft Corporation: Redmond Washington, 1989.

Milone, Michael N. *Every teacher's guide to word processing: 101 classroom computer.* Englewood Cliffs, N.J.: Prentice-Hall, 1985.

Morton, L. L. "Lab-Based Word Processing for the Learning-Disabled." *Computers in the Schools,* (8(1/3), 225, 1991.

Poulsen, Erik. "Writing processes with word processing in teaching English as a foreign language." *Computers & Education,* 16(1) 1991, 77.

Roblyer, M. D. "The Effectiveness of Microcomputers in Education: A Review of the Research from 1980–1987." *T.H.E. Journal,* September 1988, 85–89.

Schramm, Robert M. "The Effects of Using Word Processing Equipment in Writing Instruction." *Business Education Forum.* 45(5), February 1, 1991, 7.

Seymour, Jim. "Fast, Flexible, & Forward-Looking." *PC Magazine,* 7(4), February 29, 1988, 92–345.

Smith, Frank E. *Bank Street Writer Plus.* Bank Street College of Education, International Education, Inc. Broderbund Software, California, 1986.

Solomon, G. "Writing with Computers." *Electronic Learning,* November/December, 1985, 39–43.

Varblow, Judy. "Reading, Writing, and Word Processing: An Interdisciplinary Approach." *The Balance Sheet,* 72(2), Winter 1990, 22.

Watt, D. "Tools for Writing." *Popular Computing,* January 1984, 75–78.

Wang, An. *Lessons: An Autobiography.* Reading, Mass: Addison-Wesley, 1986.

Woodrow, Janice F. J. "Teachers' Perceptions of Computer Needs." *Journal of Research on Computing in Education* 23, (4), Summer 1991, 475–493.

Desktop Publishing

4

Objectives

Upon completing this chapter the student will be able to:

1. Explain what desktop publishing is
2. Describe the features of desktop publishing
3. Be familiar with a desktop publishing program and how it operates.
4. Evaluate different desktop publishing packages using standard criteria.
5. Utilize and create a repertoire of desktop publishing activities for the classroom.

Historical Background

Before the year 1450, information was transmitted orally by troubadours who traveled from place to place. They would sing ballads or recite poems concerning the news or gossip of the day. Few people could read or write, and books were scarce because they were handwritten. Reading was mainly for religious instruction or entertainment.

Then circa 1450, Johann Gutenberg revolutionized communication with the invention of moveable type. Modifying a wine makers' press to hold type, he poured hot metal into molds from which he created letters, numbers, and symbols. He placed his type and engravings containing pictures on the bed of the press, inked the surface, and placed a piece of paper on top. When the handle of the press was cranked, the pressure of the plate created an image on the paper (Figure 4.1).

Gutenberg's printing innovation gave more people the opportunity to read by making books more available. Even though, Gutenberg's methods were refined through the years, his basic concept remained unchanged for four hundred years.

In the late 1880s, Ottmar Mergenthaler invented Linotype, the first successful automated typecasting machine. This mechanical type-composing machine let the

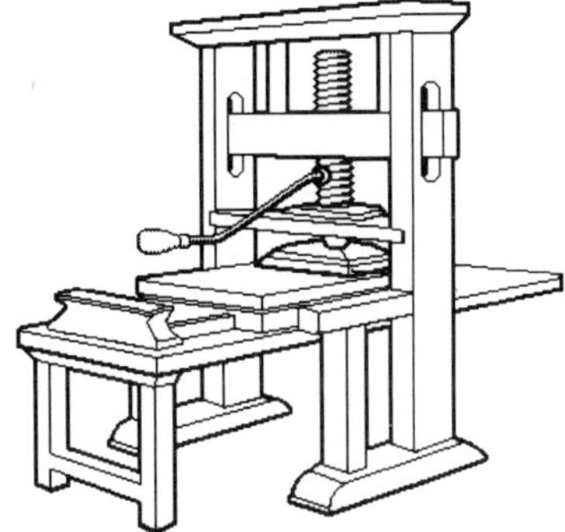

Figure 4.1
Early Printing Press
Dubl-Click Software, Inc.

operator cast an entire line of type at once by using a keyboard. It was first used to typeset the *New York Tribune* in 1886. A year later, Tolbert Lanston invented the Monotype machine that produced three characters of set type a second and was widely used for books.

The Linotype and Monotype, along with hand-set type, dominated typesetting until Intertype introduced the first phototypesetting machine in 1950. Phototypesetting replaced cast type because of its low cost, faster speed, and flexibility. "In this method, the type characters are photographically assembled on film or paper to produce negatives or positives for lithographic or photogravure platemaking" (Grolier Electronic Publishing, 1990).

The search for higher typesetting speeds resulted in the development of a method that would dispense with phototypesetting altogether by storing characters in electronic digital format. However, it wasn't until the mid 1960s that digital typesetting came into existence, and it presently coexists with phototypesetting as a standard for setting type. Digital type uses computer typesetting equipment to describe letter forms as almost invisible dots. This invention led the way for desktop publishing (DTP) a term, coined by Paul Brainward of Aldus Software.

Desktop Publishing

Desktop Publishing (DTP) means using the personal computer (in conjunction with specialized software) to combine text and graphics to produce high quality output that can be printed on either a laser printer or a typesetting machine. This multi-step process, which involves different types of software and equipment, is illustrated in Figure 4.2.

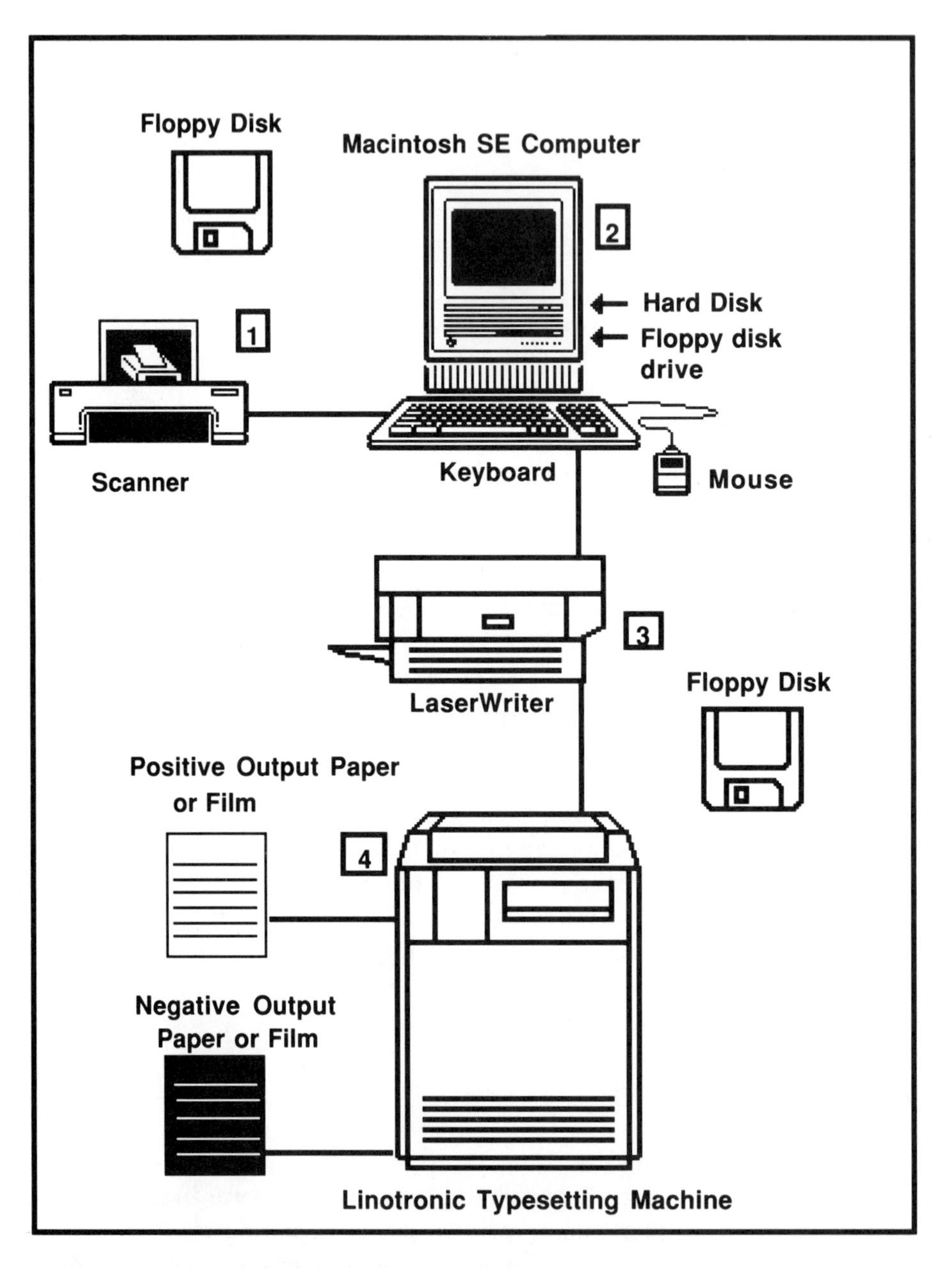

Modified from Desktop Design, Lamar, 1990.

Figure 4.2
Desktop Publishing Process
Modified from *Desktop Design* by Laura Lamar, page 6, Crisp Publications, Los Altos, CA 94022, 1990 Click Art from T/Maker Co. and Dubl-Click Software, Inc.

The computer user's first step is to create original text using the word processor and then produce illustrations using a drawing program or a painting program.

1. The DTP user inputs material using the keyboard, a scanner, a floppy disk, or video digitizer. The person can illustrate the text by using clip art, original art, or a program like Snapshot (Baseline) that captures images on the computer screen.
2. The user then transfers the product to a DTP program which has word processing, graphics features, and lay out capabilities. The user lays out the text and graphics on the screen, revising it and refining it using the DTP's capabilities.
3. At this point, the user has two choices,—printing the finished document on a laser printer or, for better quality, on a typesetting machine. If the user continues, s/he prints out the page proofs on a laser printer, makes further changes and corrections, and readies this final copy for print out.
4. The files are now sent to a service bureau via disk or electronically where the final prints are outputted from a typesetting machine.

Desktop publishing has become an all encompassing term because it can refer to fourteen Macintosh computers connected between a magazine's editorial and design department, or an IBM user running *Children's Writing and Publishing Center* to produce a newsletter on her dot matrix printer, or an eight year old creating a sign to find his lost pet. This tool is no longer the exclusive property of the skilled technician or computer programmer. By using a desktop publishing program, a person can design a business newsletter, create a banner, or produce a school newspaper. DTP lets the individual do the following: (1) create on-screen layouts, (2) use different typefaces or fonts, (3) right justify text and lay out multiple columns, (4) insert and print art and text on the same page and, (5) print camera-ready copy. The individual can take this camera-ready copy to an offset printing press, or if he has a laser printer, print it out. Publishing is now handled electronically by the computer, and DTP is revolutionary because anyone who chooses to learn it can do so.

In the past when students worked on the high school or college newspaper, each student was assigned a different task. Typically, there was a paper designer, a writer, an illustrator, a typesetter, and a "paste-up artist". Now it is possible for one person to perform all these functions by using a desktop publishing program. Desktop publishing has combined these separate tasks into one activity. There are many advantages in preparing student publications this way. DTP offers greater flexibility in designing graphics and headlines, and gives more control over the final product than ever before. The student can easily change the images, enlarge or shrink them, save them on a disk for later revision, and view the finished product early in the process. DTP is a more versatile, faster, and less expensive way to produce publications than the traditional methods because fewer people are involved and fewer revisions are necessary. DTP is a natural outgrowth of word processing, and word processing programs like the *Bank Street Writer* (New Macintosh Version) and the *Writing Center* (Macintosh and IBM versions) that have limited desktop features.

Currently, desktop publishing has become a popular phenomenon, but this was not always the case. In 1985, there were few DTP programs, and the ones available were *Pagemaker* (Aldus) and *Ready Set Go* (Manhattan Graphics).[1] These programs were designed only for the Macintosh computer, but today, there are many programs to choose from, and they exist for all computers.

The software and hardware the student needs for DTP range in price from inexpensive to very expensive. On the one hand, if the user wants to print an informal newsletter, s/he might use a program like *Children's Writing and Publishing Center* and a simple dot matrix printer. On the other hand, if the computer user is responsible for a business presentation that needed to be designed professionally, the person could use expensive scanning equipment, a program like *Pagemaker,* and create text on a full-fledged word processor. Although the resolution from a laser printer would not be as high as professional typesetting equipment, the resulting copy would be quite exceptional. Desktop programs differ in degree of complexity and features. In the following paragraphs, some of the basic characteristics of these programs will be discussed.

The Basic Desktop Publishing Features

Some of the features included in desktop publishing programs are a spelling checker, thesaurus, a fully integrated word processor, text rotation, and various graphics tools. Although the desktop programs differ in their sophistication, there are still commonalties that unite them. The commonalties we will discuss are: (1) page layout; (2) word processing; (3) style sheets and templates; (4) graphics; and (5) page view.

Page Layout

Page layout is the process of arranging the various elements on the page using DTP's page layout features. During the process, the user sets such items as the page margins, the number and width of the columns for regular text, and the position of the graphics and text. The most powerful programs like *Aldus PageMaker* and *Ventura Publishing* allow the user greatest control in page design; however these programs are sophisticated and demand a steep learning curve. There are less powerful programs like

1. This product is currently produced by Letraset USA.

Publish It Easy (Timeworks), *Springboard Publisher II* (Springboard) and *Publish-It 4 (Timeworks)* that offer a wide variety of options, requiring less learning time.

In addition to these programs, there are word processing programs like *The Writing Center* (Learning Company) and *Bankstreet Writer* (Scholastic) that have sufficient desktop capabilities to fulfill the desktop publishing needs of children from ages ten and beyond. Finally, there is the *Children's Writing and Publishing Center* (Learning Company), an excellent program for people from ages 7 to adult. This program lets the child select the document type (page layout) as shown in the following screen.

In this limited program for children, a report, story, or letter has one column of words and pictures and can be only four pages long. Furthermore, a newsletter has two fixed columns of words and pictures and can be only one page long.

A *Pagemaker* user determines the page size, sets margins, and chooses the number of columns and the width of each column. This program has master pages or templates that let the user design a standard page for every page in the document and measuring rulers and guides to help with the placement of graphics and text on the page. The majority of DTP programs let the user see an overview of the page to decide if its final design meets with the person's approval. Many present programs can resize, reshape, and reposition text, or graphics anytime, and they all have automatic page numbering.

Most page-layout programs are based on frames. If the individual wants to put text into a document, s/he either places it in the base page, an immovable frame that covers the entire page, or draws a frame and enters or imports text or graphics. With the help of a screen ruler, each program requires that the person define the shape of a text block or the size of a graphic by drawing a box or frame on the page. Once the

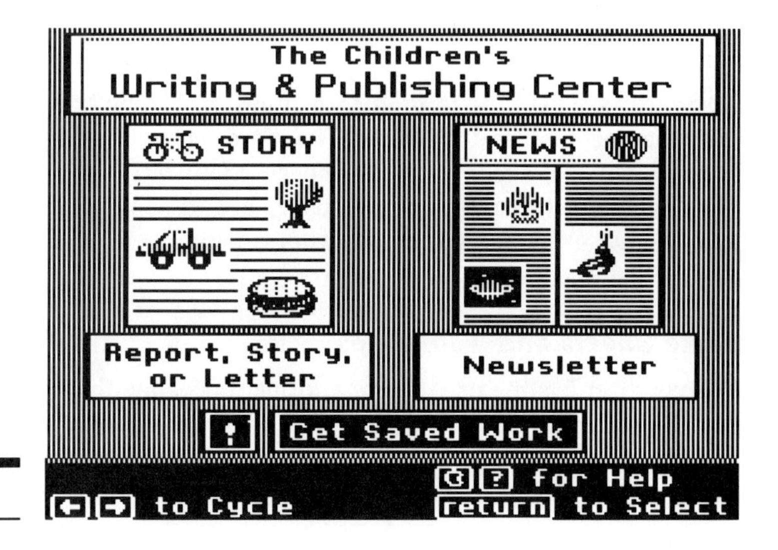

The Learning Company

frame is defined, the user imports the text or graphic to fill the space. The user can stack frames or create captions that overlay illustrations. The desktop publishing program should let the individual create as many frames as s/he wants and put them anywhere on the page. After the frames are placed, it should then be a simple matter to adjust them.

Pagemaker, the progam that set the standard for desktop publishing, is a variation on this frame-based model. In this program, the person drags the mouse to define the size of the space the text (or graphic) will fill. The *Pagemaker* user creates a frame, but in this case it is an invisible one. Next, the individual imports text or graphics by using the mouse to place the icon representing the graphic or text item on the page and then clicking the mouse for placement. After the graphic or text item is positioned, s/he can easily move the item by clicking on it, placing it elsewhere, and clicking on it again to reposition it. This method of placement leaves the page uncluttered, encouraging experimentation. Many graphics artists prefer it because they are not working with a cluttered screen and have more freedom to lift and shift graphics and text.

Word Processing

The power of the word processor varies with the Desktop Publishing program, but all DTP programs can edit and format text to some degree.

Editing. The majority of these packages let the individual enter text, edit it, and usually import documents from other word processors. The typical word processing functions are delete, insert, and copy. The majority of desktop publishing programs have spelling checkers and many have thesauruses. For the high school student, it is important that there are move, search, and replace functions.

Formatting Text. The formatting features determine how the page will look—such as the type size, font, and typefaces. The more control the user has over the text, the more professional the document will appear. Many DTP programs let the user center or align text, which makes uniform margins, and some programs let the user define the space between letters, words, and lines, which improves the readability and appearance of the document.

Style Sheets and Templates

A style sheet lets the user define a format once, one that he or she can repeat throughout the paper. For example, an individual might design a style sheet with page numbers in the right hand corner located two inches from the top of the page (so that every page in the document would have the page numbers in the right hand corner

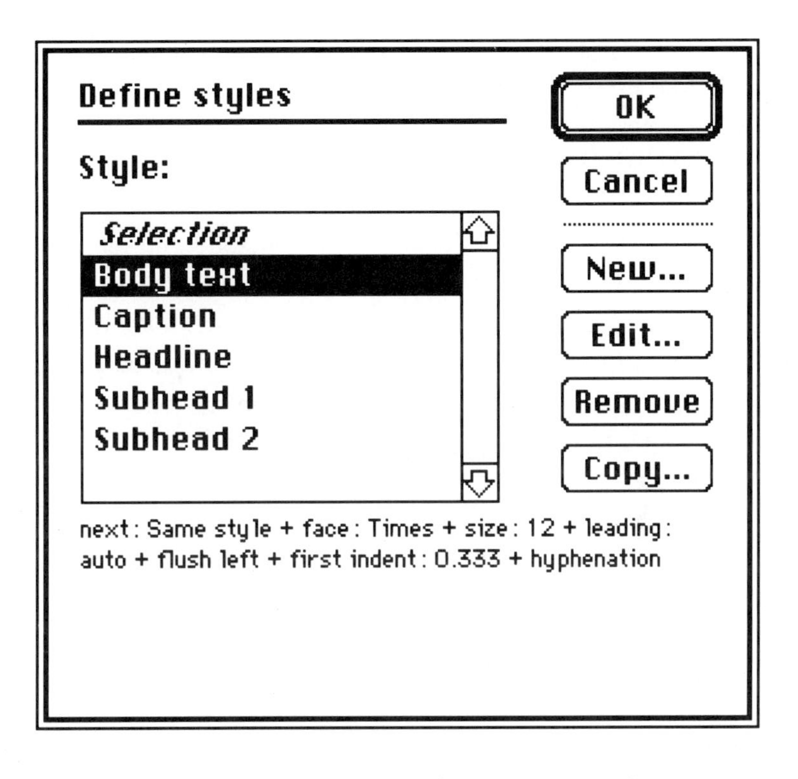

two inches from the top). If the DTP has a style sheet, the software user sets the margins, type style, line spacing, headers, footers and quotations only once and never has to reset them again. In *Pagemaker 4.0* the user defines a style using the dialog box shown above.

In this example, the style selected is "Body text" and it is defined as Times with 12 points, automatic leading, flush left justification, a .333 first indent, and automatic hyphenation. The user applies this style by selecting the text and clicking on the body text style in the following style box:

The style sheet is automatically applied to the selected text block and the result looks like this:

"The longest running- computer crime. Double-entry inventory control at Saxon Industries. A Fortune 500 company that reported profits of $7.1 million and $5.3 million in 1979 and 1980, respectively, it went bankrupt in 1982. A bogus inventory record was maintained by computer-by Saxon's Business Products Division. It was used to inflate the company's annual revenues. The double books were kept for thirteen years, and the crime might never have been revealed if the company had been profitable. Saxon was $53 million in the hole when it went under." (Rochester and Gantz, 1983, p. 117)

Quite a few DTP programs contain their own style sheets and others let the user import style sheets into their word processors. Many DTPs provide templates—guides already set up—and some companies let the user create their own templates. The following report template is from *Children's Writing and Publishing Center.*

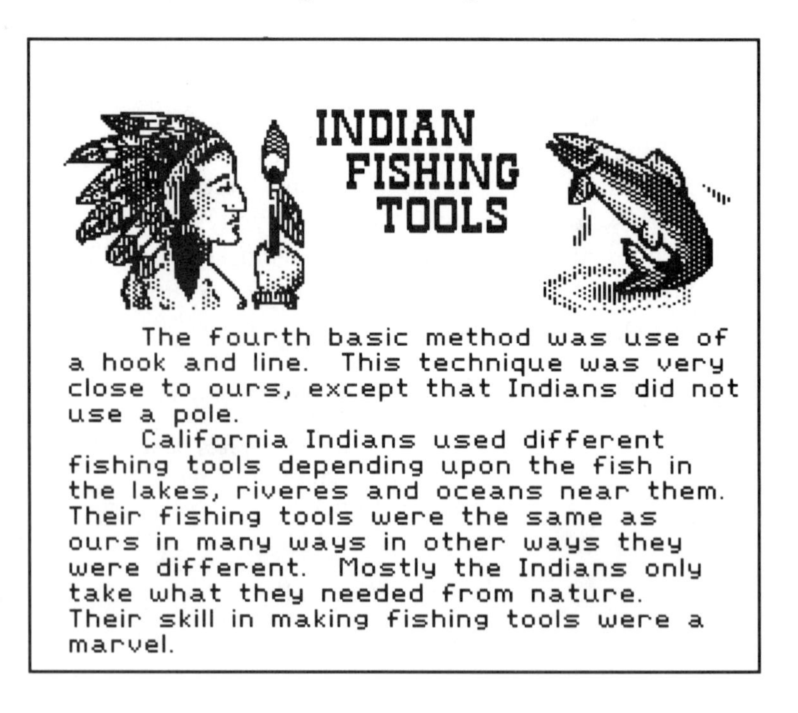

The Learning Company

Graphics

Desktop publishing programs let the individual add pictures or graphics to text either by drawing them or by importing them. A program that lets the user draw his own creations offers many tools to help in the process, including a paintbrush, a spray can, patterns, rectangles, and ovals. Figure 4.3 from *Publish It* shows the graphics and art tools that are available for the student's use.

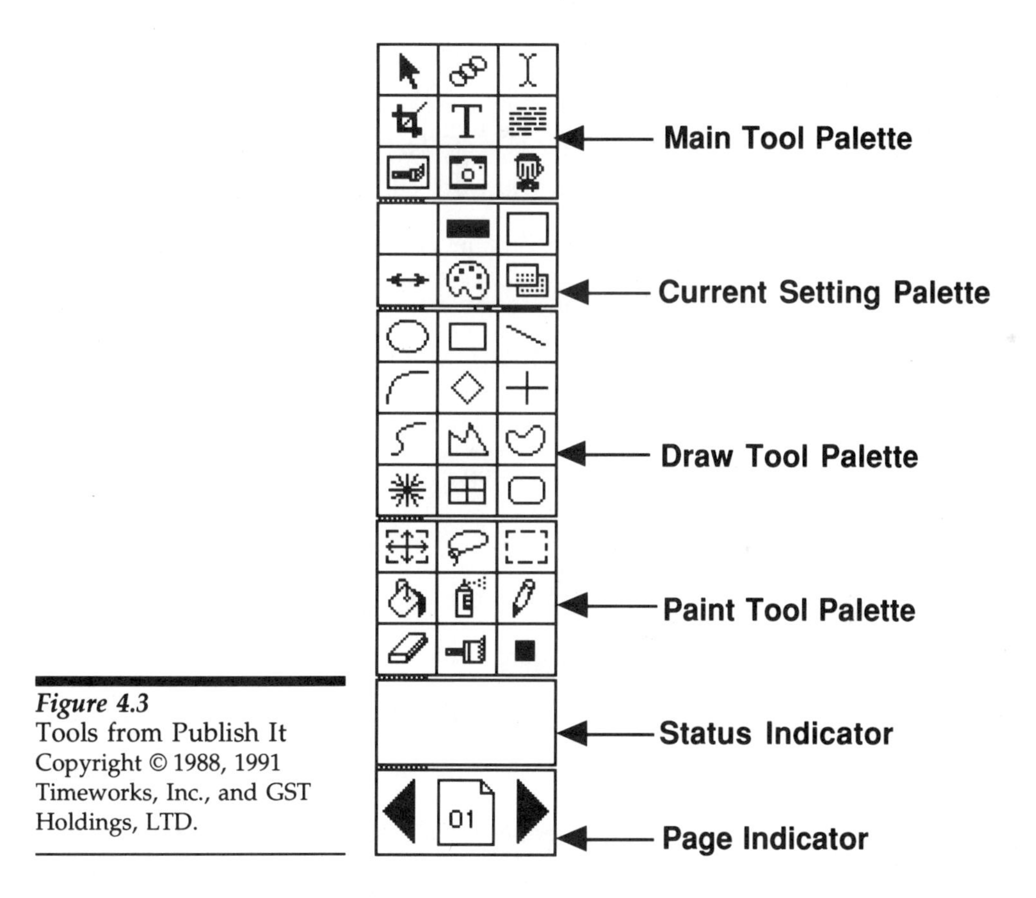

Figure 4.3
Tools from Publish It
Copyright © 1988, 1991 Timeworks, Inc., and GST Holdings, LTD.

Each tool serves a different function. Let us look at a few of the tools in the main tool palette, current setting palette, draw tool palette, and paint tool palette.

In the main tool Palette the pointer tool is used for selecting and deselecting, moving and resizing text and graphic frames. The insertion tool, a flashing point, , enters, edits, and removes text from the document. The text frame tool draws the text frames that are used to hold the text T as illustrated by the following heading:

THE NEWS

In the current setting palette the pen size tool lets the user choose a pen width from a pop–up palette of 67 different width selections. The arrowhead tool sets the style for the ends of a line, either a plain line, an arrowhead at the beginning of a line, an arrowhead at the end of a line, or an arrowhead at both ends.

The draw tool palette contains different tools for drawing object oriented graphics. The oval tool lets the person draw ovals or circles. The radial spokes tool lets the individual draw shapes with solid centers that have spokes coming out at angles.

The paint tool palette contains nine tools for painting and working with graphics. The Lasso and Region Marquee are both used to select objects or quickly erase large areas of a frame. The Lasso handles objects that are close together and irregularly shaped, while the marquee selects rectangular type areas. The eraser erases the drawing or word like an eraser on a chalkboard. The Flood Fill Tool fills an area with the fill pattern that the person selects. In Figure 4.4, this bucket tool was shown to fill one wall of the castle with a solid black, another one with a dotted pattern, and the top of the castle with gray. The spray can applies a current pen pattern, as if from a spray can of paint. This is illustrated by the pattern around the word *castle* in Figure 4.4. The pencil, a tool that draws black on white background or white on black background, drew a couple of black lines in the castle illustration. The paint brush tool, which has 32 different brush shapes and 64 pen sizes, drew a couple of lines above the castle door.

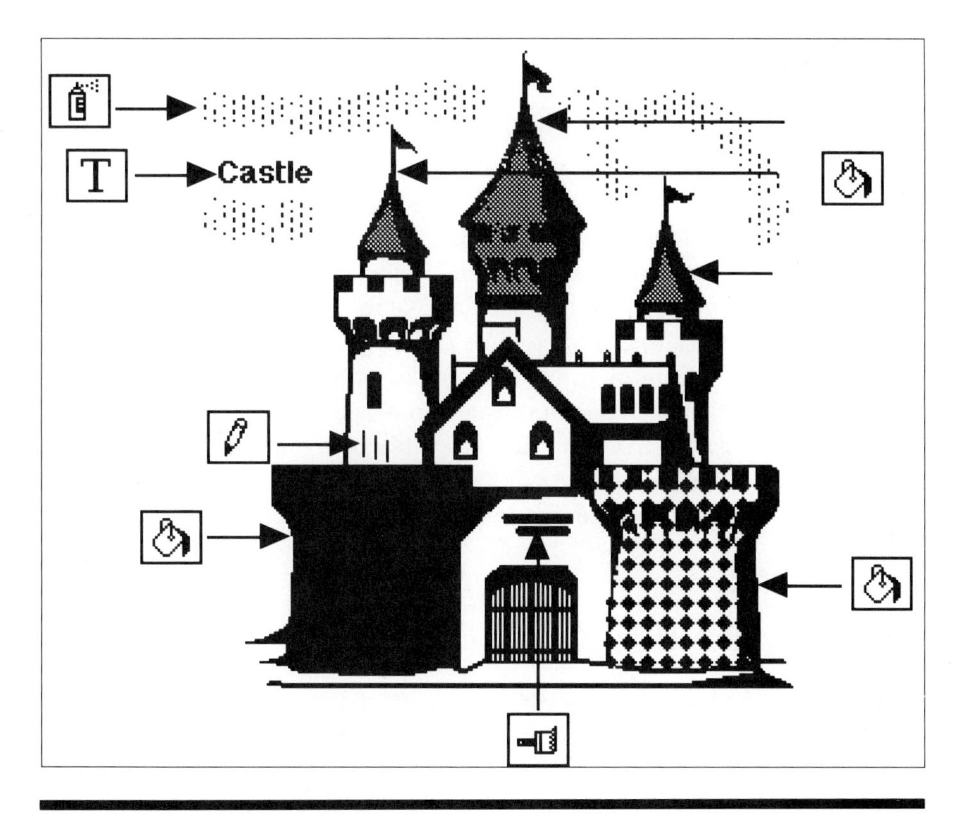

Figure 4.4
A Castle from Wet Paint Publishing
Dubl-Click Software Inc., Tools from Timeworks. Copyright © 1988, 1991 Timeworks, Inc., and GST Holding, Ltd.

Figure 4.5
Border Pattern, Wet Paint Publishing
Dubl-Click Software Inc.

Besides graphic tools, there are features that customize artwork, and that let the user reduce, enlarge, rotate, or flip a drawing, zoom in for detail, and then edit the material, pixel by pixel.[2] Some programs can trace edges and change perspective, which then can be used to produce halo effects around graphics or to outline type, or even to convert silhouettes to simple outline form. Using a desktop publishing program, a student can crop or trim away part of the image and use it as a separate graphic. S/he can also repeat or duplicate an image, thus creating, interesting designs. For example, the user can easily duplicate pictures in a regular pattern or staggered pattern. Figure 4.5 shows the same cowboy image duplicated in a regular border pattern.

A student who can't draw can import art work from other places. Most DTP programs import paint graphics or draw graphics files. Once the graphic is imported, it is important to have a text wrap feature to take care of any graphic overlay problems.

Page View

After the page layout is completed, a user invariably wants to see how it looks before printing out the document. *Children's Writing and Publishing Center* has this feature to a limited degree. The child sees the design of the page, but does not see the actual graphics or text. *The Writing Center* lets the user see what the layout will look like before it is printed with the graphics and text reduced in size. Using *Springboard Publisher,* the student can see a full page view, the actual size view, a two page spread, and even a thumbnail view of sixteen pages.

Now that the reader has some ideal of DTP features, let us look at some ways to select a good program that will meet the student's needs.

---

2. "The smallest element on a video display screen that can be manipulated to create letters, numbers, or graphics." (Freedman, 1991)

How to Choose a Good Desktop Publishing Program

There are many desktop publishing packages on the market today and they come with every imaginable feature. Among these are DTP programs that lend themselves easily to classroom use. Some programs that fit this description are *Once Upon Time, Bank Street Writer, Children's Writing and Publishing Center, The Writing Center, Publish-It, Publish It Easy, Springboard Publisher II,* and *Better Working Word Publisher.*

To choose a DTP program for the classroom, do the following: (A) Examine the hardware compatibility of the program. (B) Look at the program's general features. (C) Study the program's instructional design. (D) See how easy it is to use the package. (E) Check out the program's cost effectiveness and (F) Check out the program's technical support.

A. Hardware Compatibility

Find out what computers are available at the school. Are the computers Apple IIe's, Apple IIGS's, Commodore 64's, IBM's, or Macintosh LC's? How much memory does each machine have? Are we looking at 64K, 128K, 256K, 512K, 1 megabyte or 2 megabytes? How many disk drives are available for each machine and what kind? Generally DTP programs need two disk drives—one drive holds the program, while the other the data. What is the size of these disk drives? Are these 3 1/2 inch drives, 5 1/4 inch or a hard disk drive and a floppy disk drive? What other equipment is available? For instance, does the district have a video digitizer or a scanner?

B. General Features

How many columns can the user create for a document? *Pagemaker* creates twenty columns, the *Writing Center* creates a maximum of nine columns, while *Children's Writing and Publishing Center* creates only two columns. Is it fully What You See is What You Get (WYSIWYG)? Can the user enlarge or shrink the graphics s/he imports? If the student makes a mistake, can he or she easily change it? When the user loads a program into the computer, what is displayed on the screen? Is there an untitled document with tools or an endless series of screens? How difficult is it to change the fonts and italicize or bold face the text? How many fonts are included, and can the user mix type and font styles and sizes anywhere on the page? How easy is it to insert a piece of art in the document? What graphics tools are supplied to change the artwork that was imported or created? How extensive are the word processing features? Does the program have a find and replace feature, the ability to copy, cut and paste text, and a spelling checker and thesaurus?

There are a myriad of features to consider, but the most important question to ask is "Which ones are necessary?" For the elementary school child, the major concern should be a product that produces pleasant results; therefore a less sophisticated program is required. The high school student or novice should have a program that has more features, and thus more versatility.

C. Instructional Design

A desktop publishing program design should be straight forward. The program that has a menu bar displayed at the top of the screen is ideal for beginners. The child does not have to remember the different functions. *Children's Writing and Publishing Center* and PFS *First Publisher* have such a Menu Bar. The menu bar shown from *Children's Writing and Publishing Center* clearly displays the choices that are available from this program:

Any novice can change the font, add a picture, or use the printer by selecting the proper icon. The key to programs like *Publish-It 4,* and *Springboard II* is the flexibility of their design and the many options that are available for the user. *Publish-It* has more features and is faster than *Springboard Publisher II.* However, *Springboard Publisher II* has an outstanding starter manual and is easier to learn.

In looking at instructional design the buyer should ask the following questions: Is it a simple matter to make changes? Can the person easily delete, add or insert text? How fast is the general performance of the desktop publishing program? (A program that is very slow can waste time if the person is in a hurry to complete a job. For example, *Newsroom,* one of the first DTP programs for the elementary school, was a slow and cumbersome program, while the newer programs are much faster and more flexible.) How quick is it to change fonts, font style, character, line spacing, and paragraph justification? What flexibility does the program have in printing the newspaper? How easy is it to access the program functions? Some programs like *Springboard Publisher II* and *Publish It* have keyboard shortcuts for many of their functions, so it is not necessary to use their pull-down menus.

D. Ease of Use

The program must be easy to learn and must use simple English commands. Ask the following questions: Can the student sit down and in approximately 60 minutes be able to use this program? Are there help screens that inform the person what to do each step of the way, and are they easily accessible? Is there a menu bar across the screen so the user does not have to remember the different functions? Is there a tutorial disk or manual that takes the student through the program? How difficult is it to figure out how to use the printer setup? Can a user answer a few questions and then be ready to print immediately? Is the program tedious to use because there are too many help prompts and safety questions? Is there an automatic save feature?

E. Consumer Value

Cost has to be a major consideration in choosing a program. *Children's Writing and Publishing* can be bought for as little as $36 dollars, whereas programs like *Pagemaker* cost hundreds of dollars. Other questions to ask are as follows: If the software is protected, does the software company provide the buyer with a free backup copy? If it is unprotected, the buyer can make his or her own backup copies when necessary. (*Publish It 4* for the Macintosh is unprotected, while *Children's Writing and Publishing Center* (Apple II Version) is protected.) Does the program include templates and graphic art? (*The Writing Center, The Children's Writing* and *Publishing Center, Publish It,* and *Springboard* have templates and art included, which make these programs better value for the money.) Also, are there lab packs?

F. Support

Any reference to support, means personal as well as written help. Is the documentation sent with the program helpful, or bulky and unreadable? Can the user call someone immediately to get help on the telephone, or does s/he sit through a series of messages and wait an unbearable amount of time? Many software companies now tell the caller how many customers are before him or her and how long the wait is. It is important to get this help right away in order to use the program and not be forever frustrated. Is technical support toll free or a pay call? Is there a tutorial with the software package? Is the tutorial in the form of a manual, disk, or both? Many manufacturers provide both to simplify learning their programs. Is the manual readable, with activities, lesson plans, and an index? How easy is it to get a refund if the disk is a defective one?

Before a teacher selects a desktop publishing program, s/he should look at the pupils' needs in the classroom. From this analysis the teacher can decide what features meet these needs. From reading the list of features in this chapter, the reader can see that many factors must be weighed in order to select a DTP program.

Refer now to Appendix A for an annotated bibliography of highly rated DTP programs for the classroom. Next examine one of these programs using the following sample checklist and evaluation rating instrument.

Desktop Publishing Checklist

A. Hardware
- __ 1. Memory needed
- __ 2. Computer compatibility
- __ 3. Printer compatibility
- __ 4. Number of disk drives

B. Features
- __ 1. Comprehensive undo
- __ 2. Page size selection
- __ 3. Adjustable column size
- __ 4. Page preview
- __ 5. Graphics
  - __ a. Ruler guides
  - __ b. Resize, position, crop
  - __ c. Flip, slip, and invert
  - __ d. graphic importing
- __ 6. Text wrap around graphics
- __ 7. Word processing
  - __ a. Insert/delete
  - __ b. Search/replace
  - __ c. Copy/paste
  - __ d. Spelling checker
  - __ e. Thesaurus
  - __ f. Tabs
  - __ g. Automatic pagination
  - __ h. Hyphenation
- __ 8. Typesetting
  - __ a. Variety of type sizes
  - __ b. Different type styles
  - __ c. Variety of fonts
  - __ d. Kerning
  - __ e. Margin setting
- __ 9. Drawing/painting tools

C. Design
- __ 1. Speed of execution
- __ 2. Ease of graphics insertion
- __ 3. Simple saving function
- __ 4. Easy printing procedure
- __ 5. Number of columns possible
- __ 6. Type of page layout
- __ 7. Method of graphic importing
- __ 8. Formatting within program

D. Ease of Use
- __ 1. On-screen help
- __ 2. Tutorial disk
- __ 3. Easy printer setup
- __ 4. Minimal learning time
- __ 5. Automatic Save

E. Consumer Value
- __ 1. Cost
- __ 2. Unprotected software
- __ 3. Backup
- __ 4. Extra disk supplied
- __ 5. Templates
- __ 6. Clip art Included
- __ 7. Lab packs

F. Support
- __ 1. Technical
- __ 2. Tutorial material
- __ 3. Readable manual
  - __ a. Activities
  - __ b. Lesson plans
  - __ c. Index
- __ 4. Money back guarantee

Rating Scale

Excellent ____ **Very Good** ____ **Good** ____ **Fair** ____ **Poor** ____

Comments

After using this checklist a couple of times, the reader should be able to make a more informed decision on how to select software. Now let us explore how to use a desktop publishing program.

Learning to use a Desktop Publishing Program

This section gives the reader an overview of how a desktop program operates. It should not serve as a substitute for the program's operational manual. For illustrative purposes, let's use *The Writing Center* (Learning Company), a word processing program with some desktop capabilities. This program has many more advanced features than *The Children's Writing and Publishing Center,* Learning Company's first DTP for the schools. In the following paragraphs, the reader will see how *The Writing Center* does a layout, adds text and graphics, and refines the product to produce a print out. When the student opens the *The Writing Center,* s/he sees the following screen with three page layout options:

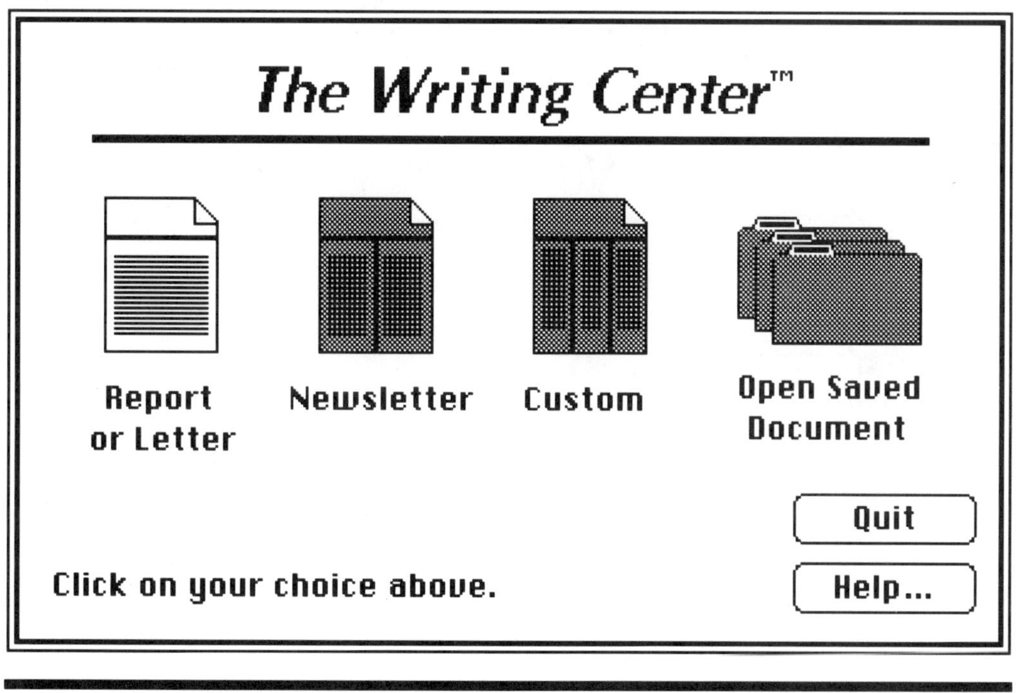

The Learning Company

The student has the option of creating a report or letter, a newsletter, or a custom document. The user chooses the custom option when he or she wants a different column size, formatting, etc. DTP programs then have the user make a series of decisions about the page layout. If the student chooses "Newsletter" on *The Writing Center*, s/he next decides whether to have a heading.

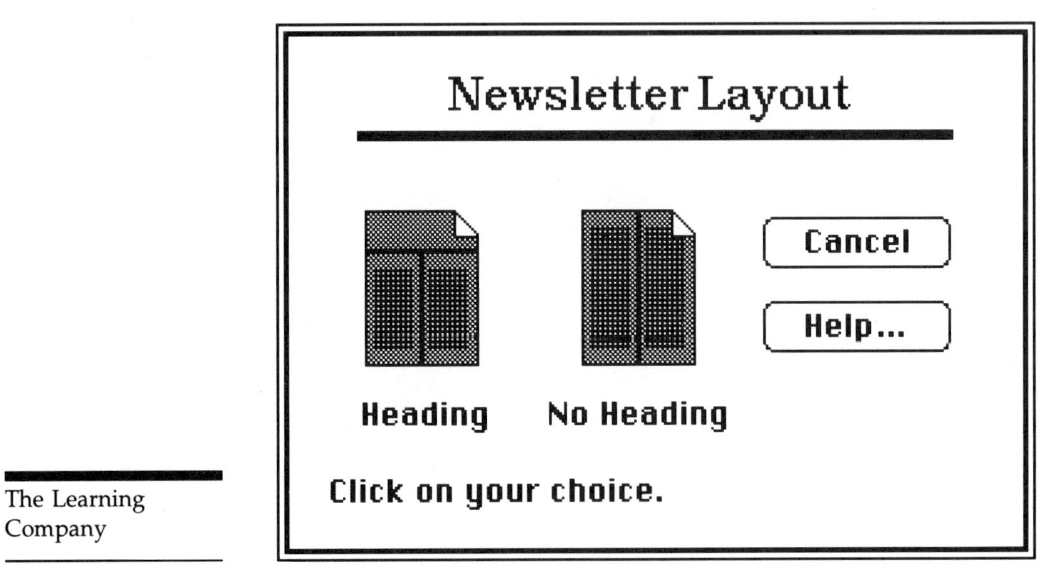

The Learning Company

If the heading is chosen, the following screen appears with a heading and body.

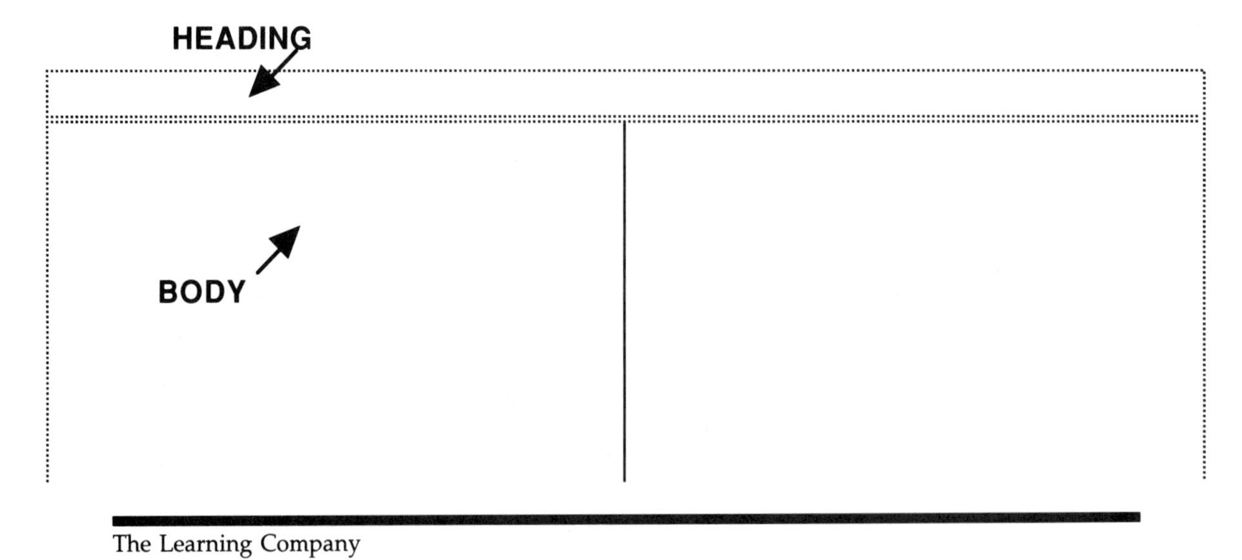

The Learning Company

During the process, the person can make changes such as margins, column sizes, page numbers, and border lines. Once these decisions are made, the student is ready to write or import text and pictures into the document. In many DTP programs, it is easier to make the changes in the word processing program and save the small changes for the DTP program. *The Writing Center* imports text from word processing documents in a text only format. This means the text looses the formatting, but this still eliminates retyping the document. In many DTP programs, for example, *Springboard Publisher II* and *Publish It Easy,* the text is in the form of text frames that can be moved as a complete unit. *The Writing Center* lets the person add text by simply positioning the insertion point anywhere s/he wants the desired text. The writer can then make any adjustments like justification, spacing, bordering, or font changes. He or she can spell check the document and use the thesaurus to find alternate words.

Occasionally the student imports graphics to illustrate a story; this usually means defining spaces or frames that the graphics will fit. In *The Writing Center,* the person chooses the picture s/he wants by clicking on it and then places it in the document. This picture then has a frame with eight "edit handles" around it. After the picture is placed, the person can resize it, move it, rotate it, or turn it sideways. *The Writing Center* has 200 pictures, that cover a range of subjects, and the user can also employ pictures from clip art collections and pictures created with other paint programs. Unlike *Pagemaker,* or *Publish It Easy,* this particular program has no painting or graphics tools of its own. The person can refine the document, creating lines, or borders to decorate the page. During this experimentation process, the student works on the actual page, but frequently needs to view the entire page. The student then activates the page preview function that displays the document in a window as shown on the following page.

Many DTP programs have a zoom feature that lets the individual see a close-up of small sections of the document.

The last step is printing the document either on a dot matrix or laser printer. The laser printer produces a professional quality copy as shown on page 103, a sample newsletter from *The Writing Center.*

Although this procedure seems straightforward, there are always compatibility problems between programs, and different programs, have different features and capabilities. Some are much easier to use and import graphics easily, while others offer more flexibility, include painting and drawing tools, and are more difficult to use.

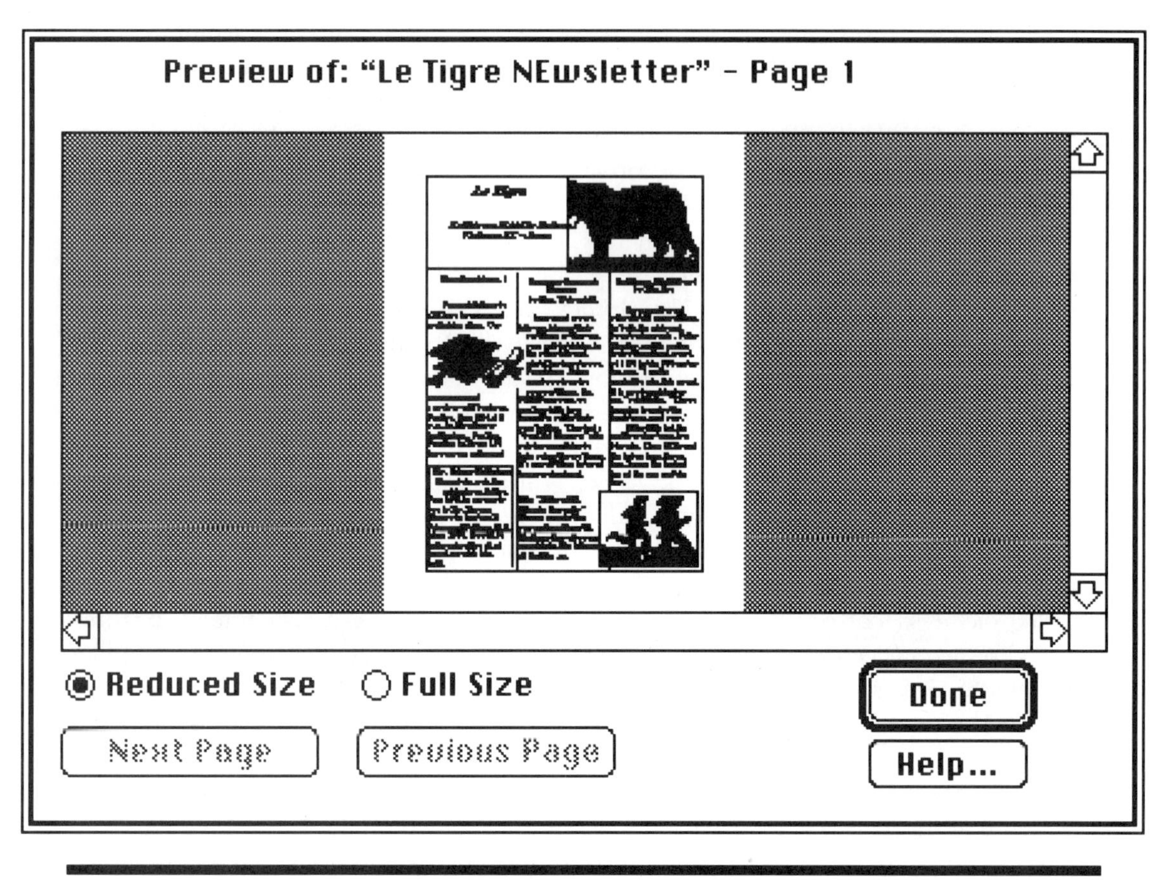

The Learning Company

Desktop Publishing Programs for the Classroom

In Appendix A there is an annotated listing of highly rated desktop publishing programs. Let us quickly review a few of these programs in terms of age level suitability. *Once Upon a Time* (CompuTeach), *KidWriter,* (Spinnaker), *Big Book Maker* (Queue) are early grade programs with desktop publishing features. *Once Upon a Time* lets children design and publish their own illustrated books. The objects in the picture set are displayed, and once the child selects a word, the program pronounces the word. *Big Book Maker* lets the student combine graphics and text to create big books, and *Kidwriter* lets the user combine graphics and text to produce a standard size book. All three programs let the students print their work to see what they have created. These programs have very limited word processing and picture handling features, but they are superior programs for the primary grades because of their low learning curve.

Le Tigre

Sullivan Middle School
Volume IX - June

Graduation !

Congratulations to all those in our newest graduating class. Our commencement exercises will begin on Sunday, June 23rd at 2 p.m. in Eisenhower Auditorium. See Mrs. Sanchez in Room 110 for your cap and gown!

Mr. Rizzo Retiring!
Please join us in the cafeteria on Friday, June 14th to say good-bye to Mr. Thomas Rizzo who has taught Science at Sullivan M.S. since 1973. He will be sadly missed by all of us and we wish him well.

Summer Support Groups:
by Mrs. Weisenfeld

In support groups, kids can discuss their problems or they can pass and just listen to the othcr kids and what they have to say. Sometimes, it is a great way to solve your problems. On CNN Newsroom, we saw how kids have learned to settle their own battles. They had a "Conflict Manager" who acted as a mediator to help solve the problems. It's a cool thing to try at home or at school.

The "Kids with Single Parents" Group meets the second and fourth Wednesday of

The Children's Writing and Publishing Center (Learning Company) and *Children's Newspaper Maker* (Orange Cherry Software) are more advanced and more suitable for grades two through six because of their better picture handling and increased word processing capabilities. Although these features are improved, they are by no means fully functioning desktop publishing programs. For example, *Children's Newspaper Center* has rudimentary word processing features, bare bones page-layout capabilities and no spell-checker. When a user graduates from this type of program, s/he might try a program like *Bank Street Writer* (Scholastic) or *The Writing Center* (Learning Co.) Both programs have better word processing features and more desktop publishing capabilities, but they lack painting and graphics tools. Programs like *Publish It Easy, Springboard Publisher, Medley,* and *PFS Choice* fill this void by providing painting and drawing tools and additional word processing and page layout features, that are useful for the middle grade student. Finally, at the high school level, a student might want to buy advanced professional programs like *Pagemaker, Ready Set Go, Personal Press, Quark Express,* or *Publish It 4* because they possess a multitude of features, file handling capabilities, and flexibility.

Guidelines for Desktop Publishing

1. Spend time planning the task and collect the items that will be included in the proposed paper or newsletter. Make a sketch or a rough layout. Review what will be communicated. Who is the audience? What approach will be best for communicating the message? Be flexible and willing to experiment. Look for consistency on each page of the document and check for balance of design. Add interest when it is needed. Organize a page around a dominant visual drawing.
2. Decide the format for the publication. Pay close attention to borders, margins, etc. Provide a dramatic graphic for the front page. When creating a headline, make this headline forceful to organize the writing.
3. Add emphasis to the work. For example, use large type size to bring across important ideas when needed. When necessary, vary the type style by using **boldface** or *italicizing*. Use blank spaces to make the designs stand out. Highlight the ideas with beautiful artwork, but do not overdo it. Let the reader's eyes focus on a particular part of the page.
4. Be careful not to clutter the page with too many elements.
5. Do not use too many typefaces because it detracts from the general feeling of what a person is writing.
6. Try to avoid white space, the part of the page where nothing appears. If it is unavoidable, surround the area with gray or black space.

7. Have the artwork face into the text.
8. Check the work thoroughly before printing out copies, and look at the printout again to apply finishing touches.

There are many activities a teacher can use with students so they are enthusiastic about writing with a DTP program. Here is a collection of five classroom activities.

Classroom Applications

Activity One: Preliminary Language Arts Skills

Objectives: The students will learn some preliminary organizational skills. At the completion of this project, they will produce a simple picture with a few lines of text.

1. Have the students bring in newsletters, newspapers, and magazines. Distribute these items around the class.
2. Divide the class into groups of five and have each group clip out text and pictures from the newspapers and magazines.
3. Next, each group chooses a picture and illustrates it with a line or two of text. For example, students can choose a headline from an article, use a graphic from an advertisement, and a line of text from the front page. The final product should communicate something.
4. Now each group uses the desktop publishing program to translate this pasteup representation. Students will have to make some substitutions depending on the graphics available from their desktop publishing program.
5. End the process by having each group display its final design and discuss it with the entire class.

Activity Two: Language Arts

Objective: The student will learn some preliminary DTP skills.

1. Have each student in the class write a story.
2. Discuss each story, talk about it, and make recommendations on how to improve it.
3. Have the students then use their scissors to cut and paste, revising their story.
4. Next, have them use the DTP program to enter their story.
5. Print out copies of each child's story for the entire class.
6. Have the students read and discuss the stories.

Activity Three: Math Stories

Objective: The students will learn how to write math word problems using their DTP program.

1. Distribute a Math Activity Sheet similar to the following:
2. Ask the students to read and solve the word problems found on this sheet.

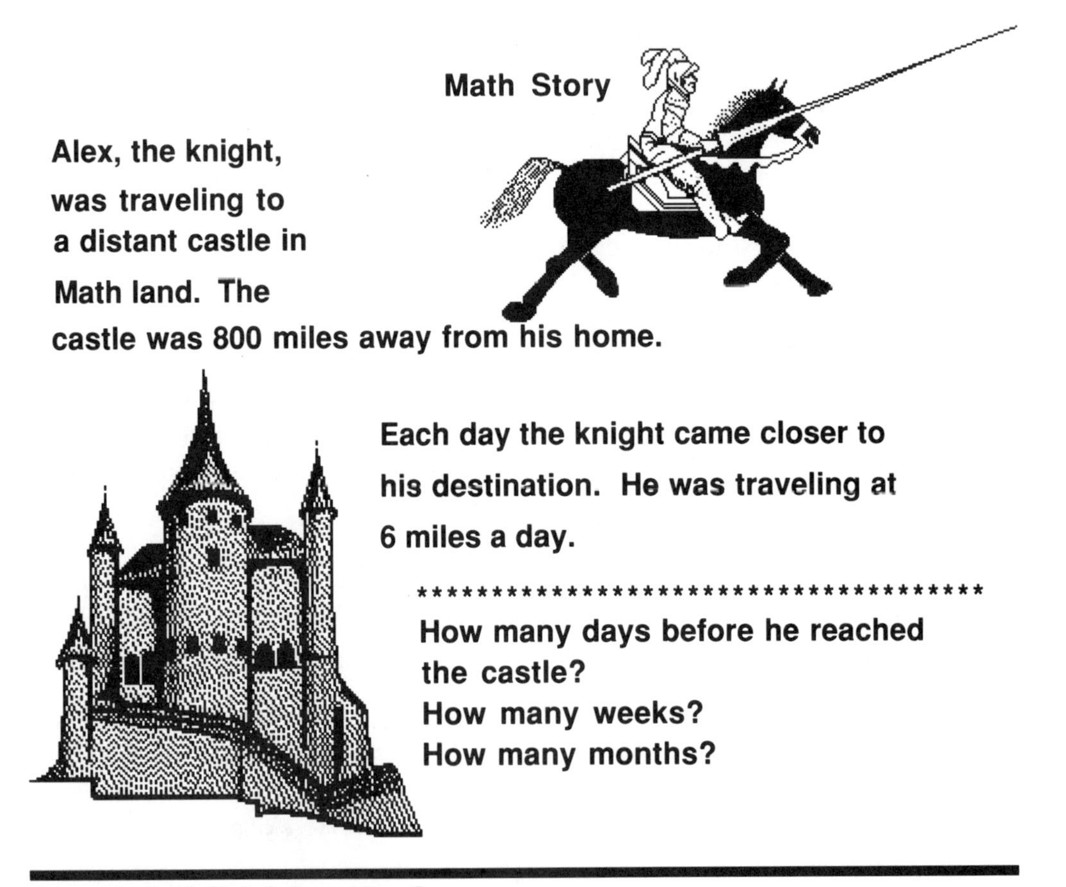

Math Story
Alex, the knight, was traveling to a distant castle in Math land. The castle was 800 miles away from his home.
Each day the knight came closer to his destination. He was traveling at 6 miles a day.
****
How many days before he reached the castle?
How many weeks?
How many months?

3. Next have the students select three pictures from anywhere and write their own word problems based on a creative story.
4. After the students have finished writing their story problems, they should take turns entering these stories into the computer.
5. Later use the print out as a math exam for class.
6. When they finish taking the exam, examine it and revise it in class.

Activity Four: Science Activity

Objective: The students will be able to design their own science lab sheet.

1. Have the students pick an experiment that they would like to do in class.
2. Design a lab sheet similar to the one that follows from *The Children's Writing and Publishing Center*:

LAB SHEET

Name: ____________

Date: ____________

Room: ____________

Question: ____________

Hypothesis: ____________

Materials: ____________

Procedure: ____________

Observations: ____________

The Learning Company

3. After the students have finished their lab sheets, discuss their work.
4. Choose one of the sheets and enter it into the computer to be printed for everyone in the class.
5. Last, have them do their experiments.

Activity Five: Newsletter Production

Objectives: The students will be able to produce a newsletter for the class. They will complete this activity after they have worked with word processing, page-layout, and graphics design.

1. Have the students bring in sample newspapers and newsletters and distribute them to everyone.

2. Divide the students into work groups and have each group be responsible for different tasks. For example, one group might write a news article on the dolphins while another group writes an editorial on a controversial issue. One group might be responsible for a "gossip column," while another handles the movie reviews. Discuss with the students the journalistic questions: who, what, why, where and when.
3. Have each work group write and revise their articles.
4. Next, talk to the class as a group and have the students write headlines and choose the pictures they want to use. Talk about the importance of visual appeal. Discuss how to be bold with headlines and how to place pictures effectively. The students should plan their placement of articles early in the process. Check their work for grammar and spelling errors. Use the following sample from Pagemaker as a model.
5. Use the desktop publishing program to enter the articles for the paper. Have students view the entire document repeatedly to check out visual appeal.
6. After the teacher is completely satisfied with the product, print out a copy of the newspaper. For later editions of the paper, rotate the tasks of the different groups in the class.
7. Students can write historical, autobiographical, or science newsletters. There is no end to the variety of newspapers or newsletters that can be created.

Additional Activities

The list of DTP activities is almost endless. Students can design awards, flyers, progress reports, questionnaires, and outlines for book reports. A sample award sheet is shown on page 110 created by using Laser Award Maker Baudville, Inc.

Summary

The computer has changed the steps involved in publishing a newsletter, magazine, or book. What was done mechanically is now handled electronically. Desktop publishing, a recent phenomenon, has altered the way school newspapers, business newsletters and advertisement sheets are produced.

This chapter traced the historical beginnings of desktop publishing. In the process, the reader learned the merits of desktop publishing. This reader discovered how easy it was for a user to produce a newsletter or lab report using one of these programs. The student became familiar with the basic features of desktop publishing and gained insight into what features to consider when selecting a program. The author presented a checklist and evaluation scale to facilitate this decision making process, along with specific ideas on how to incorporate the DTP into the classroom situation. There were five DTP activities shown that covered a range of curriculum areas.

Volume 2 Number 15 • April 25, 1992

Hill Resort to Open in Early May

Smooth Hill Resort, Hilson Properties' latest in a collection of comfortable family vacation spots, will open its doors in May of this year. Located in the Mustang River Valley, the resort is surrounded by the Hoosik Hills, which offer a variety of vacation activities year-round.

Smooth Hill Resort is reminiscent of a southern mansion, with tall white columns and gingerbread eaves, surrounded by manicured lawns and graceful willows. The resort features 180 spacious one- and two-bedroom units. Each unit sports 1-1/2 baths, 2 closets, cable TV, and a fully-equipped kitchen with dishwasher and full-sized refrigerator. Extra beds are available. Four restaurants offer variety: The Hilltop, for gourmet dining, The Captain's Table for family dining, and two snack bars, one at poolside. The resort offers child care references all year round. A small shopping arcade will meet the needs of most vacationers, including a drug store, clothing stores, and gift shop.

In the summer, vacationers can walk along 8 miles of marked nature trails that offer valley views. Nearby streams offer trout fishing with equipment rental available at the main lodge. Swimmers will find Smooth Hill's 2 swimming pools suitable for all family members, the olympic-sized pool for adults, and a smaller pool for children.

In the winter, the hiking trails become cross-country skiing routes with three levels of difficulty clearly marked. Activities for children include cross-country ski lessons, and the annual Snow Castle Contest. Smooth Hill is located within an hour's drive a 2 major downhill ski areas.

For reservations at Smooth Hill, call Getaway at (555) 555-5555. Special introductory vacation packages available.

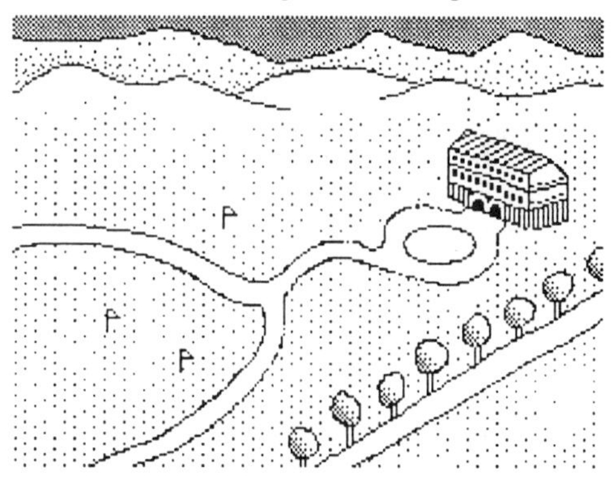

An entrance reminiscent of a Southern mansion welcomes visitors to Smooth Hill.

Weekend Scuba Diving in Niagara Falls

Fred and Harriet Brown were a just another professional couple until a recent vacation experience transformed their lives. "We had fallen into the patterns of suburban life—the same schedule, day in and day out; housework on the weekends. . .we never envisioned the impact this experience would have upon our lives," they told us excitedly.

Waterfall Scuba Diving is not new to the sporting world, although recent technological breakthroughs, such as oxygen tanks and diving helmets, have propelled the sport into an entirely new dimension. Early, more primitive, forms involved holding one's breath while plunging over the falls in a wooden barrel reinforced with steel rings. Although a favorite activity among thrillseekers, this version of the sport soon lost popularity, probably due to a steady decrease in the number of available participants.

The recent fitness craze has transformed the tourist of the past, who was satisfied at merely gazing at the falls from a safe distance or remaining sedentary on a tour boat, into an active participant. Fred and Harriet now claim, "You haven't seen the falls until you've seen them from inside."

Weekend packages are available through the Great Adventure Travel Agency, including weekend accommodations for two, a hearty meal plan, scuba gear rental, and a hospitalization plan. For more information on this new sport, please contact Getaway at (555) 555-5555.

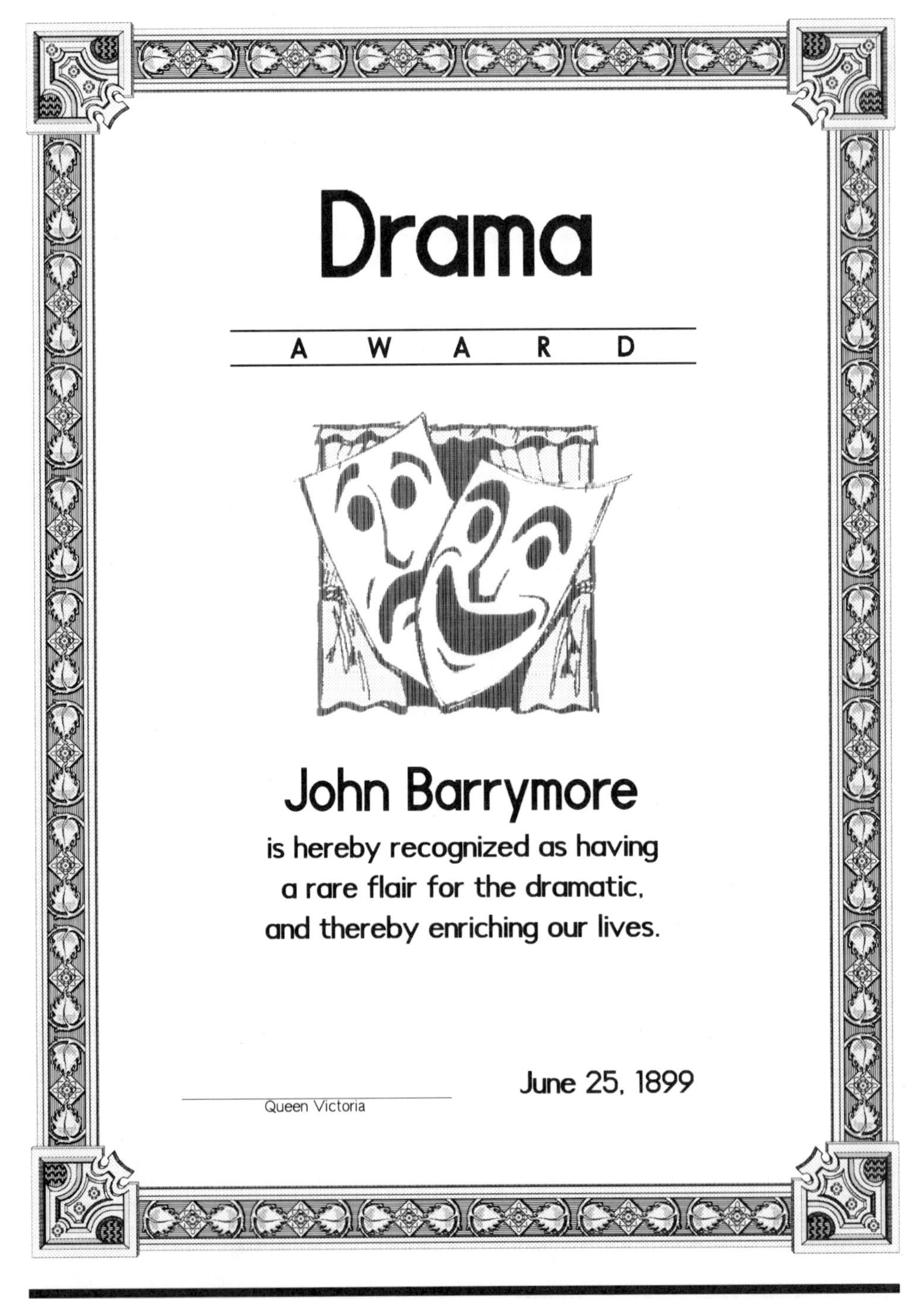

Drama
AWARD
John Barrymore
is hereby recognized as having
a rare flair for the dramatic,
and thereby enriching our lives.
June 25, 1899
Queen Victoria

Award created with Laser Award Maker, by Baudville, Inc., Grand Rapids, MI.

Let's continue by taking the mastery test, doing some of the classroom projects, and referring to the suggested readings and references.

Be sure to review the award-winning, annotated desktop publishing programs listed in Appendix A.

Chapter Mastery Test

1. Explain the difference between a word processor and a desktop publishing program.
2. What is desktop publishing? Explain its importance in education.
3. Name and describe three features of a desktop publishing program.
4. Discuss a few general rules one should follow when creating a newsletter or advertisement using desktop publishing software.
5. Which five DTP features are critical in producing a school publication? Explain your reasons.
6. When designing a DTP program, what safety features should be definitely included and why?
7. Does DTP software make the traditional methods of producing newsletter and books obsolete? Justify your answer.
8. What is a layout? Briefly discuss why it is important to take considerable time when creating a layout.
9. Explain in general terms the way a newsletter might be produced using a DTP program.
10. Briefly trace the history of DTP from inception to present day.

Classroom Projects

1. Design the following with a DTP Program
   a. Two page newsletter
   b. Advertisement for a product
   c. An award
   d. A science experiment sheet
2. Describe one desktop publishing activity and show how a teacher can use it in a classroom situation.
3. Examine two desktop publishing programs and review these programs comparing their strengths and weaknesses.
4. Learn more about DTP by interviewing someone who uses a program. Have the individual demonstrate three or four features of the program. Identify any feature that is too complicated and then discuss some way of reducing the difficulty.
5. Read two articles about DTP and then use a program. Next, prepare a report that might persuade a school district to buy this program. In the presentation, discuss the benefits of using a DTP program.

Suggested Readings and References

Assadi, B. "Publish-It Packs DTP Power" *Infoworld-Macintosh Target Edition.* S1-S5, 4 September 1989.

Beasley, Augie E. "Spreading the News with Desktop Publishing." *Media and Methods,* 27(4) 1 March 1991: 15.

Clark, Sandra. "Desktop Publishing: Alive, Well & Growing." *Media and Methods,* 27(3) 1 January 1991: 42.

Desktop Art for the Macintosh. Peoria, Illinois: Dynamic Graphics, 1986.

Field, Cynthia E. "Sneak Preview." *Incider A+,* (July 1991): 36–48.

Edwards, Keith. "Low cost Publishing for the Masses." *UNIX/world,* 8(6) (June 1991); 111.

Freedman, Alan. Fifth Edition. *The Computer Glossary.* Amacom, New York, 1991.

Hartley, James. "Thomas Jefferson, Page Design, and Desktop Publishing." *Educational Technology.* 31(1) (1 January 1991): 54.

Hickman, John. *Springboard Publisher Getting Started.* Minneapolis, Minnesota: Springboard Publisher, 1988.

Joers, Janet and L. Grimm. *The Children's Writing & Publishing Center User's Guide,* Apple Version, Fremont, California: Learning Co, 1988.

Lamar, Laura. "Desktop Design." Crisp Publications, Inc.: Los Altos, California, 1990.

Parker, R. *Aldus Guide to Basic Design.* Seattle, Washington: Aldus Corporation, 1987.

Perreault, Heidi and Lun Wasson. "Desktop Publishing: Considerations for Curriculum Design." *Business Education Forum.* 45(4) (1 January 1991): 23.

Popyk, Marilyn K. "If Gutenberg Could See Us Now: Teaching Desktop Publishing." *The Balance Sheet.* 71(3) (Spring 1990): 5.

Roth, Evan. "Designs on Desktop." *Museum News,* 70(4) (July 1991): 59.

Schwartz, R. and M. Callery. Desktop Publishing. *A+* (Now *InCider A+*) (September 1988): 26–37.

Simons, Leslie. "Desktop Publishing Software." *Home Office Computing,* (April 1989): 42–45.

Stone, Vicki L. "Getting Acquainted with Desktop Publishing: An overview of hardware and software will help you create the most productive system." *In-plant reproductions,* 41(4) (1 April 1991): 20.

Thompson, Patricia A. "Promises and Realities of Desktop Publishing." *The Journalism Educator,* 46(1) (Spring 1991): 22.

User's Manual Publish-It. (1989). Apple IIe (upgraded), IIc and IIGS Computers. Deerfield, Illinois: Publish-It, 1989.

Wasson, Gregory. "Layout for Less." *MacUser,* 7(7) (1 July 1991): 110–121.

Willis, Jerry. *Desktop publishing with your IBM PC & compatible.* Knight-Ridder Press: Tucson, Arizona, 1981.

Data Bases

5

Objectives

Upon completing this chapter the student will be able to:

1. Explain what a data base is and name its basic components.
2. Describe the basic features of a data base.
3. Evaluate data base software based on standard criteria.
4. Create and utilize a repertoire of data base activities for the classroom.

What is a Data Base?

Every day we are constantly bombarded by information in the workplace, at home, or at school. John Naisbitt in his book, *Megatrends,* writes "We are drowning in information but starved for knowledge" (Naisbitt, 1982, p. 24). Since the teacher cannot possibly retain all this data in memory, it is imperative that he or she develops skills in finding and interpreting the required information. Pupils also have to learn skills in order to organize, retrieve, manipulate and evaluate the facts they have acquired.

Whenever there is a large amount of information to be managed, there is a need for software called a **data management system** that controls the storage and organization of data in a data base. A **data base** is a collection of information organized according to some structure or purpose. It is an all encompassing term that describes anything from an address book, recipe box, a dictionary, or a file cabinet to a set of computerized data files with sophisticated data relationships. In order to understand what a data base is, the reader must be familiar with three terms: **file, record,** and **field.** The file cabinet, or data base in Figure 5.1, contains a collection of related class files where the user retrieves and stores information in a systematic way. For example, an administrator using this file cabinet might take a stack of folders out of the drawer that

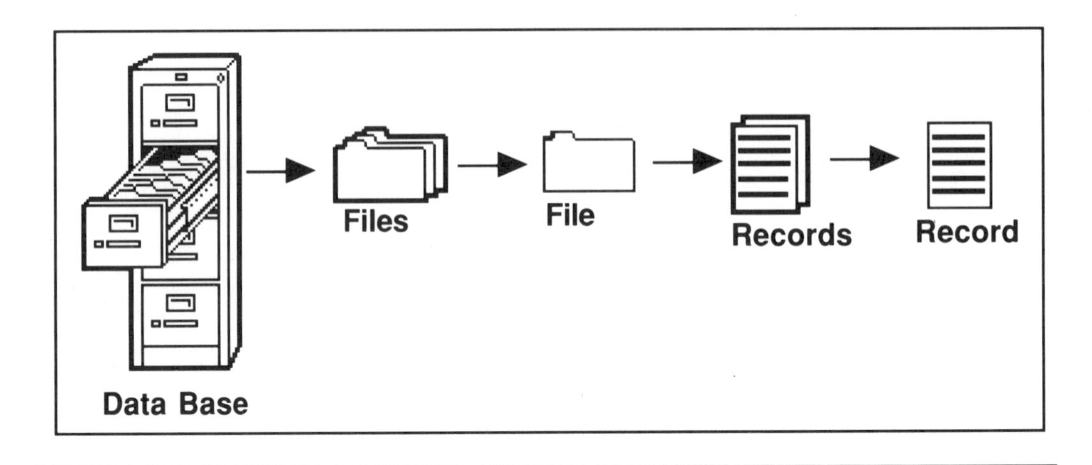

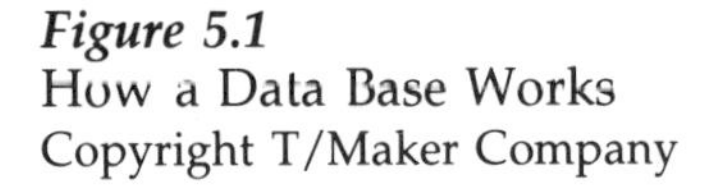
Figure 5.1
How a Data Base Works
Copyright T/Maker Company

contains the Clayton High School file. Searching through this file, s/he looks through the student records for John Doe's student record.

John Doe's record, or individual information card, is organized into five fields or categories of information (Figure 5.2) which are name, address, telephone number, birthdate, and social security number(SS).

When the administrator wants John Doe's phone number, he or she gets it from the telephone field. Each one of these fields has a label: Name, Address, Telephone, Birth Date and SS (Social Security Number), that is used when referring to the data stored in the field. For example, the field Label/Address identifies the field Address, and the information stored in this field is 333 T Street. In an electronic data base, the entire file has a name, in this case Clayton High, where the information is stored on a disk. When the individual searches for items in the electronic data base, s/he types a key term like John Doe to retrieve this record. Figure 5.3 shows six individual student records for the Clayton High School File.

Advantages of an Electronic Data Base

The computerized data base has many advantages over the file cabinet. Every data base has a method of organization that lets a person retrieve information using some key word. For example, Figure 5.3 has the Address file arranged alphabetically. The problem with the non-electronic listing of this information is it cannot be easily modified. After too many changes, the sheets of paper become unreadable and need retyping. This is not the case

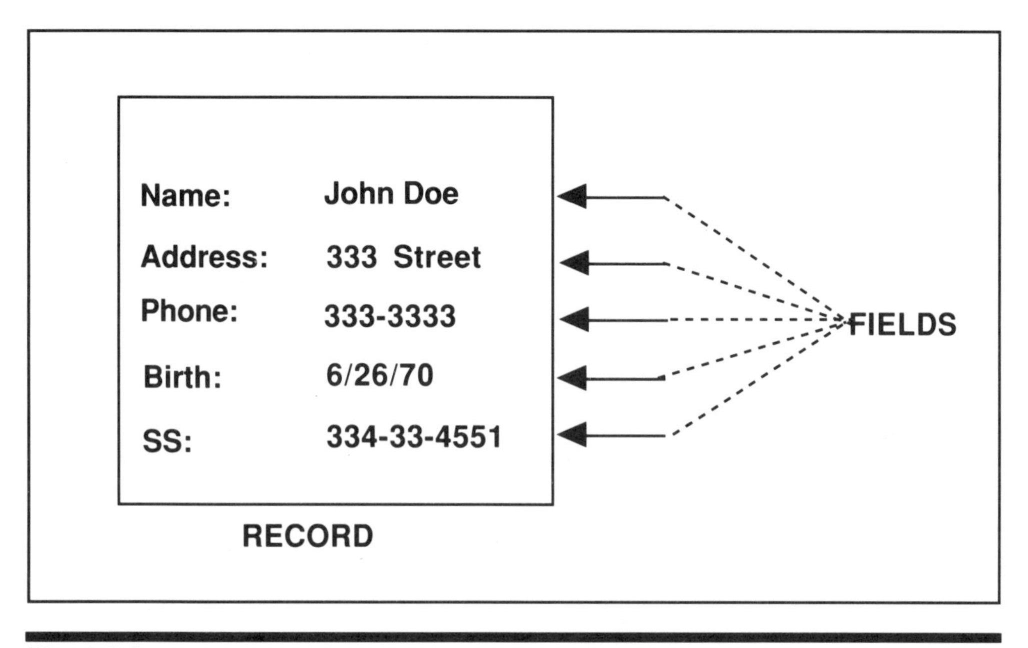

Figure 5.2
Fields

Address File (DB)

Name	Address	Phone	Birth	SS
Adams, James	333 T Street	885-2621	6/26/70	485-66-5643
Barris, Bill	456 Laguna Street	885-2621	8/27/60	387-44-4567
Davis, Jayne	234 Catalpa	234-3465	1/1/55	888-99-5643
Doe, John	455 Northridge	887-3456	3/1/70	444-66-7623
Elliot, Vicki	888 Valencia	888-4555	3/2/45	668-44-5467
Francis, Melissa	456 Cromwell Drive	264-5566	8/30/70	777-76-8888

Figure 5.3
Sample Data Base
Screen shot(s) Microsoft® Works© 1986–1990 Microsoft Corporation. Reprinted with permission from Microsoft Corporation.

with an electronic data base where the information is stored on the computer rather than paper. The computer data base also minimizes data redundancy, the same information being available in different files. When a person searches through a file cabinet, this clerk uses his or her fingers to locate key terms, which can take a long time. The electronic data base user can generate reports, retrieve files almost instantaneously, sort data in a variety of ways, edit, and print information with more flexibility and at faster speeds than by using a pencil and paper. Furthermore, there is no file that a user can physically misplace, since the files are usually in one central location and data can be shared more easily among individuals. In addition, individuals can execute file searches with only partial information; for instance, the police department is always searching for criminals with incomplete data. With only the first half of a name and a brief description, the police can search for a suspect. The only disadvantage to using a data base is its expense and the fact the existing files have to be converted into the data base format.

Computerized data bases are used daily in governmental, occupational, and professional agencies. There are virtually thousands of repositories of information, like Educational Resources Information Clearinghouse (ERIC), that students utilize for their research work. ERIC, the primary data base for teachers, is the basic indexing and abstracting source for information about education. For example, if a student is searching for **problem solving** in **primary math,** s/he would use these key words and get abstracts on the recent research articles on this topic.

How a Data Base Operates

In this section the author, using *Microsoft Works,* gives the reader an overview of how an electronic data base operates, but this discussion is not a substitute for Microsoft's documentation. For illustrative purposes, the author uses the situation where a professor needs to keep track of the software s/he has accumulated haphazardly in a closet. The professor creates a data base to make order out of this chaos, and this particular data base has one file that represents the software collection simply labeled "Software." In working with this data base, the user determines the number of fields wanted on a record. In this example, the first field is Title:

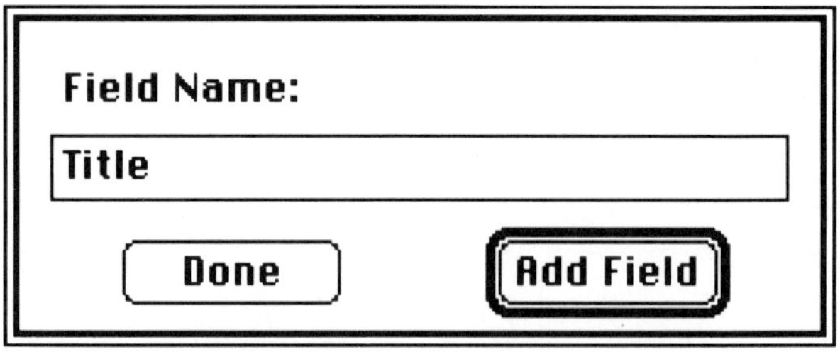

Field Name:

Title

Done   Add Field

The professor designs a record based on library referencing techniques using five fields which are **Title, Subject, Company, Copies,** and **Grade Level.** If the user wants to add or change a field, it is a simple matter. After the form or template is designed, the record is automatically saved. An example of a record follows:

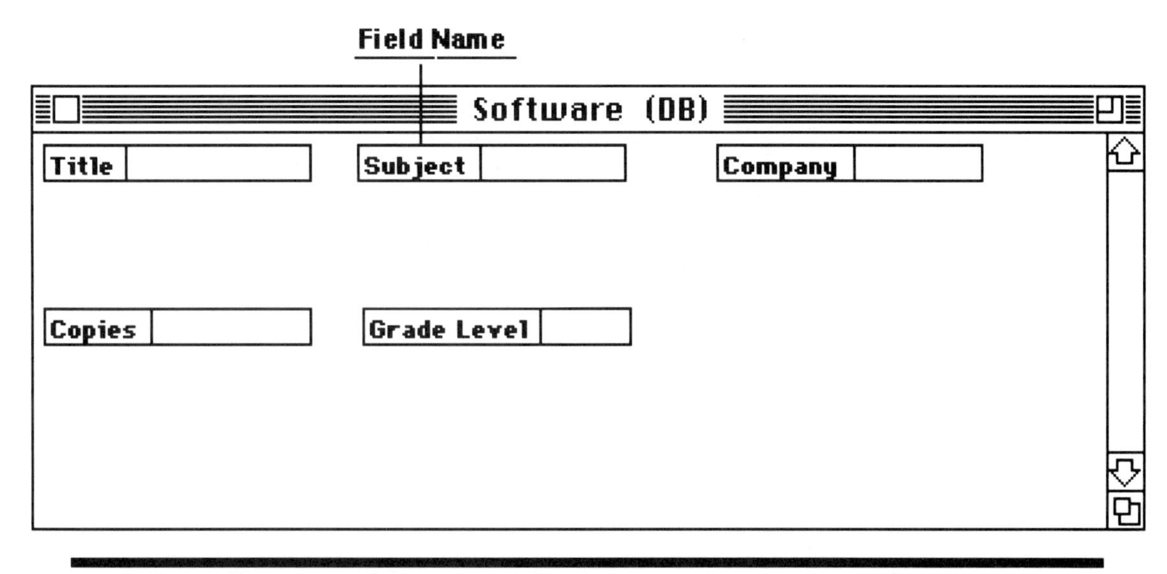

Since the structure is defined, the next step is to enter the record data for each piece of software. A completed Software File Record is shown on the following page.

The field name **Title** has the entry Word Attack Plus, **Subject** Language Arts, **Company** Davidson, **Copies** 2, and **Grade Level** 4–10. As the information is entered, the user has the option of adding or changing this information. When the one record is completed, another one is automatically generated. The user continues filling in records until s/he decides to stop or reaches the storage capacity of the particular data base file program. When the task is complete, the user has a data base file that lists ten records for the Software File (see following page).

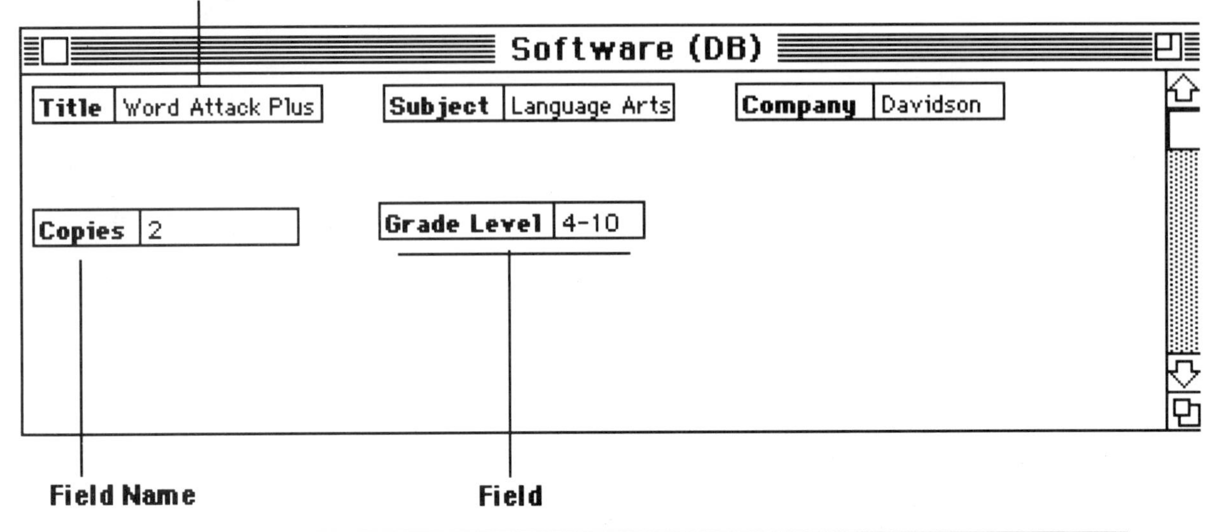

Software Listing (DB)

Title	Subject	Company	Copies	Grade
Bankstreet Writer	Word Processor	Scholastic	3	4-12
816/ Paint	Art/Graphics	Baudville	2	3-12
The Writing Center	Word processing	Learning Company	5	4-12
Compu-a-grade	Tool	Projact	8	12+
New Math Blaster	Math	Davidson	6	6-12
The Oregon Trail	Social Studies	MECC	9	5-Adult
Where in America's Pa	Social Studies	Brøderbund	3	6-Adult
Magic Slate II	Word Processor	Sunburst	4	2-6
Reader Rabbit	Lang. Arts	Learning Co.	5	K-3
Word Attack Plus	Lang. Arts	Davidson	2	4-10

Functions of a Data Base

Now that the data base is completed, the user can select or retrieve a file and sort the records. One of the major tasks of any data base is to retrieve information, and there are a variety of ways of retrieving this information.

1. The user can retrieve an entire file as shown by listing this file on the screen or printing it out.
2. A person can select only a few field headings, for example, **Software Title and Subject**:

Software Listing (DB)

Title	Subject
Bankstreet Writer	Word Processor
816/ Paint	Art/Graphics
The Writing Center	Word processing
Compu-a-grade	Tool
New Math Blaster	Math
The Oregon Trail	Social Studies
Where in America's Pa	Social Studies
Magic Slate II	Word Processor
Reader Rabbit	Lang. Arts
Word Attack Plus	Lang. Arts

3. Using a field, a student can search for one record in the data base. For example, this student might use the **Title** field to type *The Writing Center* (The student types the software title as s/he originally entered it, or it will not be retrieved.):

Software Listing (DB)

Title: The Writing Center | Subject: Word processing | Company: Learning Company

Copies: 5 | Grade: 4-12

4. The user can retrieve a record using more than one criterion such as **Company** Sunburst and **Grade Level** 4 or less. S/he can use **Boolean Operators** such as **and,** and **or** to search for more than one record.[1] For example, in this next search, a user uses the Boolean Operator **and** and searches for software that meet two criteria: (1) a word processing program, and (2) at least two or more copies. The result of this search produces two pieces of software, *Magic Slate II,* and *BankStreet Writer,* word processing programs with at least two copies available.

SoftwareListing (DB)

Title	Subject	Company	Copies	Grade
Bankstreet Writer	Word Processor	Scholastic	3	4-12
Magic Slate II	Word Processor	Sunburst	4	2-6

The Boolean operator **or** lets the user find records that meet the requirements of either criteria. In this instance, either a word processing program or a piece of software that has at least 3 copies is acceptable.

5. There are times when the data base user wants to search for a record and is not sure how to find it. For instance, suppose s/he cannot remember the name of a publisher, only that it begins with the letters "Sun." Many data base programs let the user find a record just using **data strings.** A data string is a subset of the characters within the field. If the user searches for the publisher Sunburst, the letters "Sun," and "Burst," are data strings. To find the Sunburst publisher, the person need only type "Sun" for the field name and this is enough of the word to distinguish the choice from information in other records. This type of search is often called a **wildcard search,** because the only condition that is to be met is that the first part of the title be "Sun" and the rest of the characters are "wild."

The other important function of a data base program is sorting, the ability to arrange the records in a file so that the values in a field are sorted either in alphabetical, chronological, or numerical order. Any field can be sorted, and sorting is done by field type. If the field has characters in it, it is sorted alphabetically, *A* to *Z*

1. In arithmetic, the primary operations are add, subtract, multiply, and divide, but in Boolean Logic the primary operations are AND, OR, and NOT. "Its rules and operations govern logical functions (true/false) rather than numbers" (Freedman, 1991).

or *Z* to *A*. If the field is numeric, it is sorted lowest to highest or highest to lowest. An example of a numeric sort would be the number of **Copies** from lowest to highest. Finally, a user can sort a field chronologically by date or time.

Why Use a Data Base in the Classroom?

In the past, the administrative office of a school district was the only logical place for a data base because this was the place where student records, personnel files, and school resources were located. Recently, however, the classroom teacher is beginning to use the computerized data base because there is a legitimate need for this application. S/he can use a data base to help him or her keep track of a student's progress and to store anecdotal comments on individual students. Furthermore, pupils can create their own data bases and use prepared data bases like *PC Globe+* (PC Globe Inc.) and *World Geograph* (MECC).

These data bases let the users have a vast amount of information at their fingertips. *World Geograph* lets the students observe patterns of world climate and hunger. This program has on-screen maps (Figure 5.4) graphing capabilities, and a comprehensive data base covering every independent nation in the world.

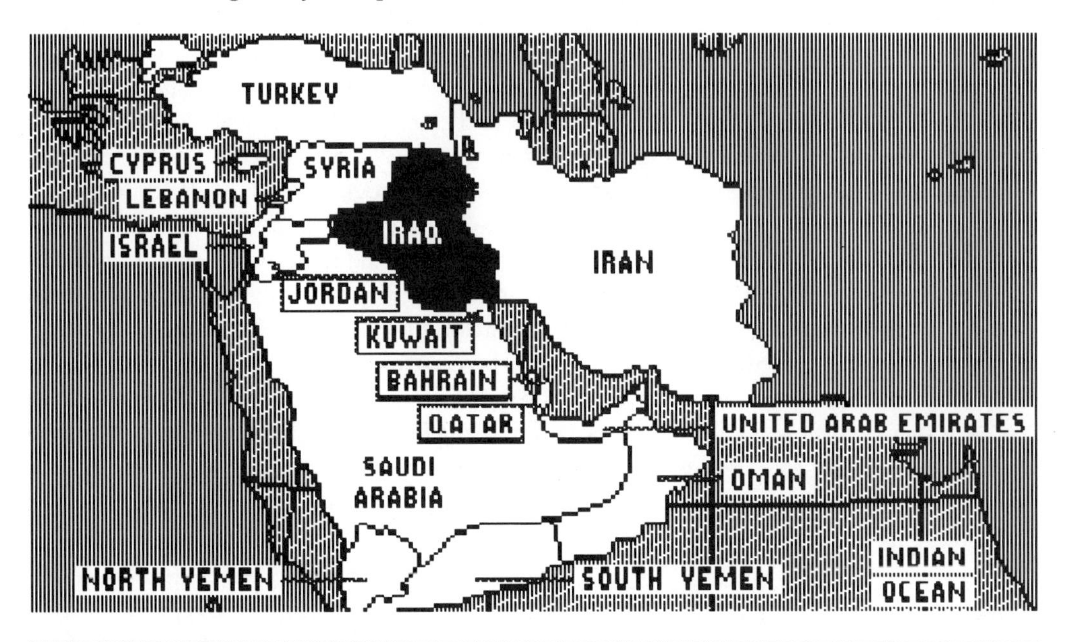

Figure 5.4
World Geograph
Courtesy of MECC

The data base is the perfect means for teaching higher level critical thinking skills, such as the ability to hypothesize, draw inferences, and use Boolean logic. For example, the students might search a data base created for the students who took a certain Dr. Gallio's Computer class. After the students develop a strategy for this search, they perform it and find out who the students are. The teacher might then ask students to hypothesize how many females received A's in this class. This time their search statement is more complex and they are looking for the following criteria. 1. Female Students and 2. Students who received an A. Following this search, the students then could be asked to draw inferences about the results of the search. They could do further searches and see if there is any correlation among other items. Besides helping with higher level thinking, a data base can aid a student who is learning content material in any of the curriculum areas. If a student understands how to manipulate a data base this student can gain deeper insight into any field of study, find patterns, draw relationships, or identify trends.

Today, students can use a data base file that they alone created or one that a teacher or software house prepared. Many times students find it more beneficial to do their own research and enter it into a design created by the teacher. The mastery of data bases takes longer than the mastery of word processing because the students must be given more experience and different types of assignments to learn how to use them. The beauty of data bases is the fact that they can be used in all content areas, and there are many data bases being commercially developed in association with the various content areas. Many of these data bases have informational files on topics such as animals, states, and countries. The manuals supplied include instructions on how to manipulate the data, student worksheets, and suggested activities. Other programs have only informational files used with data base programs such as *Professional File* or *Appleworks*. The data base programs that exist for the lower grades should be used only on an elementary level because school children cannot understand the underlying logic behind data base programs. They can, however, understand some essential concepts such as record, field, and search. It may be wise to save the complex searching for the junior high school students.

There are different factors to consider when choosing a data base program. How limited is this program in its ability to search? Can the teacher easily add or change the data in the files? Are there multiple copies of the program available? If there is a prepared data base with the product, is the content proper for the students? Is the information accurate? What is the quality of the documentation? How easy is the program to use? Let us examine these factors more closely for the purpose of making a more informed decision.

How to Select a Good Data Base for the Classroom

There are quite a few data base packages on the market today with every imaginable feature. Among these are data base programs that have been specifically designed for classroom use. The most popular programs for the schools are *Bank Street Beginner's Filer, Friendly Filer, Dataquest Composer, Easy Working, The Filer, Swift's Data Base, Professional File, FrEdBase,* and *Appleworks.* The easiest programs are the *Beginner's Bank Street Filer* and *Friendly Filer* and the most complex is *Appleworks.* Generally, the classroom data bases have fewer features and are easier to use. The features chosen for inclusion are the ones that will help students the most. Choosing a data base program for the classroom is a six step process. The following items are examined: (1) hardware compatibility; (2) general features; (3) instructional design; (4) ease of use; (5) technical support; and (6) cost effectiveness.

Hardware Compatibility

Check out the computer the school is using. Is this computer an Apple IIGS, an Apple IIc+, a Commodore 64, an IBM PC, or a Macintosh LC? (A teacher has to work within the limitations of the school's computers.) How much memory does this machine have? Does it have 64K, 128K, 256K, 512K, or 1 or 2 megabytes of memory? (Some data base programs need a huge amount of computer memory. The teacher may have to either extend the memory of the computer or not select that package.)

How many disk drives are available for each machine? Generally, most computer applications need two disk drives. However, programs like *BankStreet Filer* need only one disk drive. This program lets the user load it entirely into the computer's memory. The user can remove the program disk and insert the data file into the same drive. Because the entire data base program is in the computer's memory, the student needs only a data disk to manipulate the data. Programs such as *Appleworks* cannot be loaded into the computer's memory, and the program works more efficiently with two disk drives. What about disk drive size? Are these drives 3 1/2 inch drives, 5 1/4 inch drives or a hard disk drive and a floppy disk drive? What printers will work with this data base program?

Features of a Data Base

The features found most commonly in data base programs are (1) sorting data; (2) changing or updating data; (3) searching for specific information; (4) deleting and adding information in the file; and (5) printing.

1. Sorting Data. In review, sorting is the ability to arrange the records in different ways. A program should allow the user to name the field type easily and quickly do the sort. At the very least, the program should do the following: (1) an alphabetical sort from *A* to *Z*, or *Z* to *A*, in any appropriate character field; (2) a numeric sort from lowest to highest, and highest to lowest, in any numeric field. No matter what programs the buyer chooses, the computer user should be able to sort to the screen and the printer.

2. Changing and Updating. Every data base can update and change a file. The questions that must be asked are the following: How difficult is it to accomplish this task? Is it easy to find the record and change it? How hard is it to add a record to the file, and is it a long drawn out procedure?

3. Searching or Retrieving. Data base programs vary in the type of search criteria used to find forms in a file. For instance, there are exact matches, partial matches, numeric matches, numeric range matches, etc. In an exact match, the program looks for the forms that exactly match the search criteria. An exact match for Florence Singer would be Florence Singer or FLORENCE SINGER, whereas Mrs. Florence Singer or Singer, Florence, or FlorenceSinger would not be a match. All data base programs have exact matches, and many data base programs have partial matches. A person uses a partial match when he or she is unsure of how the information was entered into the data base or when there is an interest in records with the same information. For instance, a student might use a partial match to find Florence Singer's file by just typing in Florence or Singer. In addition, s/he might use a partial match to find the records of students who have computer experience.

The more advanced the data base, the more exotic the features. *Professional File,* an advanced program for the IBM, does quite a few numeric searches. Using this program, the user can look for items less than, greater than, or equal to a given number. The Professional File search criteria are <, >, or =. If a user wants the records found for all children who were born later than 1982, s/he would do the following: **Year: >1982.** This program has a numeric range match feature that allows the user to search for numbers within a certain range. For instance, the user might search for the dates between the range of 1988–2000.

The data base program should let the user search using multiple criteria. For instance, a computer teacher might want to search for the students eligible to take his advanced level computer course. He may use two criteria: (1) students in eleventh grade; and (2) students with computer experience. At the end of the search, the computer generates the names of students who fit these qualifications. Searching a file in some data base programs can change the file if the individual is not careful. Because of this problem, it is desirable to have a program where the search feature is separate from the add feature. The ideal program should have a way to lock files so they will not be accidentally erased.

4. Deleting and Adding. The data base program should allow the person to add or delete information in a record or field with minimum trouble. When the user adds a new field to one record, the new field is added to all the records. For example, in a software library listing, a professor need only add the field name called "publisher" once and it is automatically added to every record in the file.

5. Printing. The program should let the computer user print a neat report. The instructions for this task should be easy to follow and the print out should show the data fields that the individual wants in the report.

Advanced Features

Some programs let the user design the way the data will be displayed while others perform mathematical calculations on the data. These programs do not perform the complex functions of a spread sheet, but they let the user total simple columns of numbers or do student averages. In most cases, a data base program shows the final list or report on the screen before it is printed. *Appleworks* and *Microsoft Works* have features that let the user select fields for different records and display them on the screen all at once. There are even data bases available that store a picture with each record. The more advanced programs like *Professional File* can merge data from a data base document with a word processing document to create such things as a customized letter. Using this function, the student can generate a different copy of a word processing letter for each record in the database. This means that the computer user can produce many versions of a document, each one containing a personalized item of information and therefore this person does not have to retype the document each time.

Instructional Design

A data base program should require minimum learning time and not require hours of study time in front of the computer. The program that has a menu bar displayed at the top of the screen is ideal for beginners because the students do not have to remember the different functions. *Bank Street School Filer* (Figure 5.5) is very popular; because of its design, the user can quickly see all the major options that are available.

The key to data base programs is their flexibility of design. How easy is it to make changes and how easy is it to add a field or add information to a field in the data base program? Does the person lose the current information that already exists in the field? Does the data base program make the individual start again when s/he wants to make changes? A simpler program may make the person begin again. A more advanced data base program lets the person add fields, change field names, and rearrange a field's position with minimum trouble. What is the searching speed of the program? A program that searches very slowly can waste time if the person is in a hurry to complete a job. What flexibility is there for printing a report? Can the person be selective in printing certain columns. Is this person stuck printing the items as shown on the screen. What is the size limit of the data base? On the one hand, the program, *Friendly Filer,* has seven fields on a page and 360 records on a single sided floppy. On the other hand, *Professional File version 2.0* can theoretically have 100 fields on a page

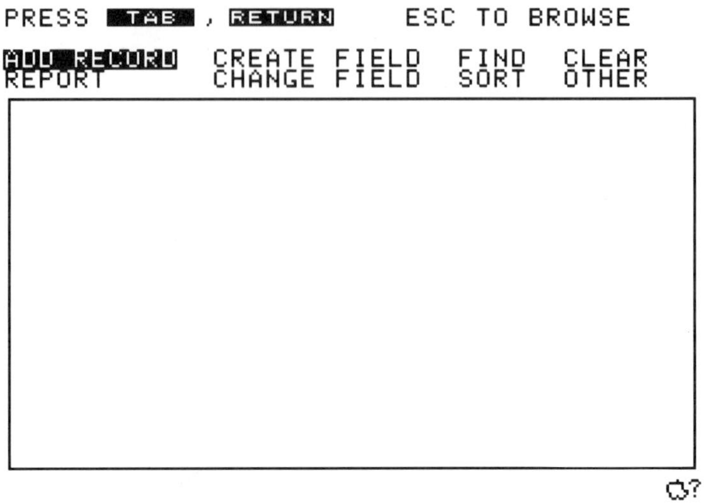

PRESS TAB , RETURN ESC TO BROWSE

ADD RECORD CREATE FIELD FIND CLEAR
REPORT CHANGE FIELD SORT OTHER

Figure 5.5
Bank Street School Filer
Sunburst Communications

and a 59,000 file size of 8 megabytes. Ask if there is a size limitation for the information in each field? *Professional File* allows 4,000 characters per page or field, while *Appleworks* has 77 characters total, including the field name. Since data base programs vary in the kinds of searches they are capable of accomplishing, what type of searches does this program have? Does the program let the student do Boolean searches? Does the searching technique fit the skills the teacher is emphasizing in the classroom?

Ease of Use

A major concern when buying a data base program is how easy it is to learn the program. It is immaterial what features it has if it is difficult to comprehend. Ask the following questions: Can a person sit down and in a reasonable amount of time use this program? Is there a tutorial disk that takes the individual through the program? *Friendly Filer* (Houghton Mifflin) uses simple English commands and has a tutorial on the disk that helps the child learn the program step by step (Figure 5.6).

Are there help screens that tell the individual what to do each step of the way? Can a person access these help screens, whenever s/he needs to use them? Are there menu bars across the screens so the user does not have to remember the different functions. Is the printer set-up easy, and can the person be ready to print immediately? Are there too many help prompts and safety questions?

Figure 5.6
Friendly Filer
From FRIENDLY FILER™ 128K. Copyright © 1989 by Houghton Mifflin Company. Adapted from FRIENDLY FILER™ 64K. Copyright 1984 by International Educations, Inc. Reprinted by permission of Houghton Mifflin Company.

Learn to Use Friendly Filer

Classroom

Teacher	Grade	Students	Room
MS ARON	K	22	103
MR DANTER	1	25	122
MRS HURLEY	2	24	114
MR DUBLIN	3	22	108
MS NUCCIO	4	26	107
MRS ALVEZ	5	23	111

Consumer Value

Because software is expensive, cost is a major consideration. Since public domain software costs very little, it is a natural alternative to commercial software. There is free software available in California through the California State Department of Education. Commercial software is more expensive, but there are many programs worth the cost. Be sure to find out if the software comes with a backup copy. If the software publisher does not supply a disk, how much money will it cost to purchase one? Many software companies let the buyer use one disk to load the software on the computers. Other companies offer an inexpensive on-site license that enables the user to make as many copies as s/he needs. Some companies have lab packs that let the buyer purchase a large quantity of software at a reduced price.

Support

Any reference to support means personal telephone or written help. Can the person call someone on the telephone at the software company and get immediate help, or does he sit through a series of messages and wait an unbearable amount of time? As mentioned previously, many houses tell the caller how many customers are before him and how long he must wait. Is the technical support toll free? Does the software package have tutorial lessons to help the beginner learn the program? Is the manual readable with activities and lesson plans? Does this book or booklet have an index? Does the program have templates or computer based files? Do the software producers have data files for various content areas? For example, *Sunburst* has a collection of prepared data bases for use on the *Bank Street School Filer.* The data bases are in such areas as Astronomy, Animal Life, Weather, Endangered Species, etc.

Data Base Checklist

Product Name ______ **Manufacturer** ______ **Appropriate Grade Level** __

A. Hardware
- __ 1. Memory needed
- __ 2. Computer compatibility
- __ 3. Printer compatibility
- __ 4. Number of disk drives

B. Features
- __ 1. Selection of field types
- __ 2. Sort
  - __ a. alphabetic
  - __ b. numeric
  - __ c. chronological
  - __ d. reverse order
  - __ e. to screen and printer
- __ 3. Deleting and adding fields
- __ 4. Search
  - __ a. alphabetic
  - __ b. numeric
  - __ c. and-or
  - __ d. using multiple criteria
- __ 5. Mathematical calculation of data
- __ 6. Mail merge
- __ 7. Display
  - __ a. Printout—screen or printer
  - __ b. Can display selected fields
  - __ c. 40–80 column display

C. Design
- __ 1. Speed of search
- __ 2. Ease of changing fields
- __ 3. Ease of adding new fields
- __ 4. Size requirements
  - __ a. field size
  - __ b. characters per field
  - __ c. no. of records in a file

D. Ease of Use
- __ 1. Help screens
- __ 2. Tutorial disk
- __ 3. Easy printer setup
- __ 4. Disk formatting within program
- __ 5. Automatic save
- __ 6. Warning questions

E. Consumer Value
- __ 1. Cost
- __ 2. Lab packs or on-site licensing
- __ 3. Backup disk

F. Support
- __ 1. Technical
- __ 2. Tutorial material
- __ 3. Readable manual
- __ 4. Lab packs
- __ 5. Templates
- __ 6. Prepared software
- __ 7. Readable manual
  - __ a. Activities
  - __ b. Lesson plans
  - __ c. Tutorial
  - __ d. Index

Rating Scale

Excellent ____ **Very Good** ____ **Good** ____ **Fair** ____ **Poor** ____

Comments

Before selecting the software, the instructor should decide which features are important for the particular class. Are there ready made published files available? From reading the list of features in this chapter, the reader can see that many factors must be weighed in selecting a data base program.

Refer now to Appendix A for an annotated bibliography of highly rated data base programs for the classroom. Next examine one of these programs using the sample checklist and evaluation rating instrument shown to the left. The checklist will make the decision easier.

Data Base Activities for the Classroom

The following exercises are meant to be used in conjunction with any data base. If a computer lab is not available, the reader can just follow this section to get an idea of what kinds of activities can be used in the classroom. The first exercise leads the user in a step-by-step introduction to a data base program. The students will need two disks, a program disk and a newly formatted disk to store their file with records.

Preliminary Exercises

1. Load the program disk into the computer and boot the machine.
2. From the Main Menu, pick the option that creates a file and gives the file a name, such as Class.
3. Type in the following field names: **Teacher, Students, Room, Grade,** and **Sex** and correct any mistakes made.
4. Using the **Add a Record Function,** type the following information for each record.

TEACHER	STUDENTS	ROOM	GRADE	SEX
Smith	23	21	K	Male
Adams	16	14	4	Female
Gramacy	17	25	3	Female
Witham	33	29	1	Female
Youngblood	21	24	K	Male

5. Add another record to the list by typing: Teacher: **Sharp,** Students: **20,** Room: **12,** Grade: **3,** and Sex: **Female.**

6. Learn how to change information in the records by changing (a) the name Smith to **Small** and his room number **21** to **24.** (b) Change the name Adams to **Allen,** and the number of students he has from **16** to **28.**
7. Next, learn how to delete a record by deleting the **Gramacy** record.
8. Alphabetize the list of records (*A* to *Z*); use the teacher's **Name** Field. Listing should look like the following:

TEACHER	STUDENTS	ROOM	GRADE	SEX
Allen	28	14	4	Female
Sharp	20	12	3	Female
Small	23	24	K	Male
Witham	33	29	1	Female
Youngblood	21	24	K	Male

9. Finally, print out the results.
10. Next, numerically sort by the Field **Grade** from highest to lowest.

TEACHER	GRADE
Allen	4
Sharp	3
Witham	1
Small	K
Youngblood	K

11. Search for the following records:
    a. Call up Youngblood's record by typing the name **Youngblood** in the **Teacher** Field.
    b. Retrieve the Allen record by typing the name **Allen** in the **Teacher** Field.
    c. Search for the Kindergarten Records by Typing **K** in the Field **Grade** and the program should find **Small** and **Youngblood.** The data base shows the records that match the specifications the user types and if there is no record, the program usually displays a 0. The user also gets a 0 if s/he types the record name different from the original entry in the data base.
    d. For our next exercises, find the records using the following two criteria— (1) all the records for male teachers (2) with exactly 21 students. Type the number **21**

for the **Students** field and **male** for the **Sex** field. For this search, there is only one record **Youngblood's.**

e. Let's choose another two criteria and find the male kindergarten teachers records. Type **K** for the grade and type **male** for the sex. In this case, there are two teachers that fit these criteria: **Small** and **Youngblood.**

12. If the data base program has a greater than (>) or less than (<) feature, find the following records.
    a. All the teachers in the classroom that have a class size greater than 20.
    b. The male teachers who have 23 or more students.
    c. The female teachers who have 18 or more students.

For practice, create another data base.

Type in the following field names: **Student, Sex, Hair Color, Birth Date.**

1. Using the add function, type the following information for each record.

Student Data Sheet

Pupil: Smith, Joan
Sex: Female
Hair Color: Brown
Birth date: 1945

Pupil: Lorenzo, Max
Sex: Male
Hair Color: Black
Birth date: 1941

Pupil: Friedman, Paul
Sex: Male
Hair Color: Black
Birth date: 1933

Pupil: Sharp, David
Sex: Male
Hair Color: Brown
Birth date: 1984

Pupil: Schainker, Nancy
Sex: Female
Hair Color: Blond
Birth date: 1950

Pupil: Friedman, Bobbie
Sex: Female
Hair Color: Blond
Birth date: 1955

Pupil: Lopez, Mary
Sex: Female
Hair Color: Black
Birth date: 1958

Pupil: Randolph, Jeffery
Sex: Male
Hair Color: Red
Birth date: 1960

Pupil: Jung, Nicky
Sex: Female
Hair Color: Red
Birth date: 1967

2. Learn how to change file names and then change the field name Pupil to Student.
3. Next, change David Sharp's birth date to 1950, Nicky Jung' s description to a male with black hair and finally, Bobby Edwards hair color to red.
4. Add the following File:
   Student: Lee, Bessie, Hair Color: Brown
   Sex: Female, Birth date: 1953
4. Alphabetize the list (A to Z) by using the Student's name and print out the list.
5. Find the following files:
   a. David Sharp
   b. All those students who are female
   c. The students who have red hair
   d. The people who are born after 1950
   e. The students who were born before 1950
   f. All the students who are female with red hair.

In the next section there are five data base activities covering different areas of the curriculum.

Activity One: General Data Base

Materials

Data base program (*Friendly Filer, Bank Street Filer,* etc.) and one computer or more)

Objective:

The student will use the Boolean operators **AND** and **OR.**

1. Discuss the use of **AND** and **OR** when each one connects two fields.
2. Have the students write out a personal data sheet about themselves and use the following sheet as a model:
3. Collect the data sheets from the students.
4. Enter the data into the computer data base.
5. Divide the class into groups of 6.
6. Divide the sheets among the three or four groups in the room.

PERSONAL DATA SHEET
1. YOUR LAST NAME
2. YOUR FIRST NAME
3. YOUR BIRTH MONTH
4. NUMBER OF BROTHERS
5. NUMBER OF SISTERS
6. FAVORITE SPORT
7. NUMBER OF PETS

7. Have the students compete against the computer in trying to find the following information.
   a. Find every record where the students first name starts with an *A* or *C*.
   b. Sort the sheets by birth month.
   c. Print a list of students who have two pets and whose last name begins with *S*.
   d. Print out the name of the student whose birth month is in August and who has one brother.
   e. Which student has two brothers?
   f. Who has the most sisters?
   g. How many students have one brother and one sister.
   h. Sort by the Last Name Field.
   i. How many people were born in August?
   j. Whose favorite sport is baseball?

Activity Two: Science Data Base

Materials

Dinosaur Data Base Form

- Data Base Program (*Friendly Filer, Bank Street Filer, Easy Working-The Filer,* etc.)
- One Computer or more

Objectives:

The students will:

- Create a dinosaur data base
- Learn about dinosaurs
- Be able to sort alphabetically
- Practice using Boolean Operators
- Sort by number

Procedure

1. Have each student read about a dinosaur.
2. After the assignment is completed, have all students use the Dinosaur Data Base Form that follows:

DINOSAUR DATA BASE FORM

NAME	HABITAT	FOOD	FEET	ARMORED

3. Following are sample data for this data base.

DINOSAUR DATA BASE

Name	*Habitat*	*Food*		*Armored*
Ankylosaurus	Land	Plants	4	Yes
Tryannosaurus	Land	Meat	2	No
Brachiosaurus	Water–Swamp	Plants	4	No
Brontosaurus	Water–Swamp	Plants	4	No
Corythosaurs	Water–Swamp	Plants	2	No
Diplodocus	Water–Swamp	Plants	4	No
Iguanodon	Land	Plants	2	No
Proceratops	Land	Plants	4	Yes
Stegosaurus	Land	Plants	4	Yes
Coelophysis	Land	Meat	2	No

4. Each student enters his or her information on the same data file disk.
5. After this task has been completed, have the students do the following:
   a. Sort the file by the number of legs in the field, highest to lowest.
   b. Using the Boolean Operator, **AND,** find out if there are any:
      1. two legged plant eaters
      2. four legged meat eaters
   c. Sort Alphabetically by Name and print out the list.

Additional Suggestions: The user can add fields such as weight, height, nickname and sort the fields by: (1) the length of the dinosaur—lowest to highest; (2) the heaviest dinosaur; (3) the dinosaur that had a bill that looked like a duck. The possibilities of fields and sorts are endless; it is only limited by the teacher's imagination.

Activity Three: Language Arts Data Base

Materials:

- Student Book Report Form
- Data Base Program (*Friendly Filer, Bank Street Filer,* etc.)
- One Computer or more

Objectives: The students will:

- Create a data base book report file.
- Learn to sort alphabetically
- Read a book

Procedure

1. Have each student read a book.
2. After the assignment is finished, have the students use the book report form that follows:

BOOK REPORT FORM

STUDENT'S NAME ____________________

1. AUTHOR:
2. TITLE
3. TYPE OF BOOK
4. SETTING:
5. MAIN CHARACTER OF THE STORY
6. SUMMARY OF THE STORY:

3. The Students will insert the proper information under each field name. The summary field needs a data base program that has a comment field. (If the data base program does not have this feature, eliminate this field name.)
4. Each student enters his information on the same data file disk.
5. After this task has been completed, have the students do the following:
   a. Search for a book they might like to read, using the search function.
   b. Have them print out a list of all the books in the data base.
   c. Have the students sort the data base alphabetically by **Title** and print out a list.
   d. Next, have them sort the data base file alphabetically by **Author** and print out the list.
   e. Find out how many students read baseball stories or biographies by using the **Find** function of the data base program.

Activity Four: Geographical Data Base

Materials:

- Student's State Data Sheet
- Data Base Program (*Friendly Filer, Bank Street Filer,* etc.)
- One Computer or more

Objectives:

The students will:

- Create a geographical data file for each state.
- Learn geographical information about each state.
- Sort alphabetically
- Search using the Boolean Operator **AND** and **OR**.

Procedure

1. Have each student in the class choose a state to research.
2. Have the students use reference books to fill out the Geographical Data Sheet shown on the following page.
3. Have the students enter the proper information under each field name.
4. Next, have the students enter their information on the data file disk.
5. After this task has been completed, have the student independently use the search function to answer *Who Am I* questions (see following page).

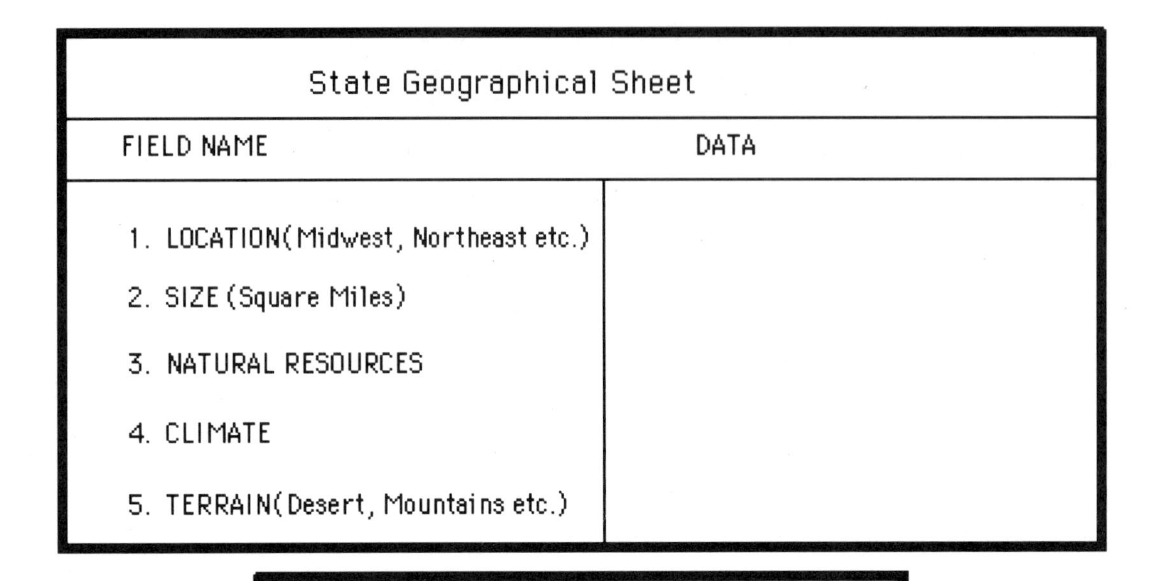

State Geographical Sheet	
FIELD NAME	DATA
1. LOCATION(Midwest, Northeast etc.)	
2. SIZE (Square Miles)	
3. NATURAL RESOURCES	
4. CLIMATE	
5. TERRAIN(Desert, Mountains etc.)	

WHO AM I

1. I am a small state.
2. I am known for my mountains.
3. I have red clover flowers.

Activity Five: Math Data Base

Materials:

- Students' State Data Sheet
- Data Base Program (*Friendly Filer, Bank Street Filer,* etc.)
- One Computer or more

Objectives:

The students will:

- Create a state data file.
- Learn statistical information about the United States.
- Sort alphabetically.
- Search using the Boolean Operator **AND** and **OR.**

Procedure

1. Have each student in the class choose a state to research.
2. Have the students use encyclopedias to fill out the following State Data Sheet.

STATE DATA SHEET	
FIELD NAME	DATA
1. CAPITAL	
2. POPULATION	
3. NUMBER OF REPRESENTATIVES IN CONGRESS	
4. YEAR OF STATEHOOD	

3. Tell them to use the encyclopedia to answer the four questions about their state and write this information in the data column.
4. The Students will complete the proper information under each field name.
5. Each student enters his information on the same data file disk.
6. After this task has been completed, have the students independently use the search function to carry out the following tasks:
   a. Search for the states that have populations over two million.
   b. Find the last state that was added to the United States.
   c. Sort the records according to population in order from lowest to highest.
   d. Sort the records alphabetically by the name of the state and print out a list.
   e. Sort and print out a list of the states by population.
7. Next, divide the class into two teams; collect each team's state data sheets.
8. The teacher reads aloud one of the state data sheets without naming the name of the state.
9. Team One then tries to guess what state or group of states the teacher is discussing.
10. Team Two checks out Team One by using the computer.

11. If Team One has answered correctly, it scores a point.
12. The teacher now draws another data sheet and reads the description.
13. Team Two now guesses while Team One checks out Team Two.
14. The first team to achieve 10 points wins.

Data Base Ideas: 1. Scheduling 2. Hobbies 3. Opinion Survey 4. Dictionary of Spelling Words 5. Planets 6. Presidents 7. World Events 8. Whales 9. Animal groups 10. Plants 11. Rocks 12. Minerals

Summary

The data base is a useful instrument that helps people deal with large quantities of data. It is an effective manager of this information and a powerful tool for learning in the classroom. The students can look for relationships with data, test hypotheses, and draw conclusions.

This chapter discussed the merits of an electronic data base and its basic features. The author presented a data base checklist evaluation form and showed the reader how to introduce a data base to the class. There were many useful classroom activities shown covering a range of curriculum areas. A Mastery Test, Classroom Projects, and Suggested Readings and References follow.

Be sure to review the award winning, annotated data base programs listed in Appendix A

Chapter Mastery Test

1. What is a data base and how could it be used in the classroom?
2. Define the following: a file, a record, a field.
3. Name and describe two ways of sorting data.
4. What distinguishes a file cabinet from a data base?
5. Discuss the advantages of using a computerized data base.
6. Discuss the factors involved in selecting a data base for a school district. Use *Appendix A* for an annotated list of data base software.
7. Name and describe three ways of searching for a file.
8. When should a student use a "wild card" search?

Classroom Projects

1. Create a prepared data base file. Using this file, do the following:
   a. Sort alphabetically from *A* to *Z*.
   b. Sort alphabetically from *Z* to *A*.
   c. Sort numerically from lowest to highest.
   d. Sort numerically from highest to lowest.
   e. Use the Boolean Operators **AND** and **OR.**
   f. Print a listing of the data base file.
   g. Add fields to the data base.
   h. Add information to the fields in the data base.
   i. Delete information or fields from the data base.
   j. Save a file.
   k. Retrieve a saved file.
   l. Print a file.
2. Examine three data bases and compare their different features.
3. Choose a grade level and create a data base activity for it.

Suggested Readings and References

Anders, Vicki and Kathy M. Jackson. "Online Vs. CD- ROM—The Impact of CD-ROM Databases Upon a Large Online Searching Program." *Online.* 12(6) (1 November 1988): 24.

Antonoff, Michael. "Using a Spreadsheet as a Data Base." *Personal Computing* 1986, 65–71.

Bachor, D. G. "Toward Improving Assessment of Students with Special Needs: Expanding the Data Base to Include Classroom Performance." *Alberta Journal of Educational Research,* 36(1) (1 March 1990): 65.

Barbour, A. "A Cemetery Data Base Makes Math Come Alive." *Electronic Learning* (February 1988): 12–13.

Bensu, Janet. "Use Your Data Base in New Ways." *HR Magazine.* 35(3) (1 March 1990): 33.

Bock, Douglas B. "Solving Crime with Database Technology." *Journal of Systems Management.* 39(10) (1 October 1988): 16.

Coe, Michael. "Keeping Up with Technology." *The Computing Teacher.* 18(5) (February 1991): 14–15.

Coulson, C. J. "Creation of Inhouse Database." *Transactions.* 17(5) (1 October 1989): 838.

Davey, Claire and Adrian S. Jarvis. "Microcomputers for Microhistory: A Database Approach to the Reconstitution of Small English Populations." *History & Computing,* 2(3) (1990): 187.

Dunfey, J. "Using a Database in an English Classroom." *The Computing Teacher.* 12(8) (1984): 26–27.

Epler, D. M. *Online Searching Goes to School.* Phoenix, AZ: Oryx Press, 1989.

Fagan Patsy J. and Ann D. Thompson. "Using a Database to Aid In Learning the Meanings and Purposes of Math Notations and Symbols." The *Journal of Computers in Mathematics and Science,* 8(4) (Summer 1989): 26.

Flynn, Marilyn L. "Using Computer-Assisted Instruction to Increase Organizational Effectiveness." *Administration in Social Work,* 14(1) (Winter 1990): 103.

Hannah, L. "The Database: Getting to Know You." *The Computing Teacher* (June 1987): 16–23.

Harris, Richard. "The Database Industry: Looking Into the Future." *Database.* 11(5) (1 October 1988): 42.

Hodson, Yvonne D. and David Leibelshon. "Creating Databases with Students." *School Library Journal* 32, LC (May 1986): 12–15.

Hunter, Beverly. "Problem Solving with Databases." *The Computing Teacher* 12 (1985): 20–27.

Lathrop, Ann. *Online and CD-ROM databases in school libraries*: readings/ compiled by Ann Lathrop. Libraries Unlimited, Database Searching Series, No. 2 (1989): 361–366.

Leonard, Jenelle. "New Data Bases for Bank Street Filer Programs." *Electronic Learning.* 8, (8) (June 1989): 45–46.

Marschalek, Douglas. "The National Gallery of Art Laserdisk and Accompanying Database: A Means to Enhance Art Instruction." *Art Education.* 44(3) (1 May 1991): 48.

Mittlefehlt, Bill. "Social Studies: Problem Solving With Databases." *The Computing Teacher.* 18(5) (February 1991): 54–55.

Naisbitt, J. *Megatrends.* New York: Warner, 1982.

Olds, Henry F. "Information Management: A New Tool for a New Curriculum." *Computers in the Schools* 3 (1986): 7–22.

Pfaffenberger, Bryan. *Democratizing Information: Online Databases and Rise of End-User Searching.* G. K. Hall: Boston, Massachusetts, 1990.

Rae, John. "Getting to Grips with Database Design: A Step By Step Approach." *Computers & Education,* 14(6) (1990): 281.

Stewart Dorothy. "Materials on Reform of Teacher Education in the ERIC Database." *Journal of Teacher Education.,* 41(2) (1 March 1990): 63.

White, Charles S. "Developing Information-Processing Skills through Structured Activities with a Computerized File-Management Program." *Journal of Educational Computing Research* 3 (1987): 355–75.

Spreadsheets and Integrated Programs

6

Objectives

Upon completing this chapter the student will be able to:

1. Define the following terms: spreadsheet, integrated software, cell, windowing, macro, mail merge, and logical functions.
2. Describe the basic features and functions of spreadsheets and integrated programs.
3. Explain how spreadsheets and integrated programs operate.
4. Evaluate different spreadsheet software and integrated programs based on standard criteria.
5. Utilize and create a repertoire of spreadsheet activities for the classroom.

Spreadsheets

In chapter 5, the reader learned that the primary purpose of the data base is data organization. In this chapter the reader examines the spreadsheet, one of the earliest applications of the microcomputer. First there is a short historical discussion, followed by an explanation of what a spreadsheet is and how it operates.

Historical Overview

In the early 1970s the microcomputer was a tool for hackers and hobbyists, but this all changed when Dan Bricklin, a Harvard student, and Robert Frankston, a MIT student, combined efforts to create the first spreadsheet, *Visicalc*. This spreadsheet, introduced in 1979, was primarily designed for microcomputers and had a small grid size and limited features. The Apple Computer was the only computer that could run *Visicalc*, so it was the first computer to be accepted by business users. *Visicalc* served as a prototype for many other programs that followed, with names such as *LogicCalc* and *Plannercalc*—all designed for microcomputers. Within a decade, the spreadsheets improved vastly, offered more features (such as the ability to create graphic displays), had faster execution speeds, and a larger grid size.

In 1982, *Lotus 1–2–3* became the leading spreadsheet initiating a new generation. It was the first integrated spreadsheet (combining several different programs) so that information could be presented in different formats. The next generation of spreadsheets had extended capabilities: a communication component, expanded spreadsheet size, and word processing. The word processor feature let the user easily explain the figures presented in the spreadsheet, while the communication component let the computers communicate with each other over telephone lines in different locations.

What is a Spreadsheet?

Every year many people use paper, pencil, and calculators to prepare their income tax forms. College students request government loans and families determine their budgets based on their income in order to predict their annual expenses. The business person keeps a record of his transactions to determine his profits and liabilities, while the scientist does mathematical calculations on experimental data. Even though a spreadsheet is thought of as a business application, a teacher uses a spreadsheet when instructing the class on how to analyze and make inferences about numerical data and when entering information into a grade book.

Components of a Spreadsheet

An electronic spreadsheet is a computerized version of a manual worksheet with a matrix of numbers arranged in rows and columns. Every spreadsheet is organized in a similar manner with two axes (Figure 6.1).

The letters across the top are used to identify the columns and the numbers along the side identify the rows.[1] At the intersection of each row and column, a box is formed called a **cell.** A cell is identified by referring first to its column and then to its row (letter, number). For example, in Figure 6.2, the first cell (A1) is in the top left hand corner, and one cell to the right is B1. By counting over to D and then counting down four cells, the user locates cell D4 where s/he places the cursor.

In the drawing the selected cell **D4** is heavily bordered and the **indicator** in the upper left hand corner displays this cell.

---

1. Spreadsheets can differ in the system used to label these rows and columns.

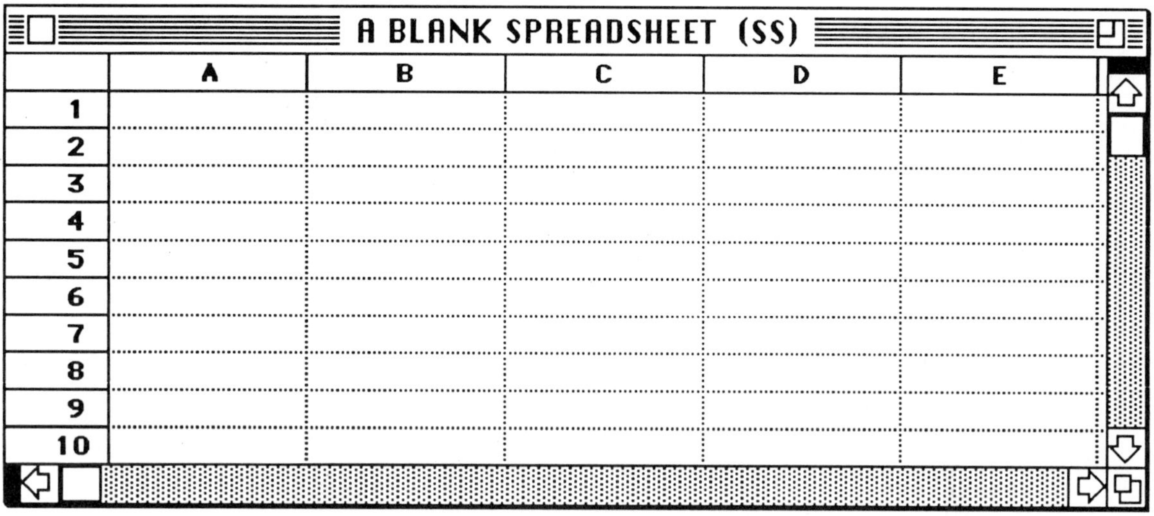

A BLANK SPREADSHEET (SS)

	A	B	C	D	E
1					
2					
3					
4					
5					
6					
7					
8					
9					
10					

Figure 6.1 Spreadsheet. Screen shot(s) Microsoft® Works© 1986–1990 Microsoft Corporation. Reprinted with permission from Microsoft Corporation.

Indicator

Then Count Down

D4

SPREADSHEET-CURSOR AT D4

	A	B	C	D	E
1					
2					
3					
4	First Count Over →			Cell D4	
5					
6					
7					
8					
9					
10					
11					

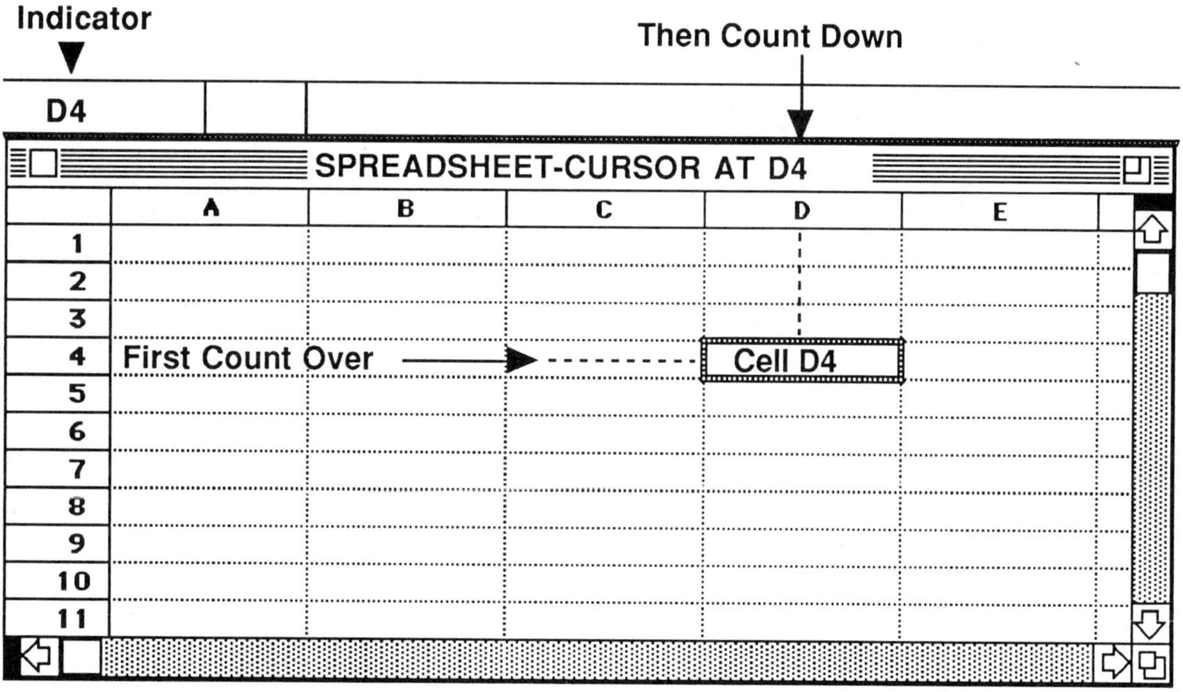

Figure 6.2 Spreadsheet Cells. Screen shot(s) Microsoft® Works© 1986–1990 Microsoft Corporation. Reprinted with permission from Microsoft Corporation.

Three types of information can be entered into any single cell: number, text, or formula. Because of the spreadsheet's ability to enter formulas, it is a powerful tool for business, science, and education.

How a Spreadsheet Operates

This section gives the reader an indication of how an electronic spreadsheet operates. For illustrative purposes, the author uses *Microsoft Works* to show a grade book example, a popular educational usage of the spreadsheet.

If a teacher uses a manual spreadsheet, he enters the eight students' names and the three quiz scores for each student. Next, using paper, pencil, and a calculator, he adds scores 99 + 97 + 86 for Richard Apple, obtaining a total of 282. He records the answer in the total column, then divides this total by 3 for an average of 94 (Figure 6.3). The teacher continues this manual procedure for each subsequent student. If the teacher makes an error or changes a score, he must recalculate everything.

Name	Quiz 1	Quiz 2	Quiz 3	Total	Average
1. Apple, Richard	99	97	86	285	94
2. Benson, Mary	85	82	76	243	81
3. Coulson, Jan	78	65	67	210	70
4. Diaz, Robert	88	85	79	252	84
5. Frank, Brad	98	88	81	267	89
6. Obrien, Keith	99	96	78	273	91
7. Sharp, David	99	94	95	288	96
8. Washington, Bill	88	87	83	258	86

Figure 6.3
Teacher's Grade Roster

Using this traditional grade book example, the author will explain the advantages of an electronic spreadsheet. After the teacher opens *Microsoft Works* spreadsheet, he sees the following blank screen:

 File Edit Window Select Format Options Chart Macro

A BLANK SPREADSHEET (SS)

	A	B	C	D	E
1					
2					
3					
4					
5					
6					
7					
8					
9					
10					

He enters the same headings, which are **Name, Quiz 1, Quiz 2,** and **Quiz 3** and **Average,** describing the contents of the cells[2]. The spreadsheet user then types the eight pupils' last names and their respective quiz scores. While entering this information, the teacher can easily make changes, corrections, delete or add any scores, and use the sort function to alphabetize the students' last names. When the task is completed, the spreadsheet looks like the one shown on the following page.

2. It is unnecessary to have a total column in this electronic spreadsheet.

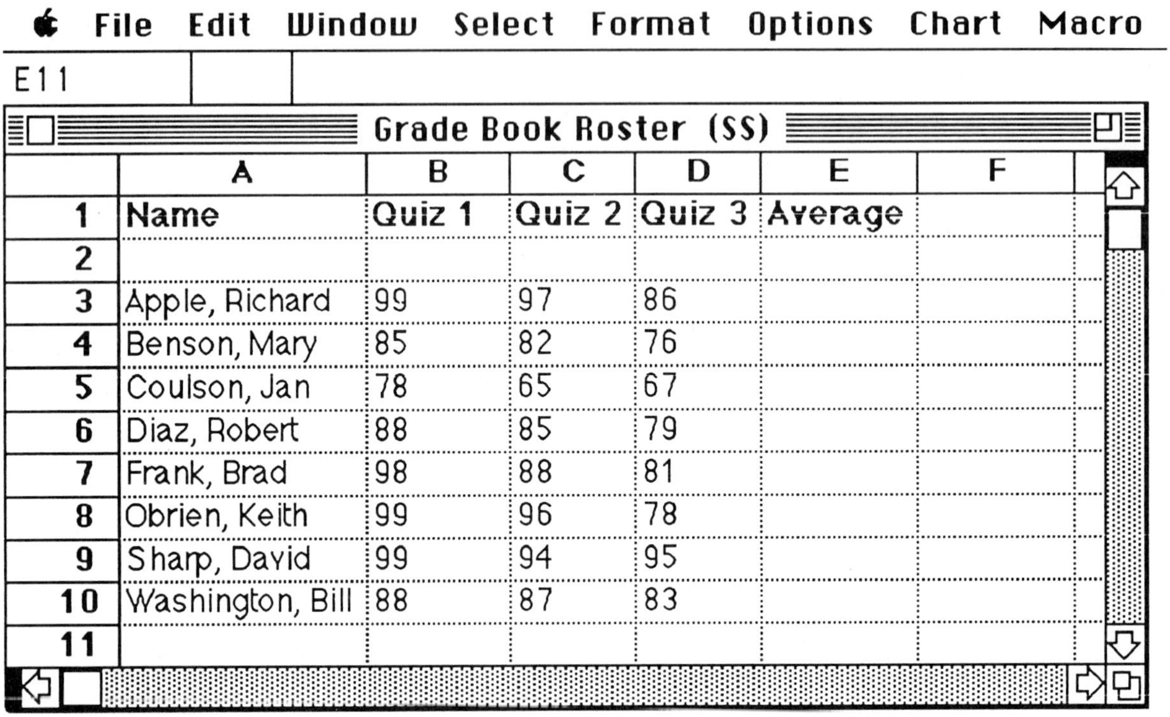

File Edit Window Select Format Options Chart Macro

E11

Grade Book Roster (SS)

	A	B	C	D	E	F
1	Name	Quiz 1	Quiz 2	Quiz 3	Average	
2						
3	Apple, Richard	99	97	86		
4	Benson, Mary	85	82	76		
5	Coulson, Jan	78	65	67		
6	Diaz, Robert	88	85	79		
7	Frank, Brad	98	88	81		
8	Obrien, Keith	99	96	78		
9	Sharp, David	99	94	95		
10	Washington, Bill	88	87	83		
11						

The beauty of any spreadsheet is the feature that each cell serves as an individual calculator that does computations quickly and accurately. Because of this, it is a simple matter for the teacher to calculate each student's average. Selecting cell **E3**, and using Microsoft Work's average formula **=Average(B3:D3),** the spreadsheet calculates the mean for numbers 99, 97, and 86 and records the answer 94 instantaneously in cell E3. The = sign begins the formula function **Average,** which tells the computer to compute an average from cell B3 to D3:

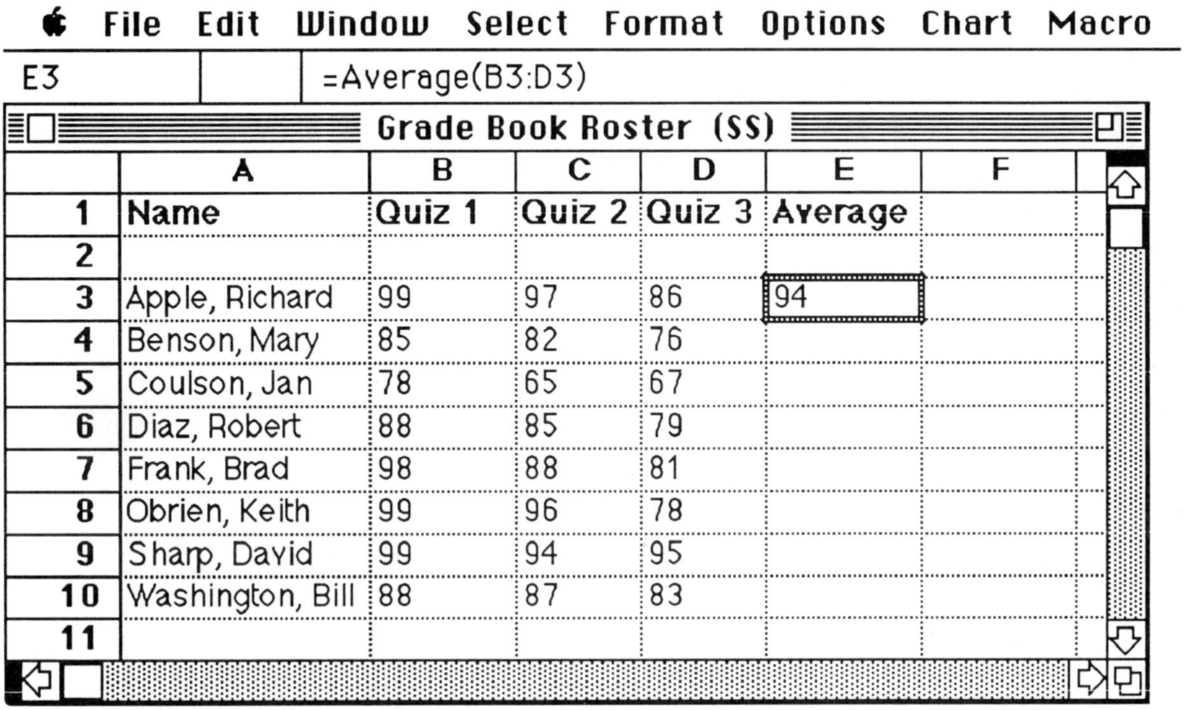

File Edit Window Select Format Options Chart Macro

E3		=Average(B3:D3)

Grade Book Roster (SS)

	A	B	C	D	E	F
1	Name	Quiz 1	Quiz 2	Quiz 3	Average	
2						
3	Apple, Richard	99	97	86	94	
4	Benson, Mary	85	82	76		
5	Coulson, Jan	78	65	67		
6	Diaz, Robert	88	85	79		
7	Frank, Brad	98	88	81		
8	Obrien, Keith	99	96	78		
9	Sharp, David	99	94	95		
10	Washington, Bill	88	87	83		
11						

When the teacher calculates the averages for the remaining pupils, he will not have to rewrite the formula, since every spreadsheet has a way of copying the original formula. In this case, the instructor selects cells **E3** to **E10,** chooses **fill down** from the menu, and the rest of the students' averages are automatically displayed in the appropriate cells as shown by the highlighted cells in column E. Using this copy function makes it easier to enter data for a large number of cells (see following page).

File Edit Window Select Format Options Chart Macro

E3 =Average(B3:D3)

Grade Book Roster (SS)

	A	B	C	D	E	F
1	Name	Quiz 1	Quiz 2	Quiz 3	Average	
2						
3	Apple, Richard	99	97	86	94	
4	Benson, Mary	85	82	76	81	
5	Coulson, Jan	78	65	67	70	
6	Diaz, Robert	88	85	79	84	
7	Frank, Brad	98	88	81	89	
8	Obrien, Keith	99	96	78	91	
9	Sharp, David	99	94	95	96	
10	Washington, Bill	88	87	83	86	
11						

In this example, *Microsoft Work's* average function was utilized to shorten the time and effort it took to type in the formula. Every spreadsheet has its own collection of functions, ranging from sum, average, to sine. *Microsoft Works 2.0* has 64 built-in functions, while *Educalc* Spreadsheet, has one function, the Sum. Generally, the more built-in or predetermined functions, the more versatile the spreadsheet.

Why Use an Electronic Spreadsheet?

There are many reasons for a teacher to choose a computerized spreadsheet over a manual worksheet. The electronic spreadsheet is faster and more flexible than the traditional methods of numerical calculation and data prediction. The teacher enters numerical data and then changes the information on the screen as often as he wants. A non-computerized spreadsheet having a matrix of rows and columns greater than 25 is cumbersome, whereas a computerized spreadsheet can have have a matrix of literally thousands of data entries. Furthermore a user merely presses a key or two and he can access any number on this spreadsheet instantaneously. An electronic spreadsheet lets the user enter numeric information, such as 33, or alphabetical data, such as John Smith, or formulas. These formulas let the user do mathematical calculations without a calculator.

A major feature of a spreadsheet is its ability to recalculate; that is, when a teacher changes the numbers in a cell, the spreadsheet automatically recalculates the other values. When a teacher corrects a simple mistake in a manual grade book, he usually has to recalculate the other values. The recalculation feature of an electronic spreadsheet lets the teacher play "What if?" analysis strategies such as, "What would happen if Johnny scored a 90 on this exam instead of a 60?"

The electronic spreadsheet lets the teacher display and print the output in many visually appealing ways. When a teacher figures the grades in a manual grade book, he is bound to make an error. As long as the teacher enters the formula correctly in an electronic spreadsheet, it is always accurate, because the spreadsheet uses this formula to perform the computations. There are many other advantages of a spreadsheet, such as the invaluable copy function that lets the user effortlessly repeat a formula once defined. Needless to say, the electronic spreadsheet has enormous advantage over a manual spreadsheet in terms of saving time and increased productivity.

Now let's look at some of the basic features of the spreadsheet and see which ones would be most useful for the classroom teacher.

Basic Features of a Spreadsheet

Protected and Hidden Cells

Many spreadsheets let the user protect a group of cells from being altered or erased and have safeguards built into the program. When the individual removes this cell protection to allow the viewer to see the data, there should be a separate command to avoid accidental erasure of data. In addition to this option, some spreadsheets let the individual take confidential information and hide it from view, and the person has the option of not printing the information in a report. If it is a good spreadsheet, the user should be able to retrieve easily the information from these hidden cells. Individuals working with secret information need complete protection of their information. They should use a spreadsheet that requires a secret password to access data.

Logical Functions

Powerful spreadsheets have logical functions that evaluate whether a statement is true or false. For example, let's say the teacher created a grade book spreadsheet with four exam grades and an average score for each student on four exams. He now wants to invite only those students into honors math who received a 97 or above as their average scores. Since the first average is in cell F4, he would enter a formula in G4 and repeat this formula for every score. With the spreadsheet program *Lotus 1–2–3,* this formula would read as follows:

@If(F4 >96, 100,0).

The formula lets a 100 represent the Honors class and a 0 represents the standard class. When the spreadsheet does its calculation, it checks to see whether the value entered (F4) is greater than 96, and if this is the case, the spreadsheet will print the first option (100) in cell G4. If the average in F4 is lower than 97, the spreadsheet will print the second option (0) in G4. The teacher then places all the students with 100s in Honors class and the ones with 0s in the standard class. Logical functions are handy for sophisticated users of spreadsheets.

Date-and-Time Functions

The date and time function is another advanced feature. If the user wants to find out how many days have elapsed between two dates in the spreadsheet cells, this function calculates the information automatically.

Macros

Macros are a group of routines or commands combined into one or two keystrokes. The user can play these routines back at the touch of a key or two. (1) The individual determines what keys s/he wants to use, such as key F12. (2) The user decides what the key will generate; for instance, F12 could print a name, address, and telephone number. (3) The individual programs the macro so that when F12 is pressed, it automatically enters the name, address, and telephone number in the chosen cell. Some macros execute their commands to a certain point, wait for the input, and then continue with the command execution.

Graphing

There are spreadsheets that generate bar or pie graphs based on the information contained in the spreadsheet. These are great visual aids, because as the data changes, the computer user can see the corresponding changes in the graphics representation.

Memory

When a user enters data into the spreadsheet, it is helpful to know how much memory remains. A spreadsheet that has a running indicator of the memory available is better than one that has a message that says the program is out of memory.

Name Cells

Some programs let the user label the cells with words instead of the short cell address. For instance, if the user has his profit in Column C, Rows 3 through 15, this person can tell the program to call these cells Profit and then can use Profit in any formula written that refers to this range.

Windows

When an individual works on a large spreadsheet, s/he cannot see the whole spreadsheet on the screen, but must scroll between sections. When the user employs the cursor to scroll around the spreadsheet, s/he can view hidden sections, and sections that were visible now become hidden. The screen is a movable window, which looks on a larger spreadsheet. If the computer user needs to compare figures on different screens, it is helpful to be able to split the screen into two or three sections, each windowing a different part of the work. By doing this, the user can see the place in the spreadsheet where s/he is currently working, can see the effect it has on cells in different locations, and can easily compare figures from different sections. If the spreadsheet does not have a split-screen option, an alternative feature is a spreadsheet with the ability to set fixed titles. A fixed title option lets the user keep a designated number of rows and columns permanently on the screen.

Attached Notes

Some spreadsheets can attach notes, a feature that is similar to having a supply of "yellow post it notes." This feature is particularly useful if the user has to remember the source of a particular idea or has to have additional information upon demand.

Editing and Sorting

When a person makes a mistake, there must be a simple way of correcting this error. S/he should be able to insert and delete rows and columns. After the information is edited to the individual's satisfaction, it is important to be able to sort that information. Sorting lets the user arrange the information in the spreadsheet alphabetically and numerically.

Advanced Features of a Spreadsheet

The more powerful spreadsheets can link other spreadsheets, have data base capabilities, and do sideways printing. The ability to link a worksheet is being able to put together more than one spreadsheet. The user gets information from one spreadsheet and pulls this information directly into his current sheet. This complicated feature is not meant for novices.

Lotus 1–2–3 (Lotus) has data base capabilities, but these functions are not comparable to a data base program. What the person has is a spreadsheet approach to dealing with data base functions. Generally printing is limited to 80 columns, or 136 if the person uses compressed type. Sometimes the spreadsheet user needs more room to fit all the columns on one sheet of paper. The best way to accomplish this is by using a utility program that lets the individual turn the print out on its side. A few spreadsheet programs have this convenience built into the program.

Copying Command

The copying command on a spreadsheet copies the contents of a group of cells from one column to another; it replicates formulas, values, and labels. The ability to copy and move from one location to another is important because it saves time on data entry.

Copy Protection and On-Line Help

If a spreadsheet program is copy protected, it is helpful if it comes with a backup copy. If it does not have a backup copy, the user will have to send for one. Another important feature is on-line help, which allows a beginner to get help on the screen when s/he uses the program.

How to Select a Good Spreadsheet for the Classroom

The spreadsheet is not only a management tool, but also a tool for learning in the classroom. The teacher can use it as a grade book, to help the students explore mathematical relationships and formulas, to improve problem solving, and to delve into social studies or scientific investigation. Spreadsheets were originally designed for adults, but there are a handful of programs that are suitable for the classroom. *Educalc* and *Kidcalc* are devised for the elementary school, while the high schools utilize *Appleworks, Microsoft Works,* and *PFS Plan.* In addition, *Easy Working, The Planner,* and *Swift Spreadsheet* are inexpensive programs that would work well in the high schools.

Choosing spreadsheet software for the classroom is a six step process. (1) Determine the hardware compatibility, (2) Study the program's features, (3) Test how easy it is to use the program, (4) Examine the program's built-in functions, (5) Investigate the program's consumer value, and (6) Check out the technical support.

Hardware Compatibility

Check out the computers in the school. Are the computers Apple IIe's, Apple IIGS's, Apple IIc+'s, Commodore 64's, IBM PC's or Macintosh LC's? How much memory do these machines have? Is there enough memory to accommodate the spreadsheets the students are using? How many disk drives are available for each machine? (Generally spreadsheet programs need two disk drives.) Do the school's computers have hard disk drives? Do the computers display 80 columns, 40 columns, or 80 and 40 columns?

Features

How is the labeling done on the spreadsheet? Can the user center the labels or move them to the left? How does the spreadsheet handle decimal points and dollar signs? If the person makes a mistake, can this user easily change the cell or cells? Can the width of the columns be adjusted? Can the individual protect the cells from being accidentally erased? Can a user hide certain cells and not print them out? How does the spreadsheet show negative values? Does the spreadsheet have any logical functions? Does it have a Date and Time function? Can a user easily find out how many days have passed between two dates entered in the spreadsheet? Does this particular spreadsheet have macros? Can the user generate bar or pie graphs? How does the spreadsheet indicate how much memory it has left? Does the spreadsheet have windows so that the teacher can split the screen into two or three sections, each displaying a different part of the work? Can the person link this spreadsheet with other spreadsheets or arrange the information in the spreadsheet alphabetically or numerically? Does the spreadsheet have enough columns and rows to meet the classroom needs?

Ease of Use

The spreadsheet is much more difficult to use than a data base program because a teacher is working with numbers and formulas. Therefore it is imperative that the teacher choose a program that is easy to use. Look for one that gives assistance while actually working with it and lets the user quickly access a help screen. *Educalc* fits these criteria because its menus are displayed across the top of the screen (Figure 6.4), and it has a tutorial program supplied on its disk.

How fast is it to edit the cells and enter the data? Can the user smoothly delete and insert rows or columns? Is it hard to copy formulas from one row to another? How does the cursor move from one cell to another?

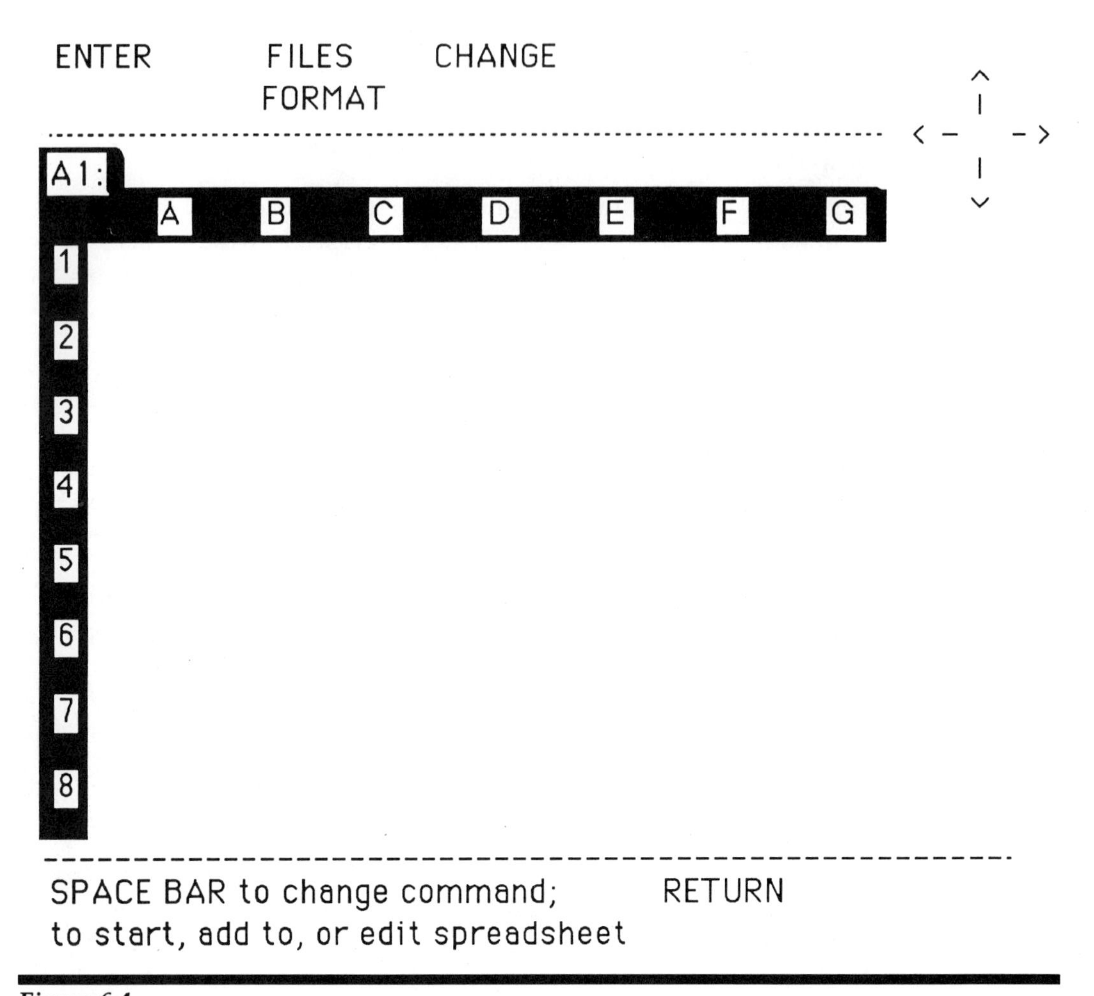

Figure 6.4
Educalc
From EDUCALC™ 128K. Copyright © 1989 by Houghton Mifflin Company. Adapted from EDUCALC™ 64K. Copyright © 1985 by Intentional Educations, Inc. Reprinted by permission of Houghton Mifflin Company.

Built-in Functions

What special functions do the students need to use in the class? For example, when students use the spreadsheet, is it to calculate sums, averages, or standard deviations? Are these particular functions present on the spreadsheet that the teacher is purchasing? *Appleworks,* an advanced spreadsheet, has 43 built-in functions, while *Educalc* has only one.

Consumer Value

Software is expensive, so cost is an important consideration. The *Swift Spreadsheet* by Cosmos and the *Easy Work Planner* by Spinnaker are bargains at $10.00. Does the software come with a backup disk? If the publisher doesn't supply a disk, how much money will it cost to buy one? Some software companies offer on-site licenses so that the purchaser can freely make copies of the software for in house use. Other manufacturers distribute lab packs, that let the software buyer purchase software at a reduced price.

Support

The software company's willingness to support their product is an extremely important factor. Can the user call someone on the telephone at the company and get immediate help? Does the person spend excessive time getting busy signals or messages that say there is a 30 minute delay? Is the technical support toll free? Does the software package come with a tutorial? Is the manual readable—with activities and lesson plans and an index? Does the program have templates? These are a few of the many questions a buyer must ask when planning to buy a spreadsheet. The checklist shown on page 158 will make the decision easier for a teacher needing a spreadsheet.

Spreadsheet Checklist

Directions: Examine the following items and determine which ones you feel are important for your class situation

Product Name ________ **Manufacturer** ________ **Appropriate Grade Level** ___

A. Hardware

_ 1. Memory needed
_ 2. Computer compatability
_ 3. Printer compatability
_ 4. Hard disk
_ 5. Number of disk drives

B. Features

_ 1. Protected cells
_ 2. Hidden cells
_ 3. Sorting
  _ a. alphabetical
  _ b. numerical
_ 4. Windowing
_ 5. Macros
_ 6. Common functions
_ 7. Formulas
_ 8. Logical operators
_ 9. Fixed titles
_ 10. Transfer to word processing
_ 11. Link to other spreadsheets
_ 12. Integration with data base
_ 13. Name ranges
_ 14. Graphing
_ 15. Flexibility of printing
_ 16. Manual recalculation

C. Editing

_ 1. Deleting and adding columns
_ 2. Change column width
_ 3. Copying labels and formulas
_ 4. Formatting of cells
_ 5. Erasure

D. Ease of use

_ 1. Help screens
_ 2. Tutorial disks
_ 3. Quick printer setup
_ 4. Easy editing of cells
_ 5. Simple command names
_ 6. Quick cell movement
_ 7. Warning questions

E. Consumer Value

_ 1. Cost
_ 2. On-site license
_ 3. Backup disk
_ 4. Lab packs

F. Support

_ 1. Technical
_ 2. Tutorial material
_ 3. Readable manual
_ 4. Templates

Rating Scale

Excellent ____ **Very Good** ____ **Good** ____ **Fair** ____ **Poor** ____

Comments

Spreadsheet Activities for the Classroom

The following exercises are meant to be used in conjunction with any spreadsheet. If a computer lab is not available, the reader can just follow this section to get an idea of what kinds of activities can be used in the classroom. The first exercise leads the user in a step-by-step introduction to a spreadsheet program. The students will need two disks: a program disk and a formatted disk to store the information.

Preliminary Exercises

1. Load the program disk into the computer and boot the machine.
2. Format a blank disk with the operating system that the spreadsheet program accepts.
3. Create a new file and give it the name **Grade Book.**
4. Begin by entering labels across the first row of the spreadsheet. Starting at cell B1, type the following labels: **Exam 1, Exam 2, Exam 3, Exam 4, Exam 5.** Place the label **Exam 1** in cell B1, **Exam 2** in C1, **Exam 3** in D1, **Exam 4** in E1, **Exam 5** in F1. Now leave Cells A1 and A2 empty and put the label **Pupils** in Cell A3. These labels will describe the contents of the cells. The spreadsheet should look similar to the following *Microsoft Work's* one:

	A	B	C	D	E	F
1		EXAM 1	EXAM 2	EXAM 3	EXAM 4	EXAM 5
2						
3	PUPILS					
4						

5. Starting at A5, enter the pupil's last names: Smith, A6, Sharp at A7, Garcia at A8, Raj at A9, Friedman at A10, Washington at A11, Reilly at A12, Hughes at A13, and Sherrin at A14.
6. Using the **sort** or **arrange** function, alphabetize these names and align each name on the left hand side of the cell.
7. Now enter the data in the Grade book. Enter Friedman's Exam 1 score as 89 in cell B5, his Exam 2 score as 46 in cell C5, Exam 3 as 69 in D5, Exam 4 as 74 in cell E5, and Exam 5 as 35 in cell F5. Now continue entering the exam scores for the remaining students; the spreadsheet should look like this:

	A	B	C	D	E	F
1		EXAM 1	EXAM 2	EXAM 3	EXAM 4	EXAM 5
2						
3	PUPILS					
4						
5	FRIEDMAN	89	46	69	74	35
6	GARCIA	45	23	75	75	34
7	HUGHES	89	43	67	67	34
8	JONES	99	45	75	75	40
9	RAJ	98	50	73	73	39
10	REILLY	56	50	67	67	32
11	SHARP	98	45	72	71	39
12	SHERRIN	78	46	73	72	34
13	SMITH	99	45	74	74	40
14	WASHINGTON	87	45	72	72	34
15						

8. Next type the label **AVERAGE** in cell G1 and enter the formula to calculate the average score for Friedman's five exams by putting the cursor on cell G5 and writing the formula. There will be variation in these formulas; for instance, if the reader is using **Appleworks,** the formula is **@AVG(B5...F5)/5,** while the formula for **Microsoft Works** is **=Average(B5:F5).** After the formula is entered, the average (62.6) should appear instantaneously in cell G5.
9. Next use the **copy** function to calculate the averages for the remaining students:

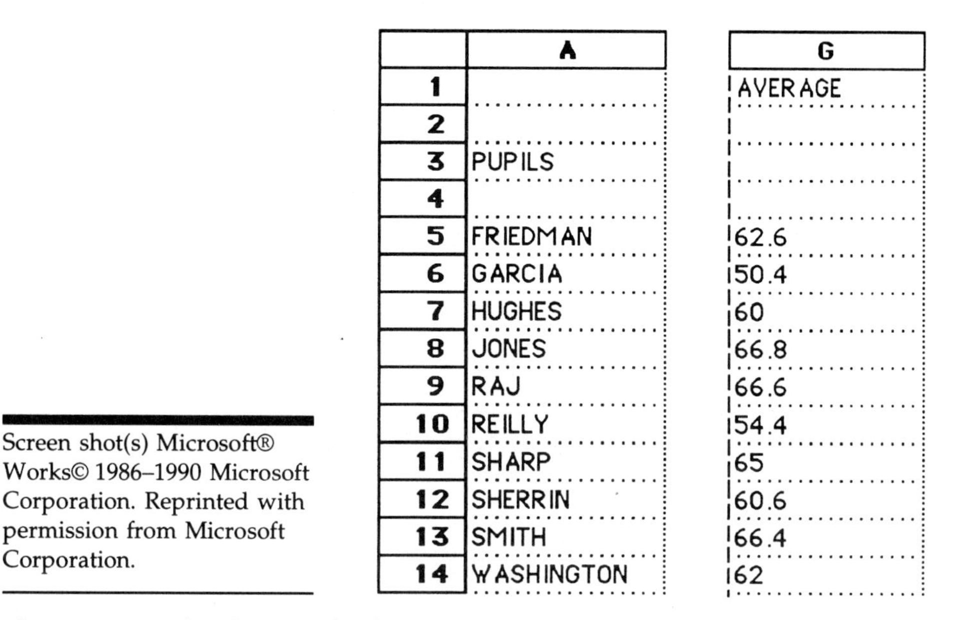

	A	G
1		AVERAGE
2		
3	PUPILS	
4		
5	FRIEDMAN	62.6
6	GARCIA	50.4
7	HUGHES	60
8	JONES	66.8
9	RAJ	66.6
10	REILLY	54.4
11	SHARP	65
12	SHERRIN	60.6
13	SMITH	66.4
14	WASHINGTON	62

10. Learn how to save the data on the formatted disk, and print it out for inspection. What follows are four ready-to-use classroom activities that test the students' ability to use successfully different features of the spreadsheet.

Activity One: Science

Objective: The students will learn about speed and how to use a spreadsheet to do simple calculations.

1. Discuss how fast an automobile can travel and the relationship between distance, miles, and time.
2. Have the students create a spreadsheet similar to the following:

	A	B	C
1	RATE	TIME	DISTANCE
2	25	0.5	
3	30	1	
4	35	2	
5	40	2	
6	45	3	
7	50	3	
8	55	4	
9	60	5	
10	65	6	
11	70	7	

3. Next pose the following question: What is the distance covered when traveling so many hours at a given speed?
4. Have the students type a formula in cell C2 that multiplies cell A2 by cell B2 and then copy this formula for cells C3 to C11.
5. After the students have accomplished this, have them examine the results and determine the answers to the questions posed. If there are not enough computers, let the students use their calculators and a pencil and paper to complete this task.

Variations The teacher can generate other spreadsheets and ask the following questions:

a. How much time does it take to travel a specified number of miles at a certain speed?

b. How much distance is covered when they travel so many hours at a given speed?

Activity Two: Mathematics

Objective: Students should be able to use a spreadsheet to help keep track of expenses.

1. Discuss the following problem with the students: The $10 Computer Club is having a fund raiser to buy software for its club. The cost of the software is $700 and the students expect to sell three raffle tickets apiece. They are selling these tickets for $3.00 each and the table shows how many tickets were sold:

$10 CLUB	DAYS OF THE WEEK							AVERAGE
	1	2	3	4	5	6	7	
1. Adams	6	4	6	2	3	4	5	
2. Barrett	5	4	4	5	0	0	3	
3. Devlin	5	2	6	2	6	1	2	
4. Johnson	2	1	4	4	2	1	3	
5. Mason	3	0	0	0	10	0	2	
6. Garcia	1	2	3	4	3	2	1	
7. Youngblood	2	3	4	5	5	7	8	
8. Sands	1	3	2	5	0	4	3	

2. Have each student create the same spreadsheet and then finish this table by calculating the average for each student.
3. Tell the students to use the logical function to determine how many club members sold 6 or more on a daily basis. Was the $10 Computer Club able to buy its software?
4. As another assignment, change the totals in the spreadsheet for any two students not selling at least 3 raffle tickets daily to 3 raffle tickets and record the value the spreadsheet recalculates.
5. Have the students compute the averages again. They are to redo the entry table again and see what the effect would be if they raised the raffle ticket price to $5.00.

Activity Three: Home Economics

Objective: The students will be able to use a spreadsheet to help them keep track of their expenditures for six months.

1. Have each student record in their spreadsheet expenditures for the following 10 items during a six month period.
2. The students should have a table similar to the following:

EXPENSES	JAN.	FEB.	MARCH	APRIL	MAY	JUNE
Food						
Telephone						
Utilities						
Rent						
Automobile Loan						
Insurance						
Entertainment						
Clothes						
Medical Bills						
Savings						

3. Use the sum formula to total each column.
4. Add an additional column to keep track of six month totals.
5. Change values in the completed table so that the students can answer "what if" questions. For example, if I cut down on my entertainment, how much more can I save a year?

Suggestions: From the savings row, create a spreadsheet that shows how much an initial deposit of $200 would grow at different interest rates and at different intervals of time.

Activity Four: The Pendulum

Objective: The student practices predicting, changing variables, and estimating. S/he will also learn how to use a formula in a spreadsheet.

Materials:
- String
- Thumbtacks
- Weights

Knowledge: The students must understand how the pendulum works.
1. Have each student enter different weights, lengths, and amplitude values. The objective is to determine what affects the pendulum's period. A period is simply the time it takes the pendulum to swing from point A to point B and then back to point A again.
2. Change the different variables by entering different numbers for each category.
3. Use a formula to figure each period for the pendulum.
4. Set up a table like the following:

Pendulum Investigations			
Length	**Weight**	**Amplitude**	**Period**

There are numerous ways to use a spreadsheet in everyday life such as for comparison shopping, calorie counting, doing income tax returns, figuring baseball statistics, and budgeting. The teacher can use a spreadsheet for a grade book, as a study aid for history, for physics experiments, and for accounting problems. The students can calculate averages and standard deviations for statistics problems and even keep track of their grades.

Since the reader now has a background in spreadsheets, let's turn our attention to the integrated program.

What is an Integrated Program?

The author previously discussed three popular applications of the computer: the word processor, the data base, and the spreadsheet. Each application was dedicated to a separate task-the word processor created and edited documents, the data base organized information, and the spreadsheet worked with numerical data.

Once the user is comfortable working with these individual programs, s/he may require software that allows for the free interchange of data. For example, s/he may need to take budget information that's stored in the spreadsheet and transfer this information to a letter that s/he is writing on the word processor. Normally, one can accomplish this task physically only by going through seven laborious steps. 1. Write the report on the word processor, leaving space for the spreadsheet table. 2. Obtain a hardcopy of the report. 3. Close the word processing application and open the spreadsheet. 4. Enter data into the spreadsheet's cells where it is manipulated. 5. Generate a printout of this spreadsheet. 6. Use scissors to cut the spreadsheet printout and paste the results onto the word processor hard copy. 7. Photocopy the report.

Cutting and pasting among applications is a time-consuming chore, necessary because stand-alone programs are not capable of communicating with other applications. There are many aspects of programming that limit the ability of these programs to address one another, and one important limitation is their different command structure. For example, the *Educalc* spreadsheet cannot electronically transfer information into the *BankStreet Writer* word processor because of their different commands. Out of this need for communication among applications emerged the integrated software program, one that combined separate programs that could communicate with one another.

In its most common configuration the integrated program includes a word processor, a data base, and a spreadsheet. *Lotus 1–2–3*, a pioneer in its field, was developed in the early eighties as a spreadsheet. It was one of the first programs to have as a part of its design a data base with some graphics capabilities. After the success of *Lotus 1–2–3,* many programs followed its example. There was *SuperCalc 3,* which integrated data base, spreadsheet and graphics, *AppleWorks* and *Microsoft Works,* programs that combined a spreadsheet with file management and word processing. Soon integrated programs, such as *Microsoft Works* expanded to include more applications such as telecommunications and graphics. ClarisWorks (Claris) has a word processor, spreadsheet, a data base, manager, communications and drawing module, while BeagleWorks (Beagle Bros.) features word processing, data base, spreadsheet, painting, and a communications module with a phone book.

The integrated programs have two common methods of integrating software, either by using the all-in-one program or an integrated series. The all-in-one software package is a single program with three or more applications, and these applications share a similar command structure. This means that many of these applications use the same commands to do the same functions. Programs such as *AppleWorks 3.0, AppleWorks GS* (Claris) and *Microsoft Works* (Microsoft Corporation) are examples of this method of integration. The major advantage of the all-in-one is ease of data transfer because each module is a component of one program. However, it has two disadvantages: (1) the program typically needs more memory than the stand alone package, and (2) the integrated program usually has a weaker module. For example, the word processing application could have limited functions compared to a standard stand-alone word processing package.

The integrated series is the other popular method of integration, and it has separate programs that have the same command structure. Because of the common command structure, the data can be easily transferred among these programs. The integrated series require less memory and offers more flexibility then the all-in-one package. The best known series of this type is *PFS* and the *Easy Working Series.*

Advantages of any Integrated Program

Why is it important to have an integrated program when the computer user can buy separately whatever is needed? Is there an advantage to owning this type of integrated software? Yes, there are definite reasons for making this decision. A buyer can purchase an integrated program for less money at a tremendous saving over buying three separate programs. This type of program is easy to use and very efficient.

Alternatives to an Integrated Program

If the user chooses not to buy this type of program, what are the alternatives?

1. He or she can use the stand alone program as it is and cut and paste when necessary. Or the computer user may be lucky and the program could have the data base or word processing capabilities needed. For example, the *Lotus 1–2–3* spreadsheet has data base capabilities, but these features are limited, compared to a stand-alone data base.
2. A user can retype the data into the separate applications. For example, s/he can reenter the data manipulated in the spreadsheet into the word processing program. This sounds like a reasonable alternative, but think how much typing this requires and how easy it is to make a typing error. Any time the user changes a number in one application, s/he is forced to retype it in another application.
3. A user can file share, which permits access to the files of the other program. Because there is little standardization among the files of programs, these files cannot be directly read. If the user wants to read these file, a special transformation program is needed. This program lets the user input a file of one type, make it conform to the file structure of another type, and then output this transformed file. The newly created file can now be used by the individual's program. Unfortunately, these transformation programs are not available for all software programs, and they are often difficult to use.

In conclusion, if the buyer is going to do the kind of work where s/he needs to transfer information from one application to another, then s/he should buy an integrated software package. However, if the user does not need to transfer data among applications, s/he should purchase a basic stand-alone application that fits the user's computer needs.

How Does an Integrated Program Work?

Let's use *Microsoft Works 2.0* tutorial example, which creates a financial report on *Pie - in-the-Sky Bakers.*

1. The tutorial creates a data base where a hypothetical person records the pies ordered and delivered as shown on this screen:

..for example, you can create a Database with your information...

PIE-IN-THE-SKY BAKERS

Pie Flavor	Ordered	Delivered
Blueberry Tart	450	450
Strawberry	783	600
Apple	98	98
Chocolate Cream	79	30
Key Lime	1,067	1,000

2. The program copies the number of pies delivered and transfers these data into the spreadsheet for manipulation. Next, the program calculates the total sales for each type of pie sold, and the report appears on the next screen:

...and then copy the key numbers to the Spreadsheet.

PIE-IN-THE-SKY BAKERS

Pies Sold	At	Total Sales
450	$6.10	$2,745.00
600	$4.95	$2,970.00
98	$4.95	$480.10
30	$5.75	$287.50
1,000	$7.95	$7,950.00
		$14,432.60

3. Using the chart function of the integrated package, the tutorial represents the data graphically as shown in the following chart:

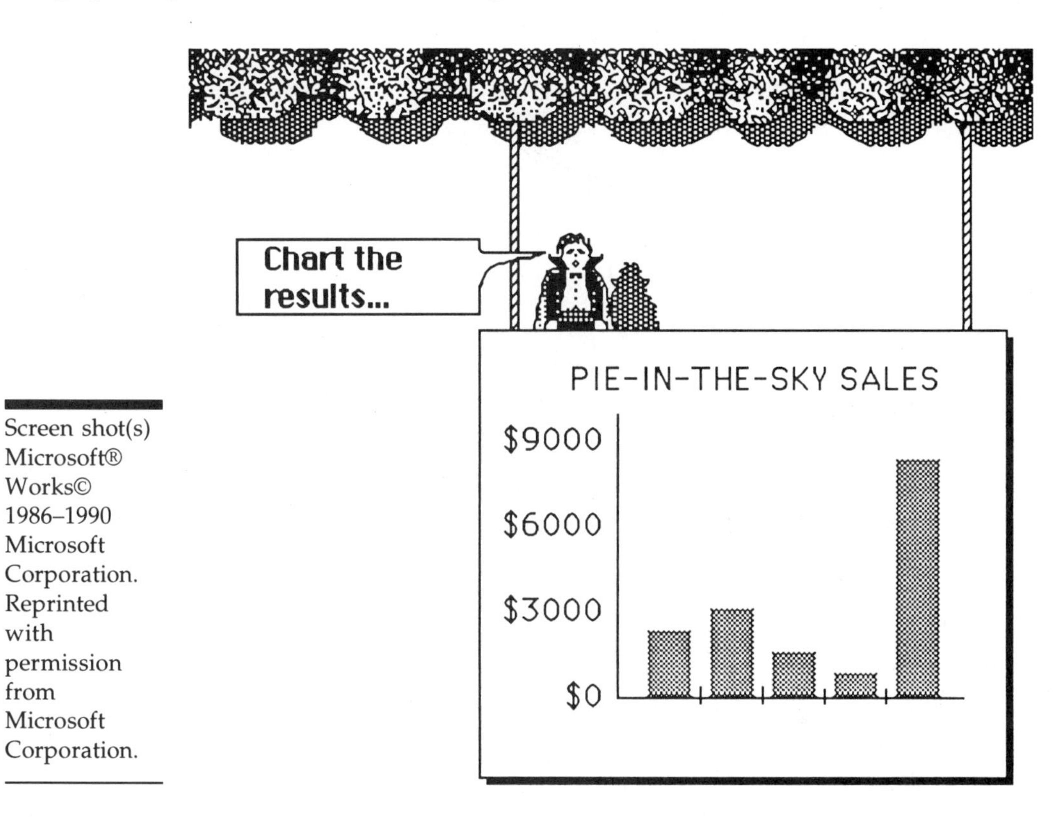

4. In the next step the computer user goes to the word processing program to write a letter about the August sales. In this report s/he highlights the Key Line pie sales and illustrates these sales by taking the chart created in step 3 and placing it in the letter as shown:

5. The person prints the report or uses a modem to send it over the telephone wires to another microcomputer or mainframe.[3] The individual receiving the report over the modem can print it or just look at it on the screen:

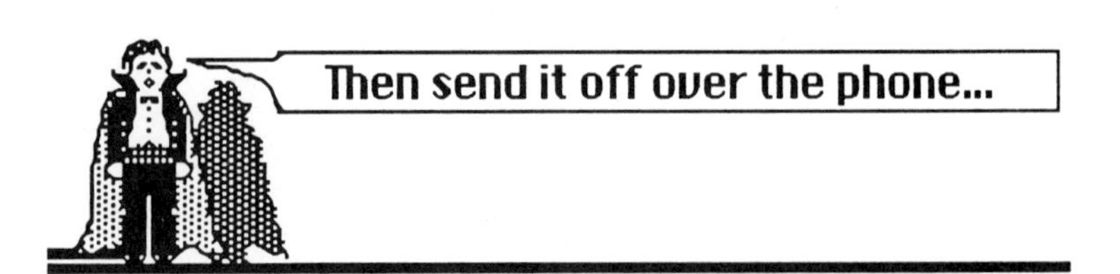

3. A modem is a device that attaches to the computer and sends its output over the telephone lines. In Chapter 11, the author will discuss the modem.

Features of an Integrated Program

When the buyer scrutinizes an integrated program, s/he is concerned with the same features in the integrated program as those in the other applications. The buyer should consider the same questions: What is the speed with which the data base sorts? How much time is needed to load a file? How fast does the spreadsheet do its calculations? How many columns and rows can the user create using the spreadsheet document? Does the word processor have a thesaurus? Besides these previously discussed features, the buyer should find out how quickly and easily each module in the integrated package shares data and if the program has mail merge and windowing capabilities. A discussion of mail merge and windowing follows:

Mail Merge

Mail merge is the ability to combine the data base information with the word processing documents to produce a customized letter or report. If the instructor wants to send out the same letter to parents of students in his or her class, mail merge lets this individual combine a form letter with a mailing list. The program automatically places each name and address in the form letter. In an integrated program, the user may have a list of names and addresses in the data base and a form letter created with the word processor. The integrated program merges the information from these applications to produce a form letter.

Windowing

Windowing is the ability to display different parts of the worksheet on the screen so that the user can work within each module window simultaneously. For example, one window might display a spreadsheet while the other window displays a graph being generated from the spreadsheet. The computer user could then change numbers in the spreadsheet and watch the effect on the graph that is redrawn with the new values.

Summary

The electronic spreadsheet, which consists of a matrix of rows and columns intersecting at cells, was developed to handle complicated and tedious calculations. In this chapter the reader became familiar with the basic features of a spreadsheet and discussed which features to consider when buying a spreadsheet program for the classroom. The author gave a spreadsheet checklist to simplify this decision making process. Next, the teacher was shown how to introduce this spreadsheet topic to the class and how to plan activities.

In addition, the integrated software package was defined as a group of programs that freely exchange data with each other. In its most common configuration, these integrated programs include a word processor, data base, and spreadsheet. Presently many graphics module. A mastery test, classroom projects and suggested readings and references follow.

Be sure to review the award winning, annotated data base programs listed in Appendix A

Chapter Mastery Test

1. What is a spreadsheet?
2. Give an example of the following terms: (a) macro, (b) cell, (c) logical functions, (d) predefined functions, (e) windows.
3. What is the advantage of being able to copy a formula in a spreadsheet?
4. Explain how a spreadsheet can be useful in determining a classroom budget.
5. Describe five features of a spreadsheet and their functions.
6. Choose two important features of a spreadsheet and show how they can be utilized in the classroom.
7. Discuss the factors involved in selecting a spreadsheet for a school district. Use Appendix A for an annotated list of spreadsheet software.
8. Explain the advantage of a spreadsheet over a calculator.
9. Give an example of a situation where an integrated software program has an advantage over a stand-alone program.
10. Explain how an integrated program works.
11. Define and give an example of windowing and mail merge.

Classroom Projects

1. Develop a spreadsheet activity for the classroom.
2. Create a spreadsheet similar to the grade book example given in this chapter, but for this example have twelve students take three exams and a final. Calculate the final exam as 40% of the grade and the other three exams as 20% each.
3. Prepare a review comparing three spreadsheets.
4. Use a spreadsheet to compare the expenses with a devised budget.
5. Outline in a lesson plan format three different ways a spreadsheet would be useful in the classroom.
6. Prepare a report on the integrated programs comparing their strengths and weaknesses.
7. List the different ways an integrated program would be useful in the school district office.

Suggested Readings and References

Allen, V. "Spreadsheets." *Electronic Learning* (April 1985): 52–53. *Appleworks Reference.* Claris, 1989.

Arad, O. "The Spreadsheet: Solving Word Problems." *The Computing Teacher,* 14(4) (1987): 13–15.

Arad, O. S. "The Spreadsheet: Solving Word Problems." *The Computing Teacher.* (December/January 1986–87): 13–15, 45.

Aranbright, Deane E. "Mathematical Applications of an Electronic Spreadsheet." *Computers in Mathematics Education*: NCTM 1984 Yearbook, Reston, Va., 1984.

Baras, E. M. (2 Ed.) *Guide Using Lotus 1–2–3.* Berkeley, CA: McGraw-Hill, 1986.

BetterWorking Eight-in-One IBM. *Manual,* Spinnaker, 1989.

Bitter, Gary. *AppleWorks in the Classroom Today.* Mitchell Publishing: Watsonville, California, 1989.

Bowman, C. Integrated Software Solves Scheduling Problems. *Electronic Learning,* (April 1985): 22–24.

Brown, J. "Spreadsheets in the Classroom." *The Computing Teacher,* 14(3) (1987): 8–12.

Brown, J. M. "Spreadsheets in the Classroom Part II." *The Computing Teacher* (February 1987): 9–12.

Duncan, Judy. "PFS: WindowWorks is a Smooth Integrator." *InfoWorld* 13(29) (20 July 1991): 63–64.

Educalc, User Guide. *Manual.* Grolier Electronic Publishing Inc., 1985.

Graggs, Tuseda A. Two Integrated Packages Appear on the Horizon. *InFoWorld.* 13(30) (29 July 1991): 13.

Harrison, David. *The Spreadsheet Style Manual.* Homewood, Ill.: Dow Jones-Irwin, 1990.

Joshi, B. D. "Lotus 1–2–3: A Tool for Scientific Problem Solving." *Journal of Computers in Mathematics and Science Teaching* 10(8) (1986–1987): 25–38.

Karlin, M. "Beyond Distance-Rate/Time." *The Computing Teacher* (February 1988): 20–23.

Luehrmann, A. "Spreadsheets: More Than Just Finance." *The Computing Teacher,* 13 1986: 24–28.

Luehrmann, Arthur. *AppleWorks Word Processing: A Hands-On Guide.* Gilroy, Calif.: Computer Literacy Press, 1987.

Makarat, Phillip. "Exchanging Files between FrEdWriter, FrEdBase, and AppleWorks." *The Computing Teacher.* 18(3) (November 1990): 17–18.

Miller, Michael J. *Microsoft Improves Works, Its Low-End Integrated Package.* InfoWorld (16 October 1989): 78.

Microsoft Works. *Using Microsoft Works for the Apple Macintosh.* Microsoft Corporation Productivity Software, Inc., 1986–1989.

Parker, J. "Using Spreadsheets to Encourage Critical Thinking." *The Computing Teacher,* 16(6) (1989): 27–28.

Parker, O. J. *Spreadsheet Chemistry.* Englewood Cliffs, N.J.: Prentice Hall, 1991.

Rubin, Ross Scott. "Integrated Software." *Incider At* (February 1991): 28–34.

Russell, J. C. "Probability Modeling with a Spreadsheet." *The Computing Teacher* (November 1987): 58–60.

Sachs, David. *Mastering Microsoft Works: A Self Teaching Guide.* New York: Wiley, 1990.

Schiffman, S. S. "Productivity Tools for the Classroom." *The Computing Teacher* (May 1986): 27–31.

Sloan, Michael L. *Working with Works.* Glenview, Ill.: Scott-Foresman, 1990.

Stang and M. Levinson. "Spreadsheets Come to School." *Media and Methods* (September 1984): 28–29.

Strickland, A. W. "Appleworks Afield." *The Computing Teacher* (November 1987): 9–11.

Strudler, N. "Adding Macro-Power to AppleWorks." *The Computing Teacher* (February 1988): 33–34.

Using Microsoft Works. *Manual.* Microsoft Corporation, 1989. "Work At Home User's Guide." *Manual.* DesignWare Plus+. Britannica Software, 1987.

Zeickhick, Allan L. "Integrated Software Comes Together." *InfoWorld* (14 August 1989): 45–56.

Software Evaluation

7

Objectives

Upon completing this chapter the student will be able to:

1. Differentiate between computer assisted instruction and computer managed instruction.
2. Define the following software terms: (a) public domain (b) shareware (c) drill and practice (d) problem solving (e) simulation (f) games
3. Name and discuss the criteria for selecting quality software.
4. Evaluate a piece of software based on standard criteria.
5. Create a plan for organizing a software library.

Introduction

In previous chapters, the reader learned about the computer as a productivity tool in the classroom—its uses as a word processor, data base, spreadsheet, and desktop publisher. This chapter's focus will be on the computer as an instructional tool or tutor.

The computer has many purposes in the classroom, and it can be utilized to help a student in all areas of the curriculum. Computer-assisted instruction (CAI) refers to the use of the computer as a tool to facilitate and improve instruction. CAI programs use tutorials, drill and practice, simulation, problem solving approaches to present topics, and test the student's understanding. These CAI programs let a student progress at his own pace, assisting him in learning the material. The subject matter can range from learning basic math facts to understanding more complex concepts in math, history, science, social studies, and language arts.

In 1950 MIT scientists designed a flight simulator program for combat pilots, the first example of CAI. Nine years later, IBM developed its CAI technology for elementary school and Florida State University had CAI courses in statistics and physics. About the same time, John Kemeny and Thomas Kurtz created BASIC, Beginner's All-purpose Symbolic Instruction Code at Dartmouth College, which provided a programming language for devising CAI programs. In the early 1960s, CAI programs ran on large mainframe computers and were primarily used in reading and mathematics instruction. In addition, computer programmers were producing simulation programs, modeled after real life situations. This earlier simulation software served as prototypes for programs today; unfortunately, most of this earlier software was tedious, long on learning theory and short on imagination, lacking motivation, sound, and graphics.

The invention of the microcomputer led to the development of improved instructional software and, indirectly, to the resurgence of interest in classroom computer usage because of public demand and the competition among companies. The software companies have employed teams of educators to enhance their products, and many textbook publishers have also become involved in producing software. The federal and state authorities, too, are studying ways to improve software.

Computer Assisted Instruction

Computer assisted instruction (CAI) facilitates student learning by using various methods. It is not one dimensional. For example, CAI can provide the student with practice in problem solving in math; it can also serve as a tutorial in history and can provide further drill and practice in English. Let us look at the different types of CAI: (1) tutorial, (2) simulation, (3) drill and practice, (4) problem solving, and (5) games.

Tutorial

The major characteristic of tutorial software is the fact that it teaches an individual new material and does not require that the student have prior knowledge of this information. A tutorial's job is to tutor by interactive means—in other words, by having a dialogue with the student. This program presents information, asks questions, and makes decisions based on the student's responses. Like a good teacher, the computer decides whether to move on to new material, review past information, or provide remediation. The computer can serve as the teacher's assistant by helping the slow learner or the student who has missed a few days of school. Furthermore, a good tutorial is interesting, easy to follow, and enhances learning by providing sound and graphics. It should have sound educational objectives, be able to regulate the instructional pace, and provide tests to measure the student's progress.

The CAI tutorials are based on the principles of programmed learning: (1) The student responds to each bit of information presented by answering questions about the material. (2) The student gets immediate feedback after each response, which means s/he knows instantaneously if the response is correct or incorrect. Tutorial lessons are called learning programs, and each lesson has a series of frames. The computer presents a frame that poses a question, to which the student gives an answer. If the student is correct, s/he moves on to the next frame.

However, there is disagreement among educators on how these frames should be arranged. Some educators are proponents of the linear tutorial, while others prefer the branching tutorial. The linear tutorial presents the student with a series of frames, each of which supplies new information or reinforces the information learned in previous frames. The student answers a question before s/he proceeds to the next frame. Every student has to respond to every frame in the exact order presented, and there is no deviation from this presentation. On the plus side, the student does have the freedom to work through the material at his or her own speed. In contrast to the linear, the branching tutorial allows more flexibility in the way the material is covered. The student does not necessarily work through the same material and the computer makes the decision of what material to present to the student. The computer presents the student with questions, then determines by the pupil's response whether to review the previous material or to skip to more advanced work.

There are many tutorial programs: Claris' tutorial for *Appleworks* shows the user how to use the integrated software program *Appleworks,* and Apple Computer has a series of tutorials for the Apple II and the Macintosh. For example, *Tour of the Apple* for the Macintosh computer illustrates how to use a mouse. Another example is *Type!* (Brøderbund), a tutorial that teaches a student how to type quickly and accurately. This tutorial has motivational drills, and diagnostic help that improves the individual's skills. The following screen is presented from *Type!* (Figure 7.1) tells the beginner to place a thumb on the space bar and gives suggestions on proper posture and position.

Simulation

In a simulation program a student takes risks as if s/he were confronted with the real life situation and yet does not have to suffer the consequences of failure. Moreover, a student can experiment with dangerous chemicals on the computer screen and not be in danger from the actual chemicals. Also, there is no expensive lab equipment to buy—the only cost is the software. Another advantage is the fact that the student does not have to wait a long period of time for a plant to grow under certain experimental conditions before he can observe the results. The student can not only observe the results, but also repeat the experiment as often as s/he wishes. Simulations save time and money, reduce risks, and work well in group situations involving decision making.

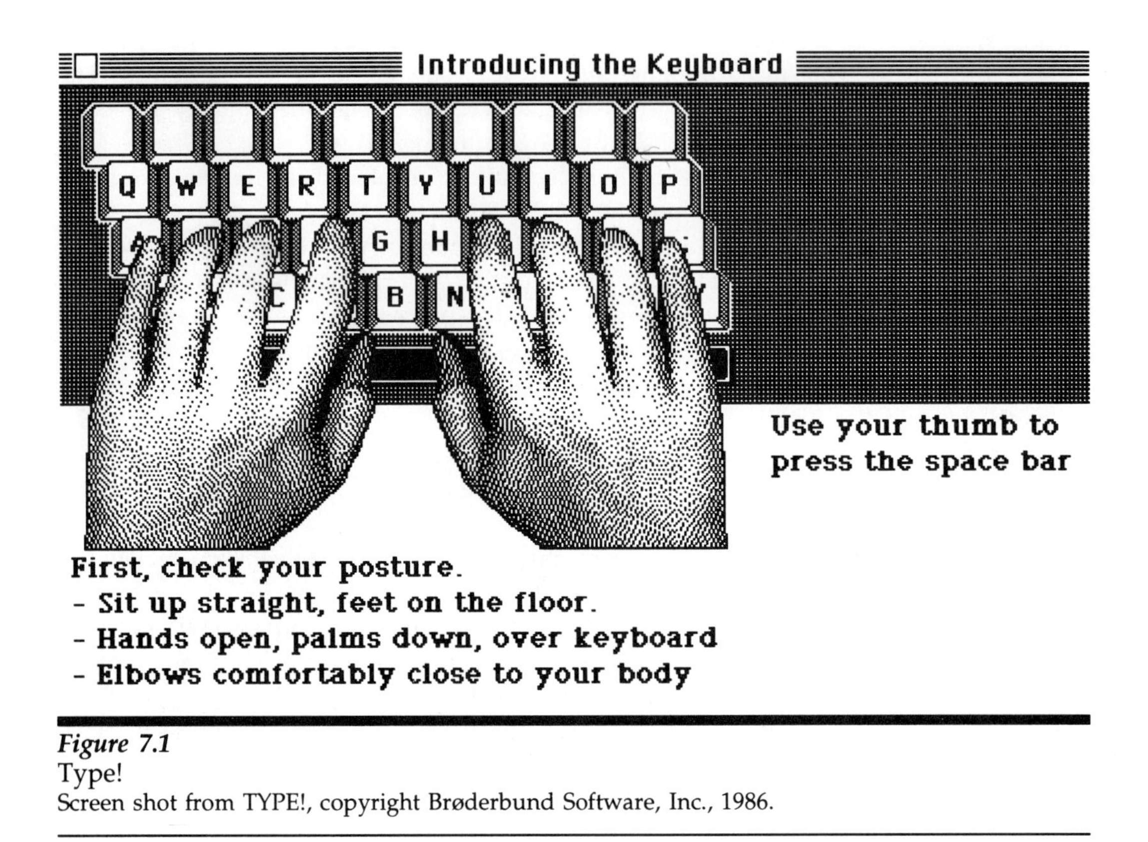

Figure 7.1
Type!
Screen shot from TYPE!, copyright Brøderbund Software, Inc., 1986.

A classic example of a simulation program is *The Oregon Trail* (MECC). The student or class uses this program (Figure 7.2, shown on page 181) to plan a trip from Missouri to Oregon in the 1840s.

The object of this program is to survive the various conditions and hardships and earn the most points. The pupil makes significant decisions before leaving on the trip by deciding whether to travel as a banker with $1600, a carpenter with $800, or a farmer with $400. The more money the student has, the more supplies and services the student has, the harder it is to earn points. The pupil must make preparations by purchasing food, ammunition, clothing, and oxen and has to decide which month to start the journey. Along the trail the class makes decisions about resting, hunting, fighting, crossing rivers, and protecting themselves from Indian attacks in order to avoid starvation, exposure, and death. In the process the class gains an understanding of what it was like to live during the pre-Gold Rush years between 1840 and 1848.

Figure 7.2
Oregon Trail
Courtesy of MECC.

Drill and Practice

In 1963 Patrick Suppes and Richard Atkinson produced drill and practice software on a mainframe computer. The computer screen displayed a problem, the student responded, and the computer provided immediate feedback. The learner stayed with the problems until s/he reached a level of proficiency and then moved on to a more difficult level. With the arrival of the microcomputer in the 1970s, this drill and practice software was widely produced in all subject areas. It was so popular that 75% of the educational software was drill and practice; however, in the 1980s many educators felt this type of software was being overused. They believed that the computer should be used for higher level thinking tasks and not as an electronic workbook. Presently most educators see the value of a good individualized drill and practice program because too much time is spent in the public schools on classroom drill and practice material. This type of drill and practice software frees the students and the teacher to do more creative work in the classroom. In many of these programs the computer serves as a diagnostic tool, giving the teacher relevant data on how well the students are doing and what work they need.

Drill and practice software helps children remember and utilize skills they have previously been taught, whereas a tutorial's primary goal is to teach the student new material. The individual must be familiar with certain concepts prior to working the drill and practice program in order to understand the contents of the program.

The typical drill and practice program design looks like the following: (1) The computer screen presents the student with questions to respond to or problems to solve. (2) The student responds. (3) The computer informs the student whether s/he has the correct answer. (4) If the student is right, s/he is given another problem to solve. If the student responds with a wrong answer, s/he is corrected by the computer. Figure 7.3 illustrates the four steps.

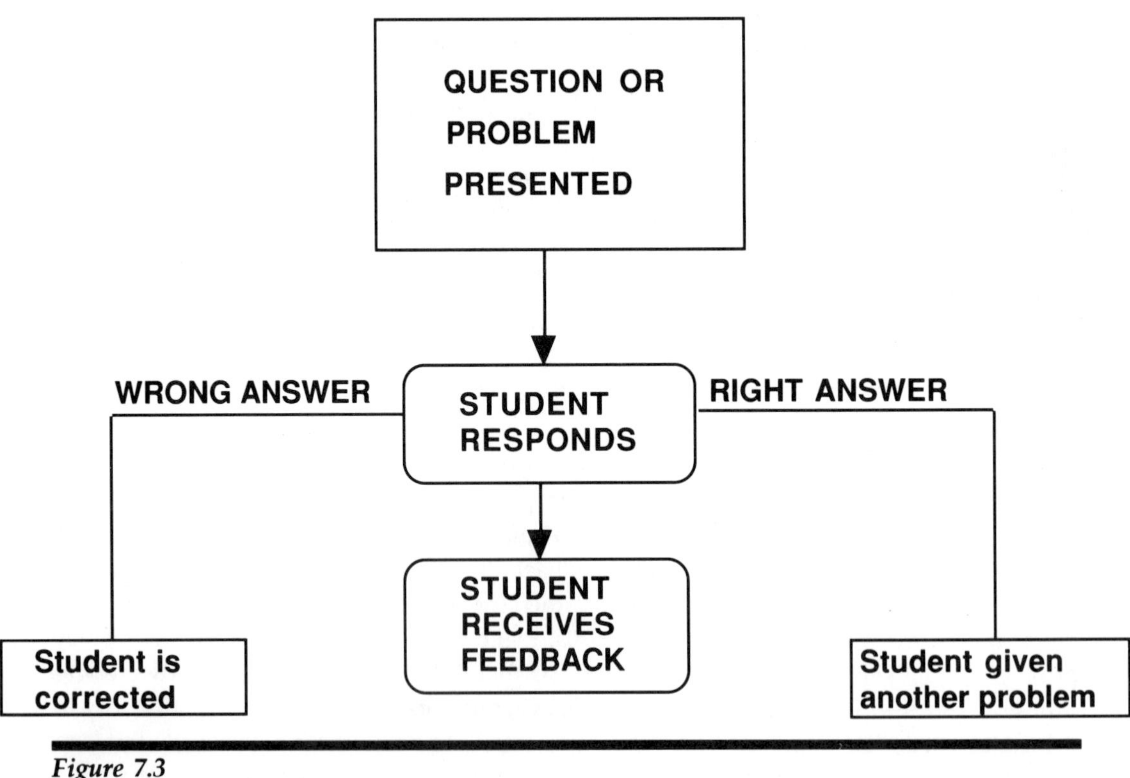

Figure 7.3
Drill and Practice Program

The computer program can handle incorrect responses by using the following techniques: (1) The computer display tells the student to try the problem again. If s/he keeps giving the wrong answer, the computer gives the right answer. The program then proceeds to the next problem. (2) The student is allowed to type only the correct response because the computer ignores all keys pressed except the right one. For example, if the problem is 1 + 1 = ?, the computer program will ignore any answer other than 2. It might beep when the student tries to type another response. (3) When a student types the wrong keys, the program displays the answer that should have been typed by the student. For example, if the student typed *salmon* instead of *cod,* the computer would type *cod.* (4) The student is given a hint when s/he responds incorrectly. If the student still misses, s/he is given a better hint. After three or four hints, the student is shown the right answer. (5) Some computer programs give the student additional information in order to help respond to a question. This type of program is similar to a tutorial program.

Drill and practice programs that utilize the capabilities of the computer are exciting because of their ingenious use of graphics and sound. For example, a program that displays a rabbit doing a jig or a boy blowing a horn has these qualities. Many drill and practice programs are games where the players are rewarded points for the correct answers. *State and Traits* (Britannica), a social studies program, has the student place states on a map and match these states with traits. When the student places a state on the map, s/he does this by moving it to the correct location. If s/he is correct, the state fills with a color and the student receives a point. If the student is wrong, s/he loses a point, the state blinks, and the computer places the state in the right location. As part of this program, the student matches such items as names, historic facts, bordering states, capitols, current facts, and land forms.

The new *Math Blaster Plus* (Davidson) is a very popular math program that uses points, certificates, animation, and coins for reinforcement. The program has four activities: Rocket Launcher, Trash Zapper, Number Recycler and Math Blaster. For example, the Math Blaster activity has the student use an arcade-like game to improve his or her speed and accuracy in solving basic math facts. The object of the game is to help the Blasternaut fly to the space stations (Figure 7.4).

The user must solve an equation before the trash alien lands on the planet. As the reader can see, the problem appears at the top, while different answers appear inside the space stations shown on the screen. The student controls the path of the Blasternaut and directs him to the correct space station. In the process, the player has to make sure the Blasternaut avoids the flying objects. If the Blasternaut touches an object, the student loses time and power. There are bonus rounds that help the Blasternaut gain points and energy.

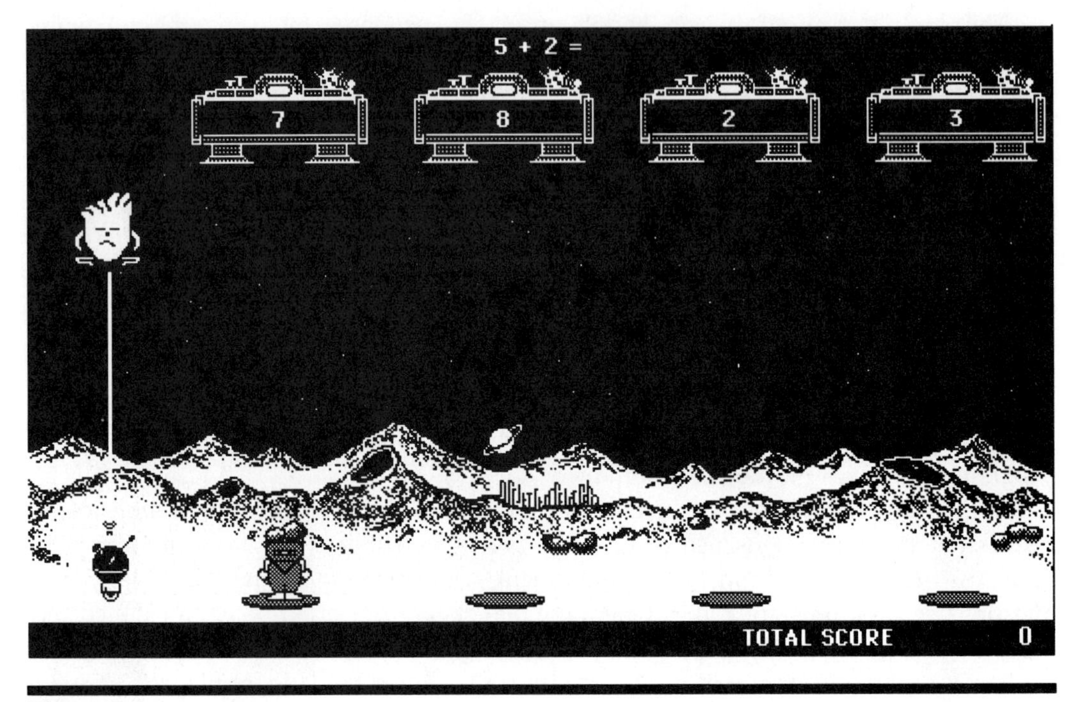

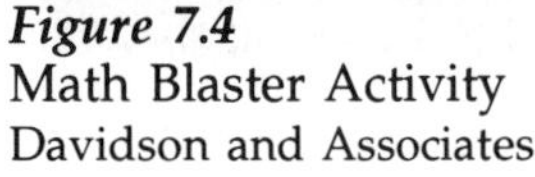
Figure 7.4
Math Blaster Activity
Davidson and Associates

Problem Solving

Problem solving skills are necessary for preparing an individual to live in a complex world, and a good way to develop these skills is to solve problems and not just read about them. Problem solving uses critical thinking skills and is not relegated to any specific content area. A problem solving program emphasizes cooperation and is suitable for small groups or individual students. There are a variety of computer programs that focus on higher level thinking. Some of the better programs are: *The King's Rule,* and *The Factory* (Sunburst), *Gertrude's Puzzles* and *Gertrude's Secrets* (Learning Company), *Where in the World is Carmen Sandiego?, Where in Time is Carmen Sandiego? Where in America's Past Is Carmen Sandiego?* (Brøderbund).

Where in the World is Carmen Sandiego? (Figure 7.5) asks the student to be a detective searching for a thief who is hiding out in one of 30 cities.

In this particular case, the student detective is told that a national treasure, the Rockettes, was stolen from New York and the objective is to capture the thief by tracking

File Edit Game Police Dossiers
New Delhi
Wednesday, 1 p.m.
Sixteen different native languages are spoken in India, including Hindi and English, which are the official languages of government and business.
Depart
Show
INTERPOL

Figure 7.5
Where in the World is Carmen Sandiego?
Screen shot from "Where in the World is Carmen Sandiego?," copyright Brøderbund Software, Inc., 1985.

the thief's movements. The detective discovers clues as s/he tracks the culprit's whereabouts and logs these clues into the crime computer. When the student detective is able to find out the identity of the criminal, the student detective issues a warrant for the person's arrest.

There are ten possible suspects and Carmen is the most difficult one to find. As a new detective, the student begins at the rookie level, but advances as cases are solved. The higher the student's rank, the harder the case the student is assigned. The student uses *A World Almanac* and a map to solve the cases.

Another example of problem solving software is the *Incredible Lab* (Sunburst) where the user plays the role of a scientist who constructs a monster in a laboratory. The student scientist makes selections from a list of chemicals, creating a monster with a green head, scaly body, and other weird parts. There are five different body parts with six possible variations, and the student (scientist) determines by trial and error and careful reasoning which chemical was used to create each part of this monster. The scientist analyzes the data, gathers more information, eliminates possibilities, and draws conclusions. To be successful, the student must record notes in an organized manner and develop a plan. The student then relates the notes to the data in the experiment, constantly devises new hypotheses, and tests these hypotheses in the next experiment.

Presently, there is a keen interest in problem software as evidenced by the number of entries in the commercial software catalogs. Teachers like this type of software because it helps students with hypothesis testing and taking notes. Similar to simulation, problem solving programs can be easily used with only one computer and 30 children. The whole class can be involved in critical thinking and making inferences. This type of software gives students more freedom to explore than the drill and practice software.

Game Programs

Game programs for the computer are classified as entertainment or educational software. The educational programs have specific learning objectives with the game serving as a motivational device, whereas the entertainment programs have playing the game as the major goal. On the one hand, educational software offers different learning outcomes, integrating the learning and the game. On the other hand, entertainment software has little academic value except that of learning a strategy for a specific game. Most CAI programs use a game format that ranges from drill and practice to logic software. For example, *Spell it Plus* (Davidson), a drill and practice spelling program, has a frog jumping over hurdles and swallowing correct answers. *Reader Rabbit* (The Learning Company), a language arts program, consists of four games that build reading skills and improve children's letter recognition, memory, vocabulary, and concentration. In *Reader Rabbit's Sorter Game* (Figure 7.6), the child matches all words that start with the letter *S*, and if the child is successful, the rabbit does a jig.

Computer games are very popular, and many educators agree that CAI programs should be designed as games. These programs (which demand that the player develop a skill, or that the students play against each other or against the computer) are motivating programs and present a challenge. The computer has to vary the presentation of material or the player will figure out a way to win every time. There are rules that the players must understand, because there is always a winner or a loser. Graphics, fast motion, and sound effects are used to enhance the program, not to distract from its educational value. A good educational game involves active physical and mental participation by the players.

Figure 7.6
Reader Rabbit
The Learning Company.

As the reader has probably gleaned from the prior discussion, most CAI programs incorporate more than one type of software in their design. For example, a program that is a tutorial may have a drill and practice element, while a simulation may have a game as an integral part of its program. When a student looks at any CAI program, he or she should try to identify the basic component of that program. For example, *Oregon Trail's* main element is simulation, with the hunting game as its game component.

Much of the software that has been reviewed can be used with the child who has special problems. The computer with its appropriate software is the suitable modality for this type of child because the computer is patient, always waits for a response, and repeatedly gives the same explanation. It is an ideal tool for individualization and remediation because the child can practice a skill as long as needed. Furthermore, the teacher can add special hardware devices to the computer to overcome the physical limitations of the learning disabled child. For example, the instructor can install a special communication board that will respond to the child's spoken command.

Children who have to stay at home can have all the benefits of CAI by using a terminal or modem that is plugged into the school computer.

Computer Managed Instruction

From the previous discussion, the reader learned how CAI directly involves the learner. This is not the case for computer-managed instruction (CMI). "The objective of computer-managed instruction (CMI) is to collect and process information to enable the instructional staff to provide the best learning environment for each student. One basic difference between CAI and CMI is the recipient of the computer information. In CAI, it is intended for the student; in CMI it assists the teacher in the management of learning." (Tolman and Ruel, 1987).

The computer in CMI is a tool that manages instruction, keeps track of the students' test scores, attendance records, and schedules, and offers diagnostic-perspective instruction in all curricular areas. CMI makes the teaching environment more organized and productive, allowing the teacher to individualize instruction. The computer directs the pupils so that they can proceed at their own pace, and it supervises instruction by telling the students to read certain books and listen to particular tapes. When the students finish their work, they then go to the computer for testing and further assignments. The students are not limited to just computer related materials; they can view movies and see previous experiments. The computer tests, grades tests and records scores so that the teacher can see and evaluate the students' progress.

CMI is based on the underlying concept that all children can learn if they proceed at their own pace and are given the proper instructions and materials. CMI can be a comprehensive program for one or more areas of the curriculum. Many computer managed instruction programs are based on pretest, diagnosis, prescription, instruction, and posttest. The results of the testing are then used by the instructor to determine the materials that are best for the individual student. With this information, the teacher can then choose the proper learning activities to aid the individual student. Let us now look at features of a more complex CMI program. (Later, the author will describe how the teacher can use the available software to manage instruction more effectively in the classroom.)

An example of a complex management system is *Classroom Management System-Mathematics,* A Science Research Associates, SRA System. This particular system is designed for pupils in the primary grades and manages math work on such topics as whole numbers, addition, subtraction, problem solving, measurement, time, geometry and money. It helps the teacher test, evaluate the student's progress, and prescribe remedial work. In addition, the teacher has a record of the student's progress. The suggestions for activities are keyed to six of the important basal math textbooks and a few SRA programs. When the teacher uses the program, she types in her name, class, and a code word that allows her to access the necessary information on her class. The teacher then makes the choice of which textbooks and materials to suggest. The teacher can also add her own activities and materials to the list. At the beginning, the student takes a pretest on the computer. If the computer survey indicates an area of need, the student is given the appropriate test to pinpoint the area of weakness. If questions are missed on this exam, a prescription is given. If the student fails again, this student must see the teacher. The teacher can customize the program, omitting tests for the class or individuals in the class. The teacher is also in charge of deciding the remediation assignments or deciding when the testing ends. The instructor can call up records, class lists, tests, status reports on individuals, class reports, group reports, and graph reports.

Many CMI packages are stand-alone packages, but some elements of CMI are being incorporated into the tutorial and drill-and-practice software. CMI can be used as a method of evaluation for special software, enabling the teacher to keep up to date on the student's progress. For example, the new *Math Blaster Plus* has a test maker that lets the teacher create and print a math test. If the teacher then wants the students to work on specific problems, she can use the editor and enter a set of problems. The program also has a record keeping device that lets the teacher keep track of every student's score. There are many utility programs that are available to help teachers in the task of recording grades and taking attendance. A superior program is *GradeBusters 1/2/3,* a grade book, attendance record machine, given top honors by such magazines as *Electronic Learning,* and *Incider.* There are teacher utility software packages that aid the teacher in producing materials for the classroom—word searches, test generators and excellent crossword puzzle makers.

In theory CMI is sound, but in practice there are some real problems. A common complaint is the disadvantage that it is difficult to set up the management module for the student. It takes time to enter each student's name and define tasks. (The teacher would normally do this over a span of months, but now with CMI she has to accomplish this task immediately.) The CMI systems are moving toward more user friendly software, but most programs are quite difficult to use. Some researchers feel there is a decrease in the interaction between the student and teacher when this system is used (Coburn, Kelman, Roberts, Snyder, Watt, and Weiner 1982, p. 48). Another frequent teacher complaint is the quality of the software. Only basic skills are being tested, using such instruments as multiple choice and true/false questions. Yet another complaint is the cost, which can be quite exorbitant for the integrated learning systems and may require considerable access to computers. Finally, the following question must be asked: How capable is the computer of truly assessing the student's performance and providing the appropriate prescription for learning? Unfortunately, CMI has not been adequately researched and the known benefits are inconclusive up to this point (Clements, 1989). Now that the reader has some idea of what Computer Managed Instruction is, let us look at some inexpensive alternatives to commercial software—Public Domain and Shareware—and spend a few moments examining the differences between these useful products.

Public Domain/Shareware

Most software programs discussed in this book are commercial. The commercial programs are expensive, and it is very costly to buy multiple copies. Fortunately, there is an alternative to commercial software—public domain software. This is inexpensive software that can be legally copied and shared with other users with no restrictions on use. Public domain is not copyrighted, and the authors choose not to seek formal rights or royalties. The buyer pays a small fee to an outfit like The Public Domain Exchange or SoftSwap, which sends the software. Also user groups pass around this software to their members. The quality of this software varies considerably. There are very useful public domain programs, but the buyer has to choose carefully and wisely. Professional programmers and teachers write these programs in their free time. The reader can find a list of some highly rated public domain programs in **Appendix A.**

Shareware is inexpensive software that may or may not be copyrighted. It lets authors send their products directly to the user. Usually the author does not have to worry about marketing or promotion costs. The user pays some nominal fee to a group like the Public Domain Exchange. Next, the user examines the program, and sees if it fits his or her needs. The computer user is then free to give the software to friends for examination purposes. If after looking over the software the parties involved are going to use the product, they must register with the owner of the product and pay another fee. A shareware fee to an author may be as low as $5 and as high as $40. The author's name and address are always on the disk. In return for the fee, the user usually gets documentation, technical support, and free updates.

Software Selection: A General Guide

In prior chapters, the author discussed different application software such as word processing and desktop publishing, and the reader learned how to evaluate these programs by using appropriate criteria. Now let's look at some general principals that apply when evaluating any software.

Choosing good software is an eight step process. The computer user should proceed as follows: (1) Know the specific software needs of his population, (2) Locate the software, (3) Research hardware compatibility, (4) Examine the program's contents, (5) Look at instructional design, (6) Check out how easy the program is to learn, (7) Evaluate the program in terms of consumer value, and (8) Investigate the technical support and cost.

1. Specific Software Needs

To make a wise decision it is essential to know the needs of the classroom. After the teacher has determined the specific requirements, he can ask the following questions: What is the grade level, and ability level? For what purpose will the software be used? Does the class need a math drill and practice program to reinforce some math skill? Does the group need a word processor or a remediation program to help the students learn something already taught? What type of software should the teacher select? How sophisticated should this software be? For example, should the program be a simple word processor for letter writing or a heavy duty word processor for book writing? After these decisions are examined, the teacher should list the features the classroom requires. On the one hand, if the teacher is teaching 1st. grade, s/he might want a word processor that does primary print. On the other hand, if the teacher is working with eighth graders, he might want a word processor that has an outliner.

2. Locating Software

The major sources of software information are software house catalogs, journals, indexes, educational organizations, and magazines. (See **Appendix D** for a listing of some of these indexes, journals, and magazines.)

Regardless what source used, the teacher should read several reviews of the software to get a different perspective. Often there is disagreement among reviewers on what constitutes "good software" because every reviewer has a priority. For example, Reviewer A may feel that ease of use is the most important factor, while Reviewer B might be concerned with features. Reviewing software is like reviewing movies. How often has the reader seen Siskel and Ebert disagree? Also, the computer user should look at advertisements for new products. The buyer can see what new products are available just by scanning the magazine ads or asking the manufacturers to send a more detailed list. The buyer might want to call the producers of the product directly to find out about some features. Software developers like Sunburst send preview copies if the recipient guarantees their safe return. There are other sources for previewing software: university software libraries, state departments of education, software clearinghouses and software publishing companies. An additional avenue is to seek out a computer enthusiast or a friend who has used the product. *WordPerfect* may be a hot selling program, but the teacher should talk to a friend who is actually using it because it might not be right for the teacher's particular situation. Computer user groups recommend good software, demonstrate it at their meetings, and have their members available to answer questions. At the very least, these groups put the user in touch with people who have the software that the buyer is using. These groups generally keep abreast of new developments in the field.

After the teacher has properly researched the type of software, he or she is ready to enter the computer store and look at the software package itself. Upon choosing a store, the instructor should make sure it is a reputable and reliable one and should also see what the store's policy is for defective disks and returns. When examining a program, check on the version number. It may be an old version that has been lying around the store for ages. Also, inspect the package and see if it is a teacher's version or a consumer version. The consumer edition will be less expensive, but it usually does not have a backup disk or an activity book. At this point, the teacher is ready to check for hardware compatibility.

3. Hardware Compatibility

Ask the following questions: Do the computers at the school have enough memory to run this program? How many disk drives does each machine have, and what size are they? Does the software program need a hard disk to run it faster and more efficiently? What equipment is necessary? Does the program require a mouse, a joystick, or a color monitor? What type of printers does the program support? Having sufficiently researched these topics, the teacher should look at the program's contents.

4. The Program's Contents

What are the objectives of this program? Are these objectives clearly stated? Does the program meet these objectives? Many programs are not logically organized and lack a theoretical base. The objectives do not have to be seen on the computer screen. However, they should be found in the documentation that accompanies this software package.

The next questions include the following: How appropriate is the program for the students? What knowledge or skills must a student possess to utilize this software program? Are the graphics and skills required reasonable for this grade level? (Be careful not to buy a program that is too easy or hard for the class.) Is the vocabulary appropriate for the grade level? (Many publishers supply readability scores that can serve as a benchmark.) How accurate is the material presented in the program? Is the program free of unnecessary computer jargon, and are the spelling and grammar correct? If it is a historical program, are the data accurate? How much time is needed to run the program?

What about the program's transmitted values? Is the program free from prejudices or stereotypes? Is there excessive violence? (It is the teacher's responsibility to make sure that the values the program represents are positive.) Now carefully examine the software's instructional design.

5. Instructional Design

There are many important factors relating to program design such as (a) learner control, (b) reinforcement (c) sequencing, (d) flexibility, and (e) appearance.

(a) Learner Control. Who controls the software program? Is it the student or the computer? Can the student move back and forth in the lesson easily? Can the student quickly return to the previous frame? Can the student escape to the menu whenever s/he wants? Can the student control the speed of the program? Does the program move the academically bright forward to more difficult problems, or is the level of difficulty the same? (It is important to use the program at more than one ability level.) How easy is it for the student to exit the program or to restart an activity?

(b) Reinforcement. How are the students reinforced? The reinforcement should be delivered in a positive way. The software should give praise and not be degrading. There should be little reinforcement for inappropriate responses. (Some programs have reinforcement for wrong answers that is more rewarding than the reinforcement for right answers.) Does the program vary the reinforcement? Is the feedback active, passive, or interactive? A student receives passive feedback when the program instructs the user that the answer is wrong or right. The student receives active feedback when there is animation on the screen like Reader Rabbit's jig (Learning Company). A program that is interactive rewards the student with a game or something extra.

(c) Sequencing. Is the instructional sequence appropriate? Does it start from the simple idea and move to the complex?

(d) Flexibility. The teacher should be able to adapt this program to small and large groups. The instructor should also be able to modify the program to meet the individual needs of the children in the classroom. For example, *Spell It Plus* enables the teacher to add spelling words to the program. Does the program provide a record of the student's progress?

(e) Program Appearance. Does the program have colorful graphics, animation, and sound? Does the sound motivate the students, or does it interfere with their learning? Are the graphics distracting or helpful? How is the screen laid out? Is it crowded or well organized? Is the full power of the computer being used? Are there too many instructions on the screen?

6. Ease of Use

Is the program easy to learn? Can the student immediately load the program and use it? Does the program use simple English commands? Can the student access a help screen whenever it is needed? Is there a tutorial disk or manual that takes the user through the program? Is the printer easy to set? Can the student answer a few questions and then be ready to print immediately? Are there help prompts and safety questions? Is there an automatic save feature? What happens when the student hits a wrong key? Must the student reload the program or does the software crash? Does the program have error messages so that the student can correct problems? Are the directions clear and concise? Can the student follow the directions on the screen without going to the documentation that accompanies the software? Are the instructions brief and to the point?

7. Consumer Value

If the buyer is a beginner or an expert, cost is a concern because some software can run into the thousands. The teacher has to decide whether that $65 word processor is really better than the $395 one. Are all the features found in that $395 package worth the cost? (Find out if there is a discount house that carries the software at a considerable saving.) Is the software protected? If it is protected, does the company supply the user with a backup disk? Are there lab packs available? (Lab packs are multiple copies of a program with one set of documentation, sold at a substantial discount.)

8. Support

How is the technical support? Can a buyer call someone immediately to get help, or does the user wait forever on the telephone? Is that telephone call toll free or is it a long distance call? Is there a tutorial with the software package? Is the tutorial on a disk or in a book form? (Many manufacturers provide both to simplify learning their program.) Is the manual readable with activities and lesson plans? (The documentation should be written for the target audience.) Is this a reputable publisher? Will the company be in business when the user is having trouble with the software product? If the teacher happens to get a defective disk, will the publisher replace it?

Shopping for software is an involved process, and using the following software checklist should simplify this task.

Software Evaluation Checklist

Program Name ______

Publisher ______

Grade Level ______ **Skill Level** ______

Subject Area ______ **Time** ______

A. Program Type
- __ 1. Drill/practice
- __ 2. Tutorial
- __ 3. Simulation
- __ 4. Educational game
- __ 5. Problem solving
- __ 6. Teacher management
- __ 7. Other ____________

B. Hardware
- __ 1. Memory needed
- __ 2. Computer compatibility
- __ 3. Printer compatibility
- __ 4. Number of disk drives
- __ 5. Hard disk
- __ 6. Peripherals

C. Program Contents
- __ 1. Objectives met
- __ 2. Vocabulary appropriate
- __ 3. Accuracy of material
- __ 4. Free of bias

D. Instructional Design
- __ 1. Learner control
  - __ a. Speed control
  - __ b. Program movement
- __ 2. Proper reinforcement
- __ 3. Self-directed program
- __ 4. Appropriate sequencing
- __ 5. Student record keeping
- __ 6. Disk crash safeguards

E. Program Appearance
- __ 1. No distracting sound/visuals
- __ 2. Animation/sound/graphics
- __ 3.Uncluttered screen
- __ 4. Material clearly presented

F. Ease of Use
- __ 1. Easy program loading
- __ 2. Simple screen directions
- __ 3. On-screen help
- __ 4. Tutorial manual
- __ 5. Easy printer setup

G. Consumer Value
- __ 1. Cost
- __ 2. Backup disk policy
- __ 3. Lab packs

H. Support
- __ 1. Technical
- __ 2. Toll free number
- __ 3. Readable manual
  - __ a. Activities
  - __ b. Lesson plans
  - __ c. Tutorial
  - __ d. Index
- __ 4. Money back guarantee
- __ 5. Defective disk policy

Comments

What is the overall rating of the software? Check one of the following

Excellent ____ **Very Good** ____ **Good** ____ **Fair** ____ **Poor** ____

Reasons for Poor Software Quality

In the teacher's quest for the "best product," s/he will find that the software quality varies. In the early days, there was a lack of sophistication in software development and naturally there were errors in the program itself. Today this is not really the case. The three reasons for poor quality software are greed, technical incompetence, and lack of instructional design.

Greed

Greed is a fact of life. Some computer developers deliberately turn out products prematurely to keep up with the competition or beat it into the market place. They rely on clever advertising, catchy titles, and deceptive marketing to get the public to buy their products. These products are so faulty that they need two or three revisions to run properly.

Technical Incompetence

Because the hardware manufacturer is constantly turning out new machines, it is very difficult for the software manufacturer to keep up with this burgeoning market. In addition, many of these new machines that are supposed to run the current software are not compatible. (The manufacturer usually makes some minor modification that prevents the existing software from working on the machine.) The software developer then finds himself with angry customers who cannot understand why their program is not working. The developer then has to make modifications and send out the revised version to all the customers. That is an expensive proposition.

Lack of Instructional Design

Many programs have good graphics, good sound, and are attractive looking. Most producers of software are able to create a sharp looking product. Yet often there is little value to the product because it is not based on sound educational theory. It is, therefore, important that educators become involved in the process. Software developers should study learning theory and apply this theory when they devise their programs. This is a crucial part of the instructional design of any first rate classroom software package. Many educational programs are no different from what might be found in a workbook. Why spend thousands of dollars producing a software program when all a teacher has to do is buy a workbook? The software program should go well beyond a standard textbook or workbook.

When the instructor has the software, the most important job remains ahead. Every teacher needs guidelines on how to organize a software collection, and the following is one approach to software organization.

Guidelines for Setting Up a Software Library

1. Choose the location for the collection wisely. It could be a classroom, library, or media center. The more central the location, the easier the access.
2. Use a data base software program to keep a record of the software. Have the software alphabetized by title and subject and, simultaneously, do an annotated listing of the software.
3. Catalog the software. There is no standardized procedure, but one of the simplest and most effective ways is to color code the software and documentation by subject area. For example, if the teacher wants to find math software on the shelf, he or she would look for the blue stickers or blue folders. If the teacher has a large software collection, this teacher or library media specialist can use the Dewey Decimal System and the Sears List of Subject Headings.
4. Decide how the software is to be stored. Is the teacher going to use hanging file folders, file cabinets, or disk boxes?
5. Protect the collection. Have security arrangements and use disk boxes, storing the disk vertically. Disks should be protected from dust, dirt, and strong magnetic fields.
6. Separate the disks from the documentation because of security reasons.
7. Devise a set of rules for software use. For example, no food or drinks in any of the computer labs. Place diskettes in their designated container.
8. Have a policy and procedures manual that will handle issues like the following: (a) Who is responsible for this collection? (b) What procedures will be used to evaluate, select, and catalog this software? (c) How will the software be checked out? (d) How does a teacher verify that the software is workable? (e) How will the teacher report technical problems? Organizing and maintaining a software library is a monumental task that requires someone to be in charge of it on a full time basis.

Let's briefly review what has previously been discussed and then answer some questions about the material, do some classroom projects, and look at the suggested readings and references.

Summary

The computer has many invaluable uses in all areas of the curriculum. Computer Assisted Instruction (CAI) software uses the computer as a tool to improve instruction, provide the student with practice in problem solving, serve as a tutor, and supply drill and practice. CAI directly involves the learner, whereas computer managed instruction (CMI) assists the teacher in managing learning. The author listed the criteria that could be applied when choosing software, using an eight step process. After these steps were examined, a software evaluation form (checklist) was presented to aid in software selection. The chapter concluded with a brief discourse on software quality, followed by guidelines for setting up a software library.

Chapter Mastery Test

1. What is the most critical step in the evaluation of software? Explain its importance.
2. Discuss three criteria that a teacher should consider when choosing software for the classroom.
3. What is the main difference between shareware and public domain software?
4. Why is feedback a crucial element to consider when evaluating software?
5. Should the student or the computer control the direction of the program? Explain.
6. What is the major difference between a drill and practice and a tutorial program?
7. Define and give an example of a simulation program.
8. Can a problem solving program also be a simulation program? Explain in detail.
9. Give the paradigm for the typical drill and practice program design.
10. What is the major difference between computer-managed instruction and computer-assisted instruction?
11. Discuss two reasons for poor quality software.
12. What are the important considerations for setting up a software library?

Classroom Projects

1. Review a piece of software using the guidelines that were given in this chapter.
2. The software evaluation form that was used in this chapter was of a general nature. Develop a software checklist for a drill and practice software program in the area of math or science.
3. Go to the library and find three or four software review forms. Write a paper comparing these forms, discussing their similarities and differences.
4. Visit a high school or elementary school software library and write a paper discussing their cataloguing system.
5. Look at a software program that runs on two types of machines. See if there are any differences in how the software works.
6. Visit the library and write a review on a public domain software program. What are the advantages and disadvantages of using this type of software program?
7. Use Appendix A or a software directory to locate several math software packages for an 8th grade class.
8. Find a published review on a piece of software in the school's collection and then write a review that compares it with the published review.
9. Form small groups in the class and have each group develop a common evaluation form no more than three pages long. Make sure there is a consensus on all items, and discuss the areas where the group did not reach a consensus.

Suggested Readings and References

Alperson, J. R. & D. H. O'Neil. "The Boxscore: Tutorials 2, Simulation O." *Academic Computing* (February 1990): 18–19, 47–49.

Berlin, D. & A. Wite. "Computer Simulations and the Transition from Concrete Manipulation of Objects to Abstract Thinking in Elementary School Mathematics." *School Science and Mathematics* 86(6) (1986): 468–79.

Bok, D. Looking into Education's High Tech Future. *Harvard Magazine.* (1985): 29–38.

Clements, F. H. *Computers in Elementary Mathematics.* Englewood Cliffs, New Jersey: Prentice-Hall, Inc. 1989.

Coburn, P., P. Kelman, W. Roberts, T. F. F. Synder, D. H. Watt, and C. Weinger. *Practical Guide to Computers in Education.* Reading MA: Addison Wesley, 1982.

Collis, B. *The Best of Research Windows: Trends and Issues in Educational Computing.* Eugene, Oregon: International Society for Technology in Education, 1990.

Collopy, D. "Software Documentation: Reading a Package by its Cover." *Personal Computing* (February 1983): 134–44.

Dede, C. "A Review and Synthesis of Recent Research in Intelligent Computer-Assisted Instruction." *International Journal of Man Machines Studies.* 24(4) (1986): 329–353.

DeMillo, Richard A. *Software Testing and Evaluation.* Menlo Park, California: Benjamin/Cummings Publishing Co., 1987.

Edward, C. Project MICRO. *The Computing Teacher.* 16(5) (1989): 11–13.

Flynn, Marilyn L. "Using Computer-Assisted Instruction to Increase Organizational Effectiveness." *Administration in Social Work.* 14(1) (1990): 103.

Haugland, Susan W. *Developmental Evaluations of Software for Young Children.* Albany, N.Y.: Delmar Publishers, 1990.

Kalmon, Ted. *Microcomputer Software: Step by Step.* Englewood Cliffs, N.J.: Prentice-Hall, 1990.

Martin, J. H. Developing More Powerful Educational Software. *Educational Leadership.* (March 1986): 32–34.

Morgan, Bill, Ed. "101 Things You Want To Know About Computers" *Educational Technology.* 10(8) (May/June 1991): 25–38.

Neuman, Delia. Edited by Farol Truett. "Computer Equity: A Model for the Library Media Specialist." *The Computing Teacher,* 18(8) (May 1991): 35–37.

Norales, Francisca O. "Students' Evaluation of Microcomputer Software." *Interface.* 13(2) (Summer 1991): 45.

Roblyer, M. D. "When is it Good Courseware? Problems in Developing Standards for Microcomputer Courseware." *Educational Technology.* (October 1981): 47–54.

Starfield, A. M. "*How to Model It: Problem Solving for the Computer Age.*" New York: McGraw-Hill, 1990.

Thomas, Rex and Elizabeth Hooper. "Simulations: An Opportunity We are Missing." *Journal of Research on Computing in Education.* 23(4) (Summer 1991): 497–511.

Titus, Richard. "Finding Good Educational Software: Where to Begin." *Learning.* (October 1985): 15.

Tolman, M. N. and A. A. Ruel. *The Computer and Education.* Washington, D.C.: National Education Association, 1987.

Vargus, Julie S. "Instructional Design Found in Computer Assisted Instruction." *Phi Delta Kappan.* (June 1986): 738–744.

White, James A. and Stephanie S. VanDeventer. "A Successful Model for Software Evaluation." *Computers in the Schools,* 8(1/3) (1991): 323.

Using the Computer in All Curriculum Areas

8

Objectives

Upon completing this chapter the student will be able to:

1. Use one computer with thirty or more children in the math, science, social studies, and language arts areas
2. Become familiar with the major software in four curricular areas

One Computer in the Classroom

The typical classroom today has one computer for thirty or more children. Some teachers store the computer in a corner encased in plastic wrap with strict rules to govern its use, while others, afraid to use the computer, let it gather dust in a remote corner of the room. In either situation, the computer is not being used to its potential. Here are seven suggestions that will help the teacher better capitalize on the computer's capabilities. These suggestions are the following: (1) Select the software according to needs of the students, (2) Collect the appropriate equipment, (3) Organize the classroom, (4) Use the team approach, (5) Know the software's time factor, (6) Encourage group participation, and (7) Integrate the Computer.

1. Selection of Software According to the Needs of the Students

As with any good instruction, an important principal is to adapt the software to the students' needs. Children within a class and at different grade levels have varied abilities, interests, and preferences, that warrant different teaching considerations and strategies. For example, if a student does not know how to type, this student will have to search for keys on the keyboard instead of being able to work with a program, thus becoming easily frustrated with the computer. At the kindergarten level, a teacher's first decision may be to instruct the students in keyboarding skills, starting with the return, escape, and arrow keys. The teacher should create a large keyboard which is placed in front of the room. Next, the teacher should arrange the students in pairs to practice the letter and number locations on a copy of the larger-size keyboard. After the students have had the experience of helping each other explore the keyboard, the teacher then directs the whole class in lessons in finding designated keys, and eventually the teacher has the children close their eyes while continuing this activity. Once the children are skillful in locating keys, they are ready to work with a typing program like *Sticky Bear Typing* (Optimum Resources). *Sticky Bear Typing* has bold graphics and three activities that use jokes, riddles, and action games to sharpen the beginner's skills in typing and keyboard mastery. In the thump game (Figure 8.1) the user challenges the robot and tries to save Stickybear from being bumped by the blocks the robot is tossing. If the user types fast enough, stickbear blocks a cube from hitting the user.

Some of the popular typing programs included in **Appendix A** are: *Mastertype* (Mindscape), *Keyboard Cadet* (Mindscape), *All the Right Type* (Didatech), *Junior Typer* (Aquarius), *Mavis Bacon* (Software Tools), and *Type!* (Brøderbund). Once the students have achieved keyboard mastery, they can spend more time working with programs instead of working on the mechanics of finding keys.

If the students in the class need to improve their problem solving abilities, there is a large range of programs available. For example, problem solving software like *Where in the World is Carmen San Diego?* (Brøderbund), could work effectively for middle

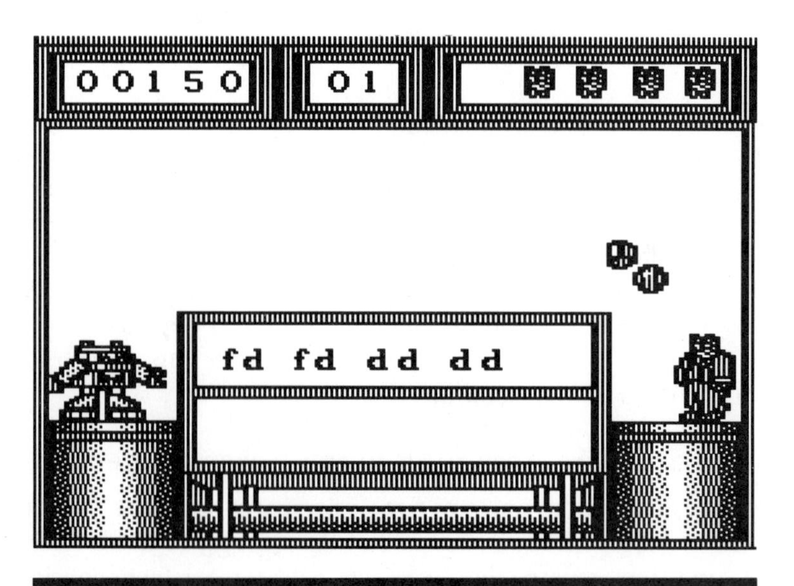

Figure 8.1
Stickybear Typing
Optimum Resource/Weekly Reader Software, 10 Station Place
Norfolk, CT 06058.

grade students in the social studies area, while *Lunar Greenhouse* (MECC) could work well for the same students in the science area. Using these programs, the students can collectively improve their critical thinking skills by taking notes, manipulating variables, analyzing the results, drawing conclusions, and offering solutions to problems.

If the class needs to study and research information about the United States, the teacher could use a data base software program like *Friendly Filer* (Houghton Mifflin). The students then create information sheets, compose questionnaires, and collect appropriate data for computer entry. Each student could research two states and input information about the state's population, capitol, number of representatives, and main crop. After information is entered into the data base, the students could search for a state where the main crop is corn. When the state appears on the screen, a student calls out its name, and the class then shades the state on a corresponding blank seat map. After the students find all the applicable states and shade them, the teacher could study the maps and discuss where the corn producing states are located. From this class discussion, the students could learn about the corn belt and why this region produces the most corn.

2. Collection of the Appropriate Equipment

When there is only one computer in the classroom, the teacher needs additional equipment to make the computer screen visible to the whole class. A portable liquid crystal display (LCD) projection panel and an overhead projector are required to project an enlarged image from the personal computer onto a wall screen. If the district cannot afford a projection panel, there is a less expensive alternative—the "T" or "Y" adapter. The teacher uses this device to split the signal coming from the class computer in order to display it on a larger television or monitor. (The Apple IIGS, also requires a modulator.) When a teacher is cramped for space, he or she can improve the situation by elevating a large television or monitor to increase visibility. This enables the teacher to introduce new software to the whole class. As an additional suggestion, the teacher can tape a transparency on the TV screen and use a grease pencil to write on the screen to illustrate a point. Furthermore, the teacher can create practice sheets duplicating a screen from a computer program and have the class work along with the presentation.

3. Organization of the Classroom

By asking certain questions, the teacher can determine the best seating arrangement for viewing the computer. Are the students going to be in their seats or on the floor? Will the pupils be placed in small groups for discussion purposes? Will they be traveling to different learning stations in the room as they use manipulatives? Are they using an instrument like a thermistor[1] to collect temperature data in different sections of the room?

4. Using the Team Approach

Many classrooms have two or three students who have been using a computer since they were very young. If the teacher has enough pupils who are familiar with the computer, these students should be organized into a team. Under the teacher's tutelage, the team can practice giving directions, solving problems, and introducing a new piece of software. After the team is experienced, the members can wear identification badges and walk around the room answering questions on the current program. In addition to reducing the number of questions a teacher receives, this team method reaches a larger number of pupils and gets them involved in helping each other.

5. Being Aware of the Software's Time Factor

The computer program's success depends not only on selecting the appropriate program for the situation, but also on knowing the program's time constraints. For instance, when the time frame is short, the teacher should not choose open-ended software because the students will be unhappy when they have to stop prematurely. *The Oregon Trail* (MECC) takes at least thirty-five minutes to complete, and the students will object to quitting, whereas *Sticky Bear Opposites* (Optimum Resources) is easier to stop and start. Therefore, in selecting a program, the teacher should make sure that the program has a save function. *Where in America's Past is Carmen San Diego?* (Brøderbund) lets the student save information for later use.

6. Encouragement of Group Involvement

At the introduction of a lesson, explain that there are many acceptable answers and that there is no one solution to a problem. Try to reduce the pupils' anxiety about their responses being evaluated. At first, involve the whole class in discussion; later break the class up into smaller groups. Ask probing questions and have these questions ready for the lesson. Ask the students for their next move, search for the reasons behind their answers, and give them time to think. The teacher should be a facilitator, letting the students do most of the talking and never imposing ideas on the class discussion. The teacher should not be judgmental in responding to the students because the students can pick up on non-verbal body language. The teacher should encourage the students to cooperate in order to promote learning and social skills. The teacher should also advance the students' thinking by making comments such as, "That is a good idea, but expand on this point."

---

1. A thermistor is a sensoring device which converts temperature changes into electrical impulses.

Let the students practice problem solving by having them solve the same problem again, checking out their hypotheses and recording their collective answers from their seats. Give the students objects to manipulate at their desks to help them answer the questions that the software is posing. For example, *Puzzle Tanks* (Sunburst) is a program that poses problems that involve filling tanks with Wonder Juice, Odd Oil, or Gummy Glue and moving this liquid over to a storage tank. At the simplest level, the program might ask the students to move 14 grams of Gummy Glue to a storage tank. For this problem the students are given a tank that can hold 7 grams and another tank that can hold 1 gram. The teacher can involve the whole class in making calculations trying to solve the problem by using measuring cups and beans at the students' desks. A favorite ploy is to divide the class into small groups that challenge each other to see which group gets the most problems correct. At the end of the day, have the children work on the computer in pairs, one partner using the computer, the other coaching and recording. This pairing encourages students to develop strategies for handling the problems inherent in the software. Organize the time the students spend at the computer by having a schedule like the following:

PROGRAM: WHERE IN THE WORLD IS CARMEN SANDIEGO

TIME	TEAMS		FINISHED
8:30-9:10	David	Scott	✓
9:10-9:30	Bobbie	Florence	✓
9:30-9:50	Jill	Judy	

The students should work on a program for a designated time interval. When their time is up, the next pair of pupils listed in the chart take a turn. If a team is absent or busy, the next available partnership will fill the void. This way the computer can be used by everyone in the class.

7. Integration of the Computer in the Classroom

The key consideration is how to make the computer an integral part of the core curriculum. The software should not substitute for the standard curriculum, but rather should complement it on a regular basis. Let's look at four different software programs and illustrate specifically how these programs can be included in classroom instruction.

If a teacher wants to improve her first grade pupils' writing skills, he might use a program like *PlayWrite* (Sunburst), which encourages creative writing and provides an opportunity for students to listen to their own written work and make revisions. When students use *PlayWrite,* (Figure 8.2) they choose costumes, expressions, and scenery for scripts. They write scripts for puppets, edit these scripts, and then are able to listen and watch the puppets perform the scripts.

Initially, the teacher and class can discuss the characters, plot, the story's purpose, and the climax. The teacher can make suggestions for script that include a recent event, a historical occurrence, a story read, or a class science experiment. Each student can work at his own desk to develop ideas for scripts, and the class can collectively brainstorm these ideas. The class then can form small groups to write their own scripts, and these scripts can be translated to the computer and viewed by the whole class.

In math, the teacher could use a simulation program like *The Market Place* (MECC) to help students improve their basic math skills. The class discovers the relationships among price, quantity sold, and income and then develops a strategy for determining the most desirable selling price, illustrated on a bar graph. The first of the three business-oriented simulations focuses on selling apples. After reading the instructions, the

Figure 8.2
Playwrite
Sunburst
Communications

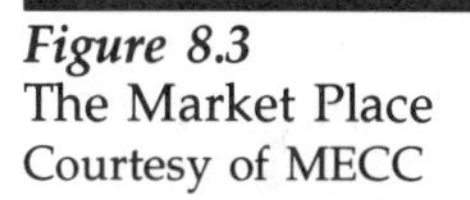

Figure 8.3
The Market Place
Courtesy of MECC

students can enter a name and set a price for the apples they will sell for that day (Figure 8.3).

A price like 35 cents per apple will not earn the class a lot of money for each apple, but the students will sell quite a few apples. At the end of the day, the students are given a report of the number of apples sold. They then discuss what effect setting a different price will have and predict the effect of the change in price on their income. Individually the students complete a sales report and, as a group they set the price for the next day. After the second day, the students individually graph the prices for apples and the income that is earned. At the end of a week, the class can be asked to determine the best price for selling apples. If the students are wrong, they can continue until they reach the best solution. At the end of this program, the best price for selling apples is displayed.

In social studies, there is a simulation series entitled *CrossCountry* (Didatech) including such titles as *USA, Texas, Canada,* and *California.* These programs are effective for teaching map reading, geography, spatial relationships, and critical thinking skills. In the program *CrossCountry California,* (figure 8.4) the students discover the geography of California by picking up commodities, that the teacher or computer selects from a list of 50. These commodities are located in cities important to California's economy. Entering the instructions given by each team, the teacher divides the class into two groups of trucking companies. If one trucking company chooses to pick up only four commodities, its mission will require about 40 minutes. However, the teacher can customize the operation of the program so that both companies have to travel the same

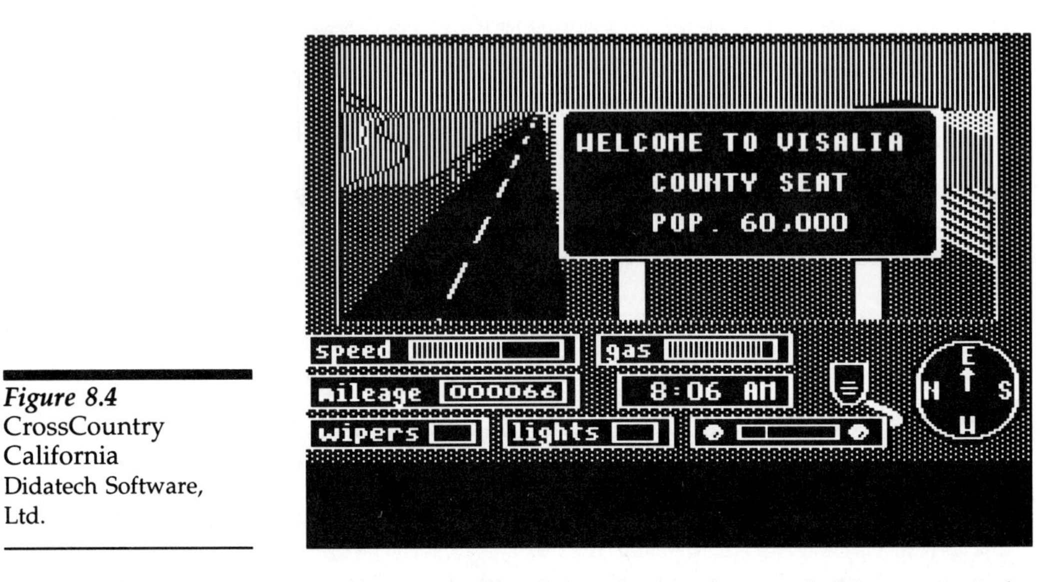

Figure 8.4
CrossCountry California
Didatech Software, Ltd.

distance. Each team's decisions are entered by the teacher, and the teams make decisions on when to eat, sleep, and get gas, on which city to travel to, and on how to get to their final destination (Figure 8.4).

Member of the teams can record the trip routes, cities visited, population, county locations, and other features. A winning team's strategy can be discussed, and each team can write a journal of the journey.

Odell Lake (MECC), is a science simulation that teaches the class about the predator/prey relationships among a group of twelve organisms found in the biological community of Odell Lake, Oregon. The members of the class are able to create a diagram of the food web of the community, based on the information they learn. The teacher works with the children by having them take notes when they use the program's "Go Explore." This option lets the students view the organism, see what it likes to eat, see what eats it, and supplies a brief description of its habits. As soon as the class becomes skilled at the "Go Explore" part of this program and knows about the different organisms of Odell Lake the students can play competitively for points. In Figure 8.5 the class must quickly decide whether the Blueback Salmon (on the right) should eat the Dolly Varden (on the left), chase it, ignore it, attempt to shallow escape, or attempt a deep escape.

In this instance, the class chose to eat the Dolly Varden, which was the wrong decision; this resulted in the Dolly Varden eating the Blueback Salmon and ending the game. This science program helps the students learn about the interrelationships among living things and helps them generalize about other biological communities.

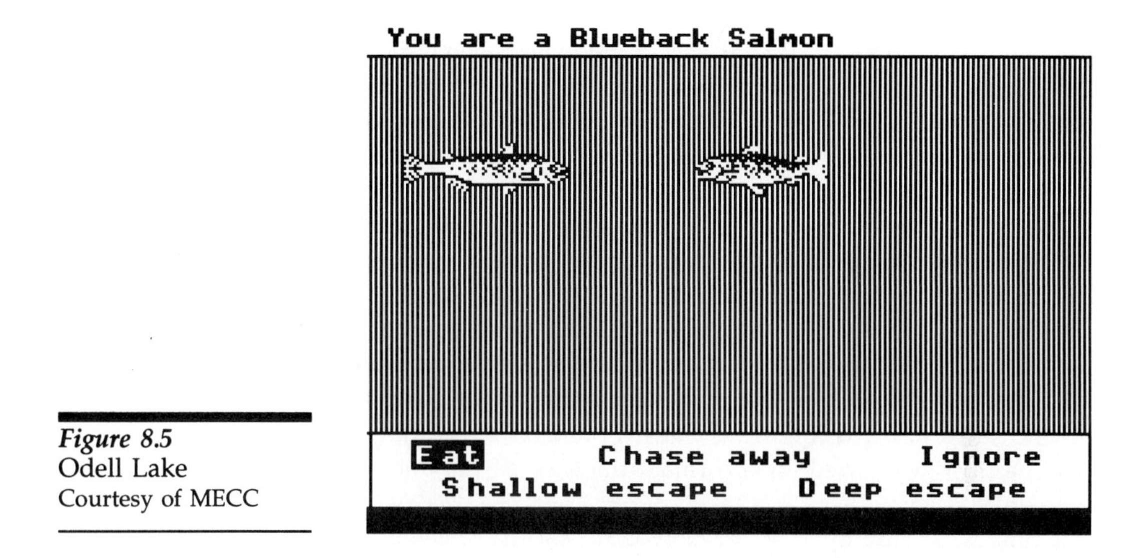

Figure 8.5
Odell Lake
Courtesy of MECC

In summation, the teacher should select the software that best satisfies the children's needs. The teacher should also take time to collect the appropriate equipment, organize the room, and use the student experts to utilize the computer effectively. The instructor should learn the software, be aware of its time limitations, know how to integrate it into the classroom curriculum, and always encourage student participation by asking the proper questions.

Now that the reader is acquainted with how to integrate the computer into the classroom, let's examine software for four different curricular areas.

Mathematics Programs

Since most computer scientists have training in mathematics, the computer is usually associated with this field. Typically, the computer is primarily viewed as a tool for programming, but it is much more than this because it is a multi-faceted instrument that can be used for learning basic skills and for developing problem solving strategies.

In the research literature there is no apparent agreement on how best to use the computer software for improving math skills or for developing higher order thinking. The individual teacher must decide how to use this math software, taking into account classroom needs. Math software is grouped as follows: drill and practice, simulation and problem solving, and tutorial.

Drill and Practice

Drill and practice math programs help students become more proficient in their math skills and concepts. These programs give the students the needed practice in a highly motivating format and assist the less academically adept child who learns at a slower pace. Programs such as *Fraction Munchers* (MECC), which focuses on fraction types, equivalent fractions, comparison of fractions, and fraction expressions, use the pacman arcade format to motivate the learners to improve their skills. The user directs the fraction muncher to "eat" numbers or fractional expressions that match a phrase that appears at the top of the screen. If the user eats an incorrect response, or is caught by a "troggle" creature, this player loses a muncher. The game automatically advances to the next level after the student successfully clears the screen of all the target values. On this new screen appears another set of equivalent fractions and target values. The following *Fraction Muncher* screen (Figure 8.6) shows a muncher, who has just swallowed an equivalent fraction for 1/5 and a troggle positioned at the top corner square.

This is an example of a good drill and practice math program because the munchers and troggles are motivating, and *Fraction Munchers* lets the user control the level of difficulty and the speed. **Appendix A** has a selection of popular drill and practice programs such as: *Math Blaster Plus* (Davidson), *Hop To It* (Sunburst), *Fay: That Math Woman* (Didatech), and *Money Works* (MECC).

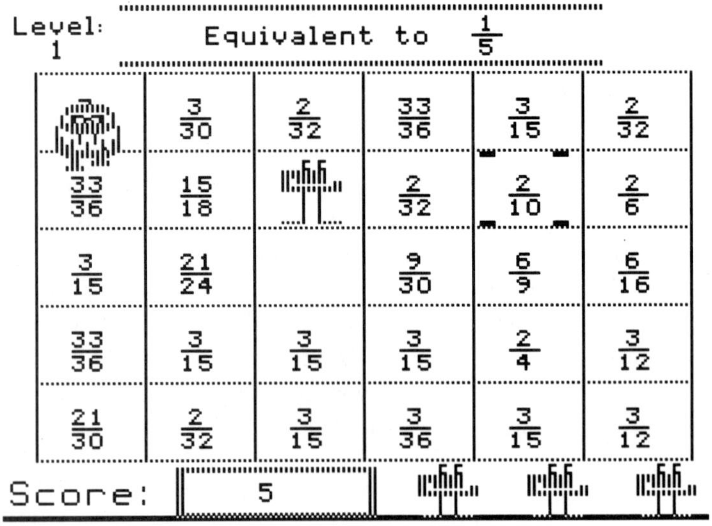

Figure 8.6
Fraction Muncher Screen
Courtesy of MECC.

Simulation and Problem Solving

In the past students thought mathematics was an abstract concept, devoid of real life meaning, but today there are math simulation programs modeled after situations that occur daily. Using vivid graphics, *The Math Shop Series* (Scholastic) challenges students to solve problems in everyday settings. As the students work in different stores, they use a wide range of relevant math skills, realizing how math pertains to the real world. The owners in the various *Math Shop* stores provide services for their customers, and they call upon the student computer users to help with these services. For example, the baker is having difficulty filling the doughnut orders, and the students' job is to adjust the donut machine so that it is properly set for each order. They use arithmetic skills to find the fractional parts of donuts. In Figure 8.7 the customer orders a total of 4 donuts, 2 glazed and 2 plain, and the students tell the donut machine to make 4 donuts with 2 glazed, for a fraction of 1/2.

The students get to choose where to begin at each store, and they receive on-the-job-training. Some stores have easy tasks, while other shops have more time consuming tasks; the task difficulty increases as the students gain proficiency. *Algebra Shop,* the most advanced program in this series, helps the students with prealgebra and algebra problem-solving skills involving factoring, squares, and square roots, whereas *Math Shop Junior,* the beginning program, helps primary students with basic addition and subtraction facts.

Problem solving software promotes critical thinking skills, and programs vary in the degree to which they accomplish this task. Most problem solving software is

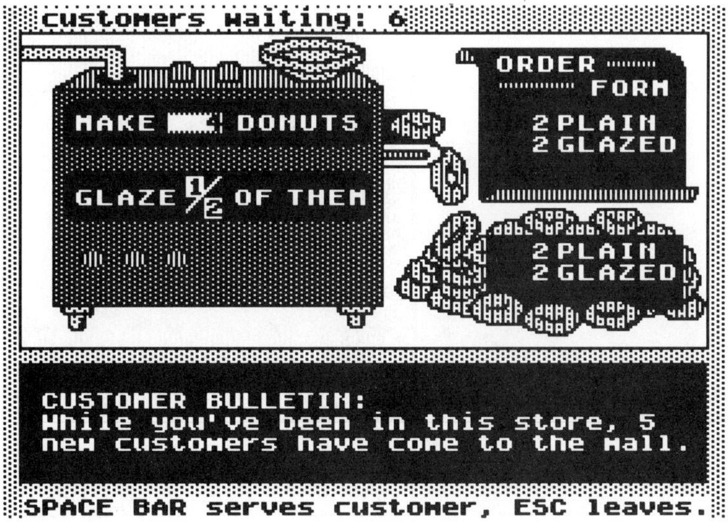

Figure 8.7
Math Shop
Scholastic Inc.

similar to simulation software because people are placed in situations where they manipulate variables and receive information on the results. For example, the program *Safari Search* (WINGS For Learning) has the students work on twelve activities that include hypothesis testing and data collection. The objective is to develop a strategy for finding hidden animals in a five-by-five matrix using the fewest moves. Let's look at the following example from *Safari Search* (Figure 8.8). Here the students use hypothesis formation and testing to find a flamingo hidden under a square. The computer gives the students clues such as "hot," "warm," and "cold," depending on the distance and direction of the hidden flamingo. The students who work at this level can open as many boxes as they want around a "warm" or "hot" response until they find the elusive bird. In this instance, the students quickly find out that "hot" means touching a side of the Flamingo,"warm" means touching a corner of the Flamingo, and "cold" means not touching the flamingo at all.

If there are only a few squares opened during the game prior to finding the bird, the teacher can use the game to predict where the Flamingo is. The teacher can also use the same game to predict the computer response on the uncovered squares when the teacher knows where the Flamingo is. After the students work with *Safari Search* a few times, they can make inferences from the different clues they receive. The students use complex judgments to determine the best two locations to choose for their first guesses. For example, looking at the above *Safari Search* screen, the teacher may ask the question: "If we get warm, what does that tell us about the location of the bird?" The teacher can

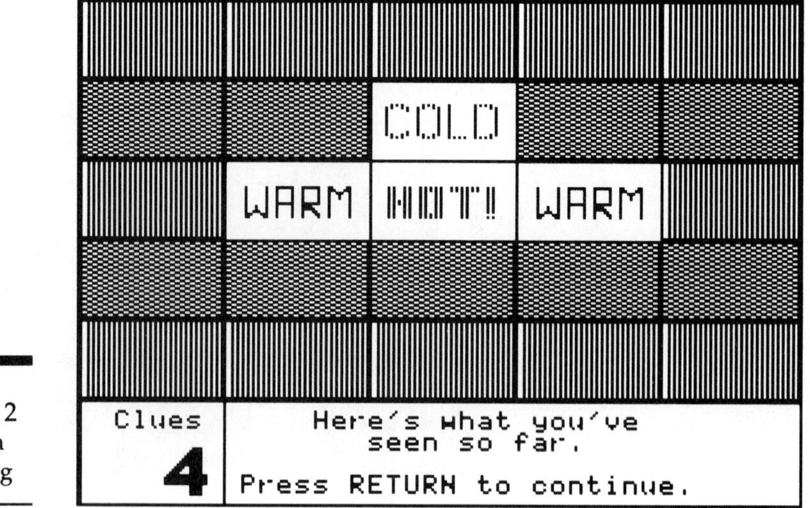

Figure 8.8
Safari Search Level 2
Used with permission of WINGS for learning

help the students develop critical thinking by showing them how to use a systematic approach to the task, thereby reducing the amount of haphazard trial and error guessing.

Safari Search has a random number generator, and there are 25 possible problems for each of the first six levels and 300 possible problems for each of the last six levels. Each of these levels uses different rules and strategies, but the strategies the pupils learn can be applied to other levels of the program.

Tutorial

A tutorial program gives the students instruction in a particular subject and serves as a well-organized teacher for the learner. A good tutorial usually starts with an overview, an explanation of the subject matter, and checks the student for understanding. The student can move through the material answering questions posed by the software. The program provides feedback for correct and incorrect responses, positive reinforcement, and a record of the student's performance. Math is a logical place for a tutorial because it lends itself to small step sequencing of material. *Alge-Blaster Plus* (Davidson & Associates) is an interactive tutorial that provides instruction on algebraic topics involving five learning activities and over 670 algebraic equations. The student learns the steps for solving equations and practices them with helpful hints for guidance. Figure 8.9 shows a graphing activity.

Students practice with points and slopes in order to develop their graphing ability. After learning these skills, the students can visualize the algebraic relationship illustrated on a graph. At the first level, the students become familiar with coordinates by location and by labeling different points on the graph. After the students are secure, they can challenge themselves against a clock to solve some computer generated problems. An integral part of this program is the *Alge-Blaster Plus* game where the students protect a space station by applying basic graphing skills.

Science

In many elementary schools, science programs used to be limited to memorization of textbook facts, and teachers did not have the time or money to collect the necessary materials for an exciting science lesson. Furthermore, science was then dependent on the teacher's interests and specific areas of expertise. Because of general lack of knowledge in science, teachers ignored many topics and most elementary students received very little science education. As a result, experimentation occurred primarily in the high school science lab, and this particular experience was usually reserved for the college bound students.

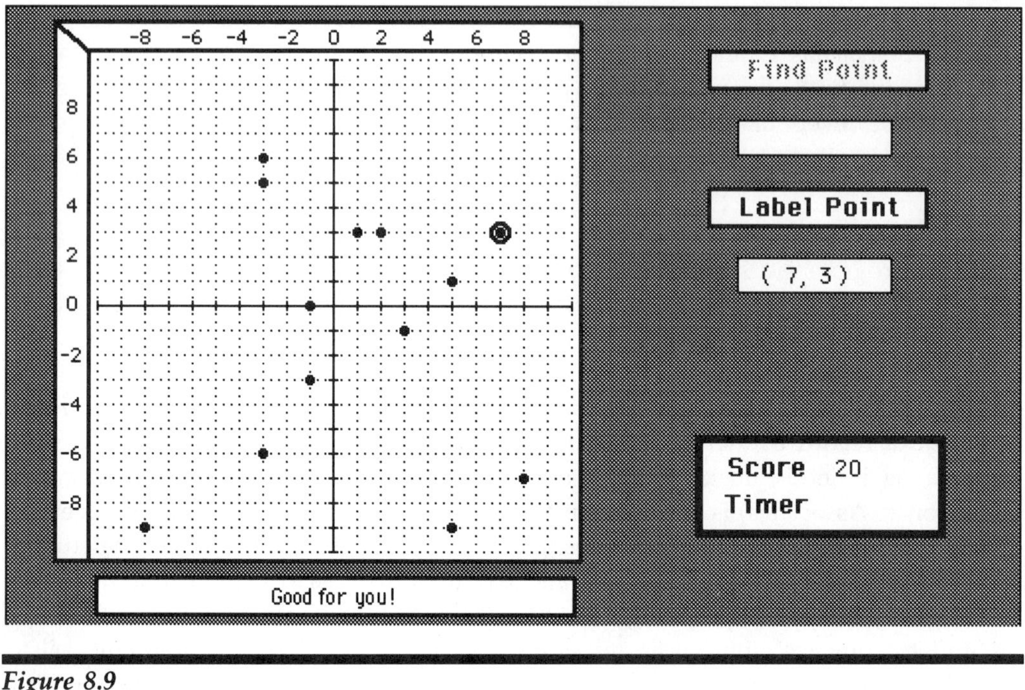

Figure 8.9
Alge-Blaster Plus
Davidson and Associates.

The computer is beginning to change this unfortunate situation. In science the student learns to investigate by classifying, synthesizing, analyzing, and summarizing data—tasks which the computer is designed to help him accomplish. The computer cannot replace the actual science laboratory, but it can simulate complex, expensive, and dangerous experiments, saving time and money. Because there is a renewed interest in science education, more schools are incorporating the computer into the science curriculum, and science software is flourishing. Publishers like MECC are producing interactive programs such as *Odell Lake, Wood Car Rally, Sky Lab, Lunar Greenhouse,* and *Discovery Lab.*

Brøderbund, another leader in the field, produces the *Science Toolkit,* a program that has a master module turning the computer into a scientific instrument. The *Science Toolkit* has external light and temperature probes that let the user perform real-life experiments. There is a thermometer, light meter, and a strip chart recorder to help the student measure an event too fast to be visible to the human eye. In addition, there is a speed and motion module, an earthquake lab module, and a body lab module. The speed and motion module has a light probe and photocell, along with a balloon powered car. The earthquake lab module has a seismograph that measures how many trucks and buses it takes to shake a house, and the body lab has a spirometer that measures a person's lung capacity.

Sunburst Communications has a temperature series, *Playing with Science Temperature,* where the students use three thermistors to monitor temperatures simultaneously in four different display modes. This program can store over 6,000 data points and has built-in statistical functions that allow the students to do calculations easily along with their measurements.

Drill and Practice Software

There is some superior drill and practice science software; however, the majority is electronic worksheet oriented, providing little motivation and no review material. An example of a good drill and practice science program is *The Body Transparent* (Britannica), which teaches the names of the organs, bones, the organ functions, systems, and diseases. The user can add questions to this program, and there are several games, each with different levels of difficulty. The student moves bones and organs to the right locations on a body and plays a function game by matching important facts to the correct parts. The following *Body Transparent* Screen (Figure 8.10) shows the user matching the word skull with the correct location on the body.

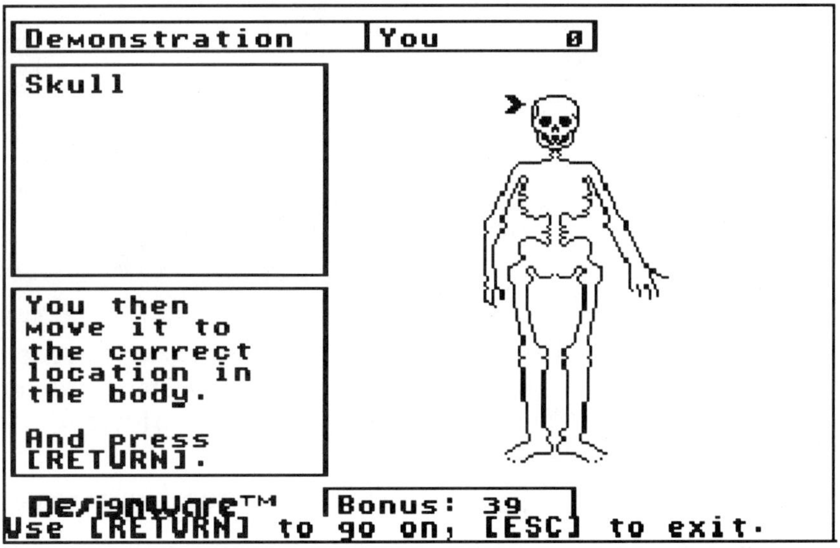

Figure 8.10
The Body Transparent
Britannica Software Inc.

Simulation Programs

Designed for repeated use, science simulation programs such as *Operation Frog* (Scholastic) have become very popular. This program simulates a frog dissection without blood and can be used as a prelude to a real dissection in the classroom. It provides an experiential understanding of the procedure used in dissecting a frog. The student dissects a frog (in simulation), dividing the organism into parts; then s/he uses a magnifying glass to examine closely each part of the frog's body. During the dissection, the student can construct the frog, part by part, reinforcing anatomy and biology. In the process, the pupil is given extensive background information on frogs.

Life and Death (The Software Toolworks), another screen dissection program, recreates the atmosphere of a medical center (Figure 8.11). The program lets the user talk with the patients, read charts, and order x-rays, ultra-sound, blood tests, and other lab work. The doctor examines, diagnoses, treats, and performs stomach surgery on

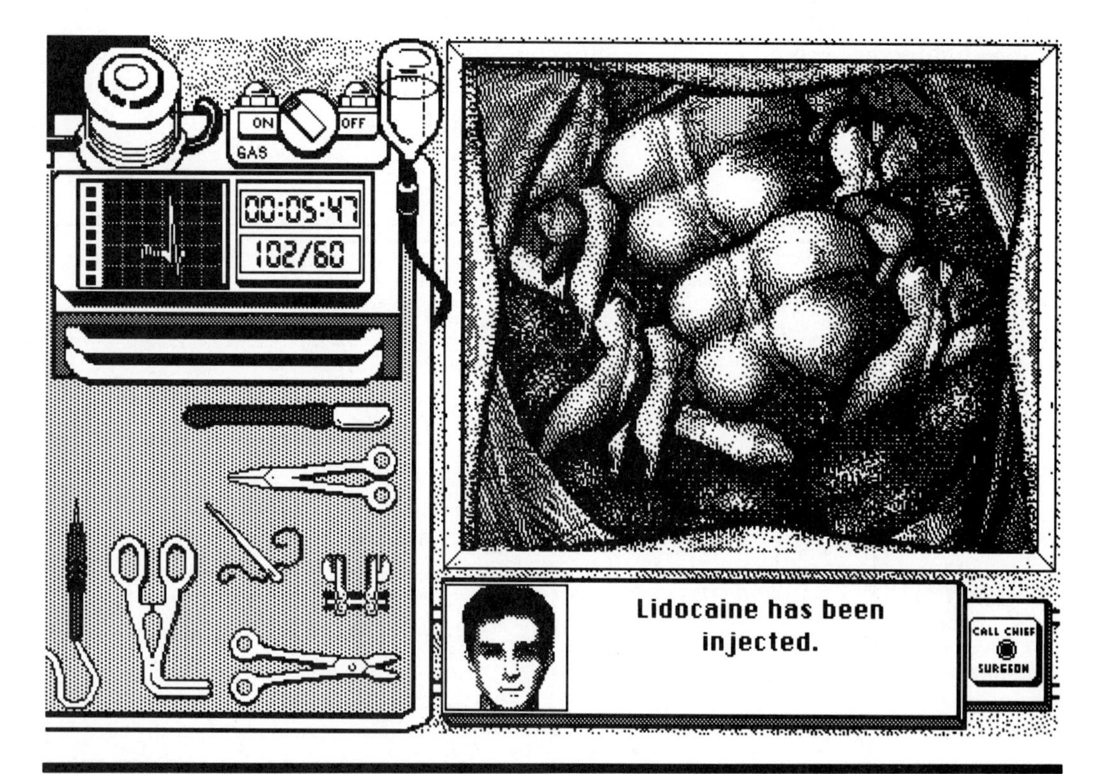

Figure 8.11
Life and Death
The Software Toolworks

patients in an interactive medical movie. The doctor makes decisions that determines whether the patient lives or dies. In the following operating room, the doctor, armed with a scalpel, operates while monitoring on-screen EKG, pulse, blood pressure, and other vital signs. *Life and Death,* which deals with stomach surgery as well as heart surgery, has excellent graphics and is entertaining, accurate, and informative. The newer version, *Life and Death II,* has a doctor performing brain surgery with the same vivid and stimulating format.

Problem Solving

The current emphasis in science is on problem solving and critical thinking as evidenced by publisher catalogs, which have increased their collection of these programs. An excellent example of a science problem solving program is *Lunar Greenhouse* (MECC), which challenges the student to raise a variety of vegetable crops in a controlled environment on the moon. Through the process of trial and error, the student discovers the effect of each variable on the crop. During the experiment, the student adjusts variables such as light, temperature, amount of water, hours of light, and amount of food, always keeping in mind the yield and days to harvest. Figure 8.12 shows the student growing a carrot crop for 79 days with a short light setting, 65° F temperature, medium watering and food.

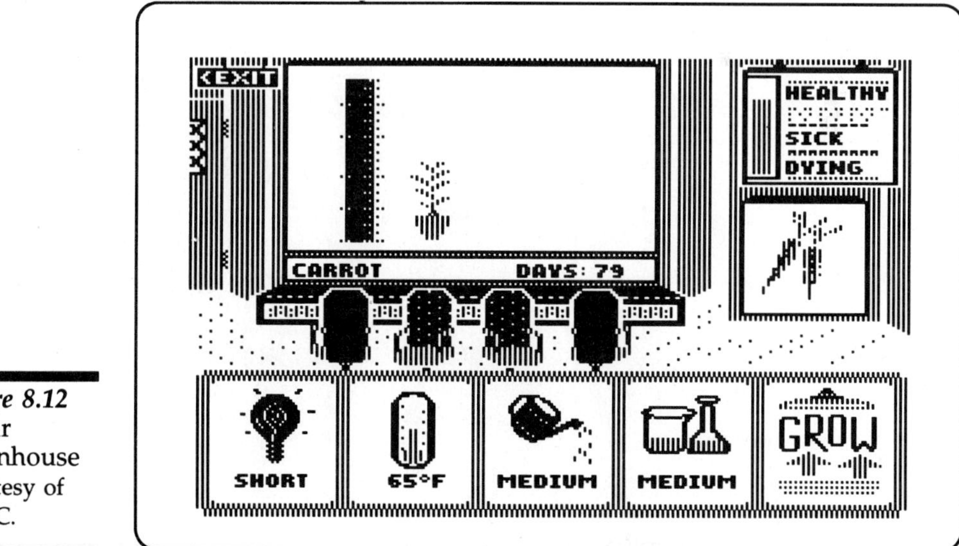

Figure 8.12
Lunar Greenhouse
Courtesy of MECC.

Tutorial

There are quite a few good science tutorials, especially at the upper elementary, high school, and college levels. *Physics* (Brøderbund) provides an introductory course in classical mechanics. It uses animations and includes over 300 problems on such topics as velocity, orbital position, kinetic energy, and potential energy. The students can use the material, chapter by chapter, looking up a particular term or leaving a marker when they are finished to continue the session at some later time. *The Human Systems Series 1,2,3,* (Focus Media) is a series that lets the students learn about the human body. Part of this program is a strong tutorial that gives numerous challenging questions, detailed graphics, stimulating explanations on how the body functions, and the important roles each part of the body plays. *The Body In Focus* (Mindscape/SVE) is a self-paced exploration of human anatomy where the students find out how the body works, understand systems and organs, and observe important mechanisms of the body. There are animated graphics that give in-depth coverage of the eight major body systems, and the student can actually see the body pumping blood and sneezing.

At the elementary level there is *Science Explorers Volume 1* for Grades 1–3 and *Science Explorers Volume 2* for grades 4–6 (Scholastic) This series lets the students explore the major science topics found in the elementary school science curricula. Before the students do their exploring, there is an interactive tutorial. In the screen from *Science Explorers Volume 1* (Figure 8.13) the student learns about the different parts of the plants.

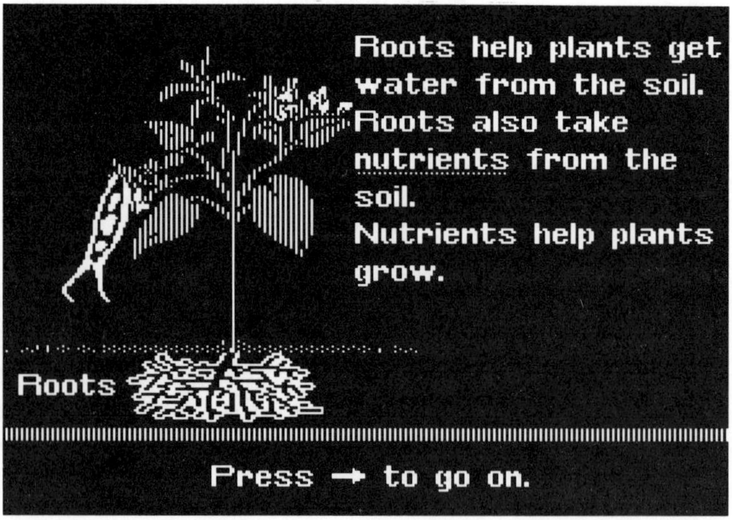

Figure 8.13
Science Explorers
Volume 1 (Plants)
Scholastic Inc.

Today the science software available is limited compared to other areas of the curriculum because it requires sophisticated programming, and its major application is at the high school level. **Appendix A** provides an annotated list of commendable science software for classroom use.

Social Studies

In social studies, the software excels at presenting current and historical events that foster class discussion and decision making. Students make decisions that affect outcomes and then they examine the consequences of these decisions. The students can experience indirectly the results of a poorly planned presidential campaign, gaining perspective on political and social realities.

Application Programs

Using application programs, a teacher can integrate other information into the social studies program. The student can use a word processor to write about any subject, the spreadsheet and graphics program to analyze statistical data and to display pertinent information, and the data base program to retrieve data and analyze the information. For example, a student using the social studies program *World Geograph* (MECC) gains access to detailed maps and a data base with more than 50 categories of information. The student can form patterns and see relationships. The lessons in the *World Geograph* teaching guide are matched to specific learning objectives and concepts.

Computer-Assisted Instruction

Using CAI programs, a teacher can integrate these programs into the social studies curriculum. First the purpose of instruction should be looked at, then the software selected. On the one hand, Teacher A may need only a drill and practice program because this teacher is interested in the simple recall of the states and their capitols. On the other hand, Teacher B needs a simulation program because Teacher B is interested in studying the causes of the Civil War. In social studies there are many excellent drill and practice and simulation programs that can be selected for each of these different purposes.

Drill and Practice

These social studies programs are easy to use, help in the retention of factual material, use a game format, and require minimal teacher supervision. In the classic drill and practice program, *States and Traits,* (Britannica) a student moves the outline of a state onto a U.S. map. If the student does this correctly, the state changes color. The quicker the correct answer, the more bonus points earned. Whenever the student answers incorrectly,

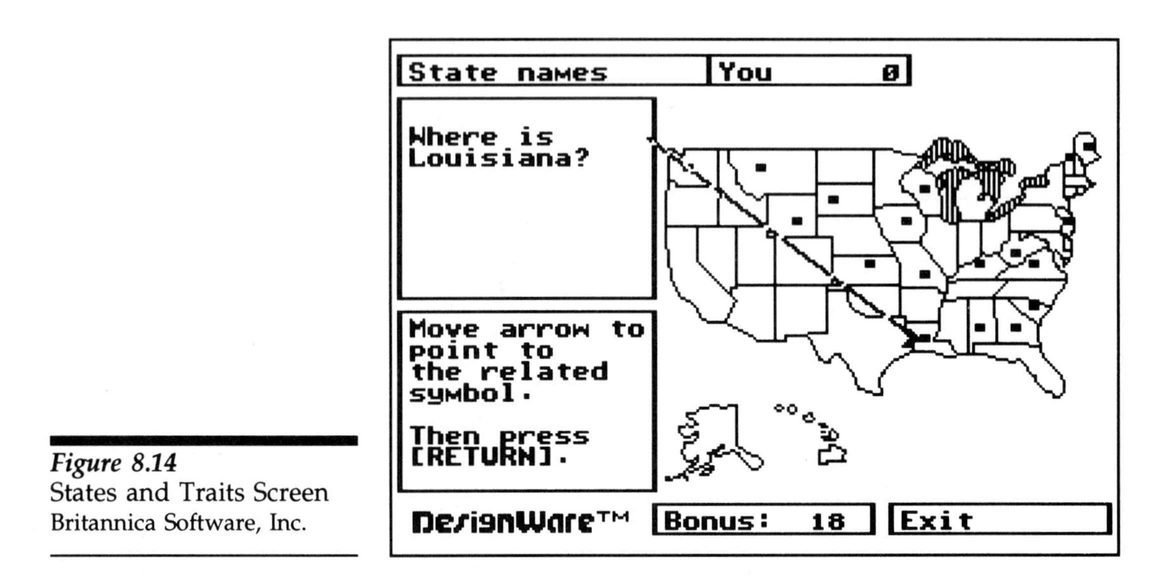

Figure 8.14
States and Traits Screen
Britannica Software, Inc.

the correct answer eventually materializes, reducing student frustration. Figure 8.14 shows a student earning 18 bonus points by locating Louisiana.

States and Traits has colorful graphics, is self-paced, includes historical information and important landmarks, and can be customized.

Simulation

A well-designed social studies simulation challenges a student to make a difficult decision concerning money, politics, or some other important factor. The Carmen San Diego series (Brøderbund), Oregon Trail (MECC), CrossCountry series (Didactech), and *Decisions Decisions* series (Tom Snyder Productions) help students gain a better understanding of different people, places, and ideas in the present or past. Students learn to use history as a basis for decision making and to distinguish between fact and opinion. In the program *Revolutionary Wars,* part of the *Decisions Decisions* series, a student plays the role of a provincial governor during a revolution, while the other students, as citizens, must decide whether or not to support the revolution. Figure 8.15 shows the students engaging in a discourse with the governor.

This program provides references from the history of the African, Latin American, French, and Chinese revolutions, giving the students insight into other historical movements for independence and freedom.

The Carmen Sandiego series has a student traveling the world, the United States, Europe, and America through the past and through time. The program *Where In Time*

Figure 8.15
Revolutionary Wars
Tom Snyder Productions, Inc.

Figure 8.16
Where In Time Is Carmen Sandiego?
Screen shot from "Where in Time is Carmen Sandiego?," Copyright Brøderbund Software, Inc., 1989.

Is Carmen Sandiego? covers many historical facts from 400 A.D to the 1950's where Carmen and her gang travel back through time to steal a valuable resource. A student detective tracks the thief and, in the process, learns about scientific inventions, famous individuals, important historical facts and different cultures. Figure 8.16 shows the student back in England in the late 1500s.

Language Arts

Language arts programs are subdivided into writing, speaking, reading, and listening categories. Because of the multitude of good language arts programs, it is easier to integrate them into the curriculum.

Writing

Writing is a difficult task, requiring higher level thinking and mechanical skills. However, in most classroom situations, writing is used in a series of disjointed activities with emphasis on self expression. The computer is an effective tool for motivating and reinforcing the necessary skills to improve a student's writing. In the next section, the author will discuss language arts software pertaining to word processors, vocabulary, spelling, grammar, and reading programs.

Word Processors

The reader learned in chapter 3 how word processors can help students save time and reduce effort by moving paragraphs, deleting sentences, and spell checking papers. The word processor not only increases students' productivity, but also gives them extra time to think about content. The author discussed word processors such as *Bank Street Writer Plus* (Scholastic), *Easy Working Writer* (Spinnaker), *Magic Slate II* (Sunburst), and *Appleworks* (Claris).

Beyond word processing, there are other programs that teach writing such as *Talking Textwriter* (Scholastic) which has a voice synthesizer pronouncing words as they are typed. This program is useful for helping the handicapped, the bilingual, and the young child. *Logo Writer* (Logo Computer Systems) combines word processing with logo. Suitable for seventh-twelfth grades, idea processors like *Think Tank* (Living Videotext) help students organize ideas by putting them in outline form making it easier for them to begin to write.

In addition, to these word processors, there are story writing programs like *Playwrite* (Sunburst), *Once Upon a Time Volumes I, II,* and *III* (CompuTeach), *Kidwriter Gold* (Spinnaker) and *Big Book Maker* (Pelican Software/Queque). In the program *Once Upon a Time Volume II,* a student has the thrill of creating his or her printed illustrated story by placing, moving, and sizing different pictures on the screen. For example, Figure 8.17 illustrates a story written by a seven year old.

Using this program, a student can improve his vocabulary by viewing, hearing, and typing words. This program stresses beginning reading and writing skills, letting the child select words, and seeing the pictures associated with them.

Figure 8.17
Once Upon A Time
Compu-Teach Educational Software.

Kidwriter Gold (Spinnaker) has an emphasis on word processing; the child selects pictures to illustrate a story, but hears no word pronunciation. In this program, a child learns the fundamentals of word processing and develops writing skills by creating and printing an illustrated story book.

Big Book Maker (Pelican/Queque) is a publishing program that lets the user print out big books in four sizes and includes a variety of graphics and fonts that the child can use to design his own pages. In the programs *Monsters* and *Make-Believe Plus* (Pelican/Queque) the children create monsters, invent dialogue in cartoon style speech balloons, and design their own big books, mobiles, or comic strips.

Comic book making programs like *Pow! Zap! Keplunk! The Comic Maker* (Pelican/Queque) and *Create with Garfield* Deluxe Version (DLM) teach reading and writing skills in a unique way. The student places people and objects on the screen in different situations and writes comic bubbles that correspond with the situations (Figure 8.18). *Create with Garfield,* similar to *Comic Book Maker,* uses the popular cartoon character,

Figure 8.18
Pow! Zap!Keplunk!
The comic book Maker
Pelican Software a division of Que, Inc.

Garfield. A child places Garfield, his friends, and props in different scenes and writes speech bubbles about these characters.

Children's Writing and Publishing Center (Learning Company) combines graphics, word processing, and page design in an easy-to-use package. With this program a child is able to create reports, stories, letters, newsletters, awards, signs, and forms.

Vocabulary

Word Attack and *Word Attack Plus* (Davidson and Associates) and *Fay's Word Rally* (Didatech) are drill and practice programs that offer a game format and are more appealing than worksheets. *Word Attack* offers five different activities for vocabulary development. In its arcade game, the student matches the designated word at the bottom (*shy*) with one of the words at the top of the screen. In Figure 8.19 (Macintosh Version) the wizard is placed in the wrong position, and the correct response is highlighted. If the user had placed the wizard under the correct response, the wizard would have shot a thunderbolt at the word *coy*. In this program, students work at their own pace, receive positive reinforcement, and print out certificates. Furthermore, the teacher has a test-maker, record-keeper, and editorial option, plus language fonts in English, Spanish, French, and German.

Fay's Word Rally, the other program, reviews sight word acquisition, sentence comprehension, and vocabulary development. The student reads a clue at the bottom of the screen, finds the word in the maze, and then drives the car to it. If the car hits the correct word, the word vanishes, and Fay waves her flag with music playing. If the player drives over the wrong word, s/he loses points. Using the picture clue trash can

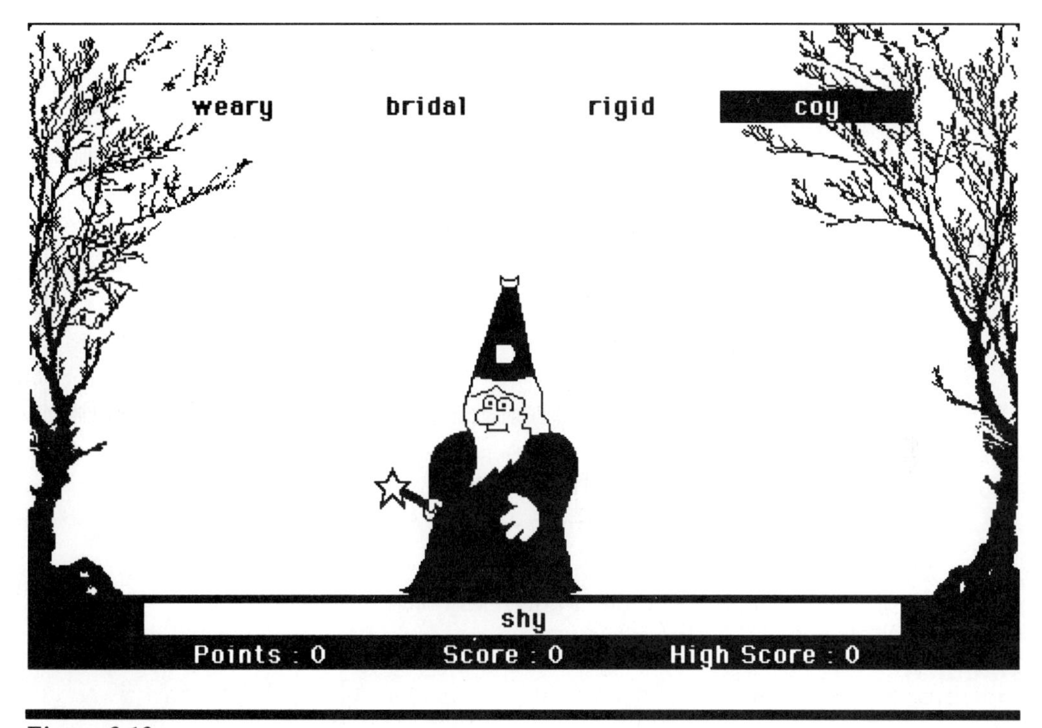

Figure 8.19
Word Attack Screen
Davison and Associates

at the bottom of the screen, Figure 8.20 shows the user about to drive the race car over the word *can.*

This program has a record keeper and an editor that allow the teacher to create a customized game.

Spelling

There are many spelling programs involving sea animals, magic castles, gulping frogs, and penny-arcade activities. *Stickybear Spellgrabber* (Optimum Resources/Weekly Reader Software) has three games in which the bear called "Stickybear" hops and juggles while the children learn how to spell. The "picture spell option" has the children spell the names of objects they see on the screen. The "word spell option" has the children unscramble letters to make words, and the "bear dunk option" has the children guess the words in the computer's memory. Since the program contains 3,500 words, the teacher can customize it. *Spell it Plus* (Davidson and Associates), which contains five

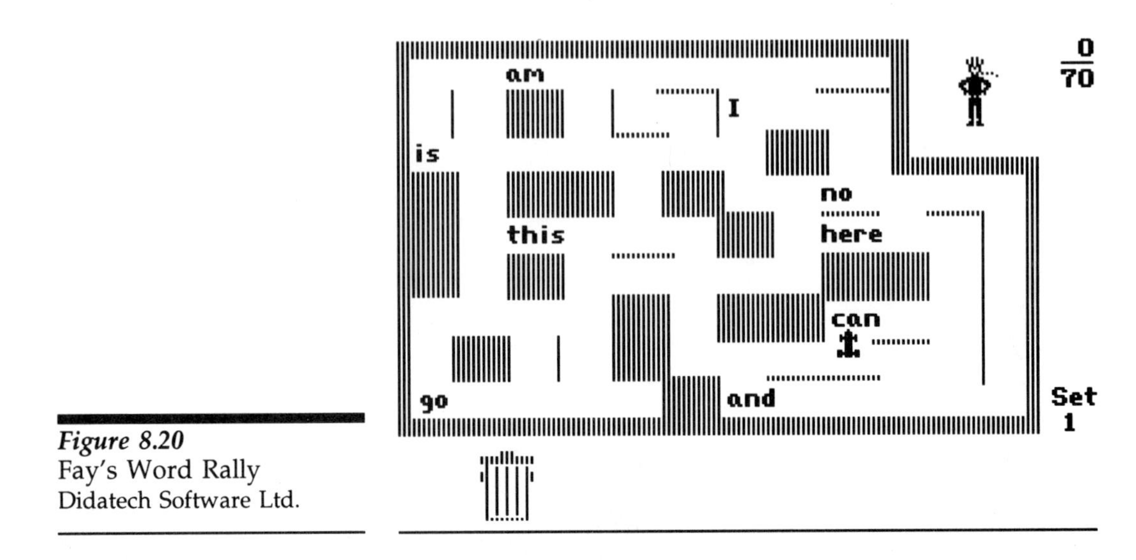

Figure 8.20
Fay's Word Rally
Didatech Software Ltd.

spelling activities, has an animated frog devour words for the correct responses. This program is suitable for middle grades to high school.

Grammar

Many of the grammar programs focus on drill and practice activities covering a range of skills from subject verb agreement to recognition of parts of speech. Other programs are tutorial, presenting grammar in a sequence of lessons. *Grammar Gremlins* (Davidson and Associates), a drill and practice program designed for the middle school, presents the rules of grammar and supplies over six hundred practice sentences with four levels of difficulty. Each level has a pretest to identify a student's weakness on a specific grammar rule, a practice activity, and a review test to show a student's progress. In Figure 8.21 the user has to decide if the word "Fly" should be capitalized.

Punctuation Rules (Optimum Resources/Weekly Reader Software), another grammar program, tutorial in nature, has for its major instructional goal the improvement of writing. This program presents a series of writing exercises for grades three through six. While the student does the exercises, s/he can view the rule related to each question by pressing the **?** Key for a help screen. Moreover, teachers can customize this program by writing in their own exercises and printing them out for later use as worksheets or study questions.

Reading

Many simulations, drill and practice programs, and tutorial programs provide reading instruction. *McGee, Katie's Farm, McGee at the Fun Fair* (Lawrence Productions)

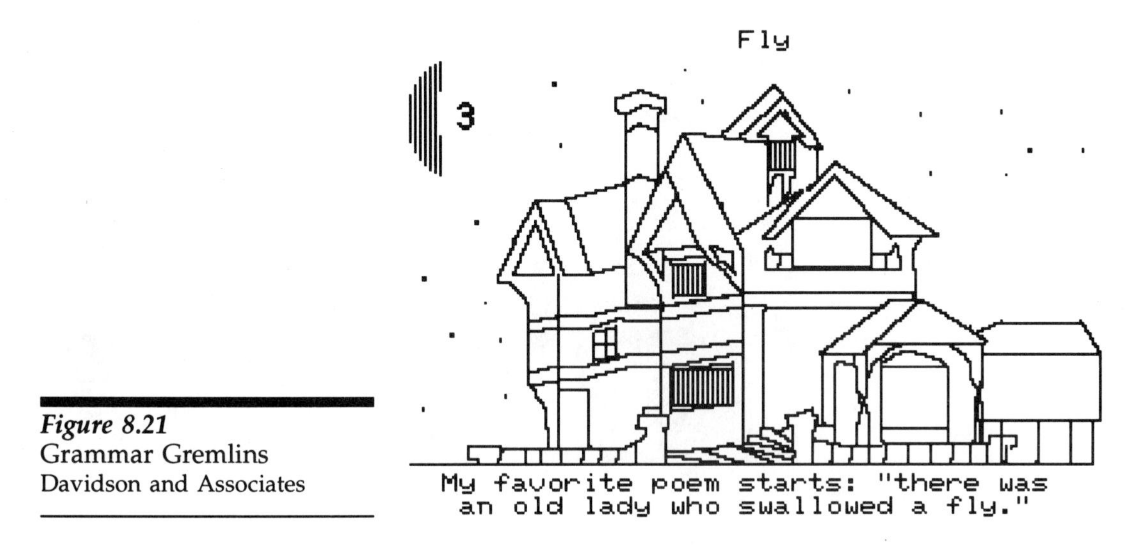

Figure 8.21
Grammar Gremlins
Davidson and Associates

and *Playroom and TreeHouse* (Brøderbund) are all suitable for the young child. The Lawrence Production programs tell a story without words and have a hypercard environment that lets the child click on objects to produce sound and movement, encouraging the child to share thoughts and feelings about the story. In Figure 8.22 McGee gives the child four options for choice—the door, sink, toilet, or shower.

Playroom, an interactive program, has elements of strategic thinking, simulation, and discovery. In the playroom, the child explores the world of letters, numbers, and time (Figure 8.23). The program is designed as a playmate for the child. It involves a clock, a computer, a mixed-up toy, a mousehole, an ABC book, and a spinner toy. For example, if a child chooses the ABC book, he can decorate a fantasy picture with people, animals, and objects or if the child chooses the mousehole, he can play three maze games.

TreeHouse, a more advanced program than *Playroom,* is built around the theme of a treehouse hideaway where a child can explore science, math, language, art, history, and music activities.

The talking version of *StickyBear ABC* (Optimium Resources/Weekly Reader Software) teaches the child the alphabet and how to pronounce words through colorful animation and sound effects. For instance, when a child presses the letter **B,** she will produce either a flying **b**ird or a flying **b**ee with the accompanying sound effects.

Figure 8.22
McGee
Lawrence
Productions, Inc.,
Street, Galesburg,
MI 49053

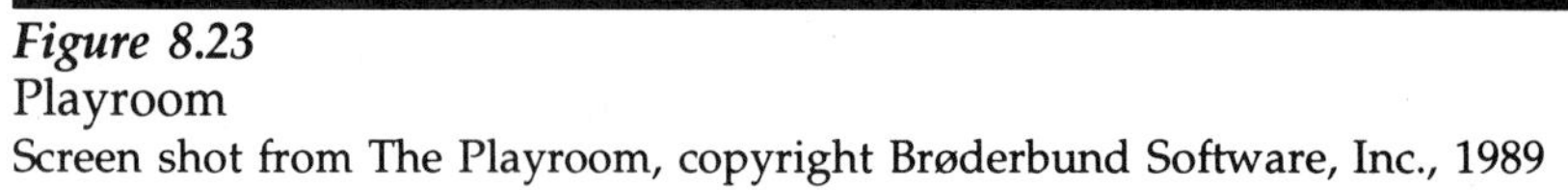

Figure 8.23
Playroom
Screen shot from The Playroom, copyright Brøderbund Software, Inc., 1989

prey		knack	lash	tab	ham
trail	rain	shave			bad
bad			calf	at	band
hack	at		crack	pain	shall
pail	trace	ace	fake	knack	paint

Figure 8.24
Word Muncher Screen
Courtesy of MECC.

Word Munchers (MECC), a drill and practice program, helps the students master vowel sounds in a pacman man game format. Figure 8.24 shows a muncher trying to eat the words that have a **short a** sound before the **troggle** (with teeth) disposes of him.

Reader Rabbit (Learning Company), another drill and practice reading program, uses a game approach where a child learns how to identify and sort letters and identify and sequence words.

Hartley has produced a series of sequential reading programs with colorful graphics and sound capabilities that teach comprehension and the ability to draw conclusions. The beginning series, *Tim and the Cat and the Big Red Hat,* follows the misadventures of the cat, Elmo, and his friend, Tim. *Chariots Cougars and Kings* covers grades 3–5, while *New Kid on the Block* covers Grades 4–6.

ACE Reporter II (Mindplay) is a graphic simulation program that lets the user become an ace reporter uncovering a story. The student reporter must get the facts on the story by reading an on-screen teletype and by having on-screen telephone interviews.

Once the reporter has placed the story in the computer, she selects a headline which indicates the main idea. The student reporter now gets a byline on the story.

The tutorial program *Your Personal Trainer for the SAT* (Davidson and Associates) uses a step-by-step approach to master the strategies for dealing with material found on the SAT. The program scores and analyzes the user's answers on sample math and verbal SAT tests. It lets the student prepare six detailed programs based on weaknesses found in the areas of vocabulary, reading, and math. Using a three dimensional chart, the user can select colleges that s/he wants to attend comparing personal SAT score with those required by the colleges selected. The following introductory screen (Figure 8.25) shows the program's options.

There is an abundance of language art software and the reader can find a list of comprehensive, annotated, award winning language arts programs in **Appendix A.**

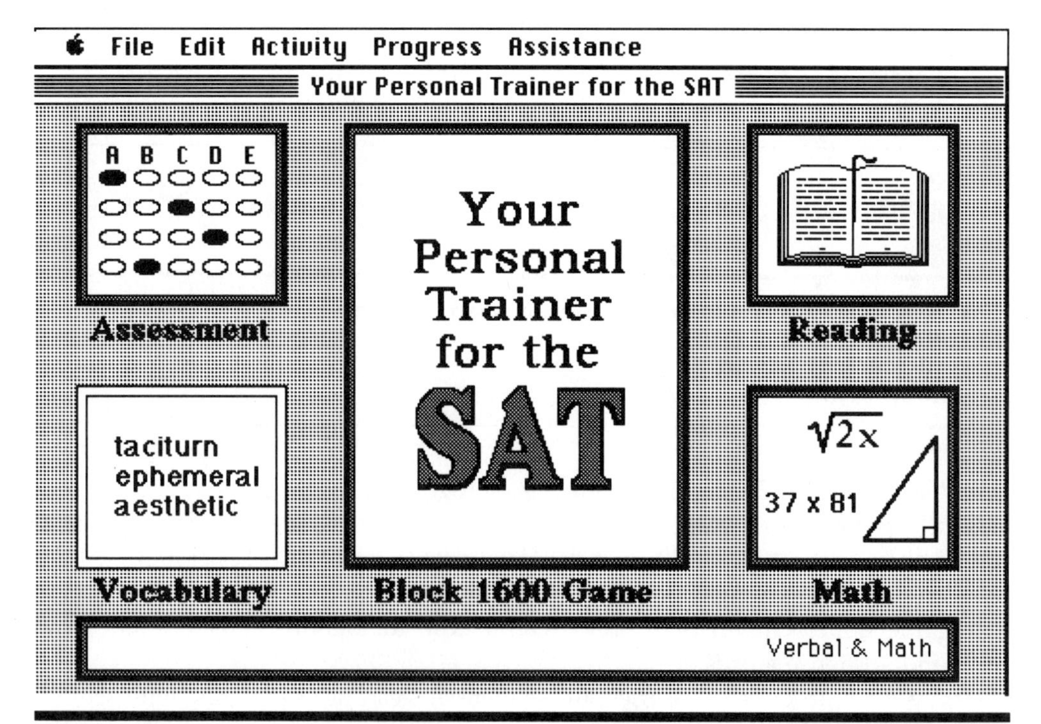

Figure 8.24
Your Personal Trainer for the SAT
Davidson and Associates

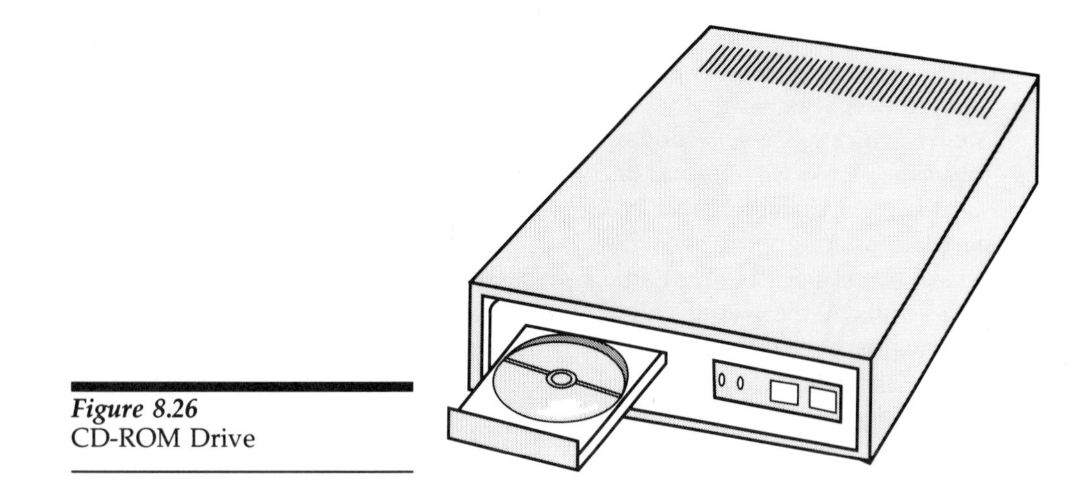

Figure 8.26
CD-ROM Drive

Compact Disk Read Only Memory (CD-ROM) Software

The CD-ROM disk drive looks like a compact disc (CD) player and it utilizes a CD-ROM compact disc format that holds text, graphics, and hi-fi stereo sound. The CD-ROM disk is similar to a CD (Figure 8.26) except that it utilizes different tracks for data storage.

Because of its reduced price, the CD-ROM disk drive and CD-ROM disks are becoming increasingly popular in the schools. A teacher can hook up a microcomputer and a compact disk drive and be able to retrieve vasts amounts of information. There are quite a few popular CD-ROM disks for the classroom—programs such as *Discis Book Series* (Discis Knowledge Research Inc.), *U.S. History on CD-ROM* (Bureau Development), *Microsoft Bookshelf* (Microsoft), *CIA World Fact Book* (Quanta Press), *World Atlas* (Software Toolworks), *Compton's Multimedia Encyclopedia* (Britannica/Jostens), *New Grolier Electronic Encyclopedia* (Grolier Electronic Publishing), *Magic Flute* (Warner New Media), *Scary Poems for Rotten Children* (Discis Knowledge Research Inc), *McGraw-Hill Science and Technical Reference* (McGraw-Hill).

For the elementary schools the *Discis Books* series has books by well known authors like Beatrix Potter that appear on the screen with the original text and illustrations, real voices, music, and sound effects. When a user clicks on a loudspeaking icon, the story begins, phrase by phrase, synchronized with the storytelling. The child can select a word and hear the proper pronunciation and syllables and also hear an explanation of any word in the text. The teacher can individualize the presentation of the story to meet the needs of the children in the class by adjusting a time delay between phrases.

At the high school level, *U.S. History on CD-ROM* contains the full text of 107 books relating to U.S. History—from the Native Americans to the present. A partial list of the books on U.S. history includes: Exploring the West, Gettysburg, Iran-Contra Affair (3 volumes), Pearl Harbor, WWII Naval Aviation, Our Country (8 volumes).

At the college level, the students might be interested in purchasing *Microsoft Bookshelf* which has a collection of references for writer including *The American Heritage Dictionary, The World Almanac and Book of Facts, Roget's II Thesarus, Bartlett's Familiar Quotations, The Chicago Manual of Style,* Houghton Mifflin's *Spelling Verifier* and *Checker,* The U.S. Postal Service's *U.S. Zip Code Directory,* The University of California Press's *Business Informations Sources* and a collection of sample letters called *Forms and Letters.* In **Appendix A** the reader will find an annotated listing of other classroom sources. Following is a chapter summary, a chapter mastery test, and a list of suggested readings and references.

Summary

The author attempted to show the reader ways to integrate the computer into the curriculum. There were suggestions given on topics such as how to select the software according to the needs of the pupils, how to collect the appropriate equipment, organize the classroom, and utilize the team approach. Next, the reader was given an overview of the programs that are available in math, science, social studies, and language arts.

Chapter Mastery Test

1. Give three suggestions that help utilize one computer with 30 children and explain each suggestion thoroughly.
2. Name two advantages of using drill and practice software to learn mathematics.
3. Give two suggestions on how social studies software can be used to teach United States history.
4. Should the teacher use language arts software to improve writing skills? Give reasons to support your position.
5. Using one computer, how can the teacher encourage the class to increase group involvement in the learning process?
6. How can the teacher teach keyboarding skills more effectively to young children?
7. What methods can a teacher use to improve problem solving skills on the computer?
8. How can the computer enhance the development of reading skills?
9. Include two examples of exemplary software and how students might use the computer in gathering, organizing, and displaying social studies information.
10. How can the teacher utilize the computer to report scientific information?
11. What procedures can a teacher use to incorporate a variety of math software into the classroom?
12. What are the advantages of using computer math manipulatives over traditional math manipulates?

Classroom Projects

1. Visit a school; then write a brief report on the criteria used in selecting the school software.
2. Devise an organizational schedule for a classrom with only one computer.
3. Using the library, discuss the problems inherent in language arts software with the existing curriculum.
4. Using the form in Chapter 7 on page 195, review five software programs on the annotated list in **Appendix A.**

Suggested Readings and References

Adams, Richard C. "Sometimes the Heat Drives You Nuts." *The Computing Teacher.* 18(7) (April 1991): 43–44.

Blanchard, Jay S. (1987), *Computer Applications in Reading.* 3rd ed. Newark, Del.: International Reading Association, 1987.

Blanchard, Jay S., and George E. Mason. "Using Computers in Content Area Reading Instruction." *Journal of Reading* (November 1985): 112–117.

Becker, H. J. "The Computer and the Elementary School." *Principal* (May 1985).

Bratt, M. "Microcomputers in Elementary Science Education." *School Science and Mathematics* 83 (4) (1983): 333–337.

Brumfit, Christopher, Martin Phillips, and Peter Skehan, Editors. *Computers in English Language Teaching: A View from the Classroom.* Oxford: New York: Pergamon Press, 1985.

Bureau of Electronic Publishing. CD-ROM Product Guide, (Spring 1991).

Caffarella, E. P. "Evaluating the New Generation of Computer-Based Instructional Software." *Educational Technology* 27(4) (April 1987): 19–24.

Cappo, Marge and Gail Osterman. "Math: Teach Students to Communicate Mathematically." *The Computing Teacher.* 18(5) (February 1991): 34–39.

Clements, Douglas H. *Computers in Elementary Mathematics Education.* Englewood Cliffs New Jersey: Prentice-Hall, 1989.

Collis, S., and Newman. *Computer Technology in Curriculum and Instructional Handbook: Courseware Evaluation.* Olympia, WA: Washington Office of the State Superintendent of Public Instruction, 1982.

Dinkheller, Ann. *The Computer in the Mathematics Curriculum.* Santa Cruz: Mitchell Publishing, 1989.

Eiser, L. "Problem-Solving Software; What it Really Teaches." *Classroom Computer Learning,* (March 1986): 42–45.

Ellis, James D. "Preparing Science Teachers for the Information Age." *The Journal of Computers in Mathematics and Science,* 9(4) (Summer 1990): 55.

Field, Cynthia. "The Lighter Side of Education." *Incider A+* (September 1991): 34–39.

Gonce-Winder, C., and H. H. Walbesser. "Toward Quality Software." *Contemporary Educational Psychology.* (12 (10) (July 1987): 19–25.

Hatfield, L. L. (1984). "Towards Comprehensive Instructional Computing in Mathematics." In

"Computers in Mathematics Education," *NCTM Yearbook,* 1–10.

Howie, Sherry Hill. *Reading, Writing, and Computers: Planning for Integration.* Boston: Allyn and Bacon, 1989.

Ignatz, M. E. "Suggestions for Selecting Science Education Software." *Journal of Computers in Mathematics and Science Teaching, (Fall 1985): 27–29.*

Kruse, T. "Finding Helpful Software Reviews." *Classroom Computer Learning.* 8(3) (November/December 1987): 44–48.

Lake, Daniel T. "Language Arts: Two Steps Beyond Word Processing." *The Computing Teacher,* 18(8) (May 1991): 30–32.

Margalit, Malka. *Effective Technology Integration for Disabled Children: The Family.* New York: Springer, 1990.

Mittlefehlt, Bill. "Social Studies Problem Solving With Databases." *The Computing Teacher.* 18(5) (February 1991): 54–56.

Nash, James, and Lawerence Schwartz. "Making Computers Work in the Writing Class." *Educational Technology* (May 1985): 19–26.

Schlenker, Richard M. and Sara J. Yoshida. "Integrating Computers into Elementary School Science Using Toothpicks to Generate Data." *Science Activities.* 27(4) (Winter 1990): 13.

Smiddie, Laura. "ERIC Resources on Using Computers to Teach the Social Studies." *The International Journal of Social Education.* 5(1) (Spring 1990): 85.

Solomon, G. "Writing with Computers." *Electronic Learning,* (November/December 1985): 39–43.

Starfield, A. M. *How to Model It: Problem Solving for the Computer Age.* New York: McGraw-Hill, 1990.

Vockell, Edward, and Robert M. Deusen. *The Computer and Higher-Order Thinking Skills.* Watsonville, California: Mitchell Publishing Co, 1989.

Wainwright, Camille L. "The Effectiveness of a Computer-Assisted Instruction Package in High School Chemistry." *Journal of Research in Science Teaching.* 26(4) (April 1989): 275.

Wepner, Shelley B. "Holistic Computer Applications in Literature-Based Classrooms." *The Reading Teacher.* 44(1) (1 September 1990): 12.

Teacher Utility Software, Graphics, Art and Music

9

Objectives

Upon completing this chapter the student will be able to:

1. Be familiar with a variety of teacher utility software.
2. Describe four types of graphics software programs.
3. Be familiar with an assortment of art and music programs.
4. Learn how to integrate art and music programs into the classroom.

Teacher Utility Software

Teacher utility programs are support tools that make the classroom teacher's work more effective. These programs are not meant for the student, but for the teacher—to help in such tasks as grade book keeping, test making, puzzle and worksheet generating, and statistic analysis. In many instances, these utility programs reduce time and improve accuracy by assisting the teacher in those chores that cannot easily be done in a traditional manner. For example, a grade book program can quickly weigh the students' grades, calculate the means, and standard deviations, assign grades, and alphabetize the student list. When looking at a utility program, the teacher should ask if the program fits his or her needs and if it saves time and results in a more effective product. In the following section, the author will examine a variety of teacher utility programs.

Grade Book

An old-fashioned grade book is useful, but an electronic one is more advantageous. Why spend hours recording and averaging grades when there are numerous grade book programs on the market today that do this burdensome task. Programs that are effective for the classroom teacher are *Gradebuster 1/2/3* and *Grade Busters Mac: Making the Grade* (Jay Klein Productions), *Apple Grader 4.0* (A. V. Systems Inc.), *Grade Manager*

(MECC), *Comput-A-Grade* (Projac), *Gradebook Deluxe* (Edusoft), *GradeQuick* (Compu-Teach), and *Gradebook Plus* (E.M.A. Software). In **Appendix A** the reader will find an annotated list of these grade book programs.

A good grade book should let the user enter student's names easily, and correct any errors. Once the teacher has typed in the students' names, there should be an option for sorting these names alphabetically, numerically, or by class standing. The grade book should let the teacher enter a large number of students for each class, record a sufficient number of grades, record absences, and flag problem students. For each score the teacher enters, there should be a scaling factor to insure that appropriate scores are figured in the student's or class's average. The program should calculate pertinent statistics—such as the range, mean, and medium scores—and should be able to save test information and produce a hard copy. An example of a grade book program (Figure 9.1), *Gradebook Plus* (E.M.A. Software) shows the student's names alphabetized, letter grades assigned, and the averages calculated for each test and each individual.

Some sophisticated grade books display data in the form of histograms, report a wide range of statistics, and have templates for parent correspondence. An example is *Grade Busters Mac: Making the Grade* (Jay Klein Productions), which has five special annotations that the teacher can append to a student scores, as well as graphing display capabilities. *Gradebook Plus V6.0* lets teachers create form letters, choose 15 user definable comments, and annotate sound to student reports. In addition, there is a report that looks like a student manual grade book.

Computers 513

Name	ID Num	1	2	Total	Pct.	Grade
Doe, Herman		89	56	145	72.5	C
Friedman, Bobbie		100	100	200	100.0	A
Sharp, David		100	100	200	100.0	A
Smith, Colleen		56	78	134	67.0	D
Washington, Bill		75	45	120	60.0	D
Average :		84	75.8	159.8	79.9	
Possible :		100	100	200		

Figure 9.1
Gradebook Plus
© 1991, E.M.A. Software, P.O. Box 339, Los Altos, CA 94023.

An obvious advantage of an electronic grade book is keeping students, parents, and administrators quickly informed about pupil performance in the classroom. However, many teachers feel that they need to maintain a pencil and paper grade book besides an electronic one, which means double entry. An electronic grade book needs a computer, and a computer is not always accessible to a teacher. When a teacher uses a traditional grade book, s/he reaches in the drawer, and there it is.

Test Makers

A test-generating program is similar to a word processor because it has standard editing capabilities such as deletion and insertion. Many of these programs have font libraries that let the user select different typefaces. There are various test formats that include true or false, multiple choice, fill in the blank, short answer, essay, and matching. A few programs have graphics editors so the teacher can integrate diagrams and pictures into the document. After questions are entered, the teacher saves them and they serve as a data base file that can be retrieved on demand. Many programs let the teacher randomize the order of the test questions and the arrangement of the possible responses to multiple choice questions. In other words, these programs produce alternate forms that serve as make-up tests or alternate tests. The majority of programs let the user print final copies of the tests along with answer sheets.

Four suitable test making programs are *Test Designer Plus* (Superschool Software), *Teacher Tool Kit* (Hi-Tech), *Multiple Choices* (Santa Barbara Softworks, S.B. Programming, Inc.), *Test It! Deluxe*(EduSoft). Figure 9.2 shows the options available from *Multiple Choices* (Santa Barbara Softworks, S. B. Programming, Inc.).

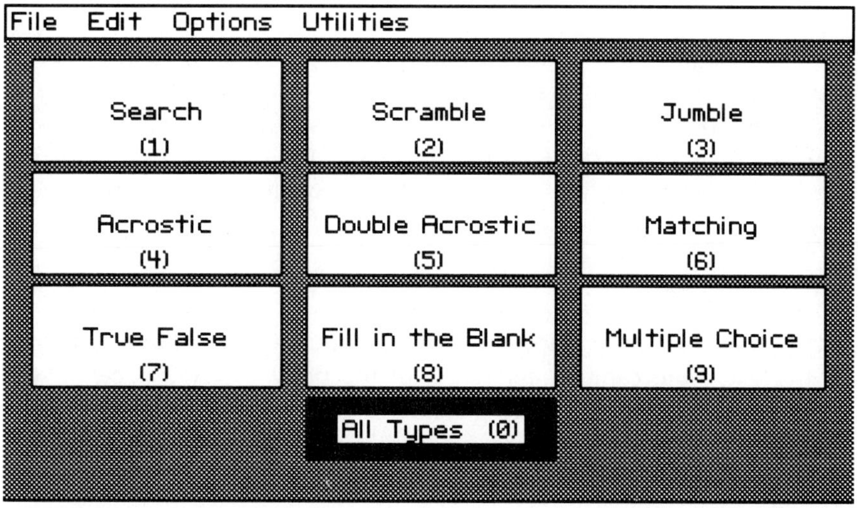

Figure 9.2 Multiple Choices © Santa Barbara Softworks, © S.B. Programming, Inc.

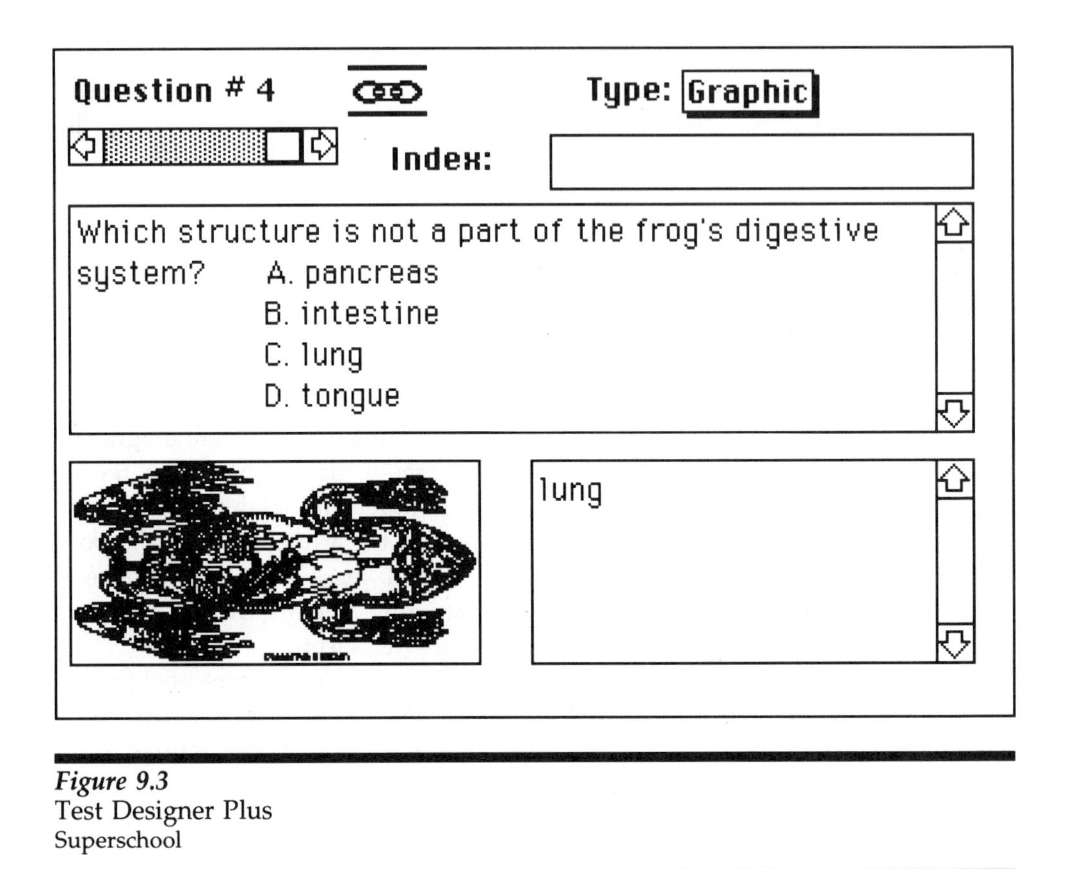

Figure 9.3
Test Designer Plus
Superschool

Test Designer Plus (SuperSchool Software) is a unique program that combines test creation with test taking, sound, and foreign languages. This program lets the teacher insert questions from a data base and then use an overhead projector to let the students take a timed test on the computer. In addition, the instructor can choose the test form needed and integrate graphics into it. Figure 9.3 shows a frog as a visual aid to the test question, "Which structure is *not* a part of the frog's digestive system?"

Puzzle Makers

Puzzle makers supply spice and provide motivation for pupils studying mundane topics such as state capitols and parts of the body. A teacher can develop a crossword puzzle for reviewing Spanish, generate a geographical crossword for studying Europe, or create a math quiz by using the equations as clues for the answers. Today there are many noteworthy puzzle generators for the classroom including *Print your Own Bingo Plus* (Hartley), *Crossword Magic* (Mindscape, A Division of SVE), *Mickey's Crossword*

Figure 9.4
Mickey's Crossword Puzzle Maker
© The Walt Disney Company

Puzzle Maker (The Walt Disney Company), and *Microzine Jr. 1* (Scholastic), an electronic periodical with a variety of programs including a classroom publishing series. There is everything from jigsaw puzzles to gameboard makers. Figure 9.4 depicting BAMBI from *Mickey's Crossword Puzzle Maker* shows the student playing against Mickey Mouse and being asked to name the fawn with whom Bambi fell in love (The Walt Disney Company).

The teacher can customize this puzzle maker to help the children learn new vocabulary words.

Drill Sheet Generators and Organizers

There are programs that produce drill sheets with answers such as *Worksheet Wizard* (Edusoft) and also programs that make flashcards such as *Make-A-Flash* (Teacher Support Software) which prints flash cards with vocabulary generated by the word processor.

In addition, there are programs that produce labels, time lines, attendance charts, and flow charts. *Timeliner* (Tom Snyder Productions) lets a teacher design and print out historical time lines of any length, showing a sequence of events. *Attendance Programs* (Hi Tech) and *Record Breaker!/Attendance* (Jay Klein Productions) let the user do monthly reports, while *MacFlow* (Mainstay) produces elegant flowcharts.

Statistical Programs

In the past, if someone wanted to do statistical analysis, he did the work by hand or on a mainframe at the university. Today there are many microcomputer programs that help the classroom teacher make calculations and analyze statistics. The majority of

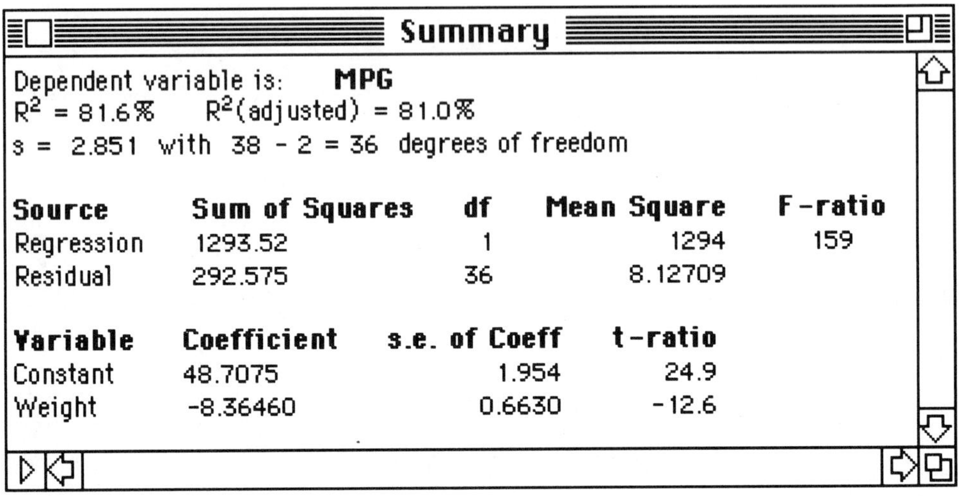

Summary

Dependent variable is: **MPG**
R^2 = 81.6% R^2(adjusted) = 81.0%
s = 2.851 with 38 - 2 = 36 degrees of freedom

Source	Sum of Squares	df	Mean Square	F-ratio
Regression	1293.52	1	1294	159
Residual	292.575	36	8.12709	

Variable	Coefficient	s.e. of Coeff	t-ratio
Constant	48.7075	1.954	24.9
Weight	-8.36460	0.6630	-12.6

Figure 9.5
Data Desk
Data Desk® Statistics and graphics program, Data Description, Inc., Ithaca, NY 14850.

these programs handle the simplest statistics like the mean and standard deviation while the more complex handle multilinear regression and factor/time series analysis. In a matter of seconds, the user can compute a regression or analysis of variance. Figure 9.5 from *Data Desk* (Data Description, Inc.) shows calculation of multilinear regression, performed simply by double clicking on the mouse.

For the Macintosh computers there are statistical programs such as *Data Desk Professional* (Data Description, Inc.), and *Fastat* (Systat, Inc.). The MS-DOS computer has *SPSS* (Spss, Inc.), and *Systat* (Systat, Inc.). The Apple II systems uses *App-Stats* and *Graphs* (Statsoft, Inc.).

In many situations the classroom teacher will not need this type of package because many of the grade book programs have sufficient statistics. However, if the instructor is doing research, or if the grade management program does not provide statistics, then this package is necessary.

Graphics Software

Just as utility programs are beneficial for the teacher, graphics are beneficial for the classroom. Pictures shape our perceptions and help us to communicate. When children first begin to read, they are always fascinated by illustrations. When a biology instructor discusses the anatomy of the body, he or she finds it beneficial to have a labeled drawing. The business person uses graphics to make important presentational points; the artist draws beautiful landscapes to make a statement. The engineer does a scale drawing to construct a bridge, the architect uses graphics to design a building, and the statistician creates charts from tables. In our society, people use pictures to educate, to communicate, to express emotions, to build, and to persuade. A picture is indeed "worth a thousand words."

The term **graphics** refers to the representation of images on a two dimensional surface. Graphics can be as simple as a pie graph or as elaborate as a detailed anatomical painting of the human body. When discussing computer graphics, the author is referring to pictures that are computer–generated on a screen, paper, or film. For discussion purposes, graphics is subdivided into four categories (1) design, (2) presentation, (3) productivity, and (4) paint.

Computer-Aided Design (CAD)

Computer-Aided Design (CAD) assists in the design of a variety of objects such as machine parts, homes, or anatomy. The computer user must have the proper computer-aided design program to accomplish this task. The architect uses software to design buildings or modify floor plans, and the plans can be saved and reused whenever needed. By using CAD software, a user can easily change or modify designs; this saves time, money, and effort. Imagine being able to work on the computer, as opposed to building the actual car, plane, or building. *Claris CAD* (Claris Corporation) can be used by students from grades ten and up to create any two dimensional geometric design, lines, arcs, and spline curves. It is a complete computer-aided design program that supports American and international design standards and facilitates drawing with a Graphic Guide System that locates an important geometric point automatically.

Many of the programs in this field are simulations that let the individual create a model car, plane, or train and show its use. For instance, CAD software allows an engineer to design a car, test it, and even rotate it to gain perspectives. *Car Builder* (Optimum Resource/Weekly Reader Software) is a simulation for education that lets the student construct, modify, and test a car. The student can do the following constructions: design the inside of the car, select the chassis length, the fuel tank, and the tires. When the mechanical selection is complete, the student can modify the body through a testing procedure that has a wind tunnel and a test track. At the end of this

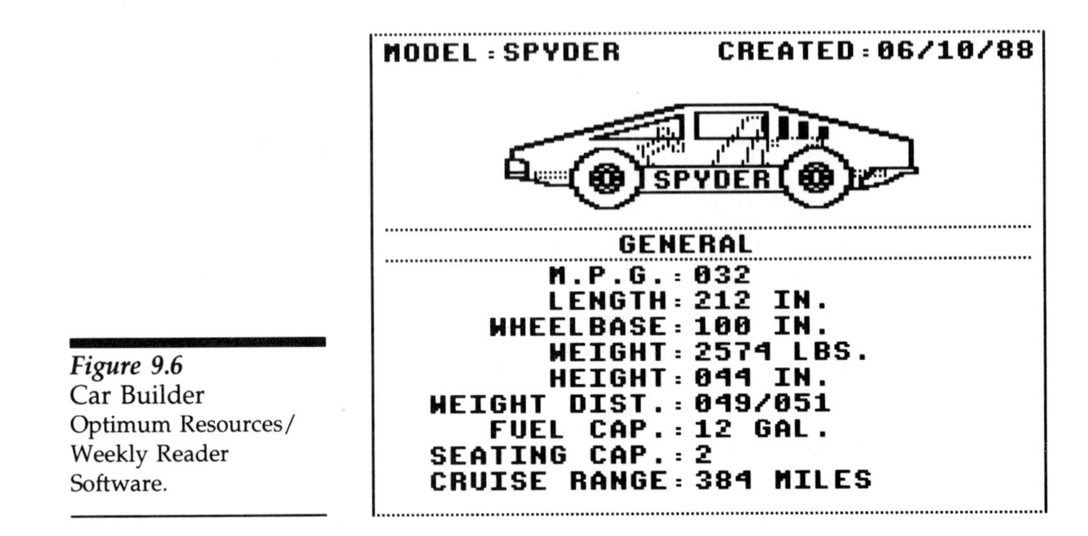

Figure 9.6
Car Builder
Optimum Resources/
Weekly Reader
Software.

testing session, the student saves the specifications of the designed car on a disk. Figure 9.6 shows the student designed car.

Glidepath (HRM Software), an educational CAD flight simulator program that comes with reproducible student worksheets, teaches the student how to reason logically and use some physics principles when designing and flying a craft. The student learns how to change flight variables such as altitude, velocity, and pitch, and learns to experiment with designed gliders or utilize the Glidepath's drawing board to design a craft. The student can also control a number of factors like wing length, wing width, and overall glider length. After the plane is designed, the student selects a terrain and runs the Glidepath simulator. The program displays the flight's progress on the screen, and there is an instant-replay option available.

Finally, *Design Your Own Railroad, Design Your Own Train,* and *Run Your Own Train* (Abracadata) provides the student with model railroad programs. Using *Design Your Own Railroad,* the student can draw layouts to scale of model railroads, which s/he can save or print. *Design Your Own Train,* lets the user create model trains, subways, buses, or trolley layouts. *Run Your Own Train* lets the student, as an engineer, traverse each layout from the top view to the inside of the locomotive.

Presentation Graphics in Business and Education

In chapters five and six the reader learned about data bases and spreadsheets and how useful these application programs were. When a teacher has data in this format, it is not difficult to create a graph from the data and use these illustrations to emphasize

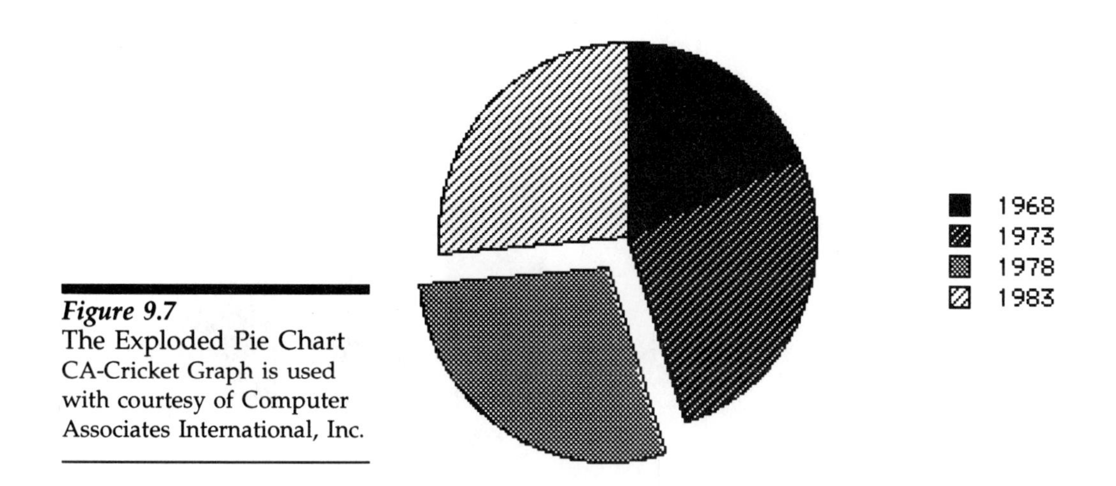

Figure 9.7
The Exploded Pie Chart
CA-Cricket Graph is used with courtesy of Computer Associates International, Inc.

key points for a presentation. These types of illustrations are called **presentation graphics** and businessmen use them all the time to illustrate salary distribution, inventory fluctuation, and monthly profitability. The images can take many forms, such as an exploded pie chart (Figure 9.7 CA-Cricket Graph) where the section that represents 1978 is separated from the pie for emphasis.

Graphs show a relationship within categories of data. In the exploded pie chart the user compares the results in four different years, with each slice representing a year. The user could have selected other graphs to illustrate the data like a bar graph to visualize the same data in a linear diagram (Figure 9.8).

A teacher can find graphics beneficial when he or she wants to see how a student performed on a series of exams. In Figure 9.9 the teacher charts Jane Smith's scores on five math tests, and by looking at the picture s/he can quickly grasp the effect of an extreme score (65) on this student's performance.

Graphing is a means of getting a clearer picture of what the data represent. In education graphing possibilities are unlimited. In science the students can graph a series of plant experiments where they alter variables such as temperature and water and record the effects on their plants. In economics or social studies the teacher might want the class to chart a stock's progress for a year or graph voting trends. In English the teacher can use the newspaper for a resource and extract different kinds of graphical data. Graphic programs such as *MECC Graph* (MECC) and *Easy Graph* (Houghton Mifflin) are suitable for classroom use. Using *Easy Graph's* tutorial, Figure

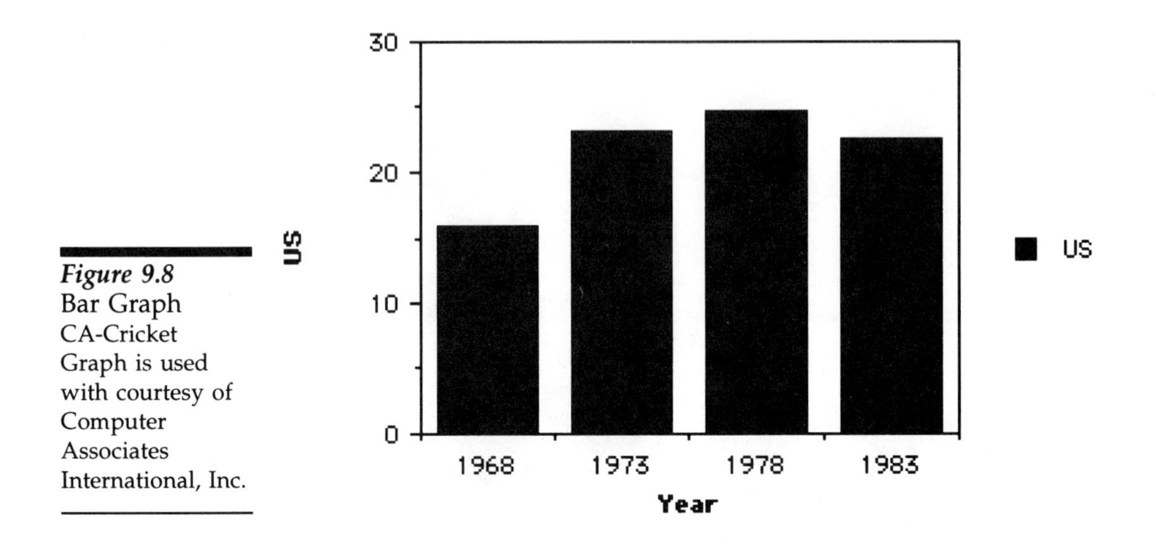

Figure 9.8
Bar Graph
CA-Cricket Graph is used with courtesy of Computer Associates International, Inc.

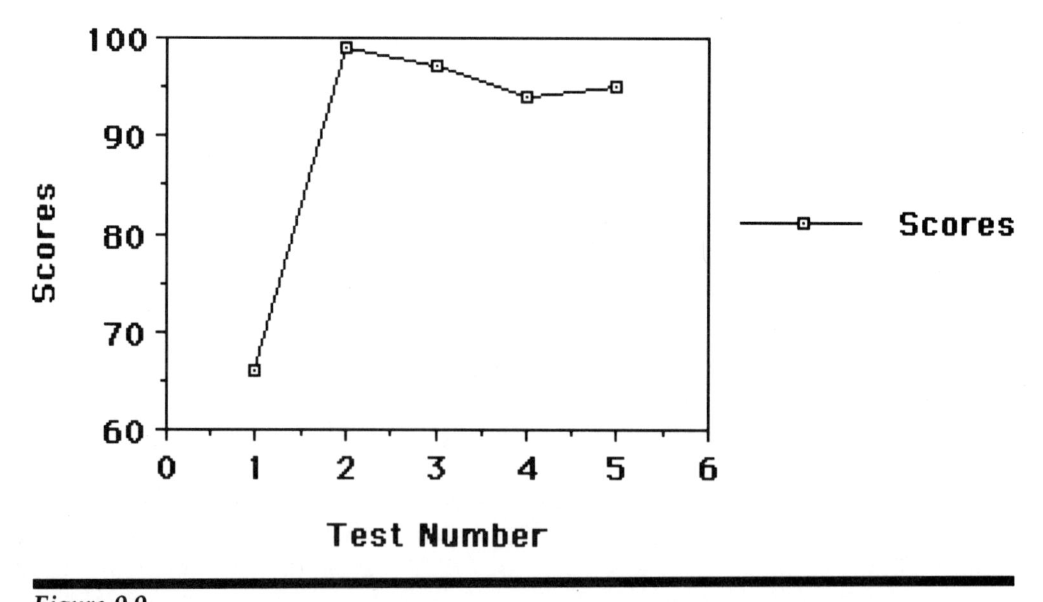

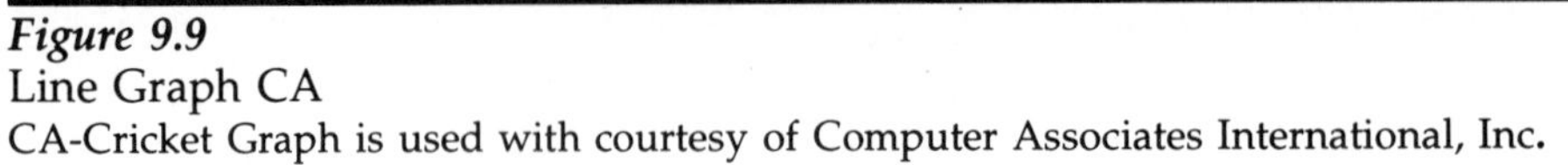
Figure 9.9
Line Graph CA
CA-Cricket Graph is used with courtesy of Computer Associates International, Inc.

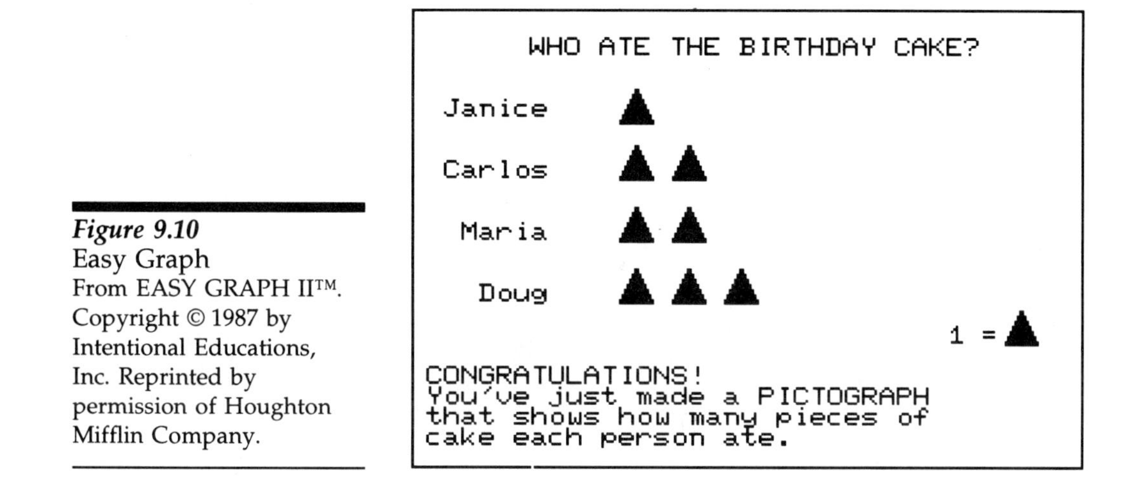

Figure 9.10
Easy Graph
From EASY GRAPH II™. Copyright © 1987 by Intentional Educations, Inc. Reprinted by permission of Houghton Mifflin Company.

9.10, the teacher or student is able to create a pictograph that determines who ate the birthday cake.

This program not only shows students how to read graphs but also teaches them the different functions of various graphs. Because of the Macintosh computer, there is a trend today toward greater usage of graphics in business and education, resulting in more software being developed.

Productivity Graphics

When the computer user wants to create an award, a poster, a banner, a greeting card or a certificate, s/he uses productivity graphics software. The best known is *The Print Shop* which lets the user create a wide assortment of multicolored graphics. This classic program has won countless awards because it is easy to use and it saves the user hours of time and effort. Figure 9.11 shows a ready-made sign from *The Print Shop.*

Since the introduction of the original *Print Shop,* there have been several versions produced. Although the concept remains the same, these programs vary in their capacity to produce color and graphics and use a laser printer. There are dozens of programs that can be used for productivity graphics, and some of the more popular are *SuperPrint*(Scholastic), *Print Magic*(Epyx), *BannerMania* (Brøderbund), *Award Maker Plus* (Baudville), *Kid Pix* (Brøderbund), *Certificate Maker* (Springboard), and *Publisher, Designer Prints* (MECC). *Award Maker Plus* (Macintosh Version) produces professional quality awards. *Microzine Jr. 1* from Scholastic's electronic periodical, lets the child design a mask. Figure 9.12 (on page 247) shows a mask designed by a nine year old who chose features to make the following face.

Figure 9.11
Print Shop
Graphic created using The Print Shop, copyright Brøderbund Software Inc., 1984.

Productivity programs have different templates, fonts, border designs and clip art. These enhancement programs are designed for users with limited artistic talent, and they have far-reaching educational benefits. The teacher can produce attractive bulletin boards, announcements, awards, interesting worksheets, and even transparency masters. The students can design their own letterhead stationery, communicating with each other by classroom mailbox.

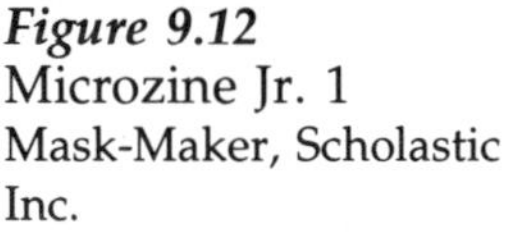

Figure 9.12
Microzine Jr. 1
Mask-Maker, Scholastic Inc.

Paint Programs

Paint programs are art-oriented rather than design-oriented, giving the user tools to draw and paint computerized pictures. There are significant advantages to drawing and painting on the computer. If the artist makes a mistake, s/he can easily rectify this situation, because there are no real paints or water colors to spill, drip, or smear. The painter simply changes the picture on the screen and instantaneously changes a color, enlarges a person, or moves an object. There are good paint programs available today including *MacPaint* (Claris), *Superpaint* (Silicon Beach Software), *Deluxe Paint II* (Electronics Arts), *Dazzle Draw* (Brøderbund), *Blazing Paddles* and *816 Paint* (Baudville), *Kid Pix*(Brøderbund), *Platimum Plus*(Beagle Bros.), *Color 'n' Canvas* (WINGS For Learning) and *My Paint* (Saddleback Graphics) all of which offer coloring and texturing capabilities. In addition to these features, paint programs have brushes of different widths and shapes, drawing tools, a mirror image function, different fonts, and an undo function. Furthermore, the images that the artist creates can be cut and pasted in any location in the document, and images can be imported from other programs. Figure 9.13 shows a screen from *Where in Time is Carmen SanDiego?* with the Leaning Tower of Pizza imported into *Superpaint*.

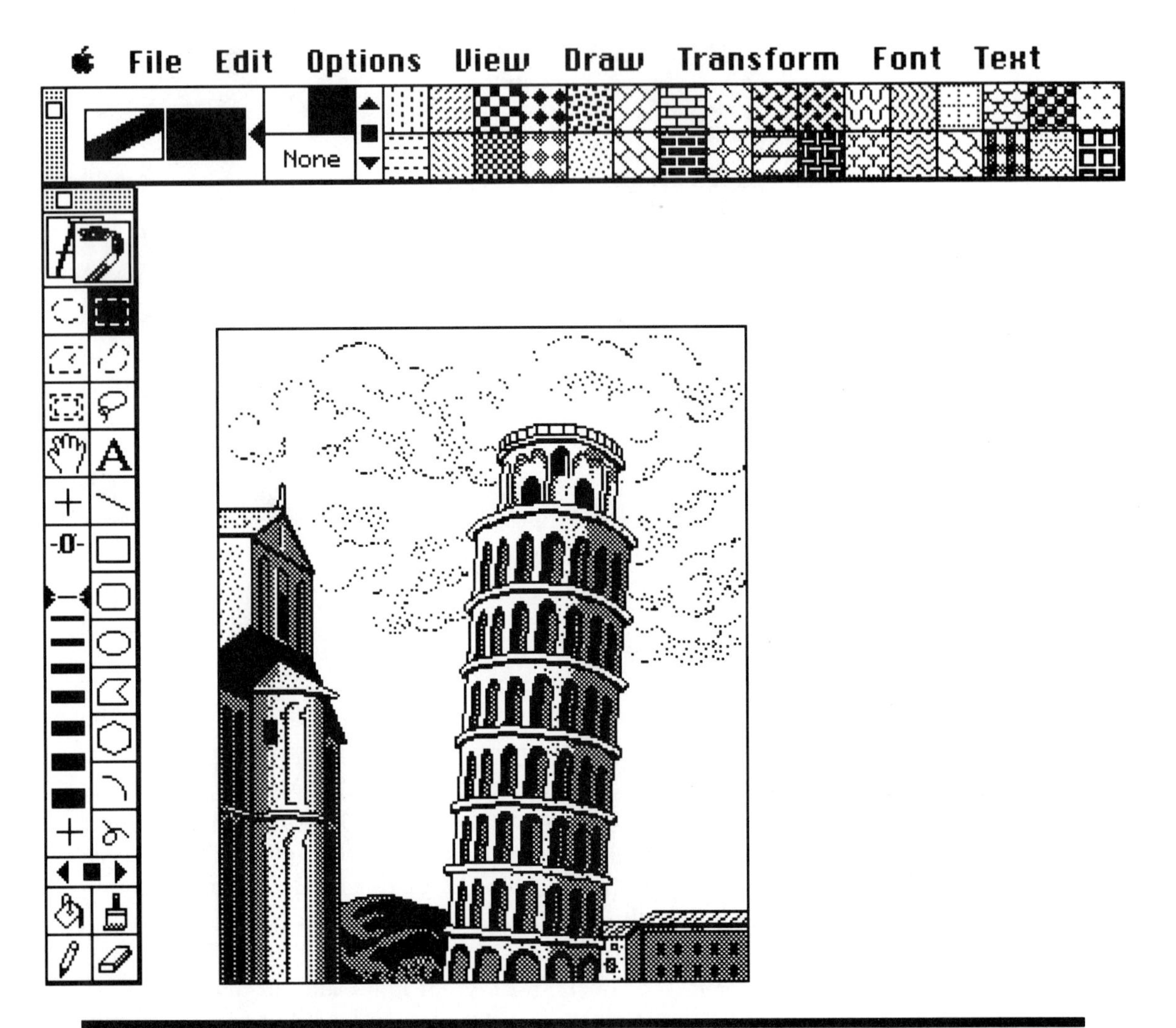

Figure 9.13
SuperPaint-Imported Picture
Screen shot from Where in Time is Carmen Sandiego, copyright Brøderbund Software, Inc., 1984. Palette from SuperPaint © 1991 Silicon Beach Software. Used with express permission of Silicon Beach Software, a subsidiary of Aldus Corporation. All rights reserved.

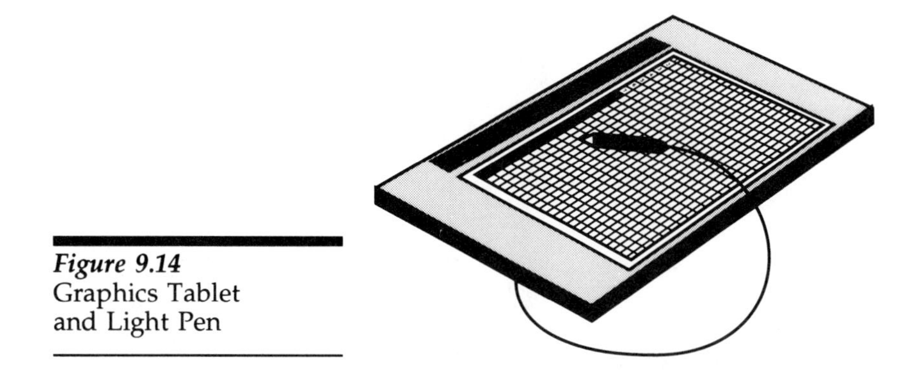

Figure 9.14
Graphics Tablet
and Light Pen

A student can draw geometric shapes, create designs, and construct miniature cities, which can be created on a color or monochrome monitor. In order to create images, the student uses an input device, such as the keyboard, or a light pen with a graphics tablet, or a digitizer. The light pen (Figure 9.14) is a pencil-shaped object that lets the user draw graphics on a tablet that is used for sketching the images, for selecting the menu items, and for moving the cursor.

The student can also use a digitizer, which converts the shades of an image into a digital representation for the computer. A digitizer can be in the form of a scanner or camera; this equipment will be discussed in the Computer Hardware chapter, number 11.

Music Education

As compared to software in other curriculum areas, music education software is scarce because there has been a lack of interest in the computer for teaching music. Nevertheless, there are programs that give instruction in playing music, composition, and music theory and programs that provide specific practice in music skills. *The Jam Session* (Brøderbund) is a musical skills program that uses high quality digitized instrument sounds combined with professionally composed music. The student, experimenting with music, plays solos and melodic passages on a variety of instruments, while the program acts as a background accompaniment that adjusts inappropriate notes.

The Miracle Piano Teaching System (The Software Toolworks) comes with a separate keyboard, built-in stereo speakers, software, and a cable connection for the student's computer. The software program customizes lessons for the student with exciting video games and popular songs. The student progresses through over 1000 lessons at an individual pace and learns how to read music and play the piano with both hands. This program has a repertoire of over 100 songs that can play in a variety of styles, including country, classical, and rock and roll.

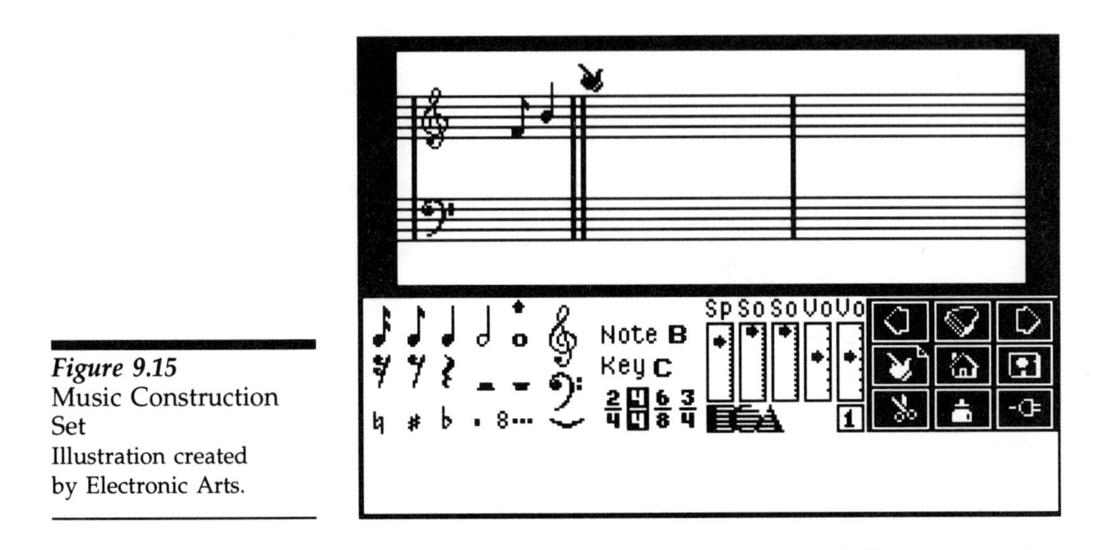

Figure 9.15
Music Construction Set
Illustration created by Electronic Arts.

Diversi-Tune (Diversified Software Research) is another music skills program that includes a selection of prerecorded music and enables the user to record his or her own songs. A keyboard-fingering diagram shows which notes are played and how long they are held. While the song is rolling on the screen, the students see with the aid of a bouncing ball the accompanying lyrics in large or small text.

MECC has produced *Music Theory,* a drill and practice program that has 18 drill activities for such skills as pitch, notation, chords, and terms. *Sound Tracks,* also produced by MECC, is a program that gives kindergarteners the opportunity to create sound and images, compose melodies, and experiment with lines, shapes, pictures, and colors. Using the keyboard with *Sound Tracks,* a child can discover a relationship between audio and visual patterns. Another music theory program, *Camus: Melodic Dictations* (Conduit), trains a students to perceive musical sounds in relation to notation. The teacher plays a short melody and the student, using the keyboard, must write the dictation in standard musical notation. The program then plays and compares the two versions. There is a musical word processor called *Music Construction Set* (Electronic Arts), that teaches a student how to arrange traditional musical symbols into compositions. The program has 16 digitized instruments and an extensive music library. The student in Figure 9.15 uses a mouse to place individual notes from a palette to a staff. In addition to instructional music programs, there is software for listening pleasure such as *Art of Fugue in D Minor* (Vol. 2) by Johann Sebastian Bach *Early Music* (Vol. 4), and *Renaissance Period (Great Wave).*

Generally, the audio quality for most microcomputers is poor; therefore music programs need a synthesizer to effectively produce good quality musical sound. Seven classroom activities that use graphic, art, and music programs follow.

Graphics, Art, and Music Activities

Activity One: Pet Data Sheet

Materials

- Student's Animal Data Sheet
- Graphing program *Easy Graphics* (Houghton Mifflin), *MECC Graph* (MECC), etc.
- One computer or more

Objectives:

- The students will learn how to:
- Do a survey
- Graph their survey, using a bar graph and a pie graph

Procedure

1. Each student surveys seven students to find out how many family pets they have.
2. Using the computer, each student creates a bar graph.
3. Each student surveys these identical students again to find out how many of their animals are dogs, cats, etc.
4. From the students' answers, they create a pie graph and a new bar graph showing this information.

Activity Two: State Data Sheet

Materials

- Student's State Data sheet
- Graphing program *Easy Graphics* by Houghton Mifflin, *MECC Graph* etc.
- One computer or more

Objectives:

- The students will:
- Read the Almanac for information
- Learn how to graph their information using a bar graph and a line graph

Procedure

1. Each student will select three states and research their annual rainfall.
2. Using the computer, the students will create a bar graph comparing the statistics.
3. The same students will track down statistics for three specific dates in the past.
4. Next the students will construct a line graph showing the changes in the data for each state over a period of time.

Activity Three: Math Riddle Card

Materials

- Student's Greeting Card
- Productivity graphics programs *Print Shop*(Brøderbund), *Superprint*(Scholastic), etc.
- One computer or more

Objectives:

- The students will find a riddle.
- The students will use a productivity graphics program to design a greeting card.
- The students will get practice in solving math riddles.

Procedure

1. The teacher gives or has each child look up a riddle.
2. Next s/he tells the pupils to design a greeting card, putting the clue for the riddle on the cover and the answer on the inside cover of the card.
3. The card should look like Figures 9.16 and 9.17.
4. Now have every child in the class solve one of the riddles.

Greeting Card Cover

A train left Chicago at 1:00 p.m. A second train left New York at 3:00 p.m. The train from Chicago traveled toward New York at 40 miles per hour. The train from New York traveled toward Chicago at 50 miles per hour. If the distance from Chicago to New York is 1000 miles, which train was farthest from Chicago when they met?

Figure 9.16
Greeting Card Cover

The Greeting Card Inside

They are the same
distance from Chicago.

Figure 9.17
The Greeting Card Inside
Clip Art Dubl-Click Software, Border-Graphics created using The Print Shop, copyright Brøderbund Software, Inc., 1984.

Activity Four: Educational Sign

Materials

- Student's Sign
- Productivity graphics programs *Print Shop* (Brøderbund), *Superprint*(Scholastic), etc.
- One computer or more

Objectives:

- The students use a productivity graphics program to design a sign.
- They will learn about design and placement of objects.
- They will discuss the reasons for not taking drugs.

Procedure

1. The teacher talks about placement and design with the students.
2. Then the pupils use a productivity graphic program to design a sign warning people not to take drugs (Figure 9.18).
3. After all students have designed a sign, discuss what makes certain signs more appealing than others.
4. Discuss the reasons why students should not take drugs.

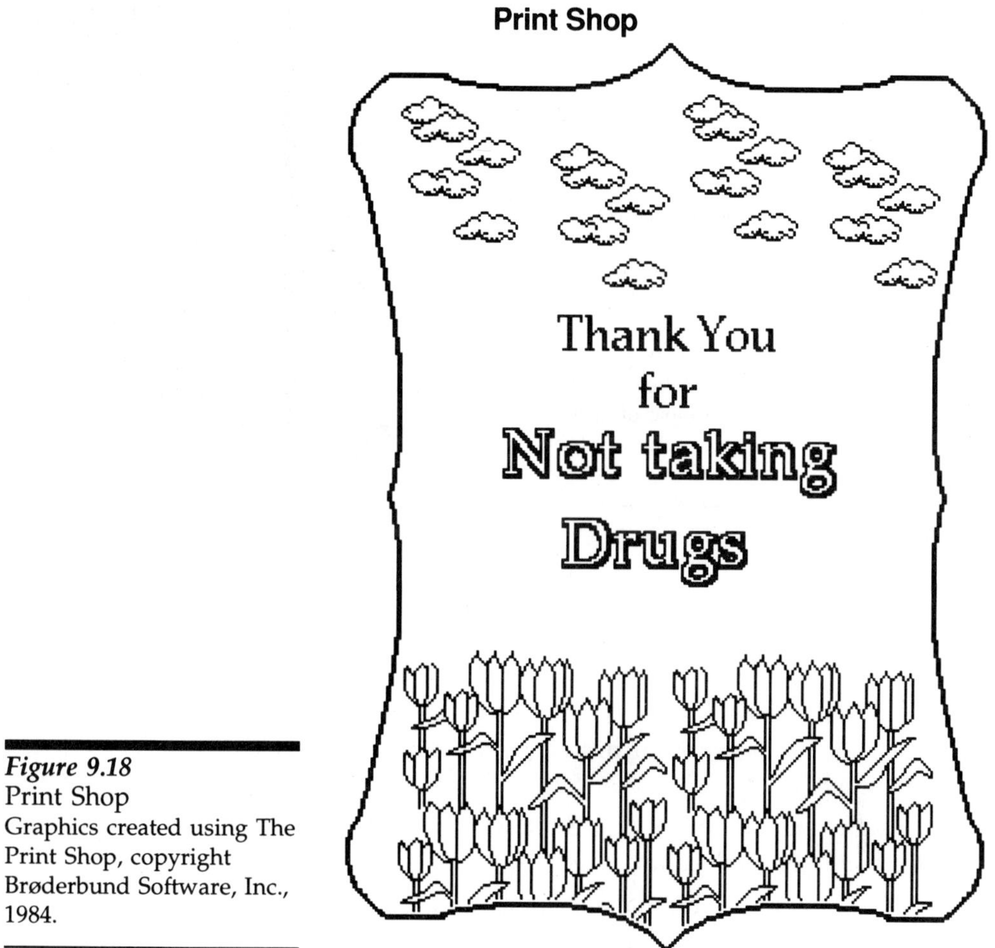

Figure 9.18
Print Shop
Graphics created using The Print Shop, copyright Brøderbund Software, Inc., 1984.

Activity Five: Math

Materials

- Paint programs such as *MacPaint* (Claris), *Superpaint*(Silicon Beach Software), *Dazzle Draw* (Brøderbund), *816 Paint* (Baudville), *Kid Pix* (Brøderbund)
- One computer or more

Figure 9.19
Drawing created using SuperPaint© 1991 Silicon Beach Software. Used with express permission of Silicon Beach Software, a subsidiary of Aldus Corporation. All rights reserved.

Objectives:

- The students will use the program and make various geometric shapes.
- They will learn about these shapes.

Procedure

1. Teach the students about different geometric shapes such as rectangles, squares, circles, etc.
2. Show the students how to use the paint program to create these shapes in some creative design like Figure 9.19.
3. Explain how to fill the shapes with color and how to repeat shapes.
4. Now have the student use the paint program to make abstract drawings.
5. When they are finished, have them print out their shapes and color them, making sure each shape has the same color.
6. Finally, display these drawings on the bulletin board.
7. As a follow-up activity, have the students do collages.

Activity Six: Music

Materials

- Music programs such as *Jam Session* (Brøderbund), *Diversi-Tune* (Diversified Software Research), *Music Construction Set* (Electronic Learning)
- One computer or more

Objectives:

- Helping the students recognize notes

Procedure

1. Draw eight bars to represent a scale on the board.
2. Turn the computer monitor away from the students and have a student play six random notes.
3. Ask the students to listen carefully to the sounds and draw the bars that represent note patterns.
4. Do this two more times so that the students can check their work.
5. Now turn the monitor toward the class and play the pattern and have them compare their pattern to the ones that are being played.

Activity Seven: "Mother, May?" Adaptation

Materials

- Music programs such as *Music Theory* (MECC), *Camus: Melodic Dictations* (Conduit)
- One computer or more

Objective:

- To improve musical comprehension

Procedure:

1. Have the students use the *Music Theory* program by MECC to improve upon their knowledge of music theory.
2. Have the class stand in a straight line in the back of the classroom.
3. Select a student at random to answer a question such as, "How many beats does a quarter note have?"
4. The student advances one step if this question is answered correctly.

5. If the student is not correct, he or she moves one step back.
6. The first student to make it to the front of the room wins.

In **Appendix A** the reader will find an annotated list of award winning teacher utility, graphics, art, and music programs A summary, a mastery test, classroom projects, and selected readings and references conclude this chapter.

Summary

Teacher utility programs are support tools that can make a teacher's job more effective. One of the most popular tools is the grade book, which lessens the time a teacher spends entering grades, computing averages, and informing parents about students' progress. Other tools that also save time and reduce effort are test and worksheet generators, puzzle makers, and statistical packages.

A good paint program lets the teacher draw without the fear of making a mistake, and a productivity program enables the teacher who is not artistically inclined to create any graphic from an award to a poster. The reader also learned that CAD programs are useful in designing room layouts, machine parts, and cars; presentation graphics produce charts and graphs that show relationships within categories of data; and music programs are an effective aide in practicing music skills and theory. The author provided seven activities for integrating graphics, art, and music programs into the classroom.

Chapter Mastery Test

1. Discuss two examples of music software and how each one can help the student in a different phase of the music curriculum.
2. What is the difference between a presentation graphics programs and a paint program? Describe the major features of each program.
3. How has the availability of paint programs on the computer affected the traditional way of drawing and painting?
4. Define CAD and discuss its primary use.
5. What is a teacher utility program? Explain how it can provide individualized instruction for a class.
6. What is a productivity graphics program? Discuss two uses for this program in the school curriculum.
7. Define computer graphics and explain its importance in today's world.
8. What are the advantages and disadvantages of using a gradebook program?
9. What is an exploded pie chart? How can a teacher use it in the classroom?
10. Explain what graphics programs are least applicable for the classroom.

Classroom Projects

1. Prepare a report showing why it is important that the school use productivity graphics.
2. Use a presentation graphics program to graphically represent Jane Smith's grades of 50, 60, 70, 88, 97, and 100.
3. Use a productivity graphics program to produce: (a) a riddle card (b) poster (c) a calendar and (d) letterhead stationery. Explain the educational value of each product.
4. Pretend your school will let you purchase only one graphics program. Will you choose a productivity graphics, presentation graphics, paint or computer aided design (CAD) package. Explain and justify the selection.
5. Create a test for the class using a test making program.
6. Evaluate three test making programs, and discuss their strengths as well as their weaknesses.
7. Use one of the many puzzle utilities to create a product for class consumption.
8. Review three gradebook programs and talk about their differences, similarities, and why you would choose one over another.

Suggested Readings and References

Adams, Richard C. "Low-Cost Graphics Tablets." *The Computing Teacher,* (11) (December/January 1984): 65–66.

Beamer, Scott. "10 Reasons Why You Need A Charting Program." *MacUser* (June 1990): 126–138.

Benton, R. and Mary Balcer. *The Official Print Shop Handbook,* Banton Books, New York, 1987.

Bunescu, Marci. "Turn Your Computer into a Music Workstation." *Electronic Learning,* (9) 5 (February 1990): 7–39.

Crotty, Cameron. "The MIDI Beat." *Incider A+.* (September 1991): 45–49.

Dumfey, J. "Ready, Set, Publish—On Your Apple II." *Electronic Learning,* (60) (September 1988): 62–96.

Eiser, L. "Print It! 101 Things to Print with Your Computer." *Classroom Computer Learning* (April 1988): 76, 77.

Eisner, L. "Test Generators: Teacher's Tool or Teacher's Headache?" *Classroom Computer Learning* (June 1988): 44–51.

Ettinger, Linda E. "Talk About Teaching Computer Art Graphics." *The Computing Teacher* (October 1983): 16–18.

Feldstein, S. "Technology for Teaching." *Music Educators Journal* 74(7) (March 1988): 33–37.

Field, Cynthia. "The Electronic Palette." *Incider A+* (August 1991): 33–39.

Greh, Deborah, Ed.D. "Graphics Gallery 6: Is It Art Yet?" *Incider A+* (September 1991): 46–48.

Holzberg, Carol S. "The Lighter Side of Education." *Incider A+* (September 1991) 34–39.

Keizer, Gregg. "Command Performance." *Incider A+* (August 1991): 41–43.

Larking, Conal L. "The New Print Shop." *Home Office Computing* (April 1990): 77.

Lodish, E. "Test Writing Made Simple: Generate Tests and Worksheets Electronically." *Electronic Learning* 5(5) (February 1986): 28, 30, 68.

Marcus, Aaron. "Graphic Design for Computer Graphics: Implications for Art and Design Educators." *The Computing Teacher* (April 1984): 59–61.

Martin, Joan, Mei-Hung Chiu, and Anne Dailey. "Science: Graphing in the Second Grade." *The Computing Teacher* (November 1990): 28–32.

Mathias, J. "Turning Data into Pictures: Part I." *The Computing Teacher* (October 1988) 40–48.

Mathias, J. "Turning Data into Pictures: Part 2." *Computing Teacher* (November 1988): 7–10, 56.

Mathis, Judi and Cathy Carney. "Easy Color Paint." *The Computing Teacher* (45) (April 1991): 46.

McCarhy. R. "Stop the Presses." *Electronic Learning* (March 1988): 24–30.

Mendrinos, R. "Computers as Curriculum Tools: Exceeding Expectations." *Media and Methods* (January/February 1988).

Schrum, L. Carton, K. and S. Pinney. "Today's Tools." *The Computing Teacher* (May 1988): 31–35.

Schwartz, R. and M. Callery. "Speaking of Graphics." *A+ Magazine* (March 1988): 73–76.

White, James, R. "Computer-Aided Design—Product Comparison." *InFoWorld* (May 28, 1990): 51–62.

Hypermedia

10

Objectives

Upon completing this chapter the student will be able to:

1. Discuss the origins of hypermedia.
2. Explain the basic hypermedia concepts.
3. Understand the basic features of hypercard.
4. Describe different types of hypermedia software.

Historical Perspective

Almost fifty years ago, Vannevar Bush envisioned an information organization and retrieval scheme that became a reality with the emergence of hypermedia. Vannevar Bush, Franklin Delano Roosevelt's first director of the Office of Scientific Research and Development, is given credit for first proposing the idea of a machine that mimics the mind's associative process. In 1945 Bush described a work station called a memex, "an extended physical supplement for man's mind, [which] seeks to emulate his mind in its associative linking of items of information, and their retrieval as a result" (Forrest, 1988). Influenced by Bush's associative linking and browsing concepts, Douglas Engelbard conducted research at the Stanford Research Institute in 1960 that led to several significant inventions, including the mouse, an on-line work environment now named "Augment" and the concept of a "viewing filter." With a viewing filter users could quickly view an abstract of a document or file, thus being able to scan a database for important information (Fiderio, 1988).

While these developments were important, it was Ted Nelson who made the most critical step in the development of the concept. He coined the term **Hypertext,** meaning nonsequential writing, and he developed the writing environment called "Xanadu" which lets a user create and interconnect electronic documents with other text information. In hypertext text, images, sound, text, and actions are linked together in nonsequential associations that let the user browse through related topics, regardless of

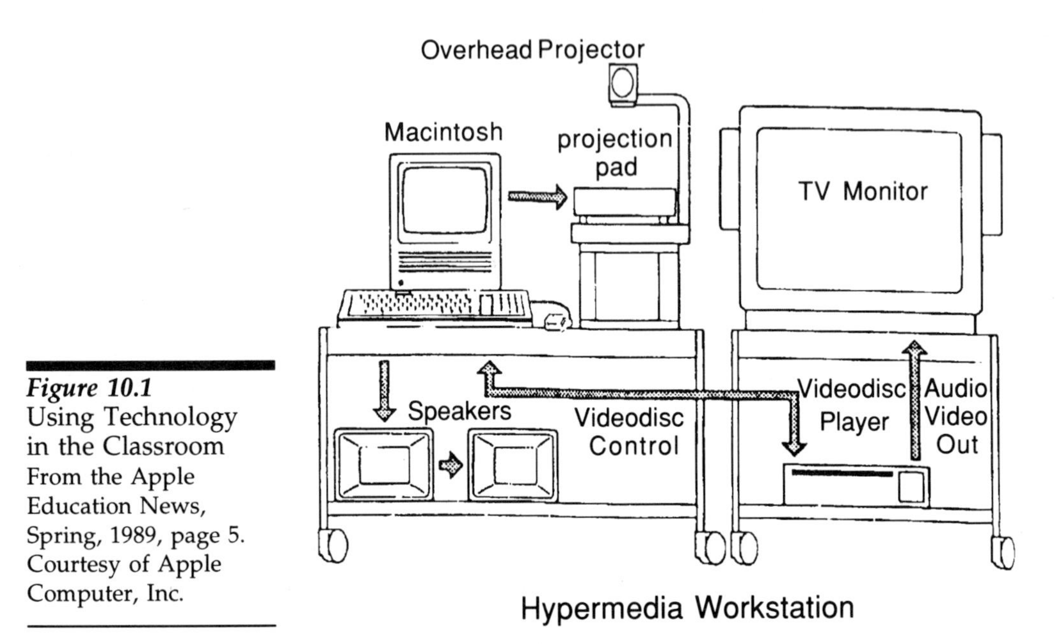

Figure 10.1
Using Technology in the Classroom
From the Apple Education News, Spring, 1989, page 5. Courtesy of Apple Computer, Inc.

the order. An example of hypertext is a computer glossary in which a user can select a word and retrieve its definition from the glossary.

A current term, **Hypermedia** is nearly synonymous with hypertext; however, it emphasizes the nontextual components of hypertext. Hypermedia uses the computer to input, manipulate and output graphics, sound, text, and video in the presentation of ideas and information.[1] When a teacher uses hypermedia, the computer directs the action, while devices such as a videocamera, video disk player, CD-ROM player, video cassette recorder, VCR tape deck, scanner, video digitizer, audio digitizer, or a musical keyboard work through the computer. Figure 10.1 is an example of a hypermedia workstation.

A computer and a monitor are the basic equipment necessary for a hypermedia presentation, with the computer acting as a controller while the monitor displays images. Depending upon their level of sophistication, teachers can add a variety of equipment and software programs to enhance the hypermedia creation. For example, they can use the videocamera to film a scene while the video cassette player records a television program, the audio digitizer transfers sounds, the scanner adds graphics or text, and the video digitizer transfers non-computer media such as photos or

1. In the literature, hypermedia and interactive multimedia are interchangeable terms.

videotape. Furthermore, teachers can use art programs like *Dazzle Draw* (Brøderbund) or *816 Paint* (Baudville) to enhance art work, a musical keyboard to enrich any musical accompaniment, and a laser printer to produce high quality images. Hypermedia components range from sound-enhanced documents that will play on any computer to a *HyperCard* stack that offers sound, animation, and color.

The purpose of this chapter is to provide an overview of hypermedia and current hypermedia software. In other words, while readers cannot expect to become hypermedia programming experts based on the information in this chapter, they will be introduced to the possibilities of hypermedia.

What is HyperCard?

The best known and one of the first implementations of hypermedia was **HyperCard,** developed by Bill Atkinson at Apple Computer. Atkinson created *HyperCard* to run on the Macintosh computer in 1987. Since then, *HyperCard* has become almost synonymous with hypermedia, although it is important to remember that not all hypermedia use *HyperCard.* In order to better understand HyperCard, let us look at some of its basic features.

HyperCard is an authoring tool that lets the user organize information, browse through, and retrieve on-screen cards that contain text, graphics, sound, and animation. A *HyperCard* application consists of a **stack** of **cards** similar to index cards; each card contains **text, graphics,** and **buttons** (Figure 10.2).

A *HyperCard* user navigates among the cards by clicking on buttons that can take the form of arrows, hands, etc. Individuals click on **buttons** to move from one card to another or to perform other actions. (Each button has a script that is written in the programming language, **HyperTalk,** and the script has a procedure it follows when a button is clicked.) For example, *HyperCard* can be used to look through the entire permanent collection of the National Gallery of Art in Washington, D.C. By clicking on a series of buttons on the Macintosh screen with a mouse, a person can see the museum's paintings by Monet in color on a monitor, view close up portions of the paintings, and, at the same time, listen to the music of Debussy. In this instance, the student or teacher is using *HyperCard* with the National Gallery of Art laser disk (Videodisc Publishing).

HyperCard comes with stacks, but users can also create their own stacks. What is unique about the program is the fact that it enables non-programmers to write their own applications without learning how to program. In addition, computer users can create stand-alone applications and develop commercial applications that can include

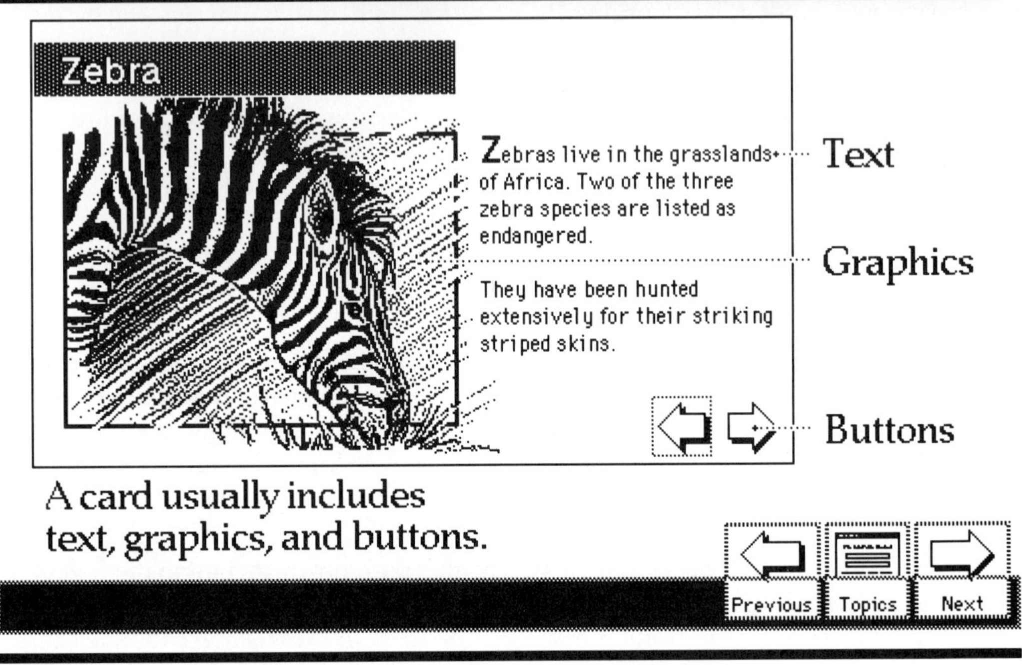

Figure 10.2 Elements of a Card.
HyperCard is a trademark of Claris Corporation registered in the U.S. and in other countries.

musical composition programs, appointment calendars, or check writing, to name only a few of the possibilities.

Let us briefly examine a few important HyperCard terms, starting with **card.** A card stores information and generally includes text, graphics, and buttons. One type of card is a **home card.** Usually when a user first open **HyperCard 2.2,** s/he immediately sees the **Welcome to HyperCard home card** (Figure 10.3), the first of five cards in this stack.[2]

The 2.2 version of HyperCard comes with five home cards: Welcome to HyperCard, which displays icons representing each stack that can be accessed, Stack Kit that takes you to advanced stacks, and Cards 3, 4, and 5—available so that users can create their own stacks. Each home card is designed to hold items that allow users

2. Even if the user does not start *HyperCard* with the Home Stack, s/he needs to have one on the disk to run *HyperCard.*

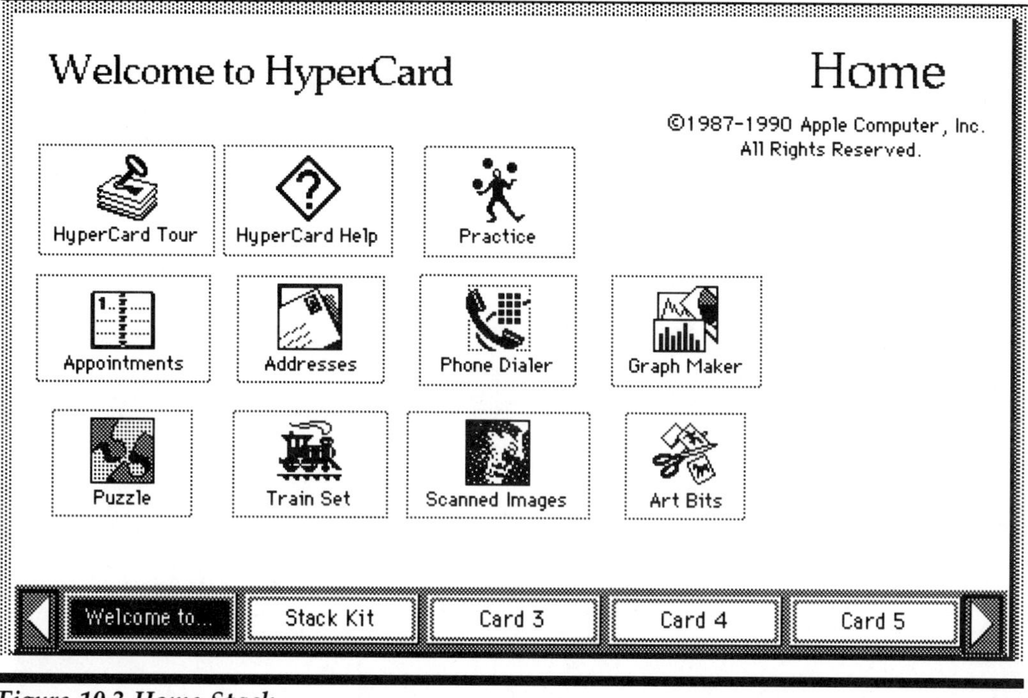

Figure 10.3 Home Stack
HyperCard is a trademark of Claris Corporation registered in the U.S. and in other countries.

to travel to all the other cards that come with *HyperCard;* that is, the home cards serve as a visual directory of the elements in the program.

A *HyperCard* user can also create cards on any topic desired, such as dogs, schedules, or address cards (Figure 10.4). This card contains the name of the person, her address, and her telephone number, identified by a graphic. On this card the information is recorded in **fields** similar to those found on a data base record. The three fields on this particular card are name, address, and telephone number, and these fields are the same for all cards created in this collection.

A collection of these cards is called a **stack,** and the icon for a stack looks like a stack of cards:

HyperCard is a trademark of Claris Corporation registered in the U.S. and in other countries.

Stack

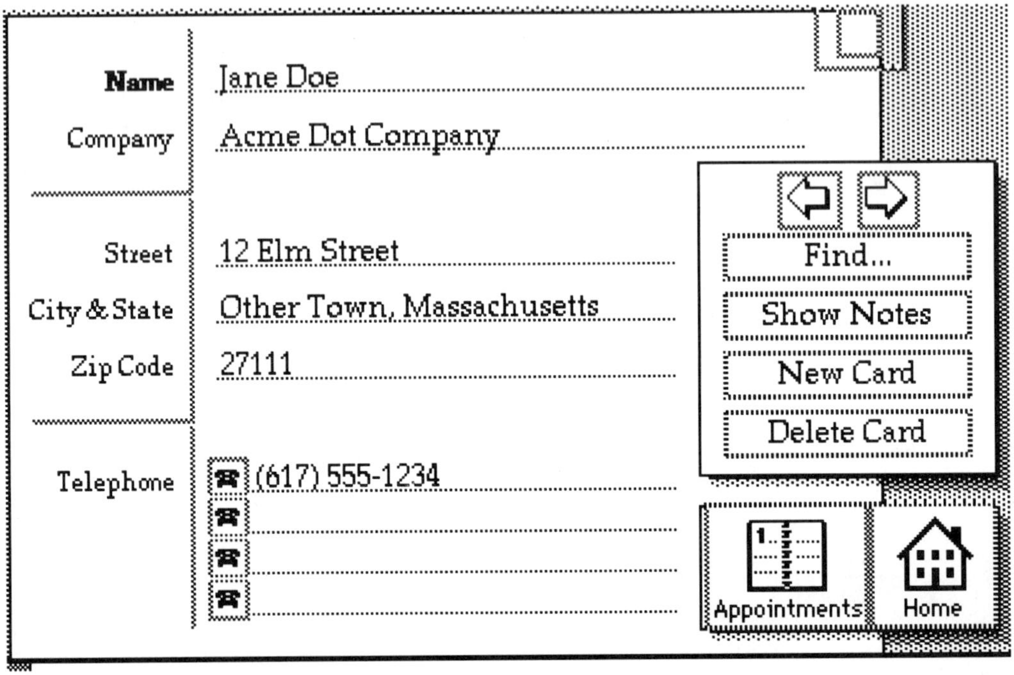

Figure 10.4
Hypercard 2.2 Address Card
HyperCard is a trademark of Claris Corporation registered in the U.S. and in other countries.

The cards in a stack are usually based on a single topic, such as endangered animals, an address book, or an airplane flying program. These cards can have the same background (text, graphics, buttons), or the backgrounds can vary with the author's purpose and imagination. The stack can teach a foreign language, take the user on a tour of a city, or the stack can be used for numerous other instructional purposes.

When an individual moves around the cards in a stack or goes to another stack, it is called browsing. There are several ways to browse: choose commands from the menu, type commands in the message box, use the arrow keys on the keyboard, or click on buttons using a **hand icon browse tool.**

HyperCard is a trademark of Claris Corporation registered in the U.S. and in other countries.

Browse Tool

The HyperCard **buttons** exist on every card and come in a variety of forms, including pop-up text, video control, text, sound control, and multi-buttons. These and other buttons are explained below.

The **pop-up text button** pops up a small window with text, and this adds extra information, definitions, or instructions to the screen without cluttering it. The **video control button** sends a command to a videodisc player, causing it to display a single, still video image or a complex sequence of images. The video can appear on a separate monitor, or if the individual uses a video overlay card, the images can replace or be integrated with the computer screen images.

A **text entry button** lets a user type a free response to a question instead of selecting an option. If the user's entry matches the pattern supplied by the program, the user receives positive feedback on the screen. If the individual gives an incorrect response, s/he is told the answer is not correct.

A **sound button** plays a sound clip when it is clicked; the sounds played may range from musical selections, to sound effects such as rain falling, to digitized sounds such as speech in English or Spanish. In the following HyperCard example (Figure 10.5), the user presses the horn button, hears a moo sound, and must respond by pressing the correct animal button.

Buttons that are **multi-button** activate a list of buttons in a special order. For example, clicking one of these buttons might give a message, change disks, and then link a card stack with a new card stack.

Figure 10.6, page 269 shows three buttons, one for mammals, one for birds, and one for reptiles. Each button takes the user to a different card in the stack. For example, the mammal button takes the user to a card where s/he can learn about mammals.

The next two screen shots show the buttons on the cards from a sample HyperCard graphics stack.

At the bottom of the Graph Maker card are the stack overview button and the home card button (Figure 10.7, page 270). The **stack overview button** takes the user to a card that gives an overview of the stack, and the **home button** takes the user to the first home card. The person uses this stack to create four types of graphs that are selected by clicking on the proper button. For instance, if the user chooses a column graph, s/he would click on this button to use the column graph card from the stack. Then the data would be entered and a graph like Figure 10.8 on page 271 would be produced.

From the explanation of *HyperCard,* the reader can see that this version is a relatively user-friendly one, although it requires considerable work. A similar *HyperCard* product is *HyperCard for the Apple IIGS,* a clone of the Macintosh version, with all the advantages and with the addition of color. *HyperCard* is currently used by numerous educators, but there are simpler authoring language tools that exist for the

Figure 10.5
Claris's HyperCard 2.2 Showing Sound Buttons
HyperCard is a trademark of Claris Corporation registered in the U.S. and in other countries.

Apple II family as well as for IBM. Some of the more useful programs include *HyperScreen* (Scholastic) for the Apple II and GS Family, *HyperStudio* for the Apple GS and *Tutor Tech* (Techware Inc.) for the Apple II Family. Others are *Linkway* (IBM Educational Systems), and *Spinnaker Plus* (Spinnaker) for the IBM computers. Many of these software packages have accompanying stackware programs developed by teachers. For example, *"So You Want to Do a Science Project?"* (CCIE) is a self-running stack developed using *HyperScreen.* The purpose of this stack is to give the students science project ideas and to take them through the experimental process step by step. Figure 10.9 (see page 271) is a sample of a screen from this teacher's program.

Creating stacks is a complicated and time consuming task that includes creating text, graphics, and buttons, and providing a complete explanation of this involved process is beyond the scope of the chapter. However, there is software used in

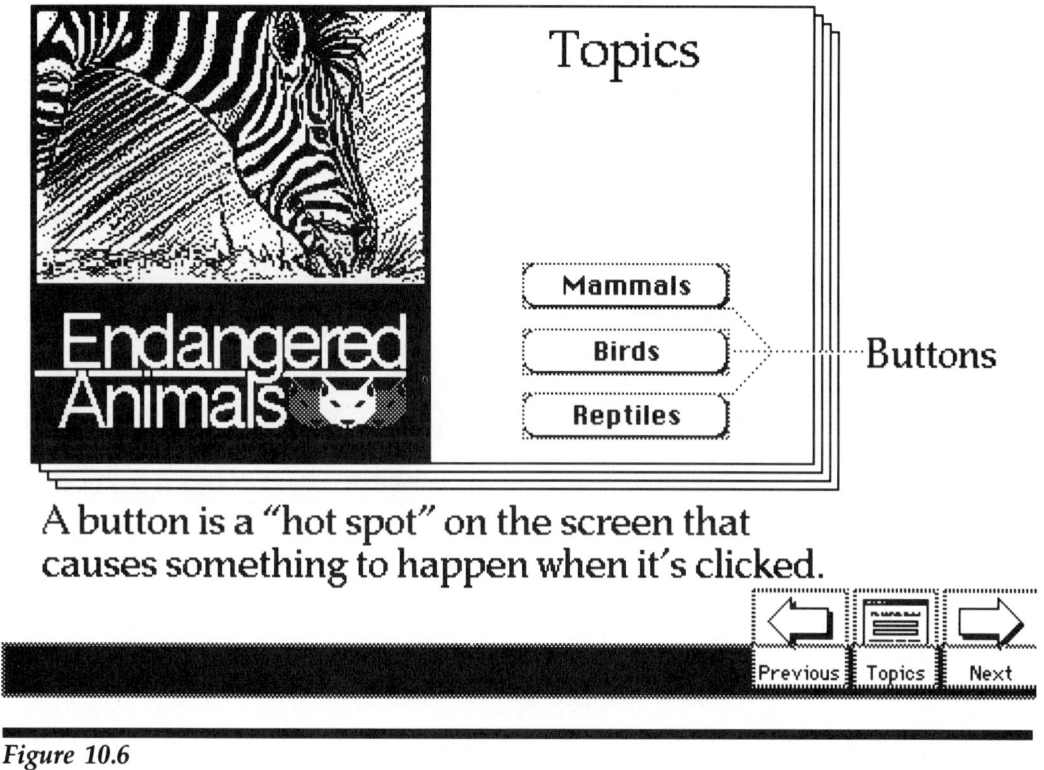

Figure 10.6
Topics Card
HyperCard is a trademark of Claris Corporation registered in the U.S. and in other countries.

conjunction with these authoring systems that helps alleviate this problem. *Modern Learning Aids* (MPG) has a multimedia presentation generator that produces hypermedia presentations on the computer with the ease of operating a VCR remote control. A typical MPG presentation might be a lesson on environmental problems caused by clearing the rain forests in Brazil. A VCR is used to present a newscast on these issues, a videodisc of an expedition down the Amazon river depicts forests, inhabitants, and sounds; digitized satellite images can be added along with text; and, finally, the additional sound of jungle music can come from a CD-ROM disc player. This system allows the author to play segments of the presentation in user-paced mode or in an automatically sequenced video presentation.

In 1991, Infotouch Marketing Corporation offered a program that does not need to use the power of an authoring program such as *Hypercard.* Infolynx, a Macintosh product, lets the user point and click to build interactive black and white and high quality color multi-media presentations without any programming or scripting. This

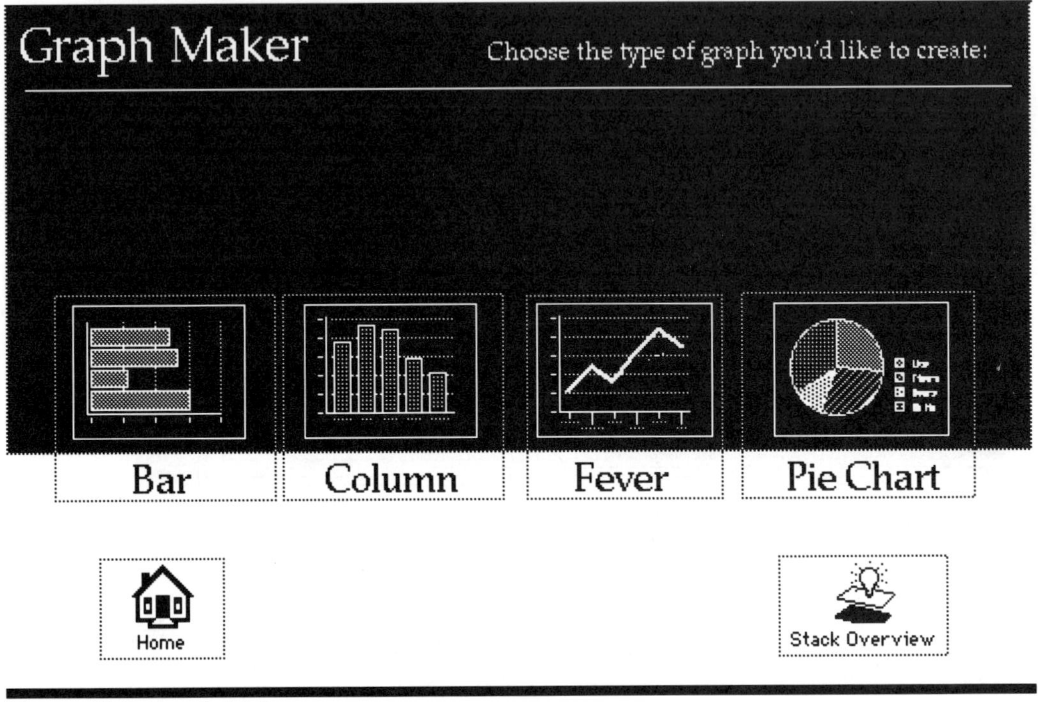

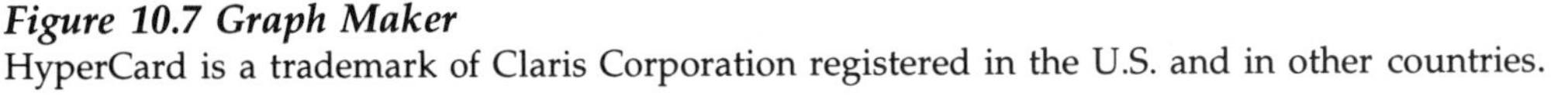

Figure 10.7 Graph Maker
HyperCard is a trademark of Claris Corporation registered in the U.S. and in other countries.

program is self launching, so the other users do not need the program to view the creator's presentation (Guglielmo, 1991). *Action* (Macro Mind) also shatters the prevailing opinion that multimedia is expensive and difficult. This program is a simple desktop presentation program designed to create on-screen presentations that tie together graphics and text that are created in the program with external sounds and graphics (Needleman, 1991).

Hypermedia Software

There is a trend for software to be hypermedia in nature, and many of the new programs like *Treehouse* are, in essence, hypermedia. Furthermore, application programs, like *The Bank Street Writer* (Scholastic) have hypermedia capabilities. Let us examine some of these diverse programs and discover what makes them particularly useful in a classroom setting.

Column Graph

Enter the labels and data to graph:

Acme Product Sales	Hyper-helper Units: thousands
Jan	19
Feb	29
Mar	32
Apr	43
May	55
Jun	53
Jul	48
Aug	44
Sep	54
Oct	62
Nov	89
Dec	96

Use this data for other graphs

Draw Graph

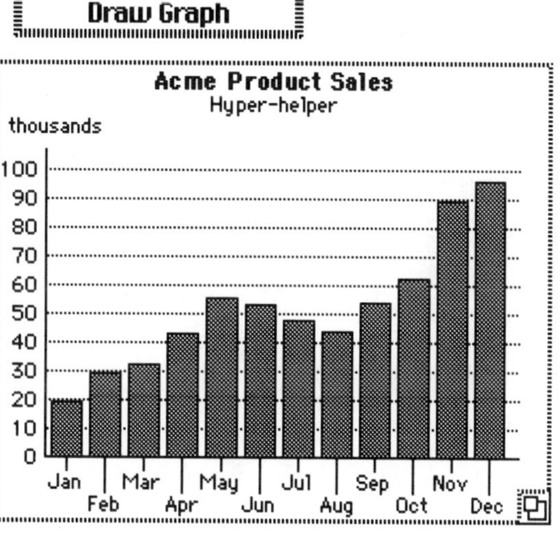

Figure 10.8 Column Graph
HyperCard is a trademark of Claris Corporation registered in the U.S. and in other countries.

Figure 10.9 Sample Card
Computer Consultants in Education.

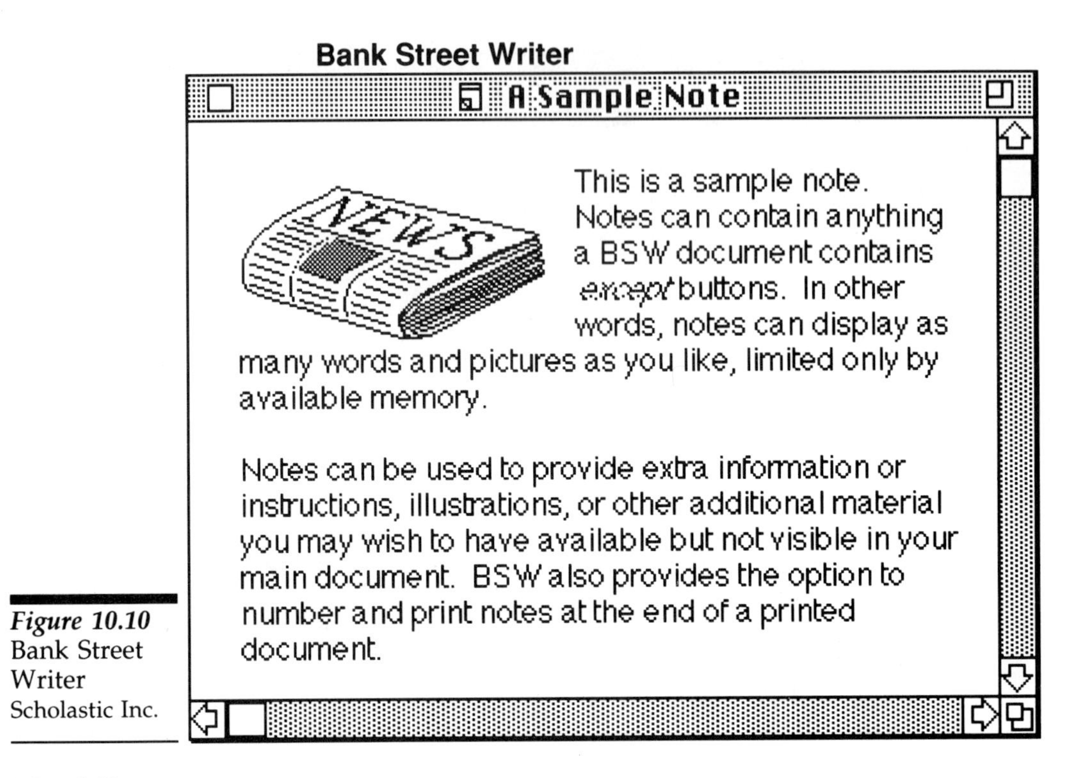

Bank Street Writer
A Sample Note
NEWS
This is a sample note. Notes can contain anything a BSW document contains except buttons. In other words, notes can display as many words and pictures as you like, limited only by available memory.
Notes can be used to provide extra information or instructions, illustrations, or other additional material you may wish to have available but not visible in your main document. BSW also provides the option to number and print notes at the end of a printed document.

Figure 10.10
Bank Street Writer
Scholastic Inc.

Word Processor

The Bank Street Writer has a hypertext button feature that lets the user turn the text into a hypermedia document. The user can insert buttons (like the sample note button in Figure 10.10) into the document and link these buttons to text, picture, sound, or voice annotation.

Literature

Hyperpole (Resource-Central: The New Yorker) is the first literary journal in hypermedia, and it is created with Roger Wagner's *Hyperstudio.* This eclectic magazine on disk contains articles in the form of stories, poems, paintings, original music, and photographs.

Social Studies

Point of View enables students to analyze historical events and write their own opinions about these events by providing the user with information from different points of view. The student can examine original documents and see or hear eyewitness testimony, essays, pictures, statistics, video, sound, and even animation. Each point of view includes information about politics, government, art, music, literature, daily life, science, technology, and other experiences. Students view charts, maps, and text that

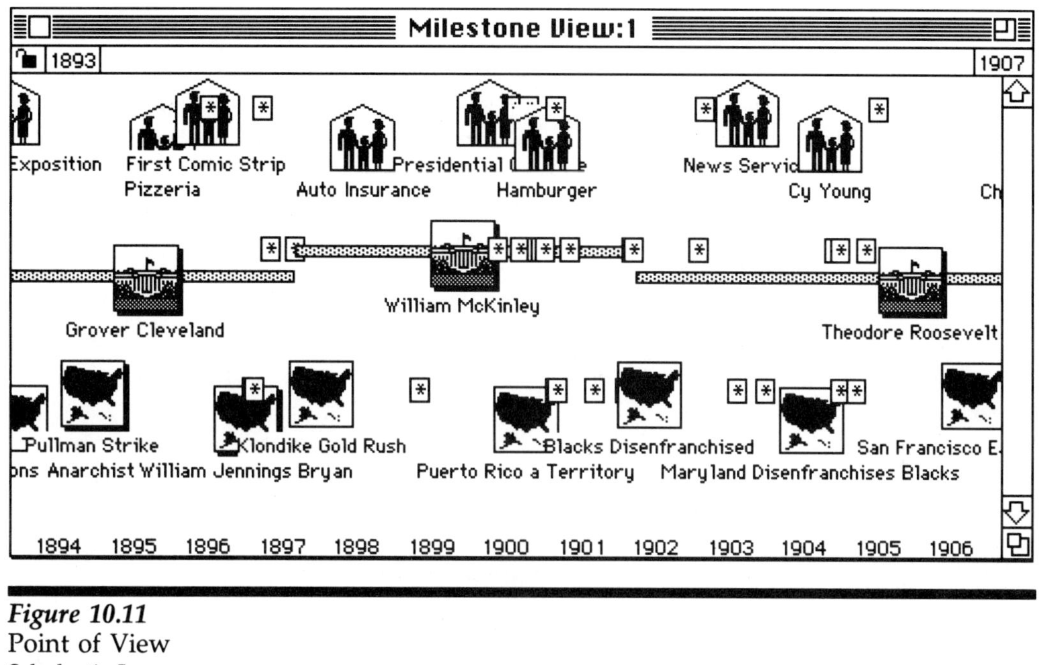

Figure 10.11
Point of View
Scholastic Inc.

can be cut and pasted into a word processing program to produce elegant reports. This program is useful to the student who wants to do historical research and to the researcher who wishes to author his own point of view for making an exciting hypermedia presentation. The program lets users integrate computer graphics, text, charts, animation, videodisc footage, and sound.

Students can access the information in *Point of View* by observing data in ten ways called "views." For example, when students choose the picture view of Lincoln, the computer displays the graphic image; and when students select the sound view, the computer plays digitized sound, as in JFK's "Inaugural Address:' "And so, my fellow Americans, ask not what your country can do for you; ask what you can do for your country." When students select a document view, they look at historical documents like the "Gettysburg Address," and when they select a milestone view, a chronological arrangement of events is displayed in Figure 10.11.

The chart and map views look at the same data in different configurations. For instance, students might look at population data as depicted in a line graph, data table, or column charts and then use a map to see this data again. The essay view is a simple word processor that lets users compose title pages or short explanations. Finally, the autoscroll feature lets users move along a time line automatically, while the presentation view is a built-in slide show feature.

Another inventive program in the Social Studies area is the Deluxe Edition of *Where in the World Is Carmen SanDiego?* This IBM version has Carmen and her gang of ten villains and new recruits stealing treasures in 45 countries all over the world. This edition features 62 animations, over 2,500 clues, digitized photo real location graphics originating from National Geographic Society slides, digitized sound, and composed music. The players learn about world geography, study facts and acquire research skills. This edition offers a higher level of difficulty than the original version because it has been expanded to include three world map representations and a 1,300 page encyclopedia of American culture and history covering such topics as science, art, music, and philosophy.

Hypermedia programs are being developed in other areas of the curriculum besides social studies. For example, there are many programs that emphasize language development and mathematical skills.

Exploration, Language Arts, and Mathematics

McGee, Katie's Farm, and *McGee at the Fun Fair* (Lawrence Productions) and *Playroom* and *Treehouse* (Brøderbund) are examples of quality hypermedia programs. The McGee series consists of early learning programs where the child clicks on various objects on the screen and these objects respond with speech and movement. These programs let the child make decisions about real life situations. In the first program McGee completes the tasks that most children accomplish in the morning: he brushes his teeth and goes to the bathroom. In the second program he visits Katie's farm to ride a horse and go fishing, pick raspberries, and gather eggs. In the most recent program McGee and his best friend, Tony, attend the summer Fun Fair and enjoy a day of entertainment: a clown twists balloons into animals, a one-man band creates music, and a guitar player strums a few chords. In the process, McGee makes quite a few friends. These programs are engaging introductions to the computer for small children and they encourage communication skills because the child discusses what is happening on the screen.

Playroom and *Treehouse* (Brøderbund) take this art form a step further. *Playroom* is directed at five and six year olds, while *Treehouse* is meant for the 6 to 9 year old age group. In *Playroom* the child can spend many hours exploring games, toys, and surprises. Every game, toy, and surprise has something to teach, and this program skillfully uses animation, sound, music, and graphics to accomplish this task. (See chapter 8 for a more complete discussion of *Playroom.*)

Treehouse, an extremely innovative program, is built around the theme of a child's on-screen tree house. This program's hideaway is filled with games and activities

Figure 10.12
The Treehouse
Screen shot from The Treehouse, copyright Brøderbund Software, Inc., 1991.

designed to help the child discover science, math, language, art, history, and music. The child is introduced to a possum who acts as his playmate, accompanying him through the program. *Treehouse* contains seven interactive games with sound effects and animations that teach a variety of skills. The main screen shown (Figure 10.12) includes activities such as a chalkboard for drawing and a calendar that reveals interesting historical events that occurred on specific dates. The child uses a mouse, joystick, or keyboard to select six objects that will lead him or her to other activities: *A Puppet Theater* (language and dramatics art), *Road Rally* (math), *Musical Keys* and *Musical Maze* (music) and *Animal Album* and *Guess My Animal* (science).

Another clever language arts program is *Superstory Tree* (Scholastic). This hypermedia program combines text, digitized sound, sound effects, music, special effects, and art. Using the program's graphics tools, students can write branching

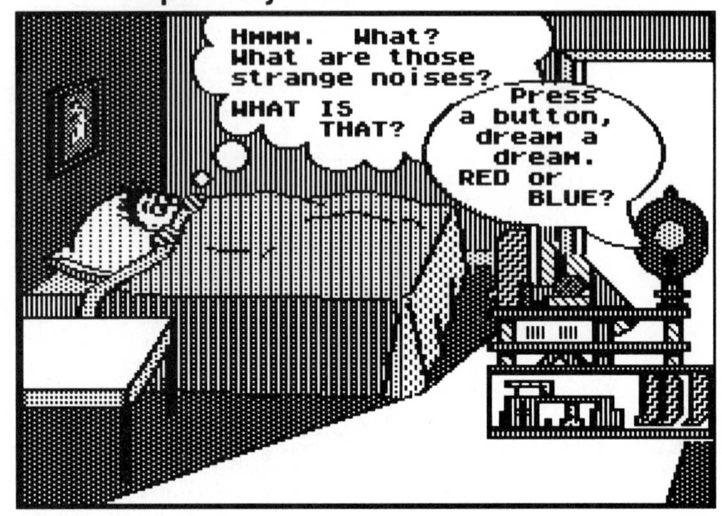

Figure 10.13
Superstory Tree
Scholastic Inc.

interactive stories with graphics, special effects, and sounds. *Superstory Tree's* interactive stories allow students to make choices that branch out to different options as illustrated by the sample screen shot (Figure 10.13) that asks the reader to make a choice between a red or a blue dream.

The new genre these days is CD-ROM based, interactive books. Brøderbund's Living Books Children's Series, *Just Grandma and Me,* a picture book by Mercer Mayer, captures the illustrations of the original book. It includes this story in English, Spanish, and Japanese, adds clever quips and dialogue, and animates the characters that fill the pages. There are hidden buttons, and if the user clicks on the same object in different places, various performances occur. Children can go through a book several times and see something different each time.

Another type of hypermedia program is the self-running demonstration.

Self-Running Demonstrations

Slide Shop (Scholastic) lets the student create audio-visual presentations on the computer as well as self-running, slide show disks, videotape presentations, printed handouts, and titles for videotapes. Figure 10.14 shows a slide produced from *Slide Shop.*

The slide includes text, clip art, backgrounds, borders, or original art that the student creates with the program's built-in graphics tools. The student's presentation can also have sound effects, music, animation, and special effects. *Slide Shop* has a sound library with music, sound effects and digitized sounds, decorative borders, a

Slide Shop

Figure 10.14
Slide Shop
Scholastic Inc.

script writer, and a clip art library. In addition to all this, a slide shop user can use other programs' clip art or Scholastic's *Sound and Graphics Boosters.*

VCR Companion, also produced by Scholastic, permits the computer user to create colorful titles, credits, and introductions for videotapes. This particular program includes fonts, full-screen graphics, animations, icons, borders, and more. The program user needs no special programming, wiring, or hardware setup to take advantage of *VCR Companion.* The student uses the regular RCA monitor cable to connect the computer and the VCR in order to add introductions, intermissions, credits, and professional-style scene transitions.

Art

In the art arena, nothing compares with *Kid Pix* (Brøderbund) as a hypermedia program for three year olds to adults. Each paint tool makes a sound—the pencil scratches, the brush ''bloops,'' and the moving tool ''vrooms'' like a truck's engine. In addition to these entertaining sounds, the color paint program contains soda pop bubbles and wacky brushes that drip paint. Many of these brushes are animated and grow into different objects. There are electric mixer tools that splash or drop big blobs of paint on the individual's creation. There are also 80 images that kids can ''stamp'' onto their drawings and unusual erasers, such as a firecracker eraser that blows things to bits. Users can even record personal messages that play every time they open a drawing if the Mac has a microphone. *Kid Pix* comes with hidden pictures (Figure 10.15) that the person uncovers by selecting the question mark option and using the eraser.

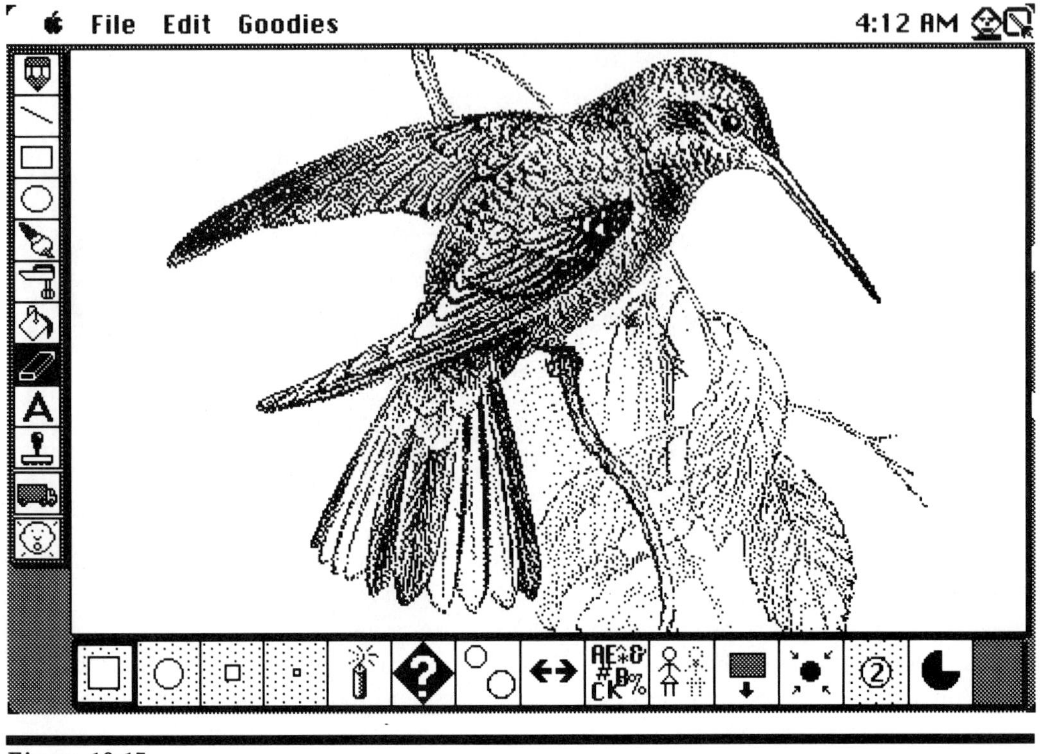

Figure 10.15
Kid Pix
Graphics created using Kid Pix, copyright Brøderbund Software, Inc.

Additionally, a child can import a variety of computer-generated images from clip art, digitized photos, *Print Shop* graphics, or pictures that are created with other paint program like *Superpaint.*

Science

In the sciences, a scintillating hypermedia program is *Interactive NOVA Animal Pathfinders* (Scholastic). Using a Macintosh computer and videodisc player, the students are able to link full-motion videos and slides from the award-winning NOVA television series to a data base of text and graphics cards. The students can work alone or in small groups to probe the science information, sights, and sounds; in the process they learn important science content and develop critical thinking skills. This program addresses topics such as animal classification, migration, adaptation, evolution, and behavior. *Animal Pathfinders* is

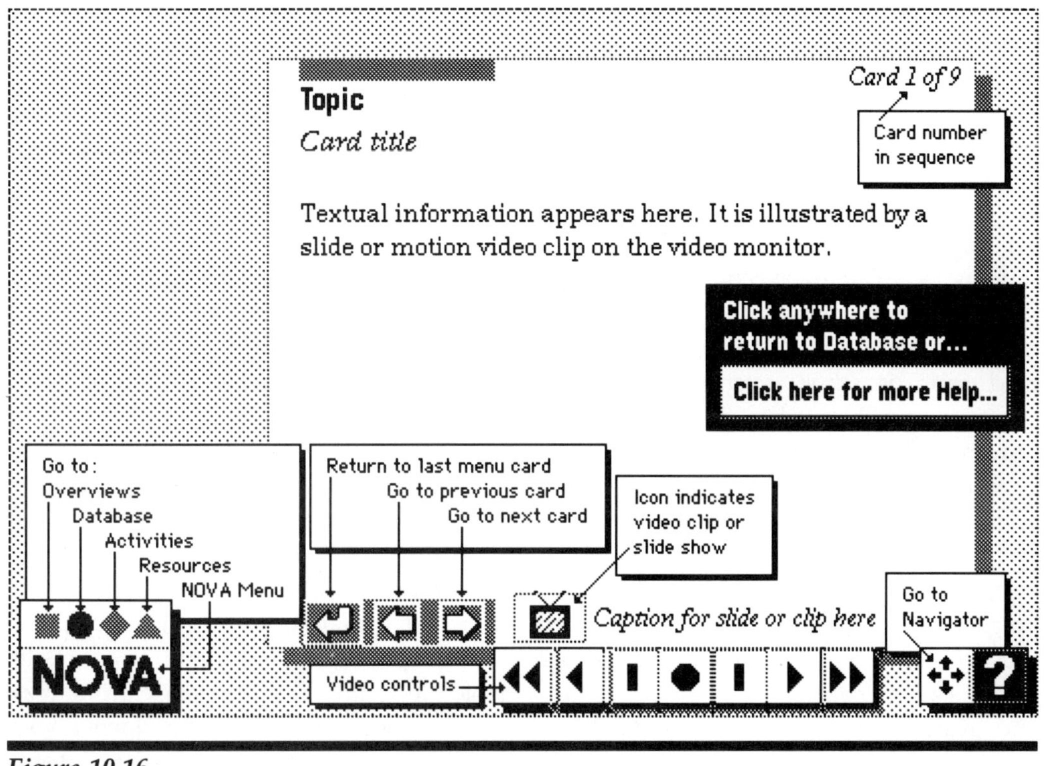

Figure 10.16
Interactive NOVA Animal Pathfinders
Scholastic Inc.

accessed through easy-to-use icons and menus where the students point and click to control the multimedia resources. Simultaneously, they view informative text or graphics on the computer screen and the related video clip or slide on the color monitor. Figure 10.16 shows schematic of the operating procedure of this program.

The next Scholastic programs in this series will focus on human reproductive biology and environmental and ecological issues.

Classroom Suggestions

The teacher or student has a rich selection of software and hardware to choose from in order to develop a first class, hypermedia presentation. For example, students can use a desktop publishing package such as *Children's Writing and Publishing Center* and *The*

Writing Center (Learning Co.) to write and illustrate stories that combine text with graphics. They can also create their own motion pictures with sight and sound by using a video disk player or by inventing their own interactive, branching stories using *Superstory Tree.* The teacher can generate a slide show which explains cell mitosis along with canned music, sound effects, and digitized human voices. A teacher can ask students to use a tape recorder to record interviews on the overcrowding of schools and make these presentations come alive with the background sounds, such as the noise of children in an overcrowded classroom. The pupils can also write audio presentations in the form of sound effects that are synchronized with words from scripts they have written.

Many other possibilities for hypermedia use in classrooms exist. The teacher can use the video camera, the camcorder, and the T.V. to prepare interesting film clips of field trips or school events. A video camera presentation can be combined with computer graphics, photographs, animation, sound, and music. Teachers or students can create videotapes with computer titles and credits using programs such as *VCR Companion* or *Slide Shop,* or digitizers such as *ComputerEyes.* For instance, the instructor might be doing a report on the different types of clouds. To make this report more interesting, video shots of the actual clouds would be recorded and a program such as *Deluxe Paint II* used to add graphic screen illustrations. In the finished hypermedia presentation, each type of cloud would have a text explanation, sound effects, and music. Finally, when students write stories in class, they may use software programs to create screens consisting of text, graphics, music, and clip art. The class can analyze and evaluate these self-running programs and use the best samples for open house presentations. In **Appendix A** the reader will find an annotated list of useful hypermedia software and hardware.

Before leaving our discussion of hypermedia, let's consider some of the benefits and problems of this new technology.

Pros and Cons of Hypermedia

Hypermedia is entertainment that may effectively mesmerize its audience with spectacular presentations. A student plugged into a workstation that has text, graphics, film clips, still photographs, sound effects, and moving maps is very likely to be an involved student! Teachers have the power to combine sound, image, and written text into their own personal productions and this is a positive attribute because of its educational implications. One of the teacher's first responsibilities is to motivate students to learn, and the hypermedia presentation addresses this concern. Using *Hypercard* products, students are not passive receptacles of knowledge; rather, they learn by following the paths and clicking on the stacks. The technology facilitates the development of research skills and encourages cooperative learning and problem solving. Reluctant readers are motivated to read and inquisitive students have the freedom to explore topics independently. All students are able to acquire depth of knowledge on whatever stack is being utilized.

Researchers like Marchionini (1988) feel there are important contributions that hypermedia systems offer for educators. First, the student has quick and easy access to large amounts of information in a variety of formats. The learner can easily use this diverse material stored in a compact form to follow paths that point out relationships between items or create their own interpretations. Second, the environment offers a high level of learner control because the user may choose predetermined paths through the lesson or paths that suit individual interests and abilities. Third, hypermedia gives the teacher and student an opportunity to change roles. The teacher can investigate tours that the learner took by using the hypermedia program and later the teacher can discuss the learner's observations with the students.

While it is obvious that there is great potential for hypermedia, there are also problems that must be addressed. One key question concerns the overburdened teacher's responsibility in this process: how is a teacher going to find the time to learn hypermedia and the time to devise hypermedia presentations? The average time to put together a decent hypermedia presentation is from 200 to 400 hours. Second, while there is general agreement that this media stimulates in depth-knowledge, whether it fosters breadth of knowledge is yet to be determined. This is a point which requires further research because it is not clear that students are receiving complete or comprehensive information. Also unclear are the implications of random learning that are possible when students determine their own program. Finally, some critics question the value of hypermedia, claiming that it is all form and little substance. Teachers who prepare these presentations do spend inordinate amounts of time and energy so that their presentations will look professional on the screen. It could be the case that this time is being diverted from attending to key content. A presentation ending with a barrage of images that have a limited connection with a topic may be a way of assuring emotional involvement, but the price may be real learning.

Fiderio (1988) believes that "Hypermedia is an immature technology with many problems yet to be solved." He describes some of the negatives: (1) There are problems developing and maintaining sound, underlying data modes, and controlled data linkages. (2) Users need guidance because they can easily become lost in obscure links in a data base before learning the subject basics. (3) Students may be attracted to tangential topics and be diverted away from subject matter that is relevant. (4) Teachers may also have difficulty in breaking the information into smaller, more organized components. (5) Other critics don't want hypermedia to substitute for books and the library. (6) The cost of hardware and the large memory requirements of hypermedia may make hypermedia prohibitive for many schools.

In conclusion, hypermedia is so embryonic a technology that research on its roles in classrooms is almost nonexistent and certainly inconclusive (Bruder, 1991). Do the benefits outweigh the problems? In the end, each individual educator must decide whether to embrace the technology of the 1990s, adopt selected hypermedia software, or cautiously await further developments.

Summary

The author discussed the origins of hypermedia and defined hypermedia as a general term for using the computer to input, manipulate, and output graphics, sound, text, and audio in the presentation of information. In the process, the reader learned how hypermedia authoring tools such as *HyperCard* operate as valuable implements for instruction. The reader also became familiar with some of the unique hypermedia software that is available for the classroom; and with suggested activities for utilizing it. Following are a mastery test, classroom projects, and suggested readings and references. In **Appendix A** the reader will find an annotated list of hypermedia software and hardware.

Chapter Mastery Test

1. What is hypermedia?
2. What are two advantages of using your own authoring tool for a hypermedia presentation?
3. Who invented *Hypercard* and why was it so revolutionary?
4. Define the following hypermedia terms: cards, stacks, and buttons. Give an example of each.
5. What is the major disadvantage of using programs like *HyperScreen, HyperCard,* and *HyperStudio?*
6. *HyperCard* has been characterized as being similar to a database. Explain this statement.
7. Discuss how you would use the button function in a *HyperCard* program. Name at least three types of buttons and give examples of each one.
8. Describe a hypermedia program available in each of the following subject areas: social studies, language arts, science, art, and mathematics.
9. Suppose you will be buying two hypermedia programs. Which two will you choose? What are the reasons for your choices?
10. Discuss the advantages and disadvantages of hypermedia in school settings.

Classroom Projects

1. Learn a hypermedia application (such as *HyperStudio, HyperCard,* or *HyperScreen*) and write a short report describing its strengths and weaknesses.
2. Explain some mathematical concept by generating your own slide show, using software such as *Slide Show.*
3. Tape record an interview on some important topic. Write a script using the speaker's words and your own synchronized sound effects.
4. Use a camcorder to record an interesting event or trip and combine this with animation, speech, and music, using one or more of the software programs discussed in this chapter.

Suggested Readings and References

Arnett, Nick. "Multimedia on the Macintosh." *InfoWorld* (9 April 1990): 79–80.

Bruder, Isabelle. "Multimedia—How It Changes the Way We Teach and Learn." *Electronic Learning* 11(1) (September 1991): 22–26.

Cable, Jeff. "Does HyperStudio Stack Up?" *A+ Incider* (September 1989): 44–48.

Camp, J and M. Cogan. "HyperCard: A Milestone in Educational Computing." *Electronic Learning,* 7(6), (March 1988): 46.

Conklin, Jeff. "A Survey of Hypertext." *IEEE Computer,* September 1987.

D'Ignazio, Fred. "Setting Up a Multi-media Classroom: A QuickStart Card." *Computers in the Schools* (Summer 1987): 10–12.

D'Ignazio, Fred. "Setting Up a Multi-Media Classroom of Today." *Phi Delta Kappan* (September 1988): 18–23.

D'Ignazio, Fred. "A New Curriculum Paradigm: The Fusion of Technology, the Arts, and Classroom Instruction." *The Computing Teacher* (April 1991): 45–48.

Field, Cynthia E. "Exploring Hypermedia." *Incider A+* (November 1990): 36–44.

Fiderio, Janet. "Grand Vision." *Byte,* (13)10, (1 October 1988): 237–242.

Finkel, LeRoy. *Technology Tools in the Information Age Classroom.* Wilsonville, OR: Franklin Beedle and Associates, Inc., 1991.

Forrest, C. "Technological Convergence." *Tech Trends* (November/December 1988): 8–12.

Goodman, Danny. *The Complete HyperCard Handbook 2.0.* New York: Bantam, 1990.

Guglielmo, Connie. "Multimedia Makers Get Point, Click." *Macweek,* 5(18) (May 1991): 22.

Jensen, Eric. "HyperCard and AppleShare Help At-Risk Students" *The Computing Teacher* (March 1991): 26–30.

Johnson, Stuart J. "MultiMedia: Myth vs. Reality." *InfoWorld,* 12(8) (19 February 1990): 47–52.

Malnig, Anita. "New Chapter for Electronic Books." *MacWeek* 6(2) (13 January 1992): 42 & 47.

Marchionini, G. "Hypermedia and Learning: Freedom and Chaos." *Educational Technology,* 28(11) (1988): 8–12.

McCarthy, Robert. "Multimedia: What's the Excitement All About?" *Electronic Learning,* 8(8) (June 1989): 26–30.

McMillan, Gordon. "Multimedia: An Educator's Link to the 90s." *The Computing Teacher* (November 1990): 7–10.

Needleman, Raphael. "'Action' Takes the Pain out of Creating Presentations." *InfoWorld,* 13(32) (12 August 1991): 1, 91.

Nelson, Theodore H. *Dream Machines: New Freedoms Through Computer Screens—A Minority Report.* Chicago: Hugo Books Service, 1974.

Nelson, Theodore H. "Managing Immense Storage." *BYTE,* January 1988.

Porter, Anne E. "Scavenged Idea and Virtual Hypermedia." *The Computing Teacher* (May 1991): 38–40.

Rogers, Michael. "Here Comes Hypermedia." *Newsweek* (3 October 1988): 44–45.

Sachs, Robert Allen. *So You Want To Do a Science Project?* CCIE. 2371 Arminta Street, West Hills, California 91304.

Stefananc, S. and L. Weiman. "Macworld Multimedia: Is It Real?" *MacWorld* (April 1990): 116–123.

Statt, Paul. "The Apple II Culture Reborn." *Incider A+* (February 1991): 37–44.

Wright, Robert. "Multimedia: What Is It?" *The MacValley Voice.* 6(10) (October 1990): 1, 6–7.

Computer Hardware and Telecommunications

11

Objectives

Upon completing this chapter the student will be able to:

1. Describe the major input devices and explain how each works.
2. Describe the major output devices and explain how each works.
3. List the salient features of the different printers, monitors, and storage devices.
4. Choose the appropriate hardware in terms of established criteria.
5. Define telecommunication and explain how it operates.
6. Describe networking and explain how a network operates.

Computer Hardware

The hardware of a computer system includes the electronic components, boards, wires, and peripherals. In contrast, the software instructs the computer hardware what task to perform. If a user has only hardware, the person is powerless to accomplish anything with the computer because it is similar to having a car without fuel. Moreover, buying hardware is a complicated and time-consuming job, that requires an examination of many factors. The computer buyer should first determine primary needs and then estimate future needs. For example, the user might be satisfied initially with *Children's Writer and Publishing Center,* but might soon require a sophisticated desktop package, such as *Pagemaker.* If the prospective purchaser wants to use an advanced spreadsheet or statistical software, s/he must buy computer hardware with ample memory. The purchaser has to spend time learning about available hardware, its capabilities, and its functions. Current magazines (*MacUser*) are helpful to alert the purchaser to the latest hardware developments because hardware changes are so rapid. The informed purchaser can save time and money by being prepared to ask appropriate questions. In the course of this chapter, the reader will look at some of the factors that most influence a buyer's decision and examine some of the basic hardware equipment available.

Input Devices

An input device gives information to the computer system so that it can perform its tasks. Years ago, the keypunch machine was the major means of input, whereas today it is the keyboard.

Keyboard

The computer **keyboard** is similar to a standard typewriter, but with extra keys such as the function keys and the numeric pad. Figure 11.1 shows the Macintosh standard keyboard with a numeric pad located on the right for quick data entry.

Although the keyboard is the primary way of entering data, it is not efficient for making screen selections. Furthermore, if the user is an inexperienced typist, he or she is more likely to make mistakes. Because of these drawbacks, computer manufacturers created pointing devices that would lessen the need for a keyboard. Today many computers use both a keyboard and supplemental pointing devices.

Pointing Devices

Light Pen

The **light pen,** one of the first pointing devices (Figure 11.2), looks like a ball point pen connected to the computer by a cable.

This instrument, used in conjunction with a video display, has a light-sensitive, photoelectric cell in its tip and sends an electrical impulse to the computer that identifies its current location. These pens are used frequently for drawing. The software traces the movement of the light on the screen, filling in the lines the user draws. The computer user can then use the light pen to select items displayed on the screen by touching the pen to the item; however, as a selection device, the light pen is not as effective as the mouse.

Figure 11.1
Computer Keyboard
© Dubl-Click Software Inc.

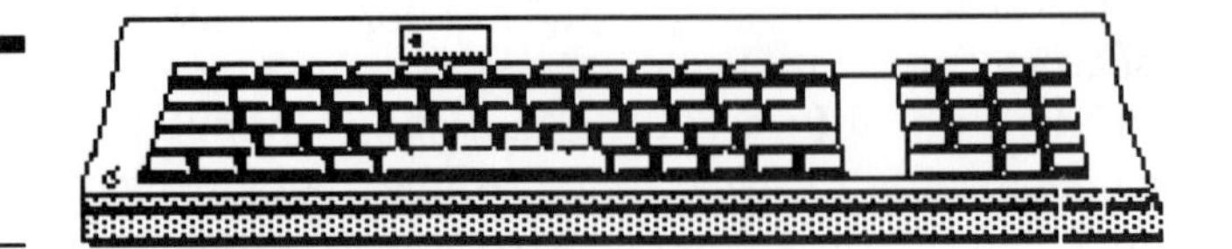

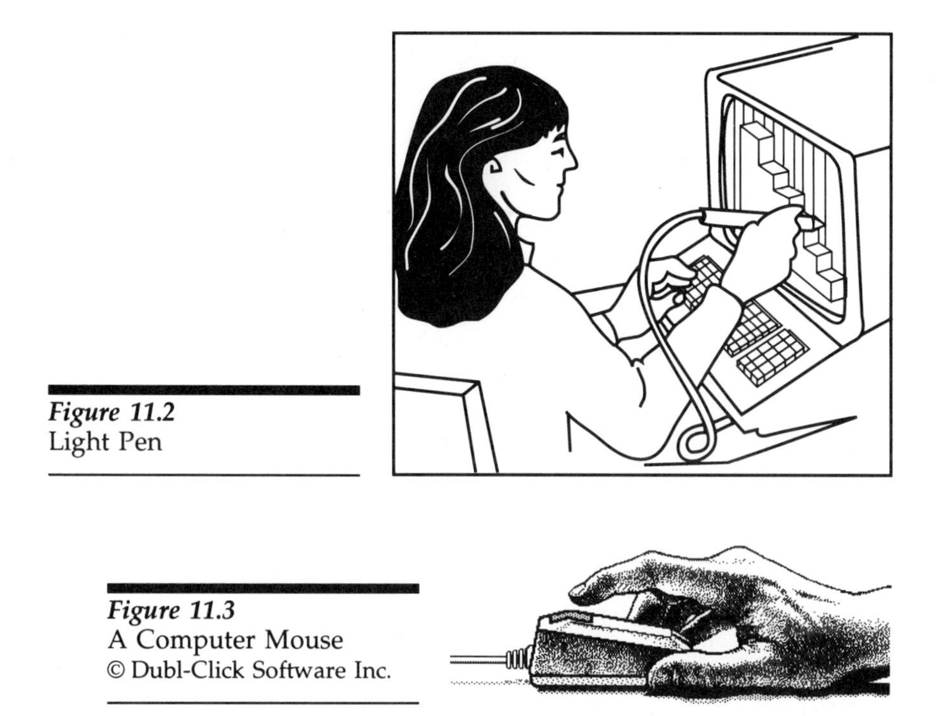

Figure 11.2
Light Pen

Figure 11.3
A Computer Mouse
© Dubl-Click Software Inc.

Mouse

Originally designed by Xerox, the **mouse** (Figure 11.3), was popularized by the Apple Macintosh computer. The original mouse was a palm-like object that looked like a box with a button on it and was connected to the computer by either a cable or a wire. Presently mouses come in different shapes and sizes, some cordless, with one to three buttons. They have two different internal mechanisms: mechanical, and optical. The mechanical mouse has a rubber coated ball on the bottom of its case, and when the user moves the mouse, the ball rotates. The optical mouse shows its position by detecting reflections from a light-emitting diode[1] and requires a special metal pad to reflect the beam.

The movement of the mouse is represented by a cursor or blinking light on the screen. For example, if the user moves the mouse to the right, the cursor moves to the right, and if the user pushes the mouse's button, the cursor is positioned at that particular location. Furthermore, the mouse can select items from a pull down menu, delete and insert text, and can be used with paint/draw software like *Superpaint*. The mouse is easy to use and install; however, it is awkward for delicate drawing and it requires space to operate. An alternative device that is stationary, requiring less desk space, is the trackball.

1. A diode is an electronic component that acts as a one-way valve used primarily as a temperature or a light sensor (Freeman, 1991).

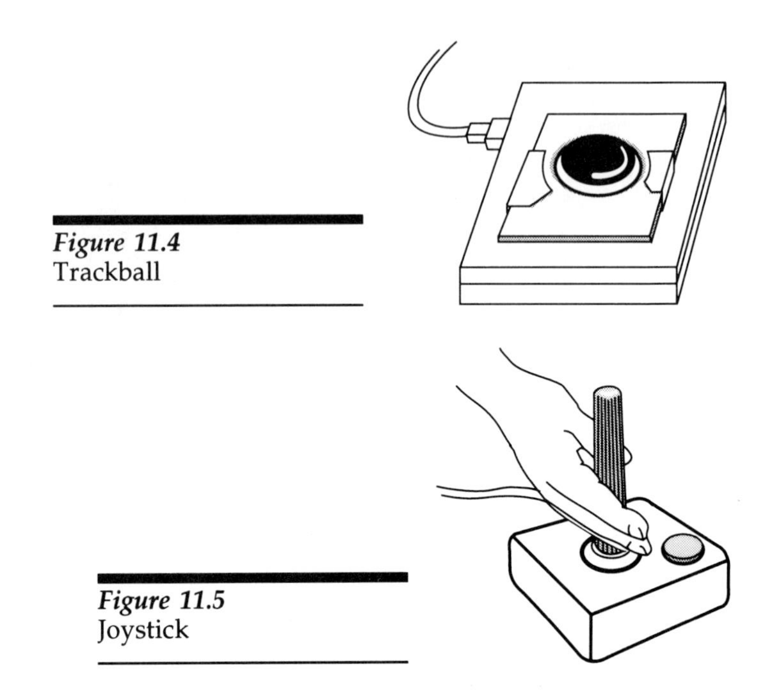

Figure 11.4
Trackball

Figure 11.5
Joystick

Trackball

The **trackball** (Figure 11.4), which does the same tasks as the mouse, operates with a rotating metal ball inset in a small, box-like device and does not require a desktop.

The user rolls the exposed part of the trackball, producing cursor movement on the screen.

Joystick

The **joystick** (Figure 11.5), a small box like object with a moving stick and buttons, is used primarily for games, educational software, and CAD systems.

Most joysticks move in a complete circle where the user manipulates the stick to position the cursor and clicks on a button to send impulses to the computer. The joystick does not interfere with the user's view of the screen (like a light pen) nor does it require the movement of an object (like a mouse). A joystick is fun to use, because of the speed with which it moves the cursor on the screen, but it is awkward in selecting items from a menu—a strength of the touch screen.

Touch Sensitive Screen

The **touch screen** is a pointing device where the user places his fingers to enter data or make selections. There are two types of screens, those designed with a pressure-sensitive panel mounted in front of the screen like *Touch Window* (Personal Touch) and those that involve the use of a special, touch sensitive monitor like the IBM *Info Window System*. The software program for the touch screen displays different options on the screen in a graphic button format, allowing the user to make a selection. For example, rather than type an answer to a multiple choice exam, the student would touch the answer button on the screen, and the screen would change in response to this action.

The touch screen offers a real advantage to handicapped students because it is fast and a natural way to enter data, to make selections, and to issue commands. Despite these benefits, a touch screen is unable to input large amounts of data and cannot point to a single character. Moreover, it is fatiguing to use for a long period of time, and the screen quickly gets fingermarked. Lessons created on one variety of touch screen may not work on another because of software incompatibility. Touch screen technology is still evolving, and in the future it may play a key role in the educational use of the computer.

Besides pointing devices, there is a wide selection of alternate input devices for use in the workplace. Many are optical scanning devices that utilize laser capabilities. The laser searches for groups of dots that represent marks, characters, or lines. It is the program and the way the computer massages the data that distinguish these devices from each other.

Alternate Input Devices

Optical Mark Reader

Initially **optical mark readers (OMR)** were designed to read penciled or graphic information on exam answer sheets. Lamps furnish light reflected from the paper, and the amount of reflected light is measured by a photocell. When a mark is blackened on a sheet of paper, the amount of light is less than if that mark were not there. The answers are scored by having the optical mark reader compare the pattern of marks on the papers with the correct pattern that is stored in the computer's memory. The optical mark reader is used by many schools and school districts to grade standardized tests. Besides grading tests, with the proper software the OMR is useful for keeping library records, for keeping attendance records and reporting grades.

Optical Character Reader

The **optical character reader (OCR)** was devised using techniques developed from the optical mark reader. Ordinarily this device uses laser technology or a light-sensing mechanism to interpret data. The OCR can read typed or printed characters directly from the original document, and advanced systems can recognize hand printing. A common application of the optical character reader is the neighborhood gas station where the attendant makes use of OCR technology when using an OCR imprinting device to process a credit card sale. The customer receives a receipt, and the service attendant forwards the heavier credit card invoice to the company's center, where an optical character reader interprets this invoice and prepares a bill. The advantage of this type of system is the fact that the person can use a source document as direct input into the computer, avoiding the inaccuracies that occur from transcribing data. Today there are many OCR devices that can be adapted to computers for less than $300.

Magnetic Ink Character Recognition Reader

The **Magnetic Ink Character Recognition Reader (MICR)** recognizes characters that use a special magnetic ink developed by the American Banking Association. All the checks issued by a bank are coded with special ink and characters so that a MICR can read them. This coding identifies a person's bank account number. MICR sorts and processes these checks and creates a bank statement for the customer. The MICR reader is also used to read and process utility bills and stock proxy statements.

Bar-Code Reader

The **bar-code reader** was first devised by the railroads to identity the location of its railroad cars. This code's most popular application is the supermarket where the majority of the products sold use the Universal Product Code (UPC). See Figure 11.6.

At the supermarket, the clerk reads the price of a product by passing a hand-held optical wand over the price label or by passing the can with the label over an optical reader. These readers are connected to computers that interpret the bar code, record the data, find the prices stored in their memory, and generate a sales receipt. The bar code reader also has many applications in a school setting. For example, library books are assigned bar code numbers that are placed on the books, a data base is created that contains the book's bar code numbers, and the students are issued library cards with bar code numbers. When a student checks out books, the librarian scans the student's library card, as well as each book that the student wants, and the computer records the

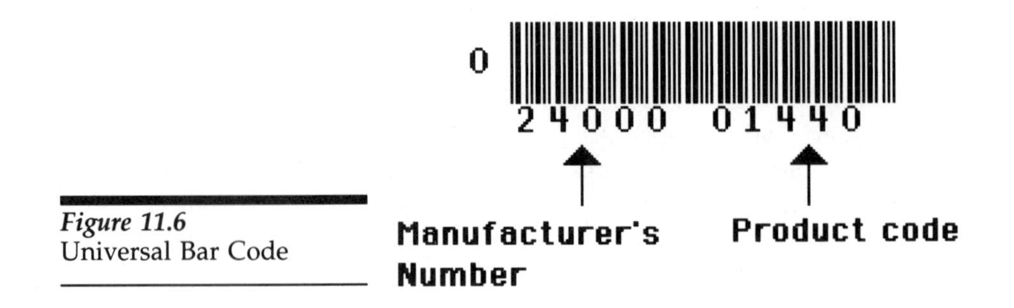

Figure 11.6
Universal Bar Code

A Sample Scan

Figure 11.7
A Sample Scan
© Logitech.

transactions. Other applications of the bar code are videodisc players and textbooks. Textbook publishers are now printing bar code in the margins of their books so that any student reading this text can wave the wand across a bar code and point at a disc player which transmits a signal to the video disc player to search and play the video portion that correlates with the text.

The Scanner

The scanner has been rediscovered because of its affordability and its usefulness for desktop publishing, optical character recognition, and faxing. The scanner has the ability to transform printed text or images into electronic images or text. Figure 11.7 is a scanned line art image from Scanman's *User's Manual.*

Scanners digitize photographs or line art and store the images as a file that can be transferred into a paint program or directly into a word processor. If the user creates a newsletter and wants to insert a picture into the text, s/he scans the picture, copies it, and then "pastes it" into the document. This input device can be in the form of a hand held scanner, or an overhead scanner, or a full size, flatbed scanner, depending upon the user's preferences and pocket book. A flatbed scanner easily scans documents, books, or periodicals because the user can open the lid of the scanner. It is more versatile than a hand scanner, which is less expensive and usually scans images that are smaller (Figure 11.8).

The **Caere** hand scanner combines scanning and optical character recognition into one small package. The overhead scans all the items that a flatbed does, as well as three dimensional objects. Scanners differ in resolution, which means the more dots the image contains, the sharper it is, and only the expensive scanners produce colors. Now let us conclude this discussion with the digital camera, graphics tablet, and the voice recognition system.

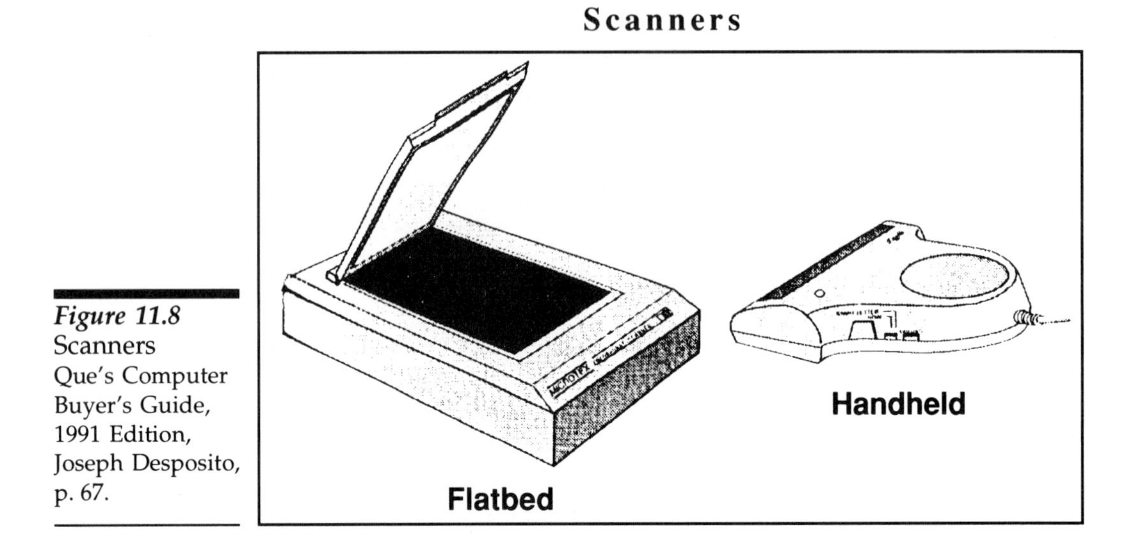

Figure 11.8
Scanners
Que's Computer Buyer's Guide, 1991 Edition, Joseph Desposito, p. 67.

Digital Camera

Logitech has a digital camera called the FotoMan that delivers eight-bit, gray-scale photo images to a Macintosh Computer without photo paper, scanner, chemicals, or film. This remarkable camera captures in a 1 Megabyte-RAM buffer and transmits these images by serial cable to the computer, where they can be saved in different formats. The company will shortly produce a color digital camera (*McManus,* 1992).

Graphics Tablet

The **graphics tablet** (Figure 11.9) is a plotting tablet that the user draws on to communicate with the computer. This device comes in different sizes, accompanied by pens or styluses. As the person draws, s/he makes contact with the surface of the plotting board, and a difference of electrical charge is detected.

An earlier, well-known graphics tablet was the *KoalaPad,* a small seven inch pad with a touch sensitive surface and a stylus. This pad let the user design endless combinations of graphic pictures easily. The graphics tablet today is widely used in art production and CAD for which there are many adaptations such as the *Light Writer.*

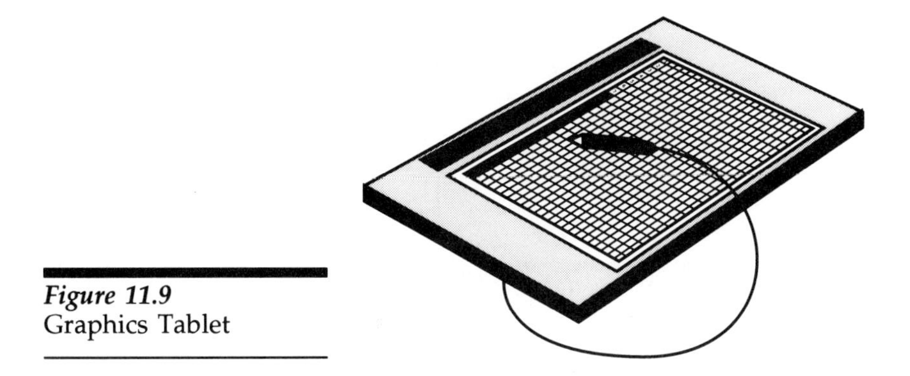

Figure 11.9
Graphics Tablet

Voice Recognition System

Still in its infancy stage, the **Voice Recognition System** shows the most potential for growth in the computer industry. This system converts the spoken word into binary patterns that are computer recognizable; it understands human speech. By speaking, the user can enter data or issue simple commands. The current systems require the user to train the system by pronouncing a few times the words that will be used. The system develops a pattern for these words and then stores them. When the user later says these words, the Voice Recognition System recognizes what is being said and performs the command. Presently there are voice recognition systems that let the user enter and store unlimited words. Using this type of system, a person then can communicate with the computer without using a keyboard or any other input device. Individuals who cannot type and handicapped persons who cannot use a handheld device will be able to operate the system.

Output Devices

Printers

When a person has finished typing a report on the computer, invariably this person wants to see a print out. One of the most notable output devices is the printer, which lets the computer user have a permanent record of his work by producing a print out, referred to as a "hard copy." Starting with the daisy-wheel printer, let us look at the most frequently used printers.

Daisy-Wheel Printer

The **daisy-wheel** is an impact printer that produces a typewritten quality print. This printer has its type characters set around a daisy-wheel (Figure 11.10), similar to a wagon wheel minus an outer ring. When the user types a character on the keyboard,

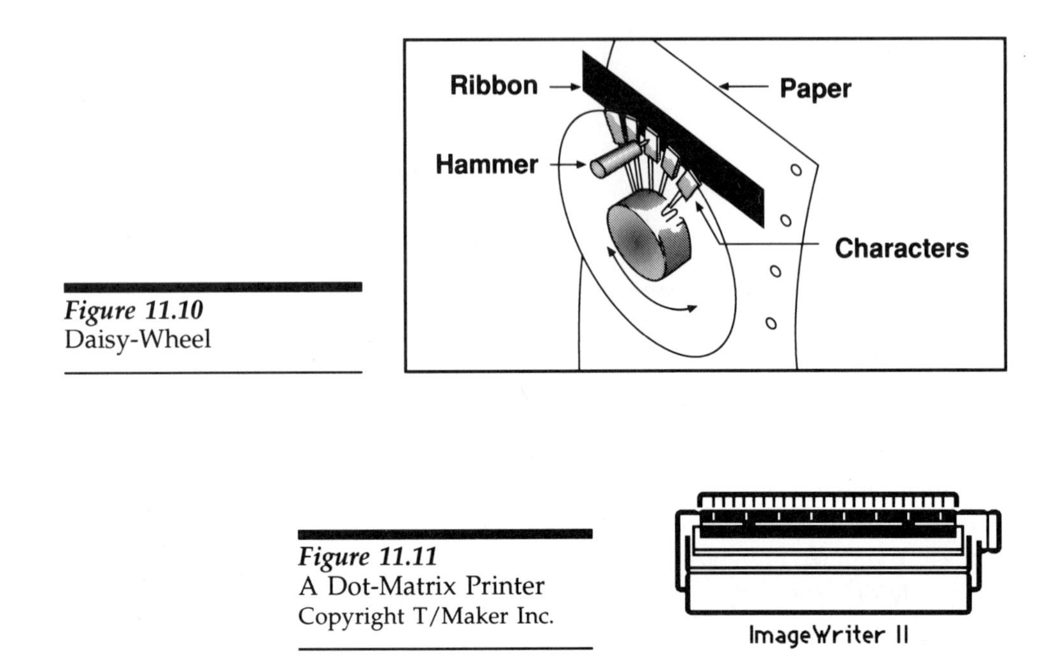

Figure 11.10
Daisy-Wheel

Figure 11.11
A Dot-Matrix Printer
Copyright T/Maker Inc.

the daisy-wheel rotates until the required character is under the hammer. The hammer then strikes the character onto the ribbon, resulting in an imprint on the paper. The daisy-wheel is mounted on the printer's frame, and the paper moves on a carriage like a typewriter. This printer can have many daisy-wheels whose typefaces are interchangeable. Because it cannot print graphics, is noisier, and is less reliable, the daisy-wheel has been superseded by the dot-matrix, ink jet, and laser printers.

Dot-Matrix Printer

For years, the **dot-matrix printer** was the most prevalent printer, but with the price reduction of laser printers and the advances in ink jet technology, this situation has changed. The dot-matrix is an impact printer, (Figure 11.11) that produces characters and graphic images by striking an inked ribbon with tiny metal rods called "pins."

When the movable print head, containing pins, is pressed against ribbon and paper, it causes small dots to print on the paper (Figure 11.12).

The print quality depends upon the number of pins the printer has; that is, a 24 pin printer produces better looking characters than a nine pin one. The majority of dot-matrix printers have a draft mode (producing grainier, less dense characters) and a near letter quality mode (NLQ) (producing print that is close to the quality of a typewriter).

Figure 11.12
Letter "A" on a Dot-Matrix Printer

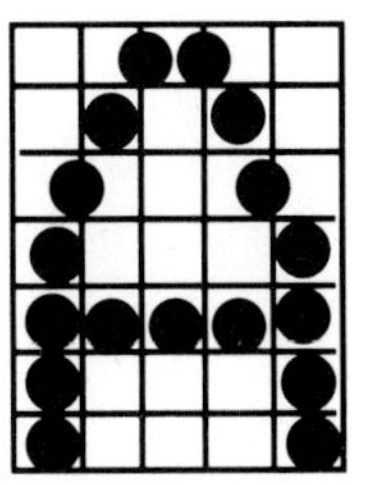

When purchasing a printer, speed is a consideration, especially when doing bulk mailing. Speed ratings for dot-matrix and ink jet printers are measured in characters per second (cps) and each printing mode has a separate rating. For example, the ImageWriter II has three modes of print quality: a draft, high speed 250 cps, a medium speed 180 cps, and a NLQ, 45 cps. For dot-matrix printers, slow speed results in better print quality.

Ink Jet Printer

The **ink jet printer** uses a nozzle that sprays a jet of ink onto a page of paper. These small, spherical bodies of ink are released through a matrix of holes to form characters. These printers produce high quality output, have few moving parts, and are quiet because they do not strike the paper like impact printers. However, the ink jet printers are slower than the dot-matrix or laser printers, and their ink can smear if the paper becomes moist.

Laser Printer

Producing near-professional quality print, the **laser printer,** (Figure 11.13) operates like a copying machine—with one important difference. The copying machine produces its image by focusing its lens on a paper, while the laser printer traces an image by using a laser beam that is controlled by the computer. Laser printers produce text and graphics with high resolution; however, the print quality is not as high as that obtained by a phototype machine used by commercial textbook publishers. There are many inexpensive laser printers on the market today, and it is becoming an increasingly popular printer.

Thermal Printer

Using heated wires, the **thermal printer** burns dots into a costly special paper. The least expensive models are slow and have poorer print quality compared to the other kinds of printers. The most useful thermal printers are miniature printers designed to produce labels, bank statements, and output in fax machines. The award-winning printer, Smart Label Printer (Figure 11.14), manufactured by Seiko Instruments produces a quality label in a matter of seconds.

Now let us turn to another category of output devices, screen displays.

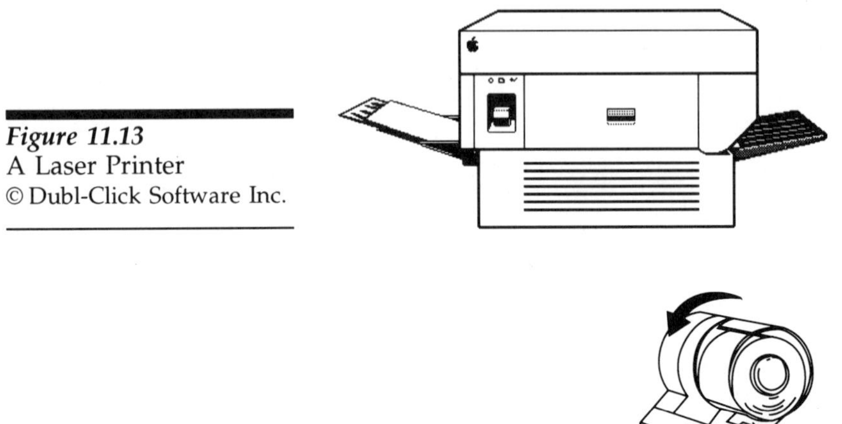

Figure 11.13
A Laser Printer
© Dubl-Click Software Inc.

Figure 11.14
Smart Label Printer
© Seiko Instruments.

Screen Displays

Cathode Ray Tube.

The cathode ray tube (CRT) is the basic element (Figure 11.15) used in a video terminal or T.V.

Figure 11.15
Cathode Ray Tube
(CRT)

There are two types of CRT screens, the standard television screen and the monitor. As a permanent display for the computer, the TV screen is inadequate because the colors tend to run together, making the picture unclear and the speed of receiving the picture slow. The television receiver does not have the capabilities of handling all the data that is being sent to it by the computer. However, in recent years, televisions have been designed to serve as video monitors.

The Monitor. As a display, the **monitor** is superior to the T.V. Although it looks like a television set, the monitor is designed to handle a wider and higher range of frequencies. There are three types of monitors: monochrome, composite, and RGB.

Monochrome. A **monochrome monitor,** the least expensive, produces output that has one foreground color and one background color. Common examples are white against a black background, green against a black background, or amber against a black background. This monitor is best used for text in word processing and business applications.

Composite Monitor. The **composite** color screen is similar to a color television set, but it can handle data quicker and has a sharper picture. This monitor accepts a standard analog video signal that mixes red, blue, and green signals to produce a color picture.

The RGB Monitor. Using three electronic guns, the **Red Green and Blue Monitor (RGB)**, generates three colors, red, green, and blue. This monitor, the most expensive, produces the sharpest images because of the separate video signals used for each of these guns. RGB monitors come in digital and analog varieties.[2] Figure 11.16 shows an RGB monitor.

Figure 11.17 represents a schematic of the inner workings of a RGB monitor.

Flat Panel Display

The **flat panel display** is a newer monitor development which will eventually replace the CRT. Found today in portable laptop computers, the flat panel uses a number of technologies (Figure 11.18).

The most commonly found flat screen displays are the plasma and liquid crystal displays (**LCD**). Used for calculators, watches, and laptop computers, the LCD is created by having a liquid crystal material positioned between two sheets of polarizing material squeezed between two glass panels. This display depends on reflected light, so the viewing angle is important; the image can disappear with the wrong angles and

2. An analog display is a "video display capable of rendering a continuous range (an indefinite number) of colors of gray shades, as opposed to digital display, which is capable of rendering only a finite number of colors." (Woodcock, 1991)

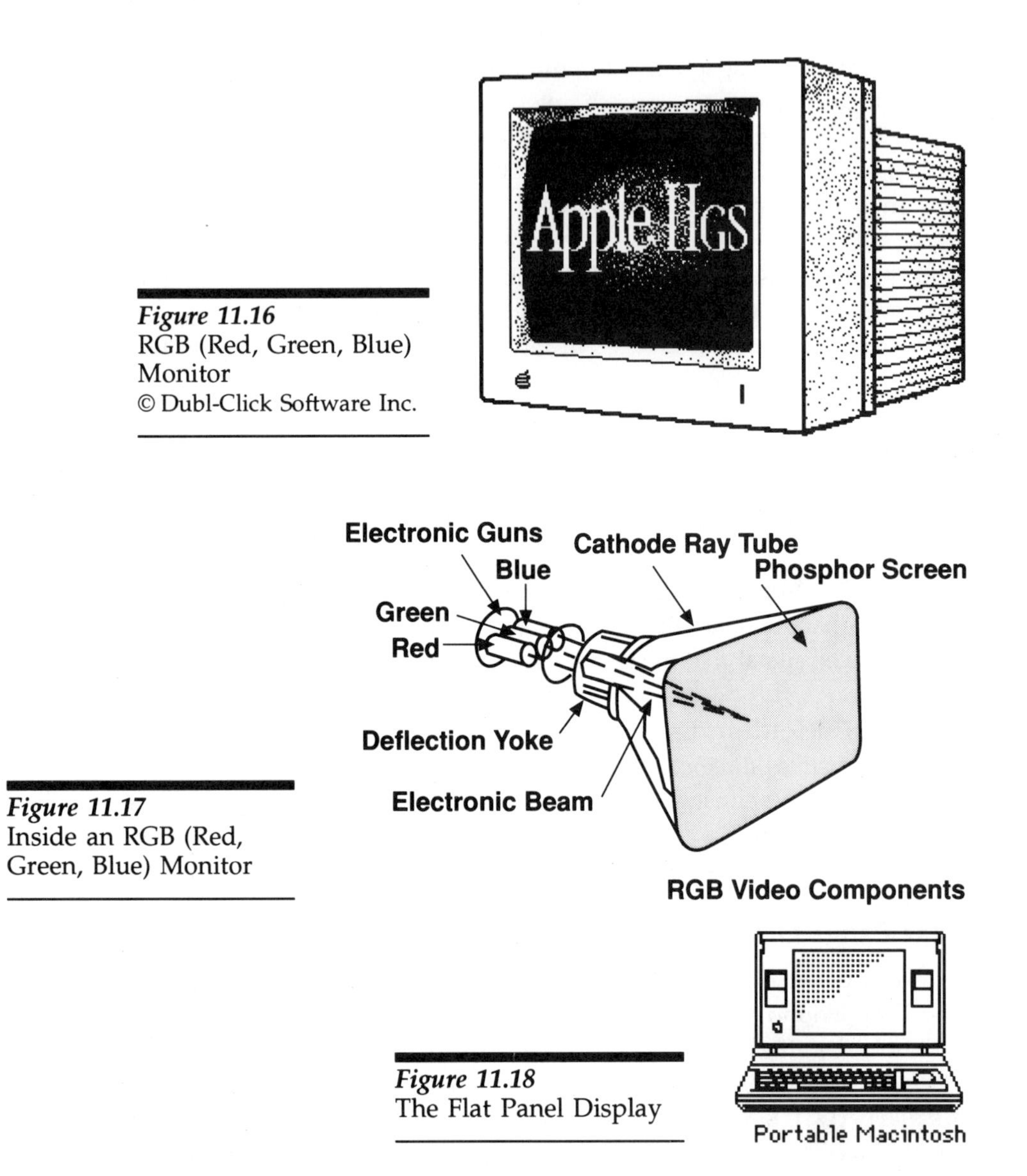

Figure 11.16
RGB (Red, Green, Blue) Monitor
© Dubl-Click Software Inc.

Figure 11.17
Inside an RGB (Red, Green, Blue) Monitor

Figure 11.18
The Flat Panel Display

inadequate adjustment of the contrast controls. Many LCD's are backlit to improve screen viewing. The plasma display is produced by a mixture of neon gases between two transparent panels, giving a very sharp, clean image with a wide viewing angle. The plasma display is found on higher end, laptop computers and is very expensive.

Another device, the projection panel, which uses LCD technology, is advantageous for business and education.

LCD Projection Panel

This **LCD panel** is important because it enables the classroom teacher to use the computer for the entire class. The LCD panel is a projector that receives computer output and displays it on a liquid crystal screen which the instructor places on top of an overhead projector. The overhead becomes the projector, displaying the programs that the computer generates on a large screen for the whole class to see. The picture can be adjusted by display adjustment and contrast controls. The projector panel looks like a piece of glass with a frame around it, and the size varies, depending upon the manufacturer.

Speech Synthesizer

Serving as another output device, the speech synthesizer is a computer chip that generates sound. This chip gives the computer the ability to search for words and their pronunciations in a data base. The computer takes this data, converts it into codes, and delivers it, allowing the computer to speak with a slight accent. However, the sound is clear enough for most people to understand what is being said. The speech quality is better if the computer has to speak only stock phrases rather than if it has to read items experimentally. Many products today use computer generated speech. For example, an automobile computer reminds the driver to shut the door or fill the tank with gasoline, a doll greets the child with "good morning." Up to this point, input or output devices were considered separate categories; now let's consider devices that perform a dual function.

Input/Output Devices

Magnetic Tape

At first, **magnetic tape** (Figure 11.19) was a popular medium for storage.

A reel of tape was usually around 1/2 inch and could store roughly 25 megabytes of data. Unfortunately, it lost favor as a medium because it was slow, unreliable and hard to access. Because of its low cost, magnetic tape is still used for long term storage and for the transfer of data from computer to computer. In the early 1980s the computer companies manufactured cassette tape drives for their less expensive personal computers and for the first laptops. Today companies manufacture floppy disk drives for their less expensive models.

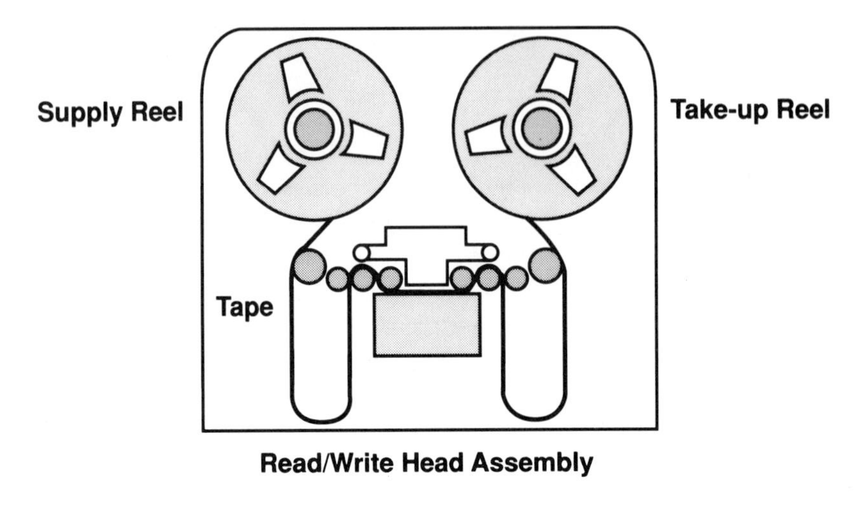

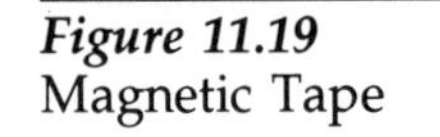
Figure 11.19
Magnetic Tape

The Floppy Disk

In the 1970s IBM introduced the eight-inch **floppy disk** (diskette) for data storage. It consists of a circular piece of plastic, oxide-coated matter enclosed in a protective jacket, similar in appearance to an audio cassette tape. When the disk is placed in a disk drive, it rotates inside its jacket, thus allowing data to be stored on it and viewed later. Using these disks, the computer operator can randomly access the data. Generally disks are available in sizes 5 1/4 inch and 3 1/2 inch. The newer 3 1/2 inch floppy (Figure 11.20) is slowly replacing the 5 1/4 inch floppy as a storage medium. The storage capacity for these disks varies, depending on the disk drive.

The disk drives can be double density or high density, with the high density disk drive designed to store more information on the floppy disk. Table 11.1 shows the disk storage capacity for some of the computer manufacturers.

A little memory does not go a long way and buyers find themselves constantly needing more auxiliary storage.

Figure 11.20
Disk and Disk Drive
Disk: © T/Maker Company
Disk drive: © Dubl-Click Software Inc.

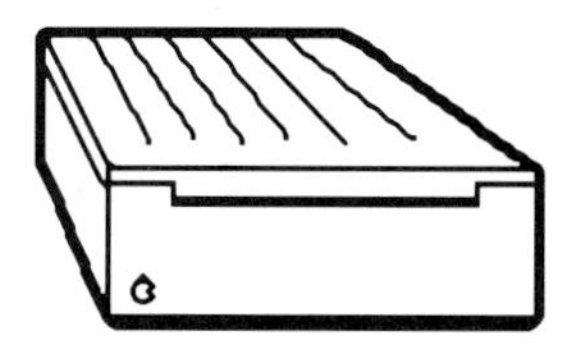

Table 11.1

Floppy Disks	Size	Double Density	High Density
Apple	5 1/4	140K	280K
Apple	3 1/2	800K	NA*
Macintosh	3 1/2	800K	1.44M
IBM & Compatible	5 1/4	360K	1.2M
IBM	3 1/2	720K	1.44M
Commodore	3 1/2	880K	NA*
Atari ST	3 1/2	720K	NA*

*NA = Not Available

The Hard Disk Drive

The **hard disk drive** provides increased storage capabilities and faster access. These disks were developed by IBM in 1973, and early ones were extremely expensive. However, with mass production of the personal computer, the hard disk drive is now available for as little as $200, and, in many cases, it is incorporated into the computer system. A fixed, hard disk usually has one or more disk platters coated with a metal oxide substance that allows information to be magnetically stored. This storage system includes the disk, a read/write head assembly, and the connections between the drive and the computer (Figure 11.21).

At first, these disk drives used fourteen inch diameter disks, but now they use 5 1/4 inch, 3 1/2 inch, and 1.8 inch diameters. In contrast to the floppy disk drive, hard disk drives hold from 20 megabytes to hundreds of megabytes of information. When looking at a hard disk, the user considers storage capacity and **seek time,** a measure of a hard disk's access speed. The smaller the numbers, the faster the disk. In the past, 65 milli-seconds was the standard access time, but today the standard is less than 19 milli-seconds.

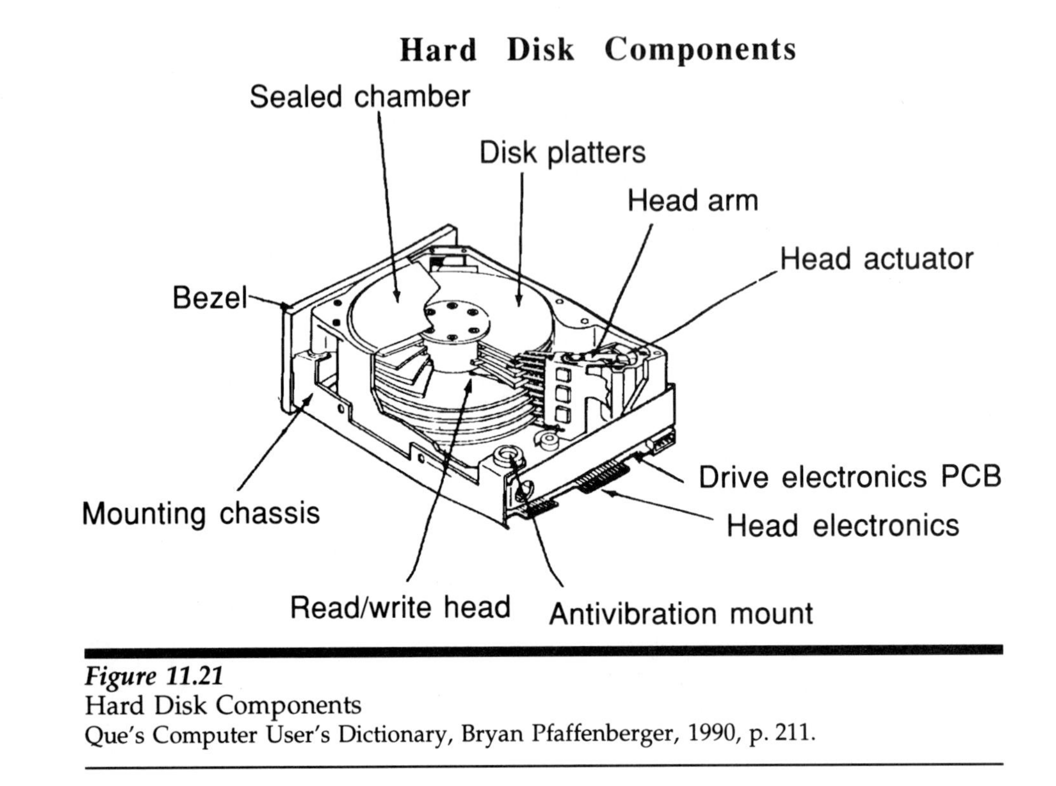

Figure 11.21
Hard Disk Components
Que's Computer User's Dictionary, Bryan Pfaffenberger, 1990, p. 211.

Optical Disks

An **optical disk** has information recorded on it by using a laser beam which burns pits into its surface, while another laser beam reads back information that it detects from these pits. Erasable, optical disks function like magnetic disks and can be recorded on repeatedly. Since the laser beam scans the disk without physical contact, the optical disk does not wear out like a magnetic disk. The disks are small, 3 1/2 inch, light weight, unaffected by dust or heat, and hold huge amounts of data. (Figure 11.22)

Because of their expense and slow access time, these disks are primarily used for storage. However, this situation could change with technological advances making these disks a viable alternative to the magnetic disk.

Figure 11.22
Optical Disk

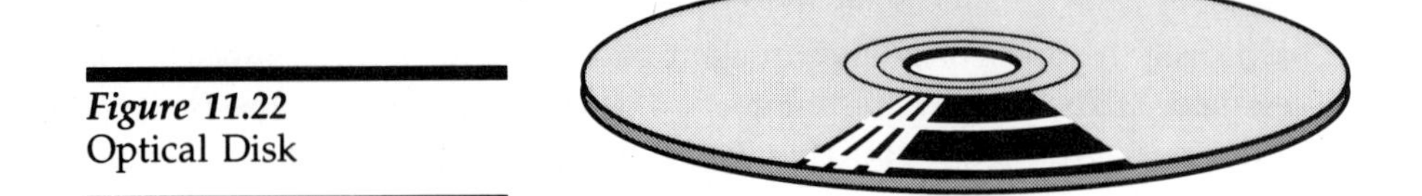

Compact Disks (CD's), Compact Disk Read Only Memory (CD-ROM), and **videodisks** are optical disks that are recorded on when manufactured and cannot be erased. CD-ROM holds text, graphics, and hi-fi stereo sound in a digital format. This disk is similar to the music CD, but it uses a different tracking system. A CD-ROM disk handles at least 600MB of data, the equivalent of 250,000 pages of text, roughly 4,285 Apple 5 1/4 inch single-sided floppy disks and fifteen 40 MB hard disks. This medium is becoming invaluable for storing large volumes of data like the *Grolier Electronic Encyclopedia.* Because of its digital signal, the CD-ROM does not handle moving pictures or a full-spectrum of color as well as a videodisk.

Using an analog signal, a videodisk is a read-only, optical disk that stores and retrieves still and moving pictures, sound, or color. Many videodisk systems were introduced in the 1970s, but only LaserVision optical disk technology survives. As of 1992, videodisks have not replaced the video tape format, but they are being used for instructional interactive purposes. A standard videodisk holds two hours of video data and provides direct access to any location on its disk.

Fax Machine

Another input/output device, the Facsimile **(Fax) machine,** lets the user transmit pictures, maps, etc., between distance locations (Figure 11.23). The fax is composed of a scanner, fax modem, and printer.

Figure 11.23
Fax Machine

This machine scans a piece of paper and converts its image into coded form for transmission over the telephone system. On the other end, a fax machine reconverts the transmitted code and prints out a facsimile of the original sheet of paper. In the 1970s the fax was slow at transmitting pages, but today it is considerably faster. The fax is one of the most popular devices for electronic mail.

Modem

The **Modem** lets two computers communicate with each other by using the telephone lines. There are three types of modems: external, internal, and acoustic coupler. Figure 11.24 shows the external and acoustic coupler modems.

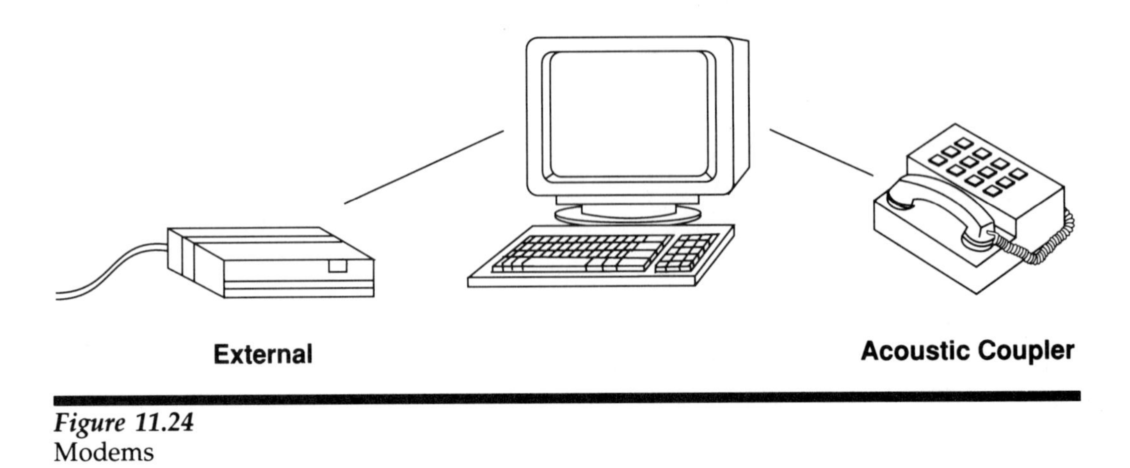

Figure 11.24
Modems

Modem comes from the words **MO**dulator/**DEM**odulator. The modem modulates the computer output to an acceptable signal for transmission and then demodulates the signal back for computer input. The modem on the first computer converts the digital signals to modulated, analog signals tones which are transmitted over the telephone lines. The modem for the second computer transforms the incoming analog signals to their digital equivalents, so that this second computer can understand it. Figure 11.25 illustrates this modem-to-modem transmission.

In order to use a modem, the person needs communication software such as *Z-term, Red Ryder,* or *Microsoft Works.* If the user loads the software, makes the correct settings, dials the other modem and makes a connection with it, then data transferral is possible. The following summary lists the devices discussed in this hardware chapter.

After perusing this table, let's consider some criteria for selecting hardware.

Hardware Selection Criteria

Memory

The first item the reader should consider is the computer's random access memory, the working memory. (See chapter two for a complete discussion of RAM.) In the early 1980s, 64K of RAM was considered more than adequate for running educational software. Today many applications have one megabyte of memory, and these memory requirement are continually increasing. Every time software publishers upgrade programs they add more features requiring more memory. For example, the Appleworks GS now needs one megabyte of RAM to run on the Apple II GS. The amount of RAM memory a computer has affects the kind of software it is capable of running. Word processing spreadsheet, and

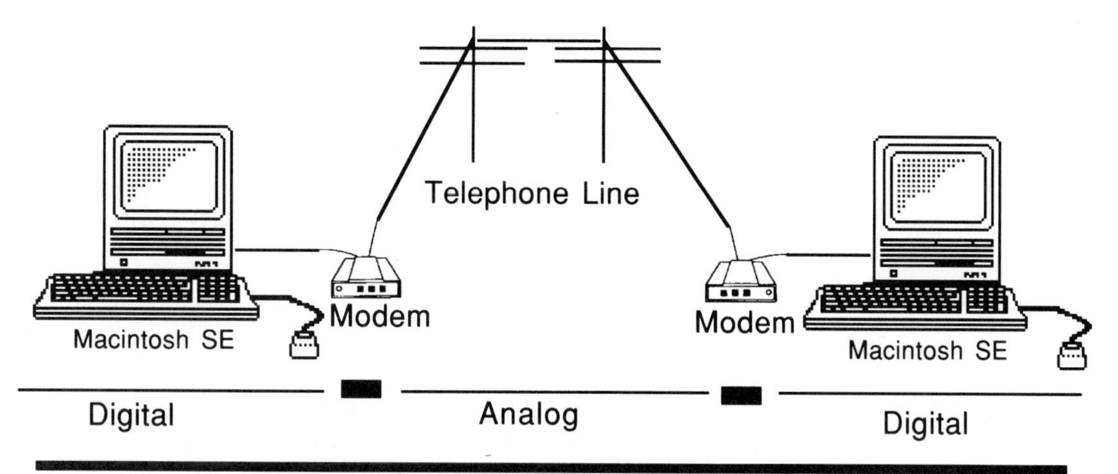

Figure 11.25
Modem–to–Modem Transmission
Wadsworth Publishing Company, © 1988.

HARDWARE SUMMARY

Input	*Output*	*Input/Output*
Keyboard	Printers	Disk Drives
Light pens	Daisy-wheel	Magnetic tape
Mouse	Dot-matrix	Floppy disk
Trackball	Ink jet	Hard disk
Joystick	Laser	Modem
Touch screen	Thermal	External
Graphics pad	Monitors	Acoustic Coupler
Voice recognition	Monochrome	Internal
Digital cameras	Composite	Optical Disks
Scanners	RGB	Erasable
Optical Markreader	Flat displays	CD-ROM
Optical Character reader	LCD	Videodisks
MICR reader	Plasma	Other Devices
Optical bar-code reader	Other Devices	Fax machine
Flatbed scanner	Projection panel	
Handheld scanner	Speech synthesizer	
Overhead scanner		

data base programs require more memory to run, whereas educational software generally needs less memory (except in the case of hypermedia software).

Expandability

Consider these questions when the computer system needs expanding. Can the memory of the computer be increased? Is the computer designed so that extra peripherals such as a modem can be easily added? Can special equipment be added to the machine for the handicapped child?

Speed

The speed at which the microcomputer accesses the instructions is another important consideration. Speed depends upon clock speed and word size. Clock speed is the number of electronic pulses per second, measured in megahertz (MHz). The more pulses the computer has per second, the faster the instructions are executed. The clock speed can vary on a microcomputer from 1 MHz to above 66 MHz. For example, the old Apple II had a clock speed of 1.0 MHz, the Apple II GS has a clock speed of 2.8, and the Macintosh LC and SE 30 have clock speeds of 16 MHz. Some programs require more speed than others; for instance, sophisticated spreadsheet programs need a faster microprocessor in order to speed up calculations.

Speed also depends upon word size, the number of bits that can be handled at one time. An 8 bit microprocessor can handle data 8 bits, while a 16 bit microprocessor can handle 16 bits. Generally speaking, a 16 bit microprocessor is faster than an 8 bit, but many educational applications still run well using 8 bit technology.

Keyboard

The user should test out the keyboard feel by sitting at it and seeing how comfortable it is to type on the keys. One computer might have impressive specifications, but typing on the keyboard may be uncomfortable. See if an extended keyboard is available. Extended keyboards have additional keys that can be programmed to perform different functions and a numeric pad that speeds up number entry.

Video Output

In every instance, there is a decision that has to be made concerning the computer monitor. The monochrome monitor works best for word processing and spreadsheets, while the color monitor is best for running educational software. The higher the resolution of the screen, the clearer the screen display. Resolution is expressed as the number of linear dots or pixels that are displayed on the screen, and the more pixels, the clearer the image or the better the resolution. The size of this monitor screen varies from five inches to 40 inches; usually a screen displays 24 or 25 lines of text.

Graphics

Find out if the computer has color capabilities. If the computer does, it will generally have high-resolution, color graphics as a standard feature. The important factor is the number of available colors.

Sound

The quality of sound is very important when playing musical compositions or educational games. Ask about the number of voices the system has. What are the octave ranges of the voices? In addition, some computers offer speech synthesizers capable of pronouncing words.

Languages

Search for a computer that supports the language that the curriculum requires. BASIC and Logo are the most popular languages for education. Many computers still have some dialect of BASIC built into the ROM. The Apple Macintosh packages *HyperCard* with its computer.

Peripherals

The teacher should study the peripherals that are needed and know the features that are available. The teacher should also read magazines to determine which ones are best to purchase. He or she should find out which peripherals have the lowest rate of repair and have the fastest access time.

Hardware Reliability and Dealer Support

There are some questions the purchaser should ask. Are the local dealers reputable? (Find a local store that can easily service the machine.) Does the store give free training on newly purchased machinery? Is there a service contract? Is the equipment warranted for a year, and is there quick turn around on computer repair? Is this computer compatible with other district computers? How easy is it to use the equipment? Is the documentation well written? Is the weight and size of the machine an important consideration? How durable is the machine? Is it too delicate for classroom use?

Ease of Operation

Is the machine relatively easy to operate? Does the user need hours to study its thick manuals? (If the user is a young child, or an easily frustrated adult, these are important factors.) Is there quality documentation for the computer? Is there free software to help the user to become acquainted with the computer?

Cost

Prices that are quoted by manufacturers are discounted, so the teacher should check the *Computer Shopper,* the local newspaper ads, and the magazines to determine the price structure of a system. Is the machine too costly compared to similar machines? Does the manufacturer include free software? The following hardware check list should serve as a handy guide in analyzing a teacher's hardware needs.

Telecommunication

After the teacher becomes experienced using the computer, s/he might want to engage in telecommunication. Telecommunication is the electronic transmission of information including data, television pictures, sound, and facsimiles. Telecommunication involves a computer, modem, software and a printer. By using these items, a friend can communicate with another friend in St. Louis, Missouri, or Paris, France, by sending and receiving anything from a manuscript to a simple message.

By subscribing to a computer service, such as the *Dow Jones, CompuServe, American Online, Dialog/Classmate, Prodigy, BRS/After Dark,* or *National Geographic Kids Network,* a user can access large data bases. Besides accessing information, many of these services provide electronic mail, information about the news, weather, entertainment, sports, and finances. Furthermore, a person can communicate with special interest groups such as a wine tasting forum. When a person joins one of these services, he or she receives a starter kit that has a subscriber identification number, a temporary password, and a manual explaining how to use the service. The majority of the services initially give free online time, but after this initiation, the charges range from $6.00 to $12.00 an hour, with an extra fee for special services such as print outs for journal articles. Most services are now going in the direction of a fixed rate each month with additional charges only for special services. *Dialog* had its beginning in the 1960s and was created to keep track of the many documents that were produced as part of the space program. It is a useful service for educators because they can access technical and scientific information. In Dialog the first service listed for access is *Education Resources Information Clearinghouse* (ERIC), the basic educational resource for research information. Another service is *National Geographic Kids Network* where middle grade students choose science units ranging from ecological issues to meteorology. For example, conducting original research on the weather, the students use the computer to record the results and share their findings with teammates via the modem. A meteorologist examines

Hardware Evaluation Checklist

Computer Type ____________________ **Model** ____________________

Manufacturer ____________________

A. Hardware Features

- __ 1. Screen size
- __ 2. Text/Graphics display
  - __ a. Number of lines
  - __ b. Characters per line
  - __ c. Resolution
  - __ d. Number of colors
- __ 3. Sound
  - __ a. Number of voices
  - __ b. Number of octaves
- __ 4. Portability
- __ 5. Keyboard design
  - __ a. Number of keys
  - __ b. Numeric keypad
- __ 6. Ease of expansion
- __ 7. Color capabilities
- __ 8. Languages
  - __ a. BASIC
  - __ b. Logo
  - __ c. Pascal
  - __ d. Other
- __ 9. Equipment compatibility
- __ 10. Networking
- __ 11. Memory (RAM)
- __ 12. Number of disk drives
- __ 13. Hard disk
- __ 14. Voice generation
- __ 15. Speed
- __ 16. Other

B. Ease of Use

- __ 1. Easy program loading
- __ 2. Flexibility
- __ 3. Easy equipment setup
- __ 4. Tutorial manual
- __ 5. Software availability

C. Consumer Value

- __ 1. Cost of basic unit
- __ 2. Cost of peripherals
  - __ a. Disk drive
  - __ b. Interfaces/cables
  - __ c. Memory expansion
  - __ d. Modem
  - __ e. Monitor
  - __ f. Printer
  - __ g. Other
  - __ h. Cost of software
  - __ i. Speech synthesizer
- __ 3. Total investment

D. Support

- __ 1. Service contract
- __ 2. Nearby dealer support
- __ 3. Readable manuals
  - __ a. Tutorial
  - __ b. Index
- __ 4. Money back guarantee
- __ 5. Warranty period
- __ 6. Teacher training

Rating Scale

Excellent ____ **Very Good** ____ **Good** ____ **Fair** ____ **Poor** ____

Comments

the student's generated data and assists these students in making generalizations about their weather study. Appendix F contains a list of commercial networks and data bases. Using *CompuServe* as an example, the author will explain how telecommunication works.

How Does Telecommunication work?

Our assignment is to use Grolier's *Academic American Encyclopedia* in order to learn about Charles Babbage, the father of computers. Before the user can access this information, the person must match the computer's modem settings, baud rate, data size, stop bits, and parity with the service's modem settings. If the settings are not identical, communication will not take place. For example, if the service has a 2400 baud rate, the user must also set his modem at 2400[3]. CompuServe has two special software packages: (1) *The Information Manager*, and (2) *The Navigator*. These programs let the user preset the user ID, password, *CompuServe's* telephone number and baud rate. For this example, the author will open the information manager and follow these steps.

1. The first screen (Figure 11.26) shows a list of *CompuServe's* General Services. Since the user is searching for Charles Babbage, Reference is selected.
2. The modem now connects to *CompuServe*'s Reference Service (Figure 11.27). There is a list of references, and the user selects *Academic American Encyclopedia*, at the top of the menu.
3. The next menu, (Figure 11.28) has five options. The user selects the last option, Search Encyclopedia (W).
4. A search screen appears (Figure 11.29, page 313) which directs the user to enter a search term, at the bottom of the screen. The user enter Babbage, Charles.
5. CompuServe matches Charles Babbage to the headings of articles in the encyclopedia. Since there is a match, information about Charles Babbage appears (Figure 11.30, page 314). If the search is unsuccessful, the user is notified that no articles were found.
6. The user can now read, save, or print this information.
7. Finally the user disconnects from CompuServe and quits the telecommunication application software.

3. The baud rate is the modem's transmission speed.

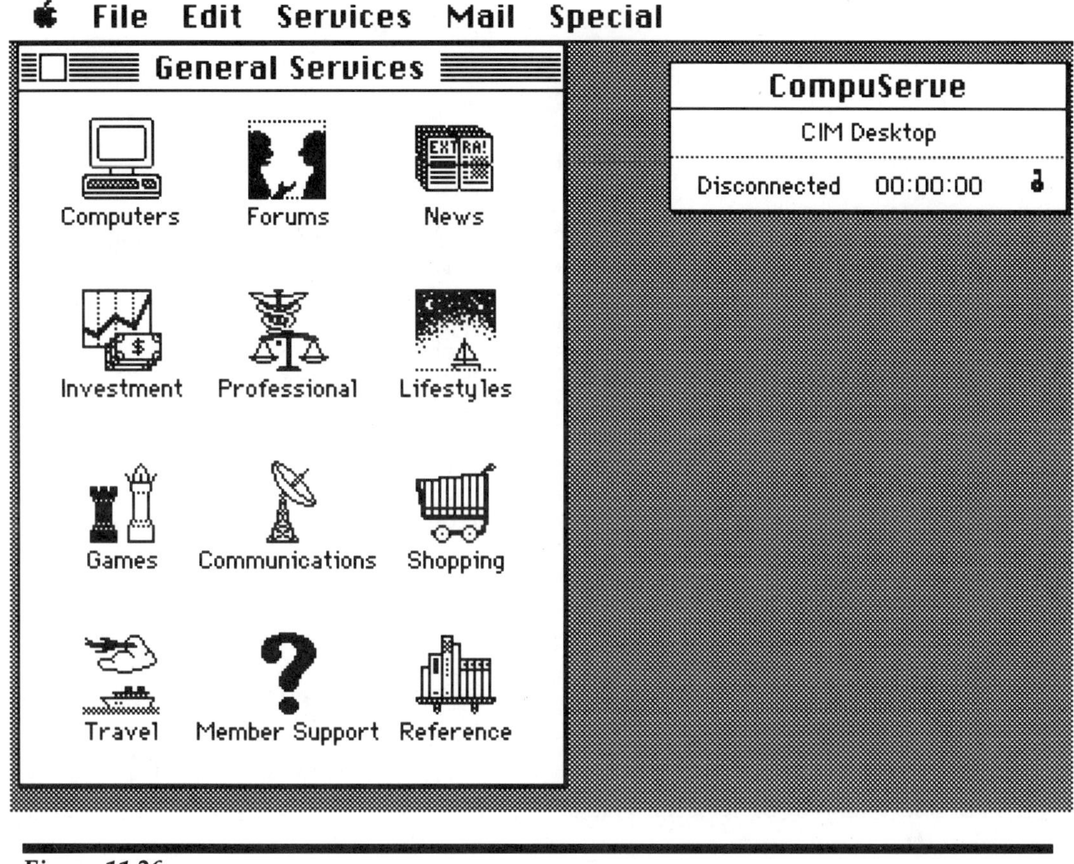

Figure 11.26
CompuServe
CompuServe Incorporated.

In addition to calling subscribed services such as *CompuServe,* the user has a host of free bulletin boards s/he can call. A **bulletin board** is a central computer that stores messages from other computers. It is often set up in a person's home, and the individual who is in charge is called a **Sysop** or **sys**tem **op**erator. The bulletin board has three individual parts: (1) A message board where the user reads or is able to post messages, (2) A library of files, where an individual can access programs ranging from graphics to public domain software and (3) Electronic mail (**E-mail**), for private communication with friends or colleagues.

KidMail and *SimuComm* are well-designed, telecommunications programs for the classroom, (SoftSwap). *KidMail* is a mail simulation that gives the students a sense of what electronic mail is like without using a modem. The students can use this program

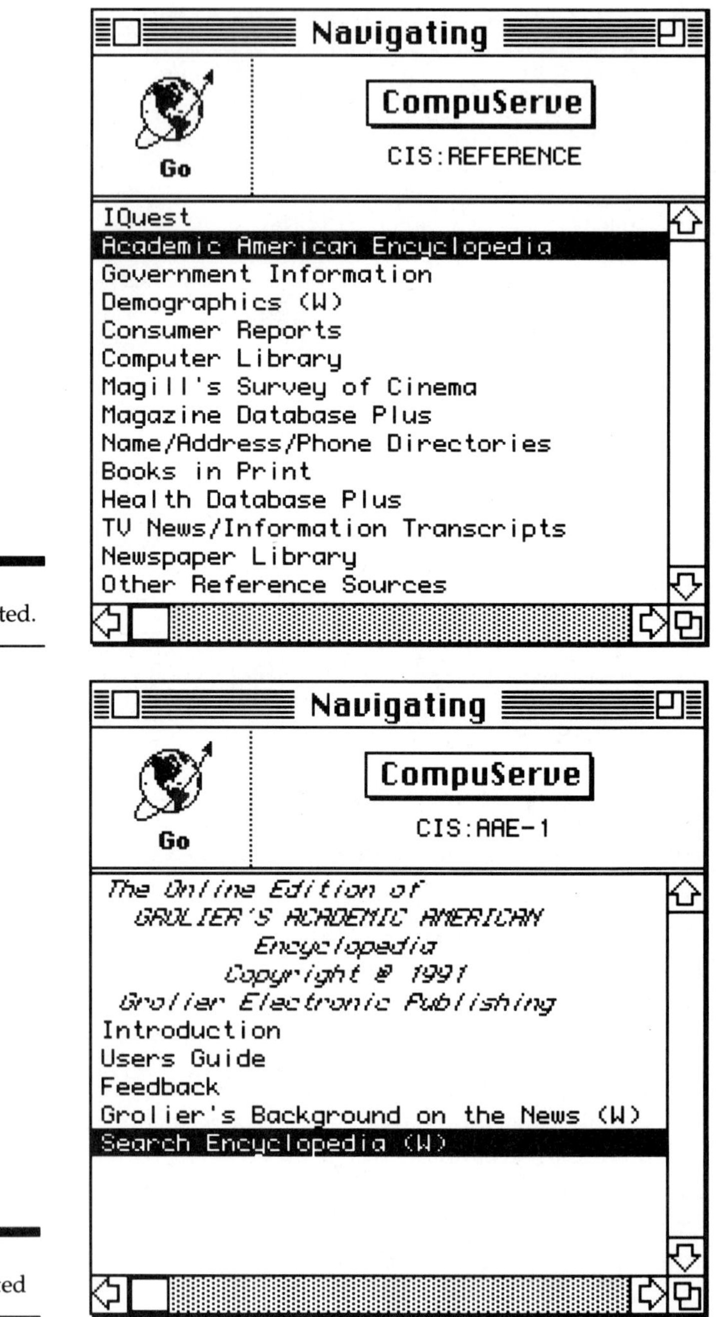

Figure 11.27
CompuServe Incorporated.

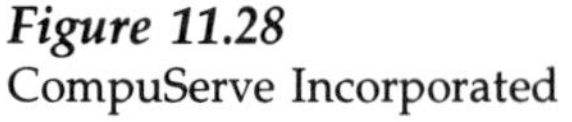

Figure 11.28
CompuServe Incorporated

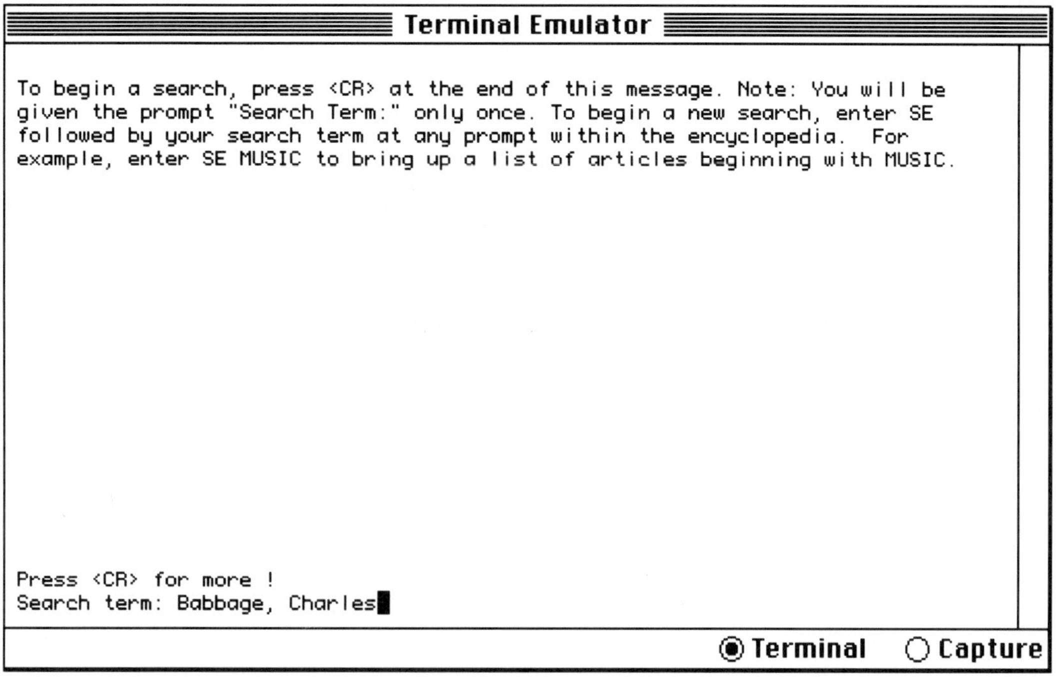

Terminal Emulator

To begin a search, press <CR> at the end of this message. Note: You will be given the prompt "Search Term:" only once. To begin a new search, enter SE followed by your search term at any prompt within the encyclopedia. For example, enter SE MUSIC to bring up a list of articles beginning with MUSIC.

Press <CR> for more !
Search term: Babbage, Charles

◉ Terminal ○ Capture

Figure 11.29
CompuServe Incorporated

to send private messages or public messages for everyone to read. *SimuComm* is a telecommunication simulation where the users make modem settings and dial as if they were really using a modem. If a modem setting is wrong, the users get gibberish on the screen. The students use the program to simulate three commonly used telecommunication services: electronic mail, a bulletin board, and an online data base.

There are numerous ways of incorporating telecommunication into the classroom; the following two activities demonstrate two ways.

Telecommunication Activities

Activity One: Language Arts

Materials

- Computer
- printer

```
Terminal Emulator

CompuServe

Babbage, Charles
--------------------------------
The British mathematician Charles Babbage, b.  Dec.  26, 1792, d.  Oct.  18,
1871, designed and built an "analytical engine," a mechanical progenitor of the
DIGITAL COMPUTER.  After graduating from Cambridge University, he was elected
(1816) a fellow of the Royal Society.  In 1827 he became Lucasian Professor of
Mathematics at Cambridge, a position he held for 12 years.  Babbage never
taught;  rather, he studied a variety of scientific, technological, and economic
problems.  In 1830 he published Reflections on the Decline of Science in
England, a controversial work that resulted in the formation, in 1831, of the
British Association for the Advancement of Science.  Two years later, Babbage
published his most influential work, On the Economy of Machinery and
Manufactures, in which he proposed an early form of OPERATIONS RESEARCH.  The
computation of logarithms had made him aware of the drudgery and inaccuracy of
human calculation, and he became so obsessed with the mechanization of
computation that he spent his family fortune in pursuit of it.  Although Babbage
never built an operational, mechanical COMPUTER, his design concepts have been
proved correct.  DAVID HOUNSHELL

Bibliography: Babbage, Charles, Passages from the Life of a Philosopher (1864;

Press <CR> for more !

(•) Terminal    ( ) Capture
```

Figure 11.30
From the *Academic American Encyclopedia,* electronic version, December 10, 1991. Reprinted by permission.

- modem
- telephone line

Objective: To send a letter using the modem

Software: Communications package and word processing software

Procedure

1. Introduce the students to telecommunications.
2. Demonstrate how the computer, software, and modem and printer work.
3. Discuss the concepts of bulletin boards, baud rates, and electronic mail.
4. Show examples of completed pen pal letters.
5. Have the students type and transmit a letter to another school, using the modem.

Activity Two: Science

Materials: One computer; RGB Monitor, printer, modem telephone line

- On-line serve
- Software: communications

Objective: To learn about the causes of chemical and physical weathering.

Procedure

1. Teach a unit on current environmental issues.
2. Have the students measure the local rainfall and its acidity level.
3. Access an on-line service and have the students discover patterns of acidity in the rainwater across the continent.
4. Let the students post their results on-line for other schools to use.
5. Have the students download information from other students and draw maps and charts.

Networking

Networking is another way that computers communicate with each other. Networking is defined as "A group of computers and associated devices that are connected by communications facilities" (Woodcock, 1991). A network can have a permanent connection, like cable, or a temporary connection made through the telephone or other communication devices. In order to have a computer network, a teacher needs to have the computers to connect or network. These computers can be Macintoshes, IBMs, or Apple II GSs. A network system generally has a file server which is a computer with a large data capacity that serves as a repository for information. The file server directs the flow of information to and from the computers in the network. An instructor needs a network card if the networking capabilities are not built or plugged into the computer, as well as cables, wires and hookups, and operating system software that gives access to the file server. Network operating system software is produced by companies such as Novell, Apple, and Lan Techs. Besides this special software and equipment, the instructor also needs **networkable** software that runs on the network.

The three most commonly known network arrangements are: the ring, the star, and the shared-bus. The ring network does not rely on a file server, and if one computer goes down in the system, the others still operate (Figure 11.31).

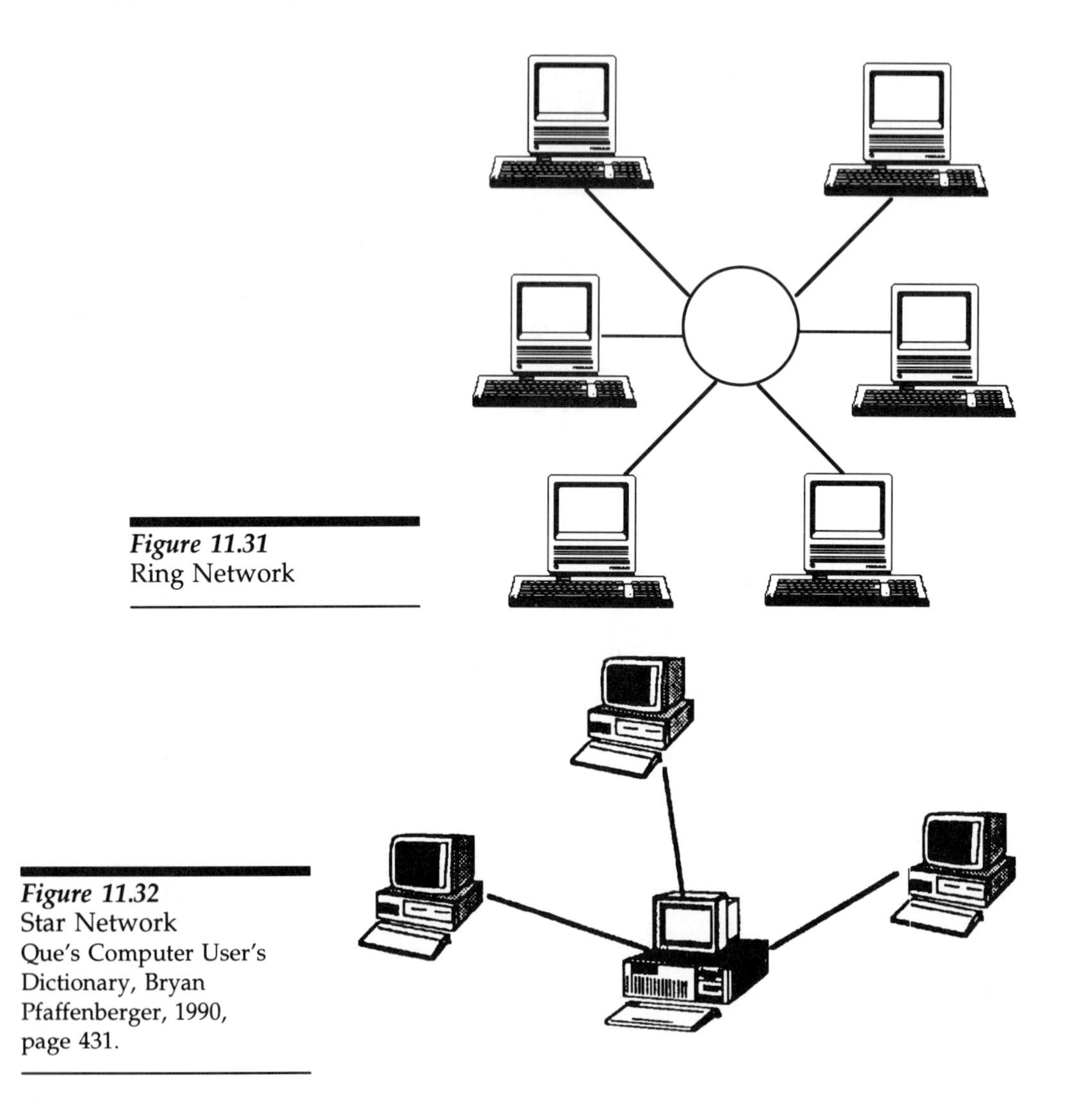

Figure 11.31
Ring Network

Figure 11.32
Star Network
Que's Computer User's Dictionary, Bryan Pfaffenberger, 1990, page 431.

This configuration is found in university administrative offices where each computer performs when needed and each computer has its own software.

The second arrangement, the star network (Figure 11.32) has a central computer or file server with several computers or terminals connected to it. The star network becomes inoperable if the file server fails.

The central computer acting as a file server has all the data in its memory, which the other computers use for processing. For example, a school computer center might use this type of network for its card catalog. The third arrangement, a bus network, uses a single bidirectional cable that acts as a "bus line" to carry messages to and from devices. Information can be stored in a central computer, but it involves complicated communication protocols to avoid data collision. Small local area networks use this configuration because it is an easier system to set up and use.

Local Area Networks (LAN), Wide Area Networks (WAN) and **Telephones** are three types of networks. (LAN) provides communication within a local area, usually within two or three hundred feet such as in an office building. For example, a school might have its card catalog stored on a file server's hard disk, accessible by other computers throughout the building. WAN provides communication with a larger area that requires miles of communication linkage, and a telephone network connects the computers using the telephones. The only difference between the WAN and the telephone network is the fact that the telephone's communication is intermittent, while the wide area network communicate all the time. Let's consider the pros and cons of this fast growing, networking industry.

Advantages

Networking establishes communication among computers and is especially helpful when people work on different floors or in different buildings. This system improves the speed and accuracy of communication because a message is not likely to be misplaced. Networking lets the user share the same software and equipment, share a word processing program, and use one laser printer. Not only does the user save on hardware, but s/he saves on software as well. A network lets the user share files with other individuals, which makes it suitable for class research. Different types of computers can communicate with each other sharing files; however, this precludes disk swapping of programs because of the different computer operating systems.

Disadvantages

The cost of this system depends upon the computer hardware, number of users, and the networking software that is bought. The price can be high for the hardware, computer training, and maintenance. Networking computers require expertise that may not always be readily available, and it is difficult to find competent technicians to repair the equipment. The district has to consider the frustration levels of the teachers because of the extra burden of learning a new system. Another disadvantage is called "computer dependency"; that is when a teacher uses this system, s/he becomes dependent on it and is at a loss if the system crashes. Furthermore, the necessary networking software is not always available. A final disadvantage is system security. An unauthorized individual can have access to the information; therefore, the user needs to protect the network.

Summary

This chapter has explored the functions and uses of the major input, output, and input/output devices. Examples of input devices included were (1) keyboards, (2) computer mouse, (3) track balls, (4) optical readers, (5) touch screens, and (6) voice input. In examining the output devices, the two most important were the printer, which gives the user a hard copy of the day, and the screen display, which shows the information on the screen. Examples of display screens discussed were the liquid crystal display (LCD) and the cathode ray tube (CRT). The major printers discussed were (1) dot-matrix, (2) ink jet, (3) laser, and (4) daisy-wheel. The dot-matrix printer has a print head with wires to create its characters; the ink jet sprays ink; the laser uses a process similar to photocopying; and the daisy-wheel uses a typing element.

The author then discussed and compared floppy disks, hard disks, and optical disks whose function is storage of data. Floppy disks and hard disks are still the most popular storage media, while optical disks are gaining influence. The author provided criteria for assisting the teacher in selecting hardware.

A mastery test, projects and suggested readings and references follow:

Mastery Test

1. Define networking.
2. Discuss the advantages and disadvantages of using networking in the classroom.
3. Name two input and two output devices. Explain how each works.
4. Name four factors to keep in mind when examining hardware.
5. Compare a laser printer with an ink jet printer.
6. Explain how a modem operates. What problems can be encountered when using a modem?
7. When is it advantageous to use a monochrome monitor, and when is it a good idea to use a color monitor?
8. Compare floppy disks and their storage capacities.
9. How are hard disks similar and different from floppy disks?
10. What are optical disks? Why are they considered the wave of the future?
11. What is a speech synthesizer? What is the relationship between speech synthesizer and voice input?

Classroom Projects

1. Have someone set up a modem in class and show how it works. If this is not possible, have students use a simulation program like *SimuComm* or *KidMail.*
2. Visit a computer store and see a visual comparison of the displays on a RGB monitor, a composite monitor, a monochrome monitor, and a flat screen, and report on their differences.

3. Take a field trip to a school that uses networking. Find out the type of network, the software being utilized, and find out how the children are using networking in the classroom. Evaluate this school's program, listing its strengths and weaknesses.

Suggested Reading and References

Bruder, Isabelle. "Schools of Education: Four Exemplary Programs." *Electronic Learning,* 10(6) (March 1991): 21–24,45.

Darrow, Barbara. "IBM Develops Prototype of Color Touch Screen for Laptops." *InfoWorld,* 13, (16) (22 April 1991): 6.

Desposito, Joseph. *Que's Computer Buyer's Guide.* Carmel, Indiana: Que Corporation, 1991.

Flyn, L. "Apple Boosts CD ROM Market with New Drive." *Infoworld* (March 1988): 31.

Fox, Jackie. "Compact Disks for the PC." *PC Today* (July 1990): 40–46.

Freedman, Alan. *The Computer Glossary.* New York: American Management Association, 1990.

Freedman, Debra. "Speech Students Learn Through Computer Technology." *The Computing Teacher,* 18(8) (May 1991): 10–14.

Greenfield, Elizabeth. "At-Risk & Special Ed. Products: Tools for Special Learning." *T.H.E.* 18(11) (June 1991): 6–14.

Holzberg, Carol S. "LCD Panels." *Electronic Learning,* 10(6) (March 1991): 46–49.

Keizer, Gregg. "In the Network Groove." *Incider A+,* 9(9) (September 1991): 40–45.

Laurie, Peter. *The Joy of Computers.* Boston: Little, Brown and Co. 1983.

Mageau, Therese. "Software's New Frontier: Laser-Disc Technology." *Electronic Learning.* 9(6) (March 1990): 22–28.

Mageau, Therese. "Telecommunications In the Classroom" *Teaching and Computers,* 7(6) (May/June 1990): 18–24.

McManus, Neil. "Logitech Digital Camera to Snap Instant Eight-Bit, Gray Scale Photos." *MacWeek,* Vol 6, No. 2, (13 January 1992): 38.

Murie, Michael. "Still Video Captures the Scene." *Publish* (August 1991): 89–98.

McCarthy, Robert. "The Advantages of Using A Network." *Electronic Learning,* 9(1) (September 1989): 32–38.

Pfiffner, Pamela. "Caere Takes OCR in Hand." *MacWeek,* 4(27) (7 August 1990): 1.

Ralston, Anthon and C. L. Meeks, Eds. *Encyclopedia of Computer Science.* New York: Petrocelli, 1976.

Ritchie, Sam. "Monitors, Monitors Everywhere: A Guide to Help You Make the Right Choice." *Electronic Learning,* 9(6) (March 1990): 32–35.

Rizzo and the MacUser Labs Staff. "Most Valuable Players." *MacUser* (March 1990): 150–170.

Roberts, Nancy, George Blakeslee, Maureen Brown and Cecilia Lenk. *Integrating Telecommunications Into Education.* Englewood Cliffs, New Jersey: Prentice Hall, 1990.

Safir, Marty. "Getting the Bugs Out of Digitizing Tablets." *MacValley Voice,* 7(6) (June 1991): 1, 5–7.

Simkin, Mark G. and Robert H. Dependahl. *Microcomputer Principles and Applications.,* Dubuque, Iowa: Wm. C. Brown Publisher, 1987.

Sippl, Charles. *Computer Dictionary.* 4th ed. Indianapolis, Indiana: Sams, 1985.

Sisneros, Roger. "Telecomputing Takes the Mystery out of On-line Communication." *Telecomputing* (Spring 1990): 15–22.

Solom, G. "Students Can Computer by Just Touching the Screen." *Electronic Learning,* 7(7) (April 1988): 50–51.

Turner, Sandra, and Land. *Tools for Schools.* Belmont, California: Wadsorth, 1988.

Waters, Crystal. "Pointing to the Best: Mice and Track Balls." *Home Office Computing* (January 1992): 48–51.

Woodcock, Joanne. Senior Contributor. *Computer Dictionary.* Redmond, WA: Microsoft Press, 1991, 14.

BASIC and Other Languages

12

Objectives

Upon completing this chapter the student will be able to:

1. Trace the major developments in the history of programming languages
2. Discuss how a flowchart works
3. Become familiar with the fundamentals of BASIC
4. Present the key arguments for and against teaching BASIC
5. Discuss an authoring language and its feasibility for classroom use

Programming Languages

Programming is the "sine qua non" for computer operations. Programming languages are sequences of words, letters, numerals, and mnemonics that let the computer user operate the computer. Each computer language has its own precise set of rules, syntax, and grammar that ordinary language lacks. In everyday language, a single word may have many meanings, but this is not the case in a computer language where no ambiguity exists. Each command can have only a single meaning.

Today, there are over 400 computer languages including their many dialects. These languages let the user achieve a multitude of tasks because no one language fits all situations. The user determines the language needed by asking the following: "Can the programmer easily use the language? Is the language available on the computer that s/he is using?" And "Is the language appropriate for the situation?" In some situations more than one language is appropriate. As different as the languages are, they all have a common base of high and low voltages represented by the 0's and 1's of the binary code. One combination of 0's and 1's, where the 0 acts as an off switch and the 1 as an on switch, tells the computer to process the data immediately, while another combination tells the Central Processing Unit (CPU) to add. The computer circuitry responds to a group of these commands and performs a variety of assignments. A machine language program composed of a pattern of 0's and 1's is far

```
10100001 00000000 00000010
00000011 00000110 00000010 00000010
10100011 00000000 00000010
```

Figure 12.1
Machine Language

removed from the language understood by human beings. Figure 12.1 shows a small program written in machine language

This program instructs the computer to read the number stored in the memory address, to add it to the number already in the CPU, and to store the sum in a memory location. Since this is an abstract language involving a notational system for 0's and 1's, the programmer can easily err preventing execution of the program.

History of Computer Languages

In 1943, when Howard Aiken built the Mark I, machine language was the only language in existence. The Mark I received its instructions from punched-paper tape that technicians fed into the computer. Mauchly and Eckert's famous Univac was more difficult to program because a group of technicians had to set thousands of switches and insert cables into the machine. Whenever a user wanted to change a program, this user had to rewire the entire machine. Because of the difficulty in using machine language, John Mauchly directed his programmers to develop a language that would let the computer user enter problems in a derived algebraic form.

This symbolic language was an improvement over machine language because the programmer could now write a problem in mathematical terms and then use a table to convert it into a two-character code. For example, a plus was coded as 07. Another computer program would then convert this code into machine language of 0's and 1's. This conversion program was a rudimentary interpreter that translated the program into machine code.

This intermediate code became outdated; nevertheless it was the first step in a long series of advances that gave the computer user the tools to write programs in a language other than machine language. In 1949, at the University of Pennsylvania's Moore School of Engineering, Mauchly and Eckert delivered a series of lectures on a proposed computer that would store programs and data electronically in memory. Maurice Wilkes, an English mathematician who attended these lectures, returned home to England to design a computer, the EDSAC, based on this stored memory concept.

The EDSAC did not use a machine code, but rather a system of mnemonics. Each time the programmer issued an instruction, it was in the form of a capital letter. For instance the letter **I** meant "read." When the user typed this mnemonic on a special keyboard, the computer received the appropriate binary instruction. Besides designing the symbols, the programmers devised a useful library of generalized subroutines for the EDSAC.[1] The programmers entered a short mnemonic command, and the computer would automatically place the subroutine in the program. Wilkes called the subroutines and mnemonics an assembly system because it assembled sequences of subroutines. This name assembly system still exists today because any language in which a mnemonic represents one machine instruction is called an **assembly language.** An assembly language program or an assembler converts the mnemonics directly into the binary sequence of the machine language. Figure 12.2 shows an example of an assembly program.

Figure 12.2
An Assembly Program Sample

```
MOV AX, TOTAL
ADD AX, VALUE
MOV TOTAL, AX
```

The top line instructs the CPU to move the contents from main memory into a memory location named TOTAL and register AX. The next line tells the CPU to add the contents in memory to the contents of AX, and the bottom line instructs the CPU to move the contents to the main memory named TOTAL. This assembly language program produces the same output as the comparable machine language program in Figure 12.1.

Assembly language is cumbersome because of its mnemonic structure. Besides, assembly language is machine specific, and a program written for one machine does not make sense on a different machine. Because of these drawbacks, prominent mathematicians such as Alan Turning and scientific researchers such as Alick Glennie worked on other languages that led to the development of high-level languages. A high-level language is farther away from the machine's operation and approximates human language, whereas low-level language like "machine" and "assembly" are nearer the machine's operation.

In 1951 Grace Hooper and a team of programmers leaped a step further by establishing a system capable of translating a program written in a high-level

1. A subroutine is an independent program that the main program calls upon repeatedly.

language. This translating program was a "compiler" that Hooper named the A–O for Autocode. The compiler was faster than the line-by-line interpreters, because it could convert an entire program in one step. This complied program could be run immediately or saved for future use. Her compiler was the first to be recognized throughout the world. In 1956, Grace Hooper and her colleagues devised another compiler called the FLOW-MATIC which permitted business people to program by using a language close to English. The market was now ready for high-level, language development because compilers could serve the function of translating entire high-level programs into machine code.

High-Level Language Development

Immediately preceding Hooper's compiler, IBM researchers created the first high-level language, **FORTRAN,** an acronym for **FOR**mula **TRAN**slation. FORTRAN has a capacity for number manipulation and formulas that is still popular today. After FORTRAN's introduction in 1957, **COBOL** (**CO**mmon **B**usiness-**O**riented **L**anguage) and **ALGOL** (**ALGO**rithmetic **L**anguage) were developed. COBOL, primarily used for business, was originally developed by the Department of Defense and later revised by Captain Grace Hooper, whereas ALGOL, primarily used for mathematics and problem solving, was designed by members of the Association of Computing Machinery and European Computer Industry Representatives. FORTRAN, COBOL and ALGOL are considered classic high-level languages, and modern languages are variations of these three.

The summary chart on the following page modified from Current Major Programming Languages by Pamela J. Milland, gives a thumbnail sketch of the major computer languages developed in the 1960s, 1970s, and 1980s.

BASIC

In the sixties, programmers designed languages such as LISP, RPG, APL, SNOBOL and BASIC because academicians were looking for a way to make computers accessible to the students. At this time, there was a scarcity of educational software, so teachers focused on computer programming. In this academic climate, John Kemeny and Thomas Kurtz created Beginner's All-purpose Symbolic Instruction Code (BASIC) at Dartmouth College. They wanted a language that would require minimal instruction and one that was easy to learn in an academic setting. FORTRAN and ALGOL did not satisfy these requirements, so they designed BASIC, which was a blend of the best of these two languages. In 1964 the students at Dartmouth College sat down at their computer terminals and were greeted by

SUMMARY CHART OF MAJOR PROGRAMMING LANGUAGES

FORTRAN (1954) FORmula TRANslator. John Backus, with a team at IBM, developed FORTRAN, the first high-level language. This language, known for its number crunching, is widely used for science, engineering, and mathematical problems.

ALGOL 58 (1958) ALGOrithmetic Language. Designed by the members of the Association for Computing Machinery and European computer industry representatives, ALGOL 58 is used for mathematical problem-solving.

COBOL (1959) COmmon Business Oriented Language. The Defense Department developed this language and Captain Grace Hooper of the U.S. Navy perfected it. COBOL is primarily used for business applications.

LISP (1960) LISt Processing. John McCarthy created this language, which is used for special applications such as artificial-intelligence.

RPG (1962) Report Program Generator. IBM created and used it to generate business reports.

APL (1962) Kenneth Iverson developed APL; it is used for scientific applications.

SNOBOL 4 (1963) StriNg-Oriented symBOlic Language. David Farber, Ralph Griswold, and Ivan Polonsky of Bell Labs devised the current version of SNOBOL, and it is still in use for text applications.

BASIC (1964) Beginners' All-Purpose Symbolic Instruction Code. T.E. Kurtz and J.G. Kemeny developed BASIC at Dartmouth College in order to teach students programming for educational and business applications.

PL/1 (1964) Programming Language 1. IBM created this language to replace COBOL and FORTRAN, which has not happened.

PROLOG (1970) PROgramming LOGic. Alain Colmerauer wrote this language at the University of Marseilles, France. It is used largely for artificial intelligence applications.

Pascal (1971) Nilaus Wirth invented Pascal, a structured programming language, to teach students how to program.

FORTH (1974) Charles Moore, the astronomer, developed this object oriented language to control telescopes. This language is growing in popularity.

C (1975) Dennis Richie created C for the Unix operating system, and it is used for systems and general applications.

ADA (1979) ADA, was named after ADA Augusta, the Countess of Lovelace, the first woman programmer. Jean Ichbiah headed a team of programmers that produced ADA, a language based on Pascal, used by the federal government for weapons system tracking.

Modula-2 (1979) MODUlar LAnguage 2. Niklaus Wirth, the author of Pascal, wrote Modula-2, a multi-purpose scientific language.

Smalltalk 80 (1980) Alan Kay developed Small Talk 80 at Xerox's Research Center. It is an object-oriented language, used for Xerox's original graphical windows system.

C++ (1983) Bjarn Stroustrup designed and implemented this object-oriented extension of C.

the famous READY> prompt; thus began an era where the novice computer user could write simple programs that were quickly executed.

After BASIC's introduction, word spread about the new language that was designed for Dartmouth's time-sharing system. By using time-sharing, several students could interact with the machine at the same time. Students now had access to the computer. They no longer had to use punched-card machines and turn their cards into computer operators, who processed the information when convenient.

In the same year, Robert L. Albrecht, a senior analyst for Control Data in Minneapolis, heard about the new language and lobbied successfully to have it become the recommended language for the secondary schools. In 1970 he started a company called Dymax that produced instruction books in BASIC and began a bimonthly paper called The People's Computer Company. Albrech wanted someone to write a similar version of BASIC called Tiny BASIC, and he commissioned Dennis Allison, a skilled programmer, to write a series of articles with guidelines for the modified version. Dick Whipple and John Arnold responded with a 2,000 octal-code of instructions, which let the Altair Computer, the first affordable microcomputer, respond to commands entered in Tiny BASIC. Albrech's magazine continued publishing new versions of BASIC submitted by its readers, and some authors released these versions through public domain. In the mid-1970s the authors of these programs began selling their versions of BASIC commercially.

Many variations appeared. For example, Tom Pittman wrote a Tiny BASIC interpreter, and Bill Gates and Paul Allen wrote a version of BASIC, using only 4K memory. For their own versions of BASIC, manufacturers wired interpreters into the

Program Instructions	Explanations
READ x,y	Reads 3 and 4
PRINT x+y	Prints 7
READ x,y	Reads 2 and 3
READ a$,z	Reads The answers is & Reads 4
PRINT a$;(x+y)*z	Prints The answer is 20
DATA 3,4,2,3, The answer is, 4	The values read and manipulated
END	Ends the program

Figure 12.3
A Structured BASIC Program
True BASIC Reference Manual, John G. Kemeny and Thomas E. Kurtz, 1988, page 44.

computer's ROM. By the middle 1980s, millions of people in the United States and abroad knew BASIC and had learned it on their own computers. The program's original designers, Kemeny and Kurtz, were upset about the compromises that had to be made in order to produce BASIC on the different incompatible machines. The computer scientists criticized the language because it lent itself mainly to short programs. Many high school teachers thought BASIC needed structure, so they abandoned it in favor of Pascal. Through the years, Kemeny and Kurtz made revisions, and in 1984, they collaborated on a microcomputer version of BASIC, TRUE BASIC that became the definitive version. BASIC was no longer a line-oriented language with little structure—It was a modern language. An example (Figure 12.3) is shown above of a structured BASIC program (taken from True BASIC by John G. Kemeny and Thomas E. Kurtz).

BASIC has improved in its sophistication, routines, and graphics. By adding statements such as Loop, Do, Select Case, it has gained more structure. Today BASIC has the ability to create data structures equal to Pascal or C and no longer has the memory limits of the earlier programs. BASIC programming has a built-in-full-screen editor with automatic syntax editing, a built-in debugger, and runs as fast as Pascal or C. BASIC has moved from an interpreter back to a compiler without sacrificing the instant feedback. The new compiler technology detects errors in programming and compiles thousands of lines of code in a few seconds. There are popular commercial programs still written using BASIC, and undoubtedly there will be future versions of BASIC.

BASIC is the language most commonly found in the schools today because it is simple to use and has English-like key words; many machines still come with BASIC installed. In the school setting, the three programming languages used are BASIC, Logo, and Pascal.

The author will now familiarize the reader with the fundamental concepts of BASIC programming and show the elements of BASIC that are common to all dialects. Graphics has been excluded from the discussion because there are too many variations in each dialect. In order to gain insight into how BASIC works, type the sample programs, run them, and save them. The programs that are shown were done on the Macintosh, using True BASIC (True BASIC Inc.) For a more in-depth discussion of BASIC, refer to the books listed at the end of the chapter.

What is a Program?

A program is a sequence of instructions that informs the computer what tasks are to be performed. The computer user must determine the order in which the computer is to perform these instructions, and the flowchart lets this user plan a program more effectively. The following narration serves as a short explanation of the basic concepts of flowcharting.

Flowcharts

The flowchart uses symbols to help the user describe the process he or she will follow to solve a problem—it is a convenient, pictorial way of communicating. Most program writers use the following symbols: the oval, the parallelogram, the rectangle, the diamond, and the circle. The oval symbol represents the beginning or end of an operation.

The parallelogram can be used for input, output statements:

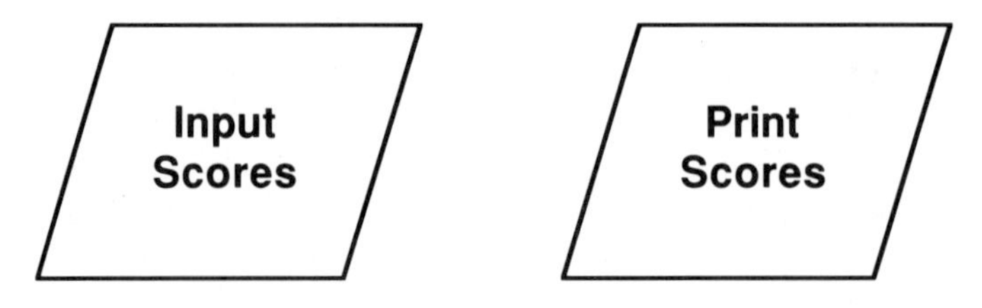

The rectangle defines variables and shows the arithmetic operations the computer will perform:

The diamond or decision symbol states a question with its choices:

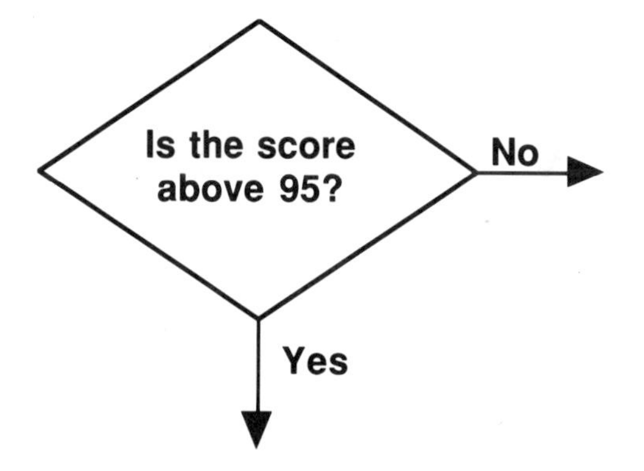

The arrows are used to indicate the direction of the flow, which is usually from the top of the page to the bottom. Figure 12.4 shows the top-down structure of a flowchart using an example from Macflow (Mainstay).

Step one, the oval, starts at the person's goal, "Draw a Flowchart." Step 2 opens a document. Step 3 adds a symbol to the flowchart. Step 4 is a decision box and asks the question, "Are you done?" If the person is finished s/he chooses, "Yes," and follows the arrow to the rectangle process box that instructs the individual to save the flowchart and exit MacFlow. If the user is not finished, s/he chooses, "No," and follows the arrow to the rectangle process box that tells the individual to add another object. This procedure continues until the user answers, "Yes," to the question, "Are you done?" After a student draws a flowchart, s/he is ready to write a program following the flowchart's blueprint.

Line Numbers

Many versions of BASIC still use line numbers to establish a sequence of instructions, and they are assigned from lowest to the highest. The programmer can type these line numbers out of order, because the computer automatically sequences them. These line numbers are usually written in in units of ten (10, 20, 30, 40, etc.) because this sequencing leaves room for the insertion of additional lines.

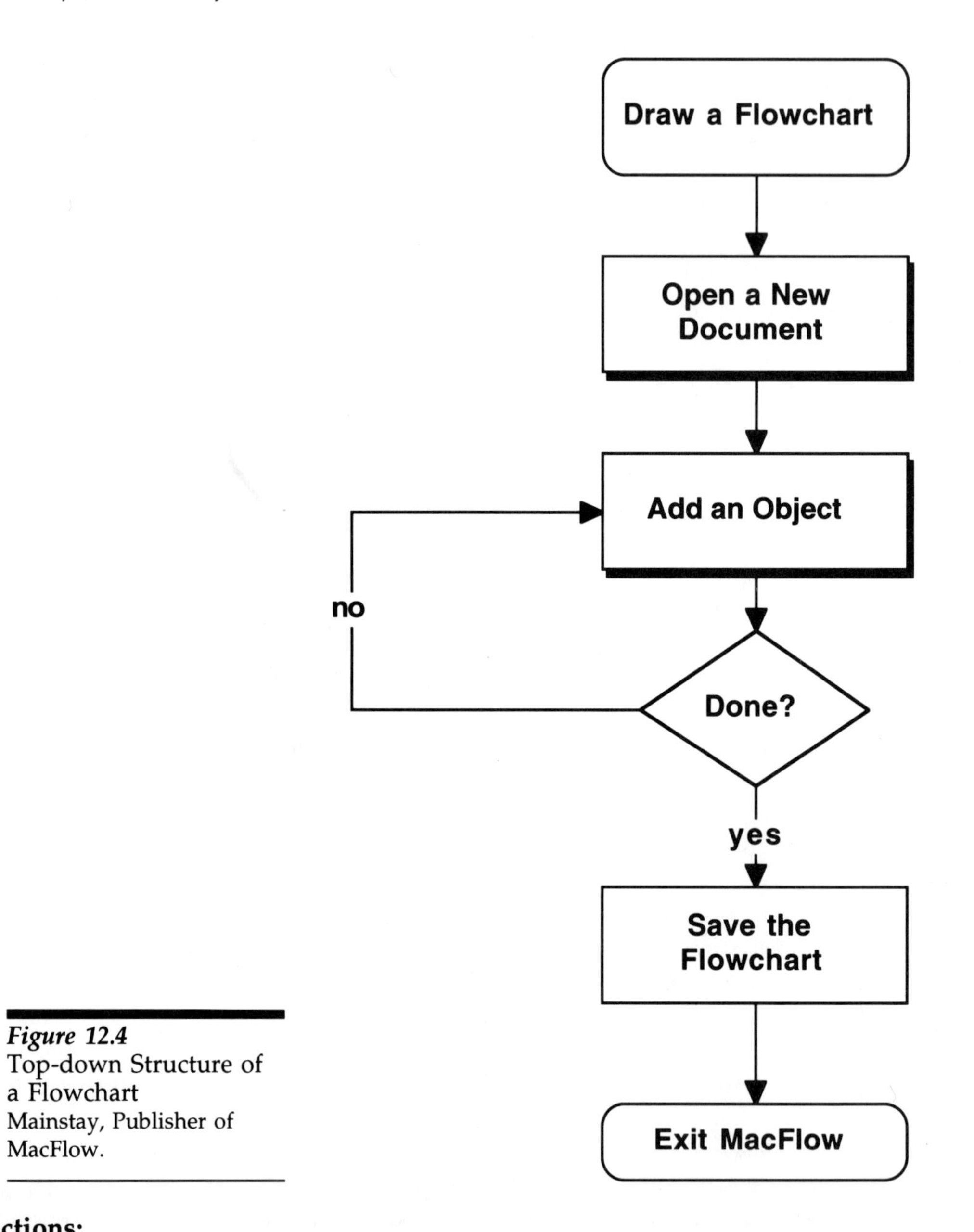

Figure 12.4
Top-down Structure of a Flowchart
Mainstay, Publisher of MacFlow.

Instructions:
When the reader types a program line-by-line, s/he must push the RETURN or the ENTER key after each line. Once the program is completed, the user should type the word RUN and push the RETURN or ENTER key.

PRINT

Background: Print displays values (or whatever may be enclosed in quotation marks) such as PRINT X or PRINT "X" Print X will print whatever the value of X is, while PRINT "X" will print just the letter X. The print statement displays any keyboard character the writer wants on the screen.

Example:

Program

```
10 Print 8*3
20 Print
30 Print 30/5
40 Print
50 Print "I am a new computer user and I enjoy using this machine."
60 End
```

Remember, type RUN and press RETURN to see the following output:

OutPut

```
24

6

I am a new computer user and I enjoy using this machine.
```

Explanation:

Lines 10 and 30: Line 10 multiplies 8 times 3, and line 30 divides 30 by 5.

Lines 20 and 40: The print statement inserts blank lines.

Line 50: Prints the sentence: I am a computer user and I enjoy using this machine.

Line 60: END terminates the execution of the program.

Instructions:

Type **NEW** and press **RETURN** to clear the program from memory. To erase the screen, type the word **HOME** (APPLE) or **CLEAR** (IBM) and then press **RETURN.**

Printing Characters

Background: To draw a picture, the programmer uses a print statement and places spaces and characters within the quotation marks.

Example

```
10 Print
20 Print" 0 0"
30 Print"   * "
40 Print" *** "
50 End
```

OutPut

```
0   0
  *
 ***
```

Explanation

Line 10: Inserts a blank line.

Lines 20–40: Prints characters which draw a face.

Line 50: Ends the program.

Punctuation Marks

Background: The semicolon (;) continues the output on the same line while the comma (,) separates the output into zones across the screen. (The Apple computer has three zones, while the IBM has five zones.)

Example:

```
10 Print"Type the following:"
20 Print
30 Print"A";
40 Print"B";
50 Print"C"
60 Print 5,10,15
70 End
```

Output

```
Type the following:

A B C
 5              10              15
```

Explanation

Line 10: Prints the sentence: "Type the following."

Line 20: Inserts a blank line.

Lines 30–50: The semicolon after letters A and B continues the output on the same line, resulting in ABC.

Line 60: The comma places the three numbers in three separate zones.

Line 70: Ends the program.

LET Statements

Background: A LET statement assigns a value to a variable and stores this variable in memory. When the person types Let X=5, the variable X stores 5 in the memory location called X. The computer displays this value when instructed to print X. Variables represent numbers, or strings. Numeric variables are represented by letter(s), A, or a combination of a letter and a number A1. Variables can change in value, as demonstrated by the following program.

Numeric Variable Example:

```
10 Print"Numbers"
20 Let X=1
30 Let Y=2
40 Print X,Y
50 Let X=3
60 Let Y=4
70 Print X;Y
80 End
```

Output:

```
Numbers
 1              2
 3  4
```

Explanation

Line 10: Prints the word **Numbers.**

Lines 20–30: Assigns X to the value of 1 and Y to the value of 2.

Line 40: Prints out the value for X and Y in two different zones.

Lines 50–60: Assigns the value of 3 to X and the value of 4 to Y.

Line 70: Prints out the values for X and Y on the same line.

Line 80: Ends the program.

String Variables

Background: A LET statement can also store string variables or words in the computer's memory. When a person types LET A$="Tom Smith", the variable A$ stores Tom Smith in its memory location. When the computer is instructed to print A$, it will display this name on the screen.

Example:

```
10 Let A$="is that Doggie"
20 Let B$="How much "
30 Let C$=" in the window?"
40 Print B$;A$;C$
50 End
```

Output:

```
How much is that Doggie in the window?
```

Explanation:

Lines 10–30: Assigns words or characters to A$,B$, and C$.

Line 40: Instructs the computer to print these strings in a prescribed order. The semicolon tells the computer to put the words on the same line.

Line 50: Ends the program.

Input Statements

Background: The INPUT statement introduces data from a keyboard. When the computer runs an input statement, it prints out a question mark and then waits for the individual to answer the question.

Example:

```
10 Print: "What is your Name?"
20 Input A$
30 Print"How old are you?"
40 Input X
50 Let F=X+3
60 Print A$;"In three years you will be";F;"years old."
70 End
```

Output:

```
What is your Name?
? David
How old are you?
? 6
David In three years you will be 9 years old.
```

Explanation

Line 10: Prints the question: What is your name?

Line 20: The input displays a question mark on next line, waits for a person's response, and stores it as a A$.

Line 30: Prints the question: How old are you?

Line 40: The input displays another question mark, waits for another response, and then stores it as variable X.

Line 50: Takes the value for X that was entered in line 40 and adds 3, then stores the variable as F.

Line 60: Prints A$, the sentence in quotes, and F's value.

Line 70: Ends the program.

IF-THEN Statements

Background: The IF-THEN Statement is a conditional statement because the action that the computer takes depends upon whether or not the statement is true. If the statement is true, the computer does what the line tells it to do. If the statement is false, the computer automatically goes to the next line.

Example:

```
10 Print"You are in a deep dark cave."
20 Print"Suddenly, a monster attacks you."
```

```
30 Print"Should you run away or fight the monster?"
40 Input A$
50 Print
60 If A$="Run" then Print "While you are running you fall."
70 Print
80 If A$="Fight" then Print "You defeat the monster."
90 End
```

Output:

```
You are in a deep dark cave.
Suddenly, a monster attacks you.
Should you run away or fight the monster?
? Run

While you are running you fall.
```

Output:

```
You are in a deep dark cave.
Suddenly, a monster attacks you.
Should you run away or fight the monster?
? Fight


You defeat the monster.
```

Explanation

Lines 10–30: Each line prints a sentence of a short story and then asks the reader to make a decision between fighting or running.

Line 40: Displays a question mark, waiting for the reader to respond with Run or Fight.

Line 50: Inserts a blank line.

Lines 60, 70, 80: If the response is Run, the computer prints out: While you are running, you fall. Next, the computer goes to line 70, inserts a blank line, ignores line 80, and ends at 90. If the response is fight, the computer ignores line 60, goes to line 70, and inserts a blank line. The computer continues to line 80, and since this statement is true, it prints: You defeat the monster. Then the computer goes to line 90.

Line 90: Ends the program.

GOTO

Background: The GOTO statement breaks into the natural sequence of the program and sends the computer to the designated line number of the GOTO statement. For example, the statement GOTO 80 means the program goes to line 80. GOTO can be used as a conditional part of an IF-THEN statement such as If A$="Yes" then GOTO 30. This means if the person inputs yes, the program jumps to line 30.

Example

```
10 Print "A GOTO statement lets ";
20 GOTO 50
30 Print "Charles Babbage was the Father of Computing."
40  Print "Ada Lovelace was his greatest suporter."
50 Print "you skip lines in a program."
60 Print "True or False John Kemeny and Thomas Kurtz created BASIC?"
70 Input A$
80 If A$="True" then GOTO 110
90 If A$="False" then Print "You are incorrect."
100 GOTO 120
110 Print "You are correct."
120 End
```

Output:

```
A GOTO statement lets you skip lines in a program.
True or False John Kemeny and Thomas Kurtz created BASIC?
? True
You are correct.
```

Output:

```
A GOTO statement lets you skip lines in a program.
True or False John Kemeny and Thomas Kurtz created BASIC'
? False
You are incorrect.
```

Explanation

Line 10: Prints: A GOTO statement lets

Line 20: The GOTO statement sends the computer to line 50.

Lines 30–40: Are never executed because of the GOTO statement in line 20.

Line 50: Because of the semicolon, it prints on the same line: you skip lines in the program.

Line 60: Prints the question, "True or False—John Kemeny and Thomas Kurtz created BASIC?"

Line 70: Waits for the person's response.

Line 80: If the response is true, the program jumps to line 110 where it is instructed to print: You are correct. It then proceeds to the next line where the program ends.

Line 90: If the statement is false, the computer ignores line 80 and continues to the next line. At line 90, it prints: You are incorrect. The program goes to the next line where it is instructed to go to line 120 and end.

Integer Functions

Background: The INT (X) rounds any number into a whole number (integer). For example, if X=42.3, then it will drop the decimal part, making X=42.

Example:

```
10 Let X= (4/2.2)
20 Print X
30 Let Y=INT (4/2.2)
40 Print Y
50 End
```

Output:

```
1.81818
1
```

Explanation

Line 10: Lets X= 4/2.2.

Line 20: Prints the value of X, which has a decimal part.

Line 30: Lets Y=the same value, but this time uses the integer function.

Line 40: Prints Y truncating its decimal part.

Random Number

Background: RND (X) picks at random a decimal fraction between 0 and 1. In many computers, the value for X is a dummy value. Computers vary in the way they randomize numbers. Some use the same value for X, while others use different values.

IBM and Macintosh Example:

```
10 Randomize
20 Print Rnd
30 End
```

Output:

```
.548508
```

Explanation:

Line 10: Instructs the computer to give a different random number each time the program is run.

Line 20: Prints a random number.

Line 30: Ends the program.

Apple Example:

```
10 Print Rnd (1)
20 End
```

Output:

```
.148596
```

Line 10: Prints a random number.

Line 20: Ends the program.

FOR-NEXT Loops

Background: Acting as a pair, the **FOR-NEXT** loop executes the statement between the FOR and NEXT statements as many times as specified in the FOR statement. The FOR statement assigns the values, while the NEXT repeats them.

Example:

```
10 For I=1 to 8
20 Print I
30 Next I
40 End
```

Output:

```
1
2
3
4
5
6
7
8
```

Explanation:

Line 10: The FOR statement instructs the computer to loop 8 times.

Line 20: Prints the value for I.

Line 30: The NEXT statement sends the computer back to print the new value.

READ-DATA Statements

Background: The **READ-DATA** statement instructs the computer to read and store a list of numbers or names. A LET statement stores one value, while a READ-DATA statement stores multiple variables. Whenever the computer encounters a READ statement, it searches for a DATA statement.

Example

```
10 Print"Name", "Score"
20 For I=1 to 5
30 Read A$,B
40 Print A$,B
50 Next I
60 Data Johnson,78,Friedman,99,Jones,89,Raj,88,Foster,78
70 End
```

Output:

```
Name            Score
Johnson          78
Friedman         99
Jones            89
Raj              88
Foster           78
```

Explanation:

Line 10: Prints name in the first zone and score in the second zone.

Line 20: The FOR statement instructs the computer to loop 5 times.

Line 30: Reads a string variable, A$ and a numeric variable, B, from line 60.

Line 40: Prints Johnson under the name zone, and 78 under the score zone.

Line 50: The NEXT statement sends the computer back to read the next two pieces of data. The program ends once the computer loops 5 times.

Since the reader now has some experience with BASIC, it is advantageous to compare three popular, high-level languages, including BASIC. All three languages show a program that computes the average of five values (Figure 12.5).

From this comparison, the reader might conclude that BASIC is a suitable language for the classroom teacher.

This concludes our mini-course on the fundamentals of BASIC programming. In Appendix G there are six, ready-to-run programs in which the reader can explore BASIC further. Since its creation in 1964, there have been many, new, high-level languages. The continued use of BASIC, a relatively old language, has sparked controversy. Within this context, let's examine some of the advantages and disadvantages of teaching BASIC.

Why Teach BASIC?

Until 1979, the computer's disk operating system was not a reality, so BASIC was a necessity. It was built into the ROM chip for most computers. Today BASIC is still on the majority of the school computers, which means that teachers do not have to buy software to program in BASIC. If it is not on the chip, it usually comes free with the

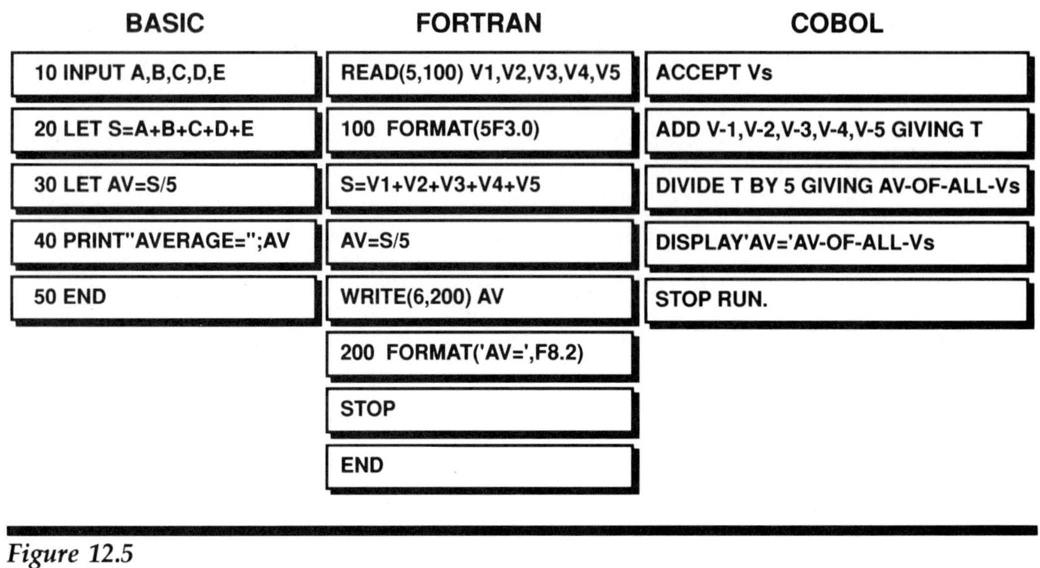

BASIC
10 INPUT A,B,C,D,E
20 LET S=A+B+C+D+E
30 LET AV=S/5
40 PRINT"AVERAGE=";AV
50 END
FORTRAN
READ(5,100) V1,V2,V3,V4,V5
100 FORMAT(5F3.0)
S=V1+V2+V3+V4+V5
AV=S/5
WRITE(6,200) AV
200 FORMAT('AV=',F8.2)
STOP
END
COBOL
ACCEPT Vs
ADD V-1,V-2,V-3,V-4,V-5 GIVING T
DIVIDE T BY 5 GIVING AV-OF-ALL-Vs
DISPLAY'AV='AV-OF-ALL-Vs
STOP RUN.

Figure 12.5
Comparison of Three Languages

computer or is available for a nominal fee. BASIC needs minimal memory and requires no special hardware, so schools do not have to make extra expenditures to teach their students BASIC. Besides being accessible, many proponents maintain that BASIC is the easiest language to learn. Nevertheless, this does not preclude it having complexities that would sustain student's interest. The enhanced BASIC versions have the ability to support graphics, color capabilities, and sound. Many teachers are familiar with BASIC, so teaching it requires no special retraining.

In spite of these attributes, BASIC has its opponents. Many feel that Pascal is superior to BASIC because of its structure, but they discount the many versions of Pascal which do not support graphics. Other opponents prefer Logo over BASIC because of its better graphic capabilities. They proclaim learning how to program graphics in BASIC is more complicated than programming in Logo. The Logo advocates concede that BASIC is easy to learn; however, it does not serve the developmental needs of the young child.

Another criticism is BASIC (Dartmouth version) teaches poor programming techniques because it does not follow the current structured programming principles. This argument does have some credence because it is more difficult for a teacher to learn a program in structured BASIC after this teacher has been programming using the older BASIC. There is a contingency of people who are opposed to teaching any programming because they feel the emphasis should be on computer applications.

The author feels that teaching BASIC is really dependent upon the individual instructor's purpose. This language does give the students and teachers an introduction to computer programming. Chances are many educators and students will not advance beyond writing a few simple programs. However, being able to program does give the teachers and students self-confidence and a willingness to explore the computer's capabilities. Presently there are many newer versions of BASIC, such as True BASIC and Quick BASIC that have made significant improvements on the older versions of BASIC. The author advocates that teaching BASIC programming using an excellent, structured program like True BASIC would be just as appropriate as using Pascal. Unfortunately, there are few books that adequately teach this BASIC, and many of the books that do teach it begin with traditional methods and introduce structure later.

At the end of the chapter, the reader can find many articles and books on BASIC. In chapter 14, there is a synopsis of the recent research on BASIC.

Learning a language is demanding, even though it gives the teacher flexibility. Authoring languages provide an alternative for converting a lesson into a program.

Authoring Languages

An authoring language is "a computer language or application development system designed primarily for creating programs, databases and materials for CAI" (Woodcock, 1991). It lets a teacher design software to meet his or her curriculum needs. By learning only a few core commands, s/he can write interactive lessons and create new programs. The user can design lessons without the countless hours of instruction necessary to learn a computer language. A single authoring language command tells the computer to execute more instructions than a command in a high-level language.

In 1959 Donald Bitzer and a team of specialists developed **PLATO** for use on a mainframe computer. PLATO, one of the earliest computer systems for educational applications, had a special authoring language called **TUTOR.** Using this authoring language, Bitzer and his colleagues produced over 200 lessons for the classroom. Expensive to produce, PLATO utilized a touch screen, and its terminal had a plasma screen that could display sophisticated graphics.

In 1969 John Starkweather and his associates at the University of California, San Francisco, created one of the oldest authoring languages, Programmed Inquiry, Learning, or Training (**PILOT**). Their purpose was to make it easy for teachers to prepare tutorial or drill and practice lessons. This program, produced and developed by Apple Computer in the early 1970s, had only eight commands. The commands usually consisted of one letter with a colon; for example, the command J: meant to jump to a special place in the program and the command E: meant to end the

```
DEFINITION ********* WRITE ****** 0 LINES

 1  T:  DEFINE THE FOLLOWING WORDS:
 2  T:  GIVE A SINGLE WORD DEFINITION.
 3  T:  PRESS RETURN WHEN YOU ARE READY
 4  A:
 5  T:
 6  T:  WHAT DOES LOQUACIOUS MEAN
 7  A:
 8  M:  TALKATIVE, WORDY, GABBY, VERBOSE
 9  TY:  EXCELLENT.  THAT IS CORRECT.
10  TN:  SORRY, THIS IS THE WRONG CHOICE.
11  E:
```

Figure 12.6
An Example of E-Z PILOT II
Permission for use granted by Hartley Courseware, Inc.

program. Since PILOT's introduction, it has been expanded by Apple into SuperPilot which has 26 commands, a graphics editor, and sound effects.

In 1983 Earl L. Kyser Jr., a systems analyst, designed a simplified PILOT (Figure 12.6) called **E-Z PILOT II** (Hartley).

Explanation: E-Z PILOT inserts line number automatically.

Lines 1, 2, 3: The letter **T:** prints the following lines:

```
DEFINE THE FOLLOWING WORDS:
GIVE A SINGLE WORD DEFINITION
PRESS RETURN WHEN YOU ARE READY?
```

The computer inserts a question mark automatically after line 3.

Line 4: A: Prepares the computer to accept an answer from the user.

Line 5: T: Prints a blank line because there are no words after it.

Line 6: T: Prints the following question, inserting a question mark, **WHAT DOES LOQUACIOUS MEAN?**

Line 7: A: Asks the user to type an answer.

Line 8: M: (match command) Compares the student's answer with the following acceptable responses: **TALKATIVE, WORDY, GABBY, VERBOSE**

Line 9 TY: Tells the computer to display the following statement if the student's response is yes.

EXCELLENT. THAT IS CORRECT.

Line 10: TN: Tells the computer to display the following statement if the student's response is no.

SORRY, THIS IS THE WRONG CHOICE.

Line 11: E: Is an end statement.

There are numerous authoring languages designed for educational use (Barker, 1987) including *CourseWriter III* and *Course of Action. Coursewriter III,* a sophisticated language designed for the IBM family of computers, requires considerable programming skill, whereas *Course of Action,* designed for the Macintosh, is considerably easier to use with its icon based menu. Authoring languages today are more powerful and flexible and are still concerned with presenting interactive information to the user. Some specialize in creating tutorial and drill and practice software, while others let the teachers develop simulations for the students. In chapter 10 the author focused on authoring languages that produced multi-media presentations. These presentations created an exploratory environment for the students.

Advantages

In many instances the authoring language, because of its simple command structure, is preferable to a programming language. The authoring language has flexibility which makes allowances for spelling and spacing errors. A teacher can easily customize lessons for the gifted, as well as the less academically-talented students. For example, the teacher may design an interactive program about the Civil War as an independent learning activity. These lessons can have graphics, sound, animation, and rudimentary record keeping capabilities. This authoring language provides a simple way to access a wide range of peripherals such as CD-ROM and videodisc players. Having these features, a teacher can create a multimedia environment using programs such as *Hyper-Studio, HyperCard* or *HyperScreen.* Advanced students can even create presentations putting a lesson in computer format. For example, a student who is learning about the Kennedy Era can have the authoring program access a videotape machine and display a clip of Kennedy delivering a speech. By using an authoring language, a teacher learns valuable information about programming the computer.

Disadvantages

Although there are several benefits of using an authoring language, there are nevertheless some drawbacks. An authoring language does not achieve the same sophistication that a general, all-purpose language does such as BASIC. An authoring language does not have full graphics capabilities nor the same flexibility in producing programs. If an authoring language is enhanced, it becomes more complicated to use than a general, all-purpose language. There is a dearth of instructional materials to help master these languages, and the user relies solely on the user manual with whatever technical support is available. Learning a programming language is time consuming, but preparing a lesson using an authoring language also requires hours of diligent effort.

Another concern is the quality of the software that the teacher eventually creates. The instructor may not be competent enough to create an excellent product, and the authoring program may be limited. Furthermore, most authoring programs run slower, so there is usually more wait time for the students.

From our discussion, the reader should have a clear picture of the pros and cons of an authoring language. Before leaving this topic completely, lets make a distinction between authoring *languages* and authoring *systems.*

Authoring Systems

In the literature authoring languages and authoring systems are used interchangeably. Equating them is incorrect because an authoring system, designed for a special purpose, is a subset of an authoring language. The authoring system is easier to use because the teacher has a predesigned template. However, it is not as flexible as an authoring language, which lets the teacher customize his or her own lessons. An authoring system has prompts that lead an individual step-by-step through its program. Like authoring languages, authoring systems do not limit themselves to drill and practice and tutorial programs, but, on the contrary, the author can create simulations, data bases for management, and adventure games. An example of an authoring system is *Test Designer Plus* (Superschool), which lets the user design tests that are presented interactively to the students.

Summary

The author initially discussed the historical development of languages, giving the reader a background on how and why BASIC became a popular computing language. The reader became familiar with how BASIC operates, its strengths and its weaknesses. Next, authoring languages, an alternative to the general, all-purpose language, were discussed as suitable tools for tailoring specific lessons to the individual instructional needs of the students. Although authoring languages such as PILOT and Easy PILOT II are easier to learn than BASIC, they still require considerable time and effort to produce a quality product. The trend now is to produce more user-friendly and flexible authoring languages like *HyperStudio, HyperScreen,* and *HyperCard.* The author concludes this chapter with some questions and classroom activities, and suggested readings and references.

Chapter Mastery Test

1. Trace the development of programming languages.
2. What are the strengths and weaknesses of an authoring language?
3. Distinguish between an authoring system, authoring language, and a high-level programming language.
4. Explain what a programming language is.
5. Why are BASIC, Logo, and Pascal popular languages in the schools?
6. List two advantages and two disadvantages of using BASIC as a programming language.
7. Give two cogent reasons why programming **should** and two reasons why it **should not** be taught in the schools.
8. What is the difference between an interpreter and a compiler?
9. What is structured programming? What is the debate concerning it?
10. What is the purpose of a Print, For/Next, and Goto statement in BASIC?

Classroom Projects

1. Create a simple BASIC program that:
    a. Displays a student's name three times.
    b. Uses a For/Next statement to count to 20.
2. Using historic references, research a programming language. Prepare a two page report that answers the following: A. How did the language originate? B. What are its features? and C. How is the language being used today?
3. Revise one of the six ready-to-run programs found in Appendix G so that it meets specific curriculum needs.
4. Using an authoring language, design a lesson for the class's specific curriculum needs.
5. Using a flowchart, plan a lesson for the computer.

Suggested Readings and References

Abernathy, Joe. "Breaking the Programming Code: Part I." *Incider A+* (June 1990): 51–56.

Abernathy, Joe. "Programming Part I." *Incider A+* (July 1990): 56–62.

Agular, Hugh. "BASIC Recursive Techniques." *Computer Language,* May 1985.

Anderson R. Bennett, H., and Walling, D. "Structured Programming Constructs in BASIC: Tried and Tested." *Computers in the Schools* (Summer 1987): 135–139.

Athey, Thomas H. *Computers and End-user Software with BASIC.* Glenview, Ill.: Scott, Foresman, 1987.

Barker, P. *Author Languages for CAI.* London: MacMillan Education Ltd., 1987.

Campbell, Tom. "Programming Power." *Compute,* 13(6) (1 June 1991): 73.

Chandler, Anthony. "Write Faster BASIC Program." *Compute,* 13(4) (1 April 1991): G–10.

Conlin, T. *PILOT: The Language and How to Use It Including Apple PILOT and SuperPILOT.* Englewood Cliffs, NJ: Prentice-Hall, 1984.

Cooper, James W. *Microsoft QuickBASIC for Scientists: A Guide to Writing Better Programs.* New York: Wiley, 1988.

Cotton, Larry. "BASIC for Beginners: Keys to BASIC Programming." *Compute!'s Gazette,* 7(11) (1 November 1989): 63.

Davis, William S. *True BASIC Primer.* Reading, MA: Addison-Wesley Publishing Company, 1986.

Dodd, Kenneth Nelson. *Computer Programming and Languages.* London: Butterworths, 1969.

Elson, Mark. *Concept of Programming Languages.* Science Research Associates, 1973.

Gates, Bill. "The 25th Birthday of BASIC." *Byte* (October 1989): 268–272.

Harter, Edward D. *BASIC-PLUS and VAX BASIC Structured Programming.* Englewood Cliffs, N.J.: Prentice Hall, 1988.

Heimler, Charles, Jim Cunningham, and Michael Nevard. *BASIC for Teachers.* Santa Cruz, Ca: Mitchell Publishing, 1987.

Horowitz, Ellis. *Fundamentals of Programming Languages.* Rockville Mo.: Computer Science Press, 1984.

Kemeny, John G. and Thomas E. Kurtz. *True BASIC, Macintosh User's Guide,* West Lebanon, N.H.: True Basic, Inc., 1989.

Levy, Steven. *Hackers: Heroes of the Computer Revolution* Garden City, New York: Doubleday, Author Press, 1984.

Milland, Pamela J. "Current Major Programming Languages." *PC Magazine* (13 September 1988): 96–97.

Nickerson, Robert C. *Fundamentals of Programming in BASIC: A Structured Approach* 2nd Edition. Boston: Little, Brown, 1986.

Poirot, J. L. and R. C. Adams. *40 Easy Steps to Programming BASIC and LOGO.* Austin, TX: Sterling Swift Publishing Co., 1983.

Ross, S. M. *BASIC Programming for Educators.* Prentice-Hall: Englewood Cliffs, New Jersey, 1986.

Spencer, Donald D. *Computer Mathematics with BASIC Programming.* Ormond Beach, FLA.: Camelot Publishing Co., 1990.

Starkweather, John. *A User's Guide to PILOT.* Englewood Cliffs, N.J.: Prentice-Hall, 1985.

Wexelblat, Richard L. ed. *History of Programming Language Design*. New York: Academic Press, 1981.

Winer, Ethan. "BASIC, Yes; Feeble, No." *PC Magazine*, 8(18) (31 October 1989): 187.

Logo

13

Objectives

Upon completing this chapter the student will be able to:

1. Trace the development of Logo.
2. Define the following terms: *primitive, procedure, recursion,* and *variable.*
3. Draw simple geometric shapes and patterns.
4. Give the key arguments for and against teaching Logo

Background

When **artificial intelligence (AI)** began in the 1950's, the researchers were looking for a language to express concepts in human words. Their first attempt was a family of languages called Information Processing Languages (IPL) whose central idea was the "list." By putting data in lists, the programmers linked concepts in the computer's memory similar to the way AI researchers think ideas are stored in the human brain. John McCarthy, a distinguished member of the artificial intelligence community, established an AI lab at Massachusetts Institute of Technology (M.I.T.) and in 1958 started working on a language that combined the use of lists with a set of symbols. He borrowed concepts from a branch of mathematics named lambda calculus and called his high-level language **LISP,** an abbreviation for "**LIST PROCESSING.**"

LISP is simply lists of symbols within parentheses, and a small section of a **LISP** program may include dozens of pairs of list defining parentheses such as (PUT(QUOTE BOAT)(QUOTE LOC)(QUOTE(9 4))). In this list, the function PUT assigns the Cartesian coordinates(9,4) to a boat's location, the function QUOTE tells the computer that the user wants to see the name of a list, not its value, and the symbol LOC is the name of the location that belongs to the symbol, boat. This language is difficult to read, but because of its structure, the user can write programs that modify other computer programs. In addition, s/he can write programs or subroutines that can refer to themselves in a process known as **recursion,** which gives the program the ability to repeat itself.

Presently, LISP is the principle programming language for AI research in the United States, and it's the second-oldest, general-purpose language in use. LISP has ease, speed, and the ability to write, run, and modify programs. Because of LISP's unique properties, it has many spin-off languages, with Logo being the most popular. Logo contains many functions found in LISP; however, Logo is less cryptic and it is user-friendly. Logo is a high-level language designed for children.

Logo

Seymour Papert, his MIT colleagues, and members of Bolt, Beranek, & Newman, Inc., created Logo. Papert, a mathematics professor, received his educational background from studying with Jean Piaget and from working in artificial intelligence. Papert felt that school age children could learn to program, and he was convinced that BASIC was too abstract for the young child. This belief motivated him to create Logo. It was a language that was originally used on the mainframe computers, but because of advances in computer technology, programs were eventually devised for the microcomputer.

In 1979 the first version of Logo was written for the Apple and the Texas Instruments 99/4 computers. Since then, there has been a proliferation of Logo versions, including Apple Logo, Logo II, and LogoWriter (Logo Computer Systems, Inc.), Logo Plus, Terrapin and Krell (MIT versions). Along with these programs, there are simplified versions like EZ Logo (MECC).

Papert's clever innovation, the turtle, was first introduced in the form of a mechanical turtle that crawled on the floor, later as a graphic on the screen. Using simple commands, the children were able to write programs that moved the triangular shaped turtle across the screen. For example, if a child gives the following commands: Forward 50, Right 90, and Forward 50, the turtle will move as follows:

Logo Software available from Terrapin Software, Inc., 400 Riverside Street, Portland, ME 04103.

WHY Teach Logo?

Why should the teacher choose Logo when BASIC is built into the ROM of most machines? What makes this investment in software worthwhile? The nature of Logo makes it a good introduction to other procedural languages like Pascal. Logo is a structured language that encourages the user to develop good programming techniques. In its initial stages, Logo is an easy language to use that lets the novice learn logic and programming in a brief time frame. Most teachers who use Logo in the classrooms create designs that can help the children learn geometric concepts and develop an intuitive sense of logical patterning.

A tool for creative exploration, Logo is also an interactive programming language that helps individuals learn from their mistakes. The user receives instantaneous feedback, allowing the child to revise the program immediately. But there are some drawbacks to this language. Since Logo handles the processing of lists and operates on numbers and words, it requires a large memory and file-handling capabilities that are appropriate for more difficult and sophisticated applications. According to the research (chapter 14), the evidence that Logo can improve problem solving and affective skill development is inconclusive.

Philosophy and Psychology of Logo

In 1980 Seymour Papert wrote the book, *Mindstorms,* in which he discussed his theories on how a computer should be used in the classroom. He felt a computer is best utilized to aid in the thinking process and not as a piece of hardware that dispenses information. He observed that CAI usually meant that the computer was being used to program the child and the child was the passive receiver of information. Papert said:

> "In my vision, the child programs the computer and, in doing so, both acquires a sense of mastery over a piece of the most modern and powerful technology and establishes an intimate contact with some of the deepest ideas from science, from mathematics, and from the art of intellectual model building." (Papert, 1980, p. 5)

According to Papert, Logo creates an environment where children are free to explore and discover. They can learn geometric concepts, actively test and retest their theories, and improve intellectual development. Papert contends that the majority of schools' mathematics programs have nothing to do with reality because the students are taught in a rote, meaningless way. According to Papert, this is the reason most children grow up hating and fearing mathematics. Logo combats this problem by letting the child experience a meaningful mathematics environment. Furthermore, Papert sees other ways that Logo can aide learning across all curriculum areas. For example, he discusses a student named Jenny who had difficulty with English grammar. When she used Logo to generate poetry, she discovered the necessity of knowing the difference between a noun and a verb in order to teach the computer how to write poetry. Because Jenny used Logo, she found a meaningless activity now meaningful.

Papert uses the term "microworld" to describe the Logo environment where the child freely experiments, tests, and revises his or her own theories in order to create a product. Using the microworld, the child better understands concepts in analytical geometry, physics, grammar, and composition. It is a playground of the mind where the computer program lets the learner explore a concept from an intuitive to a formal level. The product can be one the child wants to create to fulfill his or her needs, and the creation of this product is meaningful to the child.

Logo has been used in all areas of the curriculum, even though the majority of programs in schools have focused on it as a tool to teach mathematics. Using Logo, the students can explore mathematical ideas such as simple geometry concepts, estimation skills, and topology. A student can use Logo for problem solving when s/he breaks down a problem into smaller parts and debugs a program. In the language arts area, the student can utilize *LogoWriter,* which combines word processing with graphics, to create text for describing their Logo graphics work. Using Logo's simple, list-processing capabilities, students can teach the computer parts of speech or subject-verb agreement or poetry. In science the students can use a program like *Lego Tc Logo,* which combines Legos with the Logo programming. They can write programs that build objects, such as cars, control their movements, and, in the process, learn about physics and develop problem solving skills. Furthermore, by using commercial kits such as *The Science Toolkit* (Brøderbund) or *Playing with Science Temperature* (Sunburst) the students can use the computer as a measuring tool. They can write their own simple Logo programs and have the computer generate a chart or graph. For example, the students might plug a thermistor into a port, a device whose resistance varies with temperature, and use Logo, to write a chart-graphic procedure that produces a graph of temperature changes. In social studies, the students can use *LogoWriter* to write about geographical concepts or use Logo to create interesting maps.

Working with Logo

The following Logo introduction familiarizes the reader with the basic concepts of Logo programming. The reader should use the following examples in order to understand the full potential of this language. Type the sample programs, run them, and save them on a disk. The programs that follow are written on the Macintosh, using *Terrapin Logo* (Logo Software available from Terrapin Software, Inc., 400 Riverside St., Portland, ME 04103). When variations occur, it will be indicated in boldface type, and the *Logo Computer Systems Incorporated* (LCSI) Apple II version will be shown. In general, all Logo programs are similar, so the user should be able to make the transition from the chapter examples to his or her own version.

Instructions: Insert a copy of Logo in the disk drive, boot it, and when message **Welcome** appears, do the following:

Type ST for SHOWTURTLE and one of the following turtles appears:

LCSI Logo Computer Systems (Logo II Turtle). Logo Software available from Terrapin Software Inc., 400 Riverside St., Portland, ME 04103

Terrapin Turtle

Logo II Turtle

BACKGROUND

Logo primitives are commands built into the language itself. There are over 100 of these commands, but a novice needs to use just a few to program. The following table shows the primitives that the author will discuss in this chapter.

Primitive	Abbreviation	Explanation
SHOWTURTLE	ST	Shows the turtle
HIDETURTLE	HT	Hides the turtle
FORWARD	FD	Moves forward
BACK	BK	Moves backward
RIGHT	RT	Turns right
LEFT	LT	Turns left
CLEARSCREEN or CLEARGRAPHICS	CS or CG depends on version	Clears the screen
PENUP	PU	Does not leave trail
PENDOWN	PD	Leaves trail
HOME	HOME	Returns home

Instructions: When the reader types in one of these commands (for example, Forward) s/he gives it a numerical value, such as 50, which moves the turtle 50 turtle steps forward. Using an abbreviation for the primitive, type in the following instructions. Be sure to put a **space** between the primitive and the number and press return or enter.

1. Forward Example

FD 40

Output

Explanation: The turtle moves forward 40 steps.

2. Right Example

RT 90

Output

Explanation: The turtle turns 90 degrees, based on a 360 degree turning ratio.

3. Backward Example

BK 40

Output

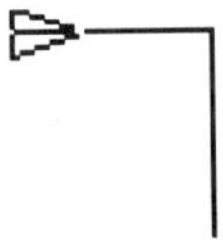

Explanation: The turtle moves 40 steps backward.

4. Left Example

LT 270

Output

Explanation: The turtle turns 270 degrees to the left, based on a 360 degree circle.

5. Combination Example

FD 40 LT 90 FD 40

Output

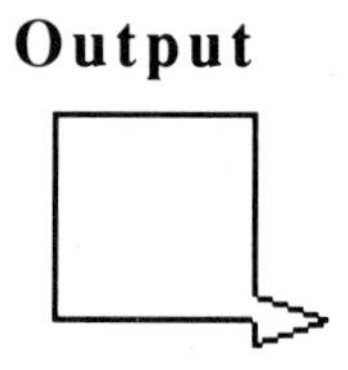

Explanation: The author gives the turtle a series of directions, which tells the turtle to move forward 40 steps, then turn left 90 degrees, and finally move forward 40. These instructions in steps 1 through 5 allow the turtle to complete the square.

Notice the turtle turned in degrees; a degree is the number used to measure the amount of a turn. The command RT 90 degrees turns the turtle right 90 degrees. When the turtle completes a square, it ends up facing the same direction. **The Total Turtle Trip Theorem** states that the turtle must turn a total of 360 degrees to go around a closed figure in order to return to its original heading.

6. HIDETURTLE Example

```
HT
```

Output

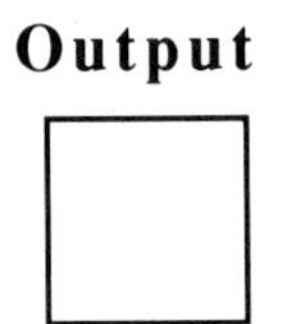

Explanation: The drawing remains, but the turtle has disappeared from the screen.

7. CLEARSCREEN or CLEARGRAPHICS Example

CS or CG (CS clears the screen for *Apple Logo* and CG clears the graphics for *LogoWriter* and *Terrapin.*)

Explanation: The drawings are cleared from the screen.

8. PENUP Example

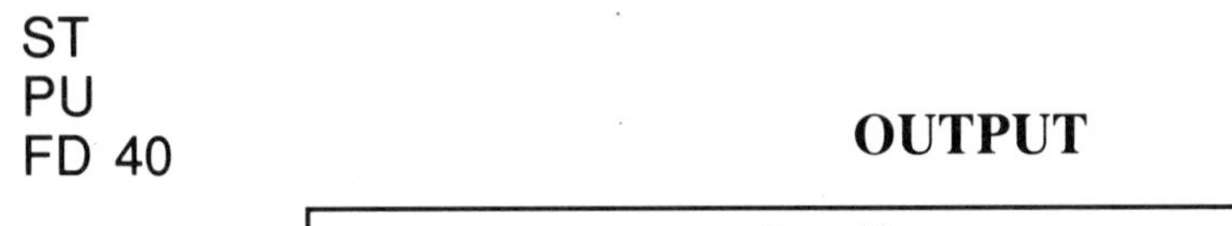

```
ST
PU
FD 40
```

OUTPUT

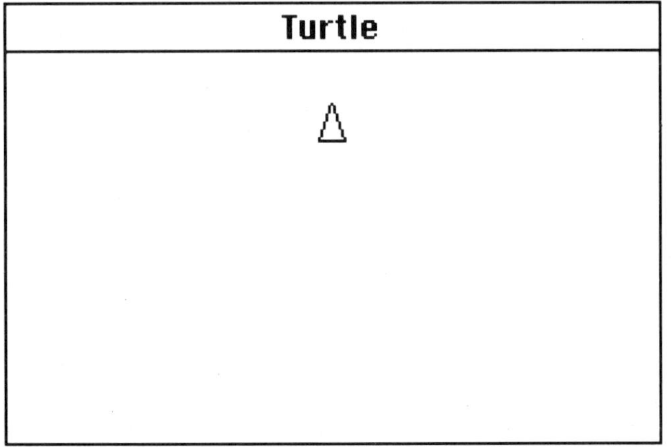

Explanation: The ST command shows the turtle, and the PENUP command tells the computer to move the turtle without leaving a trail. FD 40 moves the turtle forward 40 steps with no trail.

9. PENDOWN Example

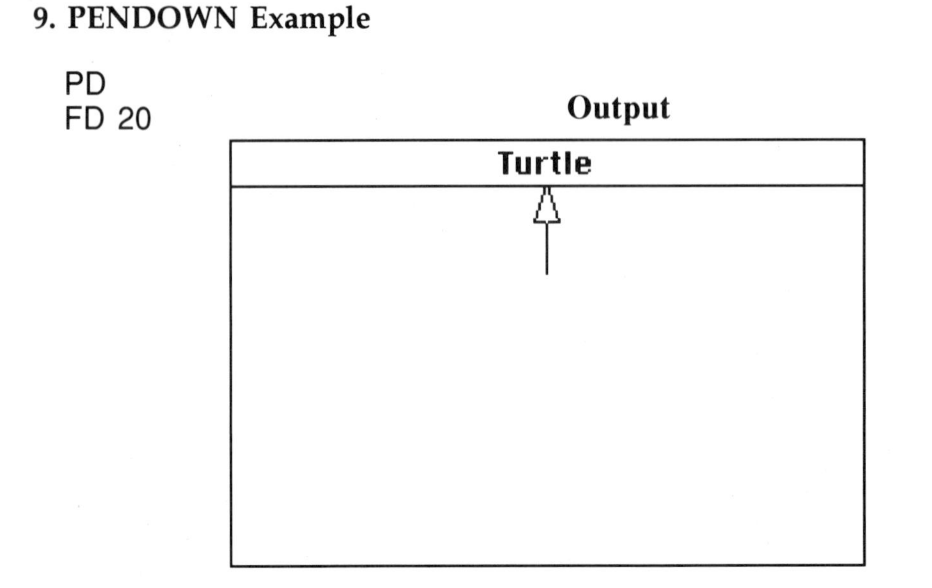

Explanation: The PENDOWN command instructs the computer to reinstate the trail, and when the user types **PENDOWN,** every command that follows will leave a trail. FORWARD 20 steps leaves a trail with 20 steps.

10. HOME Example

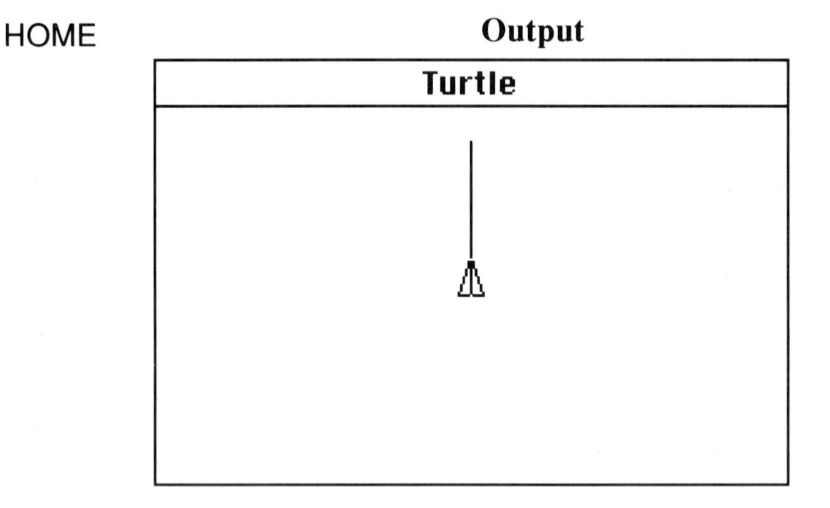

Explanation: The HOME command returns the turtle to its original position.

11. REPEAT Example

After working with Logo, the reader will notice he or she is reusing the same commands; the repeat command shortens this procedure.

Instructions: Clear the screen by typing CS or CG.

REPEAT Example

```
REPEAT 4[FD 40 RT 90]
```

OUTPUT

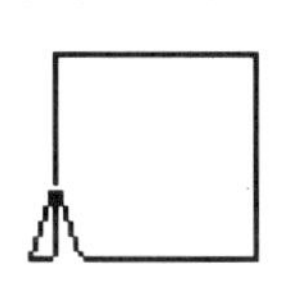

Explanation: This primitive tells the turtle to repeat the directions in the square brackets. In this example, the turtle repeats FORWARD 40, RIGHT 90 four times. When it stops, it has drawn a square. Using this repeat command, the student can draw interesting geometric patterns.

Procedures

By using these primitives, the reader can write a procedure, a set of instructions stored in the computer's memory. So far, all the turtle can do is move forward, backward, turn right and left, and use the REPEAT command to create a square. The author has not taught it how to draw a square, and if the reader types in the word square in Terrapin Logo, the program will respond "There is no procedure named SQUARE." Let's teach the turtle how to draw a square.[1]

Instructions: Clear the screen and type the following procedure for creating a square. Be sure to leave a space between TO and SQUARE.

Square Procedure Example

```
TO SQUARE
REPEAT 4[FD 40 RT 90]
HT
END
```

1. Consult the owner's manual for the specific directions for getting into the editor and defining a procedure. Some versions execute the procedure outside the editor, while others execute the procedures inside the editor.

Instructions: Type **SQUARE** to have it appear on the screen. SQUARE is a new primitive added to Logo's vocabulary which the reader can use whenever s/he wants by simply typing its name.

Output

Explanation: The **TO** tells the computer that the user is about to define a procedure and the **SQUARE** is the name given to the procedure by the user. (The user could just as easily have called the procedure SQ or Box.) In this case, REPEAT 4 tells the computer to repeat four times what is in the brackets and FORWARD 40, RIGHT 90 creates a square. The HT hides the turtle, and END ends the program. Now let's invent a design using the SQUARE procedure.

Instructions: Clear the screen and type the following:

Design Subprocedure Example

```
TO DESIGN
REPEAT 8 [SQUARE RT 45]
END
```

Instructions: After the design has been defined, type DESIGN and press return or enter.

OUTPUT

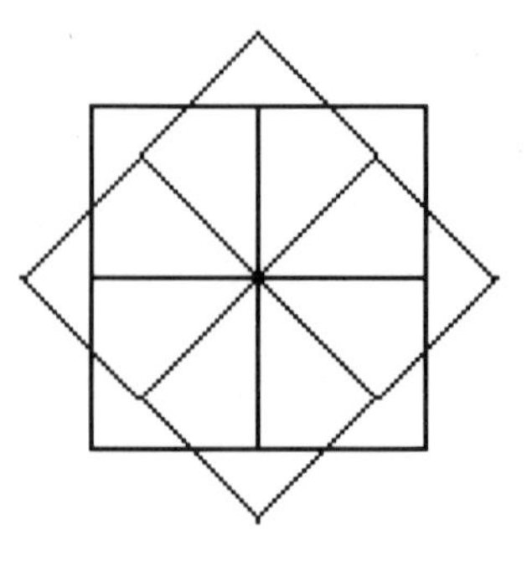

Explanation: The **REPEAT** command instructs the turtle to repeat 8 times the procedure SQUARE and turn it 45 degrees each time. For practice, the reader should create a procedure for a star or a triangle.

Logo is a powerful language because the student can use new words or procedures to define other words and can take a simple procedure to create a more complicated one. In the next example, the author will take two subprocedures that create circles and use them to create a Lazy8 superprocedure.[2]

Instructions: Clear the screen and type in the following procedure, CIRCLE.

Circle Example

```
TO CIRCLE
REPEAT 36[FD 10 RT 10]
END
```

Instructions: After circle has been defined, type CIRCLE.

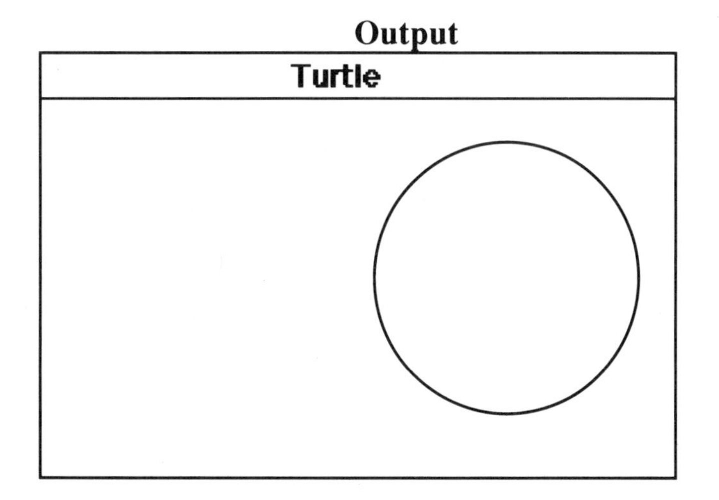

2. A superprocedure is a procedure that uses other procedures that are called subprocedures.

Explanation: REPEAT 36 tells the computer to repeat 36 times what is in brackets Forward 10, RT 10, drawing a circle that is on the right side of the screen.

Instructions: Clear the screen and type in the following procedure, CIRCLEC.

CIRCLEC Example

```
TO CIRCLEC
REPEAT 36[FD 10 LT 10]
END
```

Instructions: After CIRCLEC has been defined, type CIRCLEC and push return or enter.

Output

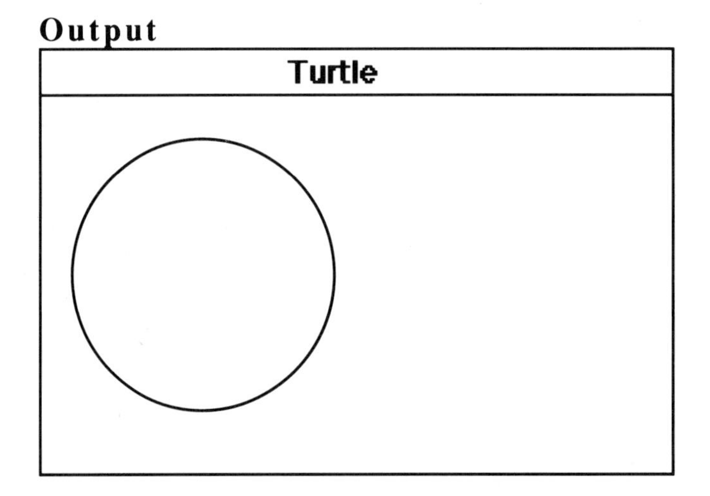

Explanation: The REPEAT tells the turtle to repeat 36 times what's inside the brackets, drawing a circle to the left.

Instructions: Clear the screen and type the LAZY8 :

LAZY 8 Example

```
TO LAZY8
CIRCLE
CIRCLEC
SEND
```

Instructions: After LAZY8 has been defined, type LAZY8 and press return or enter.

OUTPUT

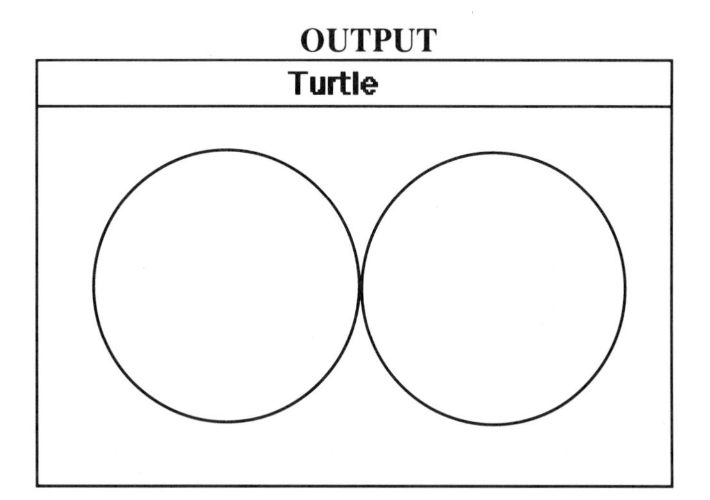

Explanation: T0 starts the procedure, **Lazy8. CIRCLE** is the first subprocedure, and **CIRCLEC** is the second subprocedure. **END** finishes the new procedure.

As the reader works with Logo, s/he should experiment and attempt more complicated projects such as designing a house. This is not a difficult task if the user breaks this assignment into smaller components or subprocedures, for example, a roof, a door, or a window. Let us begin to create a house by first defining a procedure for the body. Type the following:

Instructions: Clear the screen and show the turtle.

BODY Example

```
TO BODY
REPEAT 4[FD 80 RT 90] FD 80
END
```

Instructions: After **BODY** is defined, type BODY which shows the following:

Output

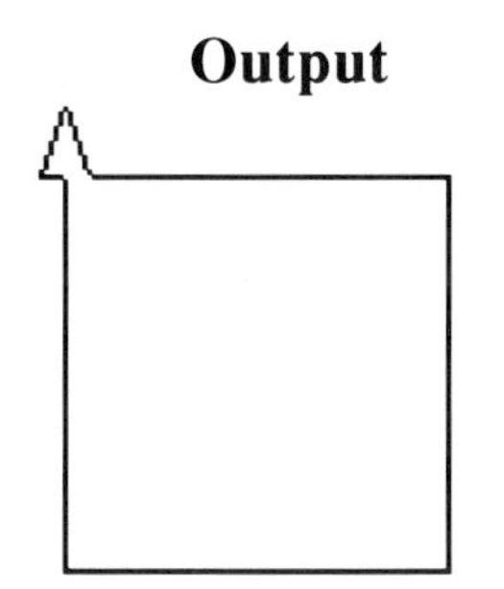

Explanation: TO starts the procedure and **BODY** is its name The repeat tells the computer to repeat what is inside the brackets, creating a square. The FORWARD 80 brings the turtle to the top, poised to draw a roof. Now the reader is ready to write a procedure for a roof.

Instructions: Clear the screen and show the turtle.

ROOF Example

```
TO ROOF
RT 45 FD 57 RT 90 FD 57 RT 135 FD 81
END
```

Instructions: After the roof is defined, type **ROOF** which shows the following output:

Output

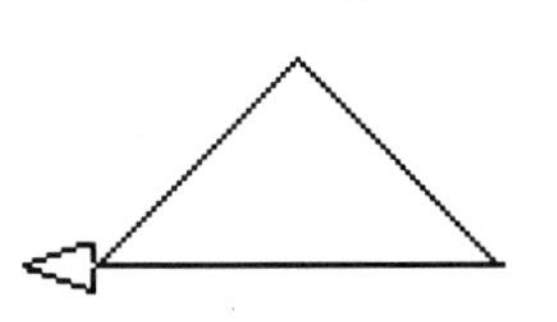

Explanation: The roof is drawn with the following series of directions:

1. Turn right 45 degrees (RT 45), go forward 57 (FD 57)—left side of roof.
2. Turn right 90 degrees, which is two 45 degree angles (RT 90), and go forward 57 (FD 57)—right side of roof.
3. Turn right 135 degrees, which is three 45 degree angles (RT 135), and go forward 81 (FD 81). Step 3's directions retrace the top side of the body completing the roof.[3]

The reader is now able to write a superprocedure that will draw a house, using the subprocedures for body and roof.

3. The roof is a right isosceles triangle whose hypotenuse (bottom side) is actually 80.6, but because of the screen's imperfections is 81.

Instructions: Clear the screen, hide the turtle, and type the following:

House Example

```
TO HOUSE
BODY
ROOF
HT
END
```

Instructions: After the procedure for house is defined, type HOUSE, and press return or enter.

OUTPUT

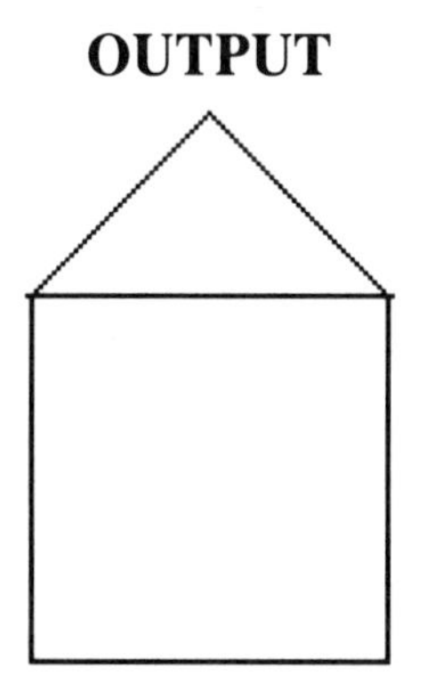

Explanation: The **TO** starts the procedure and **HOUSE** is its name. The first subprocedure executed is BODY which uses the procedure it just learned. The second procedure executed is ROOF, HT hides the turtle, and the **END** statement ends the procedure. When the reader writes a procedure, s/he is using modular programming, which breaks the problem into separate components, each of which can be programmed as a separate unit. For this example, the reader separately created two components, a body and a roof, tested them to see if they ran, then merged them into another procedure called HOUSE.

As the reader becomes experienced with Logo, s/he will create procedures to get different size squares or circles. Previously, the computer user wrote a procedure for a square size of 40, and this procedure was only applicable for this square size. If the user wanted a square size of 60, s/he had to create another procedure. To avoid writing different procedures for each new square or circle generated, the reader can use variables.

Logo Variables

Variables let the user write only one procedure to cover all cases. A variable is a part of a procedure that changes when the user tells it to change. Instead of typing the number 40 FD in the Square procedure, the user types in **:SIZE.** In the following example, the user can enter any number wanted for the size of the square to run the procedure.

Variable Example

```
TO SQUARE:] SIZE
REPEAT 4[FD :SIZE RT 90]
HT
END
```

Instructions: After the procedure is defined, type SQUARE followed by a number; for example, **SQUARE 10.**

OUTPUT

□

Explanation: The **TO** starts the procedure and the word **SQUARE** is the name of the new procedure. The colon is important because it tells the program the author is naming a variable location. The word SIZE (**:SIZE)** is the name of the variable location for this procedure. There is no space between the colon and size. The author can use any name as long as it begins with a letter or a word. For example, the user can call it **:L** or **:INPUT.** Every time a person runs this procedure, s/he types the name of the procedure with a value. The REPEAT command tells the turtle to repeat 4 times the set of actions inside the brackets, the HT command conceals the turtle and leaves the small square.

Recursion

Another powerful feature of Logo is its use of recursion, the ability of a program module to call itself. Recursion goes one step further and uses a procedure to call itself as a subprocedure. The program loops back and starts the procedure again, and this continues until the user stops the program. Clear the screen and type the following example.

Instructions: First create a square procedure like the one enclosed in the rectangle.

Recursion Example

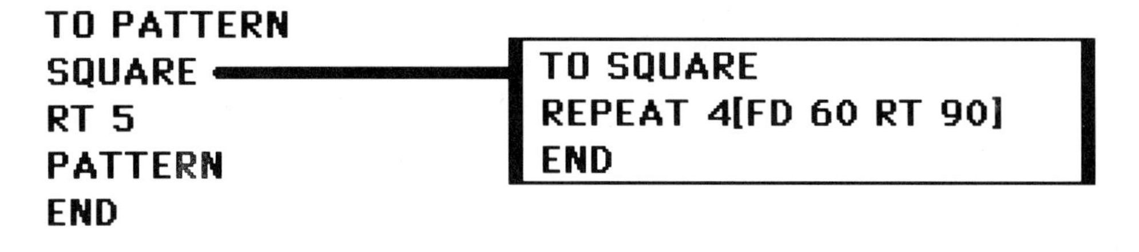

```
TO PATTERN
SQUARE
RT 5
PATTERN
END
```

```
TO SQUARE
REPEAT 4[FD 60 RT 90]
END
```

Instructions: After the superprocedure pattern is defined, type **PATTERN.**

Output

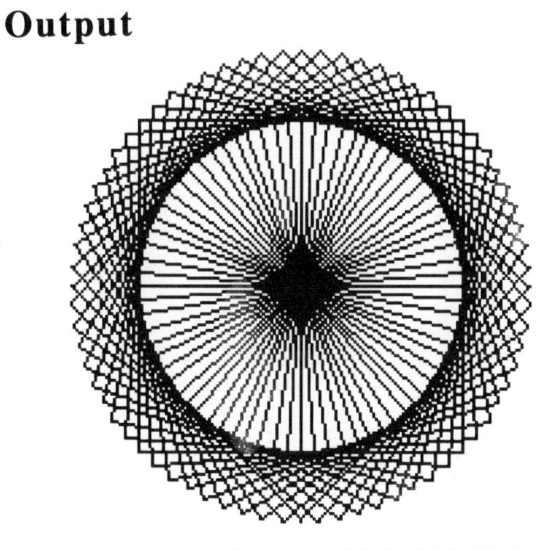

Explanation: The **TO** starts the procedure, and **PATTERN** is the name of the new procedure. The SQUARE procedure produces a square, using FORWARD 60 RIGHT 90. The instructions for this subprocedure are enclosed in the box. The command RIGHT 5 turns this square right 5 degrees, and when the turtle reaches PATTERN, it repeats the same procedure, drawing a square, and turning it 5 degrees right. The procedure then reaches PATTERN again and repeats itself. This process continues forever, and the turtle will eventually retrace its lines. If the reader hides the turtle, s/he can see it going around and around. The only way to stop this program for Terrapin Logo is to use Command G.[4] Let's do another example using the same stop command.

---

4. Use the stop command that is appropriate for your version of Logo, for example Terrapin Logo Macintosh Version uses Command G, Logowriter uses open Apple S, Apple LOGO II uses an open apple ESC.

EFFECT Example

```
TO EFFECT :SIZE
FD :SIZE RT 90
EFFECT :SIZE + 3
END
```

Instructions: After **EFFECT** is defined, type EFFECT 3. Once the turtle has retraced many of its lines, use the stop command (Command **G**) . The reader's output should look similar to the following:

Output

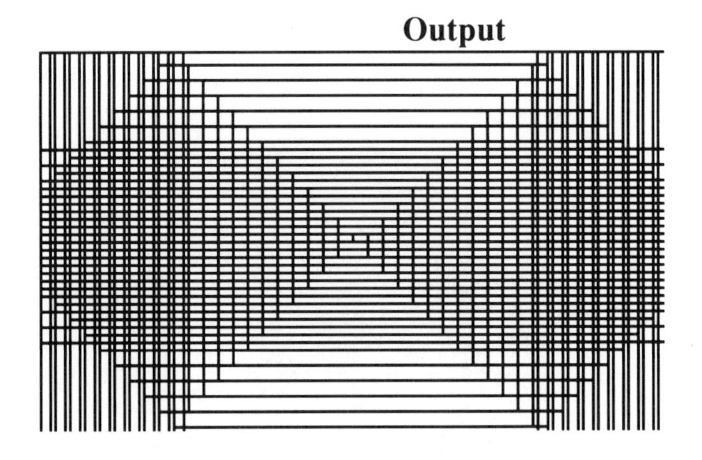

Explanation: The **TO** starts the procedure, and **EFFECT** is its name. The colon tells the program the author is naming a variable location, and the word SIZE (**:SIZE)** is the name of the variable location for this procedure. Every time the reader runs the procedure, s/he types the name of the procedure with a value. **EFFECT :SIZE +3** tells the computer to run EFFECT with its present size (3) and increase it by 3. The size will be increased by 3 every time this procedure is executed. Because of recursion, the **END** command is never reached. If the reader had not used the stop command, the program would have continued running forever.

Besides using a stop command like command G, the user can halt a procedure within a program. S/he needs to use a conditional statement such as, "If S>50[stop] or If S>50 stop." If the statement is true, then the program ends, and if the statement is false, then the procedure continues endlessly. Using the previous example including a conditional statement IF :SIZE=171[STOP], the reader should type the following example:

STOP EXAMPLE

```
TO EFFECT :SIZE
IF :SIZE = 171 [STOP]
FD :SIZE RT 90
EFFECT :SIZE + 3
END
```

Instructions: After effect is defined, type EFFECT 3.

Output

Explanation: The **TO** starts the procedure, and **EFFECT** is the name of the new procedure. The colon tells the program the author is naming a variable location, and the word SIZE (**:SIZE**) is the name of the variable location for this procedure. The **If :SIZE=171[stop]** tells the turtle to stop when it reaches a size of 171. The next line tells the turtle to go forward the number the user enters (3) and turn 90 degrees. The line **EFFECT :S+3** tells the turtle to run EFFECT and increase the size by 3, and the **END** ends the program if the value for SIZE=171.

Logo's other features

The reader should now be familiar with primitives, procedures, variables, and recursion. These powerful ideas apply to other parts of Logo, not just turtle graphics. Besides drawing pictures, Logo has many other capabilities such as letting the user work with numbers, words, and lists. In working with numbers, Logo knows how to add, subtract, multiply, and divide, and it uses the symbols +, –, *, and /. By typing **Print** the user can get it to add three numbers.

Example

Print 50+40+66

Output

156

Logo interprets a word as a series of characters with no blanks to separate them, so the user can have Logo print out words by typing.

Example

Print"Computer

Output

Computer

By working with lists, the reader can handle complex sets of information. A list is a set of words separated by blanks and enclosed in brackets [computer monitor printer scanner]. Whenever the reader works with Logo in this capacity, s/he has special commands that operate with lists of word. These commands can randomly pick out a name, a phrase or a closing message. Besides working with words, numbers, and lists, some versions of Logo can produce music. The student can then write sound effects to accompany graphics. For a more in-depth discussion of Logo, refer to the Logo books listed at the end of the chapter.

Other Versions of Logo

Originally Logo lacked turtle graphics, ran only on mainframes, and used slow printers; however, there has been dramatic improvement in Logo. Logo now has sound graphics, excellent color, and even telecommunication and data base capabilities. Starting with EZ Logo, let us examine some other versions of Logo.

EZ Logo Revised

EZ Logo Revised (MECC) is a popular program among teachers who want to introduce young children to the Logo language. It is an independent, simplified version of Logo, not relying on Apple Logo software. *EZ Logo Revised* lets the children draw with five different colors and print the pictures they create. There is a status message showing pen status, color, and available disk space. The children can control the computer and discover what turtle graphics is. They are introduced to turtle commands and movement and learn to direct the turtle's motion on the screen. *EZ Logo Revised* has a series of twenty-four activities, where the commands can be used in a variety of combinations. These activities,

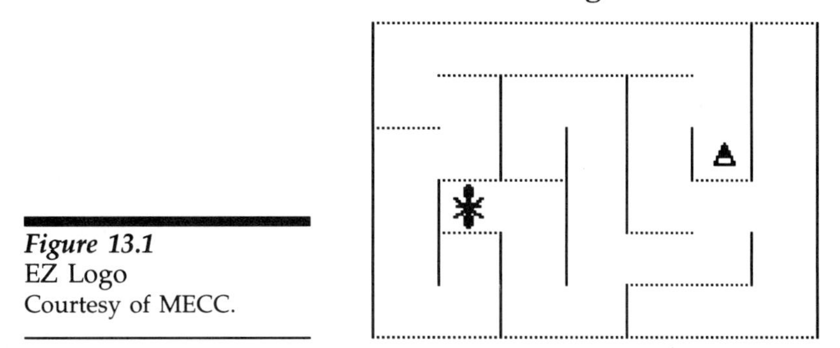

Figure 13.1
EZ Logo
Courtesy of MECC.

ordered according to level of difficulty, include such activities as maze tracing (Figure 13.1), and drawing letters, words, and patterns.

Using this program, the children can create original drawings that can be saved as procedures which are retrievable. They can learn a variety of skills: recognizing directions, estimating distances and degrees, and using procedures. Because many young children are not ready for two letter commands, *EZ Logo Revised* uses a simple set of one-letter commands. Unlike Logo, it does not have turtle degrees, number inputs, variables, and workspace management routines.

Two other noteworthy programs of a similar nature are *Logo Robot* (Scholastic) and *SeeLogo-School Version* (K-12 Micro Media Publishing). These programs prepare children for the Logo experience, whereas *LogoWriter,* a unique version of Logo, includes some special features.

LogoWriter

In 1986, LSCI released *LogoWriter,* a program that increased Logo's flexibility by combining programming capabilities with word processing. The programming part of *LogoWriter* is similar to Logo II, while the word processing component lets the *LogoWriter* user search, replace, copy, cut and paste text. In addition to these features, the programmer can change the shape of a turtle as seen by Figure 13.2 where the helicopter, rabbit, head, and body represent four shapes.

Besides using multiple turtle shapes, *LogoWriter* lets the user easily print, save and exit files. It creates animation, music, and sound effects and has a customized text editor. The student learns *LogoWriter* through a series of booklets and activity cards, and this material covers all curriculum areas. Even with these positive features, *LogoWriter* is still a more difficult program to use than Logo because of its depth of features.

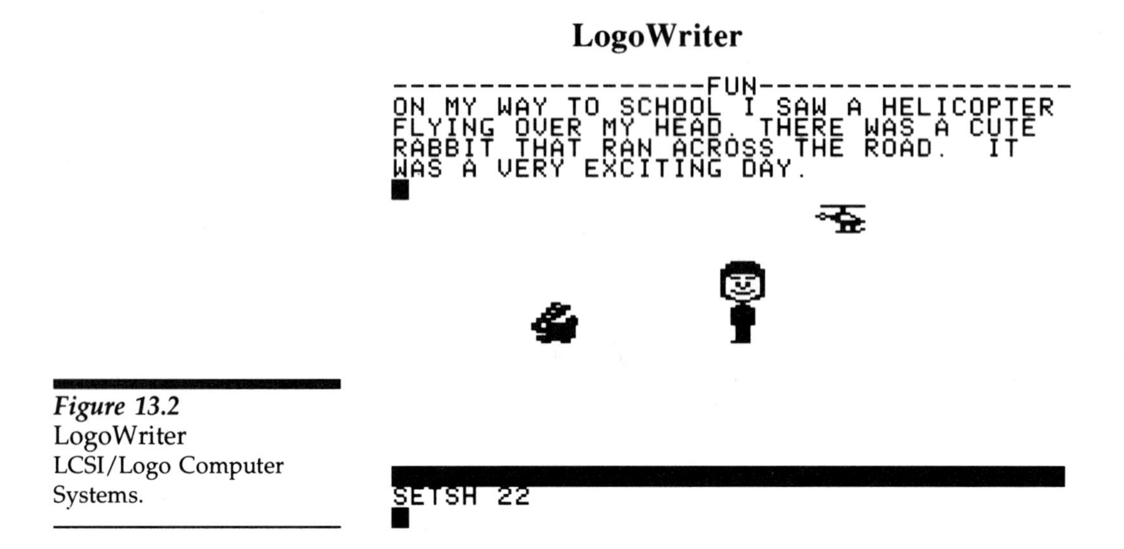

Figure 13.2
LogoWriter
LCSI/Logo Computer Systems.

The last version the author will discuss is *Lego TC Logo,* a specialized version of Logo that combines Logo programming language with Lego blocks.

Lego TC Logo

Using *Lego TC Logo,* the students build machines in the form of cars, boats, towers, and trucks which include motors, sensors, and gears. After these machines are built, the students connect them with wires and an interface box to a computer that speaks the proper dialect of Logo. Using a few simple commands, the students write computer programs to control the machines. These commands turn the motors off and on and send them in a reverse direction. *Lego TC Logo* uses primitives such as ON, OFF, and RD (reverse directions) which are appropriate for machines. Because many of the children have built objects using Lego blocks, they can progress faster when working on the computer. *Lego TC Logo* is really a relic of the early days of Logo programming when the experimenters with Logo used a "floor turtle," a mechanical robot connected to the computer by a cord. When video display terminals came along, the focus was on a "screen turtle" that was faster and more accurate than the floor turtle. Logo/Lego brings back these former days with a few differences. It allows the students to build Lego structures and create Logo programs. The students are not just restricted to a turtle, but can build all sorts of machines.

The Logo/Lego package includes an assortment of gears, wheels, motors, lights, and sensors. Students can send commands to Lego motors and lights and receive information from Lego sensors. For instance, a student writes a program, creates a Lego truck with a touch sensor, and determines whether his truck has touched an object. The program can make the truck turn to the right or reverse direction when the truck touches the wall. The students can engage in all kinds of experimentation and they can learn the importance of changing one variable at a time. They can use the scientific method as they invent their machines, and when they have problems with their inventions, they can develop hypotheses to test them out. When students use this computer-based system, they engage in data gathering, record keeping, and brainstorming sessions.

In **Appendix A** there is an annotated list of Logo software programs that are useful for the classroom.

Summary

Logo has four powerful ideas: primitives, procedures, variables, and recursion. In 1970 Logo was derived from LISP, and its principal creator was Seymour Papert. Papert's orientation toward Logo grew from Piaget's theories. According to Papert's theory, the child learns best by constructing his own knowledge, building his own programs, and developing his own designs. The child controls the computer instead of the computer controlling the child. Logo's intent is to make the student analyze what has happened and what will happen in the future. Although Logo was designed with the child in mind, this programming language can be very sophisticated. There are cogent reasons for studying Logo: 1) It is a structured language that encourages good programming techniques. 2) It is a unique tool for exploration, and 3) It is suitable, introductory language.

Chapter Mastery Test

1. Describe briefly four characteristics of Logo.
2. Briefly define primitives, procedures, and recursion.
3. Give two key arguments for and two arguments against teaching Logo in the classroom.
4. Write a program that will draw a square, a rectangle, or a circle.
5. Briefly discuss Seymour Papert's philosophy.
6. Write a Logo program that produces the design below.
7. Write a simple procedure using a REPEAT command.
8. Read procedures A and B and sketch what the turtle will draw in each case.

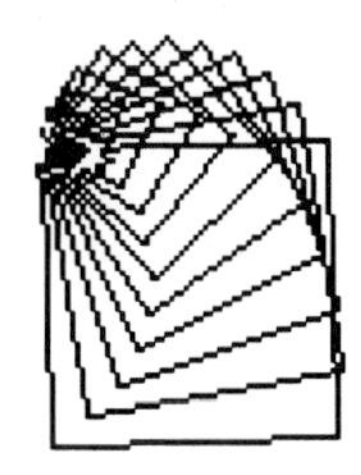

PROCEDURE A	**PROCEDURE B**
TO A	TO B
RT 90	REPEAT 4[FD 10 PU FD 20 PD FD 10 RT 90]
REPEAT 6[FD 10 PU FD 10 PD]	END
END	

9. Explain what makes *Lego TC Logo* a good teaching tool?
10. What distinguishes *LogoWriter* from Logo?
11. Explain The Total Turtle Theorem?
12. Give two advantages that Logo has over another programming language.

Classroom Projects

1. Write a procedure that designs a house with windows and doors.
2. Produce the following graphic by writing out commands.
3. Burn a maze onto a transparency, then tape it to the monitor screen. Next, play a game where the students have to drive a Logo turtle through the maze.
4. Debug the two programs on page 377. The first program produces a square, while the second procedure draws a curved line.
5. Experiment and create a design; then print it out for the class.

Program 1

```
TO SQUARE
REPEAT 4[FD 20 RT 90]
END
```

Program 2

```
TO CURVE
REPEAT[FD 10 RT10]
END
```

Suggested Readings and References

A First Course in Programming in Terrapin Logo, LogoWriter, and PC Logo. Colorado Springs, Co: Logo Curriculum Publishers, 1991.

Abelson H. & DiSessa. *Turtle Geometry,* Cambridge: MIT Press, 1980.

Abelson, Harold. *Logo For the Apple II.* Peterborough, N.H. Byte Books: McGraw-Hill, 1982.

Bitter, Gary G. *Apple Logo Primer.* Reston, VA.: Reston Publishing Co, 1983.

Cohen, Rina S. (1990, Spring). "Computerized Learner Supports in Pre-Logo Programming Environments." *Journal of Research On Computing in Education,* 22(3) (Spring 1990): 310.

Cohen, Laura. *Logo Activity Cards: Problem Solving With a Turtle Individualized.* Compton, Calif.: Educational Insights, 1985.

Dunn, S. & V. Morgan. *The Impact of Computers on Education: A Course for Teachers.* Prentice-Hall, Englewood Cliffs, NJ., 1987.

Goldenberg, Paul E. *Exploring Language with Logo.* Cambridge, Mass.: MIT Press, 1987.

Harper, Dennis. *Logo Theory & Practice.* Pacific Grove, California: Brooks/Cole Publishing, 1989.

Heller, Rachelle S. & C. Dianne Martin. *Logoworlds,* Computer Science Press, Maryland, 1985.

Hoyles, Celia. *Logo Mathematics In The Classroom.* London: New York: Routledge, 1989.

Jones, Linda. *Learning and Teaching With Logo II.* Northridge, California: California State University Northridge, September, 1990.

Kolodiy, George Oleh. Science: Logo in the Science Laboratory. *The Computing Teacher.* 18(5) (February 1991): 41–43.

Labinowicz, Ed. *The Piaget Primer: Thinking, Learning, Teaching.* Menlo Park, Calif: Addison Wesley, 1980.

Martin, Donald. *Apple Logo Programming Primer: Featuring Top-Down Structured Programing.* Indianapolis, Ind.: H.W. Sams, 1984.

Martin, Kathleen, & Donna Bearden. *Mathematics and Logo.* Reston, Virginia: Reston Publishing, A Prentice-Hall Co., 1985.

Mathinos, Debra A. "Logo Programming and the Refinement of Problem Solving Skills in Disabled and Nondisabled Children." *Journal of Educational Computing Research.* 6(4) (1990): 429.

Muir, Michael. "Talk & Draw: Logo and Artificial Intelligence." *The Computing Teacher*. 18(7) (April 1991): 31–33.

Nastasi, Bonnie K., Douglas H. Clements, M. T. Battistsa. "Social-Cognitive Interactions, Motivation and Cognitive Growth in Logo Programming and CAI Problem-Solving Environments." *Journal of Educational Psychology,* 82(1) (1 March 1990): 150.

Olive, John. "Logo Programming and Geometric Understanding: An In-Depth Study." *Journal for Research in Mathematics Education.* (22)2 (1 March 1991): 90.

Ortiz, Entrique, MacGregor, S. Kim. "Effects of Logo Programming on Understanding Variables." *Journal of Educational Computing Research.* 7(1) (1991): 37.

Papert, S. *Mindstorms: Children, Computers and Powerful Ideas.* New York: Basic Books Inc, 1980.

Papert, S. "Different Visions of Logo." *Computers in the School* (Summer/Fall 1985): 3–8.

Papert, S. "The Next Step: LogoWriter." *Classroom Computer Learning* (April 1986): 38–40.

Piaget, J. *The Construction of Reality in the Child.* New York: Basic Books Inc, 1954.

Reinhold, F. "An Interview with Seymour Papert." *Electronic Learning* (April 1986): 35–36.

Rosen, M. "Lego Meets Logo." *Classroom Computer Learning* (April 1988): 50–58.

Ruane, Pat. *Logo Activities for the Computer: A beginner's Guide.* New York: Julian Messner, 1984.

Swan, Karen. "Programming Objects to Think With: Logo and the Teaching and Learning of Problem Solving." *Journal of Educational Computing Research.* 7(1) (1991): 89.

Yoder, Sharon. "Mousing Around With Your Turtle ... Or Turtling Around With Your Mouse?" *The Computing Teacher,* 19(12) (August/September 1991): 41–43.

Yoder, Sharon. "Logo for Teachers." *The Computing Teacher* 18(8) (May 1991): 33–34.

Watt, D. *Learning with Logo.* New York: McGraw-Hill, 1983.

Watt, M. "What is Logo?" *Creative Computing* (October 1982): 12–126.

Weir, Sylvia. *Cultivating Minds: A Logo Casebook.* New York: Harper & Row, 1987.

Weston, Dan. *The Second Logo Book: Advanced Techniques in Logo.* Glenview, Ill.: Scott, Foresman, 1985.

Zaskis, Rina. "Implementing Powerful Ideas: The Case of RUN. Variation on a Simple Logo Task Introduce Students to Advanced Programming." *The Computing Teacher.* 17(6) (1 March 1990): 40.

Issues and Research: Present and Future

14

Objectives

Upon completing this chapter the student will be able to:

1. Identify and discuss major ethical issues regarding computers.
2. Describe three factors related to computer privacy.
3. Define the term **virus** and explain some precautions for preventing a virus from infecting a computer system.
4. Define **Computer Assisted Instruction (CAI)** and summarize general research findings about CAI.
5. Summarize the research findings on CAI and the following: (a) gender differences, (b) science simulations, (c) learning time, (d) word processing, (e) the learning handicapped, (f) motivation and attitude, (g) Logo and problem solving, and (h) programming.
6. Explain what artificial intelligence is, and describe its application in the classroom.
7. Explain two ways the computer can help the handicapped.
8. Extrapolate how technology will change the traditional roles in education of the teacher, students, and parents.

ETHICAL ISSUES

The computer's impact on society is similar to the technological development of the automobile. Like automobiles, computers have benefitted us in many ways. Computers have improved education, medical care, and business operations. Computers have also helped artists be more creative and allowed factories and businesses to operate more efficiently and effectively.

Unfortunately, no advance is without its disadvantages. For example, automobiles pollute the atmosphere, use resources, present parking problems, cause congestion, and even kill people. Computers, too, have their disadvantages. In this section, the author will examine some of the ethical issues or problems associated with computer technology, including invasion of privacy, computer crime, software piracy, and computer viruses.

Privacy

The concern for privacy is an issue which is not unique to computerized systems, but such systems increase the likelihood that an individual's privacy will be invaded. There are many different computerized systems, and these systems contain many different types of information. If a person lives in the United States, his or her name appears in federal, state, and local government data banks and in many private sector files.[1] The Internal Revenue Service maintains files on everyone who files tax returns. State and local governments maintain files concerning taxes and law enforcement, public and private institutions keep records on students' educational performance, and medical data banks store medical records. It is hard to determine exactly who has what information and how this information will be used.

With many different types of computerized systems, a person's financial or academic indiscretion of ten years ago may return to haunt him. Similarly, information that an individual provided for one purpose may be used for another. The computer poses a threat to an individual's privacy, and we should be concerned about the possibility of unauthorized persons or groups gaining access to personal information simply by entering a social security number into a system. For example, information about an individual could be determined, without his consent, by monitoring his financial transactions. This is comparable to what a private detective would discover by following someone around every day for a week. By looking at statements of charges from the Cigar Warehouse, Ticketron, Kids Mart, Egghead Software, and Foreign Automotive, a "computer detective" can deduce that the person likes cigars, goes to the theater, has children, and owns a computer and a foreign automobile. If bills are examined over an extended period of time, a personal, psychological, and economic profile can be developed, and this information could be used to bilk an unsuspecting individual out of huge sums of money—or even for blackmail.

Another concern regarding invasion of privacy is computer record matching, the comparison of files for the same individual stored in different governmental agencies. Law enforcement agencies use computer matching to find a criminal, officers compare the Medicare files and Social Security benefits files to identify individuals who are deceased, but still "receiving" Social Security checks. (Often relatives or other crooked individuals are forging the dead person's name and cashing the Social Security check.) Individuals who favor computer record matching believe that people who break the

1. A data bank is an electronic storehouse for data.

law should be punished, and they feel that this procedure saves the taxpayer money. Those against record matching say it uses information for a purpose different from what was originally intended. Under these circumstances, if the people who supplied the information thought that it would be used against them, they might falsify data or not give the needed information. This would impede the operation of the asking agencies, and needy individuals might not take advantage of helpful government programs.

The question of privacy became such an issue in the 1970s that a series of laws were enacted that attempted to protect privacy by controlling the collection and dissemination of information. The Freedom of Information Act (1970) gave individuals access to information about themselves collected by federal agencies. The Fair Credit Reporting Act (1970) gave citizens the right to access data about themselves, challenge it, and correct it. Under the Privacy Act of 1974, the individual could decide what data would be recorded by the government agency and how it would be used. If the agency made a mistake recording this data, then the individual must be given a method for correcting it. This act required the organization or agency to make sure the data were correctly collected, thereby preventing unauthorized use of the data. The Privacy Act also stated that data collected for one purpose could not be used for another.

The Privacy Act of 1974 was sweeping in its changes, but unfortunately it did not reach beyond federal governmental abuses. The Family Education Rights and Privacy Act (1974) regulated access to public and private school grades and anecdotal records stored in the computer. The Right to Financial Privacy Act (1978) limited how much access the government could have to a person's records stored at any financial institution, and it protected, to a lesser degree, the confidentiality of a person's financial records. Finally, the Comprehensive Crime Control Act (1984) prohibited unauthorized individuals from accessing a computer file to obtain information protected by the Right to Financial Privacy Act; it also protected any information found in a consumer agency file. The Comprehensive Crime Control Act made it illegal for individuals to modify, destroy, disclose, or use information that was stored in a government computer.

Many states have adopted laws to address the privacy issue, but litigation of violations has been very limited. In 1989, Buck BloomBecker did a study of computer security professionals and reported only 6% of the criminals were prosecuted (BloomBecker, 1989). The primary reason is that many people are unaware that their rights have been violated because the data is transferred electronically. The individuals who are aware hesitate to take claims to court because of the inevitable exposure of their private lives. In the future, there will be other laws enacted because this problem has escalated. As concerned citizens, we must continually find ways to use computer technology for our benefit while remaining vigilant for abuses.

Crime

Earlier, we discussed record matching and the controversial ways the computer can be enlisted to fight crime. Unfortunately, criminals can use computers to commit crimes such as embezzlement, unauthorized access to records, and software pirating. Now we will focus on these issues and possible ways they can be handled.

Today there are many examples of computer crime or abuse. The cost to the nation is over one half of a billion in lost time and services (BloomBecker, 1989). There are criminals who steal computers from people's homes and department stores and students who break into governmental computer files for the thrill of it. There is the case of the bank manager who manipulated customer's accounts to steal over a million dollars. We know very little about this last type of crime because very few cases have been reported, and it is feared that many of these crimes go undetected.

Some of these criminal violations are perpetrated by hackers for amusement.[2] The 414 Club was a well known example of a hacker group.[3] These teenagers' main purpose was to see who could gain entry into the best computer files. When the FBI discovered them in 1983, they had broken into different business and government computers. The Stanley Rifkin case is a perfect example of a crime perpetrated for money. Stanley Rifkin, a bank consultant, posed as a Security Pacific Bank employee to enter the wire funds transfer room.[4] He used the password number that was taped to the wall of the computer terminal to dial the Federal Reserve Bank number and transferred $10.2 million into his private account. He then withdrew the money, took it to Switzerland, and bought diamonds. This crime would have gone undetected if Mr. Rifkin had not confided in an attorney he knew. The number of these types of cases has grown over the years and will continue to grow in the future.

There are many reasons for the proliferation of these types of crimes today. A key reason is that more individuals are working with computers, so more people have become knowledgeable about computer operations. But many firms have simply ignored this growing problem. In addition, the disparity between existing computer technology and our ability to control it is widening. Finally, biased news coverage causes many people to look upon these types of thefts with greater leniency.

Software Piracy

There are thousands of illegal copies of software made in a year. The Software Publishers Association, in an in-depth study released in the U.S. in 1990, estimated that in the U.S. 2.4 billion in revenue was lost because of software piracy (Guglielmo, 1992). One

---

2. A Hacker is a technical person who is a compulsive computer user and programmer.
3. These hackers were called the "414 Club" by the FBI because their area code was 414.
4. Security Pacific Bank was formerly known as Security Pacific National Bank.

of the most popular selling computer programs is a copy program that is able to duplicate protected software. It is speculated that 20% to 50% of a typical school's software has been illegally copied. Some teachers have even sent software that was illegally copied back to the manufacturer when they had problems with it. Software piracy is a different kind of theft because people who would never think of stealing from a department store freely make illegal copies of software. They justify their dishonesty by the following rationalizations: (1) Software developers condone people making copies to get publicity for their products; (2) Software is grossly overpriced and, therefore, "fair game;" and (3) The cost of copying software is borne by the developer and not the customer. All three reasons are inaccurate. The software developer never condones illegal copying. Software is very expensive to produce and market, and the cost of copying software is borne initially by the developers, but it is ultimately paid for by the legitimate buyer (Guglielmo, 1992).

The unauthorized duplication of software violates the U.S. Copyright Law and deprives developers of the revenue they richly deserve. The law is clear: reproducing computer software without the proper authorization is a federal offense. The money paid for a piece of software represents a fee for one copy and it does not give the user the right to copy freely. There can be civil damages for unauthorized copying for as much as $50,000, as well as criminal penalties, including jail and fines. Many bills have been introduced in Congress to strengthen the copyright laws and increase the penalties for illegal copying. The software piracy issue is certain to receive continued legal attention.

The software developers themselves have produced elaborate copy protection schemes to combat this problem. Yet, for every scheme that is devised, a copy buster program is developed that will override the scheme. Trying to find a solution to this problem, many developers have removed their copy protection.

Unfortunately, schools are a major culprit in copying educational software. Why do schools copy illegally? Many schools and districts are anxious to integrate the computer into the classroom. They have limited funds and one copy for 32 children is not enough for group participation. Teachers want many copies so that they can have a group of students using the same software simultaneously. They feel copying software is like photocopying materials for their classroom. In the end, the educator is the loser when the companies cannot make a profit selling educational software. Instead, the companies divert their money to manufacturing something that is more economically beneficial. Software pirates ultimately drive smaller companies out of business.

What can districts do to dissuade teachers or students from illegally copying software? They can warn these teachers about illegally duplicating software and institute some disciplinary action when violations occur. Furthermore, the school can keep the software locked away in a restricted area and limit student and teacher access. In addition, the district can require that the teachers supervise the students when the students use the software.

In the classroom the teachers can discuss recent criminal cases or movies like *War Games* to make the students aware of the problems involved. As a facilitator, the teacher can explain the federal and state laws and the differences between a felony, a crime punishable by a year in prison, and a misdemeanor, a crime punishable by a fine or a prison term. After the students have an understanding of the seriousness of computer crimes, they can devise a computer break-in policy for the school. The teacher can then give each student a copy of this policy to study and read. Using this break-in policy, the teacher can read hypothetical cases concerning computer ethic breaches and ask the students what punishment they would use on the offender.

Teachers should further realize that there are better ways to combat their budget constraints. Buying lab packs or multiple copies of software is one answer.[5] Software purchased this way is less expensive and more equitably feasible. The district should buy an on-site license for selected programs which allows the user to make legal multiple copies and multiple loadings of a program. This is less costly than purchasing a single disk one at a time.

The schools should also move toward networking their machines. This will enable them to run a networkable piece of software over multiple machines. Educators should buy software that includes a backup copy or allows the buyer to purchase an inexpensive one. Finally, teachers should involve the students, parents, and community in earning money to buy software. In the long term, it is better to purchase the software than to steal it because the buyer receives technical support and upgrades from the publisher. Most important, it is the honorable and ethical way.

Viruses

Another harmful force in computing today is the virus, a program that infects computer files by duplicating itself. A malicious individual writes a code that is buried in an existing program. When the program is loaded into the computer, the virus replicates itself by attaching copies of itself to other programs that are residing in the system. When any person inserts an infected disk into a computer's memory, this computer's files will be infected. The reverse is also true; that is, when an individual uses an infected computer, his disk will become infected. An individual's computer can be infected by a virus electronically when a malevolent computer enthusiast creates a virus and sends it over the lines to a local network. Since the network is connected to thousands of computers, this infection is carried to all the connected computers. When the virus arrives in each of these computers, it performs the assignment it was created to do.

5. Multiple loadings refers to loading a program from one disk to several computers.

A virus program can be somewhat harmless, producing a message at weird times. But it can be a very destructive force, wiping out huge amounts of data. The virus can not only destroy files, but it can also find bank accounts with certain names and give these individuals a large sum of money. A virus is very hard to detect because it can be programmed to do things immediately or in the future. In our University Computer Lab, we had a real problem combating viruses. Every week a computer was infected with one of these culprits. We finally solved our problem by buying virus protection software. A whole industry of virus protection software such as Virex, SAM, VirusDetective, and Vaccine has come into existence to combat the different types of viruses.

Unfortunately, these anti-virus programs are imperfect at best, because new viruses are popping up all the time. For instance, in an article in *MacWeek,* Henry Norr stated that a new Mac virus had surfaced in Belgium and Holland. Called the HC virus, it infects HyperCard stacks. The effect of this particular virus is not destructive, but it can spread rapidly from stack to stack. Presently, the total number of known viruses is 34 for the Macintosh (Ward, 1992).[6] In the case of the HC virus, two leading developers of anti-virus software responded with updates to their current programs.

The best protection against virus infection is to take certain precautions, including the following: (1) Frequently back up your hard disk; (2) Down load into a single computer as opposed to a networked system; (3) Use virus protection programs to check every piece of software for a virus before loading it into the computer's memory; (4) Do not store data on a program disk; and (5) Always write-protect program disks so that they cannot be destroyed.

Security

As the reader can see from our discussion, there is an urgent need for computer security. Computer owners must take steps to prevent theft and inappropriate use of their equipment. There should be positive identification of the computer user and control over computer access.

Today, most computer facilities have some sort of security system. These facilities have means of identifying persons who will use the system so that unauthorized users will not gain access. Usually, individuals have a special card, key, password, or account number. In the elementary schools and high schools, this identification system may consist of a simple list of names. Each person on this list has a key that allows access to a computer room with bolted down machines. Unfortunately, there is a problem about users restricting the use of their keys and guarding their password information. Often,

6. According to Patricia Hoffman, antiviral researcher, "We are currently keeping track of about a thousand different computer viruses for the MS DOS computers" (Hypertext VSUM Database, 1992).

when computer users are allowed to choose a password, it is easy to remember—and easy to guess. The passwords that are typically chosen are the names of children or a spouse.

One way to avert this problem is an access code that is read from a card. The user does not have to remember this number so it can be complicated. Even if the card is stolen, the code can be changed when the theft is reported. Another way of increasing security is to require every individual to enter a special code with his or her card. Besides having these types of systems, the experts advise going a step further by checking people's personnel files for problems and restricting the number of people and the type of access to the computer. For instance, at most universities, the students and professors use the same computer center, but they are not given the same access. Typically, the students have fewer privileges than the professors.

Another security problem concerns the protection of the operating system and data that is on the computer. It is essential that security measures protect all operating systems. Unscrupulous individuals have found ways to circumvent the system and they print out a list of users' passwords, give themselves access rights they are not officially assigned, and spread viruses. For these reasons, all sensitive data should be stored and locked up when not in use. Some large companies use data encryptation to store data in a scrambled form, meaningless to anyone without a special data item called a *key*.

The computer user should also guard against natural disasters such as power surges, fire, earthquakes, and theft. At the most simple level, a good surge protector will rule out most power surges. However, disks do wear out, and fire destroys, so it is important to make backup copies and store them in a different location.

From this discussion it should be evident how important security is. How far one goes in implementing a system for security is related to its cost. Usually, the more complicated the system, the more costly it is to carry out. Security will continue to be a problem, because the number of microcomputers and microcomputer users continues to grow. For example, in the last nine years, computers found in the schools have significantly increased. In 1983–84 there were 125 students per computer in a school, but by 1989–90 there were 22 students per computer (Quality Education Data). Eventually there will be a computer on each child's desk. The teacher's main job will be to figure out how to use this technology as a powerful tool for education. A related job for the teacher will be to provide appropriate security.

Research

Because of increased access to computers, teachers are interested in the effects the computer will have on instruction. The old instructional methods may not work with this new technology, or they may require modification. In the research literature, there are many computer studies related to teaching and learning. The major purpose of this section is to highlight some Computer Assisted Instruction research findings.

Research Findings

Computer Assisted Instruction. Computer-assisted instruction (CAI) refers to applications specifically designed to teach a variety of subject areas to children and adults (Freedman, 1990). The student receives feedback from the computer, which controls the sequencing of the subject matter.

The advocates of CAI have high expectations for the computer as an instrument to help identify and meet the individual needs of the person using the program. Many studies conclude that using CAI to supplement traditional instruction is better than the instructional program by itself. Goode (1988) found that fifth and sixth grade pupils who used CAI scored significantly higher in mathematical concepts and computation than a control group who used the traditional approach. Burns and Bozeman's study (1981) showed evidence that a curriculum supplemented with CAI led to gains in achievement in some areas of the curriculum. Tsai and Pohl (1977) studied the effectiveness of the lecture approach and CAI on college students learning how to program. They found a significant difference when achievement was measured by quizzes or final exam scores. When professors used the lecture approach supplemented by CAI, it was more effective, and the lecture approach alone was the least effective method of instruction.

Gene Glass (1976, 1977) introduced a technique called meta-analysis[7] in order to get a clearer picture of the effects of computer based treatments. Other researchers followed and compiled meta-analysis studies in the area of instructional computing. Kulik's series of meta-analysis studies were the most comprehensive (Kulik, Kulik, & Cohen, 1980; Kulik, Bangert & William, 1983; Kulik, Kulik & Shwalb, 1986, Kulik, James A; Kulik, Chen-Lin C., 1987). The results of his studies showed that students who were taught using the computer scored higher on achievement tests than those students who were taught using other methods. Kulik also showed that this analysis produced different results, depending on the grade, ability level and type of instruction.

Richard E. Clark reviewed CAI and meta-analytical studies in 1985. He was critical of the research and suggested that studies by Kulik and others overestimated CAI's benefits because uncontrolled instructional methods were embedded in the instructional treatments. Clark feels that the existing evidence does not indicate that computers yield learning benefits.

---

7. Meta-analysis is a statistical technique that allowed researchers to summarize the results of a large group of research studies and identify general effects.

Roblyer, Castine, and King (1988) summarized previous literature reviews on the educational effectiveness of instructional computing before they presented their meta-analysis of recent studies. In discussing the studies from Kulik and his colleagues that were done during the early 1980s, Roblyer noted that these studies did not include microcomputer-based, research studies. This fact affects the external validity and significance of Kulik's conclusions. Roblyer, Castine, and King summarized 26 reviews of computer based instruction. They also analyzed 82 research studies that they found had adequate internal validity and sufficient data to be included in their meta-analysis. A brief rundown of their findings are these: (1) There are higher achievement results for college and adult age individuals as opposed to elementary and secondary students; (2) The computer produced the greatest achievement gains in science, with math, reading, and cognitive skills yielding effect sizes about half that size; (3) Computer Assisted Instruction software were all of approximately equal effectiveness; and (4) Lower achieving students showed more gains with CAI than students who were achieving at grade level, and these gains were not statistically significant.

Roblyer, Castine, and King's review of the research (1988) painted a very rosy picture of CAI. George Bass, Jr. (1990), however, cautioned readers about generalizing from Roblyer's conclusions. Bass felt that Roblyer neglected to identify how many of the 82 studies involved using the computer in a regular classroom situation. He said, "The independent variable in these 82 studies is not just the introduction of computer hardware, but rather the introduction of particular software on particular computers managed by particular educators. Physical equipment, instructional computer programs, and trained personnel are all factors that must be carefully described in order to determine the generalizability of research results to a specific school situation."[8]

As you can see from our discussion, the findings on CAI are inconsistent. CAI is still in its infancy stages, and there is an urgent need for additional quality research.

Gender Differences. Most gender studies try to get at the reasons for males using the computer more than females. Collis and Ollila (1986) examined the gender differences in secondary school students' attitudes toward writing on the computer. Females were significantly less positive than their male counterparts on every item that related to computers. Siann et al. (1988) studied gender stereotyping and computer involvement. They suggested there are some encouraging trends, but males still use computers more than females. Swadener and Hannafin (1987) studied the gender similarities and differences in sixth graders' attitudes toward the computer. They found that boys with higher achievement levels in mathematics also had high interest levels toward computers. The

8. George M. Bass. "Assessing the Impact of Computer Based Instruction: A Review of Recent Research." *Educational Technology*, May, 1990.

boys with low achieving scores had low interest toward the computer. This is the complete opposite of the females, with the low achieving female students having the most interest in the computer. Ware and Stuck's study (1985) explored the ways men, women, boys, and girls are pictured in computer magazines. Many stereotypic gender portrayals were cited in the 426 illustrations that were analyzed. The world of advertising portrayed computers as belonging in a male-dominant environment.

Science Simulations. Generally students learn very well with science simulation software. Linn (1986) did an experiment in which 8 eighth grade science classes used computers as lab partners for a semester. These students learned to use the computer to collect and display data and save and print out their reports. They used items such as temperature and light probes, which were attached to the computer, and the results were displayed on the computer screen. Linn found that the micro-based lab instructed students outperformed seventeen year olds who took a standardized test on scientific knowledge. In addition, these computer taught students demonstrated a very positive attitude toward experimentation.

Moore, Smith, and Avner (1980) found higher student achievement with computer simulations when the students had to interpret the results of the experiments and make decisions. If the students only had to follow directions and calculate the results, there was no difference between the experimental and control groups. Summerville (1984) and Fortner, Schar, and Mager (1986) noted similar findings.

The results of the science simulation studies are very promising (Thomas and Hooper, 1991). Even when a study shows no significant difference between students who use the traditional method and students who use the computer, this is encouraging. This means that simulations can substitute for laboratory experiments. This is advantageous because science simulations are a less dangerous, less time consuming, and less expensive method of instruction.

Learning Time. The CAI research has generally been positive regarding the time it takes to learn concepts. Dence (1980) described several studies where CAI takes less time for the students to learn than traditional instruction. Gleason (1981) reviewed CAI research and interviewed researchers. His conclusion regarding CAI was that it results in a 20 to 40 percent saving in time as compared with the traditional methods of instruction. Fisher (1983) reported that students using the computer completed their work 40% faster than when they did not have access to it.

Word Processing. There are many studies dealing with word processing and its effect on the quantity and quality of pupil writing. The evidence here is contradictory.

O'Brien (1984), Feldman (1984), and Morehouse et. al. (1987) found significant differences in favor of word processing. However, Daiute (1985) found that students wrote less with a word processor. Kurth (1987) found no differences in quality of writing or of revisions between a secondary school group that used word processing for their writing and a secondary school group that used pencil and paper. Roblyer (1988) summarized the research and said that word processing did not appear to improve the quality of writing. Hawisher (1986) reviewed the research on word processing and noted that implementation differences among the various studies could affect their outcomes. This criticism highlights the problem, not only for word processing studies, but also for other research concerning computer applications, too.

The Learning Handicapped. Most research indicates that the learning handicapped benefit from involvement with CAI. For example, Carman and Kosberg (1982) showed that there was a significant positive influence on attention-to-task behavior for emotionally handicapped children. Maser et al. (1979) investigated an alternative instructional approach to learn basic skills for the educationally disadvantaged. At the end of a three year period, they found CAI was effective in building basic skills. Other studies also support positive effects of CAI with learning handicapped (Lally, 1980; Hasselbrin, 1982; Watkins & Webb, 1981). In 1987 MacArthur et al. used computer assisted instruction with learning disabled students. Their study of fifth and sixth grade students compared the effects of paper-and-pencil and computer-delivered independent drill and practice in spelling. This study was done over a four week period with 44 learning disabled students. The researchers found that the computer-practice students did significantly better than the traditional drill students on spelling tests. The computer students spent more time on academic content and less time with their teachers than did the traditional drill students.

Motivation and Attitude. Teachers face the challenge of being able to motivate and foster a positive attitude to improve a student's chance at success in school. For example, an essential element for improving students' spelling is keeping interest high (Allred, 1977). There are many studies that report students' positive attitudes toward the computer and how computers motivate students and help them maintain high interest (Clement, 1981). Robertson (1978) found that children who had experienced failure in the past responded positively to computer-assisted programs. She concluded that the children involved in the study did not have a sense of failure over an incorrect response.

Some researchers have tried to find out if the students prefer computer-based methods simply because a computer is involved. Other research has focused on the computer's influence on student attitudes toward school and curriculum. Bracey (1982) found that students reacted favorably to computer use for instructional tasks. He reported that students who worked on the computer had a more positive attitude toward the machine than those who had not used the computer. Kulik et al. (1983) reviewed studies on students' attitudes toward the curriculum after using CAI. In three of the studies reviewed, the results were statistically significant for the CAI classroom. In their meta-analysis, Roblyer, Castine, and King (1988) found that students do not seem to prefer the computer over other media. However, there were few studies with data measuring student preferences for computer media; thus, the results are unclear. Generally, the CAI studies that focused on students' attitudes toward themselves and school learning were positive. However, there was no evidence that good attitudes toward computers resulted in better attitudes toward school achievement and work. One reason for this might be that achievement in school is not based on a simple set of variables, but is the result of a complex set of factors.

Logo and Problem Solving. There has been widespread interest among educators on Logo's effects on students. In a survey of instructional computer uses, Becker (1987) found that more than 9% of computer-using teachers in the United States use Logo. There have been numerous books written on Logo, and it has been the subject of many papers presented at conferences. However, it has been observed that only doctoral research has kept up with the interest in Logo (Pea, 1987; Walker, 1987). A number of studies attempted to determine the effects of Logo on students' self-esteem. Some of these studies found negative results and others found no statistically significant differences.

Keller (1990) completed a research review on the possible impact of Logo on cognitive development. She found that the teacher plays a critical role in the Logo environment. Some studies showed the difficulties that young children have in learning Logo (Horner & Maddux, 1985; Mayer & Fay, 1987). Grovier (1988) summarized a variety of American and British research related to Logo. She found one key factor: the studies with significant effects were the ones in which the teacher structured the learning.

The most frequent claim about Logo is that it promotes problem solving. Roblyer et al. (1988) did a meta-analysis on the effects of CAI on problem solving and general thinking. Their findings indicated that Logo showed promise as a method for developing problem solving skills, but this was not a statistical conclusion.

Pea & Kurland's (1984) research results did not give support to the connection between Logo programming and problem solving skills. Dalton (1986) compared Logo to a curriculum that was created to improve problem solving and reported that the problem solving group achieved significantly more than the Logo or control group at every level of student ability. In conclusion, the research does not show the important benefits that are supposed to occur from knowing Logo.

Programming. There are many studies that discuss non-Logo programming such as BASIC. These studies discuss the impact programming could have on different types of intellectual activities. The general conclusions from these studies are inconclusive and disappointing. There are proponents who want programming taught in the schools. Arthur Luehrmann, a well-known advocate, feels that persons who know programming can control and communicate better with the computer (Luehrmann, 1984). Many individuals argue that computer programming improves the students' problem solving (Soloway, Lockhead, & Clement, 1982; Palumbo and Reed, 1991). Still other supporters proclaim that programming should not be taught for the sake of programming, but taught instead to help children learn other subjects like math (Papert, 1980). A review of the research results on such topics as effects of programming on achievement, problem solving, and transferability are inconclusive (Collis,1990). Mayer (1986) concluded that there was no consistent evidence that learning to program had any positive impact on anything else: "There is no convincing evidence that learning to program enhances students' general intellectual ability, or that programming is any more successful than Latin for teaching "proper habits of mind."

Problems with the Research

Although there has been a considerable amount of research done in the last 20 years, there are many problems that exist with this research. Computer research is still in its infancy stage, and many CAI studies were conducted before the availability of microcomputers. In addition, many studies are not thoroughly reported in the literature, so a reader cannot tell if the conclusions drawn by the investigators are supported by the data. The analysis that Roblyer, Castine, and King (1988) performed included 38 studies and 44 dissertations from a possible 200. The rest of the studies were eliminated because of reasons such as methodological flaws or insufficient data. A good portion of CAI research is anecdotal, based on experiences and not experimental design. There is definitely a need for higher quality, computer research.

Research Generalizations

Even with these problems, there are some relevant generalizations.

1. In science, the computer is a useful tool for simulations. For example, the Army and Navy use war game simulations. The chemistry instructor uses computer based simulations instead of the chemistry lab. The flight instructor uses flight simulation software instead of flying an actual plane. A simulation program is generally less dangerous, less expensive, and less time consuming.
2. The computer is helpful for individualization. A student can progress at his own pace. If s/he needs help with math facts, the teacher does not have to act as the

tutor; the computer can. This frees the teacher to work with the same child in other academic areas. This type of individualization spreads the range of abilities in a class and allows some students to go further ahead.

3. There is general agreement that the computer does change attitudes toward the computer, school, and subjects. The computer does motivate children, and there is speculation that it might improve drop out rate.
4. The relationship between attitude and achievement is low. There is no strong body of evidence supporting the notion that a positive attitude toward the computer will result in improved achievement.
5. No substantial evidence supports the claim that studying programming improves problem solving or enhances general intellectual development. This statement is a throwback to the old argument that studying Latin improves mental acuity.
6. Modern thought leans toward using the computer as a tool or resource rather than a programming device.
7. Word processing motivates children to write. However, there was no difference in the quality of writing using a word processor or using a pencil and paper.
8. Gender studies found that boys work more frequently with the computer than girls. This appears to be a case of a culturally developed difference.

Future Trends

Now that we have examined the present research, natural questions to ask are, "What will the future bring? What are the trends for microcomputer development? Will we have more artificial intelligence applications? Will there be more telecommunication and networking in the schools? Are there going to be further developments in multimedia technologies, or is this phrase the buzzword of the 1990s?" These are some questions that we will discuss.

Computer Hardware

Recent developments such as the wireless computer, flash memory chips, and the ever changing laptop will play a more prominent role in the computer's future. Laser printers will be the dominant printing device because of drastic price reductions and superior printing capabilities.

Another major computer trend is equipment which is smaller, faster, and easier to use. Every time we turn around, we see a rash of new computers that are quicker and can run more sophisticated programs. We have witnessed a change from 1 megahertz (MHz) machines to 66 MHz machines. The memory needed to run different applications has increased. In the early eighties, most microcomputers needed only 16 kilobytes of RAM memory to run the available educational software programs. Today, there are machines that now have 16 megabytes of RAM memory. Because of their large memory, the new microcomputers are much more powerful and can perform a variety of sophisticated tasks. The cost of the memory chip has decreased in price and will continue to do so in the next few years.

Not only has memory size increased, but storage devices have enlarged their capacity to store data. The 5 1/4 inch floppy disk is fading into oblivion and the 3 1/2 inch disk that can hold 1.44 megabytes has replaced it. The trend is for smaller disks that hold more information, like the 1.8 inch ones that are available. The hard disk is more commonplace and people are initially buying hard disks with more memory capacity. A major storage device for the future is the optical disk. CD-ROM and Videodiscs are optical disks that are recorded on at the time of manufacturing and cannot be erased. These disks are becoming more commonplace because of their higher storage capacity, their sharp reduction in price, and the fact that they are not affected by magnetic fields. With a reduction in price, erasable optical disks will become an alternative to magnetic disks. These erasable optical disks have the capacity for storing hundreds of millions of bytes of information, and they do not wear out like floppy disks. In addition to these attributes, the optical disks are capable of reproducing high quality color graphics, images, and animation. This technology holds promise for interactive video which merges graphics sound with computer text by linking a video disk player with a computer, monitor, disk drive, and computer software (chapter 11, Hypermedia.)

Along with the changes in storage devices, there are changes in input devices. The movement is away from the keyboard as the primary input device. There are more touch screens, pens, and variations on the mouse. Of all the new developments, the voice recognition system seems to hold the greatest promise.

Voice Recognition Systems

The Optimum Resource Reading Program is the first interactive voice recognition reading program that is available for MS DOS compatible computers. This program was devised for reading disabled children from ages 8 to 13 and was the result of a $500,000 grant awarded to Optimum Resource by the National Institute of Child Health and Human Development (NICHHD). The research found that children using this program had significant reading gains when compared to children using traditional methods. The Optimum Resource Reading Program was tested for a year on children at six schools in Meriden, Connecticut. With this program, a computer speaks to a child and the child responds to the computer. The speaking voice of the computer is clear, precise, and as understandable as a human voice. The computer is trained to recognize the child's voice. It corrects the child when she is wrong and praises her when she is correct. The program rewards the child with games, activities, color graphics, and animated sequences. It also keeps a record of each child's progress.

In 1991, Convox Inc. introduced a voice recognition system that allows users to replace keystroke entries with spoken commands. The Voice Master Key System II works on the IBM PC and PS/2 systems. This product can recognize 64 words at a time and it can be branched to additional sets of words. The user types in the word s/he wants the system to listen for, repeats it only twice, and then types in the desired keyboard response. Now all the user does is say the word or words, for example, "check spelling," and this command will direct the word processor to check the spelling.

In 1991, Emerson & Stern Associates Inc., a research company, announced a breakthrough in speech recognition. The product Soliloquy radically differs from previous speech recognition technologies in the following ways: (1) It does not require special training and works with a single speaker; (2) It can handle continuous speech; and (3) It does not require extra hardware. This software currently runs on the Macintosh's more powerful models.

David Nagel, Senior Vice President of Apple's Advanced Technology Group, used both voice and a pen to pilot a high-end Macintosh, the Quadra 900. This system code-named Casper, has 100,000 words and unlike other systems it does not need to be trained to recognize the user's voice (Gore, 1992).

In the next two years there will be more breakthroughs in speech recognition. Many of these advances are closely linked to Artificial Intelligence. Today, the principles of AI are being used to improve the voice recognition system.

Artificial Intelligence

Artificial Intelligence is a range of computer applications that are similar to human intelligence and behavior. For instance, users can have a machine or robot with sensory capabilities that can recognize pictures and sounds. In the future, we may be able to walk up to any computer or robot and ask it a question. This robot will then ask us what kind of help we require. When we respond, the robot will call up the appropriate applications to solve the problem.

Shortly, there will be no discernible difference between the machine and an intelligent person. At UCLA and other universities, scientists are working on computer programs, and, in some instances, on robots that will emulate aspects of life such as evolution. The computer "ants" program at UCLA is a product of an infant science called artificial life. David Jefferson, a computer scientist at UCLA, feels that the ant colonies are a small step toward the creation of life itself. If these scientists are successful, there may be electronic creatures that could be considered alive and would react independently, which is both exciting and frightening. What are some philosophical questions about the dangers of producing these computer codes? At Los Alamos National Laboratory, there exists a whole repertoire of these self-reproducing computer codes. These are just variations of the so-called computer viruses that have disrupted computer networks over the last few years.

Presently there are AI systems that are designed for particular fields to make evaluations, draw conclusions, and provide recommendations. They help doctors make diagnoses on diseases and treatments, they help drill oil wells, and they aid stockbrokers in making analyses. This type of software will make a similar impact in education. The teachers are already demanding programs that are more interactive. The AI language will definitely increase the type of programs that respond like a human being. The software we will be using will be concerned with concepts and ideas. These programs will expect the student to use the computer to deal with topics that have no **yes** or **no** answer. This new and unique software will accept a range of English language commands and be easier to use. In the future all software will be radically different from what we see today.

Robots

A Robot is a computer system that performs physical and computational activities. The robot can be created similar to a human form; however, industrial robots are not designed this way. They have one or more arms that are designed for certain tasks. The advantage of a robot is the fact that it can perform many different jobs similar to the way a person might perform them. Robots are being designed with artificial intelligence features. This will enable them to respond more effectively to different situations. We can envision a robot in the classroom that will act as a teacher's aid. The robots will spend time with the students, individually drilling them in an enjoyable way on their math facts. These robots can also be used to handle dangerous chemicals in the chemistry lab or to help the disabled student with homework.

Computer Use by Handicapped Persons

There are many devices currently available that aid the disabled pupil, including a computer operated special device that helps handicapped persons communicate by telephone. Deaf children may learn to speak by matching words displayed on a screen with the sound waves for each word. There are many speech programs available that can help the blind use the computer. Additionally, blind persons have access to braille keyboards and printers. We can expect to see further developments that will aid the handicapped.

Software

Currently software manufacturers are producing talking versions of their programs, and the majority of these new programs are high quality, multimedia ones that follow sound, educational learning principles. For example, *Treehouse* (Brøderbund) is an innovative, multimedia program designed especially for children between the ages of five and nine. This exciting program is a perfect example of the kind of high quality item that is being developed. Prices for educational software and computers are being reduced, and parents are taking advantage of this by buying computers to help their children at school. Many educational programs have editors and record keeping functions. Students interact with the computer programs in a more realistic fashion because of developments in the Artificial Intelligence field. The publishing houses are moving in the direction of having software integrated with the state adopted texts. Lab packs and networkable products are now available. For example, *Wagon Train 1848* (MECC, 1991) is a Macintosh networkable product. This challenging simulation takes children on a wagon train adventure. Each child is a passenger in a wagon and makes independent decisions that affect the other members of the train.

In the future every textbook will come with a supplemental disk. A program like *Point of View* by Scholastic will be the norm, not the exception. This multi-media program combines sound, still sequences, simulation, and real life tape recordings. Let us complete our discussion by looking at what the future will hold in the field of education.

Future Trends in Education

We would all like to see computer labs in the high school and at least two or three computers with modems in each classroom. And, if a robot aid could decrease our work load considerably, there are few of us who would not order one tomorrow. Often these wonderful wish lists will never materialize. Unfortunately, schools do not have the money to buy the equipment to implement a technological based program. Besides lack of funds for equipment, a serious problem is the lack of teachers trained to manage this new technology.

At the present time, looking at our crystal ball realistically, what does the future hold? There will be increased computer use, and the computers will be smaller, faster, more efficient, and less expensive. There will be more emphasis on computer ethics and networking. The multi-media software will be more sophisticated, less expensive, more transparent, and menu and icon-based. The computer's storage capacity will be improved, allowing teachers and students to access software more easily. Every textbook that is sold will come with a supplemental computer disk.

Many states now require that teachers complete a computer course for certification. Because of this requirement, there will be more trained teachers who can integrate the computer in the classroom. However, the more sophisticated computer equipment will be found only at the college and university level. The elementary and secondary schools will not be able to afford this costly type of hardware. There will be more networkable machines rather then the stand alone variety. Advances in networking will lead to more communication between different classrooms, different schools, and school districts. One classroom will be networked with another classroom or some national or state data base. Eventually a teacher will be networking with computers in other countries. Students and teachers will commonly use desktop publishing programs as well as scanners and facsimile machines to import pictures and graphic images into their documents.

Teachers will be teaching less because the computer will have a more prominent role in the classroom. It will allow teachers to individualize instruction for the learners. There will be less drill and practice and more problem solving. More teachers will integrate the computer with video images through a laser disk player. The computer will be used with the videodisc, CD-ROM, and data base to help pupils find pertinent information.

The computer is a remarkable invention. Its possible impact on the curriculum could be staggering, but it needs to be given a chance to show what it can do for children in the schools. It is up to us as educators to inspire, motivate, and excite students and colleagues about this remarkable instrument of learning. Appendix A provides a list of useful software and hardware that the teacher should examine.

Summary

Computers are not just a passing fancy; they will be with us a long time. They have made life easier and more complicated. By using the computer, we can accomplish a great deal more, but we have to work harder to keep pace with computer technology.

Computers are responsible for new types of crime as well as some variations on the traditional ones. We now have computer embezzlement and unauthorized access to computer systems. Computer embezzlement is harder to detect than ordinary embezzlement, because computers accept keyboard entries that follow certain guidelines, whereas these entries would look very suspicious to a human. Software piracy is a problem that computer companies are still trying to resolve. Software houses have on-site licensing, lab packs, and networkable disks available, and many are dispensing with their copy protection schemes, hoping to reduce software piracy.

Computer security is a topic that is in the news often. A computer user must be concerned with protecting data from loss or unauthorized access. What is needed are proper identification of the user, authorizing passwords, equipment and disk protection, and proper backup copies of computer files. These backup copies should be kept at a different site to guard against data loss due to fire, theft, or failure of storage media.

There are many research studies on computers that examine Computer Assisted Instruction (CAI). The synopsis of research findings presented in this chapter gives a picture of the pertinent topics in this field.

In the end, we must look at the future of this exciting technology. We will definitely have smaller, faster, easier-to-use and more powerful computers. The software will be multi-media and networkable. Voice recognition, artificial intelligence, and robots will definitely play a greater role. Education will integrate computers into the curriculum as much as possible, but problems with funding and adequately trained teachers may limit what is accomplished in classrooms. We can only speculate on what will happen in the future. What we do know is that the coming years will be exciting!

Chapter Mastery Test

1. Discuss two issues related to computer privacy.
2. Describe the Security Pacific embezzlement case. Explain why computerized financial institutions are more susceptible to embezzlement than traditional ones.
3. Explain the conflict between the computer user and the software publisher.
4. Why are computer viruses destructive? List some precautions you can take to prevent one from infecting your computer system.
5. What can ordinary persons do to protect their data from fire, theft, and failure of the storage media?
6. Discuss the findings from three research studies related to CAI.
7. Does the research show that science simulations are more effective than laboratory experiences? Explain your answer.
8. Why are optical disks superior to floppy disks?
9. Why is the voice recognition system the wave of the future?
10. Define artificial intelligence and speculate on how it could be used in the classroom.
11. How can the computer help handicapped children?
12. What has slowed the use of computers in the schools? How can these obstacles be overcome?
13. Extrapolate how computers in the classroom will change the traditional roles of the teachers, students, and parents.
14. What are some future directions for computer use in the classroom? (Be prepared to defend your choices.)

Classroom Projects

1. Use the library to find an example of a recent computer crime and prepare a short report. In this report you should tell: (1) what happened, (2) how the crime was discovered, and (3) how the crime could have been prevented.
2. Research the software piracy problem. In spite of this problem, why is there a trend toward unprotected software?
3. Prepare a report on two types of computer viruses. Explain how they affect your computer and how they were discovered.
4. Compare two different surge protectors. Write a report detailing their battery life, cut off time, and resistance to power failure. Which product is the better and why?
5. Find three current examples of the computer invading a person's privacy. What are ways that these violations could have been prevented?
6. Visit the library and use the research to argue that Logo improves problem solving.

Suggested Readings and References

Bass, George M. Jr. "Assessing the Impact of Computer Based Instruction: A Review of Recent Research." *Educational Technology, May 1990.*

Becker, H. J. *The Impact of Computer Use on Children's Learning: What Research Has Shown and What It Has Not.* Baltimore, M.D: The John Hopkins University. 1987.

BloomBecker, Buck. *Spectacular Computer Crimes.* Homewood, Illinois: Dow Jones-Irwin, 1990.

BloomBecker, Buck. Commitment to Security, National Center for Computer Crime Data, 1222 17th Ave., Santa Cruz, CA 95062, telephone: 408/475–4457.

Bossone, R. M., and I. H. Polishook, Eds. "New Frontiers in Educational Technology: Trends and Issues. Proceedings of the Conference of the University/Urban Schools National Task Force." (*ERIC Document* No, 281524), November, 1986.

Bracey, G. W. "Computers in Education: What the Research Shows." *Electronic Learning* 2(3) (1982): 51–54.

Bruder, Isabelle. "Visions of the Future."*Electronic Learning* 9(4) (January 1990): 24–30.

Burger, Ralf. *Computer Viruses: A High-Tech Disease.* Grand Rapids, MI: Abacus, 1988.

Burns, Patricia Knight and William C. Bozeman. "Computer-Assisted Instruction and Mathematics Achievement: Is There a Relationship?" *Educational Technology* 21 (October 1981): 32–39.

Campbell, D. L., D. L. Peck, C. J. Horn, & R. K. Leigh. "CAI and Third Grade Mathematics." *Educational Communication and Technology Journal, (ECTJ),* 35(2) (1987): 95–103.

Carman, Gary O. and Bernard Kosber. "Research: Computer Technology and the Education of Emotionally Handicapped Children." *Educational Technology* (February 1982): 36–32.

Clark, Richard E. "Evidence for Confounding in Computer-Based Instruction Studies: Analyzing the Meta-Analysis." *Educational Communication and Technology Journal* 33(4) (Winter 1985): 249–62.

Clement, Frank J. "Affective Considerations in Computer-Based Education." *Educational Technology* (April 1981): 228–32.

Colvin, L. B. "An Overview of U.S. Trends in Educational Software Design." *The Computing Teacher* 16(5) (February 1989): 24–28.

Collis B., & Oilila. "An Examination of Sex Difference in Secondary School Students' Attitudes Toward Writing and the Computer." *The Alberta Journal of Educational Research,* 34(4) (1986): 297–306.

Collis, Betty. *The Best of Research Windows: Trends and Issues in Educational Computing.* Oregon: International Society of Technology in Education, 1990.

Daiute, C. *Writing and Computers.* Reading, MA: Addison Wesley, 1985.

Dalton, D. W. "A Comparison of the Effects of Logo and Problem-Solving Strategy Instruction on Learning Achievement, Attitude, and Problem-Solving Skills." *Dissertation Abstracts International* 47(2) (1986): 511a (University Microfilms No. 86–08596).

Dence, M. "Toward Defining the Role of CAI: A Review." *Educational Technology* (November 1980): 50–54.

Ediger, M. "Computers at the Crossroads." *Educational Technology* 28(5) (May 1988): 7–10.

Feigenbaum, E. A., and P. McCorduck. *The Fifth Generation: Artificial Intelligence and Japan's Computer Challenge to the World.* Reading, MA: Addison Wesley, 1983.

Feldman, P. R. "Personal Computers in a Writing Course." *Perspectives in Computing* (Spring 1984): 4–9.

Fisher, G. "Where CAI is Effective: A Summary of the Research." *Electronic Learning,* 82 (November/December 1983): 84.

Fites, Philip E. *The Computer Virus Crisis.* New York: Van Nostrand Reinhold, 1989.

Fortner, R. W., Schar, & J. Mayer. *Effect of Microcomputer Simulations on Computer Awareness and Perception of Environmental Relationships Among College Students.* Columbus, OH: Ohio State University, Office of Learning Resources (Eric Document Reproduction Service No. Ed. 270–311), 1986.

Freedman, Allan. *The Computer Glossary* (Fifth Edition). Point Pleasant, Pennsylvania: American Management Association, 1991.

Freedman, Warren. *The Right of Privacy in the Computer Age.* New York: Quorum Books, 1987.

Glass, G. V. "Primary, Secondary, and Meta-Analysis of Research." *Educational Researchers,* 5 (1976): 3–8.

Glass, G. V. "Integrated Findings: The Meta-Analysis of Research." In L. Schulman (Ed.) *Review of Research in Education.* Itasca, Il: Peacock, 1977.

Gleason, Gerald T. "Microcomputers in Education: The State of the Art." *Educational Technology* (March 1981): 7–18.

Goode, M. "Testing CAI Courseware in Fifth and Sixth Grade Math." *T.H.E. Journal* (October 1988): 97–100.

Gore, Andrew. "Pen, Voice Will Shape Interface." (February 3, 1992) Vol. 6, No. 5. *MacWeek,* page 1, 98.

Grovier, H. *Microcomputers in Primary Education: A Survey of Recent Research.* (Occasional Paper ITE/28a/88). Lancaster, U.K. Economics and Social Research Council, 1988.

Guglielmo, Connie. "Managers Clamp Down on Software Piracy." *MacWeek,* Vol 6, No 2, (13 January 1992): 60–63.

Hasselbring, Ted S. "Remediating Spelling Problems of Learning-Handicapped Students Through the Use of Microcomputers." *Educational Technology* (April 1982): 31–32.

Hawisher, G. E. "The Effects of Word Processing on the Revision Strategies of College Students." Paper presented at the annual meeting of the American Educational Research Association, San Francisco, California (ERIC Document Reproductions Service No. ED. 268–546), April 1986.

Haynes, Colin. *The Computer Virus Protection Handbook.* San Francisco: SYBEX, 1990.

Hoffman, Patricia, telephone (408) 988–3773, BBS (408) 244–0813.

Horner, C. M. & Maddux, C. D. "The Effect of Logo on Attributions Toward Success." *Computers in the schools* 2 (2/3), (1985): 45–54.

Keller, Janet K. "Characteristics of Logo Instruction Promoting Transfer of Learning: A Research Review." *Journal of Research on Computers in Education,* 23, (1) Fall 1990.

Kulik, James A., and C. Chen-Lin. "Review of Recent Literature on Computer- Based

Instruction." *Contemporary Education Psychology,* 12 (3) (July 1987): 222–30.

Kulik, James C. C., J. A. Kulik, & B. J. Shwath. "Effectiveness of Computer-Based Adult Learning: A Meta-Analysis." *Journal of Educational Computing Research* 2 (1986): 235–252.

Kulik, James C. C., J. A. Kulik, & P. Cohen. "Instructional Technology and College Teaching." *Teaching of Psychology* 7 (1980); 199–205.

Kulik, James A., R. Bangert, & G. Williams. "Effects of Computer-Based Teaching on Secondary School Students." *Journal of Educational Psychology* 75 (1983): 19–26.

Kulik, J. A., & C. C. Kulik. "Timing of Feedback and Verbal Learning." *Review of Educational Research,* 58 (1) (1988); 79–97.

Kurth, R. J. "Using Word Processing to Enhance Revision Strategies During Student Writing Activities." *Educational Technology,* 27 (1987): 13–19.

Lally, M. "Computer-Assisted Development of Number Conservation in Mentally Retarded Children." *Journal of Developmental Disabilities,* (September 1980): 131–136.

Linn, C. "Learning More-With Computers as Lab Partners." Paper presented at the annual meeting of the American Educational Research Association, San Francisco, CA, April, 1986.

Luehrmann, A. "The Best Way to Teach Computer Literacy." *Electronic Learning* 3(3) (April 1984); 37–42, 44.

Lundell, Allan. *Virus!: The Secret World of Computer Invaders that Breed and Destroy.* Chicago: Contemporary Books, 1989.

Maser, Arthur L., et al. *Highline Public Schools Computer-Assisted Instruction Project: A Program to Meet Disadvantaged Students' Individual Needs for Basic Skill Development: Final Report.* Research Report, July 1979, ED. 167–114.

MacArthur, C. A., J. A. Haynes, D. B. Melouf, & K. Harris. "Computer Assisted Instruction With Learning Disabled Students: Achievement, Engagement, and Other Factors Related to Achievement." Paper presented at the annual meeting of the American Educational Research Association, Washington, D.C., April, 1987.

Mayer, R. E. & A. L. Fay. "A Chain of Cognitive Changes with Learning to Program in Logo." *Journal of Educational Psychology.* 79, (3), 1987.

Mayer, R. E., J. L. Dyck, & W. Vilberg. "Learning to Program and Learning to Think: What's the Connection?" *Communication of the ACM,* 29, (7) (1986): 605–610.

McAfee, John. *Computer Viruses, Worms, Data Diddler, Killer Programs, and Others.* New York: St. Martin's Press, 1989.

Moore, C., S. Smith, & R. A. Auner. "Facilitation of Laboratory Performance Through CAI." *Journal of Chemical Education,* 57(3) (1980): 196–198.

Morehouse, D. L., M. L. Hoaglund, & R. H. Schmidt. *Technology Demonstration Program Final Evaluation Report.* Menononie, WI: Quality Evaluation and Development, February, 1987.

Norr, H. "Latest Mac Viral Infection Hits the Stacks." *MacWeek* (16 April 1991): 17

Norr, H. "Speech Recognizer Hears Through the 'Ums and Ers.'" *MacWeek* 4 (34) (9 October 1990): 5.

O'Brien, P. "Using Microcomputers in the Writing Class." *The Computing Teacher* (May 1984): 20–21.

Palumbo, David B. and Michael W. Reed. "The Effect of Basic Programming

Language Instruction on High School Students' Problem Solving Ability and Computer Anxiety." *Journal of Research on Computing in Education,* 23(3) (Spring 1991): 342–369.

Papert, S. *Mindstorms.* New York: Basic Books, 1980.

Pea, R. D. & D. M. Kurland. *Logo Programming and the Development of Planning Skills* (Technical Report No. 11). New York: Bank Street College of Education, March, 1984.

Pea, R. D. "The Aims of Software Criticism: Reply to Professor Papert." *Educational Researcher,* 16 (5) (June/July 1987): 4–8.

Parker, Donn B. *Ethical Conflicts in Information and Computer Science Technology.* Wellesley, Mass.: QED Information Sciences, 1990.

Pfleeger, Charles P. *Security in Computing.* Englewood Cliffs, N.J.: Prentice-Hall, 1989.

Rizzo, J. "Erasable Optical Drives." *MacUser* (November 1990): 102–130.

Robertson, G. *A Comparison of Meaningful and Nonmeaningful Content in Computer-Assisted Spelling Programs.* Saskatchewan, Canada: Saskatchewan School Trustees Association Research Center, 1978.

Roblyer, M. D., W. H. Castine, & F. J. King. *Assessing the Impact of Computer-Based Instruction: A Review of Recent Research.* New York: The Haworth Press, 1988.

Ruel, Allred A. *The Application of Research Findings.* Washington, D.C.: National Education Association (1987): 42–43.

Siann, G., A. Durndell, H. Macleod, & P. Glissov. "Stereotyping in Relation to the Gender Gap in Participation in Computing." *Educational Research,* 30(2) (1988): 98–103.

Soloway, E., Lockhead & Clement, J. "Does Computer Programming Enhance Problem Solving Ability? Some Positive Evidence on Algebra Word Problems." In R. J. Seidel, R. Anderson, & B. Hunter, (Eds.) *Computer Literacy: Issues and Directions for 1985.* New York: Academic Press (1982): 171–185.

Summerville, L. J. "The Relationship Between Computer-Assisted Instruction and Achievement Levels and Learning Rates of Secondary School Students in First Year Chemistry." *Dissertation Abstracts International,* 46, (3) 603a, 1984. (University Microfilms No. 85–10891).

Swadener, M., & M. Hannafin. "Gender Similarities and Differences in Sixth Graders' Attitudes Toward Computers: An Exploratory Study." *Educational Technology,* 27(1) (1987): 37–42.

Thomas, Rex and Elizabeth Hooper. "Simulations: An Opportunity We are Missing." *Journal of Research on Computing in Education,* 23(4) (Summer 1991): 497–513.

Tien, James M. *Electronic Fund Transfer Systems Fraud: Computer Crimes.* Washington, D.C.: U.S. Department of Justice, Bureau of Justice Statistics, 1985.

Tsai, San-Yun W., and Norval F. Pohl. "Student Achievement in Computer Programming: Lecture Vs. Computer-Aided Instruction." *Journal of Experimental Education* (Winter 1977): 66–70.

Ware, M. C. & M. F. Stuck. "Sex-Role Message Vis-a-Vis Microcomputer Use: A Look at the Pictures." *Sex Roles,* 13(34) (1985): 205–214.

Watkins, Marley W., and C. Webb. "Computer-Assisted Instruction with Learning-Disabled Students." *Educational Computer* (September/October 1981): 24–27.

Wright, R. "Multimedia: What is it?" *MacValley Voice,* October, 1990.

Appendix A
RECOMMENDED SOFTWARE

ART PROGRAMS

Blazing Paddles, Baudville. Apple, Commodore, Atari: Pre-K-up

Users can do color mixing, air brushing, ovals, lines, and rectangles; and the zoom feature lets them pixel edit while viewing the results at full scale. This program is so versatile that young children can use it like a coloring book, and sophisticated adults can use it like a computer artist.

Color 'n' Canvas, WINGS for Learning. Apple IIGS: Grades 1–8

The student uses two palettes for color mixing, draws freehand shapes, and adds text easily. The computer generates rectangles, triangles, and circles; any feature that is more difficult to use can be turned off. An exciting tool called "mirroring" lets the user draw a pattern, which is reflected on the monitor.

Dazzle Draw, Brøderbund. Apple II Family: Grades 3–up

Dazzle Draw is a drawing and painting program with pull-down menus and windows. Users choose from a wide range of brush widths and shapes; students can work with 16 brilliant colors, mix them, spray-paint, flood fill, cut and paste, and choose from 30 patterns. A teacher's guide contains dozens of interesting, classroom-tested projects.

816/Paint, Baudville. Apple II and GS Family: Grades 6–12

An award winning program, *816 /Paint* is a full featured, paint program with an icon menu and 12 brushes, as well as full screen painting and color animation. An educational version details 38 activities that teachers can integrate into the arts curriculum program.

Kid Pix, Brøderbund. Macintosh, Apple II Family, IBM: Pre-K-up

Easy-to-use, full-faceted, and entertaining, nothing compares with *Kid Pix* in the art area. Each paint tool makes a sound—the pencil scratches, the brush bloops, and the moving tool vrooms like a truck's engine. The color paint program also contains soda pop bubbles and wacky brushes that drip paint. Many of the brushes are animated and grow into different objects.

MacPaint 2.0, Claris Corp. Macintosh: Pre-K-up

This free-form, graphic program is extremely easy to use and works with a large assortment of word processors. Users can produce work with tools such as shapes, lines, spray paint, pencil, and paintbrush. Snapshot and magic erasure features let users retouch art.

Platinum Paint Plus, Beagle Bros. Apple IIGS: Grades 3–up

A very sophisticated paint program that lets users draw a variety of shapes and lines, using sixteen different colors. Commands are displayed in pull-down menus with dialogue boxes. Students can create many special effects: they can lighten, darken, mirror, recolor, resize, flop, rotate, and shadow.

Superpaint, Silcon Beach Software. Macintosh: Grades 5–up

Superpaint lets users combine the features of paint and draw programs in one, easy-to-use format. This approach saves money and also gives users the convenience of working with two separate programs at once. A variety of brushes and tools produce professional looking output.

AUTHORING TOOLS

HyperCard 2.2, Claris Corp. Macintosh: Grades 8–up

Developed by Bill Atkinson, *HyperCard* is an authoring tool that lets users create onscreen cards containing text, graphics, sound, and animation. Users can design various card sizes, enhance drawings, sound, and animation, and open up stacks of cards simultaneously. *HyperCard* can be used to teach programming or to create lessons.

HyperCard IIGS, Apple Computer. Apple IIGS: Grades 8–up

This program is very similar to the Macintosh Version of *HyperCard*. A special stack called *HyperMover* allows users to translate Macintosh stacks to the GS format.

HyperScreen, Scholastic. Apple II Family, IBM: Grades 7–12

This hypermedia application with graphics and sound booster packs lets users combine graphics, text, and digitized sound files. With this easy-to-use program, students will be creating cards and stacks in record time.

HyperStudio, Roger Wagner Publishers. Apple IIGS: Grades 7–12

This hypermedia authoring system for the GS is similar to *HyperCard* for the Macintosh. It comes with a sound digitizer, microphone, clip art, sample sounds, built in paint program, text recording, and text editor.

IBM LinkWay, IBM. IBM: Grades 6–up

This IBM program lets teachers and students develop multimedia presentations that combine text, color graphics, picture images, music freeze-frame, and full-motion video. The program has pull-down menus, a paint program, text editor, font editor and demonstration programs.

Tutor Tech, Techware Inc. Apple II Family: Grades 8–up

Based on the *HyperCard* idea, this program offers users pull-down menus, a graphic toolbox, dialogue boxes, cut, copy, and paste commands, text fonts, tools for drawing shapes, and a method of putting these components together.

DATA BASE PROGRAMS

Bank Street School Filer, Sunburst. Apple II Family, Commodore: Grades 5–up

This program utilizes simple, English-language commands for searching and sorting, and users can design and print custom reports. *Bank Street School Filer* includes a tutorial program, a reference manual, and a teacher's guide with detailed lesson plans and supplementary data bases.

Bank Street Beginner's Filer, Sunburst. Apple II Family, Commodore: Grades 2–6

Designed with young students in mind, *Bank Street Beginner's Filer* introduces the fundamentals of data base concepts. A simpler version of the versatile *Bank Street School Filer,* it is meant for the novice who has never used a data base.

Easy Working The Filer, Queque (Formerly Spinnaker). Apple, IBM: Grades 4–up

Easy Working The Filer is a relative to the other *Easy Working* productivity tools. These low cost productivity tools use the same command format, which means that once the user learns one program in the series, it is relatively easy to learn the other programs.

FrEdBase, SoftSwap, (Shareware). Apple II Family: Grades 9–up

FrEdBase was written by Greg Butler and was designed specifically for school use. It is a fast data base which lets the teacher use up to 18 fields in a file; it also performs two tier searches.

Friendly Filer, Houghton Mifflin. Apple II Family, IBM: Grades 3–up

With the on-screen directions there is no need to memorize commands. A cute animated introduction teaches students data base concepts and an interactive tutorial shows them how to use the product step-by-step. As an additional tutorial device, *Friendly Filer* has a set of questions to give users practice in finding information.

PFS File, Scholastic. Apple, IBM: Grades 6–up

PFS File's eight main functions are listed on the main menu: Design, Add, Copy, Search/Update, Print, Remove Select File, and Exit. While *PFS Filer* is harder to use than the *Bank Street Filer,* it does have more features and a larger record capacity. *PFS File* is a relative of *PFS Write* and works well with this word processor.

Swift Data Base, Cosmi. Apple, IBM: Grades 8–up

Swift's Data Base is an inexpensive, but high quality productivity tool that sells for less than ten dollars. On-screen menus allow users to quickly create and organize data. Users needs no experience to use this data base, but it does have sophisticated features that more expensive data bases do not have.

DESKTOP PUBLISHING

BankStreet Writer, Scholastic. Macintosh: Grades 2–up

See Word Processing.

Better Working Word Publisher, Spinnaker. IBM: Grades 8–up

A bargain desktop publishing package that is easy to use, *Better Working Word Publisher* has nine different typefaces; text styles include plain, bold, outline, underline, and italics. There are four standard columns of text. It comes with an outliner, a spelling checker, and a thesaurus. Users can easily mix graphics with text and bring images from many different clip art programs.

Big Book Maker, Pelican. Apple II Family: Grades 1–7

Big Book Maker, a very simple-to-use publishing program, lets users combine graphics and text to create big books, activity sheets, and bulletin boards. It comes with a variety of graphics and typestyles, and students can print four different size books. *Big Book Maker* uses a four key command structure: Space Bar, Return, Arrow Keys, and Escape. The documentation is excellent.

The Children's Writing and Publishing Center, Learning Company. Apple II Family, IBM: Grades 2–up

A must for elementary school children and novices, this program can have a child writing in less than an hour. The manual has a quick start section and the school edition includes a teacher's guide. It also includes an additional disk with templates and a program disk that contains pictures. Because this program is so simple to use, it is also limited.

Once Upon a Time II; Once Upon a Time III, CompuTeach. IBM, Macintosh, Apple II Family: Grades 1–7

This elementary desktop publishing package teaches students to design and publish books. There are three themes in each volume; for example, themes for *Once Upon a Time III* are Space Odyssey, Wild West, and Medieval Times. In creating pages, students arrange and delete objects. They can type up to three lines of text or may opt for text only pages.

PageMaker 4.0, Aldus Corporation. Macintosh, IBM: Grades 11–up

The desktop publishing package which launched the desktop publishing revolution, *PageMaker* gives casual users the ability to produce documents quickly. The program uses an intuitive electronic pasteboard that enables users to lay out and view text and graphics easily on a page. Several templates and predesigned publications come with the program.

Publish-It (Version 3), Timeworks, Inc. Apple II Family, Macintosh, IBM: Grades 10–up

Publish-It has an impressive array of features with an unlimited number of graphics and stories per document. The program also has an easy-to-use tutorial that gets users started immediately. Because of the breath and depth of its features, it is slightly harder to use.

Publish-It Lite!, Timeworks, Inc. IBM: Grades 8–up

This starter program is a simplified version of *Publish It.* The page layout features are easy to use and can produce a limited four page document. Three fonts come with the program, and the graphics handling is wonderful.

PFS: First Publisher (Version 2), Software Publishing Corporation (Owned by Spinnaker). IBM: Grades 9–up

Software Publishing Corporation always supports its products, and this beginning level, desktop publishing program is no exception. *PFS: First Publisher* has a simple menu across the top and artist tools along the side. The documentation is excellent.

Springboard Publisher (Version 2), Springboard Publisher. Apple II Family, IBM, Macintosh: Grades 8–up

Springboard Publisher (Version 2) is appropriate for the occasional user, the high school student, or for light office work. The program can produce small publications, memos, and flyers.

Swift Desktop Publisher, Cosmi. Apple II Family, IBM: Grades 9–up

How can a student go wrong for $9.95? This is desktop publishing for newsletters, banners, and certificates. *Swift Desktop Publisher* has on-screen menus, ten print fonts, a clip art library, built-in word processor, and text editor. It is easy to use, and a help guide and documentation are included.

The Writing Center, Learning Company. Macintosh, IBM: Grades 2–12

The Writing Center is a flexible, easy-to-use tool. It has the most popular features of *Children's Writing Center,* but goes beyond this program in scope. Children can easily design and produce a wide array of layouts and documents, including illustrated reports and stories, poems, letters, newsletters, awards, signs, cards, and calendars. Teachers can create an unlimited number of classroom instructional materials as well as parent correspondence.

EARLY CHILDHOOD

McGee, Katie's Farm, Fun Fair, Lawrence Productions. IBM, Apple GS, Macintosh: Pre-K

Children click on various objects on the screen, and the objects respond with speech and movement. In the first program, McGee completes the tasks that most children accomplish in the morning; he brushes his teeth and goes to the bathroom. In the second program, he visits Katie's farm to ride a horse and go fishing, pick raspberries, and gather eggs. In the third program, McGee and his best friend, Tony, attend the summer Fun Fair and enjoy a day of entertainment. These programs are engaging introductions to the computer for small children.

Picture Chompers, MECC. Apple II Family: Grades K–1

Using a drill and practice format, this program reinforces classification skills. Children use arrow keys or a joystick to move a pair of teeth around a grid, chomping on the items that meet a specific criteria. The objects are classified according to color, size, shape, class, design, or use. This game can be played at three levels of difficulty, with or without a timer.

Playroom, Brøderbund. Apple II Family, Macintosh, IBM: Pre–K to 1

Playroom, an interactive program, has elements of strategic thinking, simulation, and discovery. A clock, computer, mixed-up toy, mousehole, ABC book, and spinner toy allow children to explore letters, numbers, and time. Every game, toy, and surprise has something to teach; the program skillfully uses animation, sound, music, and graphics.

The New Talking Stickybear Opposites, Weekly Reader/Optimum Resources, Apple IIGS: Grades K–1

Using this drill and practice program, children learn opposites. There are roughly 20 sets of words that relate to concepts such as measurement, feeling, time and directions. These words are said more than once in a different setting. The program has excellent graphics, animation, and sound effects.

The New Talking Stickybear Alphabet, Weekly Reader, Apple, Commodore 64, IBM: Grades Preschool–3

Animated pictures and sound effects help children learn the alphabet and how to pronounce words. Each keyboard letter displays two picture examples. The Apple and IBM versions speak with an ECHO board.

HARDWARE PRODUCTS

Apple II Video OverLay Card, Apple Computer. Apple II Family:

A circuit board lets users add computer graphics to video images from a video camera, VCR, or videodisc. The professor and student can use this card to create amazing video effects. For example they can design graphic titles underneath a person who appears on the video or interesting borders around live images.

Computer Eyes, Digital Vision. Apple II Family, Apple GS, IBM:

A circuit board allows users to freeze images from a video camera and then save these images on a computer disk. Users can decorate what they save, using a program such as *SuperPrint*.

Finger Print, Thirdware. Apple II Family, Apple GS:

This card lets users press a button and dump any screen that is displayed on the monitor. It rotates, clips, and enlarges any high-resolution, low-resolution, or double high-resolution screen.

Scan Man (IBM), Scan Man 32 (Macintosh), Logitech:

This hand scanner is excellent for scanning clip art. It allows the user to scan any four inch image for inclusion in a presentation.

VideoWorks II, MacroMind. Macintosh: Grades 10–up

Professional quality animation can be produced with this program which has its own clip art and animation files, movies, and sound. The teacher can add motion to slides through clip animation features.

LANGUAGE ARTS PROGRAMS

Ace Reporter II, Mindplay. Apple, IBM: Grades 2–6

Students become Ace Reporters by uncovering who, what, when, where, and why. They read a teletype message and conduct telephone interviews to gather facts and then write their news stories, complete with headlines.

Big Book Maker, Pelican Software. Apple II Family: Grades K–4

See Desktop Publishing.

The Children's Writing and Publishing Center, Learning Company. Apple, IBM: Grades 2–up

See Desktop Publishing.

Cartooners, Electronic Arts. Apple II Family, IBM: Grades 3–8

Students practice animation techniques by choosing from 50 different characters and objects, ten backgrounds, music, and sound clips. They may put words in balloons and determine the type and direction of action. Then they arrange the frames, which can be saved, seen on screen, and printed.

Chariots, Cougars and Kings, Hartley. Apple II Family, IBM: Grades 3–4

This is a skill building series featuring Scuffy and Friends or Kittens, Kids, and a Frog. Following colorful graphics at the beginning, students read a story, then answer a series of comprehension questions that teach skills such as identifying the main idea or details. The stories are modifiable, and there is a record keeping function that serves as an excellent diagnostic tool.

Create with Garfield—Deluxe Edition, DLM. Apple II Family, Commodore 64, IBM: Grades 1–5

The student is able to create colorful Garfield cartoons, posters, and short stories. There are over 200 pieces of art, a variety of typefaces for writing cartoon captions, and a text editor for writing dialogue.

ESL Writer, Scholastic. Apple II Family, IBM: Grades K–4

Developed for Hispanic or Asian ESL students, this program has a grammar checker, spelling checker, and a word processor. Pupils type their work and the program checks it for spelling or grammar errors.

Fay's Word Rally, Didatech. Apple II Family, Commodore, IBM: Grades 2–3

Fay's Word Rally is a motivating reading and driving program that reviews sight word acquisition, sentence comprehension, and vocabulary development. The student reads a clue at the bottom of the screen and finds the word in the maze by driving the car to it. When the car hits the correct word, the word will vanish and Fay waves her flag and music plays. This program can be customized, and it has complete record keeping features.

Grammar Gremlins, Davidson and Associates. Apple II Family, IBM: Grades 3–6

Using a haunted house, *Grammar Gremlins* improves reading, writing, and language skills. The program offers highly appealing graphics and over 600 examples and practice sentences that reinforce rules about abbreviation, capitalization, parts of speech, plurals, and contractions.

Kidwriter Golden Edition, Spinnaker. Apple II Family, IBM: Grades K–4

Using the *Kidwriter* word processor, children develop writing skills and create and print their own illustrated storybooks. Children learn the fundamentals of word processing, including editing functions such as delete and insert.

Kindercomp Golden Edition, Spinnaker. Apple II Family, IBM: Pre-K–3

Kindercomp has eight exciting classroom activities, colorful pictures, and music with fun exercises. Children learn the alphabet, spelling, counting, number sequence, and simple addition. The computer user can select the difficulty level, and there is a level indicator that measures educational progress.

Monsters and Make Believe, Pelican/Queue, Inc. Software. Apple II Family, IBM, Macintosh: Grades K–6

Children create monsters and then use speech bubbles to create dialogue among them. Students can design big books, mobiles, and comic strips. A Spanish version is available. If an echo board or Cricket Speech Synthesizer is purchased, what is typed can be heard.

PickleFace and Other Stories, Hartley. Apple II Family: Grades 4–7

There are three story disks that build comprehension skills: *Pickleface, New Kid on the Block,* and *Movin' On.* Each of these appealing stories contains five chapters followed by a series of questions. Students make predictions, distinguish fact from opinion, and expand their vocabulary. Teachers can modify the story content and the questions if they wish.

PlayWrite, Sunburst. Apple IIGS: Grades 1–6

PlayWrite encourages creative writing. When students use *PlayWrite,* they choose costumes, expressions, and scenery for scripts, write dialog for the puppets, revise and edit the dialog, and then listen and watch the puppets perform the finished product.

Pow! Zap! Keplunk! The Comic Maker, PelicanQueue, Inc., Apple II Family, IBM: K–6

This program is designed exclusively for creating comic books. A word processor produces a variety of font sizes and styles, and three book size options are available. The program "speaks" the text, providing the user has an echo board or Cricket Speech Synthesizer.

Puppetmaker, Sunburst. Apple II Family: Grades K–6

This program lets the student design four types of puppets (walking, finger, paper bag, and shoe box). Children select features at the computer from numerous themes and characteristics, print out the design created, then cut and fold it.

Reading and Me, Davidson and Associates. Apple II Family, IBM: Pre-K–2

Children learn to classify objects, recognize letters, understand phonics, and read simple sentences by completing twelve simple activities that are presented sequentially. The children learn at their own pace and receive positive reinforcement in the form of certificates.

Reader Rabbit, The Learning Company. Apple II Family, IBM: Grades K–1

Reader Rabbit, an early reading program for the primary grades, uses a game approach to teach reading skills. The students learn how to identify letters, sort them into words, and then sequence words according to a specific rule. The *Talking Reader Rabbit* uses the speech capabilities of the Apple IIGS and Macintosh to pronounce over 200 three-letter words.

Read-N-Roll, Davidson and Associates. Apple II Family, IBM: Grades 3–6

Read-N-Roll is a reading comprehension program that covers main ideas, details, sequencing, inferences and vocabulary. It has more than 300 stories to focus on these five areas. One component of *Read-N-Roll* is an action packed bowling game.

Speed Reading II, Davidson and Associates. Apple II Family, Commodore 64, IBM, Macintosh: Grades 9–up

This program helps students develop their reading fluency and speed. There are peripheral vision exercises, column reading training, and timed comprehension tests. Supplementary disks are available.

Spell It Plus!, Davidson and Associates. Apple II Family, IBM: Grades 4–up

Spell It Plus! has five spelling activities that address spelling, spelling rules, and syllabication. A frog eats the words students have mastered.

Stickybear Spellgrabber, Weekly Reader/Optimum Resources, Inc. Apple II Family: Grades 1–4

Stickybear Spellgrabber has the stickybear hopping and juggling while students play one of three games: a Picture Spell, a Word Spell and a Bear Dunk. The program contains a 3,500 word list, and teachers can add their own lists of words.

Super Story Tree, Scholastic. Apple II Family, IBM: Grades 6–12

Students write branching type stories using sound, graphics and clip art, graphics tools, different size fonts, and even special effects.

The New Game Show, Advanced Ideas. Apple II Family, IBM: Grades 3–up

Similar to the popular password game, *The New Game Show* builds vocabulary. *The New Game Show* uses colorful animation, presents a wide range of subject matter, and can be played by one or two teams.

The Treehouse, Brøderbund. Apple II Family, IBM, Macintosh: Grades K–4

The Treehouse, an interdisciplinary program covering a wide range of subjects, begins where *Playroom* ends. Students explore the on-screen hideaway with seven educational games, learning about mathematics, animals, sentence structure, money, place value, and music. The program has animation, sound effects, and activities that definitely appeal to six to ten year olds.

Your Personal Trainer for the SAT, Davidson and Associates: Macintosh, IBM: Grades 8–up

This tutorial program uses a step-by-step approach to master the strategies for dealing with material found on the SAT. The program scores and analyzes the user's answers on sample math and verbal SAT tests. Users can compare their SAT scores with those required by selected colleges.

Wizard of Words, Advanced Ideas. Apple II Family, Commodore 64, IBM, Macintosh: Grades 1–up

This program has been around a long time, but stands the test of time. The *Wizard* consists of five word games which are enhanced by fire-shooting dragons, knights, jugglers, and a princess. A comprehensive word list consisting of 38,000 words is keyed to eight different learning levels.

Word Attack Plus, Davidson and Associates. Macintosh, IBM, Apple II Family: Grades 4–Adult

Word Attack Plus, a five-part vocabulary building program, is a very motivating arcade style game. Sudents use a joystick or keyboard arrows to move the hattacker directly under the word that matches the word at the bottom of the screen. Spanish and French versions are available.

Word Munchers, MECC. Apple II Series: Grade 1–5

Using a drill and practice format, students learn to identify vowel sounds. With this Pac Man type game, students move around a grid, trying to identify the right words and avoid the "Troggles."

Writer's Helper 3.0, Conduit. Macintosh: Grades 7–13

This tutorial/tool program helps students with prewriting and revision. It contains many activities for finding, exploring, and organizing a subject, as well as activities for checking structure, audience, and words.

Writer Rabbit, The Learning Company. Apple II Family, IBM: Grades 2–4

Six sequenced games with delightful animated machines teach children skills such as recognition of simple sentence parts. Children also learn to write their own stories. There is a talking version for the GS.

MATH PROGRAMS

Alge-Blaster, Davidson and Associates. Apple II Family, Commodore, IBM: Grades 8–up

This tutorial program reviews and gives practice in algebra basics. There are over 670 problems that cover different areas of algebra, and problems can be added using the Editor.

Algebra Shop, Scholastic. Apple II Family, IBM: Grades 7–10

This excellent simulation program gives practice in pre-algebra and algebra skills. Students fill customers' orders in ten different stores, practicing square roots, simultaneous equations, etc. When the students serve the customers correctly, the problems become more difficult.

Challenge Math, Sunburst. Apple II Family, Commodore, IBM: Grades 2–6

This program excites children with an alien space intruder, a dinosaur, and a mysterious mansion. Through these lovable creatures, students practice basic whole numbers and decimal operations. A teacher operation allows adjustment of the difficulty level.

Fraction Munchers, MECC. Apple II Family: Grades 4–6

Students practice their skills with fractions in a Pac Man type game by directing the Muncher to eat fractional expressions that match a target value. Children match factors, primes, multiples, equalities, and inequalities.

Hop To It!, Sunburst Communications. Apple II Family: Grades K–3

This problem solving program strengthens students' addition and subtraction skills. They help animals pick up objects that are scattered along a number line, deciding whether to add, subtract, or change the order.

Math and Me, Davidson and Associates. Apple II Family, IBM: Grades Pre-K–1

Math and Me helps with math readiness because it teaches the child about shapes, patterns, numbers and single digit addition. There are twelve motivating educational activities that are presented sequentially. This program is perfect for heterogeneous classroom use.

Math Blaster Mystery, Davidson and Associates. Apple II Family, IBM: Grades 5–up

Students work with fractions, decimals, percents, and positive and negative numbers to solve word problems. They weigh evidence, decipher codes, and search for clues. Teachers can add word problems, a test maker can print tests, and students are rewarded with certificates.

Kemeny-Kurtz Math Series: Calculus, True Basic. Commodore Amiga, IBM, Macintosh: Grades 9–16

This program has a math graphing utility, symbolic manipulator, calculator, and presentation features. Some of the topics covered are function graphing, symbolic differentiation, multiple derivatives, limits, and tangents. The strength of this program is its range of problems and the record and playback features.

Math Maze, Britannica. Apple II Family: Grades 1–6

Math Maze lets students practice math facts by picking up answers in a maze. In the first level, the student is a fly that simply travels through the maze picking up the correct answers. In level 2, the student avoids a spider and picks up the correct answers. There are 40 prepared mazes for practicing addition, subtraction, multiplication, and devision, and the teacher can customize the mazes.

Math Rabbit, The Learning Company. Apple II Family, IBM: Grades K–2

Math Rabbit has four creative games that provide practice in counting, addition, and subtraction. Students also learn about number patterns and relationships.

Math Shop, Scholastic. Apple II Family: Grades 4–6

Math Shop helps students with basic math skills like estimation, ratio, decimals, and fractions. Students work in different stores, using a wide range of "real world" math skills. There are vivid graphics and challenging exercises.

Money Works, MECC. Apple II Family: Grades 1–4

These programs give practice in money recognition, counting money, and change making. The students can make their own commemorative money, and teachers can modify the program contents.

Number Muncher, MECC. Apple II Family, Macintosh, IBM: Grades 3–up

In this Muncher program, students help the munchers hunt for numbers or numerical expressions, such as factors, primes, multiples, equalities, or inequalities. In the process of hunting, they avoid the "Troggles," creatures who will eat them up if they are not careful.

New Math Blaster Plus, Davidson and Associates. Macintosh, IBM: Grades 1–6

This new version covers addition, subtraction, multiplication, division, decimals, and percents. There are six different ability levels with over 750 problems, an editor, record keeper, test maker, and a re-take option. The clever screen design and the space age sound effects mesmerize the students.

Safari Search, WINGS for Learning. Apple II Family, IBM: Grades 3–up

Using a problem solving approach, students work on twelve safari search activities on a five by five grid. These activities provide practice in drawing inferences and making complex judgements. The object is for students to develop a strategy for finding hidden animals in the least number of moves.

Stickybear Math Word Problems, Weekly Reader/Optimum Resources, Inc. Apple II Family, IBM: Grades 2–up

This moving graphic program is aimed at building a child's word problem solving skills. There are over 150 word problems in addition, subtraction, multiplication, and division that match the progress of the user. The teacher can also add problems to meet the individual needs of the students.

Stickybear Numbers, Weekly Reader/Optimum Resources, Inc. Apple II Family, IBM, Commodore: Grades Preschool–1

This program uses over 250 picture combinations of animated balls, trains, trucks, and animals to help children learn numbers and counting. The pictures captivate children and give them "hands on" experience with computers.

SuperSolvers Outnumbered, The Learning Company. Macintosh, IBM: Grades 3–5

A character named Morty Maxwell has taken over the airwaves at Shady Glen TV Station. As a member of the Super Solvers Club, the student has till midnight to locate his hideout by solving word problems and matching clues and a secret code. This program is a fast-paced, adventure game with fabulous animation and graphics.

The Factory, WINGS for Learning. Apple II Family, Commodore, IBM: Grades 5–up

This program features colorful graphics and animation and three levels of difficulty. Students design an assembly line and use it to create or duplicate products using the program's three machines.

The Geometry Supposers, Sunburst. Apple II Family, IBM, Macintosh: Grades 8–up

Students construct any type of triangle, using their own dimensions. They take measurements and repeat experiments on different types of triangles. Each program includes one disk, backup, teacher's guide, and quick reference card. The program is based on two years of research and work with teachers.

The Treehouse, Brøderbund. Apple II Family, IBM, Macintosh: Grades K–4
See Language Arts programs.

MUSIC PROGRAMS

Camus: Melodic Dictations, Conduit. Apple II Family, IBM: Grades 9–up
The program plays short melodies and students use the keyboard to write in standard musical notation what they hear. The computer then plays and compares the input of the user with the correct version. There are four disks of varying levels of difficulty.

Concertware+, Great Wave Software. Macintosh: Grades 10–up
Users compose and manipulate music using three utilities, a music player, a music writer, and an instrument maker. They can listen to 18 different selections from Beethoven to Strauss, and these scores can be printed.

Diversi-Tune, Diversified Software. Apple II Family: Grades K–up
Diversi-Tune plays songs in conjunction with a delightful bouncing ball that lets the participants sing along. Teachers can buy prerecorded sound disks for *Diversi-Tune.* If the users buy a "Midi" musical keyboard and interface, they can connect it to the GS computer to record their own songs.

Jam Session, Brøderbund. Apple IIGS, Macintosh: Grades K–up
This program uses high-quality, digitized instrument sounds in combination with music composed by professionals. Students play solos or passages on a variety of instruments, while the program acts as an accompaniment, able to adjust for inappropriate sounds.

The Miracle Piano Teaching System, The Software Tool Works, Macintosh: Grades 3–up
This program comes with a separate keyboard, built-in stereo speakers, software and cable connection for the student's computer. The program customizes lessons for the student with action-oriented video games and popular songs. The student progresses through over 1000 lessons at his or her own individual pace, learning how to read music and play piano.

Musical Construction Set, Electronic Arts. Apple II Family Family: Grades 5–up
This classic program lets students create music and listen to it. The sheet music that the user creates and prints is absolutely outstanding! Macintosh and Commodore Versions called *Deluxe Music Construction* are available.

Music Studio, Mediagenic. Apple II Family, GS, Atari, Commodore, Commodore Amiga: Grades 6–up
With this easy-to-use program students can play, edit, and compose music on a variety of instruments. They enter the musical notes on the staff using a mouse, keyboard, or joystick.

Practica Musica, ARS NOVA Software. Macintosh: Grades 9–up
This drill and practice program teaches music theory and ear training. Students can choose from a variety of lessons in pitch reading, scales, interval, chords, melody, ear training, and melody writing. There are four levels of difficulty for each activity.

Sound Tracks, MECC. Apple II Family: Grades K–6
Using simple keyboard commands, children can create sounds and images. They compose melodies and experiment with lines,

shapes, pictures, and colors—discovering the relationships between audio and visual patterns.

PROGRAMMING

Algernon: An Introduction to Programming, Sunburst. Apple II Family, IBM, Commodore, Tandy: Grades 3–Adult

The students program a mouse called Algernon through mazes to locate a piece of cheese. The mazes range from the very simple to the complex, and the teacher can customize them.

E-Z Pilot II, Hartley. Apple II Family: Grades 10–Adult

An excellent introduction to programming, teachers can use this tool to develop interactive tutorials or stories with sound and graphics. They can individualize lessons for children who have special needs.

EZ-Logo REVISED. MECC. Apple II Family: Grades K–3

EZ-Logo is an extremely popular program among teachers who want to introduce young children to the Logo language. It is a simplified version of Logo that uses simple, one-letter commands.

How to Program in BASIC, Spinnaker. Apple II Family, IBM, Commodore: Grades 7–Up

This program covers the fundamentals of BASIC programming as well as advanced topics like graphics and sound. Students need no prior experience in order to utilize the program, and the lessons are self-paced. A "Let's Talk" feature allows users to review material or move forward.

LCSI Logo II Logo, Computer Systems Inc. Apple II Family: Grades K–up

Logo II is a full fledged computer language that provides turtle graphics and list-processing commands. The program has enhanced graphics, increased calculating speed, and complete assembly language access.

Lego TC Logo, produced by Lego Systems and purchased from Logo Computer Systems (LCSI). IBM, Apple II Family: Grades 4–Up

Students construct Lego figures that use motors, touch, and light sensors. Using simple commands, they then write computer programs to control the machines.

LogoWriter, LSCI. Apple, IBM: Grades K–up

LogoWriter has the following versions: French, Spanish, primary, intermediate, and secondary. Combining word processing with Logo, students create animated graphics to accompany their writing.

Logo Plus, Terrapin Software. Apple II Family: Grades K–up

Logo Plus has a built in shape editor that lets students create their own fantasy lands. They can write, illustrate stories, and even add music to go with the pictures drawn.

Logo Robot, Scholastic. Apple II Family, IBM, Commodore: Grades 4–8

Students can learn problem solving and critical thinking skills as they write computer programs that direct a robot to draw designs on a screen.

PC Logo, Terrapin Software. IBM: Grades K–up

PC Logo is a full-featured, computer language that can be used by beginners as well as experienced programmers. Developed by Harvard Associates Inc., *PC Logo* is a version of the language developed at Massachusetts Institute of Technology.

Seelogo—School Version K–12, Micromedia. Apple II Family: K–up

Seelogo is an introductory Logo program that includes many typical Logo program features with some new primitives added. It can place text and graphics on the same page and save several pages of a story. The 128K version prints text and graphics.

Terrapin Logo, Terrapin Software. Apple II Family, Macintosh: Grades K–up

Terrapin Logo is a full-featured, computer language that can be used for the beginner and the experienced programmer. This program is a version of the language developed at MIT. The examples used throughout the Logo chapter were generated using Terrapin Logo.

True BASIC Language System, True BASIC Inc. Macintosh, IBM: Grades 8–up

TRUE BASIC is an easy-to-use and fully structured programming language. Students write less code to solve harder problems. In fact, this elegant program can be used to generate professional-looking graphs. The examples used through the BASIC chapter were generated using *TRUE BASIC.*

Turtle Tracks, Scholastic. Apple II Family, Commodore, IBM: Grades 4–8

Turtle Tracks uses the basic elements of Logo and BASIC. The students draw simple lines or complicated designs, write melodies to go with their creations, and then save their work.

SCIENCE PROGRAMS

Audubon Wildlife Adventures: Grizzly Bears, Advanced Ideas. Apple II Family, IBM: Grades 4–12

This adventure series is a joint project of the Audubon Society and Advanced Ideas. Using four grizzly adventures, the program teaches environmental conservation, as well as information about grizzlies' size, weight, and migration. Each adventure differs slightly when it is played again, and each story builds on the knowledge gained from earlier stories.

Backyard Birds, MECC. Apple II Family: Grades 3–6

Backyard Birds is a simulation program that teaches students about birds. The student goes on a bird watching expedition and tries to identify as many birds as possible within the set time limit.

Body Transparent, Britannica. Apple, IBM, Commodore: Grades 3–10

By moving the bones and organs to the correct locations on a body, students learn about human anatomy. This program includes several games with different levels of difficulty; it has excellent graphics, a built-in demonstration, and on-screen instructions.

Car Builder, Weekly Reader/Optimum Resources, Inc. Apple: Grades 8–up

Car Builder is a scientific simulation program that lets users design a car. They select the chassis, engine, suspension, and mechanical parts and then run the car through a wind tunnel test track. Students can save the designed car or print it out for comparison with other students' cars.

Designasaurus, Britannica Software. Apple II Family, IBM, Commodore: Grades 2–up

This program has three activities: students survive as dinosaurs by going through mountains and swamps; they build dinosaurs from a collection of bones from the Museum of Natural History, or they can print out 12 different dinosaurs with complete descriptions and color these pictures. Print out options include poster size, regulation size, and a T-shirt transfer.

Discovery Lab, MECC. Apple II Family: Grades 6–9

Discover Lab introduces students to hypothesis testing and experimental design by having them create imaginary organisms. There are three levels of difficulty, and as the program increases in difficulty, the students must control more variables and analyze more complex organisms.

Learn About Animals, Sunburst. Apple: Grades K–2

In eight activities students learn about animal food, homes, and sizes. They search for these animals, write about them, create their own animals, and print masks.

Life and Death, The Software Toolworks. Apple II Family, IBM, Macintosh: Grades 6–Up

Life and Death is a dissection program that recreates the atmosphere of a medical center. Users talk with the patients, read charts, and order x-rays, ultra-sound, blood tests, and other lab work. The doctor examines, diagnoses, treats, and performs stomach surgery on patients in an interactive medical movie.

Lunar Greenhouse, MECC. Apple II Family: Grades 3–9

Students attempt to raise a variety of vegetable crops in a controlled environment on the moon with this problem-solving program. They discover the effects of each variable on the crop by adjusting light, temperature, amount of water, hours of light, and amount of food.

Odell Lake, MECC. Apple II Family: Grades 4–6

In this role playing program, the student assumes the role of different fish, learning about such things as food chains and animal interaction. Different animated animals and random events add to the excitement.

Operation: Frog, Scholastic. Commodore, Apple II Family: Grades 4–10

The students can complete a frog dissection and use a magnifying glass to examine closely each part of the organism. They are also given the opportunity to reconstruct the frog part by part. Extensive background information on frogs is provided to prepare the students for this challenging simulation.

Physics Explorer: Gravity, WINGS for Learning. Macintosh: Grades 10–up

Students explore the motion of a body under the influence of a gravitating planet. They observe Kepler's Laws and apply these concepts to the sun, earth, planets, and satellites. This program has an on-screen tutorial, experiments, and constant visual information in the form of vector displays, bar charts, and histograms.

Playing with Science Temperature, Sunburst. Apple: Grades K–7

This program allows young students to perform temperature experiments. They use up to three thermistors that are connected to the computer to measure changes in water temperature. The computer keeps track of the information. The results of the experiments can be seen in a thermometer or line bar.

Science Toolkit Plus #2, Brøderbund. IIGS IBM: Grades 7–12

This program lets pupils study earthquakes; they explore wave motion and how a seismoscope works.

The Body in Focus, Mindscape Inc. (SVE). Apple II Family: Grades 6–12

This self-paced program encourages exploration of human anatomy. Three activities help students discover how the human body operates. Using animated graphics, students actually observe the body breathing, pumping blood, and eating.

The Botanical Gardens, Sunburst. Apple II Family: Grades 4–8

Experimenting with plants under various experimental conditions, the students learn how to control variables and interpret graphs.

The Great Space Race, Hartley. Apple II Family: Grades 4–10

The students' job is to build the fastest spaceship to compete in a race. They gather information from graphs, then build the ship, test it, modify it based on additional information, and then race it.

The Incredible Lab, Sunburst. Apple II Family: Grades 3–up

Students observe an imaginary beaker that is filled with a bubbling solution and are provided with a list of chemicals. They try to discover through trial and error the effect each chemical has on the monster produced.

Wood Car Rally, MECC. Apple II Family: Grades 3–9

Students use wood cars to investigate five variables: friction/lubrication, shape, car weight, ramp angle, and length. These variables affect the distance a car travels once it leaves an inclined ramp. The students use a practice track to investigate the variables and a competition track to challenge other students with their cars.

SOCIAL STUDIES PROGRAMS

Agent USA, Scholastic, Apple II Family, IBM, Commodore: Grades 3–up

To learn geography and map reading, the students decipher clues and use math skills. They must plan ahead to save the nation from the fuzzbomb and use intelligence to decipher the clues.

Call The Parrot, Hartley. Apple II Family: Grades 3–5

An adventure game, Call the Parrot teaches direction skills and note taking. A treasure is buried in a different spot every time the child plays. The child receives clues to the treasure's whereabouts from a truthful parrot and a lying pirate, and must make decisions based on these statements.

Crosscountry USA, Didatech. Apple II Family, IBM: Grades 4–up

Students play the role of a truck driver on a mission to find certain commodities. These students need map reading ability, logic, and record keeping skills to deliver the products all over the United States. Other members of the series are *Crosscountry California, Crosscountry Texas,* and *Crosscountry Canada.*

European Nations and Locations, Britannica. Apple II Family, Commodore, IBM: Grades 3–up

Students place the nations on the map in the right locations and learn how to match historical facts with the proper country. Teachers can customize their own games by selecting current facts or ancient lore.

Headline Harry Needs You, Davidson and Associates. IBM: Grades 4–up

Harry is an ace reporter trying to outsmart saboteurs. Students uncover true news stories and attempt to get them on the front page first. This race for deadlines takes them across the country and through time. Each news assignment enriches a student's knowledge of historical and cultural events, U.S. geography, politics, sports, arts, and science.

Hidden Agenda, Springboard. IBM, Macintosh: Grades 6–12

In this simulation, the student plays the role of a president of the Central American country of Chimerica. The president's goal is to lead the country out of its economic and social problems and establish stability during a three year term.

On the Campaign Trail, Tom Snyder. Apple, IBM: Grades 7–up

This program teachers students about United States elections. The students, working in a group, assume the role of a third party candidate for president of the U.S. They explore questions concerning economy, social policies, and foreign policy, while learning how the election process works.

Point of View, Scholastic. Macintosh, IBM: Grades 5–up

This program invites students to analyze historical events and write their own opinions. *Point of View* provides the user with different points of view in the form of original documents, eyewitness testimony, essays, pictures, statistics, video, sound, and animation.

States and Traits, Britannica. Apple II Family, Commodore, IBM: Grades 3–up

This game combines geography and history, current facts, and trivia. The student learns the location of each state and its bordering states, facts about each state, the names of capitals, and the locations of major landforms and bodies of water.

The Market Place, MECC. Apple, IBM: Grades 3–9

The students set up their own business selling lemonade, apples, or tomato plants. They make advertising and pricing decisions and learn the basic economic concepts of supply and demand.

The New Oregon Trail, MECC. Apple II Family, IBM Macintosh: Grades 5–12

The New Oregon Trail program transports the user back to the 1800s. As a pioneer, a student outfits a wagon train and heads West from Independence, Missouri. If the students makes the right decisions, he or she will reach the destination and, in the process, learn about this historical time period.

The Second Voyage of the Mimi, WINGS for Learning. Apple II Family: Grades 4–8

Maya Math and *Sun Lab* are multi media simulation software programs that give the students experiences as archaeologists and astronomers. The students go with Captain Granville's crew on a voyage on the Mimi to study Mayan civilization.

Wagon Train 1848, MECC. Macintosh: Grades 5–12

The students learn what it was like to travel 2,000 miles in a wagon across the rugged frontier in 1848. This program is simple to use and it works with up to 30 Macintosh computers connected via an Apple Talk based network. This program is "groupware," software that students use simultaneously while at different computers. Wagon Train 1848 even has a "talk" feature where the players can talk to one another. The students work together; group success means individual success.

Where in America's Past is Carmen Sandiego?, Brøderbund. Apple II, Apple GS, IBM: Grades 6–12

Where in America's Past Is Carmen Sandiego? covers 400 years of American culture and regional history. The student tracks down Carmen and her band of villains by looking up clues from *What Happened When,* a 13,000 page encyclopedia of American history and culture. This popular series also includes *Where in Europe Is Carmen Sandiego?, Where in the World Is Carmen Sandiego?, Where in the USA Is Carmen Sandiego?,* and *Where in Time Is Carmen Sandiego?*

World Geograph, MECC. Apple IIGS: Grades 6–up

World Geograph is an interactive database that allows students to manipulate 55 categories of information about 177 nations. Data can be printed in graph, spreadsheet, or chart format. A similar program, *USA Geograph,* allows students to manipulate data about the United States.

SPREADSHEETS AND INTEGRATED PROGRAMS

Appleworks 3.0, Claris Corp. Apple II Family: Grades 7–up

Throughout the years, *Appleworks* has dominated the sales charts. *Appleworks* has a word processor, spreadsheet, and data base. This collection of applications solves most individual computing needs in one easy-to-use package. Excellent documentation and support are provided.

Appleworks GS, Claris Corp. Apple IIGS: 10–up

Claris delivers six popular applications in one package: (1) a word processor, (2) spreadsheet, (3) data base, (4) page layout, (5) graphics, and (6) communications. A built-in synonym thesaurus and a spell checker are also included.

BeagleWorks, Beagle Bros, Macintosh: Grades 7–up

Beagle Bros. has produced an effective integrated software package for the Macintosh. The word processing features word count, text wrap around, and irregular graphics. The spreadsheet has in-cell editing, similar to Lotus 1–2–3 and an automatic summation button like Excel. Its painting module supports color, its data base lets the user do compound searches, and its communication module includes a telephone book.

BetterWorking Eight-in-One, Spinnaker. IBM: Grades 5–up

Better Working Eight-in-One is a complete productivity tool combining eight applications: a word processor, data base, spreadsheet, outliner, desktop organizer, spelling corrector, graphics program, and communications program. It is easy to transfer work among the different applications. This program is a fantastic bargain, selling for under sixty dollars in most software stores.

ClarisWorks, Claris, Macintosh: Grades 7–up

ClarisWorks has a word processor, spreadsheet, data base manager, and a communications and drawing module. The programs work together smoothly and flawlessly. Claris has incorporated macros that make it easy to do repetitive tasks. It is an intuitive program that offers features like footnoting and mail merge.

Easy Working—The Planner, Spinnaker. Apple II Family, IBM: Grades 7–up

Another member of the *Easy Working* family, this bargain spreadsheet is carefully designed to work alone or with its word processor or data base. The planner is of high quality and was voted 1987 Product of the Year by the software publishers.

Educalc, Houghton Mifflin (formerly Grolier). Apple II Family, IBM, Commodore: Grades 7–up

With *Educalc* beginning students create, edit, save, and print their own spreadsheets in no time at all. *Educalc* has a very helpful tutorial that takes pupils through this process step-by-step. There are on-screen prompts, activity disks, and workbooks available for math, science, and social studies.

Kid Calc, E. David & Associates. Apple II Family: Grades 5–6

Designed with the young novice in mind, this program introduces the fundamentals of spreadsheet concepts. It has only six rows and three columns and is simple to use. **Kid Calc** requires DOS 3.3. The basic program runs slowly, and a quick child can actually beat the computer.

Microsoft Works, Microsoft Corp. Macintosh, IBM: Grades 9–up

Microsoft Works is an integrated software product with five tools in one. The user can work with several of these tools at one time. There is a word processor with a spelling checker, a data base, a spreadsheet with charting and drawing capabilities, and a communications program. Microsoft Corporation gives outstanding technical support and plenty of understandable documentation.

PFS Plan, Software Pub. (Now Spinnaker). Apple II Family, IBM: Grades 10–up

This *PFS* program can be integrated with the rest of the *PFS* Family of software. It is a powerful package that uses plain English, so it is not as difficult to use as the comparable advanced packages. There are numerous shortcuts to save typing time, and there is a quick entry key for automatic data entering.

PFS FIRST CHOICE IBM by PFS Software Pub. (Now Spinnaker). Apple, IBM: Grades 10–up

PFS First Choice is targeted at students and home users. *First Choice* includes a word processor, spreadsheet, graphics and data base program, and a telecommunications module. Each application is accessible through a main menu.

Swift Spreadsheet, Cosmi. Apple II Family: Grades 8–up

This bargain program has pull-down menus to guide users through the different operations and a standard spreadsheet format. When users press RETURN, the main menu is immediately called up. The documentation is on the disk.

W.O.R.K. AT HOME, Britannica. Apple II Family, IBM, Commodore: Grades 6–up

W.O.R.K is an easy to use, all in one software package that comes with three application programs: word processing, data base, and spreadsheet. This program has built-in tutorials for each program and two small manuals. Users can add, copy, move words, undo changes, and create forms.

TYPING PROGRAMS

Keyboard Cadet, Mindscape. Apple II Family, IBM, and IBM compatibles: Grades 2–12

This program is based on a best selling typing course used throughout the United States. Students look through a spaceship window and type the letters or words correctly to make them disappear from sight. The program emphasizes accuracy and speed.

Kids on Key, Spinnaker. Apple II Family, IBM, IBM compatibles, Commodore: Pre-K–5

Using three colorful games, *Kids on Keys* introduces children to the keyboard. The program stresses finger positions, letters, and numbers. It won the SPA "Certified Gold" Award and was cited in *Only the Best* as a highly rated program.

Mastertype, Mindscape. Apple II Family, IBM, IBM compatibles, Macintosh: Grades 2–12

Mastertype is an old stand-by that children and adults still enjoy. When students type the correct letters, they destroy attacking rockets. There are 18 drills for mastering finger position, accuracy, and speed. Teachers can customize games and keep track of the students' progress.

Mavis Bacon Teaches Typing, The Software Toolworks. Apple II Family, IBM, IBM compatibles, Macintosh: Grades 4–up

Mavis Bacon Teaches Typing uses animated graphics, facts from the *Guinness Book of World Records,* riddles, rhymes, and jokes. There are lessons that range from 10 to 120 minutes and a racer game that gives the students practice in building speed.

StickyBear Typing, Weekly Reader/Optimum Resources, Inc. Apple II Family, IBM, IBM compatibles: Grades K–6

There are three activities to sharpen students' skills at typing and keyboarding, including an arcade game. If the students are more advanced typists who need to review and brush up, this program can help. Pupils choose the level of difficulty and track their progress as they improve.

Type! Brøderbund. Apple II Family, Commodore, IBM, IBM Compatibles: Grades 5–12

This program has typing instruction for the beginner, intermediate, and advanced typist. One activity is an action packed race called *Type! Athlon* where the students improve their accuracy and speed by jumping hurdles. Teachers can customize the drills.

PRESENTATION GRAPHICS

Claris CAD, Claris Corp. Macintosh: Grades 10–up

This tool program offers computer-assisted design. Students can create any two dimensional geometric design, lines, arcs, spline curves, and more.

Cricket Graphics, Computer Associates. Macintosh: Grades 8–up

Cricket Graphics is a complete graphics program that offers a wide variety of chart types. It is relatively easy to use, and most high schoolers can master it.

Easy Graph II, Houghton Mifflin. Apple II Family, IBM, Commodore: Grades 3–up

Suitable for elementary school children and the novice, *Easy Graph II* is a basic graphing program. There is a step-by-step tutorial on the disk.

MECC Graph, MECC. Apple II Family: Grades 7–up

Suitable for seventh graders and above, *MECC Graph* is a more advanced tool than *Easy Graph.* Students choose the graph form and enter the information.

PFS: First Grapics, Software Publishing. IBM: Grades 8–up

This complete graphics program for the beginner lets a student create basic test and data charts.

PRODUCTIVITY GRAPHICS

Award Maker Plus, Baudville. Apple II Family, Commodore, IBM, Macintosh, Amiga, Atari: Grades 1–up

Award Maker Plus turns out professional quality diplomas, certificates, awards, and signs. Award Maker Plus has professionally designed document styles, parchment paper, and gold embossed, press-on seals to add authenticity to the teacher's creation.

Calendar Crafter, MECC. Apple IIGS: Grades K–up

Calendar Crafter is a program that prints personalized weekly, monthly, or yearly calendars. There are nine type styles, a choice of seven languages, and additional clip art.

Certificates and More, Mindscape. Apple II Family, IBM: Grades 2–up

Certificates and More creates customized certificates, game boards, calendars, and flash cards. The following templates are included: bingo card, board game, calendar, chart, checklist, flashcards, greeting card, number line, and primary paper.

Certificate Maker, Springboard. Apple II Family, Commodore, Macintosh, IBM: Grades K–up

Certificate Maker has over 200 pre-designed certificates.

Laser Award Maker, Baudville. Macintosh, IBM: Grades 4–up

Laser Award Maker produces magnificent, professional looking documents quickly and easily using the 300 dot per inch laser printer. There are over three hundred designed document styles.

Microzine Classroom Publishing. Scholastic, Apple II Family: Grades K–up

Scholastic has a series of programs from *Microzine* and *Microzine* Jr that are productivity graphics programs. These programs let teachers print their own masks, signs, awards, posters, and banners.

Scholastic SuperPrint, Scholastic. Apple II, IBM: Grades K–up

This program's features enable users to create their own graphics and place text and graphics wherever they desire. Teachers can create big books, number lines, posters, calendars, signs, banners, cards, and other classroom designs.

The Print Shop, Brøderbund. Apple II Family, Apple GS, Macintosh, Commodore, IBM: Grades K–up

A classic, the program is so easy to use that it really does not need its manual. Using the program's clip art, borders, and fonts, users can create calendars, posters, signs, banners, greeting cards, personal stationery, and advertising material. Giant size signs and calendars can be printed on the IBM version.

Scholastic Slide Shop, Scholastic. Apple II Family, IBM: Grades 4–12

Students can generate self-running multimedia presentations using this program. They create scripts on the screen and then tell the program how to run these. The program includes clip art, backgrounds, templates, borders, sounds, special effects, and drawing tools.

VCR Companion, Brøderbund. Apple II Family, IBM: Grades 6–up

This program creates colorful titles, credits, intermissions, and endings for videotapes.

The program has simple, step-by-step menus similar to *Print Shop* and includes fonts, graphics, animations, icons, and borders.

TEACHER UTILITY

Grading Programs

Apple Grader 4.0, Adrain Vance. Apple

Selling for under $45, *Apple Grader 4.0* is an inexpensive program that fulfills the needs of most teachers. The self-contained gradebook system keeps over 70,000 grades on a single disk, records letter grades, and provides statistical analysis.

Comput-A Grade, Projac. Apple II Family, IBM

A powerful grading program, *Comput-A* Grade figures grades, and prints reports for parents and children. It can handle 65 students per class and up to 99 assignments. The IBM version has 8 optional categories and allows teachers to individualize the parent message.

Gradebook Deluxe, Edusoft. Apple II Family, Apple GS

Gradebook Deluxe provides the teacher with a gradebook that handles records for 40 students per class and up to 255 grades per student. The program keeps track of missing and excused grades and calculates means, standard deviations, and grade distribution.

Grade Manager, MECC. Apple II Family, IBM

Grade Manager can handle 50 grades for up to 1088 students. The program records scores, computes grades, and prints out reports.

Gradebook Plus, E.M.A. Software. Apple II Family, IBM, Macintosh

Gradebook Plus keeps track of 8 classes with 45 students and 60 entries per student. The statistics for these entries can be displayed and changed at a minute's notice. There is a built-in, mini word processor to customize reports.

Gradebuster 1/2/3, Grade Buster Corp. Apple II, Apple GS, IBM

Gradebuster 1/2/3 is a state of the art grading and attendance program. The on-screen directions are marvelous, and there is no way the teacher can make a mistake. The grades are processed at an extremely high speed. Teachers can establish grading scales, weights, and codes for incomplete grades.

Testing Programs

Multiple Choices, Santa Barbara Softworks, S.B. Programming. Apple II Family

Multiple Choices generates word searches, scrambled words, acrostics, and double acrostics, as well as matching, true/false, fill-in-the-blank, and multiple choice questions. The program has a Macintosh look and is easy to use.

Study Mate—The Grade Booster, CompuTeach. Apple II Family, IBM, Macintosh: Grades 7–up

This program lets students develop their own tests for studying. The students enter vocabulary, geographical places, dates, and other information, edit the material, and then take tests on screen or from a print out. The program keeps track of the questions missed and can be used for retesting.

Test Designer Plus, Superschool Software. Macintosh, IBM

Test Designer Plus combines test creation with test taking. Teachers write multiple choice, true/false, completion, fill-in-the-blank, and essay types of questions. They can also integrate graphics into tests, insert questions from the user's data base, and use four foreign languages.

Teacher Tool Kit, Hi Tech. Apple II Family, IBM

Teacher Tool Kit is a very simple-to-use, inexpensive program with excellent on-line help. The instructor can produce the following: word searches, word matches, word scramble puzzles, multiple choice, true-false, or fill-in exams.

Puzzle Utilities

Crossword Magic, Mindscape. Apple II Family, IBM, Macintosh, Commodore, Atari

Crossword Magic is an extremely useful and popular product that can be utilized in all curriculum areas. This program shows the crossword puzzle on the screen and also prints it out.

Mickey's Crossword Puzzle Maker, Disney Software. Apple II Family, IBM: Grades 1 and up

Mickey's Crossword Puzzle Maker is a very creative program that lets the user solve existing crossword puzzles and design their own. In the play mode, the child types his name and selects a picture to represent him. He must then decide if he will play against the computer, another person, or just by himself. He can select a Disney puzzle with famous Disney characters, a saved puzzle, or a surprise puzzle with three level of difficulties.

Print your Own Bingo Plus, Hartley. Apple II Family

Teachers can use this program to print unique Bingo cards for classroom instruction and review in all curriculum areas. The Bingo cards can be used for new vocabulary word recognition, drill and practice, and teaching opposites.

Statistical Packages

Data Desk Professional, Data Description, Inc. Macintosh

This state of the art graphics and statistics program includes some very advanced features. It has outstanding documentation, and users can import data from spreadsheet, data bases, word processors, telecommunications programs, and text files.

SPSS/PC, SPSS. IBM

SPSS/PC is a popular statistical package for the IBM. It is menu driven and has interactive data analysis and an on-line glossary of statistical terms.

Organizational Drill and Utilities

Flowchart Maker, Mainstay. Macintosh

Flowchart Maker is an easy-to-use utility that creates flowcharts. Students place pre-drawn symbols on a page and then connect them with lines and arrows.

Letter Writer Plus, Power Up Software. Macintosh

Letter Writer Plus is a program designed to produce letters and memos. Using this program in conjunction with *Address Book Plus* desk accessory, the teacher can search for a specific *Address Book Plus* entry and paste this entry into a letter to create a mail merge.

Make-A-Flash, Teacher Support Software. Apple II Family, IBM

Using the teacher's favorite word processing program, *Make-A-Flash* prints flash cards. This program even lets the user enter his or her own math functions.

Snapshot, Baseline. Macintosh

This easy-to-use screen capture program lets users capture entire screens, user-selectable portions of the screen, windows, or menus. All the screenshot features are immediately visible on the screen.

TimeLiner, Tom Snyder. Apple II Family, IBM

The teacher is able to create time lines for all subject areas that can be up to 99 pages long. The program prints out sideways in an easy-to-read, banner format that is perfect for the classroom. *TimeLiner* comes with sample historical time lines; with minimal effort, teachers can add, edit, or merge these lines with their own time lines.

Worksheet Wizard, Edusoft. Apple II Family

With *Worksheet Wizard* teachers can create and print out individualized math worksheets for the whole class. There are five math areas covered: addition, subtraction, multiplication, division, and measurement; an answer key is supplied with each worksheet.

WORD PROCESSING PROGRAMS

Appleworks, Claris Corp. Apple II Family: Grades 10–up

See Integrated Programs.

Bank Street Writer, Scholastic. Apple II Family, IBM, Macintosh: Grades 4–up

The *Bank Street Writer* is easy to use with its on-screen prompts and tutorial. This word processor has a spell-checker and a thesaurus and comes in 20, 40, and 80 column versions. An assortment of worksheets and lesson plans are included. The Macintosh version has *HyperCard* and desktop capabilities.

BeagleWrite, Beagle Bros. (Formerly Multiscribe, by Claris). Apple II Family: Grades 6–up

BeagleWrite is a full-featured word processor with Macintosh features. It has a built-in dictionary, thesaurus, fancy fonts, and character sizes that appear on the screen exactly as they will appear in the text.

Easy Working The Writer, Spinnaker. Apple II Family, IBM: Grades 4–up

Easy Working The Writer is a relative of *Easy Working The Filer* and *Easy Working The Database.* These high quality, low cost productivity tools use the same command format, and commands are displayed at the top of the screen.

FrEdWriter, Softswap. Apple II Family: Grades 8–up

FrEdWriter is a low cost, high quality word processing program based on a public domain program called Freewriter. This program can be freely duplicated for student use, and the master disk has the documentation saved as text files.

Magic Slate II, Sunburst. Apple II Family: Grades K–up

Magic Slate is a word processor with 20 and 80 column versions available. The primary version (20 columns) has an icon based or picture menu, a variety of fonts and type sizes, and a simple command structure. Useful instructional materials are enclosed.

MECC Writer, MECC. Apple II Family: Grades 4–up

MECC Writer comes with an on screen tutorial that the student can refer to for help. The user can compose, edit, and print text from the same on-screen menu, and what the student arranges on the screen is what appears on the page.

Microsoft Word, Microsoft. IBM, Macintosh: Grades 10–up

Microsoft Word is a full featured word processor for the very sophisticated student. With advanced features such as outlining, indexing, and glossary, it is an expensive, but very worthwhile package.

The Writing Workshop, Milliken. Apple II Family: Grades K–up

The *Milliken Word Processor* includes graphic icons for easy access, document editing in the same mode, and typeface selection. Additionally, it is a memory resistant program that does not depend on the program being in a disk drive after booting. Instructional materials are included with this simple-to-use word processor.

PFS Write, Spinnaker. Apple II Family, IBM: Grades 5–up

For advanced students, *PFS Write* is a full functioning word processor with good instructional materials. The main menu has six functions: Type/Edit, Define Page, Print, Get/Save/Remove, Clear, and Exit.

Swift Word Processing Program, Cosmi. Apple II Family, IBM: Grades 10–up

This beginner's productivity tool sells for under ten dollars. The user needs minimal instruction because of the simple, on-screen menus.

Word Perfect, Word Perfect. Apple II Family, IBM, Macintosh: Grades 12–up

Word Perfect is a sophisticated, full-functioning word processor that is more difficult to learn than many other word processing programs.

CD-ROM PROGRAMS

Compton's Multi Media Encyclopedia, Britannica. IBM: Grades 2–up

The student uses this sophisticated encyclopedia in CD-ROM format to find charts, diagrams, maps, words, and articles. Entries have sound, music, speech, and animated sequences. The program is very easy to use, and the students access the contents in eight different ways.

Discis Books, Discis, Inc. Commodore Amiga, Macintosh: Grades K–6

Adding speech, sound effects, and music, this program entertains children with stories such as *Cinderella, The Tale of Peter Rabbit, Scary Poems for Rotten Kids,* and *Thomas' Snowsuit.* Students click the mouse anywhere in the story and they hear the correct pronunciation and an explanation of the story's words—as well as pronunciation in a second language.

English Express, Davidson and Associates. IBM, Macintosh: Grades 5–up

Designed for beginning English as a second language (ESL) students, this program teaches English. The students hear good pronunciation, associate speech and sentences with pictures, and acquire language naturally.

Just Grandma and Me, Brøderbund, Macintosh: Grades K–3

Just Grandma and Me is a story written by Mercer Mayer that originally appeared in a Golden Book. Brøderbund has captured the illustrations of the original book adding clever remarks, dialogue, animating characters on every page. The CD-ROM disk includes the story in English, Spanish, and Japanese.

Ludwig Van Beethoven: Symphony No. 9, Voyager Company. Macintosh: Grades K–up

This disc contains Beethoven's Symphony No. 9. and a *HyperCard* stack that discusses Beethoven's life and explains this composition.

Mammal: A Multimedia Encyclopedia, National Geographic. IBM: Grades 4–up

This on-disc encyclopedia provides information about 200 mammals. 700 color photographs, 45 clips from the National Geographic TV specials, and 600 pages of text are included in this marvelous resource.

National Geographic Kids Network, National Geographic. Apple II Family, Apple IIGS: Grades 4–6

Students conduct original scientific research about topics like acid rain and share their findings via computer with other student teams across the U.S., Canada, and other countries. A group of professional scientists help these students interpret their findings.

The New Grolier Electronic Encyclopedia, Grolier Electronic Publishing. IBM, Macintosh: Grades 5–up

This program gives students access to *The Academic American Encyclopedia,* which includes drawings, photographs, paintings, maps, and enhanced audio capabilities.

The Second Voyage of the MIMI, WINGS for Learning. Apple II Family: Grades 4–8

There are two programs in this package, *Maya Math* and *Sun Lab.* Playing the roles of archaeologists and astronomers, students serve as the crew on a voyage to study the Mayan civilization.

VIDEODISC

Bio Sci II Videodisc, Videodiscovery, IBM, Macintosh: Grades K–12.

The disc provides visual coverage of the biological sciences, containing 7,000 still images, 100 movie sequences, and 500 computer graphic diagrams.

GTV: A Geographic Perspective on American History, National Geographic/Optical Data Corp. IBM, Macintosh: Grades 5–up

Using two double-sided videodiscs containing 60 pre-programmed presentations, students explore American history.

Interactive Nova: Animal Pathfinders, Scholastic. Macintosh: Grades 5–12

Students learn about an animal's life through an hour-long NOVA documentary; there are 15 short documentaries with accompanying text/graphic cards. Students can actually hear the animals breathing and making noises.

Mist (Modular Investigation into Science and Technology), Evergreen Laser Disc. IBM, Macintosh: Grades K–5

This science resource has five subject discs that cover Air and Water; Forces, Machines, and Structures; The Senses; Living and Growing; and Materials and the Environment. A sixth disc is for teachers and provides lesson plans.

National Gallery Art Videodisc Companion, Voyager Company. Macintosh: Grades K–up

Students have access to 1,000 entries on the *National Gallery of Art* videodisc. They view still photos and motion pictures by categories, such as artist, period, date, or subject.

Windows on Science: Earth Science, Optical Data Corp. IBM, Macintosh: Grades 4–6

Students learn about geology, meteorology, oceanography, and astronomy. The three volumes cover topics like earth science, fossils, planets, space exploration, and water.

Appendix B
OPERATING SYSTEMS

APPLE DOS 3.3

Initializing A Disk

1. Put the **System Master Disk (DOS 3.3)** in the disk drive and warm boot the computer. (Press Control Open Apple and then Reset)
2. Remove the System Master Disk from the disk drive and insert a blank disk.
3. Type **NEW** and **PRESS** the **RETURN** key.
4. Type the following one line greeting program substituting your own name, and date.

10 PRINT " John Smith, 1/1/88 "
PRESS RETURN

6. Now Type **INIT HELLO** and **PRESS RETURN. (NO LINE NUMBER.)**

Running Different Programs

Applesoft=type **RUN,** one space and the filename and then press **RETURN.**

I(Integer Basic) type **INT** and press **RETURN.** The prompt sign will change and look like this **>.** Then type **RUN** one space and the **file name** and press **RETURN.** When the user wants to return to Applesoft Basic, s/he types **FP** and presses **RETURN.**

Binary files=type **BRUN** space and the **filename** and press **RETURN. Running a program in memory**=Type **RUN** and press **RETURN.**

System Commands

Catalog=Type the word **CATALOG** and then press **RETURN.**

List=Type the word **LIST** and press **RETURN**

Stop the program=Press the **CONTROL and RESET KEY** simultaneously.

Saving=Type **SAVE** the **program name** and then press **RETURN.**

Load=Type the word **LOAD** and the **program name** and then press **RETURN.**

Delete= Type the word **DELETE** the **program name** and then press **RETURN.**

Copying a File

1. Put the disk to be copied in drive one and the formatted disk in drive two.
2. Type **LOAD** a space and the **Filename comma D1** (Disk Drive 1) and press **RETURN.**
3. Type **Save** one space, the **Filename comma** and **D2**(Disk Drive 2).

If the user wants to use the copy file program that is available, s/he simply runs **Brun FID** or **Run Filem** and follows the screen directions.

Copying a Disk

1. Put DOS 3.3 in the disk drive
2. Warm boot the computer using **Control, Open Apple** and then **Reset.**
3. Type **Run CopyA**(without spaces) press **RETURN.**
4. Use the default settings pressing **RETURN** four times. To make a change, type the new number and hit **RETURN.**

5. The screen should say '—**PRESS 'RETURN' KEY TO BEGIN COPY—**"
6. Now put the original disk in the other drive and press **RETURN** for a two drive copy.

ProDOS OPERATING SYSTEM FOR THE GS

System Utilities

1. Put the System Master Disk with the Utilities on it in the disk drive.
2. Choose **Sysutil.System** and press **RETURN.**
3. The next screen displays the Utilities-**Catalog, Format a Disk, Delete Files, Copying Files, Duplicating a Disk.**
4. Once a utility is selected, the user is asked to choose the location of the disk by slot and drive or by ProDOS pathname. (A pathname is the complete name of a file. It starts with a slash, and each element of the name is separated by a slash—for example /Project/letters/Smith.)

Formatting a Disk

1. Select the **Format a Disk** option.
2. At the first screen press **RETURN.**
3. The prompt asks for the disk's location. If it is already correct, accept the default by pressing **RETURN.** If not, use the arrow keys to move and change one or both values.
4. Press **RETURN** to accept the ProDOS default.
5. The prompt asks for a volume name. Use the delete key to erase the present name and type a new name which must begin with a slash, then a letter. Do not exceed 15 characters, do not space, and use only letters, numbers and periods. For example/Computer1.
6. Press **RETURN** and a prompt will direct the user to insert the disk that s/he wants formatted in the proper drive.
7. Insert the disk to be formatted and press **RETURN.**

Cataloging a Disk

1. Select **catalog** from the Utility menu and press **RETURN.**
2. Accept the defaults, press **RETURN** two times to view the catalog.

Duplicating a Disk

Instead of using this utility, it is faster and more efficient to use a program like DIVERSI COPY (DSR).

1. Select **duplicate a disk** and press **RETURN.**
2. The screen prompt asks, "Where is your Source Disk?" If the default is acceptable, press **RETURN,** if not change it.
3. The next screen prompt asks "Where is your destination disk?" If this default is acceptable, press **RETURN.** If not, change it.
4. The screen prompt asks the user to put the destination disk and source disk in the correct drive and press **RETURN.**

Copying Files

1. Select the **Copy Files** and press **RETURN.**
2. Accept the slot and drive default and press **RETURN.**
3. If the source disk's slot and drive is correct, press **RETURN** twice.
4. If the destination disk's slot and drive is correct, press **RETURN.**
5. The screen prompt asks the user to select some or all the files on the disk. Make a selection and press **RETURN.**
6. The next screen displays a list of files, and the user selects the ones s/he wishes by pressing the space bar.

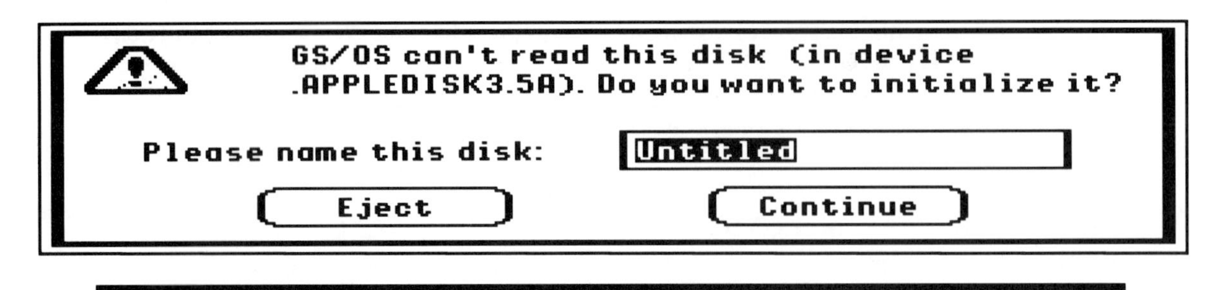
GS/OS can't read this disk (in device
.APPLEDISK3.5A). Do you want to initialize it?
Please name this disk:
Untitled
Eject
Continue

Screen for formatting a disk courtesy of Apple Computer, Inc.

7. When the user is ready to copy, s/he presses **RETURN.**

The commands Run, Stop, Save, Load and List are identical to DOS 3.3.

APPLE IIGS

This system operates similar to the Macintosh system 6.07 shown in chapter 2.

Formatting a Disk

1. When the operating system sees a blank, unformatted disk, it responds with a screen like the above.
2. If the user wants to format the disk, s/he supplies a name, and clicks continue. The name has to have letters, numbers, or periods, no spaces, and can be no more than 15 characters long.
3. The next screen prompt asks the user to choose an 800K disk format with 2:1 or 4:1 or a 400K disk. In most cases, the user selects the default **800K 2:1** and presses **RETURN.**

Making a Backup Copy

1. Insert both disks on the the desktop.
2. Drag the source disk icon on top of the destination disk icon.
3. A dialog box ask the user to confirm that s/he wants to erase everything on the destination disk and replace it with what's on the source disk.
4. When the user presses **OK,** a disk-to-disk copy takes place.

The procedure for copying a file and deleting a file is identical to Macintosh's version 6.07.

SYSTEM 7.0 FOR THE MACINTOSH

The finder looks different for System 7.0, but most of the beginning operating procedures are the same—with the following exceptions.

1. The trash is not emptied until the user empties it. The user must confirm that s/he wants to empty the file that is in the trash or it stays in the trash can when the machine is turned off.
2. The user can now open documents by dragging its icon onto a program's icon.

IBM PC/MS-DOS

Booting

1. **Cold boot** (computer off). Put the **PC/MS DOS** in the machine and then turn on the computer.
2. **Warm boot** (computer on). Put the **PC/MS DOS** floppy disk in the machine and boot the system by holding down the **Control** and **Alt** keys and then

pressing the **DEL** key. Release these keys simultaneously.

3. Press **Enter** twice to accept the current date and time defaults.
4. When the user sees the prompt screen with the current drive, for example **A>,** DOS is loaded.
5. Insert the program disk and type the name that brings up this disk.

Turning Off the Computer

1. The user should save his or her work.
2. Exit the program and return the control to **DOS A>**

Formatting a Disk

1. At the prompt, type **FORMAT** space and specify **Drive A:** or **Drive B:**
2. Press **Enter.**
3. The screen prompts tell the user to insert the new diskette in the drive specified and hit any key.

Directory

At the DOS prompt, type **DIR** and press **ENTER.** This command lists all the files on the disk.

Making a Backup Copy

Copying a disk from drive A to a disk in drive B.

1. The user types **A:** to make sure this drive is current and presses **ENTER.**
2. At the DOS prompt, type **DISKCOPY** space, type **A:** space, type **B:** and press **ENTER.** (**DISKCOPY A: B:**)
3. The screen will prompt the user to insert the disk to be copied (the source) in Drive A, and a blank disk (the target) in Drive B and then press any key to begin.

Copying a Selected File into another Disk

1. The user types **A:** to make sure this drive is current. and presses **ENTER.**
2. At the **DOS** prompt put a formatted disk in **Disk Drive B.**
3. Type **COPY** space, type the selected filename to copy, **COMPUTERS.BAS** space, type the name of the directory that will receive the copy **B:** then press **ENTER.**
4. The user should type the following: **COPY COMPUTERS. BAS B:** and press **Enter.**

Deleting a File

1. Make directory containing the file current by typing **A:** and pressing **ENTER**
2. At the DOS prompt type **DEL** press space, specify the filename to be deleted, and then press ENTER. For example **DEL COMPUTERS.BAS.**
3. This will delete the file called **COMPUTERS.BAS** located in Drive A.

Appendix C
DIRECTORY OF SOFTWARE PUBLISHERS

Advanced Ideas
2902 San Pablo Ave.
Berkeley, Ca 94702
415/526–9100
Aldus Corp
411 First Ave. S.
Seattle, WA 98104
206/628–2320
Apple Computer Inc.
20525 Mariani Ave.
Curpertino, CA 95014
408/996–1010
800/776–2333
ARS Nova Software
P.O. Box 637
Kirkland, WA 98083
800/445–4866
206/889–0927
AV Systems Inc.
1445 Estrella Drive
Santa Barbara, CA 93110
805/569–1618
Baseline
830 Broadway
New York, NY 10003
212/254–8235
Baudville Computer Products
5380 52nd St. S.E.
Grand Rapids, MI 49512
800/728–0888
616/698–0888
FAX 616/698–0554
Beagle Bros
6215 Ferris Square, #100
San Diego, CA 92121
800/345–1750
619/452–5502
FAX 619/452–6374
Bright Star Technology
1450 114th Ave S.W. 200
Bellevue, WA 98004
800/695–1860
206/451–3697
Britannica Software
354 4th St.
San Francisco, CA 94107
800/572–2272
415/597–5555
FAX 415/224–4534
Brøderbund Software
PO Box 12947
San Rafael, CA 94913
800/521–6263
FAX 415/491–6665
CCIE
23711 Arminta Street
West Hills, CA 91304
818/703–0367
CE Software
PO Box 65580
W. Des Moines, IA 50265
800/523–7638
FAX 515/224–4534
Claris Corp
5201 Patrick Henry Dr.
PO Box 58168
Santa Clara, CA 95052
408/727–8227
Compu-Teach
14924 21st Dr. S.E.
Mill Creek, WA 98012
800/448–3224
203/777–7738 Canada
Conduit
University of Iowa, Campus
Oakdale, Campus
Iowa City, IA 52242
319/335–4100
800/365–9774
FAX 319/395–4077
Cosmi
415 Figueroa St.
Wilmington, CA 90744
213/835–9687
Davidson & Associates
3135 Kashiwa St.
Torrance, CA 90505
800/545–7677
213/534–3169
Didatech Software
3812 William St.
Burnaby, B.C.
Canada V5C3H9
800/937–0063
604/299–4435
Discis, Inc.
45 Sheppard Ave. E #410
Toronto, ON
Canada M2N5W9
800/567–4321
FAX 416/250–6540
Diversified Software Research
34880 Bunker Hill
Farmington, MI 48331
313/553–9469
FAX 313/553–6441
DLM Teaching Resources
One DLM Park
Allen, TX 75002
800/527–4747
800/442–4711

E. Davidson and Associates
22 Russett Lane
Storrs, CT 06268
203/429–1785
EduSoft
PO Box 2560
Berkeley, CA 94702
800–EDUSOFT
415/548–2304
Electronic Arts
Direct Sales
PO Box 7530
San Mateo, CA 94403
800/245–4525
415/572–2787
Evergreen Laser Disc
2819 Hamline Ave. N.
Saint Paul, MN 55113
612/639–1418
FAX 612/639–0110
Grade Busters Corp
3610 Queen Anne Way
Colorado Springs, CO 80917
719/591–9815
Great Wave Software
5353 Scotts Valley Dr.
Scots Valley, CA 95077
408/438–1990
Grolier Electronic Publishing
Old Sherman Turnpike
Danbury, CT 06816
800/356–5590
FAX 203/797–3197
Hartley Courseware
133 Bridge
Box 419
Dimondale, MI 48821
800/247–1380
517/646–6458
FAX 517/646–8451
Hi Tech of Santa Cruz
202 Pelton Ave.
Santa Cruz, CA 95060
408/425–5654
Houghton Mifflin Co.
Software Division
One Wayside Rd.
Burlington, MA 01803–9842
800/633–4515
800/733–1712
IBM Educational Systems
PO Box 2150
Atlanta, GA 30055
404/988–2532
Keith A. Mitchell
PO Box 803066
Chicago, IL 6068–3066
K–12 MicroMedia
6 Arrow Rd.
Ramsey, NJ 07446
800/292–1997
202/825–8888 NJ
Lawrence Productions
1800 S. 35th Street
Galesburg, MI 49053
800/421–4157
616/665–7075
LCSI/Logo Computer Systems
PO Box 162
Highgate Springs, VTG 05460
800/321–5646
Learning Company
6493 Kaiser Dr.
Fremont, CA 94555
800/852–2255
510/792–2101
Lego Systems
555 Taylor Rd.
Enfield, CT 06082
800/527–8339
203/749–2291
FAX 203/763–2466
Mainstay
5311–B Derry Ave.
Agoura Hills, CA 91301
818/991–6540
FAX 818/991–4587
MECC
6160 Summit Dr., N.
Minneapolis, MN 55430–4003
800/685–6322
612/569–1500
Microlytics
One Tobey Village Office Park
Pittsford, NY 14534
716/248–9620
FAX 716/248–3868
Microsoft Corp.
16011 N.E. 36th Way
PO Box 97017
Redmond, WA 98073
800/426–9400
206/882–8080
Milliken Publishing Co.
1100 Research Blvd.
PO Box 21579
St. Louis, MO 63132
800/643–0008
800/397–1947 MO
MindPlay
3130 N. Dodge Blvd.
Tucson, AZ 85716
800/221–7911
602/322–6365 AZ
FAX 602/322–0363
Mindscape/SVE
Society for Visual Education
1345 W. Diversey PKWY
Chicago, IL 60614
800/829–1900
312/525–1500
National Geographic Society
Educational Services
Washington D.C. 20036
800/368–2728
301/921–1330 MD
National Geographic Society
(orders for GTV)
30 Technology Dr.
Warren, NJ 07059
800/524–2481
908/668–0022 NJ
FAX 908/755–0577
Odesta Corp (Data Descriptions Inc.)
4084 Commercial Ave.
Northbrook, IL 60062
312/498–5615
Optical Data Corp
30 Technology Dr.
Warren, NJ 07059
800/524–2481
908/668–0222
FAX 908/755–0577

Pelican/Queue
338 Commerce Dr.
Fairfield, CT 06430
800/232-2224
203/335-0906
FAX 203/336-2481

Power Up! Software Corp.
2929 Campus Dr. Suite 400
P.O. Box 7600
San Mateo, CA 94403
415/345-5900
FAX 415/345-5900
800/851-2917

Queque
338 Commerce Dr.
Fairfield, CT 06430
800/232-2224
203/335-0906
FAX 203/336-2481

Reference Software
330 Townsend Street Suite 123
San Francisco, CA 94107
415/541-0226
FAX 415/541-0509

Roger Wagner
1050 Pioneer Way Suite P
El Cajun, CA 92020
800/421-6526
619/442-0522

Scholastic, Inc.
2931 E. McCarty St.
PO Box 7502
Jefferson City, MO 65102
800/541-5513
800/392-2179 MO

Silicon Beach Software
9770 Carroll Center Road
San Diego, CA 92126
619/695-6956

Softswap C/O CUE
P.O. Box 271704
Concord, CA 94527-1704
414/685-7289

Software Publishing Corp
1901 Landing Dr.
Mountain View, CA 94043
415/962-8910

Scott Foresman
1900 E. Lake Ave.
Glenview, IL 60025
800/554-4411

Seven Hills Software
2310 Oxford Rd.
Tallahassee, FL 32304
800/627-3836

Society for Visual Education
(SVE) 1345 W. Divesey Pkwy
Chicago, IL 60614
800/829-1900
312/525-1500 IL

Software Toolworks
One Toolworks Plaza
13557 Ventura Blvd.
Sherman Oaks, CA 91423
818/907-6789

Spinnaker Software Corp
201 Broadway, 6th Fl.
Cambridge, MA 02139
800/323-8088
617/494-1200

Springboard Software
7808 Creekside Cir.
Minneapolis, MN 55435
800/654-6301

Sunburst Communications
101 Castleton St.
Pleasantville, NY 10570
800/628-8897

Superschool
1857 Josie Avenue
Long Beach, CA 90815
213/594-8580

Symantec/Edutech
PO Box 51755
Pacific Groves, CA 93950
408/372-2041
FAX 408/372-2041

Techware
P.O. Box 151085
Altamonte Springs, FL 32715
800/347-3224
407/695-9000 FL

Terrapin Software
400 Riverside St.
Portland, ME 04103
207/878-8200
FAX 207/797-9235

Timeworks
625 Academy Dr.
Northbrook, IL 60062
800/535-9497
708/559-1300
FAX 708/559-1399

Tom Snyder Productions
90 Sherman St.
Cambridge, MA 02140
800/342-0236
617/876-4433
FAX 617/876-0033

True Basic Inc.
12 Commerce Ave.
West Lebanon, NH 03784
800/872-2742
603/298-5655

Videodiscovery
1515 Dexter Ave. N. 400
Seattle, WA 98109
800/548-3472
206/285-5400

Voyager Company
1351 Pacific Coast Highway
Santa Monica, CA 90401
800/446-2001

Weekly Reader Software
Optimum Resource
10 Station Place
Norfolk, CT 06058
800/327-1473
203/542-5553
FAX 203/542-5685

WINGS For Learning
1600 Green Hills Rd
Scotts Valley, CA 95067
800/321-7511
408/438-5502
FAX 408/438-4214

Writing Tools Group
1 Harbor Drive
No. 111
Sausalito, CA 94965
812/323-1740

Appendix D
RECOMMENDED COMPUTER PUBLICATIONS

MAGAZINES AND JOURNALS

BYTE, McGraw-Hill, Inc., 70 Main St., Peterborough, NH 03458.

Computer Science Education, Ablex Publishing Corp., 355 Chestnut St., Norwood, NJ.

Computers and Composition, Michigan Technological University, Department of Humanities, Houghton, MI 49931.

Computers, Reading and Language Arts, Modern Learning Publisher, Inc., 1308 E. 38th St., Oakland, CA 94602.

The Computing Teacher, International Society for Technology in Education (ISTE) 1787 Agate St., Eugene, OR 97403–1923.

Educational Technology, 720 Palisade Ave., Englewood Cliffs, NJ 07632.

Educational Technology Research and Development, Association for Educational Communications and Technology, 1126 Sixteenth St. NW, Washington, DC 20036.

Electronic Education, Electronic Communications, Inc., 1311 Executive Center Drive, Suite 220, Tallahassee, FL 32301.

Electronic Learning, Scholastic, Inc., Box 2040, Mahopac, NY 10541–9963.

Future Generations Computer Systems, Journal Information Center, Elsevier Science Publishers, 52 Vanderbilt Ave., New York, New York 10017.

Incider A+, A+ Publishing Division of IDG Communications, 80 Elm St., Peterborough, NH 03458.

InfoWorld, InfoWorld Publishing Inc., 155 Bovet Road, Suite 800, San Mateo, CA 94402

Instruction Delivery Systems, Communicative Technology Corporation, 50 Culpepper Street, Warrenton, VA 22186.

Interact, International Interactive Communications Society, 2120 Steiner St., San Francisco, CA 94115.

Interface: The Computer Education Quarterly, Mitchell Publishing, Inc., 915 River St., Santa Cruz, CA 95060.

Journal of Computer-Based Instruction, ADCIS, Western Washington University, Miller Hall 409, Bellingham, WA 98225.

Journal of Computers in Mathematics and Science Teaching, P.O. Box 4455, Austin, TX 78765.

Journal of Computing in Childhood Education, P.O. Box 60730, Phoenix, AZ 85082.

Journal of Educational Computing Research, Baywood Publishing, Inc., Box D, Farmington, NY 11735.

Journal of Educational Technology Systems, Baywood Publishing, Inc., Box D, Farmington, NY 11735.

Journal of Interactive Instruction Development, Society for Applied Learning Technology, 50 Culpepper St., Warrenton, VA 22186.

Journal of Research on Computing in Education ISTE, 1787 Agate St., Eugene, OR 97403–9905.

Learning, P.O. Box 2580, Boulder, CO 80322.

Logo Exchange, International Society for Technology in Education, University of Oregon, 1787 Agate St., Eugene, OR 97403–9905.

MacUser, P.O. Box 56972, Boulder, CO 80321–6972.

MacWEEK, P.O. Box 5821, Cherry Hill, NJ O8034.

Media and Methods, American Society of Educators, 1429 Walnut St., Philadephia, PA 19102.

Microcomputers in Education, Two Sequan Road, Watch Hill, RI 02891.

PC AI, Knowledge Technology, Inc., 3310 West Bell Rd., Suite 119, Phoenix, AZ 85023.

PC Computing, Ziff-Davis Publishing Company, Computer Publications Division, One Park Avenue, New York, NY 10017.

PC Magazine, Ziff-Davis Publishing Company, Computer Publications Division, One Park Avenue, New York, NY 10017.

PC World, P.O. Box 78270, San Francisco, CA 94107–9991.

Personal Computing, Hayden Publishing Co., Inc., 10 Mulholland Dr., Hasbrouck Heights, NJ 07604.

T.H.E. Journal—Technological Horizons in Education, Information Synergy, Inc., 150 El Camino Real, Tustin, CA 92680.

TechTrends, AECT, 1126 Sixteenth St. NW, Washington, DC 20036.

NEWSLETTERS

Classroom Computer News, International Education, 51 Spring St., Watertown, MA 02172.

CUE Newsletter, Computer-Using Educators, Box 1854, San Jose, CA 95158.

Education Computer News, BPI, 951 Pershing Dr., Silver Spring, MD 20910–4464.

Online Searcher, 14 Haddon Rd., Scarsdale, NY 10583.

The Sloane Report, P.O. Box 561689, Miami, FL 33256.

True BASIC Bulletin, 12 Commerce Avenue, West Lebanon, NH 03784–9758.

Syllabus-An Information Source on Computing in Higher Education, P.O. Box 2716, 1226 Mandarin Dr., Sunnyvale, CA 94087.

SOFTWARE REVIEW SOURCES

Curriculum Products Reviews, 530 University Ave., Palo Alto, CA 94301.

Educational Software Preview Guide, ICCE, University of Oregon, 1787 Agate St., Eugene, OR 97403.

Only the Best, Educational News Service, P.O. Box 1789, Carmichael, CA 95609.

The Educational Software Selector, EPIE Institute, P.O. Box 839, Water Mill, NY 11976.

Software Reviews on File, Facts on File, Inc, 460 Park Ave. South, New York, NY 10016.

Technology in the Curriculum, California State Department of Education, P.O. Box 271, Sacramento, CA 95802–0271.

MicroSIFT, Document Reproduction Services, Northwest Regional Educational Laboratory, 101 S.W. Main St., Suite 500, Portland, OR 97204.

Micro, Florida Center for Instructional Computing, University of South Florida, Tampa, FL 33620.

Appendix E
PROFESSIONAL ORGANIZATIONS AND USERS GROUPS

American Educational Research Association (AREA), 1230 Seventeenth Street NW, Washington, DC 20036.

Association for Computers in Mathematics and Science Teaching, P.O. Box 4455, Austin, TX 78765.

Association for the Development of Computer-Based Instructional Systems, Computer Center, Western Washington University, Bellingham, WA 98225.

Association for Educational Communications and Technology (AECT), 1126 Sixteenth Street NW, Washington, DC 20036.

Board of Cooperative Educational Services (BOCES), Statewide Instructional Computing Network, Mexico, NY 13134.

Computer Assisted Language Learning and Instruction Consortium (CALICO), 233 SFLC, Brigham Young University, Provo, UT 84602.

Computer Information Exchange, P.O. Box 159, San Luis Rey, CA 92068.

Computer Using Educators (CUE), INC., P.O. Box 2087, Menlo Park, CA 94026.

Educational Products Information Exchange (EPIE) Institute, P.O. Box 839, Water Mill, NY 11976.

Educational Computing Consortium of Ohio (ECCO), 47777 Farnhurst Rd. Cleveland, OH 44124.

Florida Center for Instructional Computing, College of Education, University of Florida, Tampa, FL 33620.

Indiana Computer Educators, 12340 South Clinton, Fort Wayne, IN 46825.

International Association for Computing in Education (IACE), 1230 Seventeenth St. N.W., Washington, DC 20036.

International Council For Computers in Education (ICCE), Department of Computer and Information Science, University of Oregon, Eugene, OR 97403.

International Institute of Applied Technology, Inc., 2121 Wisconsin Ave. N.W. Suite 400, Washington, DC 20007.

Iowa AEDS, Educational Computer Center, 500 College Drive, Mason City, IA 50401.

International Society for Technology in Education (ISTE), University of Oregon, Eugene, OR 97403–1923.

Maryland Association for the Educational Uses of the Computer (MAEUC), c/o Catonville Community College, 800 S. Rolling Rd., Baltimore, MD 21228.

Minnesota Educational Computing Consortium (MECC), 2520 Broadway Dr. St. Paul, MN 55113.

Microcomputer Software and Information for Teachers (MicroSIFT), Northwest Regional Educational Laboratory, 100 S.W. Main, Suite 500, Portland, OR 97204.

Society for Applied Learning Technology (SALT), 50 Culpepper Street, Warrenton, VA 22186.

Special Interest Group—Computers and Social Education(SIG-CASE), National Council for the Social Studies, 3501 Newark St. N.W., Washington, DC 20016.

Technical Education Research Center (TERC), 1696 Massachusetts Avenue, Cambridge, MA 02138.

Appendix F
TELECOMMUNICATION

ON-LINE SERVICES AND BULLETIN BOARDS

America ONline, 8619 Westwood Center Drive, Vienna, VA 22182.

BreadNET, Bread Loaf School of English, Middlebury College, Middlebury, VT 05753, 802/388–3711.

BRS Information Technologies, 1200 Route 7, Lathan, NY 12110, 800/227–5277.

Champlain Valley Union High School Electronic Bulletin Board, Champlain Valley Union High School, RR2 Box 160, Hinesburg, VT 05461, 802/482–2101.

CompuServe Information Services, P.O. Box 20212, 50000 Arlington Centre Boulevard, Columbus, OH 43220, 614/457–8600.

Dialog Information Services, Inc., 3460 Hillview Avenue, Palo Alto, CA 94304, 415/858–2700.

Dialog Classroom Instruction Program, 1901 No. Moore St., Suite 500, Arlington, VA 22209, 800/334–2564.

Dow Jones News/Retrieval, P.O. Box 300, Princeton, NJ 08540, 800/257–5114.

Educational Products Information Exchange Institute (EPIE), P.O. Box 839, Water Mill, NY 11976, 515/283–4922.

Einstein, Addison-Wesley Publishing Co., Information Services Division, 2725 Sand Hill Rd., Menlo Park, CA 94025, 800/227–1936.

ERIC (Educational Resource Information Center) See DIALOG.

FrEdMail(Free Educational Electronic Mail Network) Al Rogers, 4021 Allen School Road, Bonita, CA 92002, Modem 619–292–1816 or CompuServe 76167,3514.

GEnie Online Services, 401 N. Washington St., Rockville, MD 20850, 800/638–9636.

Imagination Network, Fred D'Ignazio, Multi-Media Classrooms, Inc, 1302 Beech Street, East Lansing, MI 48823, 517/337–1549.

LES-COM-net, George Willet, 3485 Miller Street, Wheatridge, CO 80033, Modem 303–233–5824.

Long Distance Learning Network, AT& T Long Distance Learning Network, P.O. Box 716, Basking Ridge, NJ 07920–0716.

MeLink, Cathy Glaude, Maine Computer Consortium, P.O. Box 620, Auburn, ME 04210, 207/783–9776.

NASA Spacelink, Modem 202–895–0028.

National Geographic Kids Network, National Geographic, Washington, DC 20036, 202/775–6580.

National Geographic Society BBS, Educational Media Division, 17th and M ST. N.W., Washington, D.C. 20036, 202/857–7378 (300 baud) or 202/775–6738 (1200 baud).

Online Journal of Distance Education and Communications, 11120 Glacer HY. Juneau, AK 99801, 907/789–4417.

Pals Across the World, 4974 SW Galen, Lake Oswego, OR 97035, 503/697–4080 or 503/635–0338.

Prodigy, P.O. Box 8159, Gray, TN 37615–9961, 800/759–8000.

Service: FrEdMail (Free Educational Mail) 4021 Allen School Road, Bonita, CA 92002.

Special Net, National Association of State Directors of Special Education, 2021 K St. N.W., Suite 315, Washington, DC 20006, 202/296–1800.

Call 213/881–6880 for the latest listing on bulletin boards—Novation, Inc. Tarzana, CA.

Appendix G
BASIC PROGRAMS WRITTEN BY MIDDLE GRADE STUDENTS

PROGRAM 1: MY STANDING

This program provides an average for five test scores and then tells the student how many scores exceed it.

```
10 PRINT"ENTER FIVE NUMBERS."
20 INPUT V,W,X,Y,Z
30 LET A=(V+W+X+Y+Z)/5
40 LET C=0
50 IF V>A THEN LET C=C+1
60 IF W>A THEN LET C=C+1
70 IF X>A THEN LET C=C+1
80 IF Y>A THEN LET C=C+1
90 IF Z>A THEN LET C=C+1
100 PRINT "AVERAGE:";A
110 PRINT "COUNT OF INPUT VALUES THAT EXCEED AVERAGE:";C
120 END
```

PROGRAM 2: SPELLING CLUES

If the student cannot spell Abraham correctly, s/he is given three clues.

```
10 PRINT"WHAT IS PRESIDENT LINCOLN'S FIRST NAME?"
20 FOR I=1 TO 4
30 INPUT N$
40 IF N$="ABRAHAM" THEN GO TO 110
50 IF I=1 THEN PRINT " HERE IS A LETTER TO HELP YOU A"
60 IF I=2 THEN PRINT"HERE ARE TWO LETTERS TO HELP YOU AB"
70 IF I=3 THEN PRINT "HERE ARE THREE LETTERS TO HELP YOU ABR"
80 IF I=4 THEN PRINT"THE CORRECT ANSWER IS ABRAHAM."
90 NEXT I
100 GOTO 120
110 PRINT "YOU ARE CORRECT!"
120 END
```

PROGRAM 3: LOGICAL GUESSING

Developing a strategy, the student tries to guess a number between 1 and 100 in five tries.

```
10 RANDOMIZE
20 LET X=INT (100*RND) +1
30 PRINT"PICK A NUMBER BETWEEN 1 AND 100."
40 PRINT"YOU WILL HAVE FIVE TRIES TO GET THE CORRECT ANSWER."
50 FOR I=1 TO 5
60 INPUT N
70 IF N<X THEN GOTO 110
80 IF N=X THEN GOTO 160
90 PRINT "TOO HIGH"
100 GOTO 120
110 PRINT"TOO LOW"
120 NEXT I
130 PRINT "TIME IS UP. YOU HAD 5 TRIES."
140 PRINT "THE NUMBER IS ";X
150 GOTO 170
160 PRINT"YOU ARE CORRECT!"
170 END
```

PROGRAM 4: MULTIPLICATION DRILLS

The student answers a series of basic multiplication exercises and stops when s/he wishes.

```
5 CLEAR
10 RANDOMIZE
20 LET X=INT(10*RND)+1
30 LET Y=INT(10*RND)+1
40 FOR T=1 TO 3
50 PRINT"WHAT IS ";X;"X";Y
60 LET P=X*Y
70 PRINT
80 INPUT A
90 PRINT
100 IF A=P THEN GOTO 170
110 IF A>P THEN PRINT"TOO LARGE"
120 IF A< P THEN PRINT"TOO SMALL"
130 NEXT T
140 PRINT "THE ANSWER IS ";P
150 GOTO 170
160 PRINT "YOU ARE CORRECT!"
170 PRINT "DO YOU WANT TO TRY ANOTHER PROBLEM?"
180 PRINT "TYPE Y OR N."
```

```
190 INPUT R$
200 IF R$="N" THEN GOTO 220
210 GOTO 5
220 PRINT"TRY AGAIN TOMORROW."
230 END
```

PROGRAM 5: NUMBER SEARCH

In a six by six matrix, a student tries to find as many combinations equal to the given target number before the word ***stop*** appears on the screen. The student can use any math operation, as long as the numbers are adjacent.

```
10 RANDOMIZE
20 PRINT TAB(21);"TARGET NUMBER:";INT(9*RND)+1
30 PRINT
40 FOR I=1 TO 6
50 PRINT TAB(17);
60 FOR J=1 TO 6
70 LET NUMBER=INT(9*RND)+1
80 PRINT NUMBER;" ";
90 NEXT J
100 PRINT
110 NEXT I
120 FOR D=1 TO 75000
130 NEXT D
140 PRINT
150 PRINT TAB(21); "STOP!!!"
160 END
```

Appendix H
GLOSSARY

Abacus An ancient calculating device consisting of beads strung on wires or rods that are set in a frame.

ABC An abbreviation for the Atanasoff-Berry-Computer, the first electronic digital computer.

Access time The time a computer needs from the instant it asks for information till it receives it.

Acoustic coupler This type of modem lets the user insert the telephone handset into a built in cradle that sends and receives computer signals through the telephone lines.

ADA This high-level, programming language was developed in the late 1970s and named after Augusta Ada Byron, Countess of Lovelace and daughter of Lord Byron.

Algorithm Generally an algorithm is a set of instructions for a person to follow in order to solve a problem. A computer program is an algorithm that tells the computer what to do in a step-by-step manner—in a language that it comprehends.

Analog device A mechanism that represents values by physical quantities, for example, length like a slide rule, or voltages, or currents—like the differential analyzer, an analog computer.

Analytical Engine A sophisticated mechanical calculating machine that was designed by Charles Babbage in 1833. Conceived before the technology was available, it was to have been capable of storing instructions, performing mathematical operations, and using punched cards for storage.

Application program A program written for a certain purpose, like word processing.

Artificial Intelligence (AI) Using the computer to simulate the thinking of human beings.

Arithmetic Logic Unit (ALU) The central processing unit component responsible for the execution of fundamental arithmetic and logical operations on data.

ASCII Code This is an abbreviation for the American Standard Code for Information Interchange. A standard computer character set which allows efficient data communication and achieves compatibility among computer devices.

Assembler A computer program that converts assembly language programs into executable machine language programs.

Assembly language A low-level language which uses mnemonic words, and each statement corresponds directly to a single machine instruction.

Authoring language A computer language used to create educational software, such as drill and practice lessons.

Authoring system A program requiring little knowledge, one that is used to create computer-based lessons and tests.

Backup disk A second copy of a program or document.

Bar code reader An input device that scans bar codes and converts the bar codes into numbers that are displayed on the screen.

BASIC Beginner's All-Purpose Symbolic Instruction Code is one of the most commonly used high-level languages.

Baud rate The speed at which a modem can transmit data.

Binary The number system a computer uses that has only two digits, 1 and 0.

Bit An abbreviation for binary digit, either 1 or 0 in the binary number system.

Boolean logic Devised by George Boole, this system of algebra uses the operations of informal logic.

Boot The process of starting the computer.

Bug A mistake or error in a computer program.

Bulletin Boards (BBS) A computer that serves as a center for posting and exchanges information for various interest groups.

Byte A unit of computer storage which consists of eight binary digits (bits). A byte holds the equivalent of one character, such as the letter C.

Cell In an electronic spreadsheet, the intersection of a row and column.

Chip A piece of semi-conducting material, like silicon, with transistors and resistors etched on its surface.

Circuit Board A board where the electrical components are mounted and interconnected to form a circuit.

Compiler A program that translates the source code of a program written in a higher-level language like BASIC into a machine-readable, executable program.

Computer-Aided Design (CAD) Using the computer for industrial design and technical drawing.

Computer-Assisted instruction (CAI) Using the computer as an instructional tool.

Compact Disk Read Only Memory (CD-ROM) A means of high capacity storage (over 600 megabytes) which uses laser optics for reading data.

Computer-Managed Instruction (CMI) A computerized, record keeping system that diagnosis a student's progress, provides instruction, and analyzes progress.

CPS A term used to describe the number of characters printed per second by the printer.

COBOL COmmon Business-Oriented Language is a high-level language that is used for business applications.

Central Processing Unit (CPU) The "brains of the computer," where the computing takes place. The CPU is also called the processor. It is made up of a Control Unit and the Arithmetic Logic Unit.

Composite color monitor A monitor that accepts an analog video signal, which combines red, green, and blue signals to produce a color image.

Computer A machine that accepts information, processes it according to a set of instructions, and produces the results as output.

Cathode Ray Tube (CRT) This is the basis of the television screen and the typical microcomputer display screen.

Cursor The blinking light that shows the user where s/he is working on the computer screen.

Daisy wheel printer An impact printer that produces a typewriter-like quality print. This printer has its type characters set around a daisy-wheel, similar to a wagon wheel minus an outer ring.

Data base A data base is a collection of information organized according to some structure or purpose.

Data base management system Application software that controls the organization and storage and retrieval of data that is in a data base.

Debug Finding the errors in the computer's hardware or software.

Demodulation Used in telecommunication, this term refers to the process of receiving and transforming an analog signal into its digital equivalent which can be used by the computer.

Desktop A computerized representation of a person's work as if s/he were looking at a desk cluttered with folders.

Desktop publishing The use of the personal computer in conjunction with specialized software to combine text and graphics to produce high quality output that can be printed on a laser printer or typesetting machine.

Digital computer A computer that operates by accepting and processing data that has been converted into binary numbers.

Digitizer A device that translates analog information into digital information for computer processing.

Direct-connect modem A modem type that lets the user connect directly to the computer and plug into the phone jack bypassing the telephone handset.

Disk Operating System (DOS) This operating system is a program that lets the computer control its own operation. This program's major task is to handle the transfer of data and programs to and from the computer's disks.

Display The representation of data on a screen in the form of a printed report, graph, or drawing.

Documentation The instructions, tutorial, or reference material that is required to use the computer program effectively. Documentation can be on-line help or printed material.

Dot matrix printer The dot matrix is an impact printer which produces characters and graphic images by striking an inked ribbon with tiny metal rods called pins.

Download The process of sending information from a larger computer to a smaller one by means of a modem or network.

Drill and practice A type of computer instruction that lets the students practice information with which they are familiar in order to become proficient.

Electronic Mail or e-mail Transmitting messages over a communication network via the computer.

Encryption The process of coding information so that it cannot be understood unless decoded.

Execute The computer loads the machine language code of the program into memory—then carries out the instructions.

Fax machine An input/output device that lets the user transmit pictures, maps, etc., between distant locations.

Flowchart A graphical representation of the flow of operations that is needed to finish a job. It uses rectangles, diamonds, ovals, parallelograms, arrows, circles, and words.

Field A record location where a certain type of data is stored. For example, a student record might contain fields to store the last name, first name, address, city, state, and zip code.

File A file is a collection of related records.

Floppy disk Covered with magnetic coating, such as iron oxide, a floppy disk is the mass storage device used primarily with microcomputers.

Format Formatting or initializing a disk prepares a disk so the user can store information on it. During the formatting process, the computer's disk drive encodes a magnetic pattern consisting of tracks and sectors.

Function key A key located on the keyboard that the user programs to perform a specific task.

Gigabyte One billion bytes.

Graphics tablet A plotting tablet that the user draws on to communicate with the computer.

Hacker A person who is totally emerged in computer programming and computer technology. In the 1980s this expression took on a bad connotation, frequently meaning a person who secretly invades others' computers and tampers with the programs and data.

Hard copy Computer output that is on paper, film, or other permanent media.

Hard disk A fixed hard disk usually has one or more disk platters coated with a metal oxide substance that allows information to be magnetically stored.

Hardware The physical components of the computer system, which include the computer, monitor, printer, and disk drives.

High-level language A high level language is farther away from the machine's operation and approximates human language, whereas low-level language (like machine and assembly) is nearer the machine's operation.

HyperCard An authoring tool that lets the user organize information and retrieve on-screen cards that contain text, graphics, sound, and animation.

Hypermedia Hypermedia is nearly synonymous with hypertext; however it emphasizes the nontextual components of hypertext. Hypermedia uses the computer to input, manipulate, and output graphics, sound, text, and video in the presentation of ideas and information.

Hypertalk The programming language that is used with HyperCard.

Hypertext In hypertext, images, sound, text, and actions are linked together in nonsequential associations that let the user browse through related topics, regardless of the order. An example of hypertext is a computer glossary where a user can select a word and retrieve its definition from the glossary.

Initialize See format.

Inkjet printer A nonimpact printer that uses a nozzle to spray a jet of ink onto a page of paper. These small, spherical bodies of ink are released through a matrix of holes to form characters.

Integrated program An application program that combines several tasks such as word processing, and data base management in one package and allows for the free interchange of information among applications.

Integrated circuit chip (IC chip) Refer to chip.

Integrated learning system (ILS) A central computer with software consisting of planned lessons in various curriculum areas.

Interactive video This system consists of a computer, videodisc player, or videotape, and software where the student receives immediate feedback. It provides branching based on the student's performance and includes management features so lessons can be customized to specific student needs.

Interface The place where a connection is made between two elements so they can work harmoniously together. In computing, different interfaces occur, ranging from user interfaces where people communicate with programs, to hardware interfaces that connect devices and components in the computer.

Interpreter A high-level program translator that translates and then executes each statement in a computer program. It translates a statement into machine language, then runs it, then proceeds to the next statement, translates it and runs it, etc.

Joystick The joystick, a small, box-like object with a moving stick and buttons, is used primarily for games, educational software, and CAD systems.

Keyboard The computer keyboard is an input device similar to a standard typewriter, but with extra keys, such as the function keys and the numeric pad.

Kilobyte (K) The prefix means 1000. In computing, since k is based on powers of 2, kilo is used to mean 1024 or 2^{10}.

Laser printer Producing high quality text and graphic output, the laser printer traces an image by using a laser beam that is controlled by the computer.

Light pen This instrument, used in conjunction with a video display, has a light-sensitive, photoelectric cell in its tip and sends an electrical impulse to the computer, which identifies its current location.

Liquid crystal display A display that uses a liquid compound, positioned between two sheets of polarizing material that is squeezed between two glass panels.

Liquid crystal display projection panel The LCD panel is a projector that receives computer output and displays it on a liquid crystal screen which the instructor places on top of an overhead projector.

Light-Emitting Diode (LED) When charged with electricity, this semiconductor diode gives off light.

LISP Acronym for **List Processing.** A high-level, programming language, frequently used in artificial intelligence systems, that combines the use of lists with a set of symbols.

Local area network (LAN) A network that provides communication within a local area, usually within two or three hundred feet, as found in office buildings.

Logo Logo is a high-level language designed for children, one that contains many functions found in LISP.

Low-level language A programming language, like assembly language, that is close to the machine's language.

Machine language A programming language composed of a pattern of 0's and 1's which is far removed from the language understood by human beings. This is the *only* language that the computers understand.

Magnetic Disk A storage device that stores data magnetically. This information is stored in circular tracks that are divided into sectors.

Magnetic Tape A reel of tape, usually around 1/2 inch, that can store roughly

25 megabytes of data magnetically in a linear track.

Mail merge A utility usually found in a word processor that takes names and addresses from a data base and merges the information into a form letter or another document.

Mainframe computer In the early 1960s, all computers were called mainframes because the term referred to the cabinet that held the central processing unit. Today a mainframe, a multiuser computer, is a high-level computer designed for sophisticated computational tasks.

Mark I An electromechanical calculating machine designed by Howard Aiken at Harvard University and built by IBM.

Megabyte Megabyte refers precisely to the value of 1,048,576 bytes, abbreviated M or MB.

Megahertz Abbreviated MHz, it is a measure of frequency equal to 1 million cycles per second.

Memory The circuitry inside the computer that lets it store and retrieve information. Generally memory refers to the semiconductor storage (RAM) which is directly connected to the microprocessor.

Magnetic Ink Character Recognition (MICR) A character recognition system that reads text printed with a special magnetic ink. All the checks issued by a bank are coded with this special ink and characters so that a MICR can read them.

Microcomputer system A computer that uses a single chip microprocessor, one that is less powerful than a minicomputer.

Microprocessor A chip that contains the central processing unit of the computer.

Microworld It is the Logo environment, where the child freely experiments, tests, and revises his or her own theories in order to create a product.

Millisecond Abbreviated **ms,** this is equivalent to one-thousandths of a second.

Minicomputer It is a mid-level computer whose capabilities are between a mainframe and a microcomputer.

Modem Short for modulator/demodular, a device that lets two computers communicate with each other by using the telephone lines.

Modulation Used in telecommunication, this is the means a modem uses to convert digital information sent by computer to its analog form, so that the information can be sent over the telephone lines.

Monitor A video display that resembles a television set, a monitor is designed to handle a wider and higher range of frequencies.

Mouse A popular input device that is used instead of the keyboard to make menu selections.

Multimedia A subset of hypermedia, the user combines graphics, sound, animation and video.

Nanosecond Abbreviated **ns,** a prefix which represents the value 10^9, or one billionth of a second.

Napier's rods John Napier, a Scottish mathematician, invented Napier's Rods or Bones in 1617. The user was able to multiply large numbers faster by manipulating these rods.

Network A group of computers electronically connected by communications facilities. A network can have a permanent connection, like cable, or a temporary connection made through telephones or other communication devices.

On-line service A paid service that gives stock quotes, current news, magazine articles, and software, available to subscribers via telecommunication hookups.

Operating system Refer to disk operating system.

Optical Character Reader (OCR) Ordinarily this device uses laser technology or a light-sensing mechanism to interpret data. Advanced OCR systems can recognize hand printing.

Optical Disc An optical disc is a round platter that has information recorded on it by using a laser beam technology. It is capable of storing large amounts of information.

Optical Mark Reader (OMR) The OMR reads penciled or graphic information on cards or pages. Lamps furnish light reflected from the card or paper and the amount of reflected light is measured by a photocell.

Output After processing, output is the information that is sent from the computer to a peripheral device.

Pascal A high-level, structured language, designed from 1967 to 1971 by Niklaus Wirth.

Peripheral The devices that are connected to the computer under the microprocessor's control, such as disk drives, printers, and modems.

PILOT Acronym for **P**rogrammed **I**nquiry, **L**earning **O**r **T**eaching. A CAI authoring language developed by John Starkweather in 1969.

Piracy The act of copying software illegally.

Pixel Short for picture element, it is a linear dot on a display screen. When this dot is combined with other dots, it creates an image.

Plasma Screen The Plasma display is produced by a mixture of neon gases between two transparent panels, giving a very sharp, clean image with a wide viewing angle.

Presentation graphics Combining text and images, this software produces and displays graphic screens.

Printer A device that produces computer output.

Program A series of instructions designed to make a computer do a given task.

Public Domain Software It is software that is not copyrighted and can be freely copied and distributed without payment or permission.

Random Access Memory (RAM) RAM is referred to as volatile memory because of its temporary nature. Whenever an individual turns off the computer s/he loses whatever information is in RAM.

Read Only Memory (ROM) This memory retains its contents when the power supply is turned off. Often referred to as hardwired, internal memory, this memory cannot be altered or changed.

Record A collection of related fields which are treated as single unit.

Resolution The clarity or degree of sharpness of a displayed character or image, expressed in linear dots per inch.

Ring network A group of computers that communicate with each other in a ring, without a file server.

Scanner Scanners digitize photographs or line art and store the images as a file, one that can be transferred into a paint program or directly into a word processor.

Shareware Copyrighted software that is distributed free, but must be paid for if the customer is satisfied.

Simulation Software that approximates the conditions of the real world where the user changes the variables.

Site licensing A person or organization pays a set fee to run copies of a program on a large number of computers.

Software A program that instructs the computer to perform a specific job.

Speech synthesizers An output device, the speech synthesizer is a computer chip that generates sound. This chip gives the computer the ability to search for words and their pronunciations in a data base.

Spreadsheet It is a computerized version of a manual worksheet, with a matrix of numbers arranged in rows and columns, which facilitates calculations.

Star network A communications network where all the computers are connected to a file server or host computer.

Structured Programming Programing that uses a limited number of branching instructions and emphasizes modularity.

Surge Suppressor Also known as a surge protector, it protects the computer from damaging electrical surges.

Supercomputers They are the largest and fastest of the mainframe computers and have the most advanced processing abilities.

System disk The disk that contains operating software and can also be used to boot the computer.

Telecommunication Telecommunication is the electronic transmission of information, including data, television pictures, sound, and facsimiles.

Thermal printer Using heated wires, the thermal printer burns dots into a costly special paper.

Transistor An electronic gate that bridges the gap between two wires and lets the current flow.

Tutorial Similar to a tutor, this program explains new material, then tests the student's progress.

User friendly A term that means easy to learn and use.

User group A group of users of a specific type of computer who share experiences to improve their understanding of the product.

Utility programs They are programs that perform a variety of housekeeping and control functions such as sorting, copying, searching, and file management.

Videodisc Using an analog signal, a videodisc is a read-only, optical disc that stores and retrieves still and moving pictures, sound, or color.

Virus A program that infects computer files by duplicating itself.

Voice Recognition This system converts the spoken word into binary patterns that are computer recognizable; it understands human speech. By speaking, the user can enter data or issue simple commands.

Wide Area Network (WAN) A Network that uses long distance communication or satellites to connect computers over greater distances than the Local Area Network.

Word processor A word processor is a software program designed to make the computer a useful electronic writing tool that can edit, store, and print documents.

Index

A

B

C

D

E

F

G

H

I

J

K

L

M

U

V

W

X

Y

Z